DISCARDED

*Government, Technology,
and the Future of the Automobile*

REGULATION OF AMERICAN BUSINESS AND INDUSTRY SERIES

Goldschmid: Business Disclosure: Government's Need to Know

Edwards: Issues in Financial Regulation

Ginsburg & Abernathy: Government, Technology, and the Future of the Automobile

DeMott: Corporations at the Crossroads: Governance and Reform

Government, Technology, and the Future of the Automobile

edited by

DOUGLAS H. GINSBURG
Assistant Professor of Law
Harvard University

WILLIAM J. ABERNATHY
Professor of Business
Harvard University

in association with the Division of Research
Harvard Graduate School of Business Administration

McGRAW-HILL BOOK COMPANY
New York   St. Louis   San Francisco   Auckland   Bogotá   Düsseldorf
Johannesburg   London   Madrid   Mexico   Montreal   New Delhi
Panama   Paris   São Paolo   Singapore   Sydney   Tokyo   Toronto

Library of Congress Cataloging in Publication Data

Harvard Business School Symposium on Government, Technology, and the Automotive Future, 1978.
 Government, technology, and the future of the automobile.

 Consists of rev. papers and excerpts from discussions presented at the Harvard Business School Symposium on Government, Technology, and the Automotive Future held Oct. 19–20, 1978.
 Bibliography: p.
 Includes index.
 1. Automobile industry and trade—United States—Congresses. 2. Automobile engineering—Congresses. 3. Industry and state—United States—Congresses. I. Ginsburg, Douglas H., [date] II. Abernathy, William J. III. Harvard University. Graduate School of Business Administration. IV. Title.
 HD9710.U52H34   1978   338.4'7'62920973   79-14448
 ISBN 0-07-023291-1

Copyright © 1980 by McGraw-Hill, Inc. All rights reserved. Printed in the United States of America. No part of this publication may be reproduced, stored in a retrieval system, or transmitted, in any form or by any means, electronic, mechanical, photocopying, recording, or otherwise, without the prior written permission of the publisher.

1234567890   DODO   7865432109

The editors for this book were Ellen M. Poler and Susan L. Schwartz, the designer was Elliot Epstein, and the production supervisor was Sally Fliess. It was set in Palatino by The Heffernan Press Inc.
It was printed and bound by R. R. Donnelley.

Contents

PREFACE ix

PART ONE
Regulation

CHAPTER ONE
The Visible Hand 3

EDITORS' NOTE, 3

TECHNOLOGY, GOVERNMENT, AND THE FUTURE OF THE AUTOMOBILE INDUSTRY, 5
Ray Thornton

MAKING AUTOMOBILE REGULATION WORK: POLICY OPTIONS AND A PROPOSAL, 10
Douglas H. Ginsburg

DISCUSSION, 35

INNOVATION AND THE REGULATORY PARADOX: TOWARD A THEORY OF THIN MARKETS, 38
William J. Abernathy

DISCUSSION, 62

THE TECHNIQUES OF AUTOMOTIVE REGULATION: PERFORMANCE VERSUS DESIGN STANDARDS, 64
D. Q. Mills

THE EFFECTS OF OBSOLETE REGULATORY STANDARDS ON DESIGN INNOVATION, 77
Ulrich Seiffert

DISCUSSION, 84

CHAPTER TWO
The Role of Products Liability 89

EDITORS' NOTE, 89

PRODUCT LIABILITY: AGAINST POSSIBLE DISINCENTIVES TO INNOVATION GENERALLY AND SAFETY IMPROVEMENT SPECIFICALLY, 90
Hans-Viggo von Hulsen

PRODUCTS LIABILITY: POTENTIAL FOR IMPROVEMENT, 96
Daniel M. Kasper

DISCUSSION, 111

CHAPTER THREE
The Case of the Fuel Economy Standards 117

EDITORS' NOTE, 117

MANDATED FUEL ECONOMY STANDARDS AS A STRATEGY FOR IMPROVING MOTOR VEHICLE FUEL ECONOMY, 118
Richard R. John
Philip S. Coonley
Robert C. Ricci
Bruce Rubinger

THE EFFECT OF FUEL ECONOMY STANDARDS ON CORPORATE STRATEGY IN THE AUTOMOBILE INDUSTRY, 144
Kirk O. Hanson

DISCUSSION, 162

PART TWO
The Implications of Regulation

CHAPTER FOUR
Some Second-Level Effects of Regulation 169

EDITORS' NOTE, 169

THE SMALL CAR MAY BE DANGEROUS TO YOUR HEALTH! THE CONSEQUENCES OF DOWNSIZING, 171
Howard M. Bunch

DISCUSSION, 178

REGULATORY RIPPLE: A CASE STUDY, 180
Richard H. Shackson

DISCUSSION, 187

GOVERNMENT REGULATION AND THE FUTURE OF THE AUTOMOTIVE INDUSTRY, 189
Frank T. Popovich

A RISK ANALYSIS OF THE FUEL ECONOMY REGULATIONS IN THE AUTOMOBILE INDUSTRY, 196
Stephen P. Bradley
Aneel G. Karnani

DISCUSSION, 211

CHAPTER FIVE
International Trade and Domestic Regulation — 215

EDITORS' NOTE, 215

POLICIES FOR THE PROMOTION OF EFFECTIVE TECHNOLOGICAL CHANGE: A EUROPEAN POINT OF VIEW, 217
Umberto Agnelli

MULTINATIONAL AUTOMOBILE ENTERPRISES AND REGULATION: AN HISTORICAL OVERVIEW, 221
Mira Wilkins

INTERNATIONAL COMPETITION IN THE WORLD AUTOMOTIVE INDUSTRY, 259
Michael C. Pearce

THE INTERNATIONAL PRODUCT LIFE CYCLE AND UNITED STATES REGULATION OF THE AUTOMOBILE INDUSTRY, 270
Louis T. Wells, Jr.

DISCUSSION, 293

HONDA'S ENTRY INTO THE WORLDWIDE AUTOMOBILE INDUSTRY, 305
Koichi Shimokawa

DISCUSSION, 314

CHAPTER SIX
The Adversary Relationship: Regulators vs. Industry — 317

EDITORS' NOTE, 317

REGULATION AND INNOVATION IN THE AUTOMOBILE INDUSTRY, 319
Joan Claybrook

INTER-INDUSTRY COOPERATIVE RESEARCH AND THE GOVERNMENT: TWO CASE STUDIES, 334
Norman Alpert
Eugene L. Holt

DISCUSSION, 343

BEYOND AUTOCRACY: THE PUBLIC'S ROLE IN REGULATING THE AUTO, 346
Brian Ketcham
Stan Pinkwas

DISCUSSION, 365

THIRD-PARTY REVIEW, 367
D. S. Potter

TOWARD MORE EFFECTIVE ORGANIZATION FOR PUBLIC REGULATION, 372
Robert A. Leone
John E. Jackson

DISCUSSION, 390

vii

CHAPTER SEVEN
Market Forces in a Regulated Environment 391

EDITORS' NOTE, 391

ADDRESS, 393
Dave Stockman

AUTOMOBILE EMISSIONS CONTROL POLICY: SUCCESS STORY OR WRONGHEADED REGULATION? 401
Lawrence J. White

DISCUSSION, 421

CONSUMER SAFETY INFORMATION AS A GOVERNMENT POLICY TOOL, 424
Michael M. Finkelstein

DISCUSSION, 431

THE RESPONSE OF FLEET OWNERS TO REGULATION-INDUCED TECHNICAL CHANGES IN CAR DESIGN, 433
Robert Berke

DISCUSSION, 444

Appendixes 447

1. SYMPOSIUM PARTICIPANTS, 447
2. BIBLIOGRAPHY, 455

Index 461

Preface

The U.S. automobile industry has been transformed, in only a few years, from a technologically stable dominion of private enterprise into a technologically dynamic, controversial, and heavily regulated sector of the economy. Traditional market forces are now supplemented by strong external pressures for technological innovation to meet national policies and plans for energy conservation, environmental protection, and improved product safety. A large and growing number of organizations—government agencies, congressional committees, public and special interest lobbies—now have an important say in decisions that were previously handled by managers in a few firms.

This politicization and regulation of the automobile has attracted widespread publicity because virtually everyone has a stake in the process, but it has generated surprisingly little analytical or scholarly treatment, as opposed to the type of research that is conducted for presentation in advocacy documents before Congress and the regulatory agencies. With the publication of this book we can only begin to fill that gap by addressing such questions as: What has been the effect of regulation on technological innovation? On enterprise management? What practical policies can be adopted to meet future national needs with respect to energy, pollution control, and safety? What technologies will or should be available to meet these needs? How can the policy-making and regulatory processes be improved to these ends? What are the implications, for the U.S. industry and consumers, of the changing world trade in automobiles?

In order to reduce these questions to specific research topics, to be addressed in the context of automobile regulation but with useful implications for the relationship among government, industry, and technology in general, we initiated a series of five workshops at the Harvard

Business School during the 1977–78 academic year, supported by the school's Division of Research and the U.S. Department of Transportation. These sessions were organized around the implications of technological change in the automobile for (1) the regulatory process, (2) consumers, (3) the supply industry, (4) the research and development process, and (5) the United States' position in the international trade in automobiles. To each we invited about thirty people from the affected industries, government agencies, trade and consumer organizations, and academia to discuss the issues as they saw them and to identify those issues that were most promising for future research. We would solicit papers on these topics, to be given at a public symposium at the Harvard Business School in the fall of 1978.

These workshops generated more than an agenda for research. They brought together people who had previously dealt with one another only in adversary settings, such as congressional hearings and agency rule-making proceedings. As a result, they frequently revealed that public differences among the participants were based on previously unarticulated assumptions, attitudes, or factual premises; that some interests had not been fully heard in the public forums; and that no one participant commanded all the information relevant to his or her mission.

It would be gratifying but inaccurate to report that many positions were changed as a result of these meetings, however. On the contrary, it became apparent that positions on all sides had already hardened in the course of experience, and that views on seemingly narrow issues were often dictated by larger policy positions and constituency interests. This proved true, again, at the symposium at which the papers in this volume were delivered. As a result, it has become even clearer that, whatever progress we have made toward refining (much less resolving) controversies, there is much left to do

Each contribution to this volume was originally presented orally to an audience of almost two hundred invited guests at the Harvard Business School Symposium on Government, Technology, and the Automotive Future, on October 19 and 20, 1978. Under the ground rules for the symposium, assigned discussants responded first to the authors; discussion of the papers was then open to the floor. Authors were given an opportunity to revise their papers for this volume, as many of them did, in response to developments that occurred during the proceedings, and to bring them up-to-date. Discussants were given the same opportunity. The contents of this book thus represent the revised papers, together with excerpts from the discussants' remarks and the floor debate.

Although the symposium was "on the record," only the authors and discussants are identified by name here. Speakers from the floor are identified only by the sector from which they had come, such as the automobile industry, the Department of Transportation, etc. A complete list of the participants appears in an appendix to this volume.

As the foregoing description of the origins of this book suggests, an extraordinarily large number of people have contributed to it. In addition to the authors, discussants, and participants who contributed so much of their time and energy to it, we wish to express our special gratitude to: Mr. Seymour S. Feuer, Ex-Cell-O Corporation; Dr. Herbert Fusfeld, Kennecott Copper Corporation; Ms. Rhoda Karpatkin, Consumers Union; Mr. Eric O. Stork, Purdue University; Hon. John J. Fearnsides and Dr. Francis W. Wolek, Department of Commerce; and Professors Joseph L. Bower, Thomas K. McCraw, John Meyer, D. Quinn Mills, Walter Salmon, Robert B. Stobaugh, and Raymond Vernon, all of the Harvard Business School, who served as moderators for various sessions of the workshops and of the symposium. Special thanks go to Mr. William J. Devereaux of the National Highway Traffic Safety Administration for the continuing role he played, first in seeking our involvement in this project, and particularly for the very significant administrative burden he assumed in arranging participation by government officials and coordinating contractual arrangements for the conduct of the symposium.

Dr. Richard John of the Department of Transportation's Transportation Systems Center supported us in making contractual arrangements and gave technical advice and assistance. The project could not have gone forward without the gracious cooperation of Mssrs. F. James McDonald and David Potter, General Motors Corporation; Fred Secrest and Richard Shackson, Ford Motor Company; Sydney L. Terry, Chrysler Corporation; and Drs. Ulrich Seiffert and Hans-Viggo von Hulsen, Volkswagenwerk AG.

Dean Richard S. Rosenbloom of the Harvard Business School Division of Research provided essential support and encouragement for the symposium and the preparation of this book. Joan P. Curhan served admirably as Research Administrator for the symposium, ably assisted by Edward Dempsey, Edward Gillis, Robert Holz, George Oberhofer, Lawrence Ronan, and Gael Simons, students. Editorial assistance was provided by Max Hall, Robert Ross, and Eve Bamford. And Margaret Rinehart, our secretary, has been, in a word, perfect.

D.H.G.
W.J.A.

Boston, Massachusetts

PART ONE
Regulation

CHAPTER ONE
The Visible Hand

EDITORS' NOTE

When we initiated the workshops that established the agenda for this symposium, we took our subject to be the implications of technological innovation in the automobile industry. It quickly became apparent, however, that the subject could not be addressed without first studying the regulatory process by which innovation was being required and, depending upon one's view, either stimulated or retarded. Indeed, the subject of regulation—its necessity, wisdom, content, procedures, and effects—became our principal focus because it was the virtually unanimous view of the workshop participants from every sector that the existence of regulation was the dominant fact of life in the automobile industry today.

The essays in Part One (Chapters 1, 2, and 3) address directly the policies embodied in regulation today and the techniques by which government seeks to implement those policies. Those who are not already familiar with the design of the regulatory regimes for fuel economy, safety, and emissions control may wish to read first the essay by Richard John et al. in Chapter 3 for the valuable overview it contains. The essays in Part Two address the various implications of existing regulation (Chapters 4, 5, and 6), and the possibility of increasing reliance on marketplace transactions (Chapter 7) to accomplish present regulatory goals: Improved safety, pollution control, and fuel economy performance of the automobile.

In Chapter 1, Congressman Thornton reviews the general relationship between government and innovation, with particular attention to the future of the automobile industry. Next, Douglas H. Ginsburg offers an analysis of the problems that invited regulation of the automobile and suggests that innovation to accomplish regulatory goals could be stimulated by the conducting of "innovation competitions" that would draw upon the research and development capacities of enterprises that are not themselves part of the automobile industry.

William J. Abernathy analyzes the process of innovation as it has occurred in a number of industries, using a technology life cycle model. He identifies an apparent paradox, inasmuch as intense regulatory pressure can both encourage more rapid progress through incremental innovation in established products and inhibit epochal innovation by increasing barriers to the development of new technologies and enveloping existing technologies. The problem is not with regulation per se, he argues, but with its undifferentiated application to both established and potentially innovative technologies. Present regulatory policies therefore must be supplemented with programs that are more likely to yield important innovations in automotive technology.

Automobile regulation thus far has relied to a great extent upon establishing performance standards rather than mandating design specifications. The theory underlying this approach has been that the use of performance standards leaves maximum flexibility to the industry in devising its compliance strategy; innovation is encouraged and rewarded, rather than deterred, as it is conventionally said to have been in the area of housing construction. D. Quinn Mills analyzes the nature and effects of performance regulations which, when aggregated, do not seem to allow as many design options as theory would indicate. Moreover, he concludes that performance regulation imposes substantial financial risks on automobile manufacturers, generates controversies over testing procedures, and may substantially alter the competitive structure of the industry in a way that design specifications would have avoided.

Finally, Ulrich Seiffert explains the burdens that are imposed upon an automobile manufacturer by the differences in regulations from one country to another, their multiplicity in the United States context, and their testing requirements. Contrary to the implications of Professor Mills' discussion, Dr. Seiffert calls for an even greater reliance upon performance standards rather than design standards in order to preserve the possibility of design choices that enable manufacturers to use new technologies to their greatest advantage.

TECHNOLOGY, GOVERNMENT, AND THE FUTURE OF THE AUTOMOBILE INDUSTRY

Ray Thornton, *Member of Congress*

Like some of the other contributors to this volume, I once was in the business of manufacturing automobiles. I had a short career as the designer and manufacturer of a small fleet of lightweight automobiles called Handywagons in the early 1960s. As a result of that experience, I have a special admiration for anyone who can make a profit in business as an automobile manufacturer. During that time, I also developed a healthy respect for the enormous technological problems involved in automobile manufacture and a sense of awe for the complicated regulations which were just then beginning to appear. Although the 100 automobiles we manufactured were placed in full commercial operation for many millions of vehicle miles without a single instance of personal injury, those cars could not legally be sold in the United States today.

Since my short-lived venture into the field of automobile manufacturing, the automobile industry has undergone an accelerating set of changes from a private sector in which design and innovation respond to traditional market forces to an arena circumscribed and regulated by government emphasis on energy economy, safety, and a wide range of environmental considerations.

Contradictions and inconsistencies in the federal regulation of research and development in the private sector seem to be stifling the very atmosphere those policies were designed to promote and protect. The involvement of the federal government in scientific and technological affairs is not a new idea. It dates from the framing of the Constitution, where Article I, Section 8, gives the government the responsibility to protect invention and to create an atmosphere suited to innovation: "The Congress shall have power . . . to promote the Progress of Science and the useful Arts, by securing for limited Times to Authors and Inventors the exclusive Right to their respective Writings and Discoveries . . . ." What began as a federal attempt to protect the best interests of the inventor has also been responsible, however, for what is generally accepted to be a serious decline in American innovation and invention.

Restoring a balanced program designed to provide substantial rewards for innovation should be a major national goal. Federal funding of research is only one means of encouraging innovation; we also need to consider alternatives to federally funded projects. I believe that we should examine many ways of providing incentives to the private sector to accomplish needed innovation. Grants, loan guarantees, and tax incentives as well as regulation and modifications of institutional attitudes and policies may well stimulate needed innovation in the automobile industry. As a result of several hearings before my congressional subcommittee, I have become concerned that, despite government programs formulated to encourage private development of innovative techniques, we find ourselves up against regulations, and patent and antitrust policies, which actually frustrate achievement of these goals.

Leading industry and federal agency witnesses told my subcommittee that in spite of the risks of basic research in terms of dollars and time invested, many private companies do not want federal funds supporting their research programs. They pointed out that whenever federal funds support a research effort, any innovations coming from that research are patented by the government. As a result, they are available for public use—by the private developer or any of his competitors—without discrimination. This has an obviously chilling effect on federally funded private research. Indeed, even when an innovation is developed in one of these research efforts, it may never be used because it is based on a public patent. Why should a manufacturer try to market a product based on one of these patents if he knows that his competitors can use the same patent just as soon as the market is established?

Dr. Jacob Rabinow, a retired consultant to the National Bureau of Standards and the holder of 209 patents, offered simple but persuasive testimony before my subcommittee:

> During World War II, we confiscated 15,000 German industrial patents. The alien property custodian had them [and] could not give them away because any patent that is free . . . is copied by several companies. They die shortly . . . . Now the government owns 22,000 patents and it cannot give them away. Very few are used.

Dr. Rabinow's view was echoed by almost every other witness. It seems to me that we should rethink our patent policy. Ideas which are developed with federal funds are no use at all if they gather dust in somebody's file drawer.

The patent system was established to encourage private investment in research and development by taking into account the inventor's financial risk and creative investment. In recent years, however, direct participation of the government in R&D has grown to a point where today more than half of this nation's R&D effort is being conducted under government sponsorship. The resulting dual role of the government as financial sponsor and regulatory overseer raises significant questions about federal rights and responsibilities in technology development.

Along with the enormous increase in funding, we have established many new departments, agencies, and commissions with virtual autonomy in setting administrative guidelines for research and development. Confusion and complexity are the only constants in the equation, and the phrase "patent policy" has become a contradiction in terms.

Antitrust laws also hamper industrial research efforts, particularly with respect to so-called public problems. The beneficiaries of advances made on problems of pressing national importance, including abatement of environmental pollution and development of safe and economically feasible sources of energy, will be the public as a whole. Industrial inventors responsible for solving these problems can hope for little reward, as the benefits often cannot be measured in financial terms. Because such problems involve sophisticated and expensive technology, it seems reasonable to suggest a joint effort among firms—particularly in the R&D stage. Unfortunately, this cooperation is largely precluded by current interpretations of the antitrust laws.

I prepared and sponsored an effort in the House to provide a uniform patent policy. Another effort is embodied in legislation recently introduced by Senator Dole and others. This bill, entitled The University and Small Business Patent Procedures Act, would specifically allow universities, nonprofit organizations, and small businesses to obtain patent protection on discoveries they have made under government-sponsored research, provided they spend the additional private resources necessary to bring their discoveries to the public. I believe that this legislation will lower some of the primary barriers to commercialization that now exist and can help us reap the maximum benefit from the federal R&D effort.

Perhaps even more promising in its potential is the establishment by the White House of a Domestic Policy Review Committee, under Commerce Department leadership, to study issues and problems related to industrial innovation. The White House has tapped top people in some thirty agencies for this committee to lay the groundwork for developing a major legislative package that will carry the administration's support. The panel's review will proceed in two phases—a public information-gathering phase and a policy-option definition and assessment phase within the executive branch.

As part of the first phase, a series of joint seminars will be held in November 1979. The views of various constituencies—including those in the private sector—will be exchanged. Clearly the insights of groups like yours will be essential in this information-gathering process. You can provide input on the very real effects government policies have on day-to-day industrial operations.

Formation of the Review Committee is a vital step toward a reassessment of the far-reaching effects of government regulatory policies. The promise of this effort is underlined in the rationale for the committee's establishment: "Innovation provides a basis for the Nation's economic growth"; and "Federal policies have a profound impact on the innovation process." This is certainly a more realistic statement than some we have grown accustomed to hearing.

The importance of a relatively stable overall rate of innovation to a free-enterprise economy has long been recognized, and a significant reduction of innovative activity is a major contributor to a slowed and eventually stagnant economic picture. Statistics comparing the United States economy with the economies of other industrialized nations are all too familiar. The United States balance of payments in 1978, for example, reflects a $43.8 billion overall trade deficit. While it is generally assumed that oil imports are the chief cause of our economic woes, we can actually attribute at least $18.4 billion of that total to trade in manufactured goods.

The consequences—rampant domestic inflation and dollar devaluation, to name just two—are of paramount significance to our nation. The ill effects of both must be alleviated if we are to regain our formerly commanding position in the world community. By contrast with our $18.4 billion deficit in trade in manufactured goods, Japan enjoyed a $63.6 billion trade surplus in 1977.

It seems clear that current policies are not establishing economic stability and competitiveness in world trade, nor a continued growth of technological innovation. However, we are becoming increasingly aware of the problem. Policy-makers at all levels of government are beginning to recognize the critical need for answers to the questions we have about the impact of federal regulation on American innovation and invention. As a result of such attention, our awareness of concrete actions to deal with these problems is gradually but steadily sharpening.

Since the automobile plays such a dominant role in our national society and economy, it is particularly necessary to consider the future effect on innovation in formulating the policies that affect it. Just as government actions have had a large influence on the development of the automobile transportation system in times past—in areas such as highway construction, vehicle safety standards, emissions control, and fuel economy—so will future government actions continue to determine important characteristics of the automobile. The congressional Office of Technology Assessment is currently conducting a study of policy options concerning the future of the automobile, as it touches on the areas of energy, environment, safety, mobility, and cost.

The price of fuel is bound to increase. Each year as cars with poor gas mileage are scrapped and replaced by more fuel-efficient models, the annual gas savings will grow, reaching almost 10 billion gallons by 1985 over what might have been expected if the average fuel economy of new cars remained at the 1980 level. Moreover, the dismal prophesy that the

1981-to-1984 standards were likely to force the American driver into cramped, four-seat subcompacts appears to be incorrect.

What we don't know, however, is how significant the effects of innovation-related regulation may be on the export of United States technology and domestic industrial activity. We need to consider how government policies with respect to industrial R&D may undermine United States industry. The problem arises when foreign manufacturers, because of relative freedom from the restrictions of government regulation, are able to provide either more timely or cheaper versions of what began as American technology.

The topic of this discussion was to be "Technology, Government, and the Future of the Automobile Industry." If I have digressed a bit from that specific subject, it is only because of my belief that each of the factors I have touched upon is a vital component of the complex relationship between the goals and objectives of private industry and those of our nation as a whole.

I have attempted to convey our need to understand better how various policies affect the innovative process. It is clear that the innovators are the only ones who can provide those who make government policy with the hard data upon which to base our actions. Thus, it is important to incorporate the industrial viewpoint in our reassessment of policies, which may needlessly interfere with innovation in an effort to address legitimate federal concerns.

A clear definition of our problems represents the first constructive step toward their solution. We are beginning to take that step. Our hope now lies in the fact that we are and have always been a nation of innovators. We can surely work together, as we have done in the past, to attain individual as well as national goals, limited only by the reaches of our creativity and the endurance of our efforts.

MAKING AUTOMOBILE REGULATION WORK: POLICY OPTIONS AND A PROPOSAL

Douglas H. Ginsburg, *Harvard Law School*

In the last dozen years, the American automobile has become an intensively regulated consumer product, perhaps second only to drugs in the degree to which public policy determines the nature of the product. Its size, shape, performance, and consequently its price are no longer determined by market forces alone but also by federal regulatory requirements imposed in the interest of safety, pollution control, and fuel conservation. It is not surprising, therefore, that the relationship between the automobile manufacturing companies and their federal regulators is most often one of mutual wariness and suspicion and occasionally is one of distrust and resentment. Indeed, the industry and its regulators are almost continually in litigation over major regulatory decisions and their enforcement.

Meanwhile, safety, pollution, and fuel conservation timetables have had to be revised several times. Even when regulatory schedules have been met, doubts have arisen as to whether particular automobile models actually met the standards under which they were approved. And in 1977 it seems that the industry recalled—voluntarily or by order of the government safety agency—more cars than it sold. Not surprisingly, the public wants to know, and the policy-makers need to know: Is the industry deliberately thwarting the regulatory effort? Or is the regulatory system promising the public more than the industry can deliver with every good-faith effort? Who, in other words, is frustrating whom?

In the present policy environment, these questions cannot be answered. Responsibility cannot be determined, so that if automobile regulators and manufacturers are like other mortals, then both are free to pursue their self-interest under the mantle of the public interest: The regulators can substitute facile recrimination for practical regulation;

and the industry can concentrate on litigation instead of technological innovation, which is even more expensive and uncertain than a lawsuit.

Looking to the future, in which the government is sure to demand even safer, cleaner, and more fuel-efficient vehicles,[1] the question is whether we must expect more of the same. I think it is safe to predict that so long as the government's regulatory strategies remain unchanged, the path toward what Dr. Richard John has called a "socially efficient vehicle"[2] will remain a bumpy one. No one would consider that a happy prospect, and practically everyone (including myself) is ready with advice.

This essay briefly analyzes four strategic prescriptions that have been proposed by one or another participant in or observer of the process of regulating automobiles: (1) The use of taxes or subsidies to influence consumers' automobile purchasing decisions; (2) breaking up the automobile companies in order to enhance competition in the industry; (3) moving from state to federal chartering of the corporations that make automobiles, in order better to enforce compliance with regulation; and (4) to the same end, placing public representatives on the boards of directors of those corporations. The first two, I will argue, face an insurmountable practical bar; the second, third, and fourth suffer from fatal errors of logic. My own proposal, set out herein, is (5) for the federal government (i) to become significantly involved in the sponsorship of private-sector research into and development of automotive technologies; (ii) to increase the incentives for such research into and development of products or processes that can be required of automobile manufacturers in the interest of a socially efficient vehicle; and, specifically, (iii) to do so by holding "innovation competitions" along lines proposed below.

THE NATURE OF THE PROBLEM

In the model of a well-ordered or efficient market, producers and consumers bear the full costs and realize the full benefits of their production and consumption activities. Under this ideal condition, all resources are allocated efficiently, i.e., to their most-valued use. In most real-world markets, however, some of the costs of economic activity are borne and some of the benefits are realized by persons other than the direct parties to market transactions; they are externalized. This divergence between the social and the individual costs and benefits of

---

1. The Secretary of Transportation announced late in 1978 that the government will require a fleet fuel economy average of "something like 50" mpg "before the new century." (Present law requires an average of 27.5 mpg in 1985.) See *Wall Street Journal*, Dec. 6, 1978, p. 3, col. 2.

2. John, et al., "Mandated Fuel Economy Standards as a Strategy for Improving Motor Vehicle Fuel Economy," Ch. 3 *infra*.

engaging in an activity results in a misallocation of resources. When costs are externalized, people tend to engage in an activity to a greater extent than allocative efficiency would warrant; the opposite is true when benefits are externalized. To the extent that automobiles pollute and the users of automobiles are not charged for their pollution of the atmosphere, automobiles fit the case of a classic externality-producing activity.

Similarly, it is not difficult to see that automobile fuel consumption also imposes costs on parties other than the individual motorist. In the case of fuel consumption the externality is our national dependence upon imported oil.[3] Because this dependence has adverse foreign policy and national defense consequences, it has become a part of our national policy to decrease the level of fuel consumed by automobiles.

Automobile accidents also produce substantial externalities, although the linkage of the product market to the externality is not as obvious as it is in the case of pollution or fuel consumption.[4] This is because many of the costs of accidents are indeed borne by the parties to them. Motorists are injured and their vehicles are damaged in accidents, and motorists generally incur the costs of carrying accident-related insurance. Consequently, they have strong and visible economic incentives to avoid accidents and to mitigate the harm caused by accidents by investing in safety, that is, by driving carefully, and by using safety equipment.[5] It remains nonetheless true that major acci-

---

3. The alternative argument that automobile fuel consumption should be lowered simply because oil is an exhaustible resource is effectively debunked in Goldmuntz, "The Public Interest in Auto Fuel Efficiency," in 2 *Automobile Fuel Efficiency* 103 (M. Meader, Ed., Mitre Corp., 1978).

4. See generally G. Calabresi, *The Costs of Accidents* (Yale Univ. Press, 1970).

5. It is often asserted that automobile buyers and users systematically underinvest in accident avoidance—for example, by failing to use safety belts, which they could use at a seemingly trivial cost (inconvenience, delay) to themselves. This is said to be explained on the ground that people are not able accurately to calculate the expected value of a great harm (injury, death) that has a very low probability of occurring. See, for example, Kunreuther, "Limited Knowledge and Insurance Protection," 24 *Public Policy* 227 (1976); Robertson, *Urban Area Safety Belt Use in Automobiles with Starter-Interlock Belt Systems: A Preliminary Report*, Insurance Inst. for Highway Safety (1974); Tversky and Kahneman, "Judgment Under Uncertainty: Hueristics and Biases," 185 *Science* 1124 (1974). Insofar as this would provide a rationale for safety regulation, it is purely paternalistic: The state "knows better" than the citizen what is in the citizen's "true" self-interest. Paternalistic arguments are rarely able, by themselves, to justify policy in our system of government, however, because citizens (i.e., voters) are offended by them. Nor is extensive paternalism within the constitutional police power of the state; exceptions are noteworthy indeed for their narrowness. E.g., State v. Pack, __ Tenn. __, 527 S.W.2d 99 (1975), *cert. denied*, 424 U.S. 954 (1976) (snake-handling may be prohibited to protect a consenting party); 21 U.S.C. § 353(b) (1) (prescription may be required for purchase of certain drugs). Of the several courts that have upheld laws requiring motorcyclists to wear helmets, all appear to have founded their decision upon the

dent costs are imposed upon others: (1) Most personal injury victims are not fully compensated, whether they sue or settle, because they must bear their own legal costs; (2) some of the drivers involved in accidents are financially irresponsible or are not apprehended; (3) motorists are not generally charged for the costs they impose upon public services (e.g., police time) or to public property (e.g., roads, guardrails); (4) automobile accident victims consume medical resources provided at public expense; and perhaps most important, (5) the insurance premiums paid by motorists are not fully experience-rated and cannot practically be individualized, so that some of the costs of an accident are shifted permanently from the motorists involved to the class of insured motorists.

When significant costs such as these are externalized from the producers and consumers of the activity of motoring to society at large, there are only two types of societal or governmental policy responses possible:[6] One type of policy seeks to cause the externalized costs to be reinternalized to the parties; the other seeks to prohibit the externality from arising in the first instance. The choice between these alternative strategies is illustrated in the debate over fees versus standards for automotive pollutants.

In the case of pollution, the externalized costs of the activity could be reinternalized and borne by the parties engaged in automobile use by imposing a per-unit tax upon emissions, with the tax set to reflect the social cost of the externality. The full social cost of using one type of automobile that pollutes more than another would thus be reflected in the total cost, inclusive of the tax, to the private user of that automobile. The more polluting a car is, the more expensive it would be to use, and the less it would be used. Privately made decisions in this environment would lead us back to the optimal relationship between polluting and

---

potential for injury to others—usually other drivers, who could be distracted by the injury to the motorcyclist, see, e.g., State v. Mele, 103 N.J. Super. 353, 247 A.2d 176 (1968), or the state fisc, which will bear some of the medical and welfare costs of such injuries; see, e.g., Simon v. Sargent, 346 F. Supp. 277 (D. Mass.), *aff'd,* 409 U.S. 1020, 93 S. Ct. 463, 34 L. Ed. 2d 312 (1972). The few courts that have refused to indulge such heroic arguments for the existence of an externality found that the helmet laws were meant only to protect the wearer, and therefore held them unconstitutional. E.g., People v. Fries, 42 Ill. 2d 446, 250 N.E.2d 149 (1969). Consequently, I regard the paternalistic argument for automobile safety regulation as a makeweight. If safety regulation is justifiable, it must be upon externality grounds such as those instanced in the text.

6. In principle, there is also the possibility of governmental inaction, which would be indicated only if no affirmative governmental policy were cost-justified, i.e., if neither type of response discussed in the text would reduce the deadweight loss from the inefficiency of the externality by an amount greater than its administrative costs and any offsetting efficiency losses it would create. I have disregarded this possibility in deference to the obvious fact that United States policy-makers do not believe it obtains, that judgment seems intuitively plausible, and there is no independent empirical or analytical foundation for challenging it.

driving various types of automobiles, for the divergence between private and social costs would have been eliminated. Reciprocally, the purchase or use of the less-polluting automobile could be subsidized, again affecting consumer choices so as to bring about, if the subsidy is set correctly, a socially optimal level of the polluting activity.[7]

Such a system can claim two very important virtues. First, private decisions would lead to an efficient market; persons who wished to use the more polluting car would do so, and would pay for the resources—the air as well as the vehicle—they consume. Second, it is administratively straightforward. Once the admittedly difficult task of computing the appropriate tax or subsidy is done, well-established government structures for collecting taxes and disbursing subsidies could be adapted to this purpose.[8]

Applications of this principle of reinternalization through taxes or subsidies to the problems of safety and fuel consumption are just as easy to envision. Automobile manufacturers or drivers might be taxed, for instance, to reflect the costs that will be imposed on the public by accidents due, respectively, to vehicle design or incautious driving. Of course, a tax on fuel to discourage its use and relieve our national dependence upon imported oil is by now a commonplace suggestion; it is the prevailing policy in European countries.

The alternative to reinternalizing costs, controlling externalities directly, is illustrated by our present strategy for reducing air pollution from automobiles: Standards or tolerable maxima are set by a regulatory agency and automobile manufacturers are prohibited from selling cars that do not conform to the standards. This command-and-control strategy is also embodied in our approach to fuel economy and safety. In the former case, "corporate average fuel economy" standards have been set, and the manufacturer is required to meet them, under penalty of paying a fine for failing to do so. Similar performance standards are set in the area of safety, taking the form of a requirement, for example, that the vehicle be able to withstand an impact of x without sustaining occupant impact in excess of y; or, in a further extension, detailed design specifications may be laid down stating, for example, that the vehicle shall have seatbelts with webbing of a minimum width, or that a child-seating system have a head restraint of a specified height that varies with the maximum weight of the children for whom it is recommended.[9]

---

7. See Polinsky, *Notes on the Symmetry of Taxes and Subsidies in Pollution Control*, Discussion Paper, No. 515 (Harvard Inst. of Economic Research, 1970), and sources there reviewed.

8. Lawrence White's essay, Ch. 7, *infra*, more fully develops the case for a tax approach to pollution control in the specific context of automotive emissions.

9. See Federal Motor Vehicle Safety Standard (FMVSS) 209, Seat Belt Assemblies, 49 C.F.R. § 571.209-S4.2(a) (Width); FMVSS 213, Child Seating Systems, *ibid.* at § 571.213-S4.6 (Head Restraint).

The consequences of this command-and-control approach are familiar enough. Meeting the requirements adds costs that must be recovered either in the price of the vehicle, as when mandated safety or pollution control equipment must be carried, or in its attractiveness to consumers, as when cars must be made lighter and smaller in the interest of fuel economy. That is unobjectionable, of course, insofar as it reflects merely the reallocation of costs that had previously been imposed upon others. It is also understood, however, that in contrast to the reinternalization approach, all consumers' choices will be limited: One cannot pay more in order to avoid the requirements even if one would be willing to pay enough to compensate others fully for the resulting externalities—a clear welfare loss imposed now upon parties rather than strangers to the activity, but no less a loss to society for that. Furthermore, the administrative effort needed to establish command-and-control standards, monitor manufacturers, and certify that the regulated product conforms with the standards is almost certainly more costly than would be an apparatus to set and administer a tax or subsidy. Again, society is worse off.

The legislature's decisions to regulate automobile externalities by a command-and-control strategy, rather than a reinternalization strategy, cannot be attributed to ignorance of the contrasts I have mentioned. On the contrary, Congress has repeatedly and consciously chosen the command-and-control approach because it rejected some of the collateral consequences that would have flowed from a tax or subsidy approach. In the case of fuel consumption, the policy debate in Congress expressly took note of and rejected the tax approach because of its regressive distributive consequences:[10] The tax approach to pollution control has long been excoriated by editorial writers as a "license to pollute,"[11] which has ensured its political unpopularity,[12] whatever its efficiency advantages. *A fortiori* in the area of safety, it may simply have been unthinkable, at least in public, to talk in terms of a tax on, rather than a prohibition of, cars with poor safety designs; nor, it seems, would the public tolerate being fined (taxed) for incautious behavior such as driving without using a seat belt.[13]

There are, however, certain additional features of the command-and-control strategy that, as applied to automobile regulation, may not

---

10. The House voted 345 to 72 against the tax approach contained in H. R. No. 6860, 94th Cong., 1st Sess. (1975).
11. B. Ackerman, et al., *The Uncertain Search for Environmental Quality* 276–278 (Free Press, 1974).
12. White, "Effluent Charges as a Faster Means of Achieving Pollution Abatement," 24 *Public Policy* 111, 120–123 (1976) emphasizes congressional disinterest in the tax approach but establishes at the same time explicit consideration thereof.
13. Congress does not seem to have considered the possibility of subsidizing the purchase of safety-related but optional equipment.

16
Government Technology and the Automobile

have been anticipated but whose relevance can hardly be denied in the light of the last dozen years' experience. The first is that products are being required to incorporate technologies that simply do not exist at the time that the requirements are established. Before the advent of regulation, there was no incentive for a manufacturer of automobiles to develop pollution-control technologies, fuel-economizing technologies, or safety features for which, by hypothesis, there was no market demand. On the contrary, to the extent that the automobile could be built so as to externalize the costs of its use, and thereby shift the costs from consumers to society at large, a rational producer would do that.

This is clearest in the case of pollution control. A pollution-control system adds to the price of the vehicle and, at least in the state of technology as it then was, would also have cost the consumer in terms of the car's performance. Similarly, in the case of fuel efficiency, no individual consumer had any incentive to incur costs in order to lessen the nation's dependence upon imported oil by some infinitesimal degree, and therefore neither did any manufacturer. In the case of safety, motorists could express their desire for self-protection—by using seat belts, driving safely, perhaps buying an imported car that specialized in marketing safety—without concern for the control of externalities. A safety-conscious consumer would, for example, be more concerned with sharp protuberances in the interior than on the exterior of the car; or he might use studded snow tires, which provide better traction at the expense of the taxpayers who pay the costs of road maintenance. Moreover, even if motorists systematically undervalued self-protection, businessmen (like economists) would have accepted consumer preferences as a given; their task was to discover and to satisfy, not to alter preferences. Consequently, the technology needed for improved safety, fuel economy, and emissions control did not exist at the advent of regulation. And, to paraphrase Voltaire, if the technology did not exist, it would be necessary to invent it.[14]

The technology-forcing feature of automobile regulation was not merely a transitional phenomenon, however; it is inherent in the nature of the case. Regulation has taken a gradualist, progressive approach, but at any given time, the manufacturers are being required to develop for future use an improvement not extant at the moment. (Indeed, if it did exist, it would be required at the time.) This is reflected in the annual fuel-economy standards of the Energy Policy and Conservation Act (EPCA)[15] and the percentage-reduction goals, set out in 1970 Amendments to the Clean Air Act,[16] within which the Administrator of the Environmental Protection Agency (EPA) is to establish intermediate steps. In the safety field, the National Highway Traffic Safety Adminis-

---

14. "Si Dieu n'existait pas, il faudrait l'inventer" ("If God did not exist, it would be necessary to invent him"), Voltaire, *Epitres*, xcvi.
15. Public Law No. 94-163, § 502; 15 U.S.C. § 2002.
16. 42 U.S.C. § 7521(a)(3)(A)(ii).

tration (NHTSA) may not only set progressively higher standards for achievement along a particular axis, it may move to increasingly more intractable subject areas for regulation—from the strength of door locks, for example, to occupant protection under a series of evermore rigorous conditions.[17] In short, the nature of automobile regulation has placed the regulator always at the vanguard of technology, so that insisting on increasingly stringent regulation always entails requiring the industry to innovate in order to comply. Automobile regulation differs in this respect from other areas of product regulation subject to a command-and-control regime. Food and drug law or building codes, for example, if they do not actually freeze in present technology, are certainly not directed towards its replacement with superior forms.[18]

The second and related way in which automobile regulation faces a special challenge in pursuing the command-and-control strategy is that it applies to an industry that is at once highly concentrated and almost unimaginably large and important in the American economy.

The implications of concentration for automobile regulation are much like the implications for competition. Because there are so few firms, collusion among them cannot be ruled out on the grounds that the difficulty of coordination and the risks of detection would be preclusive.[19] Just as consumers can never really be assured that the product of a concentrated industry is, in price and quality, the product of competition, regulators can never be assured that the concentrated industry is not colluding in presenting a uniformly pessimistic view of the possibilities for technological innovation to meet regulatory goals.[20] Also, as in a product market with administered prices, the firms may be in tacit rather than actual collusion,[21] simply following the industry leader in developing technology or taking a position on regulation. It is to the industry's advantage, after all, to defeat or delay the cost reallocation that regulation is intended to bring about, although the firms may find

---

17. Compare FMVSS 206, 49 C.F.R. § 571.206 (Door Locks and Door Retention Components) with FMVSS 208, *ibid.* at § 571.208 (Occupant Crash Protection).

18. An analogous situation would be presented if drug regulators required drug manufacturers constantly to improve the safety and efficacy of their products (faster cures, fewer side effects) and threatened fines-per-sale or outright bans on drugs that failed to meet the regulators' schedules for improvement.

19. See Stigler, "A Theory of Oligopoly," 72 *Journal of Political Economy* 44 (1964); cf Nutter and Moore, "A Theory of Competition," 19 *Journal of Law and Economics* 39 (1976).

20. Thus, in the consent decree entered in United States v. Automobile Mfr. Ass'n., Inc., CCH Trade Cas. 72,907 (C.D. Calif. 1969), the government procured a term prohibiting the automobile manufacturers from filing joint statements on emission and safety standards before government agencies for ten years.

21. See R. Posner, *Antitrust Law: An Economic Perspective* 39–55 (University of Chicago Press, 1976); cf Turner, "The Definition of Agreement Under the Sherman Act: Conscious Parallelism and Refusals to Deal." 75 *Harvard Law Review* 655 (1972).

it politic to deny this. The denial is not credible, however, for despite the public concern for cleaner air, national oil independence, or the publicly borne costs of accidents, regulation has not changed any individual consumer's incentive to avoid the costs associated with achieving a socially efficient vehicle. Manufacturers, therefore, still have an incentive to contain the effects of regulation in order to serve consumer preferences.

Regulators cannot *know* that there is no conspiracy to thwart their efforts. Both the motive and the means exist. When they encounter frustrations in their efforts to induce innovations from the industry, therefore, it is only logical for them to wonder, sometimes aloud, whether there may not be at least a tacit agreement among firms to resist. This natural tendency to be suspicious may be reinforced by the regulators' need to give the public and Congress some explanation for their failures. "Bad man" theories have always had political appeal: They are simpler and more intelligible to the public than arguments about the limitations of science and technology or an admission that the regulators do not know when, or even whether, progress is possible because such progress is dependent upon innovations yet to be achieved. The public may well reject such statements as self-serving or an indication that the industry has captured the agencies that regulate it. This is even more likely now that the public has become accustomed to scientific progress as a way of life. In the popular mind, it seems, the space flight program demonstrated that with money and the will to succeed, any technical feat required by public policy can be accomplished. (The present extravagant effort to find a cure for cancer is another example of the consequences of this.) Furthermore, the daily press has reported that business people at very high levels in other industries have been willing to corrupt political processes at home as well as abroad in the pursuit of profits. It is not hard to see, therefore, how even earnest regulators might come to accuse the industry of doing less than it could to make technological progress toward a socially efficient vehicle and of falsely maintaining, in the meanwhile, that it is acting in good faith to build cleaner, safer, more efficient vehicles. No one can know who is right; there is no way, at present, to break the circle of charge and denial and countercharge.

The incentives at work are thus conducive to conflicts, and concentration in the automobile industry assures that result. The conflict is further exacerbated by the size and importance of the industry to the economy.[22] The government cannot credibly threaten to impose severe sanctions when the industry fails to meet a standard. To prohibit a single domestic firm from marketing nonconforming vehicles would (1) concentrate the market further in the remaining hands; and, if it is one of the big three firms, (2) have unacceptable consequences for the

---

22. See, for example, "As General Motors Goes, How Goes the Nation?", 8 *National Journal Reps.*, Jan. 3, 1976, p. 2.

national economy.[23] Therefore, the industry has not only the motive and the means to resist, it also has a degree of immunity from prosecution. Since both the industry and the government know that the Draconian sanctions now provided by law cannot be used, the industry may be readier to resist regulation, but whether it does so or not, the regulators' suspicions are raised yet another notch.

WHAT IS TO BE DONE

As can be seen from the foregoing analysis, some of the most familiar proposals for improving automobile regulation are simply inapposite to the externality and incentive structures of the problem. The tax or subsidy approach would be apposite, but it has been rejected by Congress, largely upon distributive and political grounds. Nothing that has happened since that decision was taken suggests that it would be fruitful now to reopen the debate between such a reinternalization approach and the command-and-control regulatory approach that was actually adopted. I will confine my review, therefore, to policies that are consistent with the present regulatory framework and are intended only to make it work better.

Deconcentration of the Industry

Breaking up the three major automobile companies into a larger number of smaller firms in order to enhance competition in the industry is a suggestion that long antedates the regulatory era of the automobile;[24] it is now being proposed as an antidote to the industry's perceived resistance to regulation.[25] Deconcentration of the industry would certainly reduce, if not remove, the basis on which regulators might plausibly be concerned about express or tacit cooperation among the regulatees to resist the development of new technologies for a socially efficient vehicle. That might in turn reduce the acrimony in the government-industry relationship, but it does nothing substantive to reduce pollution or to increase fuel economy and safety levels. Indeed, it would probably

---

23. Note that a less severe sanction, such as a fine levied for each nonconforming vehicle sold would, to the extent that it resulted in higher vehicle prices, have the same effect as a tax. Since the explicit tax approach to inducing technological innovation was rejected on distributional grounds, so must be the implicit tax approach represented by fines that could plausibly be imposed and thus credibly be threatened.
24. L. White, *The Automobile Industry Since 1945* 279 (Harvard Univ. Press, 1971).
25. See, for example, *Hearings on S. 1167, The Industrial Reorganization Act, Before the Subcomm. on Antitrust and Monopoly of the Senate Comm. on the Judiciary*, 93rd Cong., 2d Sess. (1974), pp. 1,841–1843, 1866–1867 (Statement of Bradford C. Snell), 2125–2126 (Statement of Stanley E. Boyle); White, "A Proposal for Restructuring the Automobile Industry," 7 *Antitrust Law and Economics Review* 89, 98, 101 (1975).

inhibit the achievement of those regulatory goals. If an industry of smaller, more numerous firms would in fact be more competitive, then each firm's incentives to satisfy individual *consumers'* preferences would be even greater than it now is; this would tend to make compliance with *regulatory* demands expressing a collective choice more, not less, difficult to obtain.

On the other hand, the government's threat to impose severe sanctions would become more credible, as they already are in the intensely competitive industries, such as food manufacturing or securities brokerage, that are subject to regulation in the quality of the products or services they sell. If there were a dozen or more automobile firms with comparable shares of the market, any one of them might plausibly be prohibited from selling nonconforming automobiles. That, however, presumes that the others do obtain the necessary technology to meet standards that were imposed before the technology existed. Where would it come from?

No one firm would have much of an incentive to develop new technologies unless assured that it would be allowed to capture market share while its nonconforming competitors remained unable to market their products. Insofar as the new technology is not a patentable device or process, there will be literally no incentive to invest in its development. Even if the innovation is patentable, however, it is not realistic to think that a patent monopoly on a device that lowers emission levels or improves fuel efficiency or safety could tolerably be extended to create a monopoly on the manufacture of automobiles. To prevent that happening, the patentee would undoubtedly be required to license use of the patented device to its competitors for a reasonable royalty. In such circumstances, a risk-averse or risk-neutral firm might well prefer not to undertake the necessary research and development at all, but rather become a licensee and pay the standard royalty if and when some other firm does indeed invent the technology (and its use becomes mandated).

In addition to being analytically unsound, deconcentration of the automobile industry would face great institutional and practical barriers. The antitrust laws now in force have never been interpreted by the courts to authorize the government to dismember firms simply because they are large or because the market in which they deal is concentrated.[26] New legislation would be required,[27] and even if it were forthcoming, I think a previous commentator is correct that "any proceeding to deconcentrate an industry by reorganizing the major firms into smaller units would probably be cumbersome, protracted,

---

26. Turner, "The Scope of Antitrust and Other Economic Regulatory Policies," 82 *Harvard Law Review* 1207, 1217 (1969).

27. For proposals for additional legislation, see Note, "The Industrial Reorganization Act: An Antitrust Proposal to Restructure the American Economy," 73 *Columbia Law Review* 635 (1973).

and indeed unmanageable."[28] In the case of the automobile industry such a proceeding could well outlive us all.

Federal Chartering

The recurring proposal that large industrial corporations be chartered by the federal rather than the various state governments has achieved renewed interest among law reformers in recent years.[29] I propose here to examine the idea only insofar as it is now being advanced with particular application to the automobile industry, i.e., as a potential solution to the problems that federal regulators have encountered in coaxing the automobile industry toward the production of socially more efficient vehicles.

At present, each state's corporation laws establish a set of formal requirements that must be met by those wishing to receive a charter to do business as a corporation with limited liability. In the formal model underlying all of these laws, the shareholders, who contribute the capital, own and ultimately direct the affairs of the corporation. The management are their hired employees and the board of directors are their representatives, responsible for overseeing management's performance. Whatever the particular business of the corporation, it is assumed that its ultimate legitimate purpose is maximizing profit in the interests of the shareholders. Both management and the directors are obliged by law to pursue this end,[30] although they are protected by a "business judgment" rule allowing them broad discretion in their choice of methods and business decisions.[31] Shareholders elect the directors who, in turn, appoint the managers. Shareholders may thus oust the directors, and by a sufficient majority can make certain types of decisions directly.[32]

---

28. R. Posner, n. 21 *supra* at 79.
29. See, for example, R. Nader, et al., *Taming the Giant Corporation* (W. W. Norton & Co., 1976); Henning, "Federal Corporate Chartering for Big Business: An Idea Whose Time Has Come?", 21 *DePaul Law Review* 915 (1972); Schwartz, "A Case for Federal Chartering of Corporations," 31 *Business Lawyer* 1125 (1976); Schwartz, "Federal Chartering of Corporations: An Introduction," 61 *Geo. Law Journal* 71 (1972); cf Cary, "Federalism and Corporate Law: Reflections Upon Delaware," 83 *Yale Law Journal* 663, 705 (1974), which recommends minimum federal standards for state chartering—an idea that President Carter has endorsed. See transcript, Public Citizen Forum, The International Inn, Wash., D.C. (Aug. 9, 1976).
30. See, e.g., Dodge v. Ford Motor Co., 204 Mich. 459, 507, 170 N.W. 668, 684 (1919).
31. H. Henn, *Law of Corporations* 483 (West Publishing Co., 2d ed. 1970).
32. See Chayes, "The Modern Corporation and the Role of Law," *The Corporation in Modern Society* 39 (E. Mason, Ed., Harvard Univ. Press, 1959):

> The analogy between state and corporation has been congenial to American lawmakers, legislative and judicial. The shareholders were the electo-

In the real world of large corporations, the formal model nowhere operates in this fashion. Because of their large numbers and fragmentation, shareholders are generally incapable of acting jointly to express their will; they can only ratify what the directors and managers have done. The directors do not usually appoint the managers but rather are appointed by them, and owe their emoluments to them. This separation of ownership and control leaves the management essentially autonomous, responsible neither to shareholders nor to directors.[33]

There is no necessary physical or functional connection between the place in which a corporation does business or has its headquarters and the state of its incorporation. In fact, approximately one-half of the large industrial corporations in America are chartered by the state of Delaware.[34] In order to maximize its franchise tax receipts, Delaware has competed most aggressively among the states to offer a package of rights and relationships in its corporation law that is attractive to incorporators. The conventional view of this competition among the states is that it constitutes a "race for the bottom," in which each state attempts to offer ever less protection to shareholders and ever more to management, since the managers in fact determine whether to retain or change the company's place of incorporation.[35] Consequently, since the turn of the century every wave of corporate abuses and the calls for reform that inevitably follow them have led to proposals for federal chartering of corporations.[36]

Federal chartering responds to the perceived problem of competition among the states by replacing it with a monopoly in the central government. It does not by itself, however, imply any particular set of rights or obligations. Nonetheless, each particular proposal for federal chartering generally entails some specification of rights and obligations for shareholders, managers, and directors designed to bring the reality of corporate governance into greater conformity with the traditional, or the proponent's own, idealized model for corporate governance. Until

---

rate, the directors the legislature, enacting general policies and committing them to the officers for execution. A judiciary was unnecessary since the state had kindly permitted the use of its own.

33. See generally A. Berle and G. Means, *The Modern Corporation and Private Property* (rev. ed., Harcourt, Brace & World, 1968). This now conventional view is criticized on analytic grounds in Manne, "Some Theoretical Aspects of Share Voting," 64 *Columbia Law Review* 1427 (1964), and is qualified on empirical grounds in M. Eisenberg, *The Structure of the Corporation* 45–51 (Little, Brown and Co., 1976).

34. R. Nader, n. 29 *supra* at 57.

35. See, for example, Cary, "Federalism and Corporate Law," n. 29 *supra*; but cf Winter, "State Law, Shareholder Protection, and the Theory of the Corporation," 6 *Journal of Legal Studies* 251 (1977).

36. The history of the federal chartering proposal is set out in R. Nader, n. 29 *supra* at 65–70.

about 1960, the reformers' ideal model was almost always the traditional "shareholder democracy" model, reflected more or less in the various state corporation laws, including that of Delaware. In the period since 1970, however, it has often been suggested that goals other than profit maximization should also be pursued by corporations; thus was born the "corporate social responsibility" movement. It effected a shift from single-minded concern with the rights and obligations of the parties to the corporation to a new emphasis on the rights of the various publics—consumers, employees, neighbors, etc.—affected by the corporation's activities and the externalities they produce.

Contemporary proposals, including Ralph Nader's book-length version,[37] therefore associate the move to federal chartering with a host of substantive obligations to be imposed upon the corporation itself. In the case of Nader's proposal, for example, federal chartering would entail not only shareholder voting on all major decisions and a redesign of the board of directors, but would also require public disclosure of a host of nonfinancial information concerning occupational safety, employment discrimination, and polluting activities; observance of an employee bill of rights; and dismemberment of corporations in concentrated markets. Criminal penalties would be used against executives and corporations to enforce the proposed Federal Corporate Chartering Act.[38]

According to Nader, federal chartering with these embellishments would bring about "more accountable managers [who] would be far less likely to make the kinds of decisions that have led to irresponsible technology, product dangers, pollution, and monopoly practices."[39] His argument is replete with references to the automobile industry meant to demonstrate a present disregard for product safety, failure to innovate, and a willingness to sponsor public relations campaigns to garner political support for the delay of emission-control standards.

It is impossible, however, to discern the connection between the problems of automobile regulation and the fact that the automobile manufacturers are state-chartered corporations. Whatever failure may be charged to the system of chartering competition among the states, it is limited in scope to the subjects covered by the state corporation laws, namely the rights and obligations of the shareholders, managers, and directors. The idea that, given control over major decisions, shareholders would move their companies toward the production of a socially more efficient vehicle must rest upon the premise that shareholders are not profit-maximizers. There is no reason to suppose, however, that individual shareholders would be any more willing than are individual consumers to set aside self-interest in the name of social responsibility.

---

37. See sources cited at n. 29 *supra*.
38. R. Nader, n. 29 *supra* at 254.
39. *Ibid.* at 254.

Nor is there any logical connection between federal incorporation and the use of disclosure requirements or substantive obligations designed to make managers more accountable to the government. Nader's linkage of them in his proposal confuses the issue. Even with federal chartering, the government would be required, in the case of the automobile companies, to issue administrative directives for the control of pollution, fuel consumption, and accidents in order to prohibit harmful externalities. The corporation would still be required to comply with those directives, although the obligation to comply might be relocated to the corporate charter. But the incentives for (non-)compliance would not have changed. If the move to federal chartering is meant to be an implicit threat to revoke an automobile company's corporate charter, that is no more credible than is the present explicit threat to prohibit one of the major automobile companies from marketing its products for failing to meet applicable standards. Moreover, any less Draconian remedy for noncompliance, such as the large fines advocated by Nader for charter violations, could be administered equally well or poorly regardless of the source of the corporation's charter or of whether the legal obligation involved is to be found in the charter or in other laws.

Board Representation

For almost twenty years, another line of American legal scholarship has urged a departure from, rather than a perfection of, the traditional model of the corporation.[40] Its reasoning begins with the proposition that a variety of interests affected by corporate decisions should be represented in the decision-making process of the corporation, generally on the board of directors.[41] These nonshareholding interests are variously said to consist of the corporation's employees, its suppliers, consumers of its products, the public-at-large, and the local publics in whose communities the corporation has major production facilities. In its most extreme form the proposed scheme of interest representation might actually exclude shareholders from representation on the ground that their connection with the corporation is purely formal, and that they can, through the mechanism of the market for shares, sever that relationship at will.[42]

In the context of automobile regulation, the most frequently heard proposal of this type calls for public (i.e., governmental) representation on the boards of directors of the automobile manufacturers. This would not require any substantial federal intervention into state corporation

---

40. This literature is reviewed in Blumberg, "Reflections on Proposals for Corporate Reform Through Change in the Composition of the Board of Directors: 'Special Interest' or 'Public' Directors," 53 *Boston University Law Review* 547 (1973).
41. *Ibid.* at 549.
42. See Chayes, n. 32 *supra* at 40–41.

laws. Special attention would have to be paid to defining the liability, as well as the authority, of a public director, however.[43]

A governmental representative would have a different and presumably a broader social outlook than his colleagues on the board representing shareholders or incumbent management. Unlike the independent outside director, who is named to the board for his financial or business acumen and who has a legal obligation to help the corporation maximize profits, the public representative on the board would be charged with monitoring the corporation and inducing it to cooperate most fully with the regulatory efforts directed at producing a more socially efficient automobile. This might be accomplished, for example, by allocating more resources to research and development of the new technologies required.

The inducing function of a public director is unlikely to be meaningful in practice, however. So long as public representation is minority representation, it would obviously be outvoted whenever a step toward achievement of regulatory goals is inconsistent with profit maximization. Such a representative would be in a position to argue that a particular decision, if made so as to further the public interest, would also be in the corporation's economic interest. However, instances in which he could persuasively argue a congruence between private and public welfare would be quite exceptional; divergence between them is in the nature of the problem.

The monitoring function is no more likely to be significant.[44] It might be objected that the public director would at least be in a position to "blow the whistle" when the board consciously takes a decision that frustrates the policies at which regulation is directed. Consider, for example, Ford's decision not to modify the allegedly unsafe Pinto design. But, on reflection, we must dismiss even this possibility. Normally, the public member would see the board confronted with close questions of business judgment that may bear ultimately and subtly upon regulatory goals, but he is unlikely to see the board of directors consciously and flagrantly deciding, vurtually conspiring, to thwart those goals. Even if management were to take a blatant decision to oppose the government on a question of safety or pollution control, managers could keep this information from the board of directors and thereby screen the public director away from any knowledge of the decision.[45] Indeed, the Pinto decision instanced above was probably

---

43. See Conard, "Reflections on Public Interest Directors," 75 *Michigan Law Review* 941, 947 (1977).

44. But cf Soderquist, "Toward a More Effective Corporate Board: Reexamining Roles of Outside Directors," 52 *New York University Law Review* 1341, 1357–1363 (1977).

45. See C. Stone, *Where the Law Ends* 131–132 (Harper & Row, 1975). A similar problem was anticipated by the Bullock Committee of Parliament, which recommended that labor unions be given representation on the boards of large

not made at the board level. The experience of the Emergency Loan Guarantee Board, which was created by Congress to administer federal loan guarantees to Lockheed and to investigate the quality of that company's management is consistent with this pessimistic view: They learned nothing of Lockheed's foreign payments practices.[46]

Perhaps the public director could be given legal authority and necessary staff to gain full access to information within the corporation as well as a general warrant to read its documents and question its officials.[47] Such a public director, however, would be a government detective placed within the company. He would function as a compliance officer for the government agencies that are dependent upon the good-faith efforts of the companies to develop new technologies. This role, however, is entirely unrelated to voting representation on the board of directors. If such on-site inspectors are desired at either the board or the operations level, it should be declared openly; inspectors should not be posed as members of the board.

Whether he is meant to be a detective or a director, however, a public representative on the board of (or otherwise within) each of the major automobile companies would not affect the companies' underlying disincentives for limiting cooperation with the regulatory effort. At most the public director might have some persuasive power within the board on close questions. The regulators and their agents on the board could still not know that there is no conscious effort to thwart technological innovations of the desired type. Worse, the whole effort might prove counterproductive if the regular board members feel that they are relieved of any obligation to question management about regulatory compliance beyond the points raised by the public member with that special responsibility, or if the public at large concludes that nothing could be amiss since their representatives would surely have known and publicized the facts.

British firms. In an attempt to ensure that the boards would not be deprived of all significance by formal delegations of power to management or reservations of power by shareholders (e.g., multinational parent companies), the committee specified certain "attributed functions" that the board would have to retain. *Report of Comm. of Inquiry on Industrial Democracy* 77, Cmnd. 6706 (1977). Any attempt to specify *ex ante* the types of information that must go to a board of directors that includes a public representative would be equally necessary but much more difficult, since the relevance of particular information to the general purpose of public board representation—furthering progress toward a socially efficient automobile—would be far from obvious.

46. DeMott, "Reweaving the Corporate Veil: Management Structure and the Control of Corporate Information," 41 *Law and Contemporary Problems* 182, 192–206 (1977).

47. See Stone, n. 45 *supra*. The constitutionality of such an authorization is unclear. The Warrant Clause of the Fourth Amendment applies to places of business in general, but there are exceptions for certain industries, such as liquor and firearms, where the long history of government oversight precludes its proprietors from forming any reasonable expectation of privacy. Marshall v. Barlow's, Inc., 436 U.S. 307, 98 S. Ct. 1816 (1978).

Government Sponsorship of R&D

In recent years policy-makers, economists, and business people have become concerned about the low level at which American industry and government are investing in basic and applied scientific research. Their concern grows out of the perception that the technological innovation that has fueled America's postwar prosperity and assured its international hegemony, both militarily and economically, cannot be expected to continue in the future given the present low level of research activity, measured both in absolute terms and relative to that in other advanced countries. Some observers therefore recommend greater government support for research, including nonmilitary applied research.[48] At the same time, businesses engaged in research-intensive fields are legitimately concerned about the entry of government into applied research relevant to civilian markets. They fear that they will find themselves competing with firms that have had the advantage of government support. They also point out problems that would arise in sorting out the proprietary rights to inventions whose development was arguably supported by both a private industry and the government. The latter problem might be avoided under another proposal for stimulating technological innovation, viz., to change the laws so that private patents may be held on the products of such jointly funded research, thereby increasing the incentive to exploit and commercialize it.[49]

The question here is whether the technologies required to further the policies reflected in automobile regulation might be created more readily if the government involved itself indirectly in the innovation support process through funding to outside contractors. If so, what collateral costs and benefits could be expected from such an involvement?

Such a program would free the regulatory process from dependence upon the research and development efforts of the automobile manufacturers, with two salutary effects. First, of course, it might enhance the rate of innovation in pollution control, fuel efficiency, and safety technologies. This would be likely even if the automobile industry is presently cooperating with the regulatory effort in complete good faith and committing to research and development every dollar with a positive marginal social benefit, notwithstanding the negative private marginal product of the investment. More groups would be involved in research efforts, bringing not just greater financial resources but also more competing imaginations to bear upon the problems.[50] The likelihood that progress will be accelerated by the creation of nonautomobile

---

48. See, for example, *Federal Incentives for Innovation, Hearings Before the Special Subcomm. on Science, Technology, and Commerce of the Senate Comm. on Commerce*, 93rd Cong., 1st Sess. (1973), especially testimony of Professor Kenneth Arrow, p. 2033; testimony of Robert J. Kuntz, pp. 67–87; and testimony of Burt F. Raynes, pp. 94–103.
49. See, for example, H. R. No. 6249, 95th Cong., 1st Sess. (1977).
50. On the relevance of the competitive spur to scientific endeavor, see generally J. Watson, *The Double Helix* (Atheneum, 1968).

industry sources of research is greater still, of course, if the automobile companies are not now giving their all to the effort.

Second, the regulators' worries about industry collusion to delay development of new technoligies would be allayed. The nonautomobile industry research effort would provide a benchmark against which to evaluate the efforts of the automobile industry.[51] If research conducted by those with an incentive to succeed did no better than that of the industry whose self-interest is disserved by technological change, there would be less reason to suspect the industry of recalcitrance, whereas the possibility that the nonautomobile industry efforts might succeed and thus embarrass the industry politically would provide a competitive spur now lacking in the structure of incentives.

Is all this necessary, however, in order to provide a benchmark or to spur competition to innovate? Lawrence White, in his analysis of the present regulatory approach to pollution control, observed that although automobile manufacturers might not make every effort to meet the standards set by EPA, that agency "by setting specific standards . . . gave the parts manufacturers, chemical manufacturers, and catalyst manufacturers a clear incentive to try to develop control systems and parts which they could sell to the automobile manufacturers."[52] Presumably, the same statement could be made now with respect to the incentives of nonautomobile manufacturers to develop fuel-economizing technologies and, in those cases where clear standards are or could be set, safety devices as well.

It is clearly not sufficient, however, to create incentives for the automotive supply and other industries to develop systems "which they could sell to the automobile manufacturers" without also creating incentives, or requirements, for the automobile manufacturers to buy such systems. In the present situation, the automobile companies have no more incentive to purchase than they have to develop new technologies that will enable them to meet regulatory goals, since the effect will in either case be to increase the cost of their product without increasing its attractiveness in the marketplace—as opposed to its attractiveness in the eyes of regulators. Thus, the automobile companies may be counted upon to reject—probably on technical grounds—offers to sell them innovations with little market appeal. The real task facing nonautomobile industry developers of new technologies, therefore, is to sell their innovations not to the automobile companies but to the regulators who are in a position to create a demand for the product by requiring that it be brought on board the automobile.

This has not actually happened to any great extent for a number of

---

51. This is a variant of the argument for government yardstick competition, such as the Tennessee Valley Authority arguably provides for the power industry. See A. Kahn, *The Economics of Regulation* 104–106 (John Wiley & Sons, 1971). It is also a feature of Louis T. Brandeis' 1905 plan for mutual savings banks to compete with the life insurance industry. *Ibid.* at 104, n. 26; see A. Mason, *Brandeis: A Free Man's Life* 152–177 (Viking, 1946).

52. White, "The Auto Pollution Muddle," *The Public Interest* 97, 103 (Summer 1973).

reasons. First, the traditional automotive supply industry is not a likely source of innovation. It is made up in large part of relatively low technology, mass production-oriented firms operating under extreme price competition. As Professor Abernathy has pointed out, these firms must emphasize productivity gains, and "there must be attendant losses in the capability for radical innovations."[53] The traditional suppliers, moreover, are not likely to risk their relationships with the automobile industry by attempting to sell to its regulators a technology or device that the industry considers inimical to its interests. If they should fail, all may be lost. Nor is the traditional supply industry, itself almost entirely unregulated, familiar or comfortable with the ways of Washington. Second, although the nontraditional suppliers that are gravitating toward the automobile industry with new primary materials and electronic substitutes for mechanical systems have greater R&D potential, they are not likely to want to alienate their prospective customers. It is surely safer to satisfy such regulation-induced demands as the industry may have for incremental improvements than to work on developing technologies capable of producing even higher levels of fuel efficiency, pollution control, or safety than are now required and then on attempting to persuade the regulators to require them.

Finally, the uncertainty surrounding such an undertaking as the invention of a product for sale to the regulators is so great that only a highly risk-preferring enterprise would undertake it. This uncertainty has two major components. The first, inherent in the research and development process generally, is the uncertainty attendant to any inventive activity—nothing may come of it. In the regulatory context, however, there is a second element of uncertainty, which is inherent in the political process, and which can cause the demand for a mandated product to be somewhat ephemeral. Consumer demand for a particular product tends to fluctuate, to be sure, sometimes rather sharply, but most often by relatively small year-to-year changes. The supplier of some optional equipment for automobiles, such as fancy wheel covers, does not realistically have to consider that demand will fall to zero next year. Experience to date with mandated products is exactly the contrary, however. In one year the supply industry manufactured 11 million seat belt interlocks; the next year the demand for these was zero because the regulation mandating them had been rescinded and there was no market demand for them. Manufacturers involved with antiskid brakes for trucks and air bags for cars have had the opposite experience, never knowing when or whether gearing up for production was a prudent course. After experience with this type of uncertainty, at least one major supply firm decided as a matter of corporate policy never again to manufacture a mandated automobile product at all.[54]

---

53. W. Abernathy, *The Productivity Dilemma: Roadblock to Innovation in the Automobile Industry* (Johns Hopkins Univ. Press, 1977).
54. This fact was reported by an official of the company at a workshop preparatory to this symposium. Under the rules of the workshop, the company may not be

Why has regulation-based demand been so inconstant? First, it is similar to monopolistic demand; it is all concentrated in one decisional authority. If that authority changes its mind, or the party in power changes, or a court reverses its decision on some procedural ground, the entire demand may be affected at once. Second, the automobile manufacturers have lent their efforts to obtaining delays and reversals of such equipment-mandating decisions as the regulators have made.

As a result, it is not realistic to rely, in the present regulatory environment, upon nonautomobile industry R&D efforts to supply the technological advances upon which the success of the regulatory program depends. Something in this environment must be changed in order to induce substantial investment by those outside the industry in the development of technologies that can then be required of the automobile manufacturers in the interest of a socially efficient vehicle. It is apparent that the direction of the change indicated must be to reduce the uncertainty presently confronting would-be innovators. Only the government is in the position to accomplish this.

A PRELIMINARY PROPOSAL: THE INNOVATION COMPETITION

Government policy may work to encourage R&D investment in either or both of two ways: By reducing the risk associated with failure and/or by increasing the rewards of success. The risk factor may be reduced to the extent that the government underwrites the researcher's investment in the first instance. The rewards of success may be increased by assuring the successful developer of a market for its product or process. In the present context, this means requiring that the automobile manufacturers adopt the innovation and either purchase it directly from the developer or pay a patent royalty or license fee for each vehicle incorporating the innovation.

A government program embodying these approaches (reducing risk, increasing reward) might take the following general form of a research and development competition: An appropriate agency of the government would identify a development goal, expressed either in terms of a performance level to be achieved by any suitable means or by research along a specific path considered to be particularly promising. It would issue a call for research proposals—possibly through informal rulemaking procedures—specifying the research or development goal, the maximum per unit cost of an acceptable innovation,[55] and other appropriate limitations.

---

identified here. For related examples, however, see W. Abernathy, "Innovation and the Regulatory Paradox: Toward a Theory of Thin Markets," Ch. 1, ns. 13–15 *infra*.

55. The articulation of this term, which would clearly be essential, would also force the sponsoring agency explicitly to value desired improvements in mileage, pollution, or safety performance; this, in turn, would require attention to

Support for the more promising proposals would be granted only up to some proportion of a realistic budget, so that each grantee would have some of its own funds invested in the project. Multiple grants would be made to establish competition among the grant recipients—the winner being the one either to meet a particular set of specifications first or to develop the most efficient innovation by a certain deadline. Regulations requiring manufacturers to adopt the first or the best submission, respectively, would then be the subject of an abbreviated, formal rule-making proceeding, so that interested parties (such as the automobile manufacturers, other research competitors, and consumers) could raise relevant objections to adopting the proposed winning innovation. Only two type of objections would be considered relevant, however: (1) Claims that the innovation does not conform to the specifications of the research grant; and (2) claims that the proposal, even if it does conform to the specifications, is technically impracticable for use in the automobile.

Potential entrants in such a competition—which would certainly not exclude the automobile companies—could evaluate the risks and rewards of participation with greater certainty than is possible at present in evaluating whether to undertake a comparable research effort. They would be reasonably assured that *some* proposal meeting the specifications of the competition would win the competition and be incorporated into the regulatory requirements imposed upon all manufacturers for some guaranteed minimum period of time, at a predetermined royalty per vehicle. They could estimate the minimum reward going to the winner on a fairly clear basis by projecting the number of vehicles on which a royalty would be paid. And, they could evaluate their prospects for success in the competition in the light of their own resources and skills, as well as those of the other competitors.

At the same time, the regulators could set the terms of the competition—the percentage and absolute maximum funding it would give the research competitors, the minimum period for which the winner would be assured that its innovation would be required, and the royalty it would be paid—in order to attract no more than an appropriate number of entrants. Clearly, government policy should not induce aggregate investments in R&D that will exceed the aggregate social benefits to be had from exploiting the resulting innovation; that would create an efficiency loss no different from the loss that may now be imposed upon society if the automobile industry makes an underinvestment in R&D directed toward reducing the externalities from automobiles.

This proposal is not without its complications. First, it may be difficult as a practical matter for policy-makers to bind themselves to require the use of the winning innovation if, shortly after a winner is

---

cost-benefit analysis early in the regulatory process, before the agency has become committed to a particular path of development.

determined, someone else should invent a superior product or process. Nonetheless, in order to offset this uncertainty, it might be necessary either to do just that or to incorporate into the terms of the competition a buy-out price that the government would pay the winner for release from the commitment to require its technology.[56]

Second, there are at present a variety of legal obstacles to be removed. The authority of the relevant agencies to fund R&D projects would have to be broadened. The Department of Transportation has only very limited authority in the National Highway Traffic Safety Act to support the development of safety-performance innovations, and it could not be used for this proposal.[57] EPA funds extensive research in the area of emissions control, but, again, under limitations that preclude an effective innovation competition.[58] Only the Department of Energy is authorized to sponsor fuel-economy research,[59] however, and this may not be the best arrangement since it is NHTSA that establishes the fuel economy standards under EPCA. Nor is it clear whether, under government contracting norms, any agency could now meaningfully bind itself in advance to incorporate a winning development into its regulations, much less agree to a buy-out price. The whole scheme might be made impractical, too, if parties making research proposals that are rejected for funding could claim a right to hearing procedures or even judicial review of the decision to reject their proposals. These potential obstacles would have to be removed by positive legislation authorizing the conduct of innovation competitions and limiting judicial review.

Third, some potential improvements in automotive technology might not be patentable under the usual standards for such protection. Therefore, unless the agency holding the competition were granted legal authority to create a de facto patent by requiring payment of royalties to the winner, in the manner described, research proposals tendered in response to its call would be heavily biased toward work

---

56. The alternative, which would create greater uncertainty for potential research competitors, would be for the agency to certify all equipment that meets or exceeds its standards; automobile manufacturers could then choose any certified device. This would have the advantages of flexibility (e.g., different devices might be preferred on different types of automobiles) and, perhaps of price competition. Whether these would exceed the programmatic costs of the resulting uncertainty cannot be known a priori.

57. 15 U.S.C. § 1395(b) (research grants to states, interstate agencies, and nonprofit institutions).

58. EPA appears to be authorized to make air pollution research grants only to "public or nonprofit private" recipients and to individuals. 42 U.S.C. § 7403(b)(3). The special emphasis that Congress directed be given to research and development for the control of automotive pollution is not similarly qualified as to eligible recipients, but grants are limited to $1.5 million. 42 U.S.C. § 7404(a)(2).

59. 42 U.S.C. §§ 5813(2)–(5) (ERDA); 42 U.S.C. § 7151 (transfer to Department of Energy).

that promised to yield a patentable product or process, even where nonpatentable innovations might be more promising from the view of social cost.

Finally, there is some uncertainty in the relevant government policy with respect to patents arising out of government-sponsored research. At present the regulations promulgated under the President's 1971 Statement of Government Patent Policy provide that the government shall "retain" the patent rights[60] to any invention made in the course of work entirely sponsored by the government where, *inter alia*, (1) the invention is intended for "commercial use . . . by the general public" or it "will be required for such use by governmental regulations;" or (2) the invention concerns the "public health, public safety, or public welfare."[61] These provisions are not mandatory where the private contractor is also a substantial sponsor of the research-yielding patentable inventions, but they are still to be followed by each agency "to the extent practicable" even with respect to such co-sponsored or cost-shared research.[62] In "exceptional circumstances" the sponsoring agency may, however, certify that it will "best serve the public interest" for a contractor to retain greater rights than a nonexclusive license in any invention that arises from the contract research.[63] It is not clear what constitutes an exceptional circumstance for this purpose, but it is at least arguable from the analysis of this paper that the public interest in advancing automobile technologies could justify an agency's invoking the exception clause in order to make a competition innovation possible.

CONCLUSION

If this analysis of the underlying problems confronting automobile regulation is accurate, it is necessary to free the regulatory process from its dependence upon the handful of regulated firms for the development of technologies that it is not in the interest of those firms to advance. If other firms in other industries now find it too risky to take up the task, the only alternative to the government's doing the necessary R&D itself—a prospect too uninviting to have been considered here—is to lower the risk and raise the incentives facing the considerable potential sources of innovation outside the automobile industry. I have proposed one method—the innovation competition—for accomplishing this. I do not doubt, that, even if the legal authority could be supplied, imple-

---

60. As Congressman Thornton explains in his contribution to this volume, government-retained patents are "public patents," and like unpatented inventions are available to anyone free of charge.

61. 41 C.F.R. § 1-9.107-3; see Statement of Government Patent Policy, 36 Fed. Reg. 16887 (1971).

62. 41 C.F.R. § 1-9.107-1.

63. *Ibid.* at § 1-9.107-3.

menting the proposal might encounter practical problems that are well beyond my ken. Perhaps it will be attractive enough, however, to warrant our considering what they are and whether they should be overcome.

DISCUSSION

ROBERT MC CABE: We generally agree with Professor Ginsburg's analysis and conclusions on most of the current proposals to make the auto industry work. His proposal for federal sponsorship of R&D by the nonautomobile companies has some merit, as long as the realities and practicalities of mass production are taken into consideration. The proposal to increase incentives for R&D within the firms has some merit, too. General Motors spent $1.3 billion on our R&D efforts last year.

What scares us is who would judge the innovations that come to mind to the federal agency? The government, I am worried, might promote research that would not have significant economic and social benefit. Ginsburg does not develop the problems that government-sponsored innovations could lead to.

I would also be concerned with the cost of government-sponsored R&D. In these inflationary times, any increase in government spending is not desirable and may not be politically acceptable. How this would be funded would be a major concern.

TIMOTHY NULTY: Professor Ginsburg missed something in his analysis. He says there are two basic approaches that the government can take for problems like fuel economy: The prices and taxes market kind of thing, and control. Clearly, Ginsburg prefers prices and taxes. I cannot say that I disagree with him, but they have been ruled out by Congress. One reason why they were voted out is the lack of conviction on the part of politicians and policy-makers that the alleged advantages of the taxing and pricing policies are all that strong. For example, one of the principal advantages which Professor Ginsburg mentions is the ease of administration. In principle, perhaps. But my experience is that this is not all that simple either.

Professor Ginsburg dismissed out-of-hand a number of alternatives to traditional regulation. This was easy for him to do because he considered extremely simple-minded varieties of the alternatives he was considering. For instance, deconcentration. There are, however, more complicated antitrust remedies that are better than simply breaking up companies—remedies that might be very carefully tailored to specific problems. One cannot dismiss these more complex remedies. Similarly for the issues of board representation and federal chartering. While Nader has carried the notion too far, the possibility that certain reforms, carefully designed, might be made easier by chartering major companies is not an intrinsically ridiculous idea.

Professor Ginsburg left out one alternative—improving consumer information. It is a variety of regulation and it is an alternative to direct command-and-control. The FTC would argue that it is a form of market incentive policy.

GINSBURG: I did fail—intentionally—to mention the role of consumer information. If consumer preferences are different from the regulator's goals, consumer information can *conflict* with the larger regulatory aims. Consumer information is fine when you are trying to accomplish a consumerist goal but is not appropriate to a regulatory goal such as the control of an externality.

Mr. McCabe's concern over the cost of government-sponsored R&D is an example of what Kirk Hanson calls "putting a new face on the issue."[1] Regarding the other problem Mr. McCabe raised—who would decide which projects are worth funding?—those kinds of decisions are being made right now by people we can all identify. Someone has to decide if passive restraints are going to be required and what kind. It is the same

---

1. See K. Hanson's essay in Ch. 3, *infra*.

MC CABE: Let me suggest that that decision-making process could be improved.

OIL INDUSTRY: Concerning Professor Ginsburg's proposal—to stimulate the development of technology via the support of research outside the automotive industry—once the emission standards were mandated by Congress, there was a great deal of innovation, both within and outside the industry, to meet these standards. The reason firms were innovative was that they were competing for profit; this in itself was a great stimulus. As we look to the near future we will see a car that is essentially pollution-free. Once the standards are there the normal competitive process can be quite effective in stimulating innovation.

In the fuel economy situation, we see much innovation not only within the auto industry, but on the part of suppliers.

Ginsburg seems to recognize the adversarial aspect of the relationship that this kind of federal sponsorship of research would further or foster. This is not the time for further sharpening of divisions between regulators and industry; this is a time for healing and coming together in order for the full innovative process to work and to make us more competitive in the world markets.

The aircraft industry provides us with one good model for this kind of cooperative approach—the direct sponsorship by the government with a particular manufacturer of a piece of research. For military purposes, specific contracts were made to achieve advanced aircraft. In this, there was a real net benefit: To the particular manufacturer receiving the contract, as well as to the public via the application of that technology to civilian aircraft. As a result, the United States aircraft industry has achieved a lead position in the world marketplace.

INNOVATION AND THE REGULATORY PARADOX: TOWARD A THEORY OF THIN MARKETS*

William J. Abernathy, *Harvard Business School*

The automobile industry has recently become the single most regulated industry and, by aggregate indicators, the new partnership between government and industry is working successfully. At the same time, much evidence suggests that the rate of innovation and technological progress in the United States automobile industry has stepped up sharply in the present decade, reaching its highest level since World War II.[1] This is a response to the recent competitive and regulatory environment in the industry: The market is now more sensitive to fuel economy; there is heightened international competition; and perhaps most significantly, intense government regulation is forcing technological change. It is important to ask, however, whether the rate and nature of current progress are sufficient to meet the energy challenge that faces us.

A recent appraisal of the energy picture suggests that energy planners have placed unlimited faith in the innovative abilities of the firms within the transportation industry to achieve "an absolute reduction in gasoline use, from 4.5 million barrels per day of oil equivalent in 1972 to 3.8 in 2000, due to improvements in fuel economy, and increased use of diesel engines."[2] This technological challenge is compounded by the

---

* Appreciation is expressed to Lawrence Ronan, for his assistance in writing and research on this essay. The discussion is based in part on an unpublished paper, "Government Procurement and the Stimulation of New Automotive Technologies," by Michael Contrarino, a Harvard graduate student. Support for this research was provided in part by DOT and by the Division of Research, Harvard University Graduate School of Business.

1. W. J. Abernathy, *The Productivity Dilemma* (Johns-Hopkins Univ. Press, 1978).
2. C. Wilson, "Energy: Global Prospects 1985–2000," *Report of the Workshop on Alternative Energy Strategies* (McGraw-Hill, 1977).

increasingly stringent standards for passenger safety and pollution from automobile exhausts, which often impose requirements that offset fuel economy gains.

Are the initiatives of the federal government and the industry really likely, then, to bring about the major innovation we will need if the impending liquid fuel crisis materializes? The purpose of this discussion is to examine the recent pattern of government initiatives and industry response to determine what these might portend for future innovation. We conclude from this analysis that strategies for dealing with the impending energy crisis will require new policies in government regulation and in industry's research and development.

PROGRESS IN THE 1970s

Industrial expenditures on research and development in the automotive industry have followed an upward trend in both current and inflation-adjusted dollars, in sharp contrast to research and development in the United States economy as a whole. Table 1-1 shows this steady increase in automotive industry R&D allocation from 1967 through 1976, as well as the increasing percentage of automotive R&D funding in the nation's total R&D spending. A brief review of achievements in fuel economy, pollution control, and safety suggests that tangible progress is associated with these rising R&D expenditures.

Fuel Economy

In response to market incentives, federally mandated fuel economy standards, and voluntary efforts of the automobile companies, the average fuel economy of all United States-produced cars has been increased by 50 percent since 1973, from 12.9 miles per gallon to more than 19 miles per gallon for 1979 models. For the most fuel-efficient, mass-produced car offered in most United States manufacturers' lines, mileage per gallon has been doubled.

It is true that some of these gains are due to the adoption of already existing technologies and a sales shift to smaller cars. But there has also been significant innovation in adapting technologies to low-cost, mass-produced cars or in introducing new concepts, components, and materials. New technologies include: Computerized electronic engine control; energy-efficient automatic transmissions; turbochargers; advanced plastics; improved ferrous metals such as high-strength, low-alloy (HSLA) steel; aluminum components; advanced lubricants; tires with lower rolling resistance; space-efficient body and chassis configurations, such as those involving transverse engine mounts; aerodynamic body designs; lighter, more fuel-efficient conventional engines; automotive diesels; and gasoline engines involving advanced fuel-charging principles like the stratified charge and Honda's CVCC engine. There are strong indications that by 1981, entirely new major

TABLE 1-1 Aggregate Industrial Spending for Automotive Research (Millions of dollars and percent of U.S. public and private R&D expenditures)

	1967	1968	1969	1970	1971	1972	1973	1974	1975	1976
$ Current	1,354	1,491	1,558	1,582	1,756	1,983	2,438	2,608	2,508	2,942
$ Constant (1967)	1,354	1,434	1,429	1,376	1,461	1,596	1,858	1,903	1,824	1,961
Percent of National R&D	8.3	8.6	8.5	8.8	9.5	10.2	11.5	10.8	10.3	11.1
Percent of All U.S. Industry R&D Spending	16.9	16.7	15.7	15.3	16.5	17.5	19.1	17.9	16.6	18.0

Sources: National Science Foundation, Science Indicators, 1977 and earlier years for figures through 1974, and Standard and Poor's Corporate Outlook, Aug. 18, 1975 and Aug. 23, 1976.

components, particularly the turbocharger and the stratified charge engine, will find broad application in United States passenger cars. A rapid rate of technological progress will probably continue at least until the 1985 fuel economy limits of 27.5 miles per gallon are reached.

Automotive Exhaust Pollution

Reductions achieved in emissions by 1978 cars over pre–1968 models range from 83 percent in hydrocarbons (HC) to 50 percent for oxides of nitrogen (NO_x). Further reductions are mandated under the Clean Air Act. These improvements in emission levels, without dramatic penalties in fuel economy, have been achieved largely through component innovations like the catalytic converter, through basic research into combustion, and through highly efficient electronic and mechanical engine controls. The development and adoption of monolithic catalytic converters enabled most United States producers to meet the interim 1975 EPA standards for hydrocarbons and carbon monoxide. In late 1976 the first three-way converter system was introduced on some Volvo lines sold in California under that state's strict standards. In 1977 General Motors and Ford also introduced such systems. Moreover, the tightening United States pollution standards and fuel economy laws, as well as the growing United States market demand for fuel economy, encouraged foreign producers to innovate in these respects with an eye toward the United States market. Honda, for example, began developing its innovative CVCC engine, which for a time eliminated the need for a catalytic converter, as soon as the direction of United States pollution policy became clear.

Safety

Important new technological features have been introduced over the last decade or so to improve the safety of United States automobiles: Seat belts, padded interiors, collapsible steering columns, body and chassis designs that offer greater structural integrity for the passenger area, and controlled crush for crash protection are a few examples. The future of the controversial air bag remains to be decided, of course, but some passive restraint will be required.

The crucial social dimensions of the safety problem, however, render it much less amenable to technological solutions than the emissions or fuel economy problems. Despite the effort expended, the generally improving trend in aggregate statistics, such as fatality rate per mile driven or per car registered in the United States has not been accelerated. Data on highway fatality trends in the United States are shown in Figure 1-1. The three milestones shown at the top of the chart signify: *a*) The onset of the so-called horsepower race; *b*) Ford's brief safety campaign (1956); and *c*) the nationally imposed 55-miles-per-hour speed

42
Government Technology and the Automobile

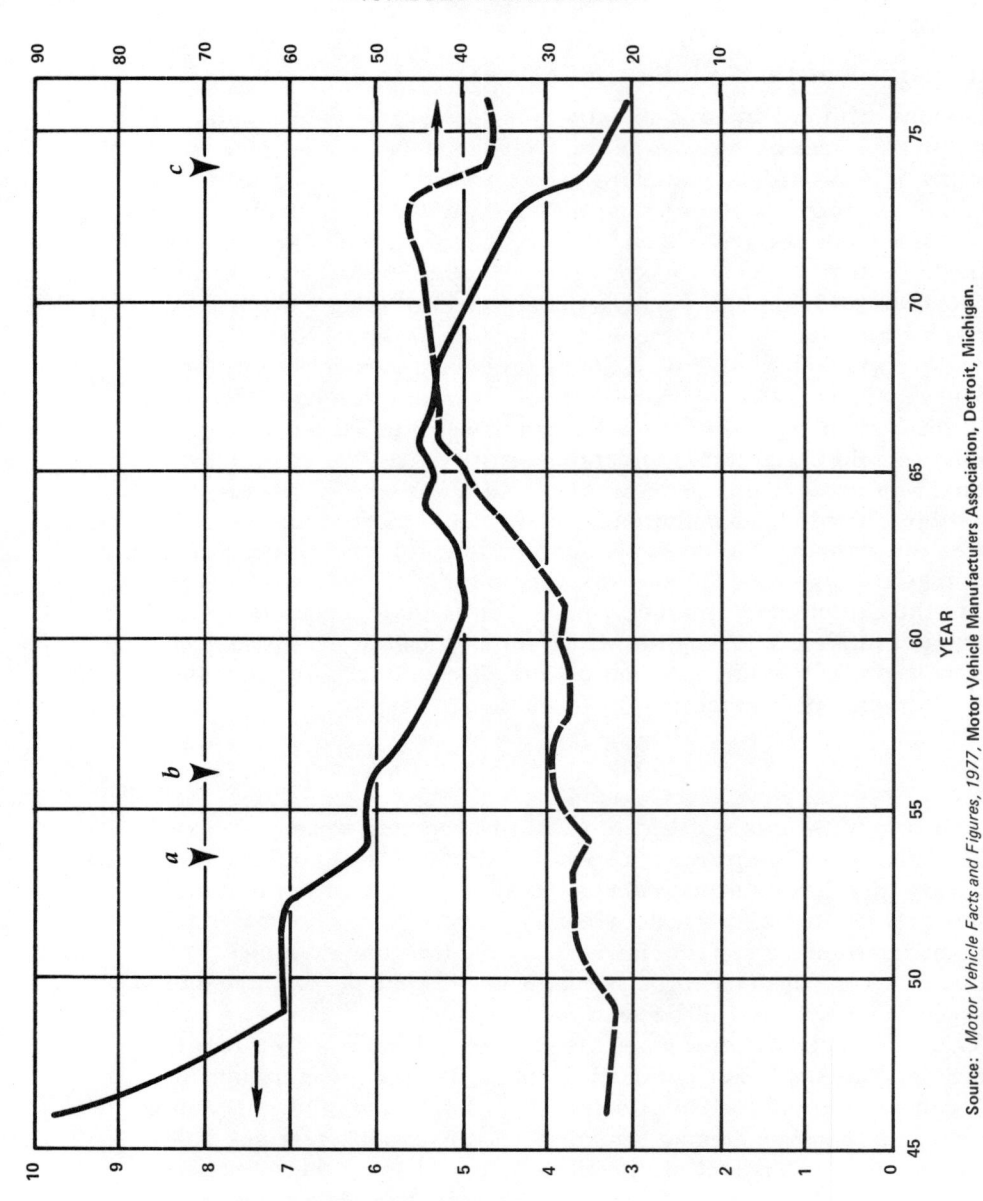

Source: *Motor Vehicle Facts and Figures, 1977*, Motor Vehicle Manufacturers Association, Detroit, Michigan.

FIGURE 1-1 Total traffic fatalities and rates: (*a*) Horsepower race; (*b*) Ford's safety campaign; (*c*) 55 mph speed limit.

limit. Only the imposition of the 55-miles-per-hour speed limit seems to have accelerated the long-term downward trend in fatality rates.

The mix of large and small cars in the United States fleet may affect safety. Injury rates may increase for a time because of the increased presence of small cars in the United States fleet. A penalty for small cars is projected even when there are fewer large cars in the total United States fleet. If the claim is correct, this is a cause for concern, even though there is now apparently a greater competitive emphasis on safety by major manufacturers. On balance, however, progress has been positive but not spectacular.

Divergence of Core Technologies

The increasing diversity in competing core automotive technologies is a subtle but important sign of increasing innovation in the automobile industry. It represents a significant reversal in the trend toward maturity. For more than fifty years, technological progress in the United States automobile industry had been marked by convergence toward a common set of basic technologies. The water-cooled, front-in-line mounted engine with independent body and chassis construction and rear-wheel drive equipped with a V-8 engine and down-draft carburetor with automatic transmission stood out as the dominant automotive configuration of the United States industry in the postwar era. It represented a flexible technology that could accommodate a wide variety of customer options and style variations without requiring fundamental modifications in the underlying set of standardized components or disrupting economies of scale. The trend is now reversed toward broadening technological diversity within more or less constant styling concepts. In engine design concepts alone, the stratified charge engine, automotive diesel, and 4- to 8-cylinder conventional engines now compete with one another. In addition, there are varied options competing for supremacy in carburetion, fuel injection, electronic engine control, emission-control technology, and body and chassis designs and materials. These are all indications that advanced technology is becoming an increasingly important competitive factor.

THE RATE OF CHANGE

The current adversarial climate between government and industry intimates that the government believes that the pace of technological change in the automobile industry is still too slow.[3] Holders of this view seem to be referring to the pace of radical or epochal changes in technology. Improvements in fuel economy, pollution control, and safety, however, are based for the most part on *incremental* innovations.

---

3. *Snail's Pace of Innovation*, remarks by Joan Claybrook before the Automotive News World Congress, Detroit, Mich. (July 13, 1977) in DOT HS-810, p. 305.

As Henry Ford II said early in the 1960s: "When you think of the enormous progress of science over the last two generations, it's astonishing to realize that there is very little about the basic principles of today's automobiles that would seem strange and unfamiliar to the pioneers of our industry."[4] The same could be said about many of the innovations of the 1970s. Two cases-in-point are the turbocharger and Honda's CVCC engine. The former uses the seventy-five-year-old principle of supercharging; the latter, the concept of stratified charge which was introduced in the first decades of this century by British engineer Henry Ricardo.

Is incremental change logically related to the kinds of federal initiatives undertaken to stimulate the development and commercialization of new products in the automobile industry? Regulatory intervention (technology pull) has been behind much of the technological change in the automobile. Federal regulation, at first arising from public concern about the effectiveness of a free market in producing certain kinds of goods and services efficiently and equitably, has recently become a pervasive factor in broadly shaping industrial performance. The federal intervention currently applied, however, does not involve the government directly in research and development to support new technology or modify existing technology (technology push).[5] Actions that might create technology include funding for basic research, direct government expenditures for the development or production of a product, and a variety of expenditures for programs that fall inbetween basic research and subsidized production such as demonstration programs and mission-oriented R&D programs leading to prototypes. The industry's allocation of R&D resources to longer-run work has reportedly declined because their discretionary capital has been channeled to meet urgent regulatory objectives.

The effects of these distinctly different types of federal initiatives on automobile technology are represented schematically in Figure 1-2. As suggested by this figure, Technology Push initiatives have ranged from modest to weak. R&D programs have generally focused on regulatory support, and survey research has centered around current technologies.[6] The differences in industry response in the three regulated areas are, therefore, largely attributable to differences in the Technology Pull initiatives of the government. Intense Technology Pull actions (i.e., regulations) may bias the innovation process. Thus, a federal strategy that relies almost exclusively on incentives for immediate progress may become a constraint upon longer-run options that are

---

4. *Ibid.* at 9.
5. See W. J. Abernathy and B. S. Chakravarthy, *Government Intervention and Innovation in Industry: A Policy Framework,* Working Paper, No. HBS 78-4 (Division of Research, Harvard Univ. Graduate School of Business Administration, 1978).
6. *Ibid.*

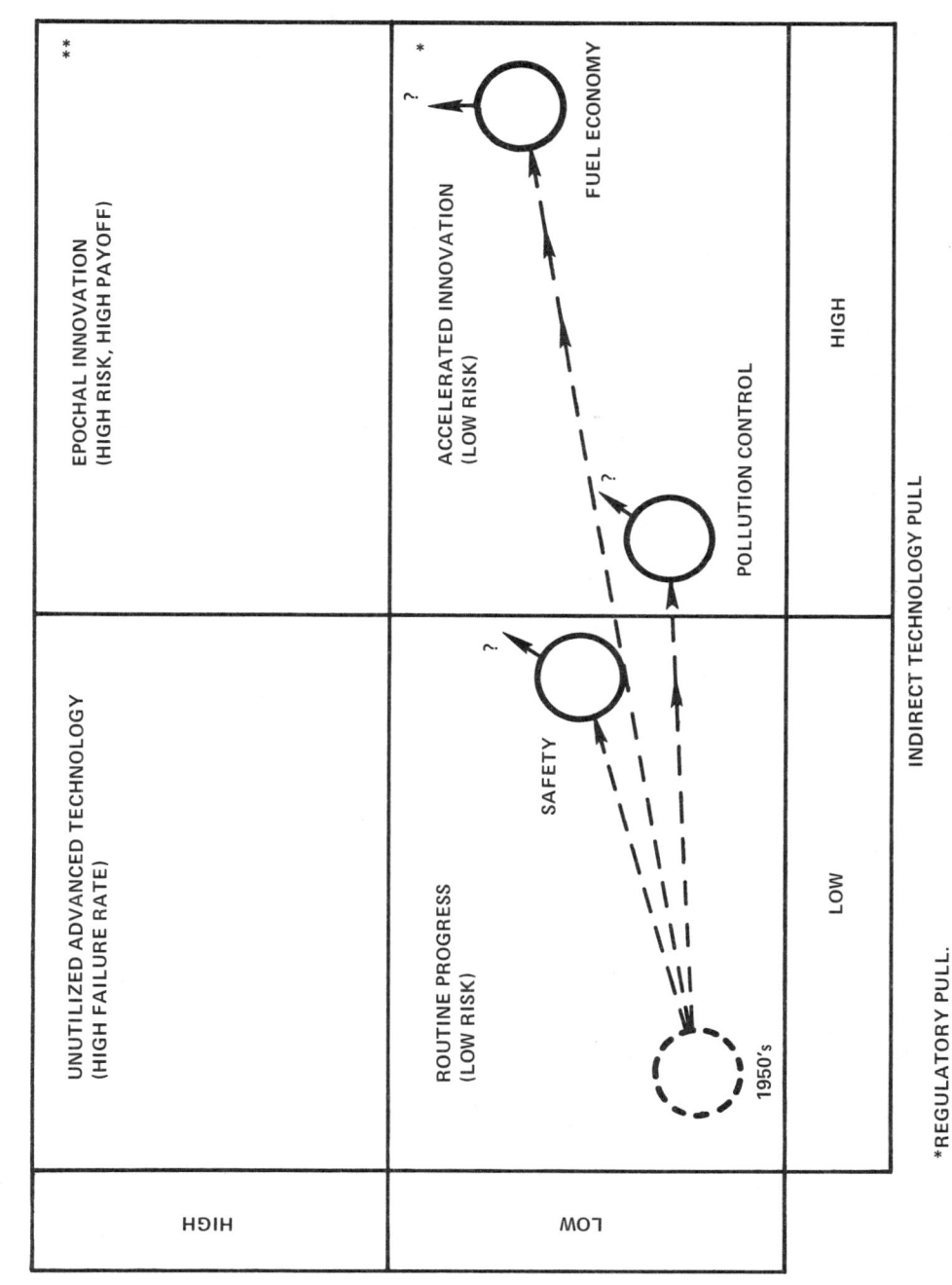

FIGURE 1-2 Effect of federal initiatives on automotive technology

*REGULATORY PULL.
**MARKET PULL.

needed for the future. And, indeed, federal regulation has hitherto stimulated only incremental changes in technology.

This suggests the following paradox: Regulation may encourage rapid incremental progress and, at the same time, constrain choices of alternative technologies (1) by diverting resources away from research into them (we call this entrenchment below); and (2) erecting barriers to the development of more epochal innovations. Existing technologies may also be enveloped by regulations tailored to current technologies, producing a regulatory fossil. To understand the possible causes of this regulatory paradox, and its potential effect on the automobile, we must first examine some aspects of the process of technological innovation in general.

TECHNOLOGY LIFE CYCLE MODEL

Technological innovation may occur in various forms.[7] Some firms seek dramatic technological breakthroughs; others forsake such radical changes and pursue incremental improvements in the existing technology. The Technology Life Cycle Model identifies factors determining which firms will be radical innovators and which will not. It depicts the condition of industrial innovation that Joseph Schumpeter, in his classic economic theory of change in capitalist economies, called "the winds of creative destruction." Figure 1-3 illustrates the pattern of product cost improvements that typically accompany the interplay of established and entering firms as new products invade established lines and evolve from inception toward maturity. According to the model, firms with younger, more labor-intensive, rapidly changing product lines are far more apt to produce radical innovations than are established, more capital-intensive, mature firms with highly developed, specialized and productive manufacturing and marketing procedures geared to the existing technology.

The *incremental* pattern of technological innovation is characteristic of progress in established, high-volume product lines, such as incandescent light bulbs, rolled steel, television receivers, refined gasoline, and automobile engines. The markets for such goods are large and well-defined. One product design dominates so that competing products derive from the same technology. Price rather than design influences market decisions. Production technology is highly efficient, capital-intensive, and specialized to the particular product. Economies of scale are very significant and play a dominant role in the competitive interaction of firms.

Change is costly in such an environment because an alteration in any one attribute of such an integrated system has ramifications in many others. The extent of investment that such firms have in the existing technology—capital, trained labor, technological know-how—further

---

7. See generally Abernathy, n. 1 *supra*.

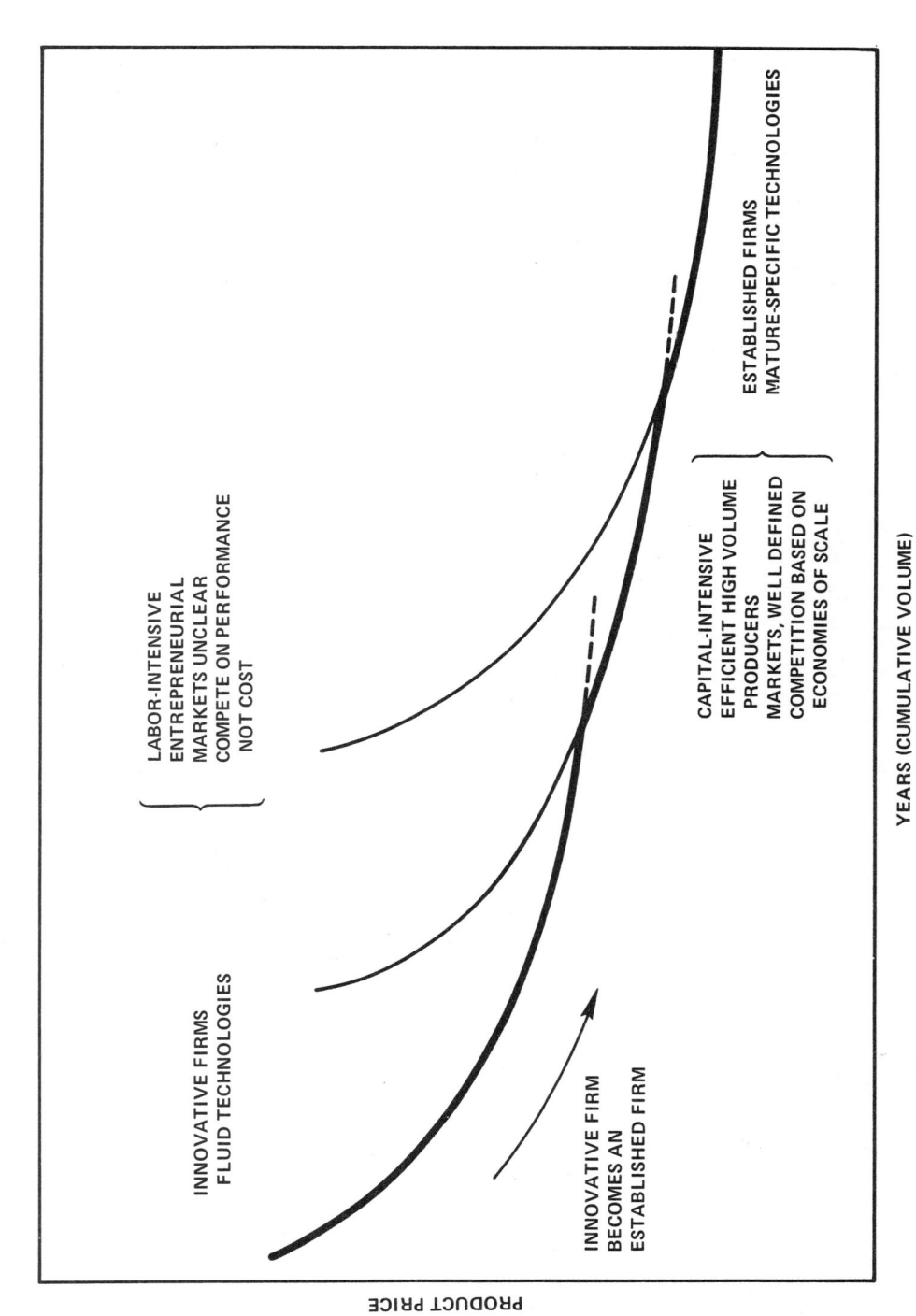

FIGURE 1-3 Evolution and competitive intrusion of technologies

discourages radical innovation. Technological change may still be frequent, but it is incremental—seeking continual refinement of the existing technology in order to increase productivity and reduce costs. Innovation, therefore, will more likely be in the process of manufacture rather than in the product itself. As in the automotive industry of the 1950s and 1960s, competition may manifest itself in less fundamental product alterations, such as styling and accessories.

Epochal innovation, however, constitutes a distinct second pattern. Since it involves the identification of new needs or a new way of meeting old needs, it is essentially entrepreneurial in nature. It competes with the existing technology on the basis of performance rather than cost. Because markets for the new product are apt to be ill-defined, and because the manufacturing process is apt to be labor-intensive and fluid, the entrepreneurial firm may continue to make dramatic changes in the new concept. Typically, such innovators come from outside the industry, unburdened, as it were, by a stake in the technological status quo. Examples of radical innovations in nonautomotive industries include such products as pocket calculators, transistors, computers, video recorders, and jet engines.

Figure 1-4 illustrates how the model applies to the entry of a new technology. In this instance, the development of electronic calculators to compete with electric and/or manual adding machines helps to illustrate the important role of thin specialty markets in the development and commercialization of a new technology. Buyers in such markets share common traits: (1) A willingness to pay high premiums for superior performance in a few limited dimensions; and (2) a willingness to accommodate some performance deficiencies in the new technology compared to its existing competitors. Aside from the risks these buyers are willing to assume, they constitute a small, affluent market.

When the pocket calculator was introduced (the upper end of the steep curve in Figure 1-4) it exhibited the basic characteristics of many other new technologies entering the critical thin market: It was costly, but it offered certain performance advantages, such as its small size, weight and low energy consumption. At the same time it exhibited basic performance deficiencies: Questionable reliability and service, the absence of a printing capability, and the necessity for the user to learn new skills. Such initial performance deficiencies in new technologies are not atypical. Consider the high fuel consumption and poor reliability of early jet engines and of advanced automotive-performance engines. Personal-sized transistor radios when first introduced had poor fidelity and frequency response. The first users of computers in the early 1950s had to accept and master an unwieldy, complex, basic logic.

There are many examples where a thin specialty market has been critically important for innovative products. The demand for high-performance cars provided a trial period for the development of turbochargers and fuel injection. Certain private consumers, who were

49
*Regulation:
The Visible
Hand*

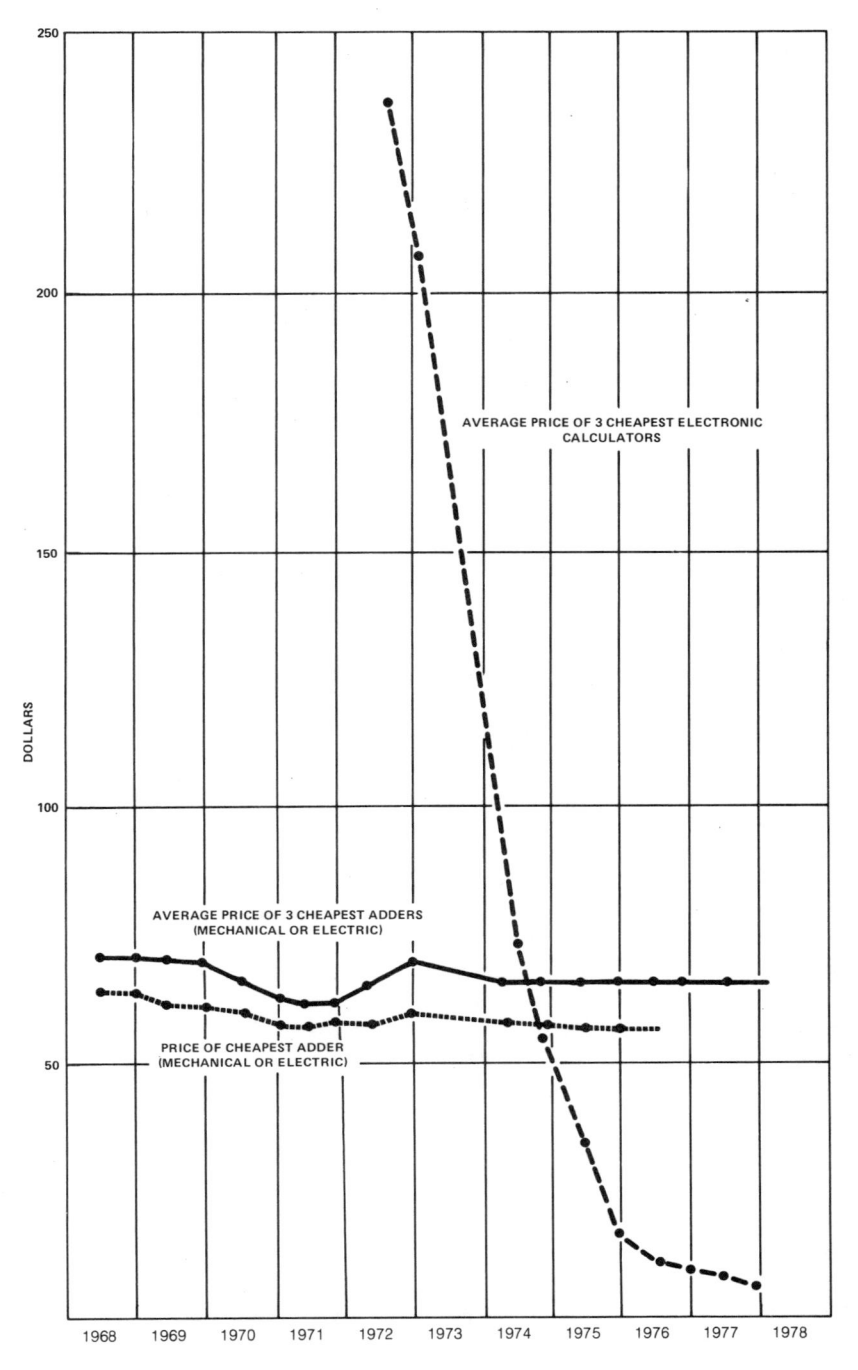

FIGURE 1-4 Price trends—electronic calculators vs. mechanical adders

willing to accept the poor performance of early ballpoint pens and pocket radios, provided those products with the initial market tests that were necessary for their further refinement and subsequent wide appeal. The critical thin market need not be composed of affluent risk-taking consumers, however, as illustrated by video recorders, semiconductors, jet engines, and computers, which were supported by both the government and industrial purchasers. Indeed the government, through its procurement programs, has been most important in creating a nurturing market, as Utterback and Murray have noted: "The major economic influence of procurement appears to have been the degree to which it enlarges the market and growth of firms, and increased the volume of production leading to regular reduction in costs and prices."[8] The Department of Defense in particular has seemed willing to pay high prices, tolerate temporary deficiencies, and accept risk to get a new product that might ultimately be ideal for its needs, as was the case with electronic components and computers.[9] The military, through its procurement programs, has been an overwhelming stimulant in the development and commercialization of many products on which the economic growth since World War II has rested.

It is important to understand how the relationship between thin, performance-oriented markets and the established mass markets affects the process of successful innovation and commercialization. At the point of introduction, the new product is very vulnerable. It is usually introduced by small, entrepreneurial firms or organizations that lack the resources to undertake major risks or to sustain high rates of R&D expenditure. The greater the established product's economies of scale and production volume, the greater is the need for robust specialty markets that nurture innovations to a stage of commercial and technical viability for competition within established markets.

The traditional concern of economic theory with simple indices of concentration in an industry as a factor of innovation may not be as crucial as the way in which concentration occurs and the question of whether or not a particular kind of concentration allows a stratified market situation to develop. Industries like textiles, shoes, and home construction, for example, may be quite deconcentrated and still not contain the specialized market segments that nurture and encourage innovation. On the other hand, more concentrated industries may be very innovative when their relevant markets include some segments that support innovation through the critical period of introduction, as identified in Figure 1-2 *supra*. William B. Capron's analysis of techno-

---

8. J. Utterback and A. Murray, *The Influence of Defense Procurement and Sponsorship of R&D on the Development of the Civilian Electronics Industry*, Report D-5 (MIT Center for Policy Alternatives, June 1977).

9. J. Tilton, *International Diffusion of Technology: The Case of Semiconductors* (The Brookings Inst., 1971).

logical change in such industries as electric power, telecommunications, and air transportation supports this interpretation.[10]

Government regulation can alter the innovation process through its effect on thin specialty markets. While the inhibiting effects of regulation can be subtle, they are nonetheless powerful and pervasive. The effects of intense regulation on the innovation process are illustrated in Figure 1-5 in terms of the Technology Life Cycle Model. The normal successive replacement of one established technology by a newer technology is shown by the two downward sloping lines on the left (*A* and *B*). An example of this process is the replacement of the obsolete, in-Line L head automotive engine by the V-8 engine in the 1930s. The V-8 engine, in turn, has become an established technology. The dotted line to the right (*C*), represents a potential competitor, under consideration at year *T*, which may replace the established V-8 engine. Possible competitors include the sterling, turbine, or electric engines.

Intense regulation may disrupt the normal patterns of interaction between the thin, high-performance markets and the established market in three distinct but related ways: (1) It may *increase barriers* to the initial development of new competing technology; (2) It may *envelop* the existing technology with regulatory requirements so that no new technology can fully satisfy the web of constraints so created; and finally, (3) by diverting all discretionary resources to improve existing technology, regulation encourages the *entrenchment* of the current technology within the industry. Figure 1-5 represents these three effects of regulation on the Technology Life Cycle Model.

Increasing Barriers

The most obvious and frequently cited consequence of regulation on the innovation process is the barrier erected to initial development of new products. This barrier results from the increase in resources, costs, and risks involved in developing and introducing new technologies. The recent and precipitous decline in the development of new drugs and chemicals following extensive regulation is well-documented and publicized.[11] Higher costs of development come from the extensive testing that is necessary to meet regulatory standards, the administrative and legal burden that attends certifications, and the greater technical challenges placed on the R&D process by regulatory demands.

Our recent casework provides an interesting example of this barrier

---

10. W. Capron, Ed., *Technological Change in Regulated Industries* (The Brookings Inst., 1971).
11. See G. E. Schweitzer, *Regulation and Innovation: The Case of Environmental Chemicals*, Program on Serv., Technology & Soc'y, Cornell Univ. (Feb. 1978); and *Science Indicators 1974*, National Science Bd., p. 104.

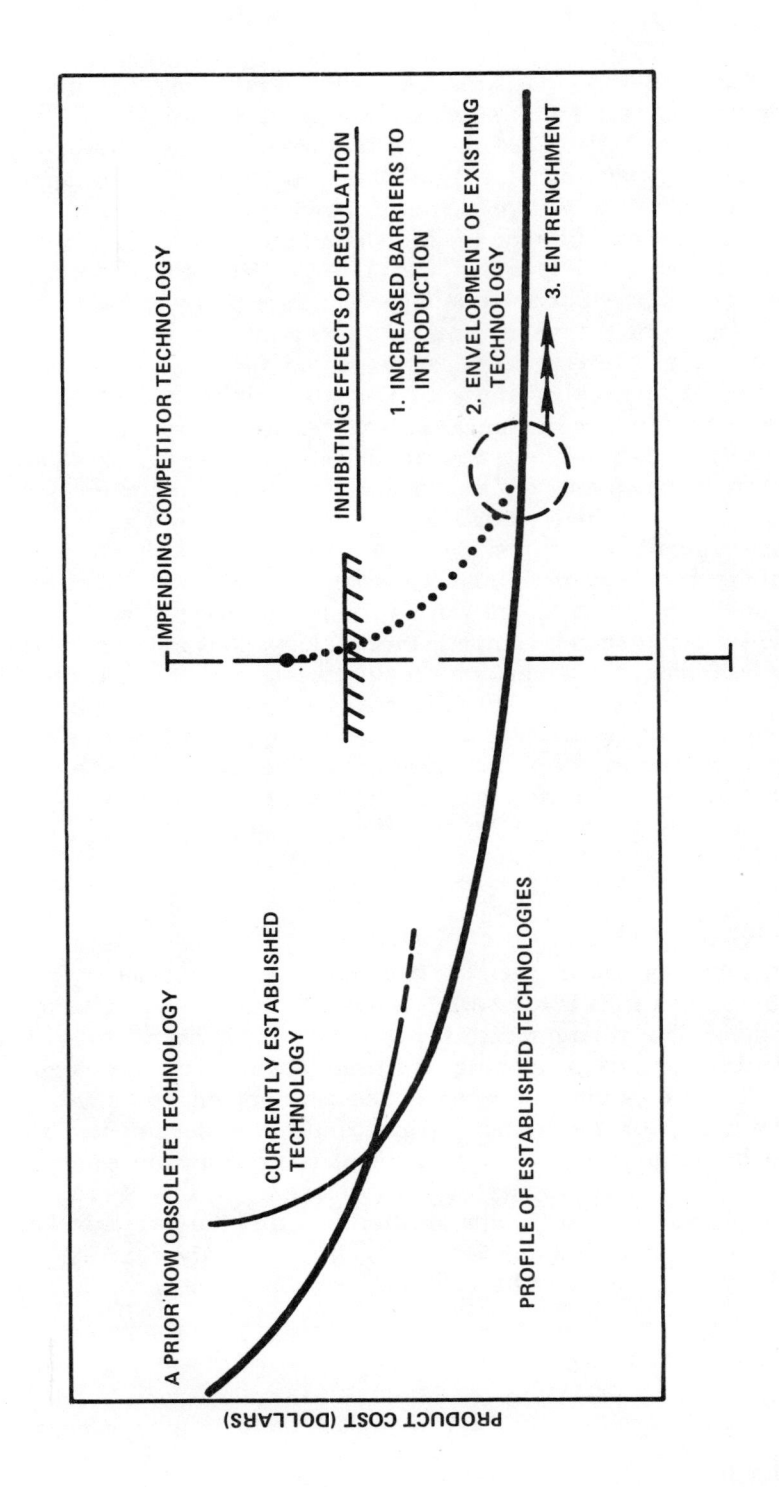

FIGURE 1-5 Effects of regulation on thin "high performance" markets

effect in the automobile industry.[12] California in the 1960s erected a regional barrier to turbocharger development that had national implications. According to market surveys, California was the largest potential aftermarket for turbochargers, but the state prohibited turbocharger installation pending certification by its Air Resource Board. Certification required a durability test of at least 30,000 miles and thereby imposed requirements that were too complicated and costly for the small firms manufacturing turbochargers. Thus, as a direct consequence of regulation, the thin specialty market that California offered for developing turbochargers for automotive passenger cars never materialized, setting turbocharger development back a number of years.

The recent experiences of several potential automotive suppliers illustrate how uncertainty over regulatory requirements, as well as increased costs, can increase barriers to the initial development of innovative components. Anticipating a requirement for antilock brakes on heavy vehicles, a number of firms began developing computerized braking devices.[13] This could not go forward, however, until the controversies raging around FMVSS 121 were resolved. Similarly, in anticipation of air bag requirements and seat belt interlock standards, supply firms invested heavily in new products that would meet these standards. According to published reports, Eaton alone invested more than $20 million in air bag development.[14] In each case, the federal programs were changed and the anticipated market disappeared or became prohibitively uncertain. According to a *Business Week* article, Rockwell International was left with a brake system exceeding market requirements and too expensive to be competitive. Rockwell subsequently announced that, as a matter of policy, it would no longer develop components for the original motor vehicle equipment market. Eaton's managers, disappointed by the sudden shift in requirements, publicly stated their concern over the viability of their investment in air bags. While still favoring inflatable air bags for all cars, Eaton's Vice President for Public Affairs, Marshall Wright, commented: "The worst thing that ever happened to air bags was their premature mandate in 1970. If DOT had played a more restrictive role in encouraging this product we are convinced that the air bag would be on the highway."[15] One major supplier has decided that, because the regulatory uncertainty is so

---

12. L. Roman and W. J. Abernathy, *The Development and Introduction of the Automotive Turbocharger: A Case of Innovation in Response to Fuel Economy Regulation*, Working Paper, No. HBS 78-43 (Division of Research, Harvard Univ. Graduate School of Business Administration, 1978).
13. "Passive Restraints: Active Controversy?", *Industry Week*, July 18, 1977, pp. 88–94.
14. "Stomping on a Brake Standard," *Business Week*, Dec. 19, 1977, pp. 88–94.
15. "Eaton Corporation Opposes Air Bag Mandate," *Automotive Industries*, July 1, 1977, p. 11.

great, it would no longer invest in R&D to meet needs that arose from regulatory requirements.

In these cases, the problem of establishing clear and certain requirements was not created by the responsible government agency (NHTSA), but was inherent in the complex nature of the political and legal context in which regulations are established. The end result, however, was to raise barriers for potential suppliers who, by initiating competitive new technologies intended to feed the innovation process.

Entrenchment

While regulation may increase barriers to new firms seeking entry into the industry with innovative technology, it may also affect the involvement of established firms in the innovation process. Steadily tightening regulatory requirements demand the diversion of more discretionary resources into programs to improve existing technologies, in effect entrenching the current technology within the industry. While this encourages more rapid incremental innovation, it may also discourage the entry of firms undertaking needed longer term advances, or epochal innovations.

An intensification of regulation, whether by adding new kinds of requirements or by tightening existing ones, requires the manufacturer to devote ever greater resources to the existing technology and market. As new requirements create new demands, R&D tasks associated with each change become more complex, costly, and subject to risks. Each change, too, becomes more costly while at the same time more changes are required. This escalation of development cost and complexity is clearly evident in the engineering interactions on new engine development:[16] New requirements and components interact with each other so that the effect on the number of subordinate design tasks, tests, and, ultimately, cost is more nearly multiplicative than additive. For example, the interaction of tough fuel economy and emissions requirements for automotive engines has led to the addition of much more complex engine-control technology and carburetion systems, as well as catalytic converters and related components. Similar effects are reported for other drive-train components.

The causes of entrenchment are subtle; their consequences, however, are vitally significant for firms in the industry. For example, to obtain the resources it needs to compete successfully in the highly regulated United States market, Chrysler has recently moved to divest itself of many of its extensive foreign operations. In Ford's recent report on the

---

16. See Russel & Nedbal, *Air-Fuel Ratio Control Using a Simple Micro-Processor*, SAE Papers, No. 770006 (1977); K. Binder, U. Kieincke and M. Zechnall, *Car Control by a Central Electronic System* SAE Papers, No. 770001 (1977); "Putting Electronics in Cars Opens Multiple Design Options," *Auto Engineering*, Dec. 1977, pp. 15–25.

state of the automobile industry,[17] it documents a need for an additional $6 billion (adjusted for inflation) above its recent, historically high rate of capital investment in order to remain competitive in North America through 1985. This figure approximates Ford's total worldwide net worth.

Envelopment

By far the most subtle influence of regulation on the innovation process depicted in Figure 1-6 is regulatory envelopment. The stream of automotive regulations in the last decade has broadened substantially from the minimum safety and pollution-control regulations of the early 1960s and late 1970s to include, among other things:[18]

- Tight maximum limits for carbon monoxide, hydrocarbon and oxides of nitrogen emissions;
- Steep energy efficiency rates, currently leading to a fleet-weighted average of 27.5 miles per gallon in 1985;
- Crashworthiness and crash avoidance requirements in respect to fire, rollover, rear and side impacts, including a 30 miles-per-hour frontal impact, interior protection and occupant restraint requirement; and
- Damageability requirements in respect to vehicle damage limits in low-speed impacts.

This is indeed a partial list. Eugene Goodson counts 237 regulatory changes pertaining to automobiles and light trucks from 1960 through 1975.[19]

Regulators have often favored performance regulations rather than design standards in order to preserve the manufacturers' freedom to innovate. They have also limited regulations to very specific objectives and based them on the best available technology. In attempting to protect the innovative process by undertaking piecemeal regulations, however, government agencies may have achieved the opposite result. They may have created a sequence of independent regulatory actions that, taken as a whole, form a tightening web of constraints that envelop the existing technology. This effect is illustrated conceptually in Figure 1-6 by the dotted circle.

Fragmented performance regulations issued by different organizations more obviously become an overall design standard when the automobile is considered as a single, integrated system. This unified

---

17. *State of the U.S. Automobile Industry* 34, Ford Motor Co. (June 13, 1978).
18. H. Herman, E. Stork, G. Manella, R. Hemphill, R. Powell, *Report by the Federal Task Force on Motor Vehicle Goals Beyond 1980* (Sept. 2, 1976).
19. R. E. Goodson, *Federal Regulation of Motor Vehicles: A Summary and Analysis*, Report to DOT (Purdue Univ., Mar. 1977).

56
Government Technology and the Automobile

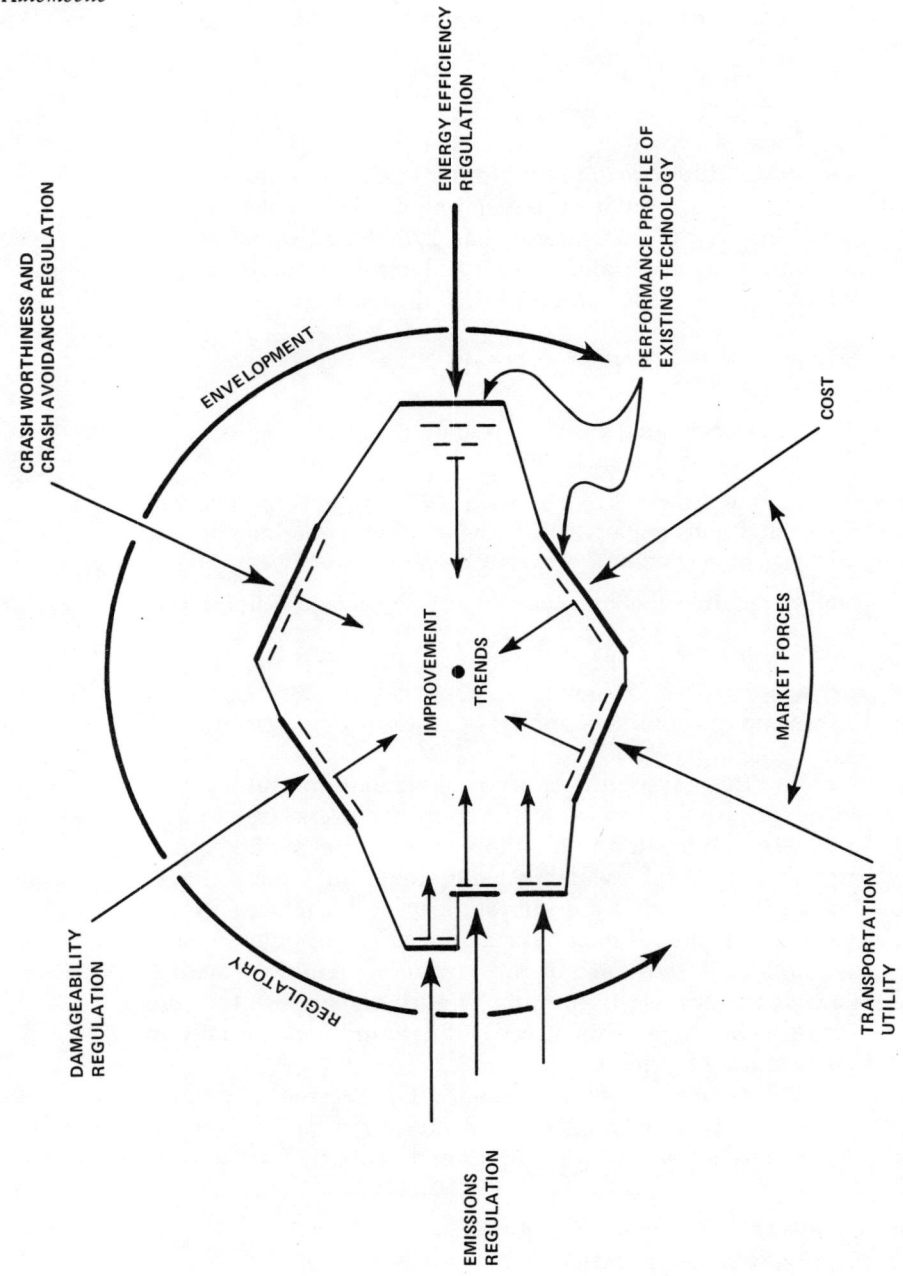

A — ENVELOPMENT OF ESTABLISHED TECHNOLOGY

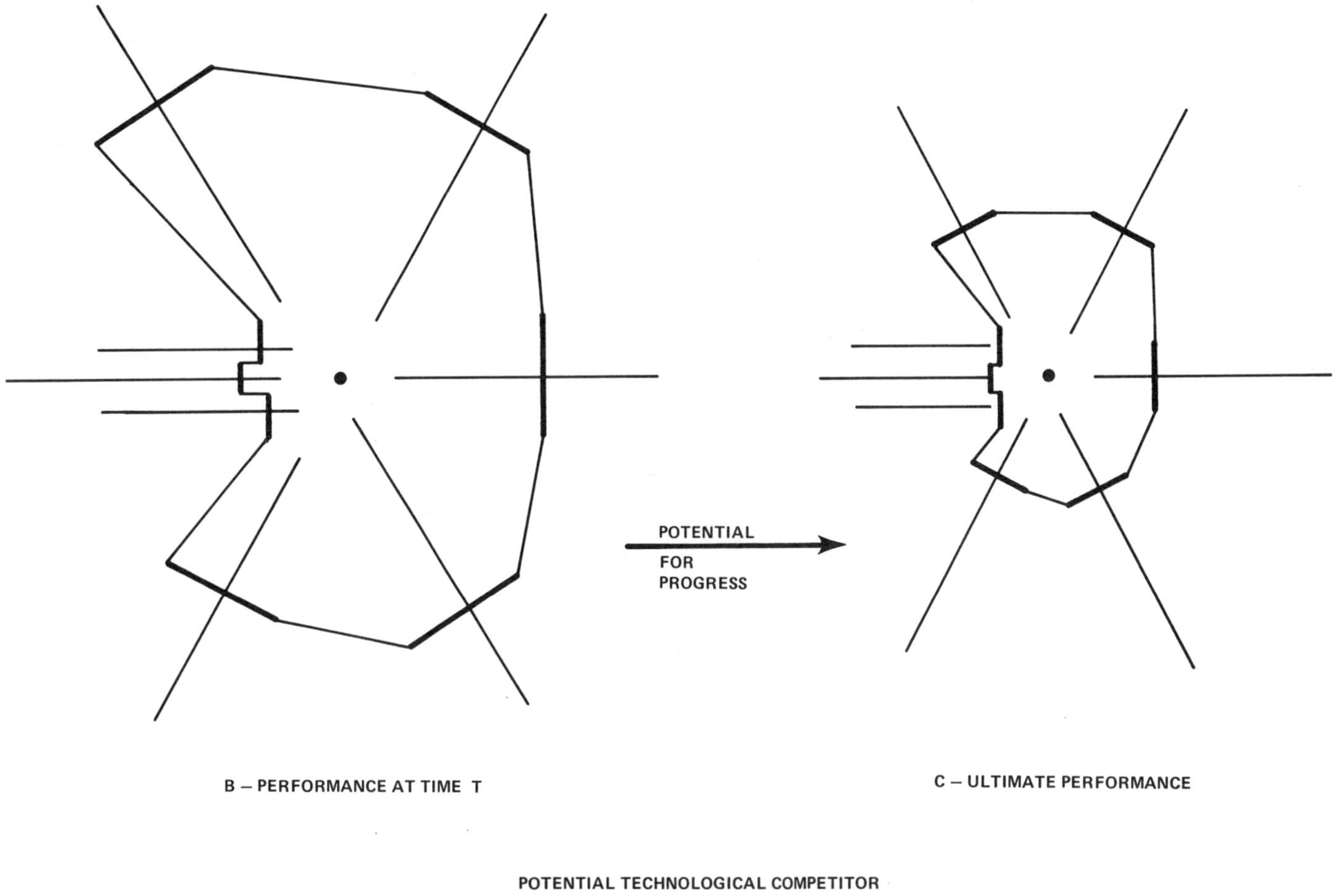

57
Regulation: The Visible Hand

B — PERFORMANCE AT TIME T

C — ULTIMATE PERFORMANCE

POTENTIAL FOR PROGRESS

POTENTIAL TECHNOLOGICAL COMPETITOR

FIGURE 1-6 Envelopment

design standard bars the entry of initially imperfect but potentially useful new technologies. The barrier effect may thwart the initial development of a new technology; envelopment bars the acceptance in established markets of such innovations as are made.

In Figure 1-6, A illustrates this concept of envelopment. An established technology, for example, the dominant design for a mid-sized United States passenger car of the 1960s, is characterized by the profile along the six axes in this figure. These six dimensions represent (1) energy utilization; (2) crashworthiness and crash avoidance; (3) damageability; (4) emissions levels; (5) transportation utility; and (6) cost. Along each dimension, a movement toward the center represents an improvement for the automotive consumer. As improvements are made over the course of evolutionary development, as suggested by the dotted interior lines, each technology will trace out a unique profile. Whereas a modest change in the underlying technology—say to downsize—may involve a minor change in the profile's shape, a more radical technological change can be expected to alter substantially the profile's basic shape. Envelopment does not inhibit all forms of progress. It does not bar incremental innovation in established technologies and, to the contrary, may encourage it. Rather, envelopment creates problems for epochal innovation and the process by which such innovation is introduced.

Consider, for example, the technology symbolized by B and C at the bottom of Figure 1-6. This represents a new technology, like the electric vehicle, that is a potential competitor for the established technology portrayed in A, Figure 1-6. Initially (at time T) this new technology offers superior performance in only one respect—for example, emissions—although once fully developed it promises performance characteristics superior in all respects to the established technology. Figure 1-6 (C) represents this ultimate state. If enveloping regulations constrain it at time T, however, the competitive developer cannot undertake the process of evolutionary improvement in the thin specialty markets that have traditionally been so important to a new product in realizing competitive performance levels. Hence, the consequence of envelopment is to limit the normal process of innovation or Schumpeterian "creative destruction."

Envelopment is not simply a theoretical issue. Although its effects are difficult to establish statistically, there is no dearth of evidence concerning its consequences in recent successful and unsuccessful innovations.

Honda introduced its highly successful CVCC engine in 1973, after a spectacular four-year research and development program.[20] Honda's CVCC program illustrates how envelopment may lead even a highly creative company to innovate incrementally. In their search for an

---

20. Tasuka Dato, Shizuo Yagi, Akina Ishizuya, Isao Fujii, *Research and Development of the Honda CVCC Engine*, SAE Transp. Paper, No. 740605 (1974).

engine concept that offered a competitive edge under impending United States and Japanese fuel-economy regulation, Honda's engineers rejected more radical engines such as the Wankel, steam, and electric. These engines were incompatible with the emissions, durability, cost, produceability, and fuel economy profiles of current engines. Honda's engineers decided to develop instead the fifty-year-old idea of charge stratification, relying on a particular combustion chamber configuration very close to the Russian production-model Nilov engine. Other automobile makers and engine manufacturers during this period were also investigating the possibilities of stratified charge technology. But their evaluations at this stage of its development led them to conclude that it had serious drawbacks in fuel economy, power output, and nitrous oxides emissions.[21] Thus, the CVCC engine was much like the competitive technology illustrated by Figure 1-6 (B). In 1973, Honda introduced the CVCC in the Japanese market. The regulatory context of this decision is instructive, for at this time, Japan, unlike the United States, had not as yet instituted emissions regulations. Consequently, Honda further refined and perfected the new engine in an unregulated environment until 1975 when it introduced the CVCC into the United States market. Honda's competitive success with the CVCC has been substantial. Recent tests suggest it is superior to competing engines of a similar size in almost all performance dimensions.

The case of electric vehicle certification under Section 212 of the Clean Air Act provided a contrasting example of blocked innovation. In an effort to encourage innovation with respect to emission requirements, Congress authorized the General Services Administration to pay a premium of more than 100 percent for low-emission vehicles to be used by federal agencies. In effect, Congress attempted to create through federal procurement policy the type of thin specialty market identified in the paper as a vital link in the innovation process. Only three manufacturers of low-emission vehicles applied.[22] All three offered electric vehicles that certainly met the emission requirement, but failed to meet other regulatory and GSA performance standards, which were based on vehicles then in use by the government. None of the applications led to Section 212 purchases. It is important to see the contradiction at work here. While the legislation provided a price incentive to support an essential but thin, performance-oriented market, it neglected to protect the developing product by relaxing regulations or standards geared toward the existing technology.

---

21. L. Ronan and W. J. Abernathy, *The Honda Motor Company's CVCC Engine: A Case Study of Innovation*, Working Paper, No. HBS 78-43 (Division of Research, Harvard Univ. School of Business Administration, 1978).

22. *Report on Low Emission Vehicle Certification Program Under Section 212 of the Clean Air Act*, Interagency Clean Car Advisory Comm., submitted to the Low Emission Vehicle Certification Bd. (Nov. 1974).

SUMMARY AND IMPLICATIONS FOR POLICY

We may summarize the argument as follows:

1. The existence of thin, high-performance markets has historically been of considerable significance in the process of innovation. The more epochal the innovation, the greater is the need for robust high-performance markets.

2. A regulatory paradox is apparent. While encouraging more rapid progress through incremental innovation in established products, intense regulatory pressure can also inhibit more epochal innovation through its effect on thin markets by increasing barriers to development of new technologies, by entrenchment, and by enveloping existing technologies.

3. Historically, government initiative has played a major role in promoting epochal innovation, particularly through procurement, indirect incentives, and support for research and development. Successful initiatives in this respect have had the effect of either creating or reinforcing the markets for high-performance products on which innovation depends. Independent initiatives are not sufficient, in themselves, to bring about epochal innovation. Neither R&D subsidies, nor direct funding (Technology Push initiatives), nor price incentives alone address all major barriers. Witness the difficulties with Section 212 of the Clean Air Act. A more comprehensive approach to both Technology Pull and Technology Push initiatives is needed, given the effect of regulation.

If national goals for the automotive sector are to include the development of epochal innovation, we need to change the current direction of government policy to better accommodate innovation. This is not to rail against regulation. Regulation has served its purpose in stimulating incremental innovations and will continue to do so. But now there is a real need to redirect policy for more selectivity and balance in its application.

Some disparage the prospects of developing incentives through procurement policies or direct R&D support, citing the failure of Section 212 of the Clean Air Act. There are, however, many hopeful precedents. Evidence suggests that the Department of Defense, through combined procurement and direct R&D support, has promoted important innovations in the motor vehicle sector. Even without intentions for commercial applications it has accomplished this through a process similar to that described earlier: The creation of a thin, performance-oriented market that nurtures a new product to a competitive stage. Table 1-2 lists seven innovations promoted by the Army's Tank-Automotive Command (TACOM).

Each innovation ultimately had important economic implications for the private sector. In addition, TACOM's advanced engine development programs may yield important future innovations.

Recent changes in the Federal Electric and Hybrid Vehicle Program

TABLE 1-2 New Products Developed with TACOM R&D Support and Their Commercial Application

Military development	Commercial use
Cold rubber polymer 41°F	Commercial tires
Rubber bushed tracks	Used on asphalt paving machines
Band tracks	Used on snowmobiles and asphalt pavers
Torsion bar suspension	Possible use on tractors and construction vehicles
Torsion bar springs	Used on motor vehicles
Automatic transmission	Used on motor vehicles
Hydromechanical transmissions	Used on cement mixers and other on-off road heavy vehicles

Source: Interviews and written communication with TACOM personnel.

(P.L. 94-413) suggest an encouraging sensitivity on the part of Congress to the kinds of policy changes suggested above. In this case, however, even with the stimulus of specific legislative action it is not clear that the thin specialty market conditions so important to innovation have been sufficiently developed and sustained to support viable technological progress in electric vehicles.

The problem is not with regulation per se, but with its undifferentiated application to both established and potentially innovative technologies. To further innovation, there is a need for real diversity in relevant markets and selectivity in the application of standards to provide both encouragement *and* support (or what amounts to the same thing, relief from constraint). The arsenal of federal policy options—procurement, tax incentives or credits, subsidies, direct R&D support, and regulatory waivers—is ample and sufficient for the task.

DISCUSSION

RICHARD STROMBOTNE: Professor Abernathy attempts to make the case that federal procurement provides enough of a market in civilian technology to foster epochal as contrasted with evolutionary technological change. However, his argument is not convincing. The Department of Defense has played a key role in aviation and engine development and in electronics technology. When we look at civilian technology, where government is not the main purchaser, the effectiveness of the procurement approach is not proven. An example is the provision in the Clean Air Act Amendments of 1970, which established a low emissions vehicle certification program. Three vehicles were proposed but none was accepted. The electric vehicle technologies which were being proposed to the federal government did not meet the needs of the user agencies.

About the fact that safety and emission requirements have the effect of offsetting fuel economy—which Professor Abernathy offered as an example of how regulation envelops and acts as a web of constraints upon innovation—the record has been that the amount of weight increase due to passive restraints, estimated in the range of 40 or 50 pounds, is probably not going to have much of an effect on fuel economy—that is about a 1 percent change in weight now and a 1 percent effect on fuel economy. On emissions, it was clear in the early part of the 1970s that standards did reduce fuel economy, but with such innovations as the catalytic converter, manufacturers will be able to improve fuel economy. In the future, we can take advantage of three-way catalysts and electronic controls.

ABERNATHY: I am not convinced that there are no offsetting fuel economy penalties for some of the emissions control regulations. I think you should look at the options that are lost in terms of new kinds of engines that won't be produced because of the added constraints.

SUPPLIER: I object to Mr. Strombotne's implication that giving away 50 pounds for any kind of a safety attribute for a car is an easy decision to make. The various wheel manufacturers in this country have each spent between $15 and $30 million over the last 2-to-3 years attempting to get around 50 pounds out of the standard vehicle. Generally regulations reduce the ability to innovate simply because companies must focus all of their resources on limited objectives.

STROMBOTNE: Of course 50 pounds is critical. Fifty pounds is 1 percent and 1 percent is about 1 billion gallons of gas which is about $600 million, but the trade-off on that is in safety. NHTSA has estimated that many thousands of lives would be saved as a result of that expenditure and the fuel costs for that saving of lives is one of the smaller costs.

SUPPLIER: In talking about technology and innovation, the key individuals are the innovators and the managers who together create a channel through which new ideas reach the market. Not enough gets through this channel because the managers, who make risk decisions, have their own constraints. We need to look at the relation between regulation and the rate of progress we can expect. Innovation in the auto industry takes a long time. Innovations must compete with what already exists and retooling for the new component is costly. Therefore, in order to guide the innovative process, we need to know now from Congress what the requirements of ten and twenty years from now will be.

THE TECHNIQUES OF AUTOMOTIVE REGULATION: PERFORMANCE VERSUS DESIGN STANDARDS

D. Q. Mills, *Harvard Business School*

A very wide range of governmental regulation affects the motor-vehicle industry. We are here concerned only with federal regulations, and only with regulation of the product, the automobile itself, which may take three forms: Regulation of safety, control of polluting emissions, and enforcement of fuel economy standards. All aspects of product regulation are not covered. The specific standards established by statutes and their application by the regulatory agencies are treated only in part. There is no concern here for whether the content of standards is appropriate from the point of view of public objectives. Nor are we concerned with the technological feasibility, costs, or benefits of particular regulations.

Instead, we deal here with a more abstract concern: The characteristics of regulation itself. We investigate the similarities and differences among varying types of regulation. We analyze their implications for innovation in the automobile industry, for they have a profound influence on the financial risks which companies must bear. We evaluate the complex mechanisms by which different methods of regulation operate over time; and predict the consequences which may logically follow from a choice of a particular mode of regulation.

It is felt that general observations about governmental regulation can be useful, and we are here involved in a surprisingly novel inquiry. Despite the recent massive outpouring of general and scholarly comment about the governmental regulatory process, one searches amost in vain for careful discussion and analysis of the techniques of regulation itself. For just as an automobile may be constructed by the use of various technologies, so may a regulatory program be based on various techniques. The consumer often directly experiences the effects of technological advances in an automobile; a sophisticated society, likewise, may respond differently to different techniques of regulation. This is especially true when the industry is as large and influential as the automobile industry.

CONVENTIONAL WISDOM

It is a widely accepted proposition about government regulation that performance standards are to be preferred to design standards. According to this conventional wisdom, this is because performance standards facilitate technological innovation while design standards frustrate it. This proposition has been the mainstay of federal regulation of the automobile for more than a decade.

The first major area of motor vehicle regulation was safety. In 1966 the Congress enacted Title I of the National Traffic and Motor Vehicle Safety Act defining "motor vehicle safety standards" as "a minimum standard for motor vehicle performance, or motor vehicle equipment performance." The legislative history of the Act commented that

> Unlike the General Services Administrations's procurement standards, which are primarily design specifications, both the interim [safety] standards, and the new and revised [safety] standards are expected to be performance standards, specifying the required minimum safe performance of vehicles but not the manner in which the manufacturer is to achieve the specified performance.[1]

The legislative history went on:

> Manufacturers and parts suppliers will thus [i.e., by virtue of performance rather than design standards] be free to compete in developing and selecting devices and structures that can meet or surpass the performance standard.

The legislative history did not present data in support of this congressional preference for performance standards. No studies of the application of performance standards to motor vehicles were cited; nor were studies of the application of design standards cited. No evidence was mentioned in either the legislative history or in the congressional hearings held in preparing the legislation.

How, then, can we explain this unqualified support by Congress for performance standards? A clue is given again in the legislative history:

> The Secretary [of Commerce] would thus be concerned with the measurable performance of a braking system, but not its design details. Such standards will be *analogous to a building code* which specifies the minimum load-carrying characteristics of the structural members of a building wall, but leaves the builder free to choose his own materials and design. Such safe

---

1. Sen. Rep. No. 1301, pp. 2713–2714.

performance standards are thus not intended or likely to stifle innovation in automotive design.[2]

During the mid-1960s considerable publicity was given to the view that building codes did stifle innovation by prescribing exactly how and with what materials housing must be constructed. Critics of construction regulations called for the development of so-called "performance standards" more readily to permit innovation in building practices, arguing that an environment allowing greater innovation would lead to lower housing costs for consumers.[3] This view of the relative merits of performance and design standards in product regulation, which remains controversial to this day in the construction industry, was apparently applied without analysis to the automotive industry. To some degree, the consequences of this preference are benign. But some are quite unfavorable to public policy, the consumer, and the companies involved. A different choice of regulatory instruments might have had more favorable results. It may not be too late. Different regulatory instruments might rectify certain difficulties if they are adopted in the future.

PERFORMANCE AND DESIGN STANDARDS: DEFINITIONS

Because of its long history, building regulation is taken as the model of all product regulation. There are two basic types of regulatory instruments for building: One is a *performance code* which sets minimum standards for the initial performance of all aspects of a structure; the other is a *specification (design) code* which prescribes specific materials and methods for certain structures. This distinction is, at best, an analytic fiction because most regulations contain a measure of both approaches.[4]

A performance standard is more difficult to define because performance depends on context. Definitions must specify whether the performance in question occurs in a controlled environment (i.e., laboratory tests), in the field under controlled conditions, or in actual use.[5] These substantial differences in definition may generate very diverse results when applied. To take an example from the automobile industry, fuel economy is likely to be much higher when a vehicle is tested in

---

2. *Ibid.* at 2714.
3. See, for example, *A Decent Home: The Report of the President's Committee on Urban Housing* (1968) (see especially Vol. 2, *Technical Studies*).
4. U. P. Gauchet and D. L. Schodek, "Incentives and Constraints in Building and The Regulatory Process," in *Research and Innovation in the Building Regulatory Process* 17–34 (P. W. Cooke, Ed., U.S. Dep't of Commerce, Nat'l Bureau of Standards, June 1977).
5. O. Richards, "Performance versus Producer-Controlled Codes," in Cooke, *ibid.*, pp. 279–284.

the laboratory conditions of a test track than in actual consumer use on the road.

CONSEQUENCES OF PERFORMANCE STANDARDS

The basic argument in favor of performance standards is that they encourage innovation. Any mechanism, design, or procedure that will meet the performance standard is allegedly acceptable, so that no bars to new technology are created by the standard.

But performance standards also have limitations:

(1) Performance standards are less precise than they appear. In order to acquire precision, they must be supplemented with design specifications and/or a detailed procedure for measuring performance. As a result, performance standards tend to be no less complex than design standards. However, the complexity in the performance standards generally is to be found in the testing procedure or design supplements accompanying the performance standard and not in the standard itself. The fuel economy standards for automobiles require only a paragraph to list. The testing procedures (with accompanying definitions) promulgated as regulations by EPA consume some 200 pages of the Federal Register.

Another example is Motor Vehicle Safety Standard Number 103 promulgated by NHTSA concerning windshield defrosting and defogging systems. The performance statement itself is a simple "requirement": "Each vehicle shall have a windshield defrosting and defogging system." To introduce precision into the statement, however, the standard refers to the requirements set out in Section 3 of SAE Recommended Practice J902, and thereby establishes a testing system. The testing procedure is in turn drawn from the SAE Recommended Practice, with exceptions involving engine warm-up speeds and duration of the warm-up period, engine speed in revolutions per minute in neutral gear, engine speed and load (not to exceed 25 miles per hour), room air changes, permissible window openings (a total of 1 inch), wind velocity (any level 0-to-2 miles per hour), etc.

(2) Performance standards may restrict innovation as much as design standards do; but in this case, the restrictiveness accompanies the testing procedure rather than the performance criterion itself.

Because the content of the testing procedure serves as a device to screen various proposed technical "solutions" to the performance criterion, the attention of manufacturers is directed not at the standards themselves, as in the case of design standards, but at the testing procedures that accompany them. Thus, a performance standard does not eliminate barriers to innovation entirely. Rather, a performance standard shifts the controversy over innovations from the standards themselves to the effects of testing procedures on innovative solutions to problems.

(3) Performance standards are often measured on an elastic

yardstick. Consider fuel economy standards. The 1985 standard of 27.5 miles per gallon seemed firm enough when it was enacted by Congress. Indeed, the automobile companies hailed this performance standard for giving them great flexibility for innovation. However, the government has continually altered the basis on which mileage tests are made. The companies charge that the EPA has changed the optional equipment items included on test vehicles, revised its assessment of driving distances in the tests, and changed humidity standards. Furthermore, through other regulations about safety and pollutant emissions, the government has made the task of meeting the fuel economy standards more difficult. According to Ford Motor Company, the result is that an automobile manufacturer's fleet that averages 27.5 miles per gallon under the most recent applications of the fuel economy standards would have averaged 30.5 miles per gallon under the previous application.

Manufacturers and parts suppliers are concerned about the inconstancy of performance standards; government regulatory authorities believe that testing procedures give them valuable flexibility. By altering testing procedures, government regulators can loosen or tighten standards as circumstances seem to require. EPA has discovered that the pollutants emitted by an automobile in actual use depend as much on how the public utilizes the cars it owns as on the manufacturers who built them. Therefore, EPA is considering changes in the testing procedures that accompany the performance standards rather than in the underlying performance standards. The Deputy Assistant Administrator for Mobile Source Air Collection Control reports as follows:

> In effect, the changes in the regulation that we expect to propose for 1980 model year cars mean that instead of making the emission test to determine compliance with the car adjusted exactly as the manufacturer says in his manual, we plan to make that test with the car's emission control and engine components set anywhere within the physical range of the available adjustment. To assure that their cars don't fail under such a testing scheme, we expect the auto designers to effectively limit the range of adjustments on their cars. And we expect that such cars, when designed and built will be much cleaner in actual use than are cars today.

(4) Performance standards, particularly some of those applied to the automobile, impose a very high degree of financial risk upon the manufacturers and parts suppliers. Financial risk is imposed in several ways, of which the most important are:

(a) Performance standards are sometimes confused with targets. A standard may be set because it embodies public objectives or aspirations. Companies can thus be placed under severe financial strain attempting to meet standards that may not be technically feasible. A design standard is theoretically subject to the same misuse; in practice however, detailed specifications would rarely be available for hitherto undeveloped technologies. Therefore, it is unlikely that they would be incorporated in standards.

This is not to criticize the establishment of technological goals for the public good. But the establishment of goals as legally binding standards involves a confusion of targets and regulations that can have unfortunate consequences.

(b) The imprecision of performance standards may also impose undue risks upon manufacturers. It is not at all uncommon for producers of a product or a system to believe that it meets an established performance criterion, only to find that peculiarities of the testing procedure (or associated design specifications) are such that the standard is not met. Of course, it is the manufacturer's responsibility to determine that it can meet relevant performance criteria before product development. Nevertheless, the ambiguities with which performance standards are stated often invite costly errors.

(c) The "elastic yardstick" with which testing of a performance standard is carried on may impose substantial risk on manufacturers. A product that was developed to meet testing requirements at one time may fail to meet changed requirements, although the performance criterion itself may have remained unchanged.

(d) The fuel-economy performance criterion creates special risks for manufacturers. The criterion is peculiar because it utilizes a fleet-wide average to determine fuel economy, rather than establishing a standard (or standards) for each product unit. As a result, a manufacturer's total business can be affected by problems with only a portion of its product line.

For example, in 1978, Ford discovered safety problems with the 1971-to-1976 Pinto model, one of the company's more fuel-efficient vehicles. Were Pintos to lose sales volume in 1978 and thereafter as a result, the fleetwide fuel economy average of Ford vehicles might drop to levels below those required by fuel economy standards. If this were to occur, Ford would possibly have had to forego production of its larger, less fuel-efficient cars in order to obtain a higher fleetwide fuel economy average. The cost to the company of such an event would be substantial.[6]

Perhaps there are analogues for such a circumstance arising under design-specific standards, but the likelihood of such an event would be far lower. The particular product in question (i.e., the Pinto) might be excluded from the marketplace, but that event could not affect the sales or production opportunity for the company's other products.

DESIGN STANDARDS WITH A PERFORMANCE SUPPLEMENT

The Congress in 1966 indicated that its preference for performance regulation in the automobile industry has some roots in its interpretation of events in the building industry. However, the building industry

---

6. W. Guzzardi, Jr., "Ford: The Road Ahead," *Fortune*, Sept. 11, 1978, p. 42.

uses performance standards in a significantly different manner than they have been used with respect to automobiles.

A provocative example can be taken from regulatory practice as it has developed in the plumbing industry.[7] Traditionally, local code authorities placed reliance upon prescriptive codes, which required certain configurations and designs, pipe sizes, and materials. This practice came to be perceived as stifling innovation and limiting opportunities for materials resource conservation and energy conservation. Most codes provided for variances to be granted by local authorities, but lacked acceptance criteria for innovations.

Performance concepts were incorporated into plumbing regulation without displacing prescriptive codes. First, a Performance Statement was developed which was composed of three elements:

(A) A Requirement of a Qualitative Nature

(B) A Criterion for Quantitative Measurement

(C) A Testing Procedure

The purpose of the performance standards is to facilitate the introduction of new technology. The certification procedure permits a manufacturer to have formal recognition that an innovation meets the performance standard. The prescriptive regulations permit the community to place reliance on proven methods and materials, and also provide the manufacturer with certainty that altered performance testing, or the ambiguity of performance regulations generally, will not prevent its product from being used in the market place. Thus, the performance concept facilitates innovation, while the prescriptive concept lessens manufacturer's risk. The certification procedure is, of course, the link between the two.

PROPOSITIONS ABOUT METHODS OF PRODUCT REGULATION

In some ways, performance and design standards are very different. In others, they are much alike. In practice, most regulations must have both performance and design elements. Even in the most prescriptive of design regulations, one can often perceive an implied performance standard. Similarly, the most general performance standards often rest upon a particular technology, the use of which is implied by the testing procedures that accompany the performance standard. And performance and design elements may be combined to create hybrid methods of regulation that may serve certain objectives well.

As a result, regulatory authorities must suit the type of regulatory programs to the public goals and to the characteristics of the industry

---

7. R. Wyly, et al., "The Evolution of the Performance Approach in Plumbing," in Cooke, n. 4 *supra* at 314–348.

and product involved. Performance regulation is different from design regulation in significant ways. Performance regulations, when accompanied by the necessary definitional elements and testing procedures, are no less complex nor lengthy than design regulations. In general

1. Performance regulations tend to favor innovation.
2. Design regulations tend to impose less risk on manufacturers.
3. Performance regulations are subject to a greater degree of ambiguity and imprecision.
4. Performance regulations tend to emphasize the short-term characteristics of materials used in products; design regulations tend to emphasize longer-term characteristics.
5. Performance regulations tend to reflect the laboratory characteristics of products; design regulations tend to reflect the in-use characteristics of products.
6. The dynamics of regulatory interaction and controversy between regulators and producers are different for the two types of regulation:
    a. Controversy regarding performance regulations most often takes the form of disputes over testing standards.
    b. Controversy regarding design regulations most often takes the form of disputes over the content of the design regulation itself.

Those propositions are not immutable. For example, there are circumstances in which performance regulation may inhibit innovation. Abernathy and Chakravarthy have pointed out that when performance standards are used to set technical targets, the financial and engineering capacity of an industry may be so strained to meet those regulations by modifying existing technologies (the least risk strategy) that attempts at radical innovation are restrained.[8] Conversely, design regulations do not, as is sometimes thought, eliminate any incentive for innovation. Much innovative activity is the result of an attempt to find a more economical means of performing a certain task. A manufacturer that can develop, or obtain by purchase or license, such an innovation has an opportunity to reduce its cost below that of its competitors. The cost reduction offers the opportunity to reduce price and so capture a larger market share, or to maintain price and thereby increase profit per unit sold. A design standard that is supplemented in such a way as to facilitate the certification of successful innovations does nothing to stifle this process.

A performance standard has a clear advantage in this case over a rigid design standard. An innovator with higher cost may nonetheless introduce a better performing product to the market if it desires. Where

---

8. W. J. Abernathy and B. S. Chakravarthy, *Government Intervention and Innovation in Industry: A Policy Framework* 35, Working Paper, No. HBS 78-4 (Division of Research, Harvard Univ. Graduate School of Business Administration, 1978).

there is a market pull for performance, the innovator may be successful despite higher costs. A rigid design standard would, however, prohibit the innovation. A design standard supplemented by a performance standard to facilitate innovation would not have this undesirable feature.

Finally, where public policy favors increasing performance, a performance standard may be used as a target to promote innovation, regardless of market pull and regardless of cost considerations (at least so far as technical considerations of regulation go). This strategy is currently being followed with respect to fuel economy and certain polluting emissions. It is likely to be a strategy that imposes high risks and high costs on manufacturers. It is also a strategy whose success has been questioned, as we shall see below.

Perhaps design standards could be adjusted to a changing target embodied in a performance standard supplement to the design standards. Such a measure might have some success in encouraging innovation. This might be a fertile field for experiments in regulatory innovation, but I know of no attempt to do this to date.

CONCLUSIONS ABOUT REGULATION OF THE AUTOMOBILE INDUSTRY

Reliance on performance standards has caused the process of motor vehicle regulation to: (1) Impose substantial financial risks on motor vehicle producers, which they have understandably sought to shift, to a degree, to their suppliers; (2) generate controversy over testing procedures; and (3) create considerable controversy over the exact meaning, in practical application, of the performance standards. A further degree of financial risk has been imposed on the manufacturers by the use of the fuel-economy and pollutant emission standards as targets for technical advance. Because financial risk falls unevenly on the various companies, the competitive structure of the automotive industry may be substantially altered.

Risk

As a political strategy, sole reliance on performance regulation in automobiles has clear advantages. As a regulatory strategy, however, it is an evasion of the responsibility owed to consumers. Risk may be shifted by the manufacturers. Initially, it may be shifted to parts suppliers, through the obligation to develop new products, materials and processes necessary for the manufacturers to meet government regulatory standards. In the short run, such costs or losses associated with risks may be borne by the suppliers or manufacturers directly, i.e., by their stockholders and employees. But in the longer run, such costs will be shifted forward in the price of the product to consumers.

Through a process of performance regulation, the government is able to stand in splendid isolation from this painful process of shifting risk and expense. Social accountability for compliance with the standards is placed solely on the industry, while the cost of compliance is ultimately shifted to consumers.

Innovation

There is a body of opinion that the targets have been largely ineffective in inducing any substantial innovation. Howard Margolis has argued with respect to pollutant emissions, that the standards in effect in 1977 "are approximately the standards for 1975 that the industry said it could and would meet before the new legislation [1970] produced by the Muskie subcommittee was ever conceived."[9] The standards set for beyond 1978 are not of this character. They assume the development of new technology, involving possibly substantial costs. The industry had not committed itself to meeting these standards. It is therefore an open question whether the targets will, in fact, induce the innovation by the companies necessary to their accomplishment.

Eugene Goodson has argued likewise. First, he has noted a marked discrepancy between announced government goals and industry implementation. This results from the process by which final regulations are established. Initial governmental proposals for regulations are published in the Federal Register. These proposals are often challenged by the manufacturers in hearings held pursuant to the Federal Administrative Procedures Act. The administrative agencies thereafter delay the promulgation of new regulations. When issued, the regulations are often revised to bear closer conformance to what is technically feasible.

Goodson argues that this procedure may be counterproductive: "It is not clear that increasingly more stringent regulations initially proposed produce a faster response [by the manufacturers] than possibly more economically and technologically reasonable standards. . . . Technological development may be impeded with a policy of setting very stringent goals which must be met in a short time frame."[10]

These arguments are not conclusive. Nonetheless, they raise doubts about the theoretical value of prospective performance standards to induce innovation. Congress has felt it increasingly necessary to qualify the performance standards established for motor vehicles by making them contingent upon economic viability. The industry and federal regulatory agencies are thereby drawn into a further adversarial stance regarding what is, or is not, economically viable. The uncertainty thereby engendered over the future application of the standards can reduce, rather than increase, the incentive to innovate.

---

9. H. Margolis, "The Politics of Auto Emissions," 49 *The Public Interest* 6 (Fall 1977).

10. R. E. Goodson, *Federal Regulation of Motor Vehicles* 1, Report to DOT. (Purdue Univ., Feb. 1977).

Performance Standards as Targets

The use of performance standards as targets has possible undesirable effects. These effects are primarily unintended consequences of the regulations. They are, however, significant matters. This article is not the place to develop them in detail, but three major elements should be mentioned.

(1) The downsizing of automobiles to meet fuel-economy standards may have a significant effect in worsening the safety record of motorists during the period when smaller vehicles share the roadways with larger automobiles. This will probably be a transition phenomenon as larger cars are phased out. But the transition could be a lengthy one.

(2) The burden of meeting governmental targets for fuel economy will probably fall unequally on the automobile producers and suppliers. It is likely that some companies will be unable to meet the governmental standards and will either leave the industry or markedly reduce their role. The result may be a further concentration of auto manufacturing and automobile parts manufacturing.

(3) Efforts to meet fuel economy targets may create bottlenecks in supply downstream from the manufacturers. For example, retooling by the manufacturers may create major capacity and labor shortages in the machine tool industry. Such bottlenecks are likely to have important inflationary consequences.

Careful evaluation of economic conditions and adjustment of the targets in governmental policy may minimize these problems. But there are also alternatives to the use of performance standards as targets. For example, the government could remove the force of law from the targets. Instead, nonbinding targets might be used to stimulate technological innovations, which, when proven, would then be given legal force as design standards.

The Relationship Between the Government and the Industry

Reliance by governmental authorities upon performance regulation is more likely to result in an exclusively adversarial stance for the government and the industry than is ordinarily the case when design standards are used. The development of performance standards in automobiles has involved exclusively the issue of what requirements are to be imposed on the manufacturers. It is not surprising that the manufacturers should attempt to minimize these requirements. Often resistance to standards proposed by the government is based on the manufacturers' legitimate concern over potential technological feasibility, costs, or consumer acceptance.

The government, for its part, lacking the technological and marketplace knowledge of the automobile companies, necessarily resorts to a negotiating stance. Initial government proposals for regulatory standards seem to be recognized by both government and industry officials as moves in a sequenced negotiation over the final form and content of the regulation.[11] In such an environment, neither the government nor the industry has any incentive to cooperate with the other to any substantial degree. The industry has nothing to gain from providing information to the government beyond that which is necessary to give credence to its bargaining position.

Government officials sometimes castigate the industry for this behavior. Eric Stork of the EPA, for example, has criticized the industry bitterly:

> The industry's tune had not changed. "This far, but no farther" continued to be the enduring chant from Detroit. Yet Detroit had cried "wolf" so many times when there had been no wolf that not many people took Detroit seriously. Not that some of Detroit's arguments did not have some validity—just as no one is always right, rarely is someone always wrong. But if someone's arguments have been shown to have been wrong often enough, and if that someone continues to predict the coming of doomsday if even one more step were to be taken toward the further tightening of emission controls, then it gets tough to give credence to any part of that protagonist's argument. That's pretty much what happened to Detroit.[12]

This is, of course, to blame the industry for a behavior pattern that is virtually required of it by the government's own choice of a regulatory method.

Design regulation permits some cooperative effort by government and industry in the preparation of regulations. In this process, both government and industry officials may learn more about the possible solutions to technological and economic barriers to the government's regulatory objectives.

Design regulation does not eliminate an adversarial stance between the government and industry. A degree of conflict is inevitable and appropriate. However, design regulation does provide an opportunity for cooperative efforts to a degree not matched by exclusive reliance upon performance regulation.

CONCLUDING COMMENTS

This paper has been focused on a narrow range of regulatory issues involving performance and design standards in the regulation of a product. Current regulation of motor vehicles is primarily by performance standards. This practice has led to certain identifiable problems. Could a more desirable mix of regulatory objectives and resulting problems be obtained by a shift in regulatory strategy from the current reliance on performance standards? I have argued that reliance upon

---

11. *Ibid.*

12. E. O. Stork, *Remarks*, The Automotive News World Congress, Detroit, Mich. (July 13, 1977).

design regulations supplemented by performance standards may facilitate innovation.

The difficulties imposed on the industry do not arise solely from the fact of governmental regulation, but to a degree from the particular choice of regulatory methods or techniques adopted by the government. Thus, some amelioration of the problems now besetting the motor vehicle industry might be achieved by innovations in the techniques of regulation, without sacrificing the constructive objectives of regulation. It is not yet possible to make convincing quantitative estimates of the degree to which changes in techniques of regulation can reduce the difficulties imposed on industry. This paper does, however, suggest the importance of future research to quantify the costs and benefits of different techniques of regulation.

THE EFFECTS OF OBSOLETE REGULATORY STANDARDS ON DESIGN INNOVATION

Ulrich Seiffert, *Volkswagenwerk AG, Germany*

The increase in motor vehicle-related standards over the past years becomes readily apparent in Figure 1-7. This trend is evident in virtually all of the countries in the world in which motor vehicles are manufactured or used in significant numbers.

Advances in technology and changing economic, social and environmental needs have made it necessary to amend existing standards. In addition, a host of new regulations have been promulgated. Simply keeping up with proposed regulations and analyzing the impact of their intricate technical details upon production and prototype development has become an extremely time-consuming and expensive task.

The multiplicity of regulations and standards together with the constant flow of proposals for new measures or detailed amendments to existing standards is, however, only one facet of a complex problem. The difficulties experienced by manufacturers selling products in a number of national markets are multiplied accordingly; national standards of different countries dealing with the same systems or components often conflict with each other. Such conflicting standards very often necessitate the design, development, tooling, and manufacture of different component parts and systems for a single type of vehicle. These activities require a commensurate investment of money and natural resources. Above all they occupy valuable development time for design and testing that would be spent more usefully on development for the future.

Society and the consumer pay the price of such conflicting and complex regulations in increased unit costs and slower technical innovation. This situation will become more widely felt in the American automobile industry as changing relationships between the dollar and other national currencies make United States motor vehicles more com-

78
Government Technology and the Automobile

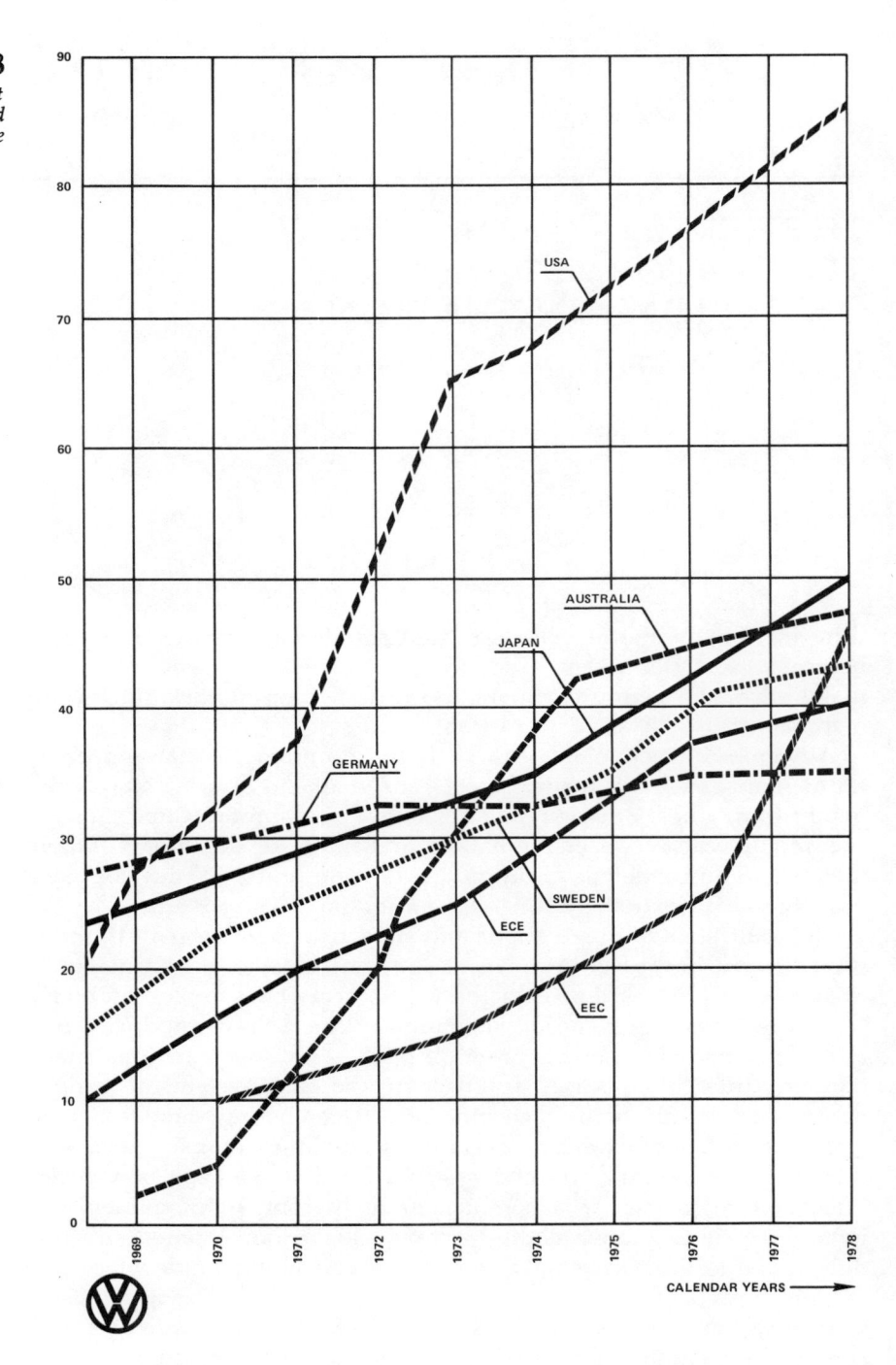

FIGURE 1-7 Standards and amendments of standards

petitive in foreign markets where different (and conflicting) standards apply.

Examples that directly affect the United States market and the American consumer will be presented. They are intended to illustrate difficulties that can arise when standards are either not carefully considered or have outlived their usefulness.

One of the testing procedures having the most significant influence upon vehicle design is crash testing. It is also the most time-consuming, most complex, and most expensive form of vehicle testing in the safety area. On a model-engine-transmission-family basis, safety testing during the development phase costs on the order of $1.5 million assuming the result of each such test is positive and no modifications to the prototype are required.

In 1968, when the original Federal Motor Vehicle Safety Standards were promulgated, one head-on, frontal, fixed-barrier crash test was required. Today compliance testing for currently applicable standards mandates 9 crash tests including head-on and 30-degree, angled frontal impacts, rear impacts, and so-called "quasistatic rollovers." (See Figure 1-8.) The requirements and conditions under which tests must be conducted to demonstrate compliance with different standards have not remained consistent with the growing number of required crash tests so that frequently a separate test is required to demonstrate compliance with each standard.

NHTSA efforts to mandate passive restraints date back to 1969. For more than four years thereafter, NHTSA held the public position that passive restraints were synonymous with air bags. These pronouncements caused the industry and its suppliers to devote millions of dollars and countless valuable man-hours to developing compatible vehicle systems that would meet the performance requirements established by NHTSA. Only after five years did NHTSA change its position to allow passive seat belt systems of different design configurations within the meaning of the standard. In 1978, the "final" rule was published regarding passive restraint systems. In general, the rule is based upon performance criteria, but there are exceptions. For example, the head injury criterion (HIC) has been established only for passive restraint systems.

The interrelationship of the HIC application to the type of restraint system, passive or active, has had and will continue to have a negative effect upon the development of passive restraint systems. A different philosophy is required. Restraint systems, or for that matter any safety device or system intended to perform a specific function, should all be subject to the same performance criteria. Thus occupant protection criteria, in this case, should be established separate and apart from the specific attributes of the particular type of system adopted and used.

Furthermore, the present rule is inconsistent and establishes a double standard with respect to performance requirements in the case of lateral impact and rollover. The rule permits compliance with these established injury criteria either by purely passive means or by the

80
Government Technology and the Automobile

FMVSS	IN EFFECT IN 1968 201 OCCUPANT PROTECTION 204 STEER. CONTR. REARW. DISPL.	IN EFFECT IN 1978 208 OCCUPANT CRASH PROTECT. 212 WINDSHIELD MOUNTING 219 WINDSHIELD ZONE INTRUS. 301 FUEL SYSTEM INTEGRITY	301 FUEL SYSTEM INTEGRITY	301 FUEL SYSTEM INTEGRITY	301 FUEL SYSTEM INTEGRITY	301 FUEL SYSTEM INTEGRITY
	FRONTALCRASH	FRONTALCRASH	FRONTALCRASH ±30°	SIDE CRASH	REAR CRASH	STATIC ROLLOVER
TEST WEIGHT	VEHICLE CURB WEIGHT	CURB WEIGHT + 2 DUMMIES + LUGGAGE	CURB WEIGHT + 2 DUMMIES + LUGGAGE	CURB WEIGHT + 2 DUMMIES + LUGGAGE	CURB WEIGHT + 2 DUMMIES + LUGGAGE	CURB WEIGHT
TEST VELOCITY	30 MPH	30 MPH	30 MPH	20 MPH	30 MPH	90° OF ROTATION WITHIN 1 TO 3 MINUTES
MINIMUM TESTS REQUIRED PER MODEL	1	1 AT 15°F 1 AT AMBIENT TEMPERATURE 1 AT 110°F	1 AT 30° LEFT 1 AT 30° RIGHT	1 LEFT SIDE 1 RIGHT SIDE	1	1 INTEGER VEHICLE 8 IMPACTED VEHICLES
SUM 1968	1					
SUM 1978	1	3	2	2	1	9

FIGURE 1-8 Crash tests and rollovers required by U.S. standards

installation of a separate lap or torso belt in addition to the passive device itself. The provision appears to be the only feasible means to circumvent the acknowledged shortcoming of the air bag in these accident modes. The requirement operates to the detriment of the consumer by permitting air bag systems to comply if an active lap belt is provided. However, generally accepted statistics clearly show that the usage rate of lap belts in the United States is approximately 20 percent. Thus, in those vehicles equipped with air bags, some 80 percent of the front-seat occupants will have no protection in lateral impacts and rollover accidents. This is but one example of how a body of standards specifically intended by Congress to be performance standards, in order not to stifle innovation and creativity, can be translated in practice into design standards, which do, in fact, limit choice and the means of solving specific engineering tasks.

One solution to this situation is the establishment of separate and uniform performance requirements for specific accident situations. Thus NHTSA could, for example, establish a requirement for the installation of a passive restraint system and, in a separate rule, establish performance requirements for frontal impact as well as lateral and rollover accident modes.

In each case research based upon controlled experiments and field accident experience would be necessary to establish reasonable and representative performance levels.

Federal Motor Vehicle Safety Standard 215 and Part 581 are other obvious examples of rule making that miss the mark. They relate to vehicle safety and damage requirements in low-speed impacts. While the primary stated purpose of the regulations is to increase vehicle safety, it appears that the principal consequence is to reduce major repair costs to the insurance industry in such impact situations. There can be no disagreement with the requirement that safety-related systems and lighting be functionally unimpaired, but the Part 581 requirements have a direct and undeniable influence on vehicle design. A number of requirements specify front and rear bumper layout, thereby limiting design freedom in terms of styling and pedestrian protection. One can only speculate about the effect of the latest moves on the part of some interest groups that indicate an intention to seek a higher "no damage" impact speed. We must ask ourselves whether the valuable man-hours, capital, and other resources would not be better spent in the improvement and upgrading of vehicle performance in other areas.

It should be understood that there can be little doubt that there is general acceptance throughout the industry of the need for uniform and reasonable performance standards relating to vehicle design. The government bears a great responsibility to proceed in a deliberate fashion and to consider carefully not only the content but also the consequences of the regulations proposed. Each proposed regulation generates substantial and costly activities throughout the automotive and related supplier industries as well as on the part of universities and private contractors to the government and industry. Each finalized standard has wide-ranging effects on research, initial design, prototype testing, final design, use of materials, tooling, quality control, production and production methods, service planning, spare parts and inventories, compliance testing at industry and governmental levels, field investigations, and, last but not least, products liability. This at times places the ultimate responsibility for inappropriate standards not on the government, which promulgated them, but upon the industry, which had no choice but to comply. The responsible authorities should not only strive to develop new standards but should carefully review and reevaluate existing standards in light of past experience and current needs.

In this context reevaluation of the following standards should be undertaken:

105—Hydraulic brake system

201—Occupant protection in interior impacts

202—Head restraints

203—Impact protection from the steering control system

204—Steering control rearward displacement

207—Anchorage of seats

209—Seat belt assemblies

210—Seat belt anchorages

219—Windshield retention

The last example that I should like to discuss are the standards for fuel consumption. Two principal approaches can be used: First, the European system, which indirectly regulates consumption via a fuel tax; and second, the NHTSA approach, which defines precise average fuel economy for manufacturers' fleets. We prefer the European approach because it gives the individual driver, the largest single factor in fuel consumption and economy, a direct financial interest in the conservation of fuel. This important motivation is not present in the NHTSA approach.

In conclusion it should be noted:

The often repeated industry request for performance standards rather than design standards should not be interpreted as a reactionary attempt to weaken the standards. The industry requests are made, rather, in the interest of preserving the possibility of design choices so that new technologies can be utilized to their greatest advantage.

If the overall goal and purpose of automotive standards is to increase occupant protection and traffic safety, to reduce vehicle emissions and increase fuel economy, and to protect and save valuable environmental resources, then we must have the foresight and, yes, the courage to revise or eliminate those standards that have outlived their usefulness or are demonstrably ineffective.

Thus, in view of the major influence of the government on vehicle design, performance, cost and allocation of resources within the industry, rule making must proceed in a deliberate fashion with:

Constant review and revision of all applicable standards based on effectiveness and actual field experience;

Elimination of conflicts between standards (i.e., fuel economy and emissions);

Clear, concise and unambiguous standards, and readily reproducible testing methods, established only after careful review and analysis of all available information;

The allowance for sufficient lead time to permit careful and thorough design activities; and

Harmonization of safety standards on an international level with a willingness to set national "pride" aside for the good of all.

DISCUSSION

JAMES GAGE: The image of performance regulation has been tarnished because regulators have attempted to force industry to meet constantly moving performance targets, a difficult task. To meet short-term objectives of regulation, the industry has used a lot of resources. Some of the objectives have been met, but others have been missed because the standards changed too quickly. Stabilizing performance targets will result in improvement in the effectiveness of performance regulation.

Performance standards should be retained because of the flexibility in design they allow manufacturers. The consumer would not accept the standardized vehicle that would result from design standards; thus, this flexibility is not only desirable but necessary. Some goals could be better met by regulating consumer behavior than by regulating manufacturers' design.

ALAN MORRISON: The two preceding essays both seem unobjectionable on one level. It is true, as noted by Professor Mills that we do not have enough information about the relative benefits of performance as opposed to design standards, and that further research, as is true in every area, may be useful. There are inevitable weaknesses in the use of performance standards and the fact that we have been using them for some time is not reason enough to continue their use without further consideration. If the construction industry is the basis for using design standards, it should not be emulated, since industry-established standards there have led to higher prices. It would be unfortunate to transfer that situation to the auto industry.

With respect to Dr. Seiffert's views, surely one would not oppose revision of regulations which are not "carefully considered" or which have "outlived their usefulness." Similarly, there may or may not have been better ways to spend time and money than on upgrading the crash provisions of Standard 215, but that kind of question can be raised about every standard. Moreover, although I agree in principle that fuel standards should not interfere with safety standards, that does not seem to me to demonstrate that we do not need both of them.

Regarding both discussions, I also asked myself whether the authors were using code words for a reversion to the free-enterprise system, in which government would have no role. Yet, Professor Mills admits his arguments are novel and only asks for more data—something no one, especially an academic, can oppose. Moreover, he carefully qualifies all of his statements regarding the relative benefits and detriments of both methods of regulation. Dr. Seiffert is even more explicit, urging us "please do not misunderstand," and that advocacy of design standards not be "interpreted as a reactionary attempt to weaken the standards." Still, even in this context, there are some troubling aspects of both presentations.

I would disagree with Professor Mills' concern for the "substantial financial risks [imposed by performance standards] on motor vehicle procedures [and] their suppliers," particularly when he cites as his example the problems with the Pinto. While no company should be asked to do the impossible, Congress is presumably aware of the costs imposed and the effect on marginal companies and recognizes that, as part of the free-enterprise system, certain trade-offs would have to be made and that some companies would suffer economically as a result of additional costs required for safety purposes. Considering the alternative of using design standards, under which it would be impossible to push the industry further unless DOT itself could create the necessary design standards, the whole process would be slowed down if performance criteria were abandoned.

I also quarrel with some of Professor Mills' characterizations in which institutions are responsible for the problems he identifies. He suggests that the government is operating in "splendid isolation from this painful process of shifting risk and expense," yet a quick examination of the debates in Congress on the Clean Air Amendments indicates that once the focus is on the proper part of government, that is not the case. Perhaps NHTSA has stood aside, but that is only because its job is not to set policy but to carry out congressional mandates. Moreover, the alternative to having Congress set specific fuel and clear air standards as performance levels would be to have Congress vote on specific design standards to achieve those results, hardly the kinds of decisions Congress is able to make. And to have Congress tell NHTSA to do it, a clear and simple objective is required and in essence, that means a performance standard.

In a similar vein, Dr. Seiffert wrongly, in my view, criticizes NHTSA for conflicts between their safety standards and those on fuel economy. If there is any fault, it lies with Congress. His suggestion of a tax on gasoline has been tried and politically has been proven unsalable.

On another level, Dr. Seiffert suggests that there are international conflicts, yet his discussion is devoid of examples. It is one thing to say that standards are different, but quite another to suggest that they are incompatible or that the incompatibility cannot be solved by a company adopting the highest safety- or fuel economy level rather than the lowest.

Dr. Seiffert also criticizes the addition of more tests, more costs, and more amendments, yet by doing so, deflects the question away from the proper inquiry, which is whether those additional tests, costs and amendments are useful or not. Finally, he suggests that performance standards "have a direct and undeniable influence on vehicle design," which, of course, is their very intent. If he means only that not all alternatives will be equally adaptable, and hence some performance standards may approach design standards, I would agree, but respond by saying that a performance standard that can easily be met in one way, and only with greater difficulty or cost in another, is still not a design standard.

GOVERNMENT (DOT): I was surprised at Professor Mills' statement that the model for performance regulation was taken from the construction industry.

MILLS: Historically, it is true. The legislative briefs for the 1966 auto regulation specifically refer to the state of affairs in construction. I looked at the construction industry to see just how similar their regulations are to those in the auto industry. Their regulations are written by local officials, not by industry people. Ninety percent of regulation pertains to fire safety; we have a good fire safety record in this country. The system is not optimal, but it does not do too badly. Further, some things have been learned from the experience in the building trades. While design standards alone restrict innovation, performance standards provide criteria too elastic, too risky, to be optimal. The best system would be to set up performance standards, then certify designs that meet the standards once and for all and to allow production to proceed without further risk to the manufacturer.

AUTO (FOREIGN): A system similar to that is used in Europe. There is close cooperation between regulators and industry; once a standard is made, firms produce designs to meet it, which are then certified by the regulators.

AUTO (U.S.): The major problem with regulation is that the ground rules change constantly—performance criteria shift, and industry bears the costs. The EPA will give us a set of test criteria, we will build a car that meets them. But, then, the EPA will say that we have built a "defeat device" that passes the test but does not meet the spirit of the law, and will change their tests around. Once a test is announced to industry, it should be retained for some minimum period, say two years; otherwise, manufacturers just cannot cope.

GOVERNMENT: Ambiguity is not an inherent part of regulation—only a function of the lack of expertise of regulators moving into an uncharted area. As expertise grows, ambiguity declines. In the aviation industry there is a refined blend of design and performance requirements that work well to ensure proper industry performance.

The spirit of any design standard can be defeated by industry. It has the expertise to outwit even an experienced regulator in any single encounter. I would much rather set up even a horribly complex test procedure than contemplate Chrysler, General Motors Corporation, and the Congress arriving at a complex of agreements over design standards for engines, catalytic converters, etc.

ACADEMIC: There is a tendency for regulated organizations to meet only the letter of regulations and nothing more. The law must, therefore, require that industry make a general effort to live up to the goals of the law and not only specific criteria spelled out in the law. Thus, the EPA is perfectly justified in changing around flawed test procedures when they are abused.

GOVERNMENT: Do you feel that it is good to allow manufacturers to cheat in meeting regulatory standards?

AUTO (U.S.): Current standards are pretty well defined and difficult to circumvent. Regulators are seldom fooled anymore. But industry needs time to react to new standards, and it needs certainty that if they meet the standards they will be allowed to sell their products. Further, some of what you would call "cheating" is merely designing to permit satisfactory performance under special driving conditions, such as passing. This type of "cheating" violates neither the letter nor the spirit of the law.

STOCKMAN: We must not forget the policy objective behind auto emission regulations—to preserve public health. Short-term tactical battles over standards cloud much more fundamental issues—namely, will reduction of auto pollution actually improve ambient air quality significantly, and will better air actually improve public health? These questions have not yet been answered satisfactorily.

If pollution control is a real problem, then a better solution than either performance or design standards might be an effluent tax. Such a tax could be updated frequently without putting industry survival on the line each time. It could also avoid the tendency of performance standards, once promulgated, to become reified and dogmatic.

CHAPTER TWO
The Role of Products Liability

EDITORS' NOTE

In this chapter, Hans-Viggo von Hulsen and Daniel M. Kasper examine the role of products liability law in regulation of the automobile, with particular reference to safety regulation. Dr. von Hulsen suggests that the law is moving toward a rule of "absolute liability" for injuries caused by products, including automobiles, and that such a rule would be a substantial disincentive to innovation in the safety area. In his view, courts and lawyers have been engaging in social engineering, with potentially disastrous consequences.

Quite the opposite may be true, in Daniel Kasper's analysis of the economic underpinnings of products liability law. In his view some changes in both the substantive and procedural law would appreciably enhance its effectiveness as a means of regulating product safety. Thus, he examines the standard for imposing liability upon a manufacturer, the contingent fee system, the state-of-the-art defense, and other aspects of tort law that may greatly affect the incentives facing producers and consumers alike.

PRODUCT LIABILITY: AGAINST POSSIBLE DISINCENTIVES TO INNOVATION GENERALLY AND SAFETY IMPROVEMENT SPECIFICALLY

Hans-Viggo von Hulsen, *Volkswagenwerk AG*

As long as a real possibility exists to avoid liability by feasible means, a large incentive is given. The traditional concept of liability for negligence, imposed only if carelessness causes harm, provides such incentives and stimulates technical progress. Technical progress leads to rising standards of care. Care and progress fertilize each other. The legal and manufacturing communities in the United States and Europe support this view unanimously.

If, however, the following demand was ever imposed on an enterprise, "either come forward with product lines which under no circumstances will harm anyone, or be liable," then such an enterprise would be absolutely liable. Such unavoidable absolute liability would necessarily paralyze all activities of the enterprise, especially design, manufacture, and quality control, and even the manner in which users are instructed to employ the products. These inevitable and disastrous consequences of absolute liability are also undisputed to my knowledge.

The borderline between incentive and disincentive affected by liability lies substantially below absolute liability. Exactly where the line falls is difficult to define. There are, however, lawyers who seem to forget the general interests of society as a whole in their pursuit of short-sighted group interests. These lawyers, who see themselves as social engineers, push much too far in the direction of absolute liability.

Having had the opportunity to follow the development of United States products liability law for ten years, I have come to the conclusion that this borderline between incentives and disincentives has not only been reached but that some aspects of United States law have already passed it. I will, therefore, remark on the development of the legal situation in the United States.

The famous California Judge Traynor stated in 1944[1] that it is not incumbent on an injured person to prove the manufacturer's negligence to hold him nevertheless liable. The judge's rationale was that the manufacturer is in a better position than the consumer to minimize the number of accidents; he can also spread the risk of injury among users of his product by buying insurance and including this cost in the price of the product. Although it was not until 1963[2] that a majority of the California Supreme Court was willing to go along with Justice Traynor, after 1963 most states soon adopted this "doctrine of strict liability," and it has become part of the famous Section 402A of the Second Restatement of the Law of Torts.

The doctrine of strict liability changes the philosophical basis of the right to compensation for injuries caused by goods and products. A right based on ethics and morals rather becomes a practice based on economics and utilitarian principles. One of the major considerations behind this changed philosophical basis was the empirical knowledge that large-scale industrial production can never be 100 percent defect-free. The best quality control can only insure a very low probability of defects. On the other hand, without serial production, the needs of the consuming public could never be met.

If the public needs the advantages of serial production, it seems reasonable to make it also pay for the loss which a single individual may suffer because a few products of a large series are defective. This can be achieved by making the manufacturer strictly liable regardless of his care. He can then distribute the damage over the price of the whole series and thereby make all who have the advantage from the product pay a small share of the improbable loss.

The costs for the compensation of damages caused by manufacturing defects (that is, deviations from the specifications set for the series) actually can be economically distributed in most cases of a large series. When the product is produced in a small series, however, damages caused by products containing a manufacturing defect cannot be covered by this principle directly. Rather a detour has to be taken via insurance. As recent practice shows, however, this detour is sometimes closed.

The new principle is even more questionable if *design deficiencies* affect the whole series. Then even in cases of large series a distribution over the series is not possible. The same is true for faulty instructions given or warnings not given with respect to a whole series of products.

The philosophical foundation for strict liability, therefore, is much less convincing if one looks beyond the relatively simple concept of manufacturing defects to the legal and economic consequences of design and concept. We must expect great care from the lawyers attempting to decide for which possibly harmful design characteristics, which

---

1. Escola v. Coca-Cola Bottling Co., 24 Cal. 2d 453, 150 P.2d 436 (1944).
2. Greenman v. Yuba Power Prod. Inc., 59 Cal. 2d 57, 377 P.2d 897 (1963).

on the other hand may be socially beneficial and useful, a manufacturer may be held liable.

The definition of design defect is presently one of the major problems confronting the United States judiciary.[3] If liability were associated with each and every design characteristic which could possibly cause harm, this absolute liability would be a strong disincentive to innovation. Published reports by some United States trade associations may be discounted as self-serving,[4] but the report of the United States Interagency Task Force on Product Liability[5] which was published in late 1977 stated:

> The Briefing Report (which was published in late 1976) found that concern about product liability has caused some manufacturers, e.g., pharmaceuticals, to forego or delay introduction of new products. The final draft of the Industry Study and other new information reaching the Task Force have supported this finding.

After discussing whether one can already speak of a generally depressing effect of product liability on the development of new and worthwhile products, the report continues:[6]

> Product liability problems may in certain industries reinforce trends against new product development and some socially beneficial products may never be developed.

Some pages further down the report again states:[7]

> Several letters received by the Task Force since January 1, 1977, indicate that the product liability problem might be more severe for certain companies in these two industries (namely pharmaceuticals and medical devices), especially highly innovative firms. . . . By reducing the amount of product innovation and causing the discontinuation of some products, product liability may have a second adverse impact. It may cause a reduction in competition within certain industries. . . .

Of special interest for the automotive industry are the remarks in the report made with respect to the Swine Flu program:[8]

---

3. The United States Interagency Task Force states in its Final Report on page VII-17 that this area (design) has caused courts extreme difficulty in formulating standards. The most prominent recent example of the judicial attempts to achieve a workable definition of design defect is to be found in the decision of the California Supreme Court rendered on January 16, 1978, in *Barker v. Lull* which, however, in my opinion is only a small step in still a long way to go.
4. E.g., *Survey*, National Fed. of Independent Business (Jan. 1971).
5. N. 3 *supra* at VI-28.
6. *Ibid.* at VI-29.
7. *Ibid.* at VI-31, 32.
8. *Ibid.* at VI-30, 31.

The recent Swine Flu program is an example of the potential impact of product liability upon the introduction of new products and its effect upon society. In that situation the President determined that the swine flu vaccine would be a socially beneficial product which was vitally necessary to protect the population against a predicted nationwide epidemic of swine flu. Congress appropriated $135 million to fund a mass immunization program. The pharmaceutical companies which were to provide the vaccine, however, refused to proceed with the production of the vaccine because they were unable to obtain adequate product liability insurance. Despite the fact that in most states manufacturers of pharmaceuticals have no duty to warn about unforeseeable risks and are not subject to liability for unavoidable risks when a proper warning is given, the companies and their insurance carriers were unwilling to assume the entire risk of the program. Their apparent rationale was that they could be subject to defense costs and protracted litigation as courts decided these issues.

The solution agreed to by the insurance carriers and Congress had the effect of shielding the pharmaceutical companies from liability other than negligence and from the burden of defending the potentially large number of claims which might arise from the program.[9]

The situation in which the automotive industry finds itself when it is directed by the government to develop protective devices such as air bags or electronically controlled antiskid braking systems closely resembles the situation of the pharmaceutical industry directed to develop new vaccines. If such devices fail, and it is impossible to make them 100 percent fool-proof, manufacturers will be sued. Manufacturers also will have to defend themselves at high expense against erroneous allegations of malfunction. Unless a solution is found comparable to the Swine Flu program which shields non-negligent manufacturers from liability, government itself also runs the risk of being drawn into liability litigation either by cross-claims or directly.[10]

Overextended product liability not only causes severe problems in such cases of directed design but will also be detrimental to the development of new, possibly beneficial, design ideas. I will mention only three aspects.

(1) For instance, some months ago a German newspaper published a small notice of a newly developed seat belt buckle:

---

9. In *Ibid.*, Chapter VI, Note 60 the following is stated:

> The National Swine Flu Immunization Program, as enacted, provides that the exclusive remedy for personal injury or death arising out of this Swine Flu Immunization Program is against the Federal Government under the Federal Tort Claim Act (28 U.S.C. § 1346(b) (1970)). . . . The Federal Government, in turn, has the right to recover all or any portion of the damages it pays which are attributable to the negligence of any program participant, including any participating pharmaceutical company.

10. This has already happened with respect to the antiskid brake standard in a case brought against the United States Government in the United States District Court for the District of Utah. Goodenough v. Omaha Porkers, et al. v. United States, Civ. Case No. C-77-0355.

New: Belts Release Automatically After an Accident

Safety belts which will never become a trap will be marketed within 4 months. A German firm has designed an automatic buckle which releases eight seconds after a car has had an accident with a velocity of more than nine miles per hour. No motorist need any longer be afraid of being burned in the car or of being drowned if his car drives into deep water. The buckle will be $25 more expensive than a conventional one.

If this newspaper report has substance, the device must be evaluated to determine whether it is useful and necessary. If it is, and if it works with the highest possible degree of reliability in its production version, the crucial question still remains whether a manufacturer can dare to incorporate it as an option into his cars. If I were asked by my management for legal advice, I would be obliged to state that the device must cause severe legal problems in the United States, not only in the very rare cases where it did not release after eight seconds or where it perhaps may have caused a premature belt release during accidents but also in many cases in which the belt was not worn at all. This device invites the fraudulent allegation that it caused a premature and dangerous belt release during the accident. Sad experience with United States litigation shows that this allegation would quickly and inevitably surface and that it would cause severe evidentiary problems to the manufacturer. These very real product liability risks diminish the incentive to introduce such possibly beneficial innovative devices.

(2) The rule of law which says that evidence of a later change of product design is inadmissible before the jury as evidence of a prior faulty design was regarded as a stimulant of innovation for general safety. Under that rule manufacturers would not be deterred from making useful safety improvements because of the fear that they might possibly lose a pending lawsuit. This rule is now being abolished by court decisions,[11] thereby reducing another incentive to innovate.

(3) The aspect of product liability law which causes the most severe problems has already been mentioned. It is the widespread uncertainty about the definition of "design defect." Manufacturers, including motor manufacturers designing a product, do not know which design characteristics of their products possibly will serve as the basis of an adverse verdict. This is an especially high risk for motor vehicle manufacturers because it takes about five years to develop a new vehicle

---

11. See CCH Product Liability Reporter No. 3280:

> Evidence that, after an accident resulting in injuries to the plaintiff, the defendant has taken precautions to prevent occurrence of similar accidents or has made changes and improvements in his products, is not competent for the purpose of originating an inference or implied admission of negligence on the part of the defendant.

Accordingly, many courts do not admit evidence on later changes. See, however, Ault v. International Harvester, CCH Product Liability Reporter No. 7055 (California Supreme Court 1974 with Justice Clark strongly dissenting).

which will then be in production for another five or more years and be on the road for ten or more years thereafter. A particular design choice, therefore, may very well be challenged in court ten-to-twenty years after it has been made.

Given the uncertainty in the United States product liability law—labelled by the Interagency Task Force on Product Liability[12] as one of the three major reasons for the product liability problems—I ask the following question: How shall engineers and lawyers now predict what will be found to constitute a design duty of today by judges and juries in ten or twenty years' time? If the legal climate in the United States with respect to product liability law continues to march along the path it has taken during the last ten years, it is no longer possible to predict anything. We were all taught that one important purpose of the law is to ensure predictability in society. We must ask ourselves whether the law continues to serve our best interests when the ability to predict is lost. This uncertainty constitutes the greatest disincentive to innovation.

Fortunately this has been noticed widely in the United States now and the Interagency Task Force has pointed to the need for the spelling out in understandable and clear rules the duty of manufacturers with respect to the design of a product.[13]

Legislation that might help to clarify these rules is under way on the federal level as well as in many states. The major part of the work to be done will, however, remain with the judges. It is our task to help the United States judiciary to find a reasonable path. This can only be achieved by a constant and meaningful discussion involving the government and its agencies, the academic world as well as practicing economists, technicians, and lawyers.

---

12. See n. 3 *supra* at XXXIX.
13. *Ibid.* at VII, 18, 244.

PRODUCTS LIABILITY: POTENTIAL FOR IMPROVEMENT
Daniel M. Kasper, *Harvard Business School*

The recent emphasis placed on products liability in the automobile safety controversy raises some important questions for industry, consumers, and public policy: Has products liability law improved safety in the past? Can it do so in the future? How will it affect product prices, industry profits, insurance premiums, user behavior, and product innovation? How will emerging changes in products liability doctrines (e.g., comparative negligence rules) affect overall safety levels? And, ultimately, how will they affect the interests and pocketbooks of consumers, producers, and insurers?

Before we can answer these questions, we must examine the basic legal and economic mechanisms of the products liability system and the relationship of that system to product safety. Only then is it possible to assess the strengths and weaknesses of the system and to evaluate its suitability for a major role in assuring consumers a safer automobile.

AN ECONOMIC OVERVIEW

Economic theory suggests that, at equilibrium, product prices will reflect differences in the relative risk of injury. That is, if two cars (Models A and B) are identical except that—due to vehicle design—users of Model A have a 1 in 100 greater probability of injury per vehicle than users of Model B, the price of Model A would be lower than that of Model B. If the average damages were estimated at $1,000 per injury, then, since $1,000 × 0.01 = $10, the price of Model A would be $10 less than the price of Model B. In addition, any risk-related price differential would be based, in part, on the likelihood of successful tort actions by those injured by the automobile. If, under present rules of law, 50 percent of the additional Model A injury victims would qualify for tort damages from the manufacturer, the manufacturer would add $5 to the price of the car ($1,000 × .005) to cover expected judgment costs, leaving Model A with a net price $5 less than the price of the safer Model B. Thus, the combined effects of lower product prices plus damage awards would give the manufacturer an economic incentive to reduce the risks of injury up to the point that the costs of further safety measures exceed the savings in revenues and damages. Expenditures of up to $5/car that increase safety enough to eliminate the probability of damage awards will be made by an economically rational manufacturer of Model A.

In reality, however, imperfect consumer knowledge of the relevant risk differentials and, more important, the massive costs to a manufacturer of contracting with purchasers and affected third parties to allocate the risk and expenditures for safety, both dictate reliance on tort liability rules to generate adequate investment in safety. Tort law thus becomes an extended form of private agreement designed to allocate losses, as much as possible, on the basis of the implicit expectations shared by the parties.

The potential cost to the manufacturer arising out of tort actions by injured users (and others) depends upon the liability rules applied by the courts. To the extent the rules accurately reflect, on average, society's demand for safety, manufacturers will receive the appropriate economic incentives to make products with the degree of safety demanded by the public. If liability rules understate the demand for safety, efficiency will be reduced as resources that should be invested in safety are diverted to other uses. When liability rules overestimate the demand for safety, similar inefficiencies result since manufacturers will devote too many resources to safety-enhancing investments.

How well do the tort liability rules reflect the demand for safety? If we assume that society seeks incentives that encourage investment in accident prevention as long as the returns are positive, it is possible to evaluate the tort liability system. But first it is necessary to review briefly the principles of tort law that underlie product liability.

NEGLIGENCE

Proof of injury alone has never been sufficient to entitle a plaintiff to recover damages from a defendant. The plaintiff also has to establish that his injuries were predominantly caused by the negligence of the defendant, that is, the defendant's failure to exercise "due care." Thus, a plaintiff could prove that his injuries resulted from a flaw in the defendant's product but still be denied recovery on the ground that the defendant had been as careful as the law required. Furthermore, in those cases where the plaintiff's own carelessness combined with that of the defendant to cause the resulting injuries, the plaintiff—with limited exceptions—has traditionally been denied recovery under the doctrine of contributory negligence.

When assessed in terms of incentives for safety, the traditional common-law fault system fares well. Under the widely accepted Hand formulation[1] of the negligence standard, a manufacturer would be held liable if the magnitude of the product-caused harm, (e.g., $1,000), discounted by the probability of its occurrence (0.01), would impose greater costs on customers (and others) than it would cost the manufacturer to take preventive actions.

CONTRIBUTORY NEGLIGENCE

Since courts have generally followed the Hand liability formulation, negligence law has encouraged manufacturers (sellers, etc.) to make cost-justified investments to prevent future accidents. This is true at least in those cases where the manufacturer was the only party able to prevent the accident for less than the expected accident costs. But in the situation where both the victim and the manufacturer could have prevented the accident for less than the anticipated accident costs, the efficiency of the common law is less clear. If the defendant manufacturer could invoke the defense of contributory negligence, which operated as a complete bar to the victim's recovery *regardless of whether the manufacturer might have been the lower cost accident avoider*, the common-law solution would be inefficient. Assume, for example, the manufacturer could have prevented the expected accident cost of $10 by an expenditure of $2, while the victim could have prevented the injury by expending $4. If the defense of contributory negligence is available, the victim is given the incentive to expend resources to avoid such accidents in the future even though the manufacturer could prevent the same accident for one-half the cost. Under Professor Posner's qualification of the Hand formulation,[2] the contributory negligence defense would not apply in this situation. According to many commentators, however, courts have not consistently limited the defense in this economically sound way, but have often permitted the defense to shield manufacturers from liability even when they were better cost avoiders.

STRICT LIABILITY

Then, in the early 1960s, the liability of manufacturers (and sellers) was broadened by the adoption of the so-called strict liability theory. Under strict liability, the plaintiff no longer needed to prove negligent conduct on the part of the defendant. Now he could recover by showing injury caused by a defect in the manufacturer's product. And the manufacturer could be held liable for harm caused by the defect regardless of how careful it had been in manufacture, distribution, and sale.

The adoption of strict products liability did not alter the inherent safety incentives of the negligence system in all cases. Returning to our

---

1. United States v. Carroll Towing Co., 159 F.2d 169 (2d Cir. 1947) (L. Hand, J.).
2. R. Posner, *Economic Analysis of the Law* (Little, Brown and Co., 1972).

original example, under strict liability the manufacturer of Model A would be held liable for all injuries caused by its defective car even though for one-half the cases it would have cost more than $10 per car to eliminate $10 worth of injuries. The manufacturer would not, in fact, make any additional investments in safety since, by hypothesis, it would be cheaper to pay the damage awards.[3]

For those cases in which the prevention costs of the victim are less than the expected accident cost and also less than the manufacturer's prevention costs, however, application of the strict liability rule would tend to reduce efficiency by inducing the manufacturer to spend more (say $4 per car to save $10 in expected accident costs) when the victim could have avoided the accident by a lesser expenditure (say $2). In negligence cases, the defense of contributory negligence provided a means for judge and jury to consider the ease with which the plaintiff could have avoided the accident. But under the strict liability doctrine, most courts have held that the negligence of the plaintiff is irrelevant (on both liability and damages issues); negligence is simply not an issue in strict liability cases. An unfortunate effect of eliminating the contributory negligence defense in strict liability cases has thus been to reduce the possibility of imposing accident-avoidance incentives on the "victim" when he could have prevented the injuries at a lower cost.

The negligence standard has not been completely superseded by strict liability in products liability cases. In cases involving design defects and duty-to-warn issues, "strict liability is virtually identical with negligence."[4] In design-defect cases, for example, many courts have recognized explicitly that the determination of whether a product design is "unreasonably dangerous" involves weighing the utility of the product against the risks it creates—exactly the process for determining negligence under the Hand formulation. The main difference between strict liability and negligence arises in the area of manufacturing defects (e.g., when the product sold does not meet its own specifications), where strict liability eases the burden of proof demanded of the plaintiff.

---

3. A potential exception, however, was identified by Posner, who argues that since the issue of whether additional accident-prevention measures are cost-justified is likely to be determined solely with reference to the existing technology, a manufacturer held strictly liable

> would compare the liability that it could not avoid by means of existing safety precautions with the feasibility of developing new precautions that would reduce liability. If safety research and development seemed likely to reduce accident costs by more than [it] cost . . . , [the economically rational manufacturer] would undertake it, and efficiency would be increased.

Since strict liability also reduces the potential victim's incentive to invest in accident-reducing research, however, strict liability will increase efficiency only in those cases where the manufacturer is likely to be a more efficient researcher than the victim. *Ibid.* at 138.

4. 4 *Interagency Task Force on Product Liability* 89.

If a defense of contributory negligence were permitted in strict liability actions, then strict liability would be just as efficient as the negligence system in terms of providing safety incentives to minimize the sum of accident-related costs. But the distribution of wealth will differ under a regime of strict liability, since it shifts the risk of loss for accidents that neither party could economically prevent from the victims to all product purchasers and, perhaps, to the stockholders of producing firms as well.

The problem of inadequate safety incentives for victims has been exacerbated under strict liability by two developments: (1) The increasingly narrow construction given to the defense of assumption of risk, which excuses a defendant from liability if the plaintiff knowingly assumes the risk of using the product in its defective condition; and (2) the extension of defendant's liability to include harms from products not fit for a "foreseeable misuse," although they may have been fit for their intended use. The erosion of these defenses prompted Richard Epstein to conclude: "A duel standard of responsibility has crept into the law. Conduct that would be sufficient to hold a person responsible for injuries inflicted upon another is ignored or overlooked when that person instead injures himself and then seeks compensation from the manufacturer. Defenses based upon the wrongful conduct of the plaintiff are by degrees being eliminated from the law."[5]

While one need not totally concur with Epstein's dire assessment of recent trends in products liability law, it is clear that doctrinal changes that remove accident-prevention incentives for victims when they are the most cost-efficient accident avoiders will lead to a misallocation of resources and to less than optimal levels of safety. Even those who question the efficacy of legal and economic incentives to encourage increased individual attention to accident prevention must at least concede the basic unfairness of imposing liability on a party (manufacturer, etc.) largely unable to prevent the harm.

The expansion of manufacturer's liability has broader economic and social consequences as well. To the extent that some products, e.g., cars, are more likely to be misused or used carelessly, liability imposed on the manufacturer for costs that could have been avoided more economically by the "victim" will tend to raise product prices—for careful and careless users alike—and lower investment returns relative to prices and returns for other products and industries. Under these circumstances, products liability amounts to a discriminatory tax levied on the basis of factors that the firm so taxed is unable to control economically. Moreover, it is not clear that holding a manufacturer liable for injuries it cannot economically prevent will actually increase overall safety. Such an approach will raise product prices, and consumers will tend to substitute other, often less safe, products, e.g., motorcycles for cars,

---

5. R. Epstein, "Products Liability: The Gathering Storm," *Regulation* (Sept./Oct. 1977).

chairs for ladders. Hence, liability rules that impose safety costs beyond that level preferred by users can be expected to encourage greater product substitution as consumers attempt to achieve by indirect means price/safety combinations denied to them by higher product prices.

COMPARATIVE NEGLIGENCE

The perceived unfairness of the contributory negligence rule in traditional negligence actions, and the growing perception of unfairness in the total abolition of the contributory negligence defense in strict liability cases, have contributed to the recent trend of courts and legislatures in adopting a rule of comparative negligence. Under comparative negligence, the plaintiff's recovery from a negligent defendant is reduced in proportion to the plaintiff's own negligence in causing the accident. In strict liability actions, a number of jurisdictions have taken the position that while the plaintiff's negligence may not be relevant to the liability issue, it is relevant in computing the appropriate damages.[6] The result in both situations is the same—the plaintiff and defendant share the burden of accident costs—in contrast to the all-or-nothing approach of traditional negligence and strict liability theories.

Because the comparative negligence rule allocates liability in proportion to fault, it will probably be considered more consistent with the "common sense" view of accident causation. It should also alleviate the unfairness of the present system of strict liability. Unfortunately, the effect of a comparative negligence rule on efficient incentives is often less desirable than that of either the traditional negligence system or a system of strict liability with a contributory negligence defense.[7] In some situations, comparative negligence will encourage both parties to invest in accident avoidance even though investment by only one would be necessary; e.g., when $10 of expected accident costs could be prevented by expenditure of $4 by either the manufacturer or the user, both will have an incentive to spend $4 even though $4 spent by either individually would be sufficient to avoid the accident. Alternatively, in such a situation neither party might invest in safety, each relying instead on the other's incentive to invest.

Nonetheless, the spread of comparative negligence is likely to represent an improvement over the present law of products liability. First, the adoption of liability rules that permit explicit consideration of the "victim's" conduct in determining damages is likely to increase users' incentives to avoid accidents and therefore to reduce the liability burden of manufacturers and distributors of products, like cars, which are

---

6. For a more comprehensive review of comparative negligence, see 5 *Interagency Task Force on Product Liability* 52 *et seq.*, and citations therein.
7. J. Brown, "Toward an Economic Theory of Liability," 2 *Journal of Legal Studies*, No. 2, pp. 323–349 (June 1973).

particularly susceptible to misuse, without diminishing the protection afforded to careful users.

Second, to the extent that present products liability rules have attenuated a plaintiff's responsibility for accident avoidance, comparative negligence should also reduce the attractiveness of products liability suits by careless plaintiffs as follows: The attenuation of defenses (under both negligence and strict liability rules) effectively increases the plaintiff's probability of recovering a judgment for the total amount of damages incurred. Comparative negligence, in contrast, reduces the *amount* of damages recoverable by a negligent plaintiff while leaving the probability of his winning *something* unchanged. Viewed prospectively, then a move to comparative negligence reduces the attractiveness of products liability suits by reducing the expected value of the damages award. If a particular plaintiff's probability of recovery under present law, despite some carelessness on his part, is 0.6 and the damages incurred are $10,000, the expected value of the verdict is $6,000; but if, under comparative negligence, the plaintiff is likely to be found 50 percent at fault, the expected value of the award would be reduced to $3,000 (0.6 × 50% of $10,000).

Finally, as discussed below, the increased willingness of courts to permit indemnity and contribution actions under comparative negligence doctrines promises a more efficient allocation of risks among those in the chain of distribution.

PRODUCTS LIABILITY IN PRACTICE: A CLOSER LOOK

The recognition that increasing manufacturers' liability will neither automatically nor necessarily result in improved safety levels and reduced accident rates is only the first step toward developing a better products liability system. The second part of the task requires closer scrutiny of the substantive norms and procedural rules of the products liability system to determine whether each moves the system toward or away from the socially efficient level of accidents and safety. Rather than review every element of the substantive and procedural law of products liability, I will concentrate on those features of the system that are most often criticized.

Jury Trials

Defendants in products liability cases often question the use of juries in such cases, primarily because they believe that juries tend to be unduly sympathetic to injured plaintiffs. Alternatives frequently suggested in lieu of trial by jury include bench trials (before a judge without jury) and some form of arbitration.

There is little empirical evidence to support the claim that jury verdicts systematically favor or overcompensate plaintiffs, relative to decisions by judges. A more immediate problem for those who advocate a move away from jury trials is the provision in the United States Constitution, and in many state constitutions and laws, that guarantees litigants the right to a trial by jury even in civil cases such as products liability suits. Still it might be possible, and more practical, to raise the court costs levied on litigants in civil jury trials to reflect their higher costs to the public. That would encourage litigants to choose less costly forms of dispute resolution, e.g., bench trials, voluntary arbitration, or negotiated settlement.

Pain and Suffering Damages

Manufacturers and other defendants in products liability cases frequently object to the damage awards for "pain and suffering." In essence, pain and suffering damages constitute that part of the award over and above the damages granted to cover economic losses such as medical and rehabilitation costs, lost wages, decreased earning potential due to disability, etc. Since it is virtually impossible to measure the value of noneconomic losses, such as the emotional damage resulting from loss of a limb, defendants tend to view awards for pain and suffering as arbitrary and, frequently, unreasonable. But neither is it fair to the injured plaintiff to deny recovery for real harms incurred because it is difficult to put a price on them. Furthermore, if the products liability system is to provide the socially optimal safety incentives, it must assess damages for all real costs caused by the product. Failure to do so will understate the social costs of defective products and thereby tend to decrease the overall level of safety.

That pain and suffering damages serve a useful purpose in providing adequate safety incentives should not, however, reduce one's concern regarding the inherently arbitrary process of determining the appropriate size of such awards. Both the fairness of the system and its efficiency as an accident reducer would be enhanced by the development of some conceptually sound, practically applicable basis for judges and juries to use in calculating the appropriate measure of pain and suffering damages. Perhaps such assistance could take the form of general guidelines with a normal or expected range for awards.[8]

Contingent Fees[9]

To many observers the problems of products liability can be traced to the system of contingent fees which, these critics argue, unduly encour-

---

8. Additional empirical research is essential in order to develop guidelines or ranges that reflect accurately and fairly the value of the essentially noneconomic aspects of injuries.
9. For a perceptive analysis of contingent fees, see M. W. Reder, "Contingent Fees in Litigation with Special Reference to Medical Malpractice," in *The Economics of Medical Malpractice* 211 (S. Rottenberg, Ed., American Enterprise Inst., 1978).

ages the filing of lawsuits and the seeking of exorbitant damage awards. The contrast is frequently drawn between the American fee system and its British counterpart where the fee is typically negotiated in advance and based on the amount of time (plus related costs) invested by the attorney, somewhat analogous to the fee-for-service principle so familiar in American (but not British) medical practice. Since the United Kingdom has a much lower incidence of products liability litigation, the critics urge, the United States should abolish the contingent fee system and thereby abate the trend toward more frequent litigation of product safety issues here.

The first point to be considered in comparing the American and British experiences is that not all of the difference in the rates of litigation is due to differences in the fee systems. Perhaps more important, there are substantial differences in the substantive liability rules that have long made it much more difficult for a plaintiff to win a products liability action in the United Kingdom than in the United States. British drug firms, for example, were not liable for injuries resulting from the sale and use of thalidomide; in sharp contrast to the situation of United States firms.

Second, even though the American contingent fee system is imperfect, it is not at all clear that the proposed changes would result in a better system. There are at least as many problems with them as there are with the present system, for less is not necessarily better in evaluating the frequency of products liability suits. If the use of a fee-for-service system prevents or discourages the filing of meritorious suits—i.e., those in which the damages could have been prevented most economically by the manufacturer—safety incentives will tend to be reduced below adequate levels. For many low- or moderate-income injury victims, the prospect of seeking a highly uncertain damage award will become much less attractive when weighed against the certainty of large legal fees under the fee-for-service system, regardless of how meritorious the attorney tells him the claim is. Since the lawyer will get his fee regardless of the outcome, and since the typical plaintiff is not capable of evaluating independently either the merits of his case or the diligence of his attorney, it is quite likely that the fee-for-service (British) system results in too little products liability litigation and economically inefficient safety incentives for manufacturers.

The advantages of the contingent fee are: (1) It gives injured parties access to court without regard to their income or wealth; and (2) it provides strong economic incentives for lawyers to do a good job for their clients. The major disadvantage of the contingent fee is that it tends to encourage nuisance or nonmeritorious litigation.

As a practical matter, the simple act of filing a products liability suit imposes substantially greater costs on the defendant than it does on the plaintiff. The defendant or its insurer typically establishes a contingent reserve against a possible adverse judgment; file searches, interviews, and other expenses are generated by the need to ascertain the validity and accuracy of the allegations and claims set out by the plaintiff; valuable management and legal staff time is diverted from other activities to respond. In short, a single legal prod by a lone plaintiff necessarily sets off a much larger and more costly response by a corporate defendant simply to find out the basic facts of the case.

This basic disparity in costs between litigants thus creates the incentive to file nuisance actions, for which the defendant's costs of settlement are less than the costs of successfully pursuing the litigation. The primary reason this situation exists is that in the United States, unlike Britain, the courts do not (as a general rule) order the losing party to pay the (reasonable) legal fees of the victor. Plaintiffs in United States courts thus have little to lose by filing such cases: If the company settles, plaintiff and attorney share the reward. If the defendant initially refuses to settle and the plaintiff can continue to increase the costs for the defendant by more than his own costs, the defendant faces a continuing economic fact of life: It is cheaper to settle than fight.

Proposals to award reasonable legal fees to the victorious party are met with the objection that such a system, like the fee-for-service system, would discriminate against low- and moderate-income litigants who could not bear the risk of paying the defendant's legal fees. But since it is essentially a lawyer's expert judgment that determines whether to file, prosecute, defend, or settle cases, a contingent fee system that required the losing *attorney* to pay the (reasonable) legal fees and costs of the victorious party—without indemnification by his client—would fully protect the rights of litigants while placing the burden of legal fees squarely on the shoulders of the lawyers, the parties in the best position to assess the probable outcome if the dispute goes to litigation. Assessment of legal costs against a losing plaintiff's attorney would eliminate the incentive to file nuisance suits since the costs of responding could be recovered by the victorious defendant. Similarly, defense attorneys would be discouraged from attempting to wear down plaintiffs by procedural ploys. At the same time, the proposed system would give victims with small claims improved access to compensation by permitting their attorney to recover legal fees in addition to the (small) claims amount. At present such cases are often turned away by lawyers because even a high percentage taken from a small award will be inadequate to compensate the attorney for the time and expense involved in prosecuting the case.

With this modification, the contingent fee system would then be in a position to carry out its important role in developing appropriate safety incentives without unduly encouraging litigation or discriminating against impecunious injury victims.

Collateral Sources of Compensation

Many successful plaintiffs in products liability suits have already received some compensation for the costs of their injuries from such sources as workers' compensation, medical insurance plans, Social Security or private insurance disability payments, or welfare. Under present law, such benefits from collateral sources do not generally reduce the liability of the defendant. Some observers conclude, however, that the accident victim should receive from the defendant only the difference between his total loss and the compensation from the collateral sources. Otherwise, they argue, the products liability judgment will result in a windfall gain to the plaintiff. Furthermore, critics charge, the prospect of "coming out ahead" by recovering more in benefits and damages than actual losses tends to convert products liability suits into a lottery, perhaps inducing litigation in the hopes of hitting the jackpot.

The overcompensation of victims can clearly encourage excessive litigation: Some victims with a lower probability of winning (p) will be encouraged to sue since the potential size of the total award (A), and, hence, the size of the expected award ($p \times A$) has increased. But if collateral income is deducted from the damage award, the cost to a manufacturer of producing unsafe products is reduced (since damages would be less than the full cost of the injury) and safety incentives weakened. Furthermore, collateral source benefits should not induce more carelessness by "victims" since carelessness which caused one's own harm would not be compensated under the socially efficient set of products liability rules discussed earlier.

The issue of collateral source income thus becomes essentially a matter of balancing policies. To the extent the benefits come from public funds financed by mandatory (tax) payments—workers' compensation, Social Security, welfare, etc.—I would favor requiring the defendant to repay those collateral sources for their outlays of public funds and denying double recovery to the victim. For those collateral source funds that come from private insurance policies purchased by the victim, the more appropriate treatment would be to ignore those sources and award full compensation to the injured plaintiff. Since the plaintiff voluntarily purchased those policies with his own funds, there would seem to be little reason to give the benefit of his foresight either to the careless defendant or to the victim's insurer. If such windfall gains are a problem for insurers, they can write policies that give them subrogation rights in such cases.[10]

Contractual Provisions

A significant products liability problem for manufacturers has been their exposure to strict liability damages in cases where the product was sold to a purchaser who modified or failed to maintain it, after which the product injured some third party. Two typical examples of this situation arise from the relationship between machine-tool manufac-

---

[10]. See generally 5 *Interagency Task Force on Product Liability* 135 *et seq.*

turers and the manufacturing firms that purchase the tools and the relationship between the automobile manufacturer and the dealer.

Since suits against machine toolmakers are generally initiated by employees of their customers (who cannot sue their employers because they are covered by workers' compensation laws), machine toolmakers have attempted to protect themselves contractually by inserting "hold harmless" clauses in their sales contracts. Such clauses bind the purchaser to compensate the manufacturer for any liability arising out of the use of the product in question. Since the major rationale of strict liability against the manufacturer is to protect the injured consumer, there seems little reason for courts to interfere with contractual reallocation of liability among parties in the chain of distribution that does not in any way impair the rights of injured users. Furthermore, such contracts probably tend to improve safety and reduce accidents by shifting the ultimate burden of liability for workplace injuries to the employer, who is typically in a much better position to prevent accidents in its own plant than is the machine tool manufacturer.

But courts have not looked with favor on "hold harmless" clauses. Nor have they been receptive to actions for indemnity and contribution—suits in which a manufacturer seeks to shift liability to, or share it with, other parties in the chain of distribution. As in the case of the contractual counterpart—the "hold harmless" clause—efficiency would be improved by permitting indemnity and contribution actions, since such suits facilitate the shifting of costs (and incentives) to the parties in the best position to prevent accidents. The spread of comparative negligence is apparently beginning to change the courts' traditional reluctance to uphold indemnity and contribution agreements. In particular, some courts have been willing to permit a tool manufacturer to recover from a user whose employee has prevailed against the manufacturer in a products liability action.[11] Similarly, automobile manufacturers and dealers have recently developed contractual indemnity arrangements to allocate products liability losses.[12]

A third form of contractual protection from products liability is the *contractual disclaimer*. Although courts and statutes disfavor them in cases involving consumer warranties, disclaimers may offer the most promising approach to a troublesome question in many products liability cases, viz., how long should a manufacturer be exposed to liability for harm caused by its products? Since most manufacturers cannot control either the use or the maintenance of their products once they have been sold, they are understandably concerned about the duration of their exposure to liability.

Given the tremendous variety of products on the market, it is virtually impossible to deal with the issue of the appropriate period of liability exposure through something as general as a statute of lim-

---

11. S. Birnbaum, "Products Liability," *National Law Journal*, Jan. 15, 1979.
12. *Automotive News*, Mar. 6, 1978, p. 1; Mar. 20, 1978, p. 1.

itations. If, instead, manufacturers could stipulate the anticipated useful life of their products, e.g., a 40,000-mile tire, they would be in a much better position to predict and control their exposure to liability. For sales from a manufacturer to intermediaries, the effect of such a useful life clause would be similar to that of the "hold harmless" clause discussed above, and again there is little reason for courts to interfere in the contractual allocation of risk among commercial parties.

The use of disclaimers in ultimate consumer markets, however, may create more difficult problems. For complex products such as automobiles, the various disclaimers could fill a small book. Tires, drive train, body, and exhaust system, for instance, would each have a different expected useful life. Nonetheless, competitive markets could be expected to keep sellers from understating the product's useful life, since an automobile with a manufacturer's estimated useful life of 12,000 miles or 12 months would be less attractive to most auto buyers than a 5-year, 50,000-mile car, comparably priced.

But, disclaimers raise other, more difficult, problems at the consumer level. Suppose that a car is driven beyond the stipulated useful life period, suffers brake failure, and injures a pedestrian. Since the pedestrian was not a party to the contract between the automobile company and the vehicle purchaser, and his safety as a pedestrian may not have been considered in the contract, he should not be bound by it. Since the pedestrian could hold the vehicle owner liable for his injuries, vehicle owners would, in principle, be forced to consider such third-party injuries in their initial choice of an automobile. It is open to serious question, however, whether courts—even if they permit disclaimers to limit purchasers' rights—would also permit a similar narrowing of third-party rights against manufacturers. If third-party cases are governed by different standards than purchaser cases, however, it is unclear how much disclaimers would benefit products liability defendants.[13] As an alternative, courts could permit an indemnity and contribution action by a manufacturer against a purchaser whose negligent use (or maintenance) of the product resulted in a third-party suit against the manufacturer. This approach would protect third-party victims while providing manufacturers and purchasers with strong incentives to consider third-party injuries when making their design, manufacture, and purchase decisions.

State-of-the-Art Defense

A similar predicament arises in design cases with the proposal to create an absolute defense for the manufacturer if the product was designed according to the state of the art within the industry at the time it was designed. Although in the absence of collusion one could assume that

---

13. For a general discussion of the contractual "solution," see 6 *Interagency Task Force on Product Liability* 1 et seq.

competition in product markets would protect purchasers against design defects, due to an industry-side lag in design standards, the problem of the injured nonpurchaser arises again, as it did in the earlier discussion of contract disclaimers. Thus, it would seem that a rebuttable presumption in favor of a defendant using state-of-the-art technology is the most that could be justified, particularly in third-party cases.

Product Safety Standards/Requirements

Safety standards and/or requirements raise additional issues of products liability. The first is whether compliance with government product standards should be a defense in a products liability action. This "solution" would be undesirable for a number of reasons. Most important, since technology changes much faster than administrative agencies can possibly adjust specifications, the effect of making such standards an absolute defense could be to slow the development of new technology without improving safety at all. Hence, it seems far preferable to treat compliance with such standards simply as evidence bearing on the issue of liability.

A second issue involves the potential effects of safety standards in creating products liability litigation. Consider the case of mandatory passive restraint systems. If the government decided to mandate a particular technology, air bags, for instance, instead of passive belts, the effect could be to spur litigation without improving overall safety. If air bags are 99 percent reliable, there will be 10,000 malfunctions for every 1 million vehicles sold. For malfunctions that occur during a collision, lawsuits are highly likely. But if malfunctions of the air bags occur when the car is in normal operation, lawsuits are also highly probable, since a malfunctioning air bag is much more likely than a passive belt to cause an accident. Thus, to the extent that the regulator's analysis ignores the different accident-causing (as well as preventing) characteristics of mandatory product safety standards, manufacturers may be forced to adopt technologies with higher exposure to products liability damages.

CONCLUSION

As the preceding analysis has made clear, the tort law of products liability is likely to play a strong and potentially positive role in the evolving regulation of automobile safety. But the system is not perfect, and changes in both the substantive and procedural law would appreciably enhance the effectiveness of the tort law as a vehicle for regulating product safety. Liability rules that take cognizance of the relative accident-avoiding costs of victims as well as producers are particularly important. In this regard, the emergence of comparative negligence is promising. Procedurally, changes in the contingent fee system could both reduce the problem of nuisance suits and give small but meritorious claims better access to the courts.

Even if adopted in their entirety, however, the proposed revisions of the tort law outlined in this paper would not satisfy those critics who view the tort system as a vehicle for compensating accident victims and allocating the accident costs to those in the best position to spread the risk of loss (typically, a defendant manufacturer or seller). Their focus on compensation of victims and risk-spreading ignores both the victim's accident avoidance costs—which may be substantially lower than those of the defendant—and the effects that compensation-oriented rules would have on the behavioral incentives of potential victims.[14]

Nonetheless, the strong contemporary social concern for compensating accident victims suggests that the immediate task is to develop a system that provides adequate compensation for accident victims without destroying their accident-avoidance incentives. The basic aim of such a system should be to provide a "safety net" for those who cause their own injuries and to protect those with insufficient reserves to tide them over from the time of the injury to the collection of damages. But the safety net should not become a magnet that attracts litigation by the prospect of recovering damages and safety net payments far in excess of actual losses. While the adequacy of the safety net clearly bears further investigation, my own suspicion is that, for many accident victims, the safety net is already in place. The combination of Social Security disability protection, Medicare and Medicaid, unemployment insurance, workers' compensation, welfare, public hospitals, and for some, Veterans Administration medical care, provides a substantial public safety net. A national health insurance program would further strengthen it. When private insurance, private charity, personal and family savings are included, I suspect that the provision of adequate compensation for products-related accident victims will not involve significantly greater costs for society.

The public policy implications of an adequate safety net for the products liability system are simple and straightforward. With adequate compensation available for accident victims, the focus of products liability should be on that which it is capable of doing best—developing and enforcing legal incentives, for users as well as producers, that move us closer to a socially efficient level of product safety. Informed with an understanding of the potentially positive role the tort system can play in product safety regulation, we are in a position to turn that potential into reality.

---

14. For a discussion of the problems of user incentives in the case of automobile safety, see S. Peltzman, *Regulation of Automobile Safety* (American Enterprise Inst., 1975).

DISCUSSION

JAN ROZENDAAL: Professor Kasper starts with the premise that the product liability system is designed to promote efficient decision-making by a manufacturer. Compensation to the accident victim is only an incident of the system; in effect, he says that product liability is a form of safety regulation.

At one time fear of product liability lawsuits was a major incentive for a manufacturer to design a safer product. Today many other incentives—expensive and embarrassing recalls, higher warranty costs, consumer complaints, federal regulation—promote that socially desirable goal.

The explosion of punitive damage awards, third-party suits, and the erosion of the bar to consequential damage claims makes the auto makers' rational calculations impossible. The manufacturer's only recourse is to price his product high enough to recover his rapidly increasing costs of legal defense, damage awards, and liability insurance premiums.

The costs to the manufacturer and thus to the consumer of attempting to regulate through products liability laws are too great and the system too inflexible. Strict liability stifles innovation and places impossible burdens on the manufacturer and the seller.

Let our liability system return to its originally intended goal of compensating the victim for his loss. And let the burden of this compensation be borne by the party who is the proximate cause of the harm. To do otherwise is to invite the possibility of the auto maker being the defendant in almost every collision case on the grounds that the car could have been built so that the injury would not have occurred. This possibility and its costs are too horrible to contemplate.

NICHOLAS ASHFORD: I will not claim to be expert in the product liability area for automobiles, but I do know a great deal about how the courts have worked in the area of toxic substances. My observation there does not conform to the view expressed that the courts have been inappropriate responders to the problems created by the dangerous nature of toxic substances. Dan Kasper's paper disturbs me because it is telling the truth about only one small section of the world. It pretends to represent a thoroughness of approach which ought to be looked at very carefully.

In chemicals, one can make a good case that the victim is highly unlikely to be at fault, for example, with harm due to the very toxic effects of materials like asbestos. The workers' compensation system has been notoriously deficient in suitably compensating the worker for harm done. What has emerged is that the courts will entertain with great pleasure products liability suits against the asbestos manufacturers because they see not only that the function of compensation is going unmet, but also that the manufacturers lack the incentives to produce safe products. Chemical companies now, as a consequence, are much more worried about products liability suits than about fire insurance. It is questionable whether products liability has had as dramatic an effect on the auto makers.

Efficiency is *not* the only socially desirable goal of products liability law. We must be clear about the difference between what the economists call a potential Pareto improvement from an actual Pareto improvement. There might be ways to get welfare maximized in terms of safety delivered; the question is, who ends up paying for it? The issue of equity is important here. We may in fact want to deliver more safety to the consumer than he is able to express his valuation for in the market. We have countless examples that people do not relate to long-term, low-probability risks. There is an entire behavioral literature on this.

I contest also the view that compensation to accident victims is the main or primary purpose of products liability. The expansion in chemical industry suits comes from a desire to increase the deterrence effect in light of the failure of regulation to move rapidly enough to change the nature of technological innovation in that area.

I next want to raise a different view of risk perception that is not captured by the insurance model; it is the choice that is faced by a firm that cannot obtain insurance or by a firm that self-insures. The decision-making model facing the firm is not a simple function derived by multiplying the probability by the size of the damage and comparing the result to what avoidance costs one may face. The choices faced by a firm are shown as Figures A and B on the next page.

These models I have drawn are distributions; and there are two distributions one worries about. One is the probability of incurring the cost of meeting a given level of protection (Figure A). The firm faces avoidance costs which are fairly predictable (i.e., a small variance), though sometimes large. The probability of a successful lawsuit as a result of not avoiding harm looks like Figure B. Insurance cuts off the tail of the distribution by spreading the economic costs over all the policyholders. In addition, limits may be placed on any single award by state law. The tail of the distribution is the place where the firms are really risk averse; this is why the chemical companies want to do away with products liability. The small probability of a very large award is something they feel strongly about. In other words, their risk aversion is not a single product of the probability times the damage, as in the Hand formula. As the damage increases, their risk-aversion increases more than linearly with the size of the award. This is the real strength of the products liability system for changing behavior.

The question of the least-cost avoider may not really be as applicable in the area of automobile safety as Kasper suggests. Who is more capable of innovating, who is more capable of coming up with a compliance response which moves the technology? I do not think in any way, shape, or form it is the victim; that is a very strong reason for not using the suggestion that we make the least-cost avoider pay.

FIGURE A

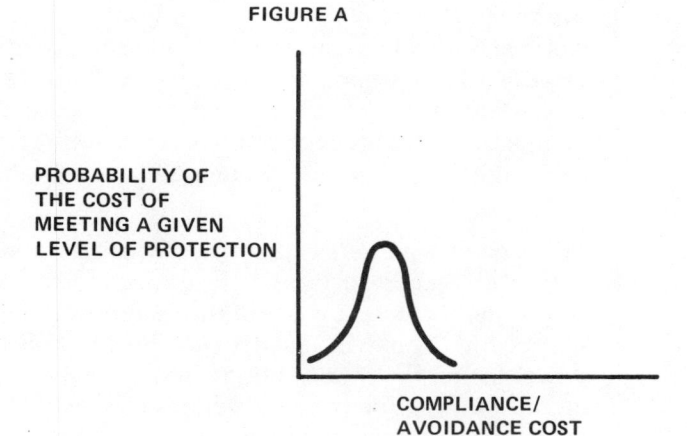

PROBABILITY OF THE COST OF MEETING A GIVEN LEVEL OF PROTECTION

COMPLIANCE/AVOIDANCE COST

FIGURE B

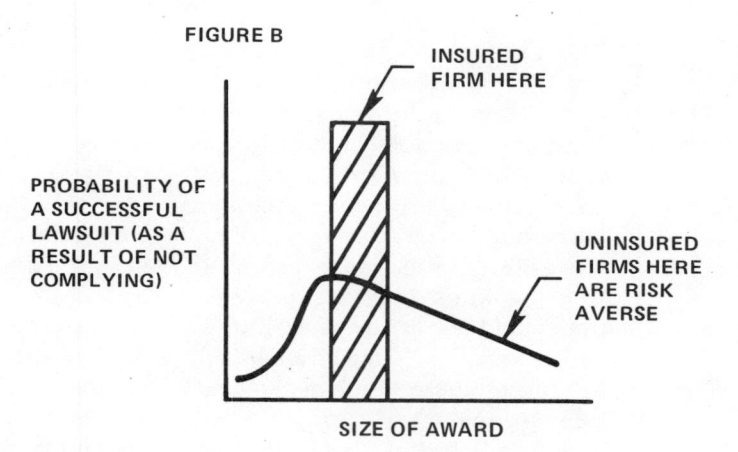

PROBABILITY OF A SUCCESSFUL LAWSUIT (AS A RESULT OF NOT COMPLYING)

INSURED FIRM HERE

UNINSURED FIRMS HERE ARE RISK AVERSE

SIZE OF AWARD

Regulation, it is sometimes said, imposes safer products on the poor than they want to purchase and, consequently, reduces their welfare. This is a misconception. In fact, if one ends up providing to the poor safer products and a safer workplace, we will not ignore the necessity to transfer to them food stamps and other forms of welfare. Their total welfare may increase!

People who undervalue their lives, like the workers in asbestos plants, will sell their lives off cheaply because they come to the world with a small bundle of goods. If you give them the right information and they perceive it, they will still sell their lives more cheaply than the son of the executive running the plant. That is economically efficient; but is it fair? We need to recognize that there is a value judgment implicit in using efficiency as a criterion of how much safety in the automobile, or on the job, or in consumer products, one ends up regulating.

Turning now to Dr. Von Hulsen's paper, is the purpose of the law to increase predictability and certainty? If you want to create incentives for technological innovation, then you do not want absolute predictability in outcome. You want some uncertainty. Technological innovation will occur when there is uncertainty as to how far one must go in protecting the consumer, and hence risk averseness in the firm in the consequence.

The Pinto case is interesting. Before it was reversed and the award reduced, the court made the calculation that on the basis of Ford's own assessment to correct the defect would have cost them X million dollars. The court awarded punitive damages just slightly over the avoidance costs that Ford could have expended. This is a signal to the firm that it is not in a firm's economic interest to avoid the costs of correction.

GOVERNMENT: The jury in Los Angeles in the *Ford Pinto* case said an interesting thing. They did not merely say $800,000, Ford's figure, was too low; they said *whatever* damage figure you set is too low.

KASPER: This tends to discourage manufacturers from using a cost-benefit analysis to figure out what the appropriate level of safety is.

GOVERNMENT: I have an idea. Let us ask Mr. Ford what he values his life at; we will use that figure as a standard.

KASPER: Are you denying the possibility that there can be such a thing as too much safety?

GOVERNMENT: Theoretically, I suppose it is conceivable. But the real question is who decides what that level is.

KASPER: Courts are deciding right now.

GOVERNMENT (DOT): We believe that there is enough diversity and competition in the United States market that products liability stimulates innovation. To the extent that one sees more concentration, then some of the problems raised by the papers becomes a greater concern; products liability exposure could hold back the state of the art in the monopolistic industry.

CHAPTER THREE
The Case of the Fuel Economy Standards

EDITORS' NOTE

This chapter is devoted to fuel economy standards. Richard R. John, et al. explain where these standards came from, how they compare and contrast with the regimes governing automobile emissions and safety, and their success to date. Although Dr. John believes that the standards through 1985 are a policy success, he suggests that their use to achieve still higher levels of fuel economy thereafter will depend upon the support of additional federal policies both to stimulate the marketability of fuel efficient motor vehicles and to mitigate the regional economic dislocations that would otherwise occur.

Kirk O. Hanson examines the effect of the fuel economy standards from another perspective, that of the student of corporate strategy. His premise is that the more regulation becomes an important factor in corporate policy-making, the more corporate decision-makers will need to understand the dynamics of the relationship between regulatee and regulator. He offers an analytic framework that will be useful for both industry and government analysts in assessing the potential effect of proposed or enacted policies on product-market strategy. As his analysis suggests, uniform standards may have quite disparate effects upon the various firms in the industry subject to those standards.

MANDATED FUEL ECONOMY STANDARDS AS A STRATEGY FOR IMPROVING MOTOR VEHICLE FUEL ECONOMY

Richard R. John, Philip S. Coonley, Robert C. Ricci, Bruce Rubinger*, *Department of Transportation, Transportation Systems Center*

This essay will review the legislative and administrative history of the mandatory fuel economy standards, and assess the potential of such standards for achieving further improvements in new car fleet fuel economy. On the basis of developments to date, we conclude that if further progress is to be achieved by the mandatory fuel economy approach, the standard will have to be supplemented by related policies to encourage research into and development of new technologies and to mitigate the economic dislocations that will attend further efficiency-seeking changes in the automobile industry.

AUTOMOBILE LEGISLATION: AN OVERVIEW

The history of the mandatory motor vehicle fuel-economy-standards legislation is closely related to the earlier legislative development of mandatory motor vehicle safety and emission standards (see Table 3-1). It is therefore instructive to understand the similarities and the differences among these three regimes.

Safety Legislation

Motor vehicle occupant safety had become a public issue by the end of the 1940s, but the concerns and potential regulations then focused on the driver. The rising death toll in the 1960s and the publication in 1965 of Ralph Nader's *Unsafe At Any Speed* dramatically sharpened public scrutiny of vehicle design as a major causative factor in motor vehicle

---

* The views presented herein are the personal views of the authors and do not represent any official position or findings of DOT.

TABLE 3-1 Motor Vehicle Regulatory Standards Governing Legislation

Product regulatory standard	Governing legislation	Political environment
Safety	National Highway Traffic Safety Act of 1966	Ralph Nader's *Unsafe at Any Speed* (1966)
Exhaust emissions	Clean Air Act of 1970	Strong public environmental movement (1970)
Fuel economy	Energy Policy and Conservation Act of 1975	Aftermath (1975) of oil embargo

safety. In response to rising public pressure, Congress passed the National Highway Traffic Safety Act of 1966,[1] which established a set of national motor vehicle safety objectives and required that the executive branch promulgate appropriate standards to achieve these objectives. Because no specific or easily quantifiable goals were prescribed in the initial legislation, it was difficult to administer. Subsequent motor vehicle emissions and fuel economy legislation, on the other hand, has been much more specific in intent and more rigorous in its expression.

Environmental Legislation

In 1965, the Congress passed legislation requiring that motor vehicle emission-control standards be promulgated by the executive branch, giving appropriate consideration to "technical feasibility and economic costs."[2] As with safety legislation, early emission-control legislation contemplated that the executive branch would both develop the standards and administer them. The Clean Air Act Amendments of 1970 represented a dramatic change from this approach. Congress itself dictated the standards in the Clean Air Act Amendments. In arriving at the 1970 standards—90 percent reduction of carbon monoxide, hydrocarbons, and nitrogen oxides by 1975 to 1976—the Congress paid minimal attention to technological feasibility and economic effects.

As the Safety Act was, in part, a legislative response to Nader's book, the Clean Air Act Amendments of 1970 were, in part, a response to the spirit of that time. During the first six months of 1970, legislation had

---

1. A background summary on automobile safety legislation is given in P. Lorange and L. H. Linden, *Automobile Safety Regulation: Technological Change and the Regulatory Process*, Ch. 2, pp. 19–23, Energy Lab., Report MIT-EL-77-036 (MIT, Oct. 1977).

2. PL 89-272, Amendments to the Clean Air Act of 1963, Oct. 20, 1965.

been prepared in the Congress to ban the internal combustion engine;[3] the administration had proposed a research effort to develop a nonpolluting engine by 1975; and editorializing on the Muskie committee hearings that led to the 1970 Amendments, the *New York Times* concluded, "A nation that can put a man on the moon in less than ten years can clean up its engines in half that time."[4]

Fuel Economy Legislation

The first congressional debates on motor vehicle fuel economy legislation occurred in 1973 in response to numerous reports of a forthcoming energy crisis, a cold winter, early summer gasoline shortages, and the October Arab oil embargo. Since that time, over 100 congressional bills have been introduced on the subject of improving motor vehicle fuel economy (see Table 3-2). The bills have covered a wide range of public policy alternatives, including gasoline and motor vehicle taxes, improving consumer fuel economy information, mandated fuel economy standards, and mandatory fuel economy labels.

Of the many proposed pieces of legislation, only three were enacted, and none of those uses the price mechanism to give consumers or producers an incentive to act in desired ways. Two of the new laws pertain to federally funded motor vehicle research and development. In 1975, Congress passed the Energy Reorganization Act (PL 93-438), providing for research and development of advanced automotive propulsion systems; in 1976, the Electric and Hybrid Vehicle Research, Development, and Demonstration Act (PL 94-413) was passed, providing for research into electric vehicle technology. Both these laws directed the expenditure of federal funding for long-term automotive research and development in areas to which industry would be hesitant to apply major resources because of the long pay-back periods. The third law, mandating fuel economy performance, was passed in December 1975 as part of the Energy Policy and Conservation Act (PL 94-163). The fuel economy standards reflected the same strategy that Congress used in the Clean Air Act Amendments of 1970: Congress dictated a precise goal—27.5 miles per gallon by 1985—and the executive branch was directed to achieve the standards.

Thus, after almost three years of debate, the Congress chose federally funded motor vehicle research and development and mandatory product regulations rather than the price mechanism (i.e., through gasoline taxes or a gas guzzler tax), as the public policy to attain improved motor vehicle fuel economy; federal actions have been primarily aimed at improving the fuel economy of the new car fleet rather than on modifying consumer behavior. Although the gasoline tax was viewed as a

---

3. H. R. No. 6599, Mar. 16, 1971 and H. R. No. 3091, Jan. 29, 1973.
4. "Fume-Free '75," *New York Times*, Aug. 23, 1970, Sec. 3, p. 12.

TABLE 3-2 Congressional Bills To Improve Motor Vehicle Fuel Economy (1973 to 1977)

Nature of proposed legislation	Number of legislative initiatives				
	1973	1974	1975	1976	1977
A. *Consumer Economic Incentives*					
Auto Gas Guzzler Tax	16	6	36		2
Gasoline Tax	2	4	13		
Gasoline Rationing		3	4	1	1
B. *Information; Fuel Economy Labeling*	2	2	1		
C. *Product Regulation*					
Mandated Fuel Economy	8	2	15		9
Relax Emissions/Safety Standards	14	14	19		1
D. *Motor Vehicle R&D*	11	5	19	4	11

potentially powerful means for reducing petroleum consumption, it was also viewed in Congress as a regressive tax that would be unpopular with voters.

This preference for product regulation over tax or other price-oriented approaches was not unanimous. Perhaps predictably, the major domestic automobile manufacturers had strongly opposed enactment of mandatory fuel economy standards. For example, Henry Duncombe, Chief Economist at General Motors, testified against imposing "regulation in an area where competition clearly can do a better job," and Fred Secrest, Executive Vice President of Operations at Ford, argued likewise for reliance upon "market forces—which allow manufacturers the flexibility to respond to consumer demand through innovation spurred by competition—rather than arbitrary standards that would tend to limit flexibility and might well deter innovation and improvement."[5]

In October 1974, the *New York Times* reported that Federal Energy Administrator John Sawhill was forced to resign in 1974 because of policy differences with the administration. He had publicly advocated a gasoline tax.[6] The basic policy of the Ford administration toward motor vehicle fuel economy improvement had been to establish a voluntary program with the industry.

In the National Energy Plan, presented to the Congress by President Carter on April 20, 1977, a "gas guzzler" tax and rebate were proposed

---

5. *Energy Conservation Working Paper, Sen. Commerce Comm. Hearings* (Dec. 10, 1974), p. 174.
6. "President Ford announces forced resignation of Federal Energy Administrator John C. Sawhill . . . ," *New York Times*, Oct. 30, 1974, p. 8.

on the grounds that present mandatory fuel economy standards were insufficient to assure needed petroleum conservation. A graduated excise tax would be imposed on new automobiles and light trucks whose fuel economy failed to meet the applicable fuel economy standard under existing law. The proposed gas guzzler tax and rebate are still being debated in the Congress.[7]

Finally, Charles Schultze, current head of the Council of Economic Advisers, explained in his 1976 Harvard Godkin Lectures why public regulation of the private sector is inherently difficult and how it might be made more effective.[8] His main thesis was that regulatory laws have attempted to force people and businesses directly to do certain things rather than to encourage them through more indirect methods. He suggested, as an alternative, the increased use of market-like incentives, such as tax and transfer arrangements, that would enlist private interests in the pursuit of public goals.

Thus, the debate on the efficacy of price mechanisms versus product regulation for improving fuel economy continues. Mandatory fuel economy standards are now the law, however, and, unless and until changed, must be observed.

STANDARD SETTING IN THE THREE REGIMES COMPARED[9]

As we have seen, in each of the three major motor vehicle policy areas—fuel economy, emission control, and safety—the Congress has selected product standards rather than taxes or some sort of monetary incentive scheme as its major policy instrument. A comparison of assigned responsibilities and the structure of the motor vehicle regulatory standards (see Tables 3-3 and 3-4) shows that the nature of the product standards is quite different for each of the three areas, however.

Safety

In the initial regulation of the motor vehicle, the National Traffic and Motor Vehicle Safety Act of 1966, Congress gave the executive branch the authority to set practical safety performance standards and goals. The burden of proof as to what was "practical" was on the executive branch. NHTSA was to prescribe practical performance goals, which were to be promulgated within the constraints of the Federal Administrative Procedure Act. Under this Act, proposed administrative standards are subject to interagency and public comment, and can be

---

7. "Conferees Agree to Penalize Makers of Gas Guzzlers," *Congressional Quarterly Weekly Report*, Sept. 30, 1978, p. 2714.
8. C. Schultze, *The Public Use of Private Interest* (Brookings Inst., 1977).
9. A summary of the characteristics of motor vehicle standards is provided in J. Heywood, et al., *Regulating the Automobile*, Energy Lab., Report MIT-EL 77-007 (MIT, Nov. 1977) in Ch. 1, "The American System of Regulating the Automobile," by L. H. Linden and D. Iverach, pp. 1-1 through 1–53.

TABLE 3-3 Comparison of Assigned Executive and Congressional Responsibilities in Federal Regulations for Fuel Economy, Safety, and Emissions

In the Case of Safety (National Traffic and Safety Act, 1966):

Congress gave the executive branch authority to set performance standards with the constraint that they be "practical."

Burden of proof on agency.

NHTSA prescribed performance goals which are subject to public hearings and can be contested by all "concerned" parties.

In the Case of Emissions (Clean Air Act of 1970):

Congress mandated numerical emission goals (e.g., $NO_x = 0.41$ gm/mile).

Congressionally mandated numerical goal can legally be contested only on constitutional grounds.

In the Case of Fuel Economy (Energy Policy and Conservation Act, 1975):

Legislation combines strategies of legislatively prescribed and agency prescribed performance goals.

TABLE 3-4 Structure of Motor Vehicle Regulatory Standards

Standard	Characteristics	Comments
Safety	Equipment performance	1. Little flexibility to manufacture 2. No motive to provide innovative technology
Emissions	Vehicle performance	1. No particular equipment required by regulation 2. Near-term technical fix
Fuel economy	Fleet performance	1. Allows flexibility to manufacturer 2. Final new car fleet average fuel economy is a function of consumer behavior

challenged on a variety of grounds, including inflationary and environmental effects.[10] In contrast, a numerical goal mandated by Congress can only be legally contested on constitutional grounds.

The Safety Act required that automotive safety standards be performance standards; however, because formulating a single motor vehicle safety performance standard was so difficult, the administering agency (i.e., NHTSA), defined performance standards for specific items of motor vehicle equipment such as headlights, side structure, and so forth. These standards are therefore referred to as *equipment performance standards*. The manufacturer must improve the specified equipment on each vehicle to the mandated minimum performance level. Little flexibility is allowed. In order to attain higher levels of safety, new standards must be added, but the burden of proof that these new standards are warranted rests with the administrating agency. The manufacturer has no incentive to use innovative technology beyond the requirements called for by the agency except insofar as it might reduce cost or minimize consumer discomfort.

Emissions

In the Clean Air Act Amendments of 1970 and the Energy Policy and Conservation Act of 1975, the Congress set numerical values for emission and fuel-economy-performance goals, assuming what had been an executive branch function. A key motivating factor in this procedural change was the Congress's and the public's growing displeasure with the unresponsiveness of the industry to national goals.[11]

The Clean Air Act Amendments of 1970 set numerical limits, on a specified timetable, for each of three major pollutants emitted by the automobile—carbon monoxide, hydrocarbons, and nitrogen oxides. The standards were to be met by each vehicle produced, and all vehicles produced in a given year were to meet the same standard. The legislation did not require any particular equipment; the legislation only required that the standards be met. The role of the administering agency, in this case the EPA, was to enforce the standards; the burden of proof was on the manufacturer to show that the emission standards had been or could not be met.

The emission-control standards have encouraged the industry to develop near-term technical fixes that could be implemented within the time constraints of the standards. The technology that is adopted may not, however, be the most effective overall; e.g., early emission-control

---

10. The role of the Federal Administrative Procedure Act in establishing the framework within which the regulatory process must function is developed in E. Goodson's, *Federal Regulation of Motor Vehicles—A Summary and Analysis* (Purdue Univ., Mar. 1977) (prepared for DOT).
11. Margolis, "Another View of the Politics of Auto Emissions Control," in Heywood, n. 9 *supra* at Ch. 5.

technology resulted in a significant fuel economy penalty. The legislatively mandated motor vehicle performance standards, in general, do offer more flexibility than the administratively mandated safety equipment performance standards in that they can be gradually tightened, thus giving the manufacturer an incentive to develop new technology.

Fuel Economy

Finally, the Energy Policy and Conservation Act of 1975 combines performance standards mandated by Congress and performance goals prescribed by an agency. The mandatory fuel economy portion of the Energy Policy and Conservation Act prescribes passenger car fuel economy standards for model years 1978, 1979, 1980, and 1985, and directs the Secretary of Transportation to set passenger car fuel economy standards for model years 1981 through 1984, as well as for light trucks and vans. Consideration must be given to: (1) Technical feasibility; (2) economic practicability; (3) the effect of other standards; and (4) the need to conserve energy. The passenger car fuel standards were set by Congress at 18 miles per gallon for model year 1978, 19 miles for 1979, 20 miles for 1980, and 27.5 miles for 1985.

The new car fleet fuel economy performance standards are, from the manufacturer's viewpoint, the most flexible since they allow the manufacturer to phase-in new technology development over different motor vehicle lines. The ability to phase-in new technology is particularly important in consideration of both technical and market risks.

HISTORY OF THE FUEL ECONOMY PROGRAM[12]

Background

During the early 1970s, studies and programs were undertaken by the executive branch on the subject of improved motor vehicle economy (see Appendix A), which affected the form and administration of the mandatory fuel economy standards. Nonmandatory fuel economy programs complemented ongoing congressional debates on mandatory fuel economy standards.

In June 1971, the Office of the Secretary in DOT completed an internal study of opportunities for transportation energy conservation.[13] The motor vehicle fleet was the most promising target. During 1972, an interagency task force consisting of participants from DOT, EPA, the National Aeronautics and Space Administration, and the Department of Defense prepared a summary, *Energy Research and Development Goals,*

---

12. A summary of the administrative history of fuel economy regulation is presented in Goodson, n. 10 *supra* at 14–29.
13. *New Technology Initiatives,* Internal Report, (DOT Office of the Assistant Secretary for Sys. Dev. & Technology, June 1971).

for the White House Office of Science and Technology. The Transportation Panel of this task force concluded that motor vehicle fuel economy could be significantly improved by 1980 with no major changes in vehicle functional characteristics.[14] These findings were confirmed in the 1974 DOT/EPA *Report to Congress on the Potential for Motor Vehicle Fuel Economy Improvement*. The DOT/EPA Report to Congress had been congressionally mandated as part of the Energy Supply and Conservation Act of 1974, which required that DOT and EPA assess the feasibility of a 20 percent improvement in new car fuel economy by 1980. The report concluded that rather than 20 percent, a 40-to-60 percent improvement could be obtained by 1980. These findings became a critical technical input for President Ford's Voluntary Fuel Economy Program and for the mandatory program subsequently enacted by Congress.[15]

Influenced in part by the DOT/EPA study, President Ford announced to Congress in October 1974 a goal of 40 percent improvement in new car fuel economy by 1980.[16] In his State of the Union Message in January 1975, President Ford indicated industry agreement to a Voluntary Fuel Economy Program. The voluntary program was in effect from January 1974 to April 1976, when the Mandatory Fuel Economy Program replaced it. The final report on the Voluntary Fuel Economy Program (April 1976) concluded that industry product programs then in progress would meet the planned target of 40 percent improvement by 1980.

In March 1975 the White House Energy Resources Council, chaired by Secretary Rogers Morton, requested that DOT establish an interagency task force to study long-range goals for the motor vehicle fleet that would be compatible with national environmental, safety, and economic objectives. The final report from this study, *Report by the Federal Task Force on Motor Vehicle Goals Beyond 1980*, was issued in November 1976, and concluded that a goal of 100 percent improvement in motor vehicle fuel economy by 1985, compared to model year 1973, was achievable. This finding was compatible with the goal of 27.5 miles per gallon adopted in the Mandatory Fuel Economy Program.

It is clear from the congressional hearing records on mandatory fuel economy standards that Congress had little faith in the efficacy of any voluntary program.[17] Mandatory fuel economy legislation did pass as

---

14. *Research and Development Opportunities for Improved Transportation Energy Usage*, Report No. DOT-TSC-OST-73-14, (Transportation Energy Panel, Sept. 1972).

15. N. 5 *supra* at 1 and 8.

16. President Gerald R. Ford, "The Economy," address before a Joint Session of Congress., Oct. 8, 1974, in *Weekly Compilation of Presidential Documents*, Oct. 14, 1974, pp. 1239–1247.

17. *Energy Conservation and Oil Policy, Hearings Before the House Interstate and Foreign Commerce Comm., Subcomm. on Energy and Power* (March/May 1975), Pt. 2.

part of the Energy Policy and Conservation Act (PL 94-163) in December 1975. This formally killed the voluntary program.

The mandated fuel economy numbers were based, in part, on projections made in the DOT/EPA study. Heywood et al., argue, however, that the 1985 fuel economy standards set by Congress were arbitrarily "chosen principally for their symbolic value—a doubling of the economy of existing new cars."[18] Available evidence suggests that this was not the case. At least five years of agency and congressional background work had been performed prior to passage of the mandatory fuel economy legislation. The data used were the best available.

Rule-Making Process

The Energy Policy and Conservation Act (EPCA), Public Law 94-163, enacted December 25, 1975, amends the Motor Vehicle Information and Cost Savings Act to include a new Title V, "Improving Automotive Efficiency." This Title requires the Secretary of Transportation to define and implement a program for improving the fuel economy of new automobiles in the United States market. On June 22, 1976 the authority to administer the program was delegated by the Secretary of Transportation to the Administrator of NHTSA.

NHTSA's responsibilities under the Act can be divided into four major areas: (1) To establish and enforce motor vehicle fuel economy standards; (2) to grant exemptions from applicable standards; (3) to review and assess reports from the automobile manufacturers; and (4) to report to Congress on the fuel economy program. In the process of fuel economy rule-making, the NHTSA follows the pattern required by the Administrative Procedure Act;[19] other federal agencies, industry, interested groups, and private citizens are requested, through the Federal Register, to comment on the fuel economy proposals. From these comments, and other available data, NHTSA acquires information that will contribute to the final rules.[20]

---

18. N. 9 *supra*.
19. 5 U.S.C. § 553 as amended.
20. *First Annual Report to Congress* 25–27 Automotive Fuel Economy Program, NHTSA (Jan. 1977). As part of the fuel economy rule-making process, NHTSA is required to: 1) Prepare an engineering draft of the proposed rule, describing technical specifics; 2) Prepare a rule-making support paper (RSP), preliminary impact assessment (PIA) and draft environmental impact statement (DEIS) if needed. The RSP provides technical basis for the PIA; 3) Prepare a legal draft of proposed rule-making action; 4) Obtain concurrence of the Secretary and complete interagency coordination; 5) Publish a Notice of Proposal Rule-making (NPRM) in the Federal Register; 6) Collect comments from interested parties; hold public hearings as appropriate; 7) Incorporate information and comments into rule-making documentation; 8) Prepare a final draft of proposed rule-making action; 9) Obtain concurrence of the Secretary and complete interagency coordination; and 10) Publish the rule in Federal Register.

In support of the fuel economy rule-making process, NHTSA has an ongoing research and analysis program which is, in part, carried out by DOT's Transportation Systems Center, under the direction of the NHTSA Associate Administrator for R&D, Office of Passenger Vehicle Systems. The objectives of this program are to develop, maintain, and update the data base and analytical tools necessary for rule-making and policy formulation activities in the area of automotive energy conservation.[21] The philosophy and goal of the rule-making process are to maximize information gathering by interaction with all affected and interested parties.

Passenger Car Rule-Making

Under the provisions of the Energy Policy and Conservation Act, the Secretary of Transportation (authority has subsequently been delegated to the Administrator of NHTSA) was required to develop fuel economy standards for 1981-to-1984 model year passenger cars and for light trucks (under 8500 pounds gross vehicle weight). The major actions undertaken by NHTSA on the standards for the 1981-to-1984 passenger car and the 1980 and 1981 light truck are summarized in Appendix B. An advanced notice of the rule-making on the 1981 through 1984 standards was issued in September 1976; the formal notice of rule-making was published in February 1977; and the final rule was published in the Federal Register in June 1977.

The sequence of rule-making actions in the 1980-to-1981 light truck standards followed those on the 1981 through 1984 passenger cars. A questionnaire was issued in March 1977 requesting information from truck manufacturers to help in the standard-setting process. This questionnaire took the place of the advance notice of rule-making. The formal notice of rule-making was issued in December 1977, and the final rule was published in the Federal Register in March 1979. Thus, the two separate rule-making activities each required about twelve months to complete. Both involved significant interaction among the administering agency (NHTSA), the public, and the automotive industry.

Eleven groups participated in the 1981-to-1984 passenger car hearings, held in March 1977. Five were automobile manufacturers and four were "funded" public interest groups (Citizens for Clean Air, Inc., Public Interest Economics Foundation, Environmental Defense Fund, and Public Interest Campaign). These hearings represented the first application by the Secretary of Transportation of a new program to fund public interest groups that might otherwise be unable to participate.

The industry in general expressed concern with the financial, marketing, and, to a lesser extent, technical risks associated with the proposed standards. For example, Henry Duncombe of General Motors testified:

---

21. *Second Annual Report to Congress* 33, Automotive Fuel Economy Program, NHTSA (Jan. 1978).

Technical feasibility is not the key issue here today—cars on the market already exceed 27.5 mpg. The major uncertainty will be the potential losses of auto sales caused by fuel economy standards. It seems safe to say that the more rapidly the fuel economy standards are raised, and the higher the 1985 standards, the greater the risk will be if there is a decline in the rate of replacement of the existing fleet.[22]

The four "funded" public interest groups had different interests. A consultant for Citizens for Clean Air, testified:

> The particles in the diesel exhaust contain several known or suspected carcinogens. Dieselization (to improve fuel economy) will trade the carbon monoxide problem which we know in our cities for a particulate problem which we do not know. We find it hard to believe that EPA will long allow such an engine to emit carcinogenic materials without improving controls.[23]

(Because of uncertainty about potential health effects, the final rule-making decisions on both passenger cars and light trucks assumed negligible diesel penetrations.) Walter Adams of the Public Interest Foundation indicated concern about the lack of competition and innovation in the automobile industry:

> Since World War II American automobile manufacturers, particularly the "Big Three," have had a record of innovative lethargy and unprogressive sluggishness. They have lagged, not led, in the battle to develop cleaner, safer, and more fuel efficient cars. The Government should adhere to its (proposed) fuel economy standards so that the industry will then proceed to do that which it has previously demonstrated it is capable of doing when faced with a national crisis and national challenge.[24]

Other public interest groups presented statements on the health, safety, and consumer impacts of the standards. In the light truck hearings, concern was also expressed about the potential industrial employment impact of the proposed standards.

Following the hearings and subsequent submissions, the final rule was published in June 1977. The proposed and final fuel economy standards are compared in Table 3-5. (The notice of proposed rule-making, issued in February 1977, indicated a possible range rather than a single value of fuel economy.) The values in the final rule tended to be on the high side of the original projections.

---

22. H. Duncombe, *NHTSA hearings on 1981–1984 passenger car fuel economy* (Mar. 22, 1977).
23. W. D. Balgord, *ibid.* (Mar. 22, 1977).
24. W. Adams, *ibid.* (Mar. 22, 1977).

TABLE 3-5 Passenger Automobile Fuel Economy Standards, 1981–1984

Proposed in Notice of proposed rule-making (mpg)		Final standards (mpg)
1981	21.5–22.5	22
1982	22.5–23.5	24
1983	23.5–25.5	26
1984	24.5–26.5	27

Two weeks later, at the July 1977 Senate Commerce Committee hearings on automobile fuel economy, the Big Four automobile makers testified that they would meet the fuel economy requirements of the law, i.e., the new 1981-to-1984 passenger car fuel economy standards.[25]

In March, however, representatives of the industry had said they could *not* meet the proposed standards. Elliot Estes, President of the General Motors Corporation, explained the industry dilemma:

> In dealing with the government—and in raising questions and explaining the possible difficulties and costs, we have reinforced the negative image that many people have of us—I don't know how it can be avoided.
>
> In all honesty, we have contributed to this lack of credibility because we wanted to see some promising results with real hardware before we predicted our ability to make progress to meeting some of these standards and rules.
>
> Early last year (1976) we were saying that we didn't know how to meet the 27.5 miles per gallon fuel economy average for 1985 except by building 92% Chevettes. That was the case at the time, and, in saying so, I didn't mean that we were not working to do better. Now we are going to take the risk that we can meet the required fuel economy average in the 1980s and still provide a reasonable mix of attractive vehicles that will meet most of our consumers' transportation needs.[26]

---

25. At the Senate Commerce Committee hearings on automobile fuel economy, July 1977, Herbert Misch of the Ford Motor Company said: "We will meet the fuel economy standards recently set by the Secretary of Transportation at levels substantially more stringent than we anticipated."
Sidney Terry of Chrysler similarly confirmed that his company would meet the law: "We at Chrysler have made our commitment to meet the requirements of the law. We are well along in a multi-billion dollar program to redesign every vehicle we now make and to introduce a new line of lighter more fuel-efficient passenger cars."
Frederick Stewart of American Motors put it quite simply: "There is no question as far as American Motors is concerned too, Mr. Chairman, we will meet the standards."
Finally, GM's Dr. Henry Duncombe quoted GM President Elliot Estes, saying: "Now we are going to take the risk that we can meet the required fuel economy average in the 1980s and still provide a reasonable mix of attractive vehicles that will meet most of our consumers' transportation needs."

26. E. Estes, *Remarks*, Automotive News World Congress (June 1977).

Thus, in the summer of 1977, the automobile manufacturers indicated that although there were major financial and market risks, they felt they could meet the mandated 1980-to-1985 fuel economy standards with a "marketable product mix."

Light Truck Rule-Making

The 1981-to-1982 light truck fuel economy rule-making indicates the likely course of future fuel economy rule-making activity. As the proposed passenger car and light truck fuel economy standards become more stringent,[27] the required changes in product design and the associated manufacturing processes will be seen to cause significant changes in the nature and regional distribution of the motor vehicle industry workforce. In November 1977 a draft of the proposed 1980-to-1981 light truck fuel economy rule-making was sent out for interagency review as required in the rule-making process. Despite the legal requirement of confidentiality, the draft proposal was leaked to industry officials. In the industry's view, the proposed standards were quite restrictive. The industry reacted with a massive lobbying effort to modify the proposal before it became public. White House, congressional, and agency officials were contacted, including Treasury Secretary Blumenthal, Commerce Secretary Kreps, and Secretary of Transportation Adams. Despite this lobbying, the light truck fuel economy standards in the notice of rule-making, issued in December 1977, were basically unchanged from the draft that had leaked to industry.[28]

Prior to and during the January 1978 light truck public hearings, the manufacturers publicly disclosed possible plant closings. Chrysler indicated that it had been forced to postpone the conversion of its Jefferson Avenue plant in inner-city Detroit because of uncertainty on truck standards.

> We had planned to convert the Jefferson Plant to van production at a cost of $50 million. In the process, we would keep more than 3,000 jobs in the city of Detroit. We have been forced to delay that project until the question of truck standards is settled. We can't go ahead and commit millions of dollars to build vehicles that we know can't meet the regulations NHTSA is planning to impose on us.[29]

27. The NHTSA Five-Year Plan for Motor Vehicle Safety and Fuel Economy Rule-making indicates that NHTSA plans to perform the necessary analysis and issue notices of proposed rule-making and final rules for model year 1985 and 1986 passenger automobiles and for model year 1982 through 1984 light trucks in 1979; during the 1985 and 1986 passenger car rule-making activity the existing fuel economy standards for model year 1984 will be reexamined.
28. S. Freidman, "Leaks Let Carmakers Zero In on Fuel Rules," *Detroit Free Press*, Jan. 6, 1978; H. Kahn, "Tough Truck MPG Rules Stir Washington Ruckus," *Automotive News*, Dec. 19, 1977, p. 1.
29. Chrysler comment at *NHTSA Light Truck (1980–1981) Hearings* (Jan., 16–17, 1978).

The arguments in the light truck public hearings and submissions were in marked contrast to those of the earlier passenger car hearings. Whereas 11 groups had participated in the passenger car hearings, 31 groups participated in the light truck hearings. The notice of proposed rule-making on the passenger car standards resulted in 48 responses to the public docket; the light truck rule-making brought in 326 responses.

Where testimony and submissions at the passenger car hearings had pertained to the technical and marketing risks associated with the standards, and to the potential health effects of diesel particulates, the presentations at the light truck hearings pertained primarily to potential unemployment and particularly to minority unemployment. For example, V. Lonnie Peak, Jr., a member of the Board of Trustees of New Detroit, Inc. said:

> In Detroit, who is affected? I am not here to wage a battle for Chrysler and other truck manufacturers. This is a battle for poor and black people. These people are the "who" that will be so severely affected. They are the ones who work in the plants. Heavy industry is a major employer of black and poor people. Blacks are not heavily employed in plastics. Blacks are not heavily employed in aluminum. Blacks are not heavily employed in aircraft production. Twenty-eight percent of all auto industry employees are black Americans, but in the cities the majority of assembly line workers are black.[30]

Gerald Smith, President of the Detroit Chapter of the National Association of Black Social Workers, Inc., had this to say about the situation:

> It stands to reason that aluminums and plastics are the building materials of the future if automobile companies are to successfully build lighter, more economical vehicles. Few minorities and women have skills or hold jobs in the aluminum/plastics industries, as compared with the vast network of steel industries involved in producing automobiles. As vehicle production moves away from dependence on the urban located steel industry, toward the suburban located aluminum/plastics industries, urban job displacement will follow.[31]

Following the hearings and submission of additional information, the final 1980-to-1981 light truck standards were published in the Federal Register in March 1978. A comparison of the standards as originally proposed and the final standards (see Table 3-6) shows that the final fuel economy values were considerably less severe than those proposed before the hearings. Industry and congressional reactions to the final standards were generally positive. General Motors and American

---

30. V. L. Peak, Jr., New Detroit, Inc., *NHTSA Light Truck Hearings* (Jan. 17, 1978).
31. G. Smith, Nat'l Ass'n of Black Social Workers, Inc., *ibid.* (Jan. 6, 1978).

TABLE 3-6 Comparison of Proposed and Final Light Truck Fuel-Economy Standards (Without Captive Imports)

Model year	Proposed rule (mpg) 2-wheel drive	Proposed rule (mpg) 4-wheel drive	Final* rule (mpg) 2-wheel drive	Final* rule (mpg) 4-wheel drive
1980	19.2	16.2	16.0	14.0
1981	20.5	17.7	18.0	15.5

* The actual standards include the following provisions:
    If EPA does not approve use of slippery oils in testing by January 1, 1980, then standard may be reduced 0.5 mpg.
    No reliance on dieselization was made in establishing the technological feasibility of meeting those standards.
    All domestic trucks under 8500 lb. gross vehicle weight are included; manufacturers may not include imported vehicles (captive imports) in calculating new fleet average.
    Manufacturers using only truck type engines (i.e., International Harvester) granted special one-time standards.

Motors asserted that they could meet the new light truck standards in 1980 and 1981; Ford repeated an earlier announcement that they would spend $600 million to keep Ford light trucks as industry leaders in fuel economy; and Chrysler indicated that, although the 1981 light truck standards demand an increase in fuel economy beyond their current capability, they had every intention of meeting the standards in both years.[32]

"ECONOMIC PRACTICALITY" AND FUEL ECONOMY

Background

The Energy Policy and Conservation Act requires that the fuel economy standards set for light trucks and for passenger cars be "economically practical." In the rule-making on the 1981-to-1984 passenger car standards, a standard was considered economically practical if it was "within the financial capability of the industry, but not so stringent as to threaten substantial economic hardship for the industry." NHTSA therefore analyzed several economic areas that would directly affect the industry's financial capability to convert to the production of fuel economical cars, which included making a projection of total car sales and thus potential revenue. In addition, NHTSA analyzed the economic effects of the standards on the consumer by comparing the decrease in lifetime operating costs (discounted to present value) resulting from improved fuel economy with the increase in motor vehicle prices associated with implementation of fuel efficient technology.

This cost-benefit analysis concluded that consumers' savings in gasoline and maintenance costs would be greater than the new car price

32. "DOT Sets Final Truck MPG Rules," *Automotive News*, Mar. 20, 1978, pp. 101–103.

increase required to cover costs attributable to the fuel economy standards. Potential macroeconomic impacts were also analyzed, including the effect of the mandated standards on the GNP, unemployment, and the Consumer Price Index. The change in these indices due to the imposition of the standards was small: "Essentially insignificant, amounting to much less than one percent of the value of these indicators."[33] A macro-analysis of the motor vehicle material supply industries was also provided, concluding that "downsizing and material substitution would imply either slightly retarded or slightly accelerated growth rates."[34]

In the rule-making for 1980-to-1981 light truck standards, the consideration of "economic practicability" came to include a much more specific assessment of the possible effects of plant closings and relocations associated with meeting the standards as originally proposed.

Community/Regional Economics

There is increasing national concern about the possible impact of federal regulations on inner cities, low-income households, and minority employment. This concern will be reflected in future rule-making activity. The substitution of light-weight materials and more sophisticated power plant technology are considered potential threats to minority and inner-city employment. United Auto Workers Vice President Marc Stepp recently proposed to the House Subcommittee on Labor Standards that legislation be enacted to govern plant relocation and closings to include advance notice of an impending plant shutdown with an intensive effort to provide alternative employment for affected workers—mobility assistance to make it easier for workers victimized by economic dislocation to relocate.[35]

A recent directive from the Office of Management and Budget also states that executive branch agencies shall prepare urban and community impact analyses of proposed policy initiatives.[36] Fuel economy regulations would be covered by this directive.

Industry Competition and Structure

The manufacturers' ability to generate the capital necessary to fund the changeover to fuel economical motor vehicles is strongly dependent on

---

33. *Rulemaking Support Paper Concerning The 1981–1984 Passenger Automobile Average Fuel Economy Standards,* DOT/NHTSA (July 1977).
34. *Ibid.,* p. ES-15.
35. Marc Stepp, UAW Vice President and director of the Union's Independent Parts Supplier Department, before the House Subcommittee on Labor Standards and to the Automotive News World Congress. "UAW Official Cites Grief Caused by Plant Closings," *Automotive News,* Aug. 28, 1978, p. 9.
36. *Circular No. A-116 to the Heads of Executive Departments and Establishments on Agency Preparation of Urban and Community Impact Analyses,* Office of Management & Budget (Aug. 16, 1978).

the general economic climate—to which new car sales are very responsive—and the marketability of the new products. Since the state of the economy and automobile sales have been cyclical, the requirements to meet mandated standards by specific dates—independent of the state of the economy—considerably increase the manufacturers' financial risk. Financial risk is greatest for the smaller manufacturers who do not have the same access as larger companies to capital resources to carry them through an economic downturn.

In its *1977 Annual Report,* Chrysler Corporation complained:

> These standards impact more heavily on Chrysler Corporation than on its two larger competitors . . . . The effect of these unreasonable standards is to have the government strengthen the competitive advantage of the largest manufacturers.[37]

The Ford Motor Company likewise complained:[38]

> It is ironic that the cumulative impact of government regulation may be to strengthen the position of GM and the imports and possibly weaken domestic competition in the automotive industry.

In a recent study, *The Contributions of Automobile Regulations,* NHTSA questioned the industry statements on the effects of regulation on industry structure:

> It has been charged that despite efforts by some Government agencies to prevent concentration in industry, the regulators are fast bringing the automobile industry to the point where only the largest companies can survive. This assertion is easily refuted by the figures in [Table 3-7], which shows the share of the market enjoyed by each manufacturer since the NHTSA regulations first became effective. As the table demonstrates there is no discernible trend in percent of market for any individual producer, much less an overall movement toward concentration.[39]

The available information suggests that, to date, the motor vehicle regulations have had little effect on industry competitive position; however, both Chrysler Corporation and the Ford Motor Company have expressed concern about their financial future because of the necessity for maintaining a continuing capital investment program, whatever the state of the economy. It will remain for the future to assess the validity of these concerns.

Inflation/Trade Balance

Rule-makers will continually have to reassess the positive and negative effects of mandated fuel economy standards on inflation and on the

---

37. Chrysler Corp., *1977 Annual Report,* p. 6.
38. *State of the U.S. Automobile Industry* 32, Ford Motor Co. (June 13, 1978).
39. *The Contributions of Automobile Regulations* 19–20, NHTSA/DOT (June 1978).

TABLE 3-7 Percent of Total U.S. New Car Registrations*

Year	GM	Ford	Chrysler	AMC	Imports
1968	46.7	23.7	16.3	2.8	10.5
1969	46.8	24.3	15.1	2.5	11.3
1970	39.8	26.4	16.1	3.0	14.7
1971	45.2	23.5	13.7	2.5	15.1
1972	44.2	24.3	14.0	2.9	14.6
1973	44.5	23.5	13.3	3.5	15.2
1974	41.9	25.0	13.6	3.8	15.7
1975	43.3	23.1	11.7	3.7	18.2
1976	47.2	22.5	12.9	2.5	14.9

* Reproduced from the *Contributions of Automobile Regulations*, Table 5, p. 21.

balance of payments. In a White House meeting (April 1978), business leaders, including representatives of the motor vehicle industry, identified regulation as a significant causal factor in inflation. Since that time the domestic automobile manufacturers have proposed—as one element in the fight against inflation—that (1) the 1981-to-1983 passenger car standards calling for 2 miles-per-gallon annual increases in fuel economy be reexamined; (2) the 27.5 miles-per-gallon standard not be raised because of the attendant cost and risk; and (3) the 1982-to-1984 light truck standards reflect the load-carrying function of trucks and be increased at a slower rate than cars.

In order to reduce the capital requirement necessary to meet the mandated standards, the domestic manufacturers are sourcing components from overseas suppliers rather than producing them domestically. For instance, Chrysler Corporation will purchase more than $200 million in components from its newest partner, Peugeot-Citroen for use in a new line of front-drive compacts.[40] On the other hand, the massive capital investments being made to meet the standards are resulting in improved domestic productivity. Therefore the net inflationary and trade effects of mandatory fuel standards remain unclear.

Energy Conservation Costs vs. Benefits

Secretary of Commerce Juanita Kreps has indicated the need for better understanding of the regulatory process: "For each federal regulation it is essential to ask: What does it cost? What benefits are we buying? Do these costs and benefits accurately reflect our priorities? Is there a way to achieve the same benefits at lower cost."[41]

---

40. "Peugeot to Supply FWD Parts for '81 Chrysler Small Cars," *Automotive News*, Sept. 11, 1978, p. 4.
41. J. M. Kreps, U.S. Secretary of Commerce, "Why We Need a Regulatory Budget," *Business Week*, July 31, 1978, p. 14.

The industry has argued that in setting the level and rate of introduction of fuel economy standards, NHTSA should consider a cost-benefit analysis. General Motors, in their response to NHTSA's request for information on the 1984-to-1986 passenger automobile, has suggested that a study be done to "find the point at which the financial resources used in fuel production is close to the financial resources used for conservation per gallon produced or saved over the life cycle of the vehicle."[42]

As fuel economy standards are increased, the incremental petroleum savings become less—a doubling of fleet fuel economy from 25-to-50 miles per gallon saves only one-half as much fuel as a doubling of fleet fuel economy from 12.5-to-25 miles per gallon—and, in the absence of significant technological innovation, the incremental costs become greater. Determination of the level of fuel economy at which fuel production costs equal fuel conservation costs would require information that does not currently exist, however. Further, it is not clear that energy replacement production costs are the best measure of energy conservation benefits. It is clear, however, that as the fuel economy standards are made more stringent, rule-making will increasingly involve assessments of total consumer, industry, labor, and societal risks compared to the total benefits of petroleum conservation.

CURRENT AND PROJECTED TECHNOLOGICAL INNOVATIONS CONTRASTED

Current Technology Available

By 1985 the projected domestic new car fleet average fuel economy will be more than double its 1973-to-1974 value of about 13 miles per gallon. This increase will have been accomplished with relatively small changes in motor vehicle functional characteristics; interior passenger and baggage volume and performance will be about the same as at present. The 1975 industry predictions that mandatory fuel economy regulations would require a fleet of subcompacts have not come to pass. The fuel-efficient motor vehicle technologies now being commercialized in the United States market were developed, in large part, by Western European and Japanese motor vehicle manufacturers and suppliers in an environment of high fuel prices and horsepower taxes. The advanced electronic control technology currently being adopted, while not derived from the foreign auto industry, has been derived from technology developed in other industrial sectors.

---

42. H. Kahn, "GM Cites Difficulties to Clear in Meeting MPG Rule for '80s," *Automotive News*, Aug. 28, 1978, pp. 1 and 43. The article quotes from the nonconfidential portion of GM's response to NHTSA's fuel economy questionnaire, Docket FE 76-01-N3, "General Motors Corporation on Request for Information on Passenger Automobiles Questionnaire for Vehicle Manufacturers," August 7, 1978.

The existence of fuel economy standards has unquestionably accelerated the commercialization and transfer of existing technology. The first round (1977 to 1982) of motor vehicle weight reduction was achieved by downsizing. In the next round (1982 to 1985) there will be increased emphasis on material substitution in body panels, structural members, and powertrain castings. However, the incremental weight changes associated with material substitution are smaller than those associated with the original downsizing programs.

The first round improvements in powertrain efficiency have been associated with engine resizing; four- and five-speed transmissions have been substituted for three-speed transmissions, while turbochargers have been used to preserve vehicle passing and acceleration performance. In the second round, more sophisticated actuators, sensors, and on-board micro-processors are being incorporated for more accurate engine control and improved fuel utilization. Diesel penetration is being increased with associated uncertainties in the health effects of diesel exhaust emissions. As in the case of weight reduction, the incremental improvements in powertrain efficiency are becoming more difficult to achieve.

Projected Technology Requirements

No Western European maker has a corporate sales-weighted average fuel economy as high as our 1985 requirement (27.5 miles per gallon), although a number of individual production models are higher.[43] The available fuel efficient motor vehicle technology in Western Europe and Japan is *rapidly being used up.* If the nation chooses to increase motor vehicle fleet fuel economy further after 1985 it appears reasonable to ask the question: Will the anticipation of more stringent fuel economy standards be sufficient to generate the new technology required for another round of rapid and significant increases in fuel economy?

This question is controversial. Some say that the motor vehicle industry has the necessary resources and that it can be stimulated into action through product regulation. Others say that without knowledge of whether the regulation is feasible, the government is not in a position to make regulations stick; i.e., if the automobile companies say "no," the government has to have some basis for saying "yes."[44] According to this view, the possibility of more stringent fuel economy

---

43. "Europe Way of 1985 CAFE Regulations," *Automotive News*, Sept. 25, 1978.
44. Statement of Dr. Kenneth Arrow, Professor of Economics, Harvard Univ. and President of the American Economic Ass'n, *Federal Incentives For Innovation: Hearings before the Special Subcomm. on Science, Technology, and Commerce of the Sen. Comm. on Commerce*, (Aug. 31, Sept. 4, 1973) Serial No. 93-57, pp. 20–33. Dr. Arrow testified that: "In fact, without a knowledge of whether the regulation is feasible or not, the Government is in no position to make such a regulation. There has therefore to be independent research, if for nothing else, merely to establish the feasibility . . ." (p. 26).

standards may even be a deterrent to innovation since in developing new technology the industry will only be increasing the government's basis for demanding higher standards. Therefore, unless fuel economy improvement continues to be a marketable feature, the motivation for industry to show that it can exceed the 1985 mandated fleet average of 27.5 miles per gallon is likely to be small.

The sources of motor vehicle technology are being depleted. If the nation chooses—on the basis of an assessment of the benefits and costs—that motor vehicle fuel economy should be further increased, the motor vehicle technology base, including safer lightweight structures and more fuel-efficient powertrains, must be replenished.

SUMMARY

Effects to 1985

PETROLEUM CONSERVATION

Mandatory fuel economy standards have proved to be a powerful instrument for stimulating improvements in new car fleet average fuel economy and in achieving the societal goal of decreased petroleum consumption. New car fleet average fuel economy will have doubled in the period from 1975 to 1985 with a resulting annual petroleum savings of 2-to-3 million barrels per day by the early 1990s.

REJUVENATION AND MODERNIZATION

The accelerated capital spending required to meet the mandatory standards has provided the domestic motor vehicle manufacturers with a unique opportunity to modernize and rejuvenate their aging manufacturing facilities and put into place a more efficient and productive physical plant than previously existed.

COMPETITION

The mandated standards have resulted in the domestic production of motor vehicles that may not only capture a significant segment of the domestic small car market, but may also be competitive in the world market.

MARKET AND FINANCIAL RISK

The ability to generate the new capital necessary to fund the accelerated changeover to fuel economical motor vehicles is strongly dependent on the general economic climate and market acceptance of the new products. The financial risk is greater for the smaller manufacturers, who do not have the same access as the larger companies to capital resources to carry them through an economic downturn.

Prospects Beyond 1985

TECHNOLOGY GENERATION

The projected doubling of motor vehicle fuel economy by 1985 will have been accomplished, for the most part, by the use of mass-produced technology that had already been commercialized in Western Europe and Japan. It is not clear, however, whether the anticipation of more stringent standards in the post–1985 period will, by itself, result in the allocation of resources—trained manpower, equipment, and capital—to the generation of new motor vehicle technology at a rate sufficient to achieve significant additional gains in fuel economy during the second decade of regulation. If fuel economy is to be increased, additional efforts—on the part of the industry and the government—will be required to replenish the technology base.

POLICY ALTERNATIVES

Mandatory fuel economy standards have proved to be a powerful and flexible instrument for increasing motor vehicle fuel economy, and are, therefore, likely to be employed again if the nation wishes to achieve further gains in fuel economy. As the mandated standards are increased, however, the resulting changes in motor vehicle design and manufacturing processes may have increasingly serious effects on certain industrial sectors, regions of the country, and segments of the work force. Since it is not possible at the start of rule-making to assess properly all the impacts of a regulatory decision, continuous reappraisal of proposed standards will be required as new information and knowledge is provided by interested parties. If, in the post–1985 decade, mandatory fuel economy standards are to continue to be useful as a strategy for stimulating fuel economy improvements, they will have to be supported by other federal policies both to stimulate the marketability of fuel economic motor vehicles and to mitigate the effects on affected groups in and outside the industry.

APPENDIX A FOR "MANDATED FUEL ECONOMY STANDARDS AS A STRATEGY FOR IMPROVING MOTOR VEHICLE ECONOMY"

Executive Branch Activities on Motor Vehicle Fuel Economy—1970 to 1976 (Non-Mandatory Fuel Economy Program)

Date	Action	Comment
June 1971	DOT study to determine major *transportation energy conservation opportunities*	The motor vehicle represented major opportunity to conserve energy in transportation.
Sept. 1972	DOT/EPA/NASA/DOD participated in study on "*Energy Research and Development Goals*" for White House Office of Science and Technology	Report projected that automobiles could achieve 30-to-40% fuel economy improvement and still meet emission goals.
Nov. 1972	EPA published report on *Fuel Economy and Emission Control*	Major findings were that vehicle weight is most instrumental factor affecting fuel economy.
Jan. 1973	*Auto Energy Efficiency Program* established at DOT's Transportation Systems Center	Program aimed at assessing auto industry's ability to improve fuel economy.
Oct. 1973	Arab oil embargo	Organization of Arab Petroleum Exporting States announced oil boycott.
Dec. 1973	EPA published the 1974 *Gas Mileage Guide*	Result of voluntary fuel economy labelling program.
Feb. 1974	Washington Energy Conference	Program of international cooperation to deal with world energy situations. New energy ethic to promote conservation.
June 1974	Request from Federal Energy Administration to auto manufacturers on feasibility of voluntary fuel economy program	Auto manufacturers asked to respond to feasibility of achieving 30% fuel economy improvement by 1985.
Aug. 1974	Industry response to FEA's request on feasibility of 30% fuel economy improvement by 1985	Motor industry responded positively to FEA request.
Oct. 1974	DOT/EPA Report on *Potential for Motor Vehicle Fuel*	Report concluded that 40-to-60% improvement could

Date	Action	Comment
	Economy Improvement (120 Day Study)	be obtained in motor vehicle fuel economy by 1980. Became critical technical base for voluntary program and subsequent mandatory standards.
Oct. 1974	Congressional Address by President Ford on *The Economy*	Announcement of a goal of 40% improvement in new car fuel economy by 1980. Goal based on *120 Day Study*.
Jan. 1975	Initiation of *Voluntary Fuel Economy Monitoring Project* in DOT	Project aimed at monitoring industry's progress toward fuel economy goal of 40% improvement.
Jan. 1975	State of Union Message	President Ford announced agreement by the manufacturers on the voluntary fuel economy program.
Mar. 1975	DOT Secretary Coleman asked by White House to head task force on *Motor Vehicle Goals Beyond 1980*	Task force to study long range goals compatible with environmental safety, and economic objectives.
Sept. 1975	FEA announced possibility of increases in fuel economy goals	Auto makers were achieving large gains in fuel economy, and administration wanted to continue voluntary program in spite of congressional pressure.
Dec. 1975	*Energy Policy and Conservation Act* signed into law	Legislation called for 20 mpg in 1980 and 27.5 mpg in 1985. Over 100% improvement in fuel economy levels compared to 1973–1974 values.
Apr. 1976	Dept. of Transportation's *Monitoring Report on Auto Voluntary Fuel Economy Program*	Final Report on voluntary program concluded that future product programs would meet 1980 goal of 40% improvement.
Nov. 1976	Report by the *Federal Task Force on Motor Vehicle Goals Beyond 1980*	Report concluded that goal of 100% improvement in fuel economy by 1985 was achievable.

APPENDIX B FOR "MANDATED FUEL ECONOMY STANDARDS AS A STRATEGY FOR IMPROVING MOTOR VEHICLE FUEL ECONOMY"

AFEP Second Annual Report
(Summary of Rule-Making Activities for FY' 77)

Docket No.	Description	Publication date NPRM*	Comments closing date NPRM	Final EIS**	Published final rule
FE 76-01	1981-1984 Passenger Automobile Standards	2/22/77	4/12/77	6/1/77	6/30/77
FE 76-02	Reduction of Passenger Automobile Fuel Economy Standards	10/26/76	12/27/76	***	11/14/77
FE 76-03	Nonpassenger Automobile Standards 1979	11/26/76	1/10/77	3/3/77	3/14/77
FE 76-04	Exemption from Average Fuel Economy Standards	12/9/76	1/24/77	***	7/28/77
FE 76-05	Vehicle Classification	12/20/76	1/19/77	***	7/28/77
FE 77-02	Manufacturers of Multistage	2/9/77	3/9/77	***	7/28/77
FE 77-03	Automotive Fuel Economy Reports	4/11/77	5/11/77	***	12/12/77
FE 77-05	1980-1981 Nonpassenger Automobile Standards	12/15/77 Public Hearing 1/16-17/78	1/30/78	3/15/78 (DEIS draft available to public 12/12/77)	3/15/78

* Notice of proposed rule-making.
** Environmental Impact Statement.
*** Not applicable.

THE EFFECT OF FUEL ECONOMY STANDARDS ON CORPORATE STRATEGY IN THE AUTOMOBILE INDUSTRY*

Kirk O. Hanson, *Harvard Business School*

Between 1973 and 1978, the automobile industry faced increasingly stringent regulations regarding the fuel economy of motor vehicles. Concern for declining fuel economy in the early 1970s produced EPA requirements for the disclosure and reportage of the gas mileage of individual models. In the wake of the oil embargo of 1973 and 1974, the major automobile makers agreed to a voluntary program to increase fleet average fuel economy by 40 percent by 1980. Unwilling to grant President Ford the credit for improving fuel economy, and desiring to limit energy usage by automobiles even further, Congress passed mandatory average performance standards in December 1975 in the Energy Policy and Conservation Act. In July 1977, DOT Secretary Brock Adams issued corporate average fuel economy standards (CAFE) for the years 1981 to 1984, completing a schedule of mandatory average performance standards for the 1978-to-1985 period. In so doing, he rejected at least two alternative proposals for the 1981-to-1984 interim period: (1) A Ford Motor Company proposal for small increases in the earlier years; and (2) a "straight-line" proposal for equal increments from the 1980 standard of 20 miles per gallon to the 1985 standard of 27.5 miles per gallon, which were set in the Energy Policy and Conservation Act (see Figure 3-1). Finally, in recent months, proposals have been debated for more stringent average performance standards and for minimum performance standards (through excise taxes or an outright ban on gas guzzlers).

---

* This discussion presents preliminary findings of a research project on the impact of regulation on corporate strategy. The research has been supported in part by the Division of Research, Harvard Business School. The author is grateful for the assistance of Associate Professor Michael Lovdal and Research Associates Terry Cauthon Soltys and Karen Tracy.

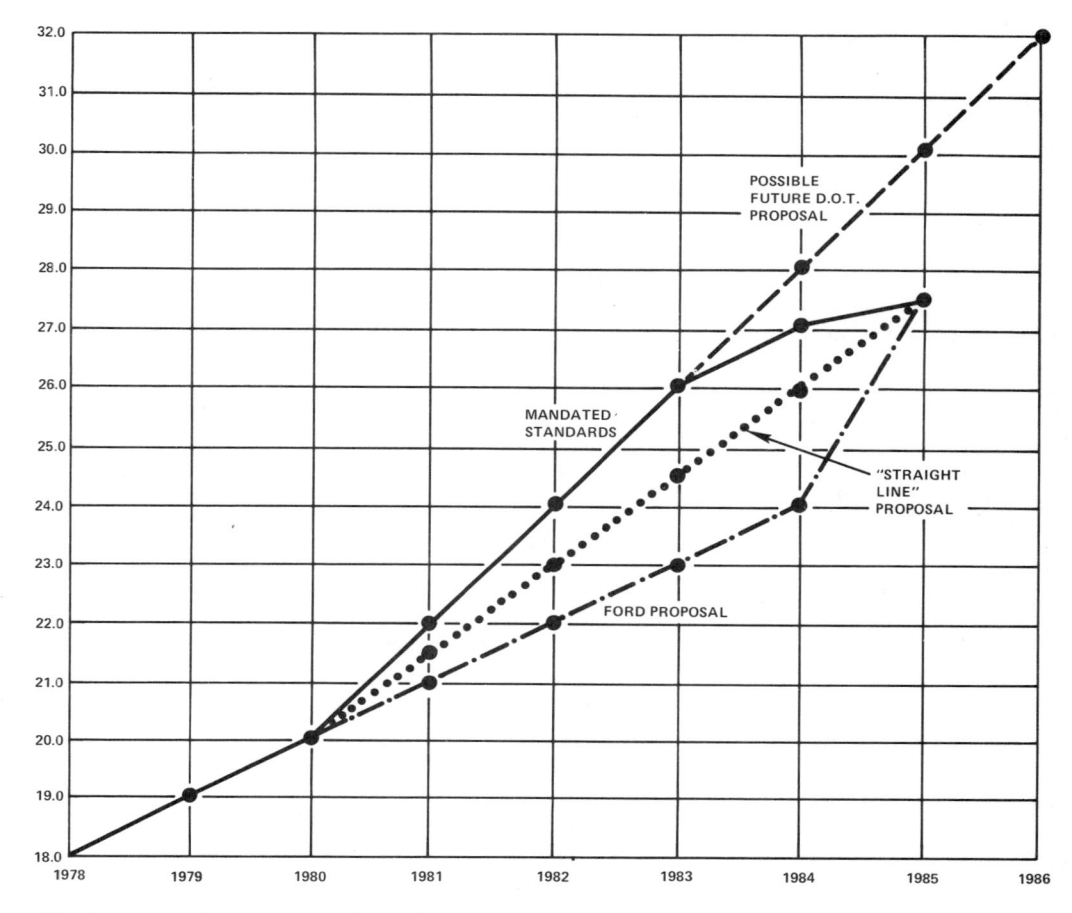

FIGURE 3-1 CAFE proposals and standards for passenger cars

Because of these rapid changes in the regulatory atmosphere, corporate executives must contend with considerable uncertainty about the eventual shape and severity of fuel economy standards. Joan Claybrook, Administrator of NHTSA, announced to an industry gathering in July 1977: "We should look forward as the horizon is etched with optimistic signs; instead of 27.5 mpg, it is not unrealistic to seek 40 or 50."[1]

How the automobile manufacturers respond to this increasingly stringent regulation of an important feature of their product offers an important case study of the effects of regulation on corporate strategy. The more regulation becomes an important part of corporate policy-making, the more corporate decision-makers will need to understand the dynamics of the interaction between regulatee and regulator.

---

1. *The Snail's Pace of Innovation*, remarks by Joan Claybrook, Administrator of NHTSA before Auto News World Congress Detroit, Mich. (July 13, 1977).

CHANGES IN THE STRATEGIC ENVIRONMENT

Fuel economy standards have changed the environment in which the major automobile companies operate in three fundamental ways. First, it has made fuel economy, traditionally a minor product attribute, a major competitive characteristic. Second, it has added to and altered the risks associated with existing product-market strategies. Third, it has made the public policy process a part of the firm's strategic environment: Firms may now gain competitive advantage by influencing the public policy process, just as they can by taking action in the economic market place.

Strategic Product Characteristics

Fuel economy standards have made the fuel efficiency of automobiles a product characteristic with a substantial effect on the competitive strength of firms in the industry. Although the automobile firms have argued that fuel economy was already a "marketable attribute before regulation," public policy developments have undoubtedly intensified competition in this dimension.

The automobile makers did not all start from the same fuel efficiency baseline in seeking ways to meet CAFE standards. Their fleet average fuel economy figures for 1974 and 1975, before mandatory standards were passed, differed substantially (see Table 3-7). General Motors was traditionally positioned in larger, fuel expensive cars; Ford, with its popular Falcon, Mustang, and Maverick models, had been stronger in the small, fuel efficient car segments which would be an important part of the strategy for meeting CAFE standards. But General Motors gained significantly in the 1975 model year through the widespread introduction of the fuel-saving catalytic converter. In early 1975 General Motors had also begun a major program to redimension all its models, reducing its average car by several hundred pounds. General Motors seized at least a year's head start on its competitors in thus downsizing its fleet.

When fuel efficiency emerged as a prominent product characteristic, certain resources were needed before automobile makers could compete in the race to increase fuel economy. These included the financial strength to support rapid product innovation, knowledge of specific technologies and materials which would be used to improve mileage,

TABLE 3-7 Fleet Average Fuel Economy Performance: Passenger Automobiles (Miles Per Gallon)

Model year	GM	Ford	Chrysler	Other*	Average
1974	12.0	14.4	13.8	20.1	14.0
1975	15.4	13.3	15.8	21.2	15.9

* All other U.S. manufacturers and imports.

and the organizational and managerial expertise to manage the efforts for complying with the new standards. Like other resources, these were unevenly divided among competitors in the industry. General Motors appears to have had the advantage of greater experience with the diesel engine; Ford had an advantage with the PROCO engine, a unique design using direct cylinder fuel injection. Chrysler, already strapped for financial resources, found itself needing billions more dollars to support major unanticipated model redesigns. Economies of scale also favored General Motors which had significantly larger production runs over which to spread the costs of crash technological development programs and extra retooling expense.

Competition in any regulated product or process characteristic raises two new concerns for corporate management. First, the firm competes with the regulatory standard itself and wins if the standard is met. Second, the firm competes with other firms in the industry by trying to comply with the regulatory standard most efficiently and most effectively. Design standards which restrict the firm's choice of ways to meet the requirements may minimize firm-to-firm competition. Performance standards, even *average* performance standards, in which individual firms have considerable leeway in how to meet the standard, enhance firm-to-firm competition.

Alteration of Strategic Risks

Management personnel in the automobile industry are very familiar with the management of risks: Risks required to develop a new technology, risks when major financial commitments are made in the face of possible economic slowdowns, and the uncertainties when new models are offered to the public. But the regulatory process alters the types of risk calculations and the risk tradeoffs from those management normally makes in setting strategy.

In selecting strategies for complying with CAFE standards, the automobile makers must cope with four distinct types of risk: Technological, market, financial, and regulatory. Three dimensions of risk are familiar, although they are altered by new regulatory initiatives. First, because rapid improvements in fuel economy demand the use of untried technologies, there exists a substantial *technological risk* that the chosen system will not perform as anticipated. Ford estimates that it must develop "high-risk programs" to overcome what would otherwise be a "10% shortfall to the 1975 (CAFE) standards." Second, the need to alter significantly the design and characteristics of the automobile creates a much higher than usual *marketing risk* that consumers will simply refuse to buy certain models. General Motors Vice President Henry Duncombe, speaking at DOT hearings on the interim fuel economy standards, emphasized the importance of market risk: "The major uncertainty surrounding future gasoline consumption will be the potential losses of auto sales created by fuel economy standards. Those of us in the industry have learned the costly lesson to never underestimate the independence of American consumers . . . ."[2] Third, the massive capital outlays required to achieve increases in fuel economy heighten considerably the *financial risks* management is compelled to embrace. The fourth, regulation, introduces a novel *regulatory risk* which is often more serious than the others. The regulatory ground rules are not fixed; as they change the task of complying with one particular standard, such as fuel economy, also changes. The severity of CAFE standards may be altered by the particular test procedures or enforcement standards adopted as well as by further congressional action. Furthermore, regulatory developments in other areas, particularly in emissions control, may make more difficult the achievements of particular CAFE objectives. Ford has expressed particular concern for standardizing testing procedures because of the crucial role testing procedures play in determining compliance with standards and in formulating policy.[3]

General Motors' difficulty in securing emissions certification for its 1980 model front-wheel drive compacts is a good example of the inhibitory effects of regulatory risk. EPA, which had not yet finalized the Federal Testing Program under which the 1980 models would be certified, would not begin certification of General Motors' models fearing some loopholes might remain in the procedure. Although certification was finally accelerated, regulatory risk had jeopardized General Motors' plans to market this car in the spring of 1979.

What is most significant in this analysis of risk and regulation is that risk calculations change rapidly in response to day-to-day regulatory developments. In selecting a particular technological or marketing strategy for meeting CAFE standards, for example, the major manufacturers must construct and constantly update risk profiles for each important product decision. Table 3-8 illustrates one type of risk matrix which companies could use in analyzing risk tradeoffs. The risk profile will differ from firm to firm depending on the starting point, the resources, and preferences of the firm.

Competition in the Public Policy Process

The third major change in the strategic environment of the automobile makers is the increasing competitive importance of the public policy process itself. As long as firms in an industry do not see significant competitive advantage to be gained through the adoption of a particular standard, or through the selection of one rule over another, the public policy process remains relatively unimportant from a strategic point of

---

2. H. L. Duncombe, *Statement of General Motors Corp. to NHTSA on 1981-to-1984 Passenger Automobile Average Fuel Economy Standards* 6, Wash, D.C. (Mar. 22, 1977).

3. *Ford Motor Company Response to NHTSA Questionnaire on 1984–1986 Passenger Car Fuel Economy*, pp. 5–6.

TABLE 3-8 Sample Risk Matrix

	Technological risk	Market risk	Financial risk	Regulatory risk	Payoff MPG
Downsizing, round I	Low	Moderate	Moderate/high	Low	High
Downsizing, round II	Low	High	Moderate/high	Low	Moderate
Dieselization	Moderate	Moderate	Moderate	Very high	High
PROCO engine	Moderate	Moderate	Moderate	Low	Moderate
Turbocharging	Low	Low	Low	Low	Low
Materials substitution	Low	High	Moderate	Low	Moderate

Source: Author's estimates.

view. But once, as Robert Leone[4] has pointed out, individual firms recognize that the burdens and opportunities imposed by regulation are significant and unevenly divided, firms begin to consider the public process itself as another setting in which to pursue a competitive advantage. The public policy process becomes a second arena in which the firm must compete if it is to survive.

Corporate positions toward safety and emissions legislation and rule-making were rarely differentiated. Working together, often through the Automobile Manufacturers Association and its successor, the Motor Vehicle Manufacturers Association (MVMA), the major automobile firms pursued positions which they felt represented their common interest. With fuel economy, however, the automobile makers clearly believe they are affected in different ways. As a result, they take different political positions toward some proposed statutes and rules.

IMPACT ON PRODUCT-MARKET STRATEGIES

Fuel economy policies have brought about fundamental changes in the industry's strategic environment, which, in turn, has forced observable shifts in strategy. Among the most important changes are the following:

Market Segmentation

Traditional definitions of industry market segments are being challenged as fuel economy standards alter basic characteristics of the product. Inertial weights of domestic cars have ranged from approximately

---

4. R. Leone, "The Real Costs of Regulation," *Harvard Business Review* 57–66 (Nov.–Dec. 1977).

2,250-to-5,500 pounds during the past few years. Most industry observers have noted five distinct market segments, within this range: Subcompact, compact, intermediate, standard, and luxury. It is estimated that by 1985, inertial weights may range from 2,000 to about 3,500 pounds. Can today's five distinct segments be clearly differentiated and separately merchandised within that narrower range? Most industry observers conclude there will be some blurring between the full-size and the intermediates or perhaps between segments in the lower range.[5]

If existing competitive patterns are disrupted, there will be a rapid repositioning of body styles and perhaps the definition of entirely new market segments. The automobile makers' greatest fear of altered model definitions relates to the fact that the vast majority of annual sales are replacement sales. If the consumer returning to replace a five-year-old model cannot find a model he considers comparable, he may be more likely to consider the products of another manufacturer.

Already the sequenced downsizing of General Motors' fleet has caused some confusion. In 1977 General Motors' downsized standard models were approximately the same length and weight as the intermediates, and in 1978 the downsized intermediates were approximately the same dimensions as the compact models.

The competitive impact of a realignment of market segments is impossible to predict. It is clear that both General Motors and Ford are committed to maintaining the existing segments as much as possible. General Motors has announced that a second major downsizing scheduled for all models between 1982 and 1985 will be much less severe than planned. Ford is counting on the PROCO engine to make it unnecessary to substantially redefine today's segments: "PROCO . . . is preferred over further vehicle downsizing as a CAFE improvement because it significantly improves fuel economy of 5 and 6 passenger family cars and thus protects a very critical portion of the new car market."[6]

A second effect of fuel economy standards is the reduction in model variety offered by the major manufacturers. The absolute number of different domestic models, defined as those which are merchandised separately, has declined from 325 models in 1975 to 294 models in 1976, 275 in 1977, 259 in 1978, and 247 in 1979.[7] The vast capital investments made necessary by CAFE standards and by cost pressures already squeezing the car design and development process have encouraged the use of common parts and component systems in different models produced by different divisions of the same manufacturer. Some alternative models from the same manufacturer are almost identical "under the skin."

---

5. For example, GM Design Vice President E. Rybicki.
6. N. 3 *supra* at 4.
7. *Automotive News*, Oct. 2, 1978, p. 1.

Product Mix

Since the time of Alfred Sloan, General Motors' President or Chairman from 1923 to 1956, full-line strategies have enabled manufacturers to provide an appropriate product no matter which way consumer preference shifted in a particular year. A manufacturer who chooses to produce cars in larger sizes, must sell smaller cars to meet fleet average mileage standards. This creates a more competitive environment in which each manufacturer competes segment-by-segment with other manufacturers. General Motors must sell Chevettes in competition with Pintos and subcompact imports. Ford must sell its Fairmont models in competition with General Motors' compact models. No segment can be ignored for a model year. CAFE standards have threatened some of the traditional advantages gained by the full-line strategy of the major automobile makers.

The need to sell smaller models has caused automobile makers to make special efforts to market them:

> Ford Motor Company has undertaken substantial efforts in recent years to increase our leadership position in small car sales including allocating the majority of our advertising resources to small, fuel-efficient car lines, offering dealer and salesmen incentive programs at the retail level, offering numerous special value programs giving away popular optional equipment, and a variety of pricing strategies favoring small cars and fuel-efficient powertrains. . . . Competitive actions would indicate that this also has been an industry strategy.[8]

General Motors denies having adopted such a delibarate strategy:

> Since the effectiveness in moving people from one class to a class with higher fuel economy is greatly dependent upon the acceptability of the product, product pricing, and the consumer environment, advertising and dealer incentives can only be used effectively as extensions of these other factors and not as a market motivating tool unto itself.
>
> GM has not used such strategy to improve fleet average fuel economy. GM would incorporate such measure only to meet a current need on a case by case basis. Our major effort is to increase the attractiveness and value of our subcompact and compact models.[9]

Nevertheless, it is clear that General Motors has already found several special "cases" in which to employ such a strategy. Fearing that imports, particularly Japanese imports, were taking too large a share of the subcompact and compact car market, General Motors and Ford both priced their subcompact models, the Chevette and the Pinto, at unusu-

---

8. N. 3 *supra* at XVII-1.
9. *General Motors Response to NHTSA Questionnaire on 1984–1987 Passenger Car Fuel Economy*, p. 53.

ally low levels for the 1978 model year. They also adopted a differential pricing system whereby models sold in the western states, where Japanese imports are strongest, were priced lower than in other parts of the country. Even with price increases, made possible by the rising exchange rate of the yen, the domestic subcompacts remained "underpriced" by past standards.

The demands of segment-by-segment competition are particularly severe when a specific model fails to sell or when a competitor introduces a completely redesigned model in competition with carryover designs in a manufacturer's own line. Both cases occurred in the fall of 1978. Charges that the Pinto subcompact is a fire hazard in rear-end collisions have sharply curtailed sales. Ford has therefore concluded that it must sell large numbers of Pintos in the 1979 and 1980 model years if it is to meet CAFE standards. Ford has therefore been forced to lower Pinto prices below cost to move them. Faced with continuing bad press in late summer 1978, Ford announced additional dealer incentives on Pinto sales totalling $325 per car. A completely redesigned subcompact will not be introduced until 1981.

Product mix strategies of the major manufacturers are being changed in another way, too. The massive capital investments necessary to redesign models are causing all makers except General Motors to consider withdrawing from particular market segments, giving up the traditional full-line strategy. Chrysler, unable to afford the redesign of all its models in a short time, has let some segments drift until redesigns can be accomplished. Ford Motor Company has been considering pulling out of some segments entirely.[10]

Pricing

Pricing strategies have changed significantly to serve the heightened segment-by-segment competition brought on by CAFE standards. Ford admits it has used "relative pricing," a euphemism for selling below cost, to hold onto and increase subcompact market share in competition with foreign imports. Some analysts estimated that General Motors was losing $200 to $300 for every 1978 Chevette sold at the fall 1977 introductory price. The rapid appreciation of the Japanese yen later relieved this situation, and General Motors raised its Chevette price several times during the model year.

Traditional financial strategies have also been upset by the flood of regulatory measures. Whereas General Motors typically sought to maintain a 20 percent rate of return on investment (or about 10 percent on the

---

10. Henry Ford II comments: "We have discussions every week about whether we should compete across the board with GM. As of now, we're going to meet them across the board. But there are a few exceptions. . . . It's hard to say what part of the market we would withdraw from. . . . If you don't have the money, you have to pick and choose." Remarks, June 12, 1978, New York.

selling price of the average car), recent returns have slipped. General Motors reports that it has absorbed approximately $100 per year in cost increases not passed onto the consumer during the past several years. In 1977, a banner year, General Motors' average return on sales was 6 percent, and its return on investment was 21 percent.

Because General Motors has functioned as the price leader in the industry, pressures on General Motors to trim its profit margins fall even more heavily on the other major manufacturers which do not enjoy comparable margins to begin with. Many executives complain that investors in the automobile industry, and not consumers, are bearing the cost of industry regulation, thereby producing uncertain effects on capital formation.

Geographical Markets

With increased regulation in the United States and slower market growth in all of North America, opportunities abroad have taken on greater importance. Ford's dominant worldwide position has been extremely valuable. General Motors also seems to have given more prominence to the world automobile market in its planning. General Motors Overseas Operations (GMOO) have been strengthened and moved from New York to corporate headquarters in Detroit to insure greater coordination and attention.

Chrysler, on the other hand, facing the critical capital shortage brought on by CAFE laws, has been forced to pull out of Europe and other international markets. The sale this year of its European operations to Peugeot and the sale of partnerships in several other international units to other automobile companies signal the end of Chrysler's role as a world-wide automobile company. American Motors Corporation, needing significant financing and more markets for its successful Jeep lines, is negotiating an agreement with Renault for cost-sharing at some United States manufacturing facilities that will produce both American Motors and Renault models, and for marketing Jeeps in Europe.

Strategic Flexibility

In the preregulation days, future product plans were formulated no more than forty-eight months before model introduction. Under the pressure of CAFE standards, future product planning has been pushed back at least twice as far. This extremely long-term planning in response to the regulatory climate demands, in both the long and short run, significantly greater flexibility than was previously necessary. The larger firms with significantly greater financial strength can, in effect, buy this flexibility by investing simultaneously in several alternative technologies. The smaller and less sound firms must make much steeper bets on fewer technologies.

In 1977, for instance, flush with the success of downsizing its standard or full-sized cars, General Motors announced that it would redimension all its models not once but twice by 1985 in order to meet CAFE standards. The downsized intermediates, introduced in the fall of 1977, did not sell as well, but demand for the diesel engines General Motors offered on a few models was spectacular. General Motors therefore began crash programs to develop and introduce diesels in many new configurations. In mid-1978 the company announced that the second round of downsizing, previously announced, would be less severe than anticipated and that the company would rely more on the diesel to increase fuel economy. Uncertainties still exist for General Motors' plans, obviously. Further strategic shifts will be necessary if problems with diesel emissions cannot be remedied, if consumers cool on the diesel engine, or if CAFE standards for 1984 to 1986 are substantially raised.

IMPACT ON POLITICAL STRATEGY

Among the most clearly defined changes in the content of the political strategy pursued by the major automobile makers in the most recent two to three years are: A rejection of the "stonewalling" strategy pursued by most firms in the 1965-to-1973 period; an increasing commitment to the public interest and a concurrent decline in the ideological content of positions taken; the development of differentiated political strategies unique to each firm; an increasing attention to enlisting the support of other interest groups for positions taken; an attempt to tie positions taken to broader national problems of public concern; and the use of a more open and candid style to reduce some aspects of regulatory risk. Each of these developments is described below.

An End to Stonewalling

During early debates on safety and emissions regulation, the automobile industry replaced its habitual "low-profile" or "head-in-the-sand" political posture with another pattern that it came to regret. The industry frequently responded to proposed standards or rules by taking the following series of positions: (1) "Technologically, it can't be done;" (2) "the standard demands technology which has not been fully developed in production volumes and cannot be relied on;" (3) "it can be done, but costs will be so high that it is not justified;" (4) "it can be done, and costs may not be that high, but such regulation violates our nation's commitment to free enterprise;" and (5) "okay, we'll do it." Claims that standards were technologically unfeasible and too costly proved unjustified in a number of cases and severely undercut the credibility of the industry. In the mid–1970s the automobile companies exhibited considerably greater political sophistication: Strategies are more complex and differ from company-to-company.

Public Commitment to the Public Interest

Throughout the late 1960s and early 1970s, the common argument pursued by the automobile companies in regulatory discussions was firmly grounded in a commitment to free enterprise. The automobile companies were criticized for maintaining a greater commitment to self-interest in a free-enterprise system than to such public interest as highway safety or pollution control. The proposed standards were designed to rectify that situation.

But in the 1970s, particularly in the case of fuel economy, the automobile companies emphasized a strong commitment to energy conservation and to increasing the fuel economy of American automobiles. General Motors Chairman Thomas Murphy reflected on the experience of the auto industry:

> The only arguments and proposals we should even consider taking to Washington—or advancing in our public speeches—should be those that place the heaviest emphasis on the factual, scientific and legal merits of our position. Our objective, no less than government's, must be the public interest.[11]

Differentiated Strategies

The major automobile makers have been less likely to take identical stands on proposed standards and rules relating to fuel economy than they were on safety and emissions issues. Two 1978 examples will illustrate this development.

In the summer of 1978 all three major domestic automobile makers opposed provisions in draft energy legislation which would have imposed severe excise taxes on low mileage cars (termed "gas guzzlers") and which would have banned gas guzzlers entirely. General Motors and Ford rely on big car sales for much of their volume and a substantial percentage of their profit and consequently preferred the tax to the ban. Chrysler, weaker in standard and luxury models than Ford and General Motors, preferred an outright ban on gas guzzlers.

In their submissions to NHTSA (August 1978) in response to discussions about whether to raise the 1984-to-1985 CAFE standards above their current levels, the big three automobile makers took different positions. Chrysler, most threatened by CAFE standards, pressed for a lowering of all 1981-to-1985 CAFE requirements. Ford, in a better posi-

---

11. Quoted in *Fortune*, Sept. 11, 1978, p. 48.

tion than Chrysler, but worried over the rapid rise of 2 miles per gallon per year in the 1981-to-1983 period, recommended once again that 1981-to-1984 CAFE standards rise by 1 mile per gallon per year, with a 3.5 miles per gallon jump in 1985. General Motors, in the strongest position on fuel economy, simply stated the company's opposition to raising the 1984 and 1985 standards.

An incident in the spring of 1978 furnishes the second example. Ford and Chrysler encouraged NHTSA to approve a new elliptical tire for use on passenger cars; the two companies were prepared to offer the tire as a fuel-saving option when 1979 models were introduced in the fall of 1978. General Motors, which uses "made-to-specification" tires rather than the standard models Ford and Chrysler planned to buy from Goodyear, would not have been able to offer the fuel-saving option at the same time. General Motors opposed approval of the tire, claiming it did not save fuel and was potentially unsafe. By the time NHTSA investigated General Motors' claims and rejected them it was late May—too late for Ford and Chrysler to introduce the tires in September.

Differences in political strategy are not always the result of competitive analyses. Often the major automobile makers simply evaluate the momentum of political events differently. When the Energy Policy and Conservation Act was being considered in 1975, Ford, the United Auto Workers, and the National Automobile Dealers Association concluded that some form of fuel economy measure would be passed, and so came out in favor of the mandatory average performance standards rather than an alternative proposal for excise taxes on gas guzzlers. General Motors and Chrysler believed both measures could be defeated in the legislative process and that, in any event, President Ford would veto them. However, President Ford signed the legislation after Congress passed it. Perhaps his decision was made easier by the split in the industry's position.

Building Political Coalitions

American business, acutely aware of its lack of credibility in political processes, has increasingly sought the support of nonindustry groups. The early 1978 consideration of light-duty truck CAFE standards for 1980 and 1981 clearly illustrates the point. All the major manufacturers believed compliance with the strict proposed standards was impossible without removing some model offerings from sale. Initial appeals by General Motors and Ford for relief from the proposed standards attracted some attention but did not influence NHTSA's plans. Chrysler, however, noted that the standards would make it necessary to close their Detroit Jefferson Avenue Plant, which employed many recently hired disadvantaged minority persons. On this point, Chrysler found they could muster a coalition of groups including the Detroit Urban League and the NAACP in opposition to the severe truck standards. This need for outside support even united labor and management on the same side in opposition to regulation. In mid–1977, the automobile makers and the United Auto Workers lobbied side-by-side against the strict emissions standards. Confronted with this broad opposition, NHTSA backed down and approved more lenient standards.

Tying Positions to Critical Issues

During the early 1970s the major automobile makers recognized that arguments about the need for "free enterprise" and for "managerial autonomy" did not capture the support of legislators or their constituents. Instead automobile company positions are increasingly tied to external issues which the companies have concluded are of greater concern to the general public—increasing inflation, unemployment, and government bureaucracy. Early in 1978 Ford Motor Company called for a moratorium on all federal regulations tying it to the problems of inflation. Chrysler tied its opposition to the light-duty truck standards to unemployment and minority opportunity. Thus the issue of regulation is no longer "shall we clean up the environment?" but rather "can we accept more inflation as a result of regulation?" A similar strategy of changing the face of an issue was used successfully by a broad business coalition in defeating the Consumer Protection Agency Bill in 1978. The coalition made the issue one of "do we want more government bureaucracy?" rather than "do we want more consumer protection?"

Speaking to the Sixty-First Annual Convention of the National Automobile Dealers Association in February 1978, NADA President Robert P. Mallon urged a two- or three-year moratorium on further regulations as an economic stimulus: "We need something to get things moving . . . . The country is calling for dynamic leadership. A moratorium would produce just the effect we need."[12] In a White Paper submitted to the government in late June 1978, Ford tied its concerns directly to public policy fears over increasing concentration of the automobile industry and to lost jobs: "It is ironic that the cumulative impact of government regulation may be to strengthen the positions of GM (which already has half the market) and the imports (which are contributing heavily to the nation's balance of payments and unemployment problems) and possibly to weaken domestic competition in the automotive industry."[13] In a late September 1978 speech General Motors Chairman Thomas Murphy tied concern for overregulation to the currently popular "Proposition 13" movement: "By directing the momentum generated by the tax revolt toward a sensible rejection of wasteful government regulation and excessive government involvement, the entire American economy and every American family depending upon it could and would benefit profoundly."[14]

---

12. Quoted in *Automotive News*, Feb. 27, 1978, p. 1.
13. Quoted in *Automotive News*, July 3, 1978, p. 3.
14. Quoted in *Automotive News*, Oct. 2, 1978, p. 32.

More Open Style

Fuel economy laws force the major domestic manufacturers to embrace untested technologies subject to possible future regulation. Recognizing the risks involved, General Motors has begun "floating" future product plans long before they are irrevocable commitments. There are several advantages to such a political strategy. First, the company at least appears to be a more open and candid organization. Second, it focuses public attention and debate on particular new technologies; opposition, if it is to arise, should emerge at an earlier stage in the technological development process, thereby giving General Motors greater warning of potential conflicts. Third, it creates a constituency of suppliers who have made plans to provide the materials and technology needed, and customers who are anxiously awaiting the new offerings. Should technological or regulatory snags develop in the later stages, General Motors can probably count on some allies in the regulatory review process.

In early 1978, General Motors announced its major program to introduce diesels in the 1980s. General Motors also let it be known that major financial commitments must be made to the plan by late 1979; this puts the regulators on notice that they should act soon if the nitrogen oxides or particulate problems of the diesel may rule out its use.

ORGANIZATIONAL CHANGES

Product-market strategy and political strategy are only two aspects of overall corporate strategy that need to be studied in light of extensive government regulation. Among the most intriguing remaining issues are those concerning the effects of regulation on the structure of the firm. Internal data are generally unavailable from published sources. Nevertheless, we may assume that when product-market strategies are shifted as dramatically as they have been by the fuel economy laws, significant internal organizational changes must result. Among the changes one might expect to find are the following:

New Planning Organizations

The short-term focus of most automobile industry planning in the past has been drastically extended. Instead of a forty-eight-month horizon, the manufacturers are now coping with an eight- to ten-year horizon. One could expect to find the reorganization of planning units or the creation of new planning groups to cope with these new demands.

Strengthening of Government Relations Organizations

It is obvious that the complex strategic calculus and gaming with government that the automobile firms now engage in demand a highly trained and proficient staff. Increased numbers and raised status of government relations staff are likely results. Furthermore, the top executives of the government relations staff must increasingly be tied into the strategic apparatus of the firms, in order to advise on product-market strategy and to aid in setting political strategy. One would expect to find the top government relations executives in a more prominent role, perhaps serving on the executive committee.

Weakening of Decentralized Organization

The pressures towards commonization of components and engineered systems in car models make the independence of car divisions less functional. One would expect to find engineering tasks performed on a more centralized basis, with fewer prerogatives left to the divisional staffs. Since 1973 General Motors has developed what they call "project centers" which, following a pattern common in the airframe industry, bring a team of engineers together to design all the common parts of certain models. Such a development may have ripple effects throughout the organization, increasing centralized decision-making and reducing the power of the divisional executives.

Strengthening of Research and Marketing Organizations

As the automobile firms are forced to embrace increased technological and market risk due to CAFE standards, one would expect to find a heightened importance given to the research and marketing staffs. Both must be more creative and more flexible if the firm is to meet CAFE standards. A simultaneous downgrading of the importance of the styling staff might also result.

Executive Changes

Any industry whose external environment has been altered as drastically as that of the automobile industry in the past ten years needs significant changes in leadership. Executives who have spent their lives operating in an environment centered in Detroit, with considerable freedom of decision, find it extremely difficult to function in an environment of regulation and externally imposed strategic constraints. One would therefore expect to find a pattern of increased executive replacement, early retirements, and voluntary transfers as the executive ranks are realigned to put in place executives capable of formulating strategy in the new environment.

TOWARD AN ANALYTIC FRAMEWORK

The firm must manage its relationship with two separate but equally important portions of its environment—the economic market and the public policy process. Each environment presses upon the corporation in characteristic ways so that threats and opportunities continually arise from each environment. The public policy environment itself functions as a kind of second market wherein the corporation can seek to advance its own interests, engaging in a kind of competition with other interest groups, with legislators, and with regulators, to influence the final shape of statutes, rules, and enforcement strategies. The actions the corporation takes to influence the workings of each environment are called strategy—market strategy and political strategy. The two environments are mutually dependent, constantly influencing conditions in one another. Developments in the public environment alter conditions in the market environment, creating new threats and opportunities for the firm every bit as real as those which emanate from the normal workings of the market.

We can suggest a series of questions a firm might ask itself in assessing the potential effect of a proposed or enacted policy on product-market strategy. Government analysts should be concerned with the answers to these same questions for every firm in an industry:

1. What type of new competitive characteristics are established by the proposed policy? Are all the firms affected equally?

2. Where does the firm begin the new competitive battle created by this statute or rule? Are competitors far ahead?

3. What resources are important to competing in this new dimension? Does the firm have more than competitors?

4. What effect does the statute/rule have on risk associated with existing strategies pursued by the firm?

5. What effect does the statute/rule have on existing patterns of market segmentation, product design, product mix, pricing, geographical markets, and needed strategic flexibility?

Finally, our analysis allows us to understand the decision-making process by which firms determine which political strategies they are to pursue. The political calculus is performed in terms strikingly similar to those which determine market strategy. As shown in Figure 3-2, the strategists consider the effect of the proposed or enacted public policy on the firm and the momentum the proposed policy has in the political process. The strategist then considers what resources the firm has at its disposal to intervene in the process by which the policy is being developed. Two considerations related to values are important: How does the proposed statute or rule relate to values or desires of the strategist himself or the committee which is considering a political strategy, and how does the proposed statute or rule relate to considerations of the "public interest" and notions of the socially responsible role of the firm? Beyond these considerations, the strategist will weigh tactical questions in choosing what techniques should be used to implement the political strategy selected.

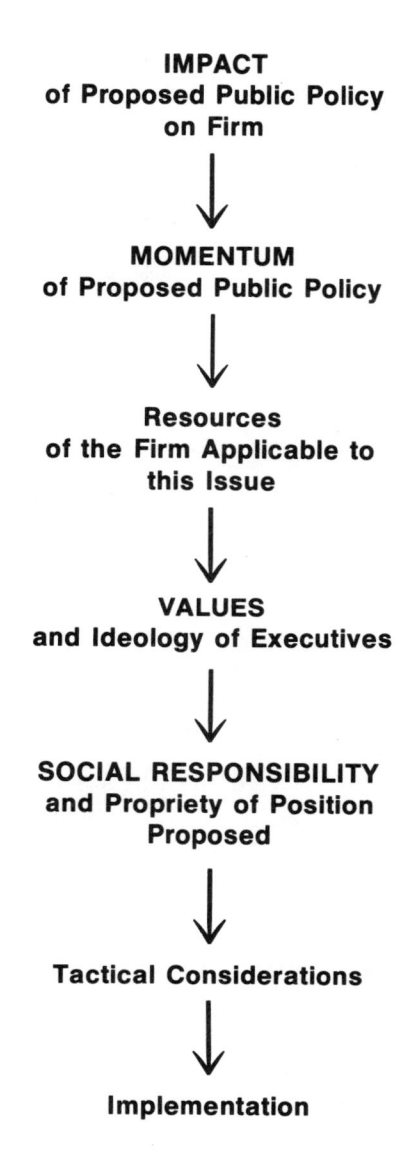

```
        IMPACT
of Proposed Public Policy
         on Firm
            │
            ▼
       MOMENTUM
of Proposed Public Policy
            │
            ▼
       Resources
of the Firm Applicable to
        this Issue
            │
            ▼
        VALUES
 and Ideology of Executives
            │
            ▼
 SOCIAL RESPONSIBILITY
 and Propriety of Position
        Proposed
            │
            ▼
  Tactical Considerations
            │
            ▼
      Implementation
```

FIGURE 3-2 Formation of corporate political strategy

The case of fuel economy regulations and strategies for dealing with them in the automobile industry also suggests the following propositions about the content of corporate political strategy: When faced with a public policy demand that so strongly affects the competitive conditions in the industry, corporate political strategy will become (1) less ideological and more pragmatic; (2) more differentiated from other firms in the same industry and more closely tied to the economic self-interest of the individual firm; and (3) more constituency and coalition oriented.

DISCUSSION

ROBERT MCCABE: The authors underplay the international competitive position of the United States auto industry. Our world car is far from competitive. We believe that regulation has clearly hurt our worldwide competitive position.

Dr. John implied that the only major reason for fuel economy gains was federal regulation. I am glad that Mr. Hanson pointed out that the industry in 1974 had agreed to voluntary fuel economy standards and that we were well along with product programs and different components to try to implement them at the time that the government passed the fuel economy requirements. Still, General Motors, in order to meet the 1980 fuel economy goal which we agreed to voluntarily, had to improve its fuel economy 53 percent.

Regarding standards to be proposed for beyond 1985, we would like to see a cost-benefit analysis done, comparing the incremental conservation gains with the impact of the regulations on the United States economy.

Dr. John has also stated that fuel economy technology has come largely from Western Europe and Japan. I would just say that General Motors and the United States auto industry have contributed also, in particular, the throttle-body injection system, electronically controlled fuel injection, and General Motors' big contribution—the catalytic converter—which is important to both fuel economy and emission control. However, our analysis shows that R&D dollars at some point, we are not sure where, are better spent in synthetic fuel development than in fuel economy innovations. We believe this point could be reached in the mid–1980s. He also failed to mention that all of these innovations are costing the consumer somewhere in the area of $800 more than a pre–1970-to-1978 car.

Mr. Hanson developed very well some of the issues of the impact of regulation on corporate strategy: The alternations in the competitive environment and in the product-market strategies, and the development of company strategies to deal with legislators and regulators. His scenario of the declining profit margins was probably accurate.

I would like to emphasize the tremendous capital investments that are required of us to meet all of these standards. Last year General Motors spent $3.6 billion just in new plant and equipment, and new product programs like downsizing. Our current estimates are scaring the hell out of us; the estimates we are making say $5 billion a year by the early 1980s—just for General Motors alone—to meet the requirements to get to the 1985 fuel economy standards. We do not know where that money is going to come from. Our profit margins are deteriorating and we scarcely made $3.6 billion last year. Chrysler is spinning-off overseas subsidiaries. To an FTC man this should be cause for concern.

Finally, General Motors definitely has what Hanson calls a more "open style" now in our product programs. We are trying very hard to tell our story to the appropriate public forums. This forum here is no exception.

To summarize: The auto industry acknowledges that some government regulation is necessary to meet society's needs. But creativity has been stifled in many areas because of regulation. Many companies are having to put their entire effort into meeting regulations and thus cannot do any independent innovating. We would emphasize that the cost-benefit analysis should be applied and that the competitive nature of the industry, both domestically and worldwide, should be preserved.

TIMOTHY NULTY: I agree with Dr. John's rather pragmatic conclusion that society will demand and require higher mileage after 1985. It will be hard to do it. The easy technological solutions have possibly been exhausted. The auto industry will be more sophisticated in resisting greater demands from the government. The whole thing will get messier and more difficult. What should we do about this? Dr. John does not say. And this is true, too—there are no easy answers.

The reference in Mr. Hanson's discussion to the experience of other regulated industries is very interesting. Granted that regulation in the auto industry is significantly different from traditional regulation of power, electricity, trucking, railroads, etc., which involve prices as well as specifications of products and services; however, there are similarities at least to the initial experience, the initial strategic behavior of the firms when they were first subjected to regulation. More work needs to be done on these parallels.

AUTO (U.S.): None of the discussants or writers has talked about the most obvious thing of all—letting the price of fuel go up and taxing it. If you want to save gas or oil, it is obvious that if you increase the price of gas in a way in which people can plan for, you will change the driving habits of the public. Then the auto makers would not have to puzzle as to what kind of cars to build to get people to buy. They would know what to plan for.

ACADEMIC: Dick John, has there been any consideration given to total energy use in automotive transportation rather than the technological measure of the fuel economy of individual vehicles, and to a set of policies that would derive from that—which would include changes in the price of fuel—rather than the single-minded and imprudent route of fuel economy standards? We have the post–1985 possibility that even the fuel economy standards we have on the books may not be met.

JOHN: The Congress decided, after much debate, that what the public wanted was mandated fuel economy standards and so told the executive branch to carry them out. Thus far, we have had a fairly good first act. Notwithstanding Mr. McCabe's saying that General Motors would have done it by itself, I truly doubt that.

The reason I brought up Western European and Japanese technology is not that General Motors has incorporated this into their cars, but rather that the world knew in 1975 that that source of fuel economy technology existed. We do not know that going into 1985. We do not know where the technology is. So what

I have said is mandated fuel economy standards are the likely path that Congress will choose on the basis of the last five years of experience. What I am telling the policy-makers is from what we can see there are going to be some problems. And it started with the light truck hearings, and it will get more and more difficult. Therefore, policy initiatives have to be started into other areas and I do not think it will be price mechanisms, or tax incentives, or rehabilitation/relocation. It will be a package and we will get there to 1995 in the stumbling way the democratic process works.

OIL INDUSTRY: We could go beyond the standards set for 1985 with current technology. You see this in cars being sold in United States markets today. Weight reduction is extremely important here, I think. The advanced powerplant is important, too, but maybe not as much as weight reduction.

JOHN: My concern really was manufacturing process technology. What are the motivations for the industry to make the investments into manufacturing process technology if indeed the goal of increasing fuel economy beyond 1985 is not clear. I agree with you that this is a time for a coming together. If the nation selects a redoubling of the fuel economy by 1995 it is hard to see how the industry can do that on its own without support in a whole variety of areas starting with the price mechanism.

AUTO (FOREIGN): In Europe we think that the consumer has a more important role, for example, in fuel economy. In United States legislation the consumer is not taken too much into consideration, for example, his buying of other car sizes, the move to vans or light trucks. I do not know how much of your increase in sales in this area is due to the downsizing of cars and decreasing the overall fuel economy.

ACADEMIC: Fuel economy emerges as a somewhat different issue from fuel consumption and the problems dealing with it turn out to be substantially different from those of auto safety.

GOVERNMENT (DOT): Auto safety is not a different problem. Look at no-fault auto insurance.

CONSULTANT: Mr. McCabe mentioned that research efforts should be directed toward development of synthetic fuels. Is that based on displacing the use of petroleum as a strategy for the country?

MCCABE: By taking the weight out of the car we have gotten a good return on our R&D expenditure in the sense of getting good fuel economy gains. However, for additional spending we figure on getting one-tenth of a mile per billion dollars of investment. At this point those dollars are better spent for the development of synthetic fuels, either as a supplement or replacement.

HANSON: We can learn a great deal from other regulated industries. We see a pattern of initial response which is probably not that different from what we have seen in the auto industry: Initial outrage, emphasis on ideology, the challenge to internal logics that have developed within a particular industry or firm—all regulators are ignorant that size is necessary for value in automobiles, for example. When this logic is challenged by regulation, you get the response that it is Them versus Us; you get united industry action. Only later, does one see an increasing sophistication on the part of the firms, and the firms differentiate their strategies when they realize that there are competitive possibilities in the political realm, as well as in the marketplace.

PART TWO
The Implications of Regulation

CHAPTER FOUR
Some Second-Level Effects of Regulation

EDITORS' NOTE

The four essays in this chapter concern the future effects of present regulations. What are the likely consequences, direct and indirect, intended and inadvertent, of what we, as a nation, are requiring of the automobile?

Clearly, the regulatory regime with the greatest potential impact upon the automobile and the automobile industry is that governing fuel economy. Merely casual bystanders can see that, unlike most safety standards and the pollution control regulations, the requirement of greater fuel economy is reshaping the automobile—"downsizing" it, in present parlance.

Not so visible effects may be waiting down the road, however, as the industry struggles to meet ever-higher average fuel economy standards. Insofar as these induce the manufacturers to emphasize diesel engines, they raise questions about the health effects of diesel particulates. These questions are probably not going to be answerable, through medical research, for many years to come.

The move to smaller, lighter automobiles may also have effects upon occupant safety. In the first essay in this chapter, Howard M. Bunch projects that the effect of downsizing will be an increase of almost 6 percent in automobile occupant deaths and injuries. Fuel economy, that is, will impose a safety penalty.

According to Richard H. Shackson, fuel economy also conflicts with emissions controls: "Control of emissions reduces fuel economy." The result of these and other interacting regulatory requirements, he argues, is that automobile manufacturers must move to electronic engine controls if they are to meet all the standards. This may work severe dislocations in the automotive service sector, reduce the level of competition now obtaining, and raise the consumer's cost of repairs.

Frank T. Popovich analyzes the effects of continuing materials and parts substitutions as automobile manufacturers seek to build safer, cleaner, and especially more fuel-efficient (lighter) vehicles. Some supplier industries will suffer, while others will profit, from the changes. If further safety and noise regulations require adding back some of the possible weight reductions, however, and if consumers shift in greater numbers to light trucks and utility vehicles, the result may be a 1985 sales-weighted vehicle weight about the same as it is today.

Finally, Stephen P. Bradley and Aneel G. Karnani use a risk analysis model to assess the relative financial impacts of fuel economy standards on each of the major United States automobile manufacturers. Using a variety of alternative assumptions or scenarios, they derive consistently significant projections which show that the domestic manufacturing firms will be affected in quite different ways. Will the domestic industry in 1985 consist of four, or three, or two manufacturers?

Each of these papers will be greeted with controversies that will be settled, if ever, only in the future. Regardless of those particular controversies, however, the papers taken together hold an important lesson about the nature of regulation: Some of its most significant effects may be unintended and unwanted. Indeed, they may be felt in areas far removed from those ostensibly being regulated, and they may frustrate other policies, conceived and executed elsewhere in the same government, that are of equal or greater importance to the public interest.

THE SMALL CAR MAY BE DANGEROUS TO YOUR HEALTH! THE CONSEQUENCES OF DOWNSIZING

Howard M. Bunch[*], *Highway Safety Research Institute, the University of Michigan*

Major and dramatic changes will be occurring in the structure of the private passenger automobile in the years ahead. Most of these changes will occur in direct response to governmental regulation. To those involved in evaluating and studying passenger car safety, an important implication of governmental regulation has been its effect on population injury and death. While there is good reason to applaud the purposes of fuel economy legislation, we should also recognize some of the potentially negative implications of this legislation. For example, downsizing of the passenger car to meet the mandatory fuel economy standards may have negative effects upon occupant safety. Our purpose is to isolate, insofar as possible, the effect of vehicle size changes upon the death statistics at that point in the future when the vehicle fleet is primarily composed of units meeting the 27.5 miles-per-gallon standard.

There have been numerous evaluations of the differences between "small" car and "large" car safety. In a 1977 study of the problem, McLean[1] stated that there would be a 35 percent increase in fatalities during the decade ending in 1985 because of the increasing fleet of smaller cars colliding with older and heavier vehicles. The study did not make the injury projections, however, for an environment that included only vehicles made to comply with the more stringent fuel economy standards.

---

[*] Significant support in the preparation of this paper was received from Dr. Robert L. Hess, Mr. James O'Day, Dr. Richard Kaplan, and Mr. William McCormick, all with the Highway Safety Research Institute.

1. R. McLean, *Lightweight Versus Heavyweight—The Contest of the Future*, Soc'y of Automotive Engineers, Passenger Car Meeting, SAE Paper, No. 770809 (Sept. 26–30, 1977).

In a most interesting study, Carlson[2] also projected an increase in injury statistics as a reduced-weight fleet is introduced into the system. But he predicted that the increase would be nearly eliminated as the vehicle size differences disappear. Carlson concluded that the fuel savings (in dollars) will be greater than injury cost (in dollars) when the stabilized condition occurs. Carlson treated age as a linear term in his model, however. He did not make any adjustments to accommodate the effects on accident statistics of an older driving population.

The issues of how changing vehicle size will affect accident statistics are complex; the interests of special groups will be severely affected; and, significant sums of money—billions of dollars—are at stake. For example, the insurance industry will be negatively affected by downsizing. It is in their financial interest to prevent any destabilizing events in accident-loss ratios. Such a trauma will have a significant impact on their short-term profits. Likewise, the established automobile industry is against downsizing changes because compliance forces the redirection of some profits to plant reinvestment, rather than to the stockholder.

Other sectors of the economy are in favor of the change. The aluminum industry and the plastics industry, for example, see the vehicle redesign requirements as an opportunity for their products to penetrate the market because the need to reduce vehicle weight will encourage material substitution. A case can be made that NHTSA would be especially pleased if it could be proved that no additional injury exposure results from reducing vehicle weight. With such a proof NHTSA would be able to align itself, without difficulty, with other segments of the federal government on the issue of mandatory fuel economy standards.

As present legislation now stands, the most stringent fuel economy standards, emissions standards, and safety standards will have been implemented by the 1986 model year. To assure ourselves that the majority of the passenger car fleet would meet those standards, 1995 was selected as our evaluation year. By then at least 85 percent of the vehicles will be 1985 model year or later, and at least 98 percent will be 1980 model year or later.

Table 4-1 shows the economic and demographic projections for 1995 used in our analysis. By 1995, the total United States population will be 250 million. There will be significant changes in the age distribution: About 52 percent of the population will be over 35 years of age. This is a segment increase of 10 percent over the 1975 profile.

We estimate that there will be 161.3 million drivers in 1995—an increase of 25 percent over the 1975 count. We also project that over 65 percent of the drivers will be over 35 years of age, as compared with about 55 percent in 1975.

---

2. W. Carlson, *Empirical Crash Injury Modeling and Vehicle-Size Mix*, DOT-HS-803-348 (May 1978).

TABLE 4-1 U.S. Economic and Social Projections, 1975 and 1995

	1975 (actual)	1995 (projection)
Population (millions)	213.5	250.0
Distribution, by age		
<24 years old	43%	36%
25–34	15	12
35–54	22	29
>54 years old	20	23
	100%	100%
Licensed drivers (millions)	128.8	161.3
Distribution, by age		
<24 years old	23	17
25–34	23	17
35–54	32	42
>54 years old	22	23
	100%	99%[a]
Passenger autos (millions)	106.7	136.0
Annual miles traveled, per auto	9,635	9,635

[a] Total < 100 due to rounding.

Source: *U.S. Statistical Abstracts,* Systems Design Concepts, Inc., Stanford Research Inst.; Bureau of the Census.

Our projections for passenger automobile counts are derived from an average of published estimates. The 1995 passenger car population is projected to be 136 million units, an increase of about 27 percent over the 1975 count.

We assume for the study that the average automobile's annual vehicle miles traveled (VMT) will remain unchanged at slightly over 9,600 miles. We point out, however, that many think there will be significant increases in VMT/auto. One source,[3] for example, projected a range of 9,305 to 12,800. The mid-range was estimated at 11,410 VMT/auto.

There is no doubt that the manufacturers are being confronted with severe redesign problems as they prepare for compliance with the fuel economy standards. To determine the car population's physical attributes in 1995, we made an analysis of General Motors' plans for future vehicle redesign. Figure 4-1 presents a time schematic through the 1985 model year of their redesign program. One observation stands out: Most of General Motors' *basic vehicle redesigns through 1985 have already been introduced.* The exception is the compact vehicle which will appear

---

3. *Technology Assessment of Changes in Future Use and Characteristics of the Automobile Transportation System,* Office of Technology Assessment, U.S. Congress. Background report by Systems Design Concepts, Inc. prepared in Jan. 1978.

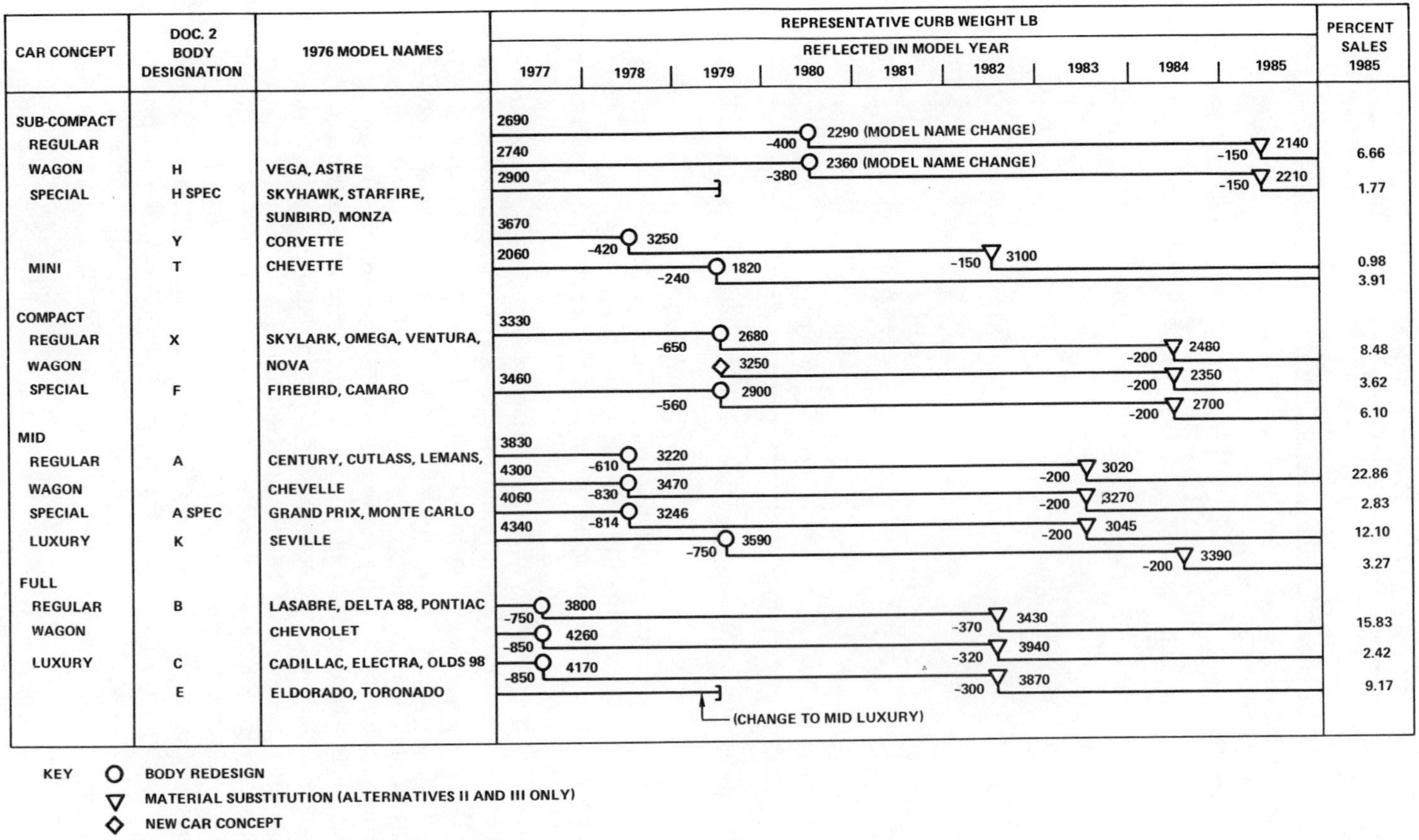

FIGURE 4-1 Time-phased introduction of GMC weight-reduction technology

Source: GMC; "Data and Analysis for 1981 – 1984 Passenger Automobile Fuel Economy Standards."; DOT, NHTSA, 1977.

KEY:
- ○ BODY REDESIGN
- ▽ MATERIAL SUBSTITUTION (ALTERNATIVES II AND III ONLY)
- ◇ NEW CAR CONCEPT

in its redesigned form in 1980. Further weight reductions will come from material substitutions.

General Motors expects to meet the 1985 fuel economy standards with vehicles that weigh between 1,820 pounds and 3,940 pounds. This is in contrast to a 1976 model year weight range of 2,060 pounds to 5,110 pounds. The average weight in 1985, on a sales-adjusted basis, is expected to be almost exactly 3,000 pounds.

We let the General Motors projected sales profile in 1985 represent the United States car population in 1995. First, General Motors has over 50 percent of the market and differences in size mix from other manufacturers would be pretty much balanced out, over all. Second, all presently legislated regulations will be in effect by 1985, and there would be no need for further size reductions after that date.

Another assumption was that the driving habits and attitudes of each age group will remain consistent through 1995. That is to say, there will be the same propensity for people to have accidents twenty years from now as there is today.

A final assumption was that fatality statistics will adequately represent changes that will occur in all injury statistics.

The analysis presented here was made on the basis of three accident scenarios. The scenarios were:

A single-vehicle accident;

A car-versus-truck accident; and

A car-versus-car accident.

The data files we used consisted of about one million police–reported accidents in the State of Texas for the years 1975 and 1976. (Our analysis was based on a 5 percent random sample of accidents, and on one of the scenarios (car/car), we only looked at the 1975 data.)

Table 4-2 is a prediction of the propensity for an accident, by type, as a function of driver age. As indicated earlier, we assumed that this propensity will remain constant through 1995.

TABLE 4-2 Relationship Between Driver Age and Passenger Car Accident Involvements, by Type of Accident (Number of automobile accident involvements per year per 10,000 licensed drivers in each age group)

Driver age (years)	Single vehicle	Car vs. truck	Car vs. car
<24	163	195	867
25–34	70	128	543
35–54	37	89	378
>54	23	92	339

Accident type column spans Single vehicle, Car vs. truck, Car vs. car.

Source: Calculated from police-reported accidents in Texas, 1975 and 1976.

Table 4-2 clearly shows the higher probability of all types of accidents involving younger drivers. But the age/accident relationships are different for different accident types. For example, only about 8 percent of single vehicle accidents involve drivers over 54 years of age. But nearly 16 percent of the two-car accidents involve drivers over 54 years of age.

Based on data shown in Table 4-2, we expect that there will be declines in the number of accident involvements per licensed driver in the years ahead because of the increasing age of the driving population. Assuming that all of our earlier assumptions will be correct, we estimate that there will be about 660 automobile involvements in police-reported accidents per 10,000 licensed drivers in 1995. This compares with about 710 in 1975. The projected decline is about 7 percent.

Table 4-3 shows the calculated vehicle occupant fatalities per 10,000 vehicle accident involvements for the 1975 (or standard) fleet and for a 1995 (or downsized) fleet. The downsized fleet is estimated to have only vehicles whose weights were less than 4,000 pounds. The data generally indicate a greater probability of fatality/accident involvement in the downsized fleet.

Table 4-4 shows the estimates for the number of fatalities that will occur in 1995 with the downsized fleet if all of the earlier assumptions are valid. For comparison, the table also projects what the estimated number of fatalities would be if no downsizing occurred. The table shows that *with the downsized fleet there will be an increase in the fatality rate of about 6 percent (5.6 percent).* If we assume the traditional linear relationship will exist between injuries and deaths, then we can expect the same 6 percent increase in injuries as well.

Of course in the years ahead, there will be further changes in the safety characteristics of automobiles and in the transportation system in general. We have held these factors constant in our analysis in order to

TABLE 4-3 Estimated Number of Vehicle Occupant Fatalities Per 10,000 Vehicle Accident Involvements

Age of vehicle driver	Single vehicle	Car vs. truck	Car vs. car
Standard Fleet (vehicle population existing in 1975)			
<25	139	41	18
25–34	136	38	20
35–54	163	42	21
>55	280	71	32
Downsized Fleet (projected vehicle population existing in 1995)			
<25	145	43	18
25–34	139	32	20
35–54	176	47	23
>55	274	84	37

(Type of accident column spans Single vehicle, Car vs. truck, Car vs. car)

Source: Calculated from Texas accident data, 1975–1976.

TABLE 4-4 Estimates of Passenger Car Occupant Fatalities in 1995[a] with Fleets of "Standard-Weight" and with "Downsize Weights" by Driver Age and Type of Accident (hundreds of deaths)

Driver age	Single vehicle	Car vs. truck	Car vs. car	Total
Standard Fleet				
<25	63	22	43	128
25–34	27	14	31	72
35–54	41	25	54	120
>54	24	25	41	90
Total	155	86	169	410
Downsized fleet				
<25	66	23	43	132
25–34	27	12	31	70
35–54	44	28	59	131
>54	24	29	47	100
Total	161	92	180	433

[a] Assumes the following conditions: No passive restraint system; 9,635 VMT/auto; 161.3 million licensed drivers.
Source: Estimated from analysis of Texas accident data, 1975–1976.

isolate, insofar as possible, effects of the single factor, vehicle downsizing. Among these changes are the introduction and use of passive restraint systems in all passenger automobiles by the 1984 model year. By 1995, most of the passenger car population should be so equipped. It is expected that the devices will have major impacts on injury and death statistics. DOT estimates that air cushions (one form of passive restraint) would reduce fatalities in front, side, and rear crash modes by 43 percent.[4] If the estimates are correct, then we could make an approximate 40 percent reduction in the number of fatalities shown in Table 4-4.

This reduction would be partially, if not completely, offset by the anticipated increase in VMT/auto. If the projected VMT/auto of 11,410 were to be a reality in 1995, there would be an approximate increase of about 19 percent in the projections shown in Table 4-4.

Whatever the final VMT/auto relationship, or the benefits that result from passive restraint systems, we believe that, as matters now stand, at least 6 percent of the fatalities that occur in 1995 will be the direct result of downsizing of the vehicle. This translates into approximately 1,300-to-1,700 lives each year, plus an even larger number of nonfatal injuries. These numbers represent significant economic loss and increase in human tragedy.

---

4. *Interagency Task Force on Motor Vehicle Goals Beyond 1980*, Vols. 1 and 2, DOT (Sept. 1976).

DISCUSSION

CLARENCE DITLOW: Dr. Bunch's discussion on small-car safety assumes a constant level of technology in safety. Small car safety will be improved, however, as cars are downsized. The Center for Small Car Safety has been looking at this problem for years. Three years ago and again last year, we worked for better side-impact protection. The old standard, when cars weighed an average of 3500 pounds, was that cars had to resist side impact forces of twice vehicle weight or 7000 pounds, whichever was less. Smaller cars have reduced the effectiveness of this standard so that it now needs to be upgraded. Significant upgrading is in the works for the restraint system standard and others as well. Dynamic tests are being developed. In sum, mandated safety improvements will act to offset the safety problems associated with downsizing.

DON RANDALL: I have a question for Mr. Bunch. Did you consider, in making your projections, the effects of consumers retaining old cars longer due to regulation, the availability of fuels, front-wheel drive, the mix of trucks in the total fleet, or modal switch?

BUNCH: Future improvements in safety could be applied to a standard-sized fleet as well as to a downsized fleet, so their effects on the *relative* performance of the two fleets cancel out. We controlled for all such effects in our analysis in order to look solely at the effects of downsizing on safety.

ACADEMIC: Howard, where did your numbers come from? You have no downsized fleet in equilibrium from which to draw data.

BUNCH: We constructed our data base from the Texas accident file, selecting only accidents involving cars of 4000 pounds or below, simulating an equilibrium fleet. We controlled for all factors that would affect small and large fleets equally. We assumed a replacement of large cars in the present fleet with light trucks and vans in the 1990s.

TRADE PRESS: With regard to safety improvements, there may be safety innovations which affect only the performance of small cars, introducing a new effect into Howard's simulations.

ACADEMIC: Howard raises the question, how does society calculate the costs and benefits of trading lives for fuel economy? How do you calculate that?

ACADEMIC: The correct trade-off to look at is not lives versus economy, but rather savings in fuel economy versus the dollar cost of safety improvements to completely eliminate additional loss of life.

BUNCH: Because of future safety improvements, this 6 percent increase in fatalities may be 6 percent of a rather low number and thus may represent a perfectly acceptable trade-off.

REGULATORY RIPPLE: A CASE STUDY

Richard H. Shackson[*], *Ford Motor Company*

The technology of electronic engine controls has been forced, or at least accelerated, by a series of regulations. This discussion traces its origin and forecasts its possible impact on other parties. While neither the Congress nor the executive branch administrators have mandated the use of such technology, a combination of regulations now interact virtually to require it to be widely used in the near term.

The major government requirements include:

- Increasingly stringent new car emission requirements that can approximate a 95 percent reduction from uncontrolled levels.
- The Energy Policy and Conservation Act requirements of steeply escalating fuel economy improvements, representing an improvement of almost 100 percent in 10 years.
- Regulations by EPA limiting the adjustments that can be made to carburetors and engine controls.
- The need for reduced in-use emissions which have been above standard due to tampering.

The first two of these requirements, emission and fuel economy standards, were conceived independently and administered by different agencies. Alone they might not have led to widespread electronic engine control technology. Taken together, however, they gave manufacturers little choice. Control of emissions reduces fuel economy. In order to minimize the fuel economy degradation due to tighter emis-

---

[*] Mr. Shackson is now with the Energy Productivity Center of the Carnegie-Mellon Institute of Research.

sions standards, manufacturers can be expected to utilize technologies which precisely control air/fuel ratios, exhaust gas recirculation (EGR) flow rates, and spark timing. This leads them inevitably to electronic engine controls and three-way-catalyst technology.

The third major government requirement, adjustment limitations, is designed to ensure that vehicles which have been certified at a given emissions level are not readjusted in a way which leads to poorer emissions performance. In the past manufacturers have provided manual adjustments on vehicles to permit compensation for manufacturing tolerances on new cars and for wear on vehicles in service. Under the new regulations, if provided at all, these adjustments must yield emissions that still meet standards even in the worst possible combinations. The problems in meeting the standard at any degree of adjustment will increase substantially as 95 percent emissions reduction is required. Electronic engine controls offer the promise of solving this problem by continually adjusting itself for both wear and production variation.

Tampering can still erode the effects of good design. EPA inspection data of vehicles in use suggest that tampering has been the major cause of excessive in-service emissions. Customers tamper with the preset controls chiefly in an attempt to improve driveability and/or fuel economy. This is at the expense of emissions performance. Electronic engine controls will remove much of the incentive for such tampering because fuel economy and driveability will be continually optimized at required emission levels by such controls. Further, these controls will reduce the opportunity for adjustment. There is simply no place to insert a screwdriver or a wrench in an electronic circuit.

As a result of these pressures, most manufacturers are reported to be implementing some form of electronic control program. The growth rate of this technology is impressive. Chrysler's Lean Burn System was introduced in 1976. General Motors, which introduced computer control on 4,000 of its 1978 California cars, announced recently that the system would be on all California cars in 1980 and on all gasoline-powered cars sold in the United States in 1981. Ford used electronic controls in the Versailles and in 2.3-liter California Pintos and Bobcats in 1978, and a second-generation system will be used on many LTDs and Mercurys in 1979.

This suggests that by the mid– to late–1980s, more than one-half the cars on the road will have some form of electronic controls. Moreover, by that time, 20 million or more cars will be beyond the 5-year, 50,000-mile emissions warranty applicable to those components of electronic control systems specifically designed to reduce emissions.

In order to understand the second-order impacts of these systems it is necessary to know a little more about the technology. Electronic engine control systems consist of (1) a group of sensors that measure engine parameters and operating conditions; (2) a "black box" computer that receives input from these sensors; and (3) actuators that adjust the engine to desired settings governed by the black box. For example, sensors might measure crankshaft position, ambient air temperature, barometric pressure, manifold pressure, EGR flow, coolant temperature, throttle position, and oxygen content in the exhaust gas. The black box reads this information and calculates the appropriate spark timing, air/fuel ratio, EGR valve position, etc., to optimize fuel economy and driveability while staying within emission standards. The black box then signals actuators to make the necessary adjustments. These control functions can be updated, up to thirty times each second to give almost instantaneous monitoring of engine performance.

Advanced concept black boxes with self-diagnosis and memory capability are under development. These will not only regulate engine performance but will also "remember" the count of problems to aid in diagnosis of difficult intermittent malfunctions.

What can go wrong with these electronic control systems? The design intent is that those systems should not require attention. Each of the components is highly reliable, and the systems might not require scheduled maintenance. Recognizing the real world, however, where a large number of components, wires, connections, etc. are jostled in the harsh environment of an automobile engine compartment leads one to anticipate difficulties. Consequently, manufacturers are now training service technicians, developing electronic diagnostic testers, and providing for modular replacement of control components.

The black box itself cannot be repaired at a service establishment. While it is possible that a service technician could visually spot a poor connection or a pinched wire, most diagnoses will require a functional analysis of the complete system using a testing device. At present, the black box must be replaced. However, remanufacturing programs are under development to reduce net repair costs. Most of the sensors are modular throw-away parts. The materials, specifications, testers and replacement parts are all available to the aftermarket.

Ford is developing a tester for each of its electronic engine control systems which can be used to check out each circuit with one plug-in to the system. The operator follows a checklist of procedures to perform the diagnosis. A new tester will be needed for most of the next several model years. These testers will be available to service establishments at prices of $400 to $1,000. Ford is also working on automatic or computerized testers which will be faster, will reduce the chance of operator errors, and can be preprogrammed to accommodate new systems. These, of course, will be much more expensive initially; they may reduce costs, however, by being applicable to more than one model year through the use of alternate tapes.

Improved fuel economy is only one of the very real benefits the car buyer will reap from this technology. Starting and driving performance will be improved. This performance will not degrade either as the vehicle ages, because the electronic control system will compensate for changes in the car's performance over time.

Air quality will also benefit because of the ability of the electronic controller to maintain emission performance as the vehicle ages. This characteristic was overlooked as the Congress was drafting the 1977 Amendments to the Clean Air Act. As a result, many consumers will soon be subjected to an expensive, inconvenient, and unnecessary mandatory inspection program which may do little to improve air quality. The issue is a good example of the need to consider the interaction of regulations as well as their direct impacts.

The EPA recommended, and Congress required, air quality implementation plans including mandatory emissions systems performance testing for all vehicles in regions failing to achieve ambient air quality standards. Car owners whose vehicles fail an emissions test will be required to have their cars repaired until the car passes a subsequent test. Our analysis indicates that EPA has overestimated the potential emissions reduction of this procedure by as much as a factor of three, even for the preelectronically controlled cars where tampering was prevalent. But for electronically controlled engines it is likely that this costly, time-consuming program will have almost no effect on air quality because of the self-correcting feature of the controls, the lack of incentive for tampering, and the difficulty of doing so.

A third impact of this technology, which is a great deal harder to estimate, will be experienced by the service industry. Diagnosis and repair of electronic engine controls could be viewed simplistically as new business, unrelated to existing service operations. It is unlikely, however, that the consumer will view it as such. If a car does not run as it should, the owner is not likely to be able to determine in advance whether the problem is in the electronic controls, fouled spark plugs, or a dirty carburetor. Owners are more likely to go to a service establishment which can diagnose and correct any of the problems regardless of cause. It is probable, therefore, that the tuneup and carburetor business will go to those service establishments which are also capable of diagnosing electronic control problems.

In 1975 an estimated 57 million tuneups were performed in the United States, exclusive of those done by department store service establishments or directly by individual owners. Of these 57 million, approximately 38 percent were performed by service stations, 33 percent by independent garages, 28 percent by new vehicle dealers, and 1 percent by fleet owners.

Table 4-5 shows the size distribution of service stations and independent garages and the way in which they participate in the tuneup business. Although almost one-half of these establishments have annual repair sales of less than $40,000, only one-fifth of the tuneups are done by this segment. Over one-third of the tuneups are done by the largest one-fifth of the establishments—those with annual sales in excess of $100,000. It would appear therefore, that some concentration of this business has already occurred. The capital requirements of new diagnostic equipment may result in additional business for the larger

TABLE 4-5 Distribution of Engine Tuneups by Shop Size[a]

Annual repair sales volume	Distribution of engine tuneups (car only)	Distribution of independent garage and service stations
Up to $40,000	21%	42%
$40–$60,000	16	14
$60–$100,000	26	21
Over $100,000	37	23
	100%	100%

[a] Independent garages and service stations by amount of annual repair dollar volume.

Comment:
   Most of the tuneups are done by the larger stations. Many of the smaller service outlets do not currently perform engine tuneups.

   These data include:
      Discount/Department Stores
      Mass Merchandisers
      Do-It-Yourself

These data are for 1975. The introduction of breakerless ignition and lead-free gasoline, which became widespread with the 1975 model year, are expected to reduce substantially the need for engine tuneups.

firms. The service industry will probably change in several ways. For the first five years, the electronic control business will probably be handled largely by dealers, for at least two reasons: (1) The potential applicability of the 5/50 emissions warranty; and (2) the availability of trained technicians and diagnostic equipment. The dealer will require testers for only one manufacturer's products and has greater financial incentive to make the capital investment.

Ford's recent experience in California is illustrative. The manufacturer of the tester used for certain 1978-model-year Ford products has found that essentially all Ford dealers in that state have purchased these testers. Not a single tester has been bought by a nonfranchised facility.

As vehicles begin to exceed the statutory 5/50 warranty period, there will be an increasing incentive for independent service establishments to attract this business. Several responses can be expected:

- Diagnostic equipment manufacturers (which have been provided with specifications for each model year) will develop "universal" diagnostic equipment capable of dealing with products of more than one manufacturer. This process will be simplified by the maturity of the control systems so that less year-to-year change occurs.

- Module remanufacturers will solicit black box unit exchange business from independent shops.

- A new specialty establishment, analogous to AAMCO or Midas, may emerge.

- The resulting distribution of business will certainly not be confined to dealers. It will probably shift away from the smallest independent shops, for whom investment in the tester may not be warranted.

Several sectors of government have expressed concern about these effects of the regulation-induced move toward electronic engine controls. Three examples will illustrate this point. First, in its summary of emissions progress for 1976, the EPA stated:

> In practice, a specialized diagnostic instrument might be required for GM vehicles, a completely different one for Ford vehicles, etc. While the impact of this diversity on new-car dealers might be slight, the impact on the rest of the service industry would be most significant. It is not realistic to expect all independent service organizations to be able to afford to buy and store several different types of specialized electronic diagnostic equipment. If the independent service industry cannot service most kinds of vehicles, as it does today, their business may be negatively affected. Not having the capability in the service industry to deal with a wide range of vehicles could also have a negative impact on Inspection and Maintenance (I/M) programs. A requirement that service compatibility be considered in the initial design and development of electronic control systems has obvious trade secret and antitrust problems. Thus, how to service electronic controls in the field raises unanswered questions.

Second, in March 1977, Jonathan Rose, then Deputy Assistant Attorney General of the U.S. Department of Justice, testified at an EPA hearing concerning emission warranties. Mr. Rose pointed out that an expanded, comprehensive, mandatory service warranty could significantly impede the ability of independent service stations and garages to compete with the service departments of dealers franchised by automobile manufacturers. Thus, he said, concentration in the automobile aftermarket—auto repair, service, and parts dealers—could increase substantially, and the advantage of free competition could be lost.

Finally, in its report on auto repair costs the U.S. Department of Transportation expressed the view that modular replacement will mean unnecessarily higher consumer costs. As yet electronic engine controls can only be serviced by modular repairs.

While manufacturers have scrambled to improve the technical capability of service personnel and are investing heavily in developing and implementing diagnostic equipment to ensure that electronic engine controls do not become a customer repair problem, they run the risk of being criticized for taking actions which could make it difficult for the rest of the repair industry to compete.

The national interest seems to have gotten lost. No one has the responsibility to assess the whole system of trade-offs between an excessively broad interpretation of the 5/50 emissions warranty coverage, modular replacement, cost of repair, and competitive environment in the repair industry. In this case we may be lucky. The service industry may be sufficiently innovative and resilient to absorb the abrupt change without serious dislocations; EPA may recognize the improved in-service emission performance before a whole new testing bureaucracy is in place; and DOT may agree that modular replacement is not all bad. But this is only the first case. What will be the secondary impacts of diesel and programmed combustion (PROCO) engines, of extensive use of plastic and aluminum body parts, of turbochargers and selective valve disabling, of front-wheel drive?

What can be done to anticipate and minimize impacts of these emerging technologies? On the regulatory side, there are at least two obvious options:

- The regulatory analysis review, required on all major regulations under Executive Order Number 11420, could include a set of criteria for analyzing the secondary and tertiary impacts of a specific technology which goes far beyond the agency's narrow congressional mandate.

- Alternatively, the interagency review process could be specifically directed at identification and study of questions.

The "Catch 22" here, of course, is that analysis is already required and generally done by agencies on all "major" regulations. But it is the agency itself that determines which of its regulations are so identified. It is possible, therefore, that an agency could be totally unaware of the down-the-road impacts of what it might consider to be a "minor" technology or a simple rule change. In the meantime, a combination of stringent performance standards and a very rapid pace of implementation now effectively mandate the inclusion of much new hardware on cars. The widespread effects of mandating much hardware must be studied. There is neither time nor resources, however, to study these questions and delay may jeopardize compliance.

DISCUSSION

CLARENCE DITLOW: We agree with Mr. Shackson that electronic controls are a valuable innovation which could lead to greater efficiency, lower emissions, and better performance. However, they could also lead to monopolism in repair, high module replacement costs, and sophisticated techniques for evading emission standards. The EPA and the California Resource Board are looking at electronics' emission performance in the highway performance portion of their tests to forestall this latter development. Abuse of electronic systems could be prevented by sharing more information between manufacturers, repair shops, and consumers. We need independent diagnostic centers and better dialogue between the groups I have mentioned in order to realize the full potential of diagnostics and overcome the mutual suspicions of the three groups.

DON RANDALL: Cars are not being built to be diagnosed, and repairmen have not the expertise, or the necessary diagnostic equipment, to repair these new, more sophisticated vehicles. We need a moratorium on regulation until the repair industry can catch up. I/Ms are a good way to mitigate these problems. They could perform the function of enforcing federal emission noise, fuel economy, crash worthiness, and safety standards, but more importantly, they could diagnose repair problems, thereby taking a major burden off repair shops. A 10 percent reduction in losses now associated with the private vehicle system would save consumers at least $2 billion a year and cost only $1.5 billion for initial installation.

Our national priorities need to be reassessed. Annually we expend on passenger costs for autos more than ten times the passenger costs expended for all air, rail, and water. Yet the federal government seems unwilling to devote adequate resources toward training programs for auto mechanics. We desperately need to improve the skills of our current mechanic population. We also need to train a large number of new entrants.

DEALER: What I/M system do you envision?

RANDALL: We are studying the problem now. The system could be very low cost; Arizona's system cost only $100,000 of public money. The rest was put up by private interests that would have operated the inspection program profitably. Consumers would pay about $7 per inspection in any such system.

SUPPLIER: How would you integrate I/M programs and the need for training of new mechanics that would be required under such a system?

RANDALL: There is a pilot study under way on that question, too. The problem is that training could not be incorporated effectively into high schools, since teenagers lack the motivation necessary to persevere in such a program.

GOVERNMENT REGULATION AND THE FUTURE OF THE AUTOMOTIVE INDUSTRY

Frank T. Popovich, *Director, Automotive Services Group, Data Resources, Inc.*

Early in the 1970s, automotive material and component suppliers of the United States were called upon to assist the vehicle producers in the formidable task of meeting the severe federal regulations that were to be mandated as early as the mid-1970s and would surely continue beyond. Suppliers were encouraged to develop new products or to modify existing ones so that the industry could build safer, cleaner, and more fuel-efficient vehicles. As a result of this new regulation of the automobile, the suppliers were forced to reexamine their product lines; to recognize and to isolate those product lines that could be threatened; to strengthen their position by developing new or modified products; to recognize and isolate new business or profit opportunities; and to make some risky investment decisions.

A review of some activities in the major industries contributing to the automotive sector during the last seven years reveals a history of rapid and imaginative responses to a rapidly shifting market.

- The iron and steel industry has traditionally supplied about 85 percent of the material needs of the motor vehicle industry. Fully 35 percent of their iron- and steel-making capacity is available for Detroit's needs, providing added peaking capacity when required. In response to regulation-induced changes in the automotive industry, the steel industry moved subtly but defensively to develop new families of lighter weight, high-strength steels which were nevertheless easy to form and weld. They developed new families of corrosion-resistant steels including one-side, zinc-coated steels and prepainted steels that retain excellent formability characteristics.

- The aluminum industry developed light-weight alloys to ameliorate problems of handling, forming, and joining the metal as well as difficulties of aging. They moved swiftly into the passenger car bumper market and, to a lesser extent, into the markets for hang-on body panels and light-weight engine castings.

- The battery industry developed maintenance-free, virtually life-time batteries.
- The plastics industry overcame severe problems of painting and applying plastics to the design of components traditionally made from both ferrous and nonferrous metals.
- The zinc industry kept plastics from intruding into their traditional markets by providing corrosion-resistant coatings and thin-wall, light-weight castings.
- The rubber industry developed longer lasting tires with increased tread wear.
- The oil industry contributed lubricants that reduce friction more effectively and do not break down as rapidly as conventional lubricating oils.
- The coatings industry provided new water-based paints that eliminated the need for air-polluting solvents.
- The glass industry manufactured thinner and lighter high-strength glass.

New products were also born of this technological ferment. The catalytic converter was introduced to clean emissions; the turbo charger was added to increase the efficiency of the engine and to keep it quiet; fuel injection systems were developed to improve fuel efficiency; new electronic monitoring and control systems were designed to increase efficiency and vehicle power equipment utilization; and new families of diesels were introduced to improve fuel economy and reduce operating costs.

Although the automobile market is huge and the changes have been rapid, some broad trends are already becoming apparent. We can begin to make projections about the nature of the vehicle market seven years from now, in 1985. As shown in Table 4-6 some very dramatic trends are evident in the design of the passenger car. The dramatic decline in the large car was apparent before the energy crunch in late 1973.

As Table 4-7 shows, the mix of lighter trucks and buses (less than

TABLE 4-6 Passenger Car Size Mix % of All Cars Sold in Model Year

	Wheel base			
	Under 101 in.	101–111 in.	112–119 in.	Over 119 in.
1971	22	18	21	39
1974	24	24	23	29
1978	26	36	27	11

TABLE 4-7 % of All Trucks/Buses Sold in Model Year

| | \multicolumn{4}{c}{Gross vehicle weight} ||||
	Under 6,000 lb.	6,000– 10,000 lb.	Subtotal under 10,000 lb.	Over 10,000 lb.
1971	60	23	83	17
1974	60	25	85	15
1978	37	53	90	10

10,000 pounds) is getting heavier and the mix of heavier trucks and buses (over 10,000 pounds) is getting lighter.

Table 4-8 shows the mix of all vehicles, 1971 to 1977. It shows that the domestic passenger car, representing only 60 percent of the vehicle market, is continuing the downtrend in size of the past 15 years. Looking at the truck mix in context, we see larger and heavier trucks becoming a larger regiment of the United States vehicle fleet.

What then, can we expect in terms of total vehicle weight—which can be equated to material requirements and ultimately to fuel economy? The average vehicle weight in the 1978 model year was 4 percent heavier than in 1971.

In future years, changes will be necessary. Therefore, new products will be developed, and marginally useful or successful products will be abandoned. More money will be invested; some investment decisions will pay off, while others will be written off; some will hold market position; and others will gain or lose. Some specific changes we can expect to see in the next seven years are listed on page 192.

TABLE 4-8 Total Vehicle Mix (%)

| | \multicolumn{5}{c}{Passenger cars (Wheel base)} ||||| \multicolumn{4}{c}{Trucks/buses (GVW)} ||||
	Under 101 in.	101– 111 in.	112– 119 in.	Over 119 in.	Total	Under 6,000	6,000– 10,000	Over 10,000	Total
1971	19	15	18	32	83	10	4	3	17
1974	18	18	18	23	77	14	6	3	23
1977	19	27	20	8	74	10	14	2	26

TABLE 4-9 Vehicle weight (lb.)—Sales Weighted Mix

	Passenger cars	Trucks/buses	Total
1971	3,300	5,165	3,615
1974	3,510	5,100	3,880
1978	3,250	5,130	3,745

- Electric vehicles will be introduced in quantities that could represent about 3 percent of the passenger car market.

- The rubber industry will feel the effects of downsizing passenger cars as we move to smaller wheels and tires. Elimination of the spare tire will reduce tire needs by almost 20 percent.

- The steel and glass industries moving rapidly into lower weight, high-strength, thinner products will find that these applications will reduce their capacity requirements by 20-to-30 percent. They will be getting more mileage from the same raw material production capacity for the same vehicle component applications.

- The light truck producers will produce lighter trucks in their mix. Some assembly operations will be moved into this country eliminating captive imports. More trucks will be produced with diesel engines to increase fuel economy. As the consumer demands, manufacturers will produce larger, heavier trucks.

- Dramatic changes will be made in the mix of passenger car engine cylinder count, moving from 8-to-6-to-4. The 400+-cubic-inch-displacement (CID) engine will move out of the passenger car in 1980 to 1981 and the 300+ CID engine will move out of the passenger car in the 1981 to 1982 model year.

- The turbo charger will supplement the power of the smaller engine for both gasoline and diesel engines in passenger cars and trucks.

- New families of small diesel engines will move under the hood of the passenger car if the emission standards are manageable. These engines provide better fuel economy and, more important, permit Detroit to produce passenger cars large enough for those 11 million American families of 5 or more to travel in 1 rather than 2 cars.

- Domestic passenger car producers will have large volumes of smaller, front-wheel drive vehicles of sizes and types in market segments heretofore dominated by imports. With 88 percent of the passenger car market supplied by 4 producers and 12 percent of the market supplied by 17 producers, competition will be severe.

- Some foreign vehicle producers will join Volkswagen in setting up shop in this country as they establish a market base that is large enough to support this operation. Stamping plants and engine lines will follow.

Some products will be threatened by changes in the automotive industry. The shedding of the catalytic converter, as the diesel engine emerges, will threaten markets for stainless steel. The absence of spark plugs in the diesel and the need for fewer plugs on smaller gasoline engines will threaten spark plug producers and their material suppliers. The steel industry will be concerned with new developments by the paint and coatings industry which could move newly developed one-side, zinc-coated steel out as fast as it moved in. The aluminum industry must convince Detroit that price and availability will not be insurmountable problems. The plastic and elastomer industries will need to continue their efforts to provide products that can deal with higher temperatures under the hood, higher impact, and greater structural demands.

In terms of overall materials use, where are we headed?

Starting with the vehicle market segments again, let us examine the profile of materials—used in that average 111-inch wheel base, 3,500-pound American-made car sold in the 1978 model year. Table 4-10 shows the material profile of the domestic passenger car, comparing steel-oriented manufacturing (1978) and aluminum-oriented and plastic-oriented manufacturing (1985).

The rather substantial decline in material required to produce the 1985 domestic passenger car is noteworthy. What this tells us is that with the 7 percent increase in passenger car sales projected for the next 7 years (12 percent for all vehicles), suppliers must improve their market penetration at least 13 percent just to stay even in terms of material shipments to produce the passenger cars sold. Not every supplier will be able to do this; some will get hurt.

Our raw material price, and scrap-loss or yield estimates indicate an interesting comparison in raw material costs. This should not be looked upon as the only cost effectiveness criterion for selecting materials,

TABLE 4-10

	1978 Pounds	1978 %	1985[a] aluminum oriented Pounds	1985[a] aluminum oriented %	1985[a] plastic oriented Pounds	1985[a] plastic oriented %
Material Profile—Domestic Passenger Car						
Steel and iron	2,725	77.7	1,995	70.1	1,872	68.0
Polymer	235	6.7	199	7.0	368	13.4
Aluminum	119	3.4	257	8.9	110	4.0
Other	429	12.2	396	14.0	394	14.6
Total	3,508	100.0	2,847	100.0	2,734	100.0
Estimated raw-material cost per lb.	$0.35		$0.38		$0.36	
Per vehicle	$1,228		$1,106		$992	
Material Required to Manufacture 10 Million Cars						
Material required for 10 million[b] (×1,000 tons)	21,900		18,100		16,900	
Change in material requirements			−17%		−23%	
Estimated scrap loss	20%		20%		19%	

[a] Assumes a vehicle powered by a 4-cylinder 140 CID turbocharged engine.
[b] Reflects total car weight × 10 million cars + 20% scrap loss.

however. We must also look at manufacturing costs, productivity, equipment utilization, investment costs, and cost penalties associated with rendering obsolete or reducing the utilization of existing in-place equipment and facilities before we can make judgments in regard to cost effectiveness. Probably even more important, we should look at the British Thermal Unit content of materials over a life cycle span. These inquiries tell us that the 1985 passenger car will probably come in with a profile somewhat between the extremes we see here.

Now, let us turn to the total market, again placing the passenger car in its proper prospective by recalling that the domestic passenger car represents only a little more than one-half of the market.

If the current trends in vehicle mix continue, we can expect the average vehicle weight to be as shown in Table 4-11. In this scenario, we projected a 65 percent share of the vehicle market for passenger cars in 1985, compared with a 74 percent share in 1978, and an 83 percent share in 1971, continuing the apparent trends.

Here we see a vehicle weight that is about 7 percent under the 1978 weight. If the total vehicle market grows 12 percent in the next 7 years as projected, material and component suppliers can expect to increase their shipments by 5 percent. The vehicle weight projected here is only 4 percent less than it was in 1971.

Taking another approach, if we assume that the vehicle mix has stabilized with passenger cars taking 74 percent of the market in 1985 as in 1978, the vehicle weight can be expected to be as shown in Table 4-12. Here we see that compared with 1978, the 1985 vehicle weight is down 12 percent—exactly offsetting the increase projected for vehicle

TABLE 4-11   Vehicle weight (lb.)—Sales Weighted Mix

	Passenger cars	Trucks/buses	Total
1971	3,300	5,165	3,615
1974	3,510	5,100	3,880
1977	3,250	5,130	3,745
1985	2,700	5,040	3,520

TABLE 4-12   Vehicle weight (lb.)—Sales Weighted Mix

	Passenger cars	Trucks/buses	Total
1971	3,300	5,165	3,615
1974	3,510	5,100	3,880
1978	3,250	5,130	3,745
1985	2,700	5,040	3,308

demand in which case we have a zero material growth scenario. This means dog-eat-dog just to stay even in terms of market position.

We have assumed in our scenarios that passenger car weights as well as truck weights will move down, while the passenger car portion of the vehicle mix will hold at current levels or will continue the decline based on recent trends. These assumptions will be critical to the overall vehicle weight average, as we have seen.

Additional regulations will be implemented in the next seven years, covering passive restraints, noise control, and perhaps life cycle costs and fuel economy standards for trucks of certain sizes or weights.

The addition of passive safety restraints alone could add 40 pounds to the passenger car. The implementation of new noise standards could add about another 60 pounds or more. Adding 100 pounds brings us to within 40 pounds of the vehicle weight we had in 1971. There are also some other not-so-apparent factors to consider. As we know, quality standards for materials and components have been getting increasingly tighter. Synonymous with quality is yield or scrap loss plus added inspection costs. As we hear more and more about product liability, these quality standards can be expected to become even more rigid. A 1 percent increase in scrap loss implies the use of another 40 pounds of raw material to make the same components for one passenger car or 50 pounds for one truck—multiply these by 15 million!

If we end up in 1985 looking at a sales-weighted vehicle weight that is about the same as it is today, I leave it up to you to draw your own conclusions as to where we will be at that time. A congenital optimist might conclude that had it not been for the federal regulations in regard to fuel economy, we would have vehicles weighing much more than they would be otherwise.

A RISK ANALYSIS OF THE FUEL ECONOMY REGULATIONS IN THE AUTOMOBILE INDUSTRY

Stephen P. Bradley, *Professor, Harvard Business School*
Aneel G. Karnani, *Harvard Business School*

On December 27, 1975 the Energy Policy and Conservation Act was passed by Congress requiring all automobile manufacturers to establish a schedule of improved fuel economy for new car sales in the United States. The current regulations require that the fleet-weighted average fuel economy, in miles per gallon, for each manufacturer meet or exceed the specified minimum standards given in Table 4-13.

This paper is based on a study that was carried out under the auspices of the Transportation Systems Center of DOT to develop a risk analysis model of the automobile industry in order to assess the impact of these Automotive Fuel Economy Standards (AFES) on each of the four major United States automobile manufacturers.[1] The purpose is to report some of the findings of the study and to present an overview of the methodology developed. The basic approach of the study was to use data supplied to the DOT by the automobile manufacturers or estimated by the DOT, in order to synthesize the overall impact on the financial performance of each of the manufacturers. The conclusions are, of course, contingent upon the accuracy of the data available about the manufacturers and the validity of the assumptions of the model.

Risk analysis involves the computer simulation of a business for the purpose of evaluating a specific strategy by explicitly taking into account the most important uncertainties in the environment faced by the business. The uncertainties are combined using the Monte Carlo simulation approach to obtain risk profiles, or probability distributions, of various key summary measures of performance.

---

1. S. Bradley and A. G. Karnani, *Automotive Manufacturer Risk Analysis: Meeting the Automotive Fuel Economy Standards* (Task 5 Only), DOT Contract, DOT-TSC-1333, for H.H. Aerospace Design Co., Inc. (June 30, 1978).

TABLE 4-13 Automotive Fuel Economy Standards for New Car Sales (Fleet Weighted by Manufacturer)

Actual	Required
1974—14 mpg	1978—18 mpg
	1979—19 mpg
	1980—20 mpg
	1981—22 mpg
	1982—24 mpg
	1983—26 mpg
	1984—27 mpg
	1985—27.5 mpg

In order to structure the risk analysis for the context under study, uncertainty has been categorized into two types: Contextual (or exogenous) and intrinsic (or endogenous). Contextual uncertainty arises from two sources: (1) Economic conditions; and (2) marketing conditions. Sources of endogenous uncertainty include a wide range of technological and manufacturing conditions. The several sources of uncertainty interact in this risk model to have a single effect on the financial performance of each manufacturer studied.

One of the effects of AFES is to "enrich the price range" of cars. That is, the price of small cars decreases while the price of large cars increases in order to sell a mix of cars that will meet the fuel economy standards. This, in turn, causes the contribution margin (i.e., the portion of sales price per car that goes to cover general and administrative costs and profit) on small cars to decrease and that for large cars to increase. Therefore, although the AFES are a burden to all manufacturers, they tend to be less burdensome (favor in a competitive sense) to manufacturers with a full product line. Therefore, the AFES tend to favor the larger manufacturers. This statement should be interpreted in a relative sense; that is, the AFES hurt the larger manufacturers less than they hurt the smaller manufacturers. The net result is that the AFES will tend to increase industry concentration.

The model also represents significant factors which affect manufacturers in the environment under study. It is found, for instance, that uncertainty in the costs of implementing the various fuel economy measures is a source of greater risk than the technological uncertainty associated with these measures. Another finding is that the decrease in variable manufacturing cost (i.e., those costs that vary with production volume) due to downsizing of automobiles is more than enough to offset the increase in capital costs due to downsizing. Hence, the AFES allow all manufacturers to increase contribution margins by downsizing without fear of losing demand to manufacturers that choose not to downsize.

198 METHODOLOGY

In this study, we carry out *conditional risk analyses* whereby each situation is analyzed as if the contextual uncertainty has been solved. We assume fixed values for the variables which are the source of contextual uncertainty. This is called "defining a scenario." Conditional on each scenario, several different cases are examined by assuming different values of the variables which are the source of endogenous uncertainty. We also examine the "probability case" in which only probability distributions of the endogenous variables are known. The model then produces probability distributions for various summary measures of performance for each of the manufacturers. It is necessary to carry out the analysis conditional on a scenario so that the contextual uncertainty does not overwhelm the extraordinary risks imposed by having manufacturers meet the AFES.

In this paper, we discuss four major United States automobile manufacturers labeled G, F, C, and A which are as close approximations to the North American passenger car operations of General Motors, Ford, Chrysler and American Motors, respectively, as possible given the data available to us and the objectives of the study. The four major United States automobile manufacturers are obviously very complex organizations. It is clearly unreasonable to expect to capture the full complexity of their operations in a model based solely on available data. Since much of the required data is confidential and not released by the companies, various approximations and assumptions have been employed.

The first step in our approach is to formulate a simulation model of the four automobile manufacturers acting in their business environment. Constructing such a model in detail would require a large amount of data that is proprietary to each of the manufacturers. However, since this type of data is simply not available, almost all the data used in this study is taken from publicly available documents.[2] Most of these data have been provided directly by the manufacturers but in aggregate form; some of the financial data are inferred from publicly available aggregate data; and finally, a few items of data are based on the judgment of industry experts.

The analysis is carried out in 1976 dollars which is roughly equivalent to assuming that the inflationary increases in factor costs are equal for all factors. However, it should be pointed out that this approach to inflation overstates cash flows in the future as a result of overstating depreciation tax shields.

---

2. In addition to Annual Corporate Reports, see *Rulemaking Support Paper Concerning the 1981–1984 Passenger Auto Average Fuel Economy Standards*, DOT/NHTSA (July 1977); *Data Analysis for 1981–1984 Passenger Automobile Fuel Economic Standards*, Summary Report and Documents 1-4, DOT/NHTSA (Feb. 1977); Wharton EFA, Inc., *An Analysis of the Automobile Market: Modeling of the Long-Run Determinants of the Demand for Automobiles*, prepared for DOT, TSC (Feb. 1977).

Because of the approximate nature of the data input to the model, the results generated by the model should be interpreted with some caution. The model should be used to analyze the *relative* impact on the manufacturers due to the AFES. "Relative impact" refers to the impact on a manufacturer relative to either that on the other manufacturers or relative to his own initial position.

SIMULATION MODEL

The simulation model estimates the financial performance of the manufacturers' given assumptions about (1) their strategy for meeting the AFES; and (2) the resolution of the contextual and endogenous uncertainties. We first describe the assumed strategy of the manufacturers and then give an overview of the model. A more detailed description of the model including the mathematical equations and the precise data used is given in the full report of this study.[3]

Assumed Manufacturers' Strategy

It is assumed that the manufacturers will implement the following measures in order to meet the AFES: Downsizing, material substitution, technological improvements in transmissions, lubricants, accessories, aerodynamic drag, and rolling resistance. If, after implementing fuel economy measures, the fleet-weighted average fuel economy (in miles per gallon) for a manufacturer is equal to or exceeds the AFES for that year, then the manufacturer is assumed to produce the same product mix as in the previous year. Otherwise, the manufacturer is assumed to change his product mix in order to just meet the AFES. That is, the manufacturer will produce a larger proportion of small cars. It is also assumed that each of the manufacturers will have to change car prices in order to sell the resulting product mix.

A few other alternatives available to the manufacturers are not considered in developing the simulation model. For example, reduction in acceleration performance is not considered although smaller engines are assumed concomitants of downsized cars. In addition, either diesel engines or stratified charge engines could be used to improve fuel economy. However, in the time frame of this analysis, the market penetration of these engines is assumed to be quite limited. Finally, if the manufacturers have to change their product mix to meet the AFES, they will certainly increase promotion and advertising to sell the changed product mix. If the resulting margins remain approximately unchanged, this refinement need not be included in the model.

It is assumed that the manufacturers will not raise significant new equity financing. The capital investments are assumed to be financed out of retained earnings and increases in long-term debt. Cash inflows

---

3. See Bradley and Karnani, 1978, n. 1 *supra*.

are used to retire long-term debt or invested in other opportunities within the corporation. As a surrogate for these other opportunities, cash inflows are invested in interest-bearing securities, which are represented in the model as negative debt. In reality, a manufacturer will not use cash inflows in such a manner. This assumption is merely a convenient manner of keeping track of the cash-use/cash-generation ability of the manufacturer.

The Model

The model can be divided into seven modules which are schematically represented in Figure 4-2. Starting with the first year in the period under analysis, the model progresses forward in time, calculating the performance for each manufacturer for each year. Some important particulars regarding the calculations within selected modules are as follows:

Calculations within the Marketing Module assume that the foreign manufacturers' product mix and the domestic manufacturers' market shares remain constant over time. This assumption is made because there are no estimates available as to how these factors might change over time. Moreover, while doing sensitivity analyses, we examine the effect of changing this assumption.

For Fuel Economy Module calculations, the module first calculates the fleet-weighted average fuel economy using the previous year's product mix. If this average is equal to or exceeds the AFES for that year, then the manufacturer's new product mix is assumed to be the same as the previous year's mix. Otherwise, this product mix is changed to just meet the AFES. The output from this module is the new product mix for each manufacturer.

The input to the Variable Cost Module consists of the following data of each manufacturer: Material cost per pound, direct labor cost per car, schedule for implementing the fuel economy measures, and the change in variable cost due to implementing these measures.

For the Price Module almost all the concepts, assumptions and data are adapted from the Wharton EFA (WEFA) model and its forecast of automotive demand through 1985.[4] This module determines the product mix produced by each manufacturer, and hence, by aggregation, the product mix supplied to the market. If the product mix supplied is the same as the mix estimated by the WEFA model, then the price differential to sell this mix is the same as that assumed by the WEFA model. Otherwise, the price differential is changed so that the product mix supplied is the same as the product mix desired by consumers. This new price differential is calculated using a set of equations adapted from the WEFA model; these equations pertain to the price cross-elasticities between size classes. In keeping with the assumptions made

---

4. See Wharton EFA, Inc., n. 2 *supra*.

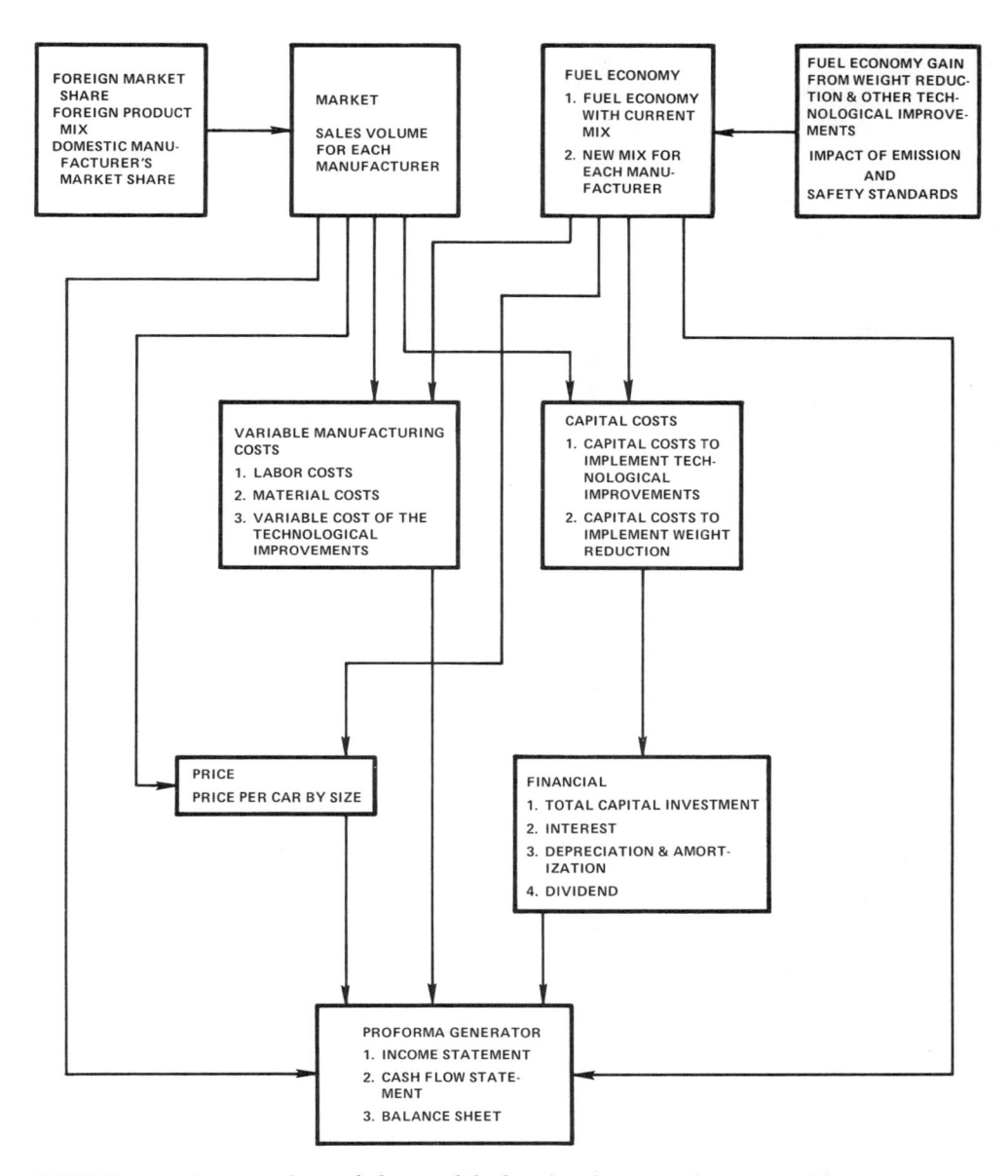

FIGURE 4-2 An overview of the model showing input and output of each module

in the WEFA model, and since our analysis is carried out in 1976 dollars, we have assumed that the real average car price remains constant over time. The exact mathematical procedure for using these equations is rather complicated and explained in detail within the original report.[5]

---

5. Bradley and Karnani, 1978, n. 1 *supra*.

Financial Module calculations assume that "other capital investments" (i.e., not related to fuel economy improvement) for a manufacturer are constant over time. It would be preferable to use a more sophisticated projection of capital expenditures; however, such projections are not available.

Property, equipment, and toolings are depreciated on a straight line basis using assumptions developed in a separate DOT study. In reality the manufacturers undoubtedly will use accelerated depreciation for tax purposes. However, any increase in accuracy that would result from a more complex treatment of depreciation and taxes would not be sufficient to warrant the increased complexity. Liabilities have been classified into equity, retained earnings, and long-term debt. Equity capital and dividends paid are assumed to remain constant over time.

The Pro Forma Generator Model calculates the income statement, balance sheet, and sources and uses of funds statement for each of the manufacturers. The module first calculates the so-called fixed costs. Interest, depreciation, and amortization are obtained from the Financial Module. Retirement fund and nonincome taxes are considered to be fixed costs. Selling and administration, research and development, and maintenance, repair and rearrangement are considered to be semivariable costs. The fixed and variable components of these costs were estimated for each manufacturer based on historical data using simple regression.

NOMINAL SCENARIO

Under the Nominal Scenario all the data, except the data related to fuel economy measures, are set at the best available one-point estimates, or nominal values. Within the Nominal Scenario four cases are examined: Nominal, optimistic, pessimistic, and probabilistic. We later separate the impact of technological uncertainty from that of manufacturing uncertainty. All analyses are carried out for the period 1977 to 1985.

Nominal Case

In this case we use nominal data for the fuel economy-related variables also. Highlights of the results are presented in graphic and tabular form; the detailed financial statements are not included here in order to save space. Figure 4-3 and Table 4-14 indicate the fuel economy achieved by the four manufacturers if each manufacturer implemented all fuel economy measures according to the reported schedules, but maintained their 1976 product mixes.

None of the manufacturers can meet the AFES without changing the product mix after 1981. Thus, the manufacturers will be forced to produce more small cars and fewer large cars. The large cars will thus become more expensive; the small cars will thus become less expensive.

Some Second-Level Effects of Regulation

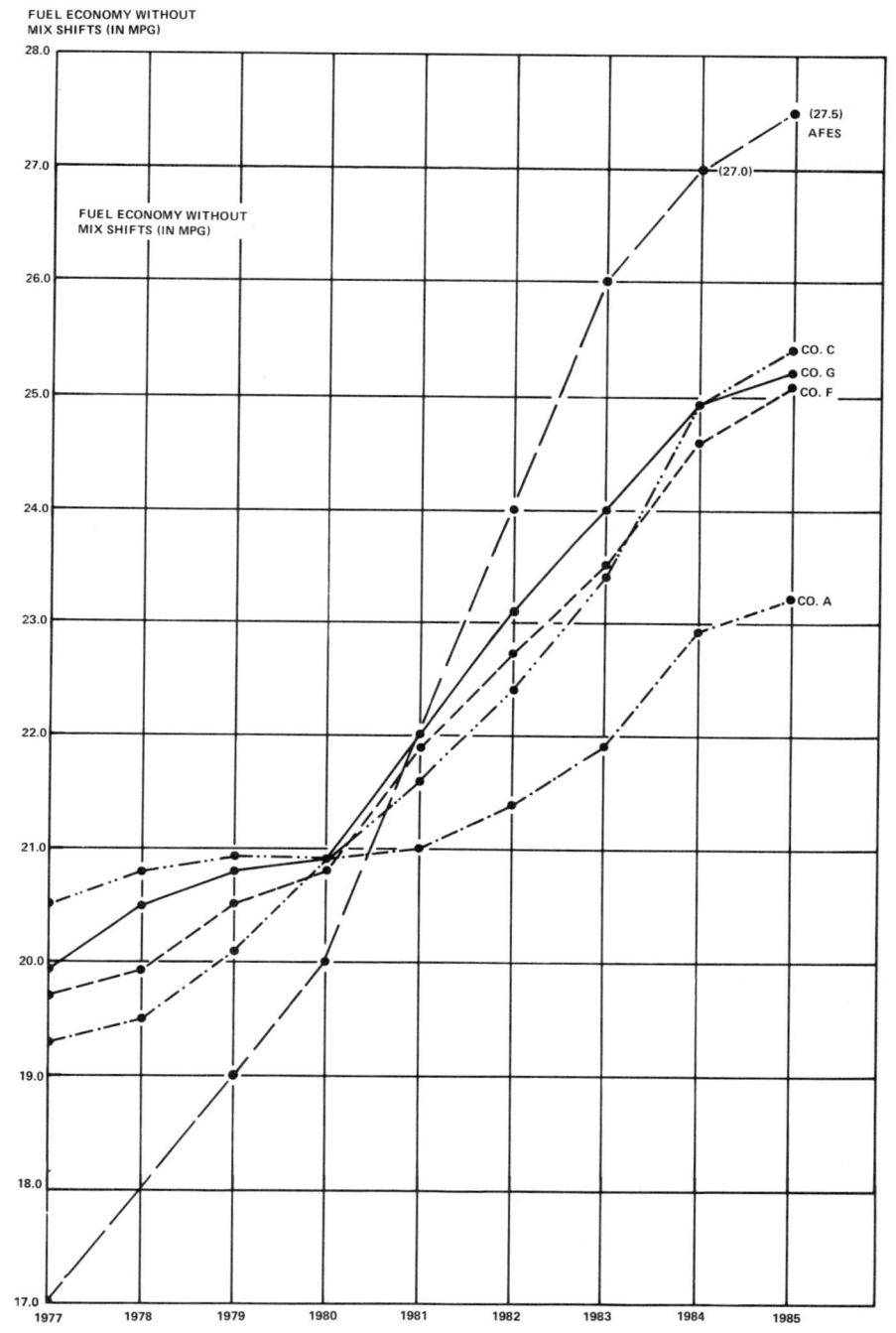

FIGURE 4-3 Nominal case results: Fuel economy achieved without mix shifts

TABLE 4-14 Nominal Case—Market Characteristics

	Full size	Mid-size	Compact	Subcompact
Mix produced in 1977	0.19	0.27	0.23	0.32
Mix produced in 1985	0.11	0.23	0.25	0.40
Price in 1977	7,924	6,315	4,747	3,866
Price in 1985	7,569	7,184	4,949	3,689

Figure 4-4 shows the after-tax profit and the net cash inflow while Table 4-15 summarizes the financial position in 1985 for each of the four manufacturers. Company G performs relatively well: Its after-tax profits and net cash inflow are positive and increase steadily throughout the period. Company F performs well with increasing profits and cash inflows except for one year, 1979. Return on sales figures for 1985 suggest that Companies G and F are both in very healthy positions. Both have generated significant amounts of cash which must have been

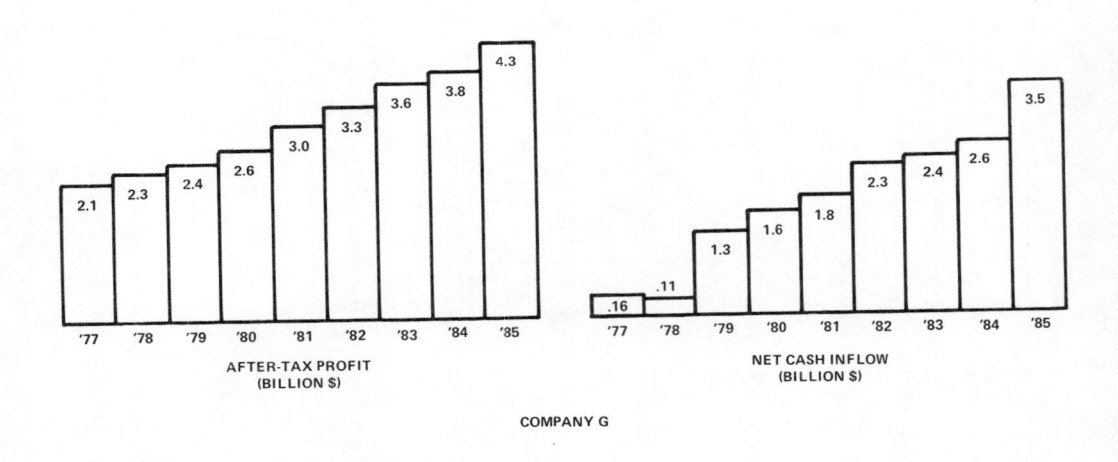

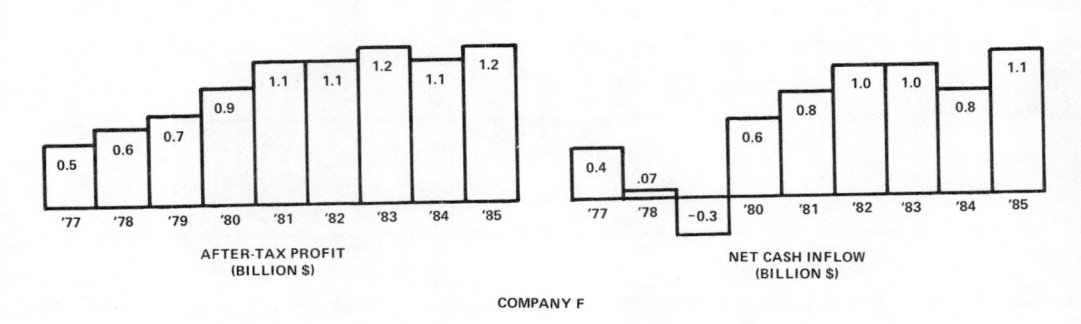

COMPANY G

AFTER-TAX PROFIT (BILLION $): '77: 2.1, '78: 2.3, '79: 2.4, '80: 2.6, '81: 3.0, '82: 3.3, '83: 3.6, '84: 3.8, '85: 4.3

NET CASH INFLOW (BILLION $): '77: .16, '78: .11, '79: 1.3, '80: 1.6, '81: 1.8, '82: 2.3, '83: 2.4, '84: 2.6, '85: 3.5

COMPANY F

AFTER-TAX PROFIT (BILLION $): '77: 0.5, '78: 0.6, '79: 0.7, '80: 0.9, '81: 1.1, '82: 1.1, '83: 1.2, '84: 1.1, '85: 1.2

NET CASH INFLOW (BILLION $): '77: 0.4, '78: .07, '79: -0.3, '80: 0.6, '81: 0.8, '82: 1.0, '83: 1.0, '84: 0.8, '85: 1.1

FIGURE 4-4 Nominal case results: Financial performance 1977–85

invested elsewhere in the corporations. While the AFES are a burden to all manufacturers, they are not terribly damaging to Companies G and F.

Company C, however, makes a loss throughout the period, though its losses decrease fairly steadily. In 1985 it does make a slight profit; its

Some Second-Level Effects of Regulation

COMPANY C

AFTER-TAX PROFIT (BILLION $)

'77 -.25, '78 -.22, '79 -.16, '80 -.13, '81 -.03, '82 -.03, '83 -.02, '84 -.04, '85 .05

NET CASH INFLOW (BILLION $)

'77 -.23, '78 -.49, '79 -.25, '80 -.50, '81 -.08, '82 -.03, '83 -.04, '84 -.30, '85 .08

COMPANY A

AFTER-TAX PROFIT (MILLION $)

'77 -74, '78 -80, '79 -54, '80 -35, '81 -23, '82 -32, '83 -49, '84 -60, '85 -60

NET CASH INFLOW (MILLION $)

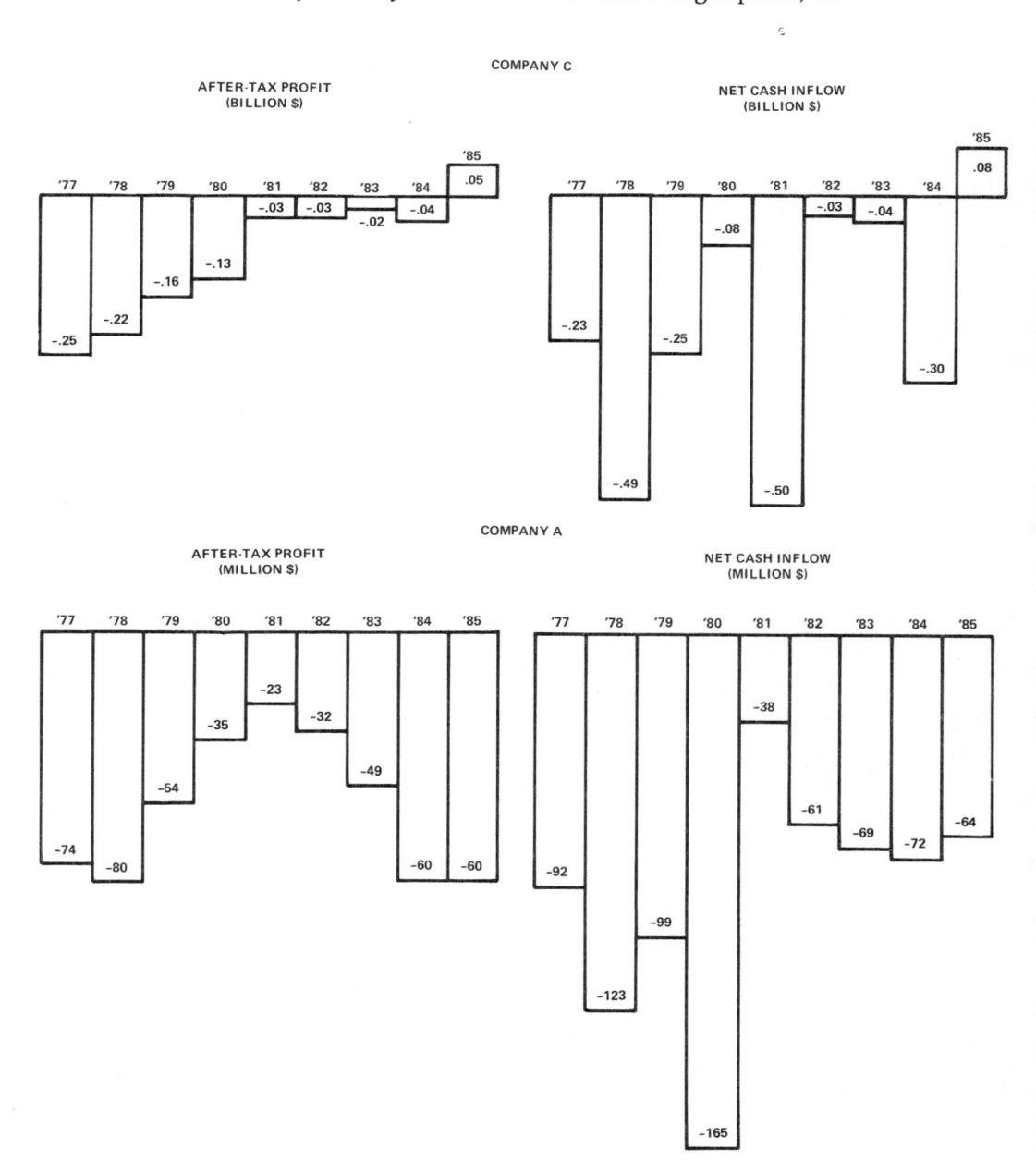

'77 -92, '78 -123, '79 -99, '80 -38, '81 -61, '82 -69, '83 -72, '84 -64, '85 -165

FIGURE 4-4 (Cont.)

TABLE 4-15 Nominal Case—Financial Position 1985

	Company G	Company F	Company C	Company A
Sales (million cars)	5.9	2.7	1.6	0.25
Breakeven (million cars)	2.7	1.4	1.5	0.35
Revenue (billion $)	29.9	11.9	7.2	0.87
After-tax profit (billion $)	4.3	1.2	0.05	−0.06
Return on sales %	14.4	10.1	0.7	−6.9
Equity capital (billion $)	0.39	0.12	0.23	0.04
Retained earnings (billion $)	27.1	10.8	0.59	−0.30
Long-term debt (billion $)	−15.2	−4.7	2.5	0.88

return on sales is less than 1 percent. Its cash inflows are significantly negative throughout the period, except for a small positive inflow in 1985. Company C has a debt/equity ratio in 1985 of 3.0 which is clearly impossible considering industry practice. Even if Company C could substantially reduce the amount of capital required by reducing investment, it would still have to find some way of raising a significant amount of capital.

Company A fares even worse making significant losses throughout the period. In 1985 its retained earnings and stockholders' equity is negative; long-term debt is very high. Such a capital structure is clearly an untenable position. What would undoubtedly happen is that before 1985, Company A would have had to take some actions to raise equity capital, cutdown on investments and losses, sell other assets, or close down some operations. The model indicates that some drastic action will be essential but, of course, does not forecast what that action will be.

Optimistic and Pessimistic Cases

In the *optimistic case,* it is assumed that fuel economy gains from the various technological improvements are higher, while costs associated with these improvements are lower than estimated by Department of Transportation. In the *pessimistic case,* fuel economy gains are less and costs are higher than estimated by DOT. Values actually used in the model were decided upon in consultation with industry experts.

Due to space restrictions we present for these two cases only the long-term debt position in 1985, which is an indicator of cumulative performance for the period 1977 to 1985. It can be seen from Table 4-16 that Company G is better off by 5.9 percent in the optimistic case compared to the nominal case. But in the pessimistic case it is worse off by 30.2 percent compared to the nominal case. This should be interpreted to mean that the downside risk of being off in our estimates is very high. This holds for the other three manufacturers as well.

Probabilistic Case

We assume in this case that fuel economy-related variables are distributed according to a truncated normal distribution. The form and the parameters of the distribution are based on the judgment of an industry expert. Once again, we report only the distribution of the 1985 long-term debt position for each manufacturer (see Table 4-17).

Results obtained in the probabilistic case correspond well with the results of the earlier cases studied. The 0.1 fractile corresponds fairly well to the optimistic case and the 0.9 fractile corresponds to the pessimistic case. As we would expect from the earlier remarks about high downside risk, the median values are well above the nominal case values.

Technological and Manufacturing Risks

Technological risk is the risk due to the uncertainty in the fuel economy gains that will be achieved from the various fuel economy measures.

TABLE 4-16 Long-Term Debt Position in 1985

	Optimistic case	Nominal case	Pessimistic case
Company G	−16.1	−15.2	−10.6
Company F	−5.4	−4.7	−1.9
Company C	2.3	2.5	3.4
Company A	0.80	0.88	1.22

TABLE 4-17 Long-Term Debt Position in 1985 (billion $)—Probabilistic Case

	Fractiles				
	0.1	0.25	0.5	0.75	0.9
Company G	−15.7	−14.0	−12.7	−11.1	−9.7
Company F	−4.7	−4.0	−3.5	−2.7	−1.9
Company C	2.4	2.8	3.1	3.4	3.8
Company A	0.87	0.95	1.04	1.11	1.23

TABLE 4-18   Debt Position in 1985 (billion $)

Costs Related to Fuel Economy Measures

		Opti-mistic	Nominal	Pessi-mistic	Opti-mistic	Nominal	Pessi-mistic
Fuel Economy Gains	Optimistic	−16.1	−14.9	—	−5.4	−4.8	—
	Nominal	−16.4	−15.2	−9.8	−5.4	−4.7	−2.2
	Pessimistic	—	−16.3	−10.6	—	−4.5	−1.9
		Company G			Company F		

Costs Related to Fuel Economy Measures

		Opti-mistic	Nominal	Pessi-mistic	Opti-mistic	Nominal	Pessi-mistic
Fuel Economy Gains	Optimistic	2.3	2.6	—	0.80	0.86	—
	Nominal	2.2	2.5	3.8	0.81	0.88	1.15
	Pessimistic	—	2.0	3.4	—	0.93	1.22
		Company C			Company A		

Manufacturing risk is the risk due to the uncertainty in the costs of implementing these measures. In the above analysis, we have varied fuel economy gains and costs of the measures simultaneously. We have thus assessed the joint effect of the uncertainties in the technological and manufacturing domains. We now separate the two effects by separately varying fuel economy gains and costs of the measures. The results of this analysis are given in Table 4-18.

As shown in Table 4-18, the model indicates that the risk due to uncertainty in manufacturability is higher than the risk due to technological uncertainty. The variation in a column is the variation in performance as fuel economy gains vary, assuming that the related costs remain constant. Thus, variation in a column is an indicator of risk due to technological uncertainty. Similarly, variation in row is an indicator of risk due to uncertainty in manufacturability.

ANALYSIS OF DIFFERENT SCENARIOS

In this section we examine different scenarios, while the values of fuel economy-related variables are assumed to be the nominal values.

Increased Capital Expenditure Scenario

A recent report[6] produced by DOT and conversations with their personnel led us to suspect that the data input for the Nominal Scenario discussed earlier might lead us to underestimate the capital expenditures of the manufacturers. Table 4-19 compares the capital expenditure

---

6. *Ibid.*

TABLE 4-19 Cumulative Capital Expenditures for 1978–1985 (billion $)

	Company G	Company F	Company C	Company A
Revised estimates[a]	23.4	12.9	5.04	0.72
Nominal case	15.8	6.56	3.29	0.68

[a] These figures are for North American passenger car operations only and are based on M. Anderson and J. Blair, *The Impact of Federal Regulation on the Financial Structure and Performance of the Domestic Motor Vehicle Manufacturers* (DOT, May 1978).

estimates for the period 1977 to 1985 based on the above report[7] with the output of the model for the Nominal case.

The revised estimates and the Nominal case results agree to within 5 percent for Company A. For Companies G, F, and C, however, the difference is very large. In this scenario the input data relating to capital expenditure are adjusted so that the total capital expenditure for the period 1977 to 1985 for each manufacturer is equal to the revised estimates given in Table 4-19. Table 4-20 summarizes the results for this scenario.

Considering the capital structure in 1985 under this scenario, we see that Company G is in a strong position. It has liquidated all its debt and has built up a credit balance of $7.4 billion. Company F is also in a strong position with a debt/equity ratio of 0.28. Companies C and A are both in clearly untenable positions. Both have negative stockholders' equity and high long-term debt. Both the companies would have had to take some drastic actions to avoid reaching such positions.

Three Final Scenarios

The results for the Nominal and the Increased Capital Expenditure Scenarios are illustrative of more extensive analysis that was obtained for three additional ones: (1) An *Ideal Scenario,* with downsizing and material substitution but presumed on a more nearly voluntary basis, without strict regulatory AFES standards; (2) a *Foreign Penetration of Mid-Size Car Market Scenario;* and (3) an *Economic Risk Scenario.* The latter scenario tests three different assumptions about overall demand changes in the United States market, an increase and a decrease in demand by 5 percent of projections in each year and an assumption that demand is more cyclical.

Results with the ideal scenario suggest that under the assumptions of the model, downsizing is economically profitable while material substitution has no significant economic impact. That is, material substitution causes the weight of the car to decrease while the material cost per pound is increased; the net result of this is that the material cost per car

---

7. *Ibid.*

TABLE 4-20 Increased Capital Expenditure Scenario Financial Position 1985

	Company G	Company F	Company C	Company A
Sales (million cars)	5.94	2.71	1.62	0.25
Breakeven (million cars)	3.00	1.97	1.87	0.36
Revenue (billion $)	29.9	11.9	7.2	0.87
After-tax profit (billion $)	3.57	0.62	−0.14	−0.07
Return on sales (%)	11.9	5.2	−1.9	−8.0
Equity capital (billion $)	0.39	0.12	0.23	0.04
Retained earnings (billion $)	22.75	7.26	−0.52	−0.33
Long-term debt (billion $)	−7.41	2.07	4.5	0.93

decreases. However, this decrease is almost exactly offset by the increase in capital cost.

For the Foreign Penetration of Mid-Sized Car Scenario, Companies G, F, and C perform worse, with Company G being the most affected. Company A is relatively unaffected by the foreign penetration of the mid-size car market. This is understandable since such a penetration would reduce the competitive pressure in the small car market; and since Company A is mostly in the small car market, it is not hurt by this move of foreign manufacturers.

The Economic Risk Scenario yields different outcomes for the three market projections. As is to be expected, all the manufacturers perform better under the high demand scenario, and worse under the low demand and cyclical demand scenarios. The results yield another, and more interesting conclusion. For Companies G and F the effect of persistently low demand is much more significant than that of cyclicality. For Company C the effects of low demand and cyclical demand are equally significant. While for Company A the effect of cyclical demand is more significant than that of low demand. Thus, cyclicality in demand is more critical for the smaller manufacturers than for the larger manufacturers.

DISCUSSION

E. S. BROWER: As Mr. Popovich told us, there are going to be changes in materials, a loss of capital, and a real scramble in the raw materials business. At the same time there are new markets and new products and I think that that is a very positive and definite opportunity.

Radical innovation may lead to vertical integration by the automobile companies, however, because they have to get as much fuel economy as possible by a combination of things. Suppliers may become manufacturing organizations rather than design organizations.

POPOVICH: The Toyota-Datsun-Honda trio could end up with facilities in this country very quickly. Each has established a market base to support assembly production and the three together could support an engine plant, which means more opportunities for suppliers in this country. There are 17 automobile passenger car suppliers in America who share 88 percent of the market. There have to be some mergings or joint activities because of economies of scale problems. Chrysler made a commitment to buy 1 million engines from Japan in a 5-year span. If you take .25 million engines a year and add these to the Volkswagen commitment of another .25 million, it is the equivalent of two engine lines, or $700 million in job opportunities moving out of the country. The three Japanese producers could offset this loss in the next 7 years.

RICHARD STROMBOTNE: Mr. Popovich does a service by pointing out the growing importance of light trucks. Looking at the projected high growth rate of the light truck and recognizing that light trucks tend to last 14 years as compared with 10 years for cars, we see the light truck fleet growing to something like 55 million, plus or minus 5 million or so, by 1990. That is from about 20-to-25 million today. Our estimates of weight reduction are substantially higher than those of Mr. Popovich, however, and thus we would reach different conclusions about the average weight both in passenger cars and light trucks by 1985.

Professor Bradley has concluded that fuel economy standards will tend to increase industry concentration; his analysis is convincing although it will have to be expanded in detail. The nominal scenario that he discussed is not based on the final assessment of the manufacturers' ability to increase fuel economy in the early 1980s, which NHTSA produced last year. It is based on earlier documentation. Thus it does not include what we thought was a critical difference in assumptions about the use of smaller engines in passenger cars. Professor Bradley's assumptions are important in the derivation of the estimation of the role of market shifts in cash flow and the ability of manufacturers to meet the fuel economy standards.

I would like to emphasize that weight reduction does not necessarily mean small cars. Light cars, yes. Our analysis shows that manufacturers should be able to meet the 1985 standards by keeping the same mix of car sizes we have now but by redesigning, downsizing, using different materials, using the improved automatic transmissions being developed, and having some reduction in engine horsepower to vehicle weight ratio. Technology is not limited to small engines. We have seen in recent years that auto manufacturers can eliminate 600-to-800 pounds in each car. General Motors' standard size car redesign in 1977 was successful. We will see more of this in the front-wheel drive cars coming out in the next few years.

ACADEMIC: My hope is that the risk model, if pursued by DOT, could focus the debate on the points that we disagree on. Even if the data we used were out of date, they demonstrated that Chrysler was indeed headed toward difficulties, which the European divestiture shows. It is an indication of their need to raise capital.

SUPPLIER: It was pointed out that Chrysler needed $8 billion, not $5 billion, and by selling their entire European operation they only came about a third of the way toward raising this money. The kind of study Professor Bradley made would have more value had it been done in inflating (current) dollars, because that is what the industry has to work with.

BRADLEY: I agree that the capital needs are understated because of the constant dollar; part of the problem was a lack of data. The common interpretation of equality and equity in regulation is that you should set the regulations and apply them equally across the board. The alternative view of regulations is that they should be applied in a way by which competitive differences are considered, but there is a problem of administering such a system.

ACADEMIC: All the readings I have done tend to confirm the finding Professor Bradley has made, that regulation tends to exagerate the strengths and weaknesses of firms in the marketplace.

CHAPTER FIVE
International Trade and Domestic Regulation

EDITORS' NOTE

Even a close observer of the domestic automobile industry may know little of the world trade in automobiles. Imported cars have never taken much over 20 percent of the United States market, and the American manufacturers have long found it more advantageous to manufacture overseas for, than to export to, overseas markets.

The world trade in automobiles may now, however, be on the verge of a substantial change. Regulation-induced downsizing and other changes in the American product line may invite more direct competition with foreign manufacturers (in both the United States and other markets), and accelerate the trend toward international standardization of parts. On the other hand, some regulations, particularly those respecting safety and pollution control, may act as nontariff barriers to trade. Which effect will dominate the other is by no means clear at this time.

In this chapter, Dr. Umberto Agnelli shares with us a European point of view, one that has been shaped by a history of greater orientation to international issues. This is a trenchant and sensitive review of the "last five or six years of debate [that] have questioned just about every aspect of the automobile industry." While recognizing the need for some differentiation based upon different national environments and their needs, Dr. Agnelli emphasizes the danger that world markets will be Balkanized by regulation.

Through an historical survey of the multinational operations of automobile manufacturers, however, Mira Wilkins demonstrates that the configuration of the worldwide industry has always been a reflection of government interventions, broadly conceived to include trade policies. United States policy-makers now face a new dilemma, she argues, for our regulatory policies, combined with our commitment to free trade and low tariffs, could give an *advantage* to imports and thereby have adverse effects on the United States' balance of payments and domestic employment.

Michael Pearce contrasts the United States government's relationship to the automobile industry with that of other governments, which tend to be concerned more with employment levels or export promotion than with consumer protection or energy conservation. These differences, and the emergence of some less developed countries as manufacturers for world markets, may lead the United States to adopt a more protectionist attitude toward the domestic industry, he suggests. In any event, they make it increasingly unrealistic to think about domestic policy issues without an eye on world market developments.

According to Louis T. Wells, Jr., application of the "product life cycle" theory to the automobile industry shows that regulation is likely to be a minor factor in retarding a long-term process that leads to the United States being a substantial importer of automobiles. The American industry will not disappear, but it will be under greater competitive pressure. Unfortunately, perhaps, innovation may not be an effective means of competition in the future, unless international antitrust policies keep the world market open to new entrants.

If they do, there will be much interest in the story of Mr. Honda who, as told by Koichi Shimokawa, used innovation—in technology, in management, and in marketing—to build Honda Motor Company into an international best seller. As the foreword to that essay says, "It is an instructive article for those who believe that innovation in the automobile industry does not pay."

POLICIES FOR THE PROMOTION OF EFFECTIVE TECHNOLOGICAL CHANGE: A EUROPEAN POINT OF VIEW

Umberto Agnelli, *Vice Chairman and President, FIAT*

In the last few decades innovations in the automobile sector—and particularly in the European automobile sector—have fostered (1) the evolution of the *product* in attempts to adapt to a diversified market; and (2) the evolution of *production processes* to satisfy better the consumers' demands for quality on the one hand and the employees' demands for better working conditions on the other. The evolution of the product itself has been a tough and risky task in which even the deepest commitment rarely brings immediate results. Manufacturers who sought new solutions most vigorously may have gained in public esteem but this improved image has rarely earned them anything extra to speak of in terms of profits. And yet there has never been so much talk of the need for innovation in the automobile field in order to keep pace with the heaps of demands from the authorities, the consumers, the workers, and so on, creating uncertainty in the day-to-day working of the individual firm even beyond the normally difficult decisions which must be made in this sector of industry.

Anyone familiar with the automobile industry knows that almost all of the crucial policy decisions reduce to investment decisions. And also that in a firm which has been in existence for a number of years, a new investment—however considerable—can only partly alter the qualitative mix of the existing assets. The risk for the company may be great, and the effort massive, but sometimes the overall effect is relatively modest compared to the original expectations.

Balancing great expectations with economic realities is a problem for consumers of automobiles as well as for producers. Around the world, people's expectations vis-à-vis the automobile have been numerous and are still increasing. On the other hand, the growing use of cars—

and the dependence it fosters—produces serious social, political, and economic problems. This tension is the product of a number of factors.

First, there is an increasing sensitivity on the part of governments to the emergent problem of how to cope with a cumbersome population of cars. In the United States, for example, the automobile population is around one-half the human population. This concern has led to the promulgation of increasingly severe antipollution measures, safety regulations, and petrol consumption standards.

Second, there is increasing sensitivity on the part of consumers who favor the car as a useful machine but dislike it as an object which eats up public space and resources and cuts heavily into the family budget in terms of the initial investment and day-to-day running costs. This feeling has led to the creation of consumer associations and to the various measures concerning product liability.

Third, increasing pressure on the part of the workers in the automobile industry to reduce boring, repetitive, production-line tasks calls for the introduction of new technologies and production practices.

These last five or six years of debate have questioned just about every aspect of the automobile industry. We should not forget that some people have even begun to believe that the death of the motor car is at hand. This debate has had a salutary effect. In Europe, at least, it has separated the real criticisms from the superficial caviling. It has clarified the distinction between what is feasible and what is merely desirable; it has distinguished ideas with practical potential from a relatively amorphous mass of emotional reactions; it has sharpened our understanding of the costs and benefits; and has, at least in part, reconciled us to the automobile.

This means that the time is fast approaching for a new phase of innovation. For an investment to be approved in the automobile industry, there must be sufficient likelihood at the outset of ten years of life for bodywork and perhaps twenty years of life for the mechanicals. At this moment, just when we are emerging from that phase of existential questioning during which all aspects of the automobile have been reexamined, one is aware of a desire that regardless of whether they derive from such external sources as legislative authorities, public opinion, or the unions, or from internal sources within the management of the industry itself, the whole bundle of new policies to regulate the automobile should add up to an organic whole, providing a clear guideline and a stimulus for investment decisions for a considerable period of time.

When these favorable conditions are lacking (as is often the case nowadays), the costs of taking mistaken decisions is bound to fall on the consumer, either directly, in that he buys a product which is more expensive than it ought to be, or indirectly, in terms of taxes and day-to-day expenditure.

Innovation is a process which has some of the characteristics of biological evolution. The right environmental conditions must be present in order to preserve the valid adaptations to an environment which is continually changing. In our own case, we require an abundance of that creative talent which proposes new solutions; and this is a rare resource. But in our experience, the most tricky phase is that which runs from the original idea to the first concrete results. This phase calls for a management which is prepared to accept the risks inherent in any new process, with the will to overcome the difficulties involved in getting novel solutions accepted both inside and outside the factory, and the ability to coordinate the human and material resources required to make the idea a success. The experience of the last few decades shows that if the automobile is to mature and progress, we must be in a position to guarantee that the system will be both stimulating and rewarding.

I am firmly convinced that the external system of restrictions we have had in Europe, which tend to reward limited consumption, has stimulated innovation in the search for solutions which are both cost-efficient and effective in meeting the requirements and the expectations of the authorities and of the consumers. But each time policy-makers outside the industry have tried to influence technical decisions (for example, the Italian fiscal system based on engine capacity and the number of cylinders), this has had a negative effect, preventing the manufacturer from combing the market for the most suitable solutions to his problems.

This leads me to the conclusion that there is a considerable risk that the increasing complexity of standards and legislation, arising out of the need to meet a multiplicity of requirements, may well become a means to ends which are a far cry from the original intention of the initial regulations. For example, the regulations proposed in the fields of consumer protection and environmental conservation are genuinely useful; but they could also be used to set up artificial barriers to markets, or to accelerate a process leading toward centralized economic planning. I feel we should make it an objective to be able to defend specific "automobile-based cultures" which are the expression of a particular relationship between man and the automobile, against the pressures calling for total standardization. A system of limitations which is the same for everybody is probably impossible.

It is very difficult to predict how the requirements of governments, consumers, and trade unions will define and direct the process of innovation in the automobile world. What is certain, however, is that these forces cannot be the same throughout the various automobile-manufacturing areas of the world. Different environments will therefore bring into being different types of innovation. Only after the test of time will we be able to know how such innovations may be applied or adapted elsewhere. In Italy, for example, the requirements of the unions are imposing on us the need for innovation in *production processes* in bodywork shops. As a result, my country is ahead of others in this field. In other countries, a greater awareness of consumer protection problems is stimulating innovation in reliability and durability of components. It is inevitable that these differing experiences will eventually come to be offered—already well-tried and relatively risk-free—to other manufacturers throughout the world.

The only guarantee which we as automobile manufacturers must demand, however, is that the various forces involved in regulating the processes of innovation should use *the correct functioning of the market* as their yardstick. This means giving up the illuministic temptation to force the automobile along technocratic paths of carefully constructed, increasingly detailed, and precise standards which permit only one bureaucratically foreordained outcome.

MULTINATIONAL AUTOMOBILE ENTERPRISES AND REGULATION: AN HISTORICAL OVERVIEW*

Mira Wilkins, *Professor of Economics, Florida International University*

The automobile industry is made up primarily of multinational enterprises that have foreign investments in manufacturing, assembly, selling, and servicing. Table 5-1 indicates the largest of these companies and their multinational involvements. Suppliers are also multinational.[1] Specific markets, by contrast, are national, those within the European Economic Community perhaps excepted.[2] Governments set

---

* The author wishes to acknowledge the splendid research assistance of Mr. George Oberhofer. Dr. Hiroko Sakai, Messrs. James Boxall, William Krist, Stephen Merrill, and Ms. Johanna Shelton also provided information and ideas.

1. Initially, I had hoped in this paper to consider in depth the internationalization of supplier industries. Space considerations made this impossible. I am going to confine myself to passenger cars. However, the multinationalization of suppliers should be recognized as an important underlying aspect of the same activities by the car companies. For example, the German firm, Robert Bosch, produced automobile ignition systems in the United States before World War I; in 1915 the Swedish company, SKF began production in the United States of ball bearings for the American automobile industry; by the 1920s, the leading United States and British tire producers had foreign plants; parts makers followed American automobile companies abroad in that decade; and so it went. Included in a recent United Nations list of major world enterprises are such suppliers of the automobile industry as ITT; the leading tire makers; Robert Bosch; Bendix; TRW; Guest, Keen and Nettlefolds; Borg-Warner; Eaton; Dana; Lucas Industries; and Budd. See L.F. Franko, *The European Multinationals* 9,164 (Greylock Publishers, 1976); M. Wilkins, *Maturing of Multinational Enterprise, American Business Abroad from 1914 to 1970* 75 (Harvard Univ. Press, 1970); United Nations, Economic and Social Council, *Transnational Corporations in World Development* 288–311 (New York, 1978).

2. While the European Economic Community has free trade within it in automobiles, national regulations still define individual markets. Thus, for example, Fiat can attribute the rise of the French share in EEC automobile production to

TABLE 5-1 Foreign Business of Major Motor Vehicle Producers (Sales of Over $3.5 Billion) End 1976

Rank by sales[a]	Company	Nationality	Government ownership (percentage)	Total consolidated sales (millions of dollars)	Foreign sales: Exports from home country As percentage of total consolidated sales	Foreign sales: Sales of overseas affiliates to third parties As percentage of total consolidated sales	Foreign assets as percentage of total assets	Foreign earnings as percentage of total earnings	Foreign employment as percentage of total employment
2	General Motors	United States	—	47,181	—	24	12	18	—
4	Ford Motor	United States	—	28,840	—	31	40	45	51
14	Chrysler	United States	—	15,538	—	28	33	22	47
20	Renault	France	100	9,353	—	45	—	—	—
24	Daimler-Benz	Germany, Federal Republic of	14[b]	8,938	39	21	—	—	17[c]
26	Volkswagenwerk	Germany, Federal Republic of	40	8,513	62	—	—	—	32
34	Toyota Motor	Japan	—	7,696	35	—	2	—	15[c]
38	Peugeot-Citröen	France	—	7,347	19	28	—	—	16
42	Nissan Motor	Japan	—	6,584	41	25	6	—	15
72	Fiat	Italy	—	4,658[d]	—	—	—	—	19
82	British Leyland	United Kingdom	100	4,178	36	18	—	—	12
102	Volvo	Sweden	—	3,615	44	24	—	—	27

Source: United Nations, Economic and Social Council, *Transnational Corporations in World Development* (New York, 1978).

[a] Ranked in descending order of total consolidated sales; rank of major industrial corporations.
[b] Kuwaiti interest.
[c] Estimated.
[d] Parent company sales.

tariffs and taxes; provide incentives; and establish safety, emission, and conservation standards. Costs in building and operating cars vary by country, and people still think of "American," "German," "French," and "Japanese" vehicles. Thus, while enterprises extend themselves internationally, governments and popular viewpoints remain national in both policy and vocabulary.

None of this is new. Indeed, the automobile industry has participated in international business almost from its inception. Ford—now probably the most international of the car companies in terms of foreign assets as a percentage of total assets (see Table 5-1)—exported in 1903 the sixth car it built.[3] From the 1890s, races and exhibitions attracted participants from many countries.[4] Trade journals reported industrywide events beyond national arenas.

PRE–WORLD WAR I

In the pre–World War I context government regulation meant the Red Flag Law, tariffs, and, to a lesser extent, taxes. These government interventions had an impact, but the differences between the European and United States automobile industries seemed to have been shaped more by economic and geographic than by regulatory factors. Indeed, the handcrafted, highpowered luxury cars predominated in countries where skilled labor was available, where there were wealthy consumers, and where markets were small. The mass-produced car was a product of the United States, where the cost of skilled labor was high, where there was a vast potential demand—because the country was physically enormous and per capita income was the highest in the world—and where the price of gasoline was undoubtedly the lowest in the world. (America was an exporter of oil products.)

The birthplace of the passenger car was in Germany, where the Daimler and Benz models of 1885 to 1886 were the first commercially viable gasoline-powered products.[5] Early French units included the Panhard & Levassor (built on a Daimler license), the Delaunay-Belleville, and the Renault. In March 1899, Louis Renault and his brother founded Société Renault.[6] Peugeot also began building automobiles in France in the 1890s.[7]

"national policies." See Fiat, *Reports of the Board of Directors, 1977*, 7 (Apr. 1978).

3. M. Wilkins and F. E. Hill, *American Business Abroad: Ford on Six Continents* 1 (Wayne State Univ. Press, 1964).
4. A. Nevins and F. E. Hill, *Ford: The Times, The Man, The Company* 191, 194 (Charles Scribner's Sons, 1954), for examples.
5. *Ibid.* at 125.
6. D. Landes, *Unbound Prometheus* 446 (Cambridge Univ. Press, 1969); and for more details, S. Saint-Loup, *Renault de Billancourt* (Paris, Le Livre Contemporain, 1956).
7. J. M. Laux, "Managerial Structures in France," in *Evolution of International Structures* 99 (H. Williamson, Ed., University of Delaware Press, 1975).

In Britain, where railroad interests feared competition from steam (and later, gasoline) carriages, the automobile industry was slower to emerge. A "Red Flag" Law of 1835 set a maximum speed of 4 miles per hour on all free-moving, self-propelled vehicles and required that they be preceded by a man carrying a red flag! When that law was finally repealed in 1896, a licensee of the German Daimler enterprise, Daimler Motor Co., Ltd., was the first to manufacture cars in England.[8]

At the dawn of the twentieth century, European-made automobiles were handsome, handcrafted, chiefly high-powered units, designed for the wealthy.[9] In the United States, the elite of Newport, Rhode Island, drove the elegant and expensive French vehicles. At the turn of the century, European automobile output was greater than American.[10] The cars were sold in limited, high-income markets in the United States and Europe. That Daimler licensed producers in France and England already indicated segmentation of national markets.

The United States developed an indigenous automobile industry behind a 45 percent ad valorem tariff.[11] American-made products were initially inferior to their European counterparts. Thus, a contemporary described the 1902 Olds as having a "coughing, spitting, one-cylinder engine that seemed to be suffering the final stages of shaking palsy."[12] The Olds was by no means an isolated instance of poor construction.

As late as 1906, United States imports exceeded United States exports of cars and parts in dollar value ($4.2 million versus $3.5 million). Figures on the number of cars exported in 1906 are not available, but the quantity was probably larger than the 1,106 cars that were imported, since United States exports were relatively low-priced and imports higher priced. In 1907, when the dollar value of United States passenger car exports surpassed imports, the average price per automobile exported was $1,709, while the average price per car imported was more than twice that, or $3,436.[13] As Ford Motor Company and others initiated volume production, the quality of cars on this side of the Atlantic improved. From 1907, and for the next half century, America was a net

---

8. Wilkins and Hill, n. 3 *supra* at 10; *Harper Encyclopaedia of the Modern World* 681 (R. Morris and G. Irwin, Eds., Harper & Row, 1970).
9. U.S. Tariff Comm'n, *Tariff Information Surveys, Automobiles* 7 (Washington, 1921), notes that they were "chiefly high powered." This report will henceforth be cited as *Tariff Commission Report–1921*.
10. D. W. Fryer, *World Economic Development* 459 (McGraw-Hill, 1965); Wilkins and Hill, n. 3 *supra* at 8.
11. *Tariff Commission Report–1921*, p. 13.
12. Cited in Wilkins and Hill, n. 3 *supra* at 9.
13. *Commerce and Navigation of the United States for 1909* 173, 493–494. In 1906 imports of cars were $3.8 million, and parts $.4 million, making a total of $4.2 million. In 1907 imports of cars were $4.0 million, parts $.8 million, totaling $4.8 million. In 1907 exports of cars were $4.9 million, parts $.6 million, totaling $5.5 million.

exporter of passenger cars, measured both in number of cars and in dollar value.

United States wages were higher than those in Europe, and the American industry substituted machinery for labor in making automobiles. What emerged in the United States were mass-produced "cheap cars" made with interchangeable parts, assembled on a moving assembly line. The products were designed to reach a large domestic market—rugged vehicles, easily repaired. The concept became entirely distinct from that which had arisen in Europe. Behind the high protective tariff wall, the United States industry introduced economies of scale and economies of speed of production, and prices declined accordingly.[14]

Certain European firms gave up the American market. The British exported to their colonies, almost exclusively.[15] The French remained large exporters, but did not sell large quantities in the United States.[16] By contrast, the German Daimler firm's affiliate, the Daimler Manufacturing Company, jumped over the American tariff wall and in 1905 began manufacturing American-made Mercedes at a factory in Long Island. The car was advertised as a "faithful reproduction in materials, workmanship and design of the foreign car." Offered at $7,500, it was $3,000 less than the "Foreign Mercedes."[17] In 1909, the Italian Fiat Company began production of its luxury cars in Poughkeepsie, New York.[18]

The output of Mercedes and Fiats in the United States is unknown, but when the Mercedes factory burned down in 1913 it was not rebuilt. The war in Europe in 1914 was undoubtedly one reason; a second was the development of a fully competitive American industry; and a third was, as the historian for Mercedes-Benz reports, that the American Mercedes was "no match for the German Mercedes."[19] The 1913 United States tariff had nothing to do with the decision not to reopen, for while the United States rate of duty was lowered to 30 percent for cars under $2,000, the high-priced Mercedes was still subject to a 45 percent levy.[20]

---

14. A. D. Chandler, *Visible Hand* (Harvard Univ. Press, 1977), emphasizes throughout the U.S. accomplishments of economies of speed.
15. *Tariff Commission Report–1921*, p. 11.
16. *Ibid.* at 10. In 1913 French exports were larger in dollar value than American ($45 million v. $33 million). This, of course, was due to the fact that the French exported high-priced and the Americans low-priced cars. Of the few U.S. imports in 1913, the French furnished about 50 percent. *Ibid.* at 12. J. Rousseau, *Histoire Mondiale de l'Automobile* 118 (Paris, 1958), says Renault had "agencies" worldwide, including America, in the pre–World War I years.
17. *The American Mercedes* (Daimler Mfg. Co., 1906).
18. L. T. Wells, Jr., "Automobiles," in *Big Business and the State* 231, 295 (R. Vernon, Ed., Harvard Univ. Press, 1974).
19. F. Schildberger, "75 Years of Mercedes-Benz Ties with the United States," *Mercedes-Benz in Aller Welt* 213 (Stuttgart, Daimler-Benz, 1963).
20. *Tariff Commission Report–1921*, p. 13, gives tariff history.

Fiat's Poughkeepsie plant was sold to the American Duesenberg Motor Company in 1918.[21] United States imports of finished cars declined from 1,305 units in 1910 to a mere 708 in 1914. In 1914, automobile imports were barely .3 percent of United States production.[22]

By contrast, United States passenger car exports reached about 7.5 percent of production in 1914.[23] Ford Motor Company already had factories in Canada (started in 1904 to 1905) and England (built in 1911 to 1912), where its initial models were replicas of the United States-made units. The Canadian facility gave Ford the opportunity to penetrate a market that was protected by a 35 percent tariff. While England was not circled by a tariff, transportation costs warranted local production. By 1914, then, the Ford Model T was not only in first place in the United States (where it sold for $440)[24] but in Canada and England as well.

Europeans looked in awe to the American automobile industry. By 1914, more private automobiles were in use in the United States than in all the rest of the world.[25] Even before World War I, some European car makers had begun to imitate United States production methods and to use American machine tools.[26] In England, William Richard Morris (later Lord Nuffield) produced the Morris-Oxford car in 1913, designed to compete with the Model T.[27] On the Continent, where the automobile companies built vehicles solely for the very wealthy, however, costs of purchase, ownership, and operation (including gasoline and taxes) were far higher than in the United States.

During World War I, the United States automobile industry continued to perfect mass production methods, and the importation of cars essentially stopped. Between 1914 and 1919 the number of passenger cars in use in the United States quadrupled.[28] Meanwhile, in 1915, the first of the popular British "small cars,"[29] the Morris-Cowley, was introduced in England. French and Italian industry remained unchanged, while the industry in Germany was virtually destroyed by the war.[30]

---

21. Wells, "Automobiles," n. 18 *supra* at 295.
22. *Tariff Commission Report–1921*, p. 8.
23. *Ibid.*
24. Wilkins and Hill, n. 3 *supra* at 18–20, 51, 53, 435.
25. Based on figures given in W. W. Rostow, *The Stages of Economic Growth* 170 (Cambridge Univ. Press, 1960).
26. *Tariff Commission Report–1921*, p. 9.
27. Wilkins and Hill, n. 3 *supra* at 51.
28. Based on figures in Rostow, n. 25 *supra* at 170.
29. G. Maxcy and A. Silberston, *The Motor Industry* 99 (London, Allen & Unwin, 1959).
30. *Tariff Commission Report–1921*.

THE INTER-WAR YEARS

International Trade and Domestic Regulation

At the end of World War I, the United States automobile industry had no rival. Domestic output was higher than ever before. Exports in 1920 reached 16.1 percent of production. Imports continued to be negligible (about one-tenth of 1 percent of United States output, three-quarters of which came from Canada).[31]

The 1920s were years of triumph for United States automobile companies. Mass production had been achieved before World War I; now, for the first time, mass consumption matched it as the United States became the world's first mass market for passenger cars. The decade began with the Ford Model T capturing 55 percent of all car sales; the Runabout sold for a mere $260 at the end of 1924. General Motors, which had been formed in 1908, decided to provide cars to satisfy the taste of every consumer and recognized that Americans wanted more than basic transportation. Thus, although General Motors' cars were mass-produced, they offered variety in styling, as well as comfort, accessories, and power.

The American "love affair" with the automobile had begun.[32] By 1929, there was 1 car for every 5 Americans;[33] that year 4.5 million passenger cars were sold in this country,[34] and United States motor vehicle production equaled 85.3 percent of world output.[35] American automobile makers (Chrysler joined the leaders in 1925) developed sales and service networks. Credit was made available to finance car purchases.

Although the United States tariff was lowered in 1922 to 25 percent (or to a duty equal to that imposed by the country from which the import came but not to exceed 50 percent), imports remained under one-tenth of 1 percent of United States production.[36] No foreign pro-

---

31. *Ibid.* at 8, 12. In 1920 the average value of cars imported from Canada was less than $700, from France $2,600, and from Great Britain $3,600. *Ibid.* at 12.
32. On the price of Ford cars, see A. Nevins and F. E. Hill, *Ford: Expansion and Challenge 1915–1933* 264 (Charles Scribner's Sons, 1957). This volume and A. Nevins and F. E. Hill, *Ford: Decline and Rebirth, 1933–1962* (Charles Scribner's Sons, 1963), give an excellent picture of Ford and the U.S. automobile industry in the interwar period. On General Motors, see A. Sloan, *My Years with General Motors* (Doubleday, 1964), and F. Donner, *Worldwide Industrial Enterprise* (McGraw-Hill, 1967). On the U.S. industry in general, see Federal Trade Comm'n, *Motor Vehicle Industry* (Wash., 1939) (henceforth cited as *FTC Report*). See also A. D. Chandler, Jr., *Giant Enterprise* (Harcourt, Brace & World, 1964).
33. The per capita ownership figures are based on data in Rostow, n. 25 *supra* at 171.
34. *FTC Report*, p. 29.
35. *Ibid.*, p. 36.
36. U.S. Tariff Comm'n, *Summary of Tariff Information, 1929, on Tariff Act of 1922* 750 (Wash., 1939).

ducer of cars could compete in the American market. Barriers to entry lay in the major United States companies' efficiencies (economies of scale), their product designs, and their extensive marketing organizations, all of which were more effective than tariff protection.[37] With the depression of the 1930s, United States automobile sales sank.[38] But American automobile companies still had little to fear from foreign competition,[39] and in June 1934 the tariffs on automobiles were effectively reduced to 10 percent.[40]

In the early 1930s, the 7-horsepower British "baby" Austin car was produced, under license, in western Pennsylvania. Austin advertised that "big" United States cars cost about 2 ¼ cents per mile (for gas, oil, and tires) to operate, while its automobile was a bargain to run at three-quarters of a cent per mile. Depression notwithstanding, the baby Austin (the initial cost of which was $5 more than the Ford Model A) did not prove popular; its small size made it a butt for American cartoonists' and gagmen's ridicule.[41]

The United States was, in the 1920s and 1930s, the world's largest exporter of cars (see Table 5-2). United States producers could not fill foreign demand through exports alone; Ford and General Motors found that to serve foreign markets they had to have their own assembly and manufacturing plants located abroad. By 1929, United States automobile companies had sixty-eight foreign assembly plants.[42]

Because of the obstacles to trade, United States assembly operations in the largest foreign markets soon were transformed into manufacturing facilities. These foreign barriers to trade included tariffs and taxes,

---

37. Nonetheless, the U.S. tariff did motivate Rolls Royce to manufacture cars in Springfield, Mass., between 1921 and 1929; A. W. Soutter, *The American Rolls Royce* 44, 90 (Mowbray Publishers, 1976). In 1929, a Rolls Royce executive was quoted as saying that if automobiles went on the free list, the Springfield plant would close. *U.S. Sen. Comm. on Finance, Tariff Act of 1929, Hearings*, 71st Cong., 1st Sess. (1929), p. 828. It was, however, the prospect of new tooling expenses for the Phantom II and the stock market crash that was behind the decision to discontinue production in 1929. Soutter, *American Rolls Royce*, p. 118. Assembly operations continued into the 1930s. *Ibid.* at 135–137.

38. See figures in Chandler, n. 32 *supra* at 4.

39. Alvan MacCauley, however, representing the National Automobile Chamber of Commerce and the Packard Motor Car Co., testified in 1929 that complete removal of duties might result in an "invasion of the American market by foreign made cars." *Tariff Act of 1929, Hearings*, pp. 823, 824, 840. Ford Motor Company came out, as it had for years, for free trade. *Ibid.* at 840.

40. See Reciprocal Trade Agreements Act, June 12, 1934, PL 316, in *Statutes at Large 1933–1934*, 73rd Cong., 2nd sess. (1934), p. 944.

41. G. E. Domer, "The History of the American Austin and Bantam," 14 *Automobile Quarterly* 404–429 (1964). In 1930, 8,558 Austins were sold in the United States (Sir Herbert Austin had hoped for between 50,000 and 100,000 that year); in 1931, 1,279; 1932, 3,846; 1933, 4,726; 1934, 1,300. *Ibid.* at 417, 418, 422. "Tell me, do you get into that car, or do you put it on," was a typical response. *Ibid.* at 414.

42. *Tariff Act of 1929, Hearings*, p. 822.

TABLE 5-2 Exports of New Cars and Car Chassis (in Thousands of Units)

	U.S.	Canada	U.K.	France	Italy	Germany
1929	340	65	39	39	24	5
1932	41	10	32	14	6	9
1937	229	44	78	20	26	52
1938	162	40	68	19	18	65

Source: G. Maxcy and A. Silberston, *The Motor Industry* 228 (George Allen & Unwin, 1959).

and in the 1930s, exchange restrictions along with government local purchase requirements—in short, regulatory rather than market barriers. To be sure, Europeans also rejected United States imports because of "inadequate roads, expensive fuel, and meager repair facilities."[43]

In the inter-war years, automobile makers in Canada and Europe adopted mass-production methods. Canadians followed the United States pattern and built the North American-type car. Because of the Canadian tariff, the "Canadian market" remained separated from that of the United States. Nonetheless, by 1929, 83 percent of the cars, trucks, and parts made in Canada were produced by subsidiaries of United States enterprises.[44] To obtain economies of scale, these subsidiaries exported automobiles to Australia, New Zealand, South Africa, and, in some cases, to South America.[45]

Britain had abandoned free trade in 1915 and imposed a 33 1/3 percent tariff on automobiles imported from outside the Empire.[46] At war's end, it retained this tariff; in 1919 the British Board of Trade estimated that with "the adverse exchange, freight, packing, and insurance charges," the British passenger car was protected to the equivalent of an 88 percent surcharge.[47]

The British horsepower tax shaped that nation's industry, further defining and protecting it. British car designers offered a small-bore, long-stroke engine which met the tax formula requirements and thus minimized annual taxes for the buyer.[48] These engines obtained better gas mileage than the United States-type car. With high-priced fuel in England, this gave them a further advantage there. Even though it produced in England, after 1924 Ford Motor Company fell far behind

---

43. The quotation is from W. H. Nelson, *Small Wonder, The Amazing Story of the Volkswagen* 31 (Little, Brown and Co., 1950).
44. Wilkins, n. 1 *supra* at 75.
45. From Canada, Ford exported to Commonwealth markets, while General Motors exported to Commonwealth markets and to South America.
46. Wilkins and Hill, n. 3 *supra* at 62–63.
47. *Tariff Commission Report–1921*, p. 11.
48. On the horsepower tax see *ibid.* at 142, and Maxcy and Silberston, n. 29 *supra* at 49.

Morris and Austin, which had copied United States assembly-line methods of production to make small, low-priced, low-powered units, with low costs of operation. Ford ultimately realized that if it were to sell in Britain, it could not market a North American-type vehicle, and had to undertake major design modification. Thus, in 1932, Ford introduced the Model Y, the first car specifically designed by it for a foreign market.[49]

British economists believe the horsepower tax, which imposed the special design requirements, retarded British car exports.[50] Exports were further hampered by the overvaluation of the pound, especially in the period 1925 to 1931. In short, by the 1920s, the British had adopted United States methods of mass production; government policies greatly affected engine design and, incidentally, probably served to impede exports.

French industry also imitated United States production techniques: Citroen introduced a "popular" car in 1919; by 1922, "mass-produced," "light" cars were offered by the principal French manufacturers, including Renault and Peugeot.[51] The French government set a 45 percent tariff.[52] To penetrate the French market, Austin Motor Company licensed the French production of "Rosengart" vehicles in the late 1920s.[53] By the end of 1931 the French customs duties on automobiles and parts reached more than 90 percent ad valorem.[54] Ford began manufacturing in France in 1934.[55] That same year, Simca (a successor to a Fiat dealership) started to build Fiats in France.[56] Soon the French imposed import quotas,[57] and like the British, the French market became distinct.

---

49. Wilkins and Hill, n. 3 *supra* at 241.

50. For this view, see Maxcy and Silberston, n. 29 *supra* at 49, and G. C. Allen, *British Industries* 156, 171 (5th ed., London, Longman, 1970). The argument was that Britain suffered in overseas Commonwealth markets, where the standardized, high-powered, large-engined American cars were more appealing. For the opposite view, see R. B. McKern, "The U.S. Automobile Industry in the World Market," in *Manager in the International Economy* 439 (R. Vernon, Ed., Prentice-Hall, 1972). McKern suggests that British development of light small cars with "high-efficiency" engines in response to the horsepower tax "doubtless aided British exports." This may have been true in the long run. It was not true in the short run.

51. Wilkins and Hill, n. 3 *supra* at 112.

52. *Tariff Commission Report–1921*, p. 14.

53. Domer, n. 41 *supra* at 405.

54. See *Report to the Board of Directors,* Ford SAF, Dec. 31, 1931, in Accession 606, Box 4, Ford Archives, Dearborn, Mich.

55. Wilkins and Hill, n. 3 *supra* at 248–250.

56. *Harper's Encyclopaedia*, n. 8 *supra* at 755.

57. See *letter from Maurice Dollfus to C. E. Sorensen,* Feb. 4, 1936, Accession 38, Box 32, Ford Archives. In March 1936, Dollfus was writing Sorensen (March 25, 1936 in *ibid.*):

In 1924, Adam Opel A.G., which began to make cars in Germany in 1898, resumed post–World War I operations, adopting United States mass-production methods, but making a small car. That year Opel became the leader in the German automobile industry; in 1929, General Motors instantly obtained first place in this German industry when it purchased control of Opel.[58] Tariffs, foreign exchange restrictions, and then government-imposed national content requirements made local production imperative.[59] In 1931, to remain competitive, Ford started to manufacture cars in Germany. (It had had an assembly plant there since 1926.)

At the Berlin automobile show in February 1933 the new Chancellor, Adolph Hitler, promised to reduce German automobile taxes and to start a formidable road construction program.[60] At the March automobile show the next year, Hitler was more explicit. Automobiles should not be merely for the privileged. Hitler proposed a "Volkswagen," a cheap dependable car for "millions of new purchasers," a standardized, all-German car.[61] This was a Model T concept. The car envisaged by Hitler was not actually produced until after World War II, although prototypes were made in 1938. Throughout the 1930s, therefore, General Motors Opel retained first place in the German market.[62] It is a paradox often encountered that governmental protection of *national* industry meant protection of a unit of a multinational enterprise based elsewhere.

Everywhere on the European continent in the early 1930s, tariffs and nontariff barriers blocked international trade in automobiles. "Can a manufacturing plant be made to pay when output is confined within the limited areas which national tariffs are building up?" the chief executive of the British Ford operation asked plaintively in December 1933.[63] It was a good question. In different countries in Europe, multinational corporations produced models that had no interchangeable

---

> I should mention that the fact that our present frame is American is a handicap, both from the point of view of cost and from the point of view of 'nationalization' of our product. Besides we shall probably not be permitted to import frames in 1937.

58. Wilkins and Hill, n. 3 *supra* at 138, 207.
59. *Ibid.* at 232, 233, 247.
60. In June 1931, to cover part of the serious German deficit, a heavy tax had been placed on gasoline (*E. C. Heine to F. S. Thornhill Cooper*, June 9, 1931, British Ford Archives, Langley, England). There was also a steep tax on new cars registered. On Hitler's speech see Wilkins and Hill, n. 3 *supra* at 270. Nelson, n. 43 *supra* at 29, says that Hitler in this 1933 speech proposed a popular car. The reports that we have read of the speech do not indicate this.
61. Wilkins and Hill, n. 3 *supra* at 272; *Volkischer Beobachter*, Mar. 9, 1934; *New York Times*, Mar. 9, 11, 1934. Nelson, n. 43 *supra* at 35, puts this 1934 show in January; it was in March.
62. On German car registrations, see data in Accession 507, Box 95, Ford Archives.
63. Quoted in Wilkins and Hill, n. 3 *supra* at 248.

parts. Each European nation set tariffs, taxes, and standards that provided obstacles to trade and economic integration. Each promoted its own industry. These regulations shaped and defined markets. The multinational enterprises simply conformed to them.

Vehicles produced in the United States for a mass market, where gasoline prices were relatively low and distances great, came to be totally different in design from the "small" cars sold in Europe. There, costs of operations were high; low-powered and light cars conserved gasoline; distances were not great; and automobile ownership remained limited. The Canadian market—although it had the same products as that of the United States—could not benefit from integration with the United States market because a tariff "protected" the inefficiencies caused by the absence of scale production by United States subsidiaries in Canada. Table 5-3 indicates the costs of direct annual taxes, taxes on fuel, and compulsory insurance of a comparable car traveling a comparable number of miles per year in the immediate pre–World War II period. It shows vividly that government-mandated costs of operating a vehicle in the United States and Canada were far below those in Europe.

Throughout Europe the railroad and the bicycle were more common forms of transportation than the passenger car. In 1939, in the United States, 1-in-5 persons had a car (roughly the same as in 1929); in Canada about 1-in-9; in France 1-in-20; in Great Britain 1-in-23; and in Germany, 1-in-56.[64] Mass-production techniques had arrived in Europe in the interwar years, but mass consumption had not.

Elsewhere around the world, in Latin America, Asia, and South Africa, assembly plants were built by Ford and General Motors. Automobile production was started in the Soviet Union (with Ford's technical assistance). In Australia and Japan, the foundations for car manufacturing were established.

During World War I, the Australian government had prohibited the import of car bodies, to save shipping space. Australians began to manufacture car bodies, and in the post–World War I years, the Australian government protected the new industry with a high tariff. From 1925, Ford assembled cars and manufactured bodies in Australia.[65] General Motors in 1926 started assembly in Australia and in 1931 acquired Holden Motor Body Builders Ltd. In 1928, three-quarters of all automobile registrations in Australia were North American-type cars and every 1-in-14 persons had a car, a ratio bettered only by the United States, Canada, and New Zealand.[66]

In Japan, Ford and General Motors began assembling cars in 1925 and 1926, respectively. In 1930, only 458 motor vehicles were manufac-

---

64. Based on figures in Rostow, n. 28 *supra* at 171.
65. Wilkins and Hill, n. 3 *supra* at 124–128.
66. U.S. Dep't of Commerce, Bureau of Foreign and Domestic Commerce, *The Automotive Market of Australia* 1–2 (Wash., 1929).

TABLE 5-3 Annual Direct Taxes, Taxes on Fuel, Compulsory Insurance Costs—1939

North America	Index (U.S. = 100)	Europe	Index (U.S. = 100)
U.S.	100	U.K.	400
Canada	85	France	292
		Germany	231

Source: Society of Motor Mfrs. and Traders, *The Motor Industry of Great Britain 1939* 141, based on a 1,500 cc car, traveling 8,000 miles per year.

tured in that nation, all by Japanese producers. Imports (mainly those of Ford and General Motors) dominated the market. During the 1930s, Japanese manufacturing emerged with Nissan and Toyota. American enterprises wanted to manufacture in Japan, too, but Japanese government regulations effectively barred the United States firms from doing so.[67]

In summary, by the eve of World War II, North America had mass production *and* mass consumption of automobiles. In 1937, despite the spread of automobile manufacturing, the United States still accounted for 76 percent of world motor vehicle output.[68] Europeans had imitated United States production techniques, and devised distinctive products suitable for national market conditions (in many cases determined by government regulation), but their home markets remained small and Europe still did not have mass consumption of passenger cars. Outside of Europe and North America, a number of countries had automobile assembly plants; Australia and Japan had the rudiments of manufacturing, fostered by national government policies.

1945 to 1970

The manufacture of civilian automobiles virtually ceased worldwide during World War II. In its aftermath, major alterations in passenger car markets took place as world trade and investment resumed and as a new world economy was established with the dollar as the key currency. Change occurred in a world where United States international economic policy pressed for a "free market oriented trade and investment system."[69]

---

67. M. Wilkins, "The Role of U.S. Business," in *Pearl Harbor as History, Japanese-American Relations 1931–1941* 360–361 (D. Borg and S. Okamoto, Eds., Columbia Univ. Press, 1973); and M. Wilkins, "American-Japanese Direct Foreign Investment Relationships 1930–1952," 1978 typescript, publication forthcoming.
68. *FTC Report*, p. 36.
69. S. D. Cohen, *The Making of United States International Economic Policy* 29 (Praeger, 1977).

Europe was plagued by a severe dollar shortage. Governments there would not allow scarce dollar resources to be spent on automotive imports from the United States. The British government set an export target of one-half the cars produced in that country; when this was met, the target was raised to two-thirds.[70] In 1947, the British government revised its prewar horsepower tax, and the next year introduced a new automotive tax structure designed specifically so as not to impede British exports.[71] The 1949 devaluation of the pound provided a further impetus to British car sales overseas. That year, the United Kingdom replaced the United States as first in world exports of new cars.[72] By 1950, only 25 percent of the cars made in England were sold in the domestic market. The leader in British industry, and British exports, was paradoxically Ford of England, which exported to the world, including the United States.[73]

The British automobile industry became one of that nation's principal postwar growth industries.[74] In 1952, the two leading British-owned producers, Austin and Nuffield, merged to form the giant British Motor Corporation, after further mergers to become British Leyland (1968). From 1949 through 1955, British industry continued to lead the world in car exports,[75] spurred on by government pressures. High purchase taxes notwithstanding, domestic consumption of automobiles also rose to new records.[76]

On the continent, recovery from the wartime disaster was slower. The French government nationalized the largest enterprise, Renault. Fiat resumed its leadership in Italian production. And both Renault and Fiat expanded internationally, establishing new foreign subsidiaries.[77]

After the war, German industry lay in ruins; but it was not by any means certain that the Allied powers would permit industrial recovery. Nevertheless, the plant the Germans had built for Volkswagen, situated in the British-occupied zone, was in limited production by 1945, using its prewar designs.[78] Henry Ford II liked the idea of acquiring the Volkswagen company, but the idea of Ford ownership died when the complexities of ownership and the liabilities of that company became apparent—some 337,000 Germans had made payments on cars they had not received[79]—and when one senior Ford executive sneered, "You call

---

70. Wilkins and Hill, n. 3 *supra* at 364.
71. Allen, n. 50 *supra* at 171–172.
72. Maxcy and Silberston, n. 29 *supra* at 17, 228.
73. Wilkins and Hill, n. 3 *supra* at 363, 365, 381, 382.
74. Allen, n. 50 *supra* at 158.
75. Maxcy and Silberston, n. 29 *supra* at 228.
76. Allen, n. 50 *supra* at 157.
77. Franko, n. 1 *supra* at 103.
78. Nelson, n. 43 *supra* at 332.
79. Wilkins and Hill, n. 3 *supra* at 368; Nelson, n. 43 *supra* at 3–4.

that a car?" Even the German Heinz Nordhoff, whom the occupying forces put in charge of the plant late in 1947, initially had only disdain for the bug-like creation.[80]

Nordhoff's baptism in the automobile industry had been with General Motors' Opel. Using his experience with "American practices," Nordhoff set about improving the product, reducing the noise, coping with "flimsy" construction, improving the engine, and going beyond basic transportation to provide more comfort and attractiveness with improvements in upholstery and paint work. Drawing on his experience with the General Motors subsidiary, Nordhoff insisted on developing a marketing and service organization to spur Volkswagen sales. When Volkswagen started to export to the United States in the 1950s, its representatives were warned that British and other imports had entered the United States market, yet failed to sustain their momentum due to inadequate distribution organizations.[81] Volkswagen did not repeat their mistake. In 1956 German car output and exports exceeded that of the British, and German automobile exports became the largest in the world;[82] by 1961, Volkswagen's foreign sales alone surpassed total British car exports.[83]

How much did the regulatory environment on the European continent influence the expanding automobile industry? Until 1959, the French protected their industry with high tariff walls and maintained a quota on imported cars.[84] Professor Louis T. Wells suggests that through its ownership of Renault, the French state was able to encourage exports, influence product size in the direction of smaller units, affect plant location, restrain price increases, and set a pattern for wage settlements.[85] Until 1961, Volkswagen was entirely state-owned, but its management seems to have been insulated from state intervention. Of course this became especially true after 1961, when state ownership dropped to 40 percent.[86] In the 1930s Volkswagen had been under state ownership, receiving state subsidies and endorsement. The influence of the regulatory environment in the postwar period seems more distant.

Unquestionably, the formation of the European Economic Community in 1957 had more impact on the automobile industry in Europe than any other single governmental action. The Treaty of Rome provided for a Common Market, made up of six nations: Belgium, Netherlands, Luxembourg, Germany, France, and Italy. By 1968, free trade in

---

80. Nelson, n. 43 *supra* at 117, 121.
81. *Ibid.* at 140–147, 172, 174.
82. Maxcy and Silberston, n. 29 *supra* at 223, 227, 228.
83. Compare Nelson, n. 43 *supra* at 332, and Allen, n. 50 *supra* at 178.
84. Wells, "Automobiles," n. 18 *supra* at 234.
85. *Ibid.* at 238–239.
86. Nelson, n. 43 *supra passim* and Wells, "Automobiles," n. 18 *supra* at 239–241.

goods within the European Economic Community had been achieved, while a common external tariff of 17.6 percent protected passenger car producers inside the 6-country market.[87] The effects were extraordinary. In 1958, the first year of the Common Market, France imported from other European Economic Community countries 1 percent of the cars sold there, Italy 2 percent, and Germany 7 percent. In 1970, French imports from other European Economic Community nations had risen to 16 percent; Italian European Economic Community imports were 28 percent, and German 25 percent of the domestic market. Free trade over borders within the European Economic Community meant that Europe was becoming an increasingly integrated market,[88] and most important, that producers could take advantage of economies of scale. The return to convertible currency throughout most of Europe by 1959 also contributed to growing international trade. So, too, rising European affluence in the 1960s added purchasing power.

In the late 1950s, and especially in the 1960s, for the first time western Europe entered an age of mass consumption of automobiles. Increasingly, car company executives in Europe considered marketing problems and established sales and service networks. As automobiles were designed to meet mass market needs, Europeans concentrated on small, low-priced units, with low costs of operation and maintenance. Quality became important. Part of these product developments were influenced by economic concerns, such as the high cost of gasoline in Europe; part by road conditions; and part by the regulatory environment. European gasoline taxes continued to be higher than American; progressive registration fees on vehicles, according to engine capacity, influenced car size and weight, as well as engine design. In Germany, particularly, the government's continued commitment to building *autobahns* meant the need for passenger cars that could cruise at high speed, yet were economical on fuel use.[89] The economic, geographical, and regulatory environment that influenced product design protected European producers from United States import competition long after the dollar shortage had turned into a dollar glut. American multinational corporations could, however, and did, invest within the European Economic Community, gain the advantages of the large protected market, manufacture appropriate products, and remain fully competitive.[90] Ford, General Motors, and Chrysler all invested heavily in manufacturing facilities within the European Economic Community.[91]

---

87. The 17.6 percent went into effect July 1, 1968. Data from EEC Washington office.
88. Wells, "Automobiles," n. 18 *supra* at 246.
89. McKern, n. 50 *supra* at 445, 447; Motor Vehicle Mfrs. Ass'n, *1972 Automobile Facts and Figures*, p. 67.
90. Wilkins, n. 1 *supra* at 404.
91. General Motors and Ford expanded their prewar German manufacturing. Ford sold its French plants to Simca; Chrysler by 1963 had obtained control of Simca.

In the 1950s, cars produced in England and on the European continent—even by multinational corporations—had no interchangeable parts. In the 1960s, multinational enterprises recognized that if output in Europe were to benefit from economies of scale and specialization, interchangeability was obviously desirable. Moreover, if Britain were to join the Common Market, as it first sought to do in 1961, standardization and interchangeability of parts would be essential. In 1968, European automobile production for the first time since the early years of the century exceeded United States output.[92]

In the 1950s and 1960s automobile production in the United States remained the highest of any *single* nation in the world. This country had the world's greatest domestic market. In the immediate postwar period, both General Motors and Ford considered introducing a light car, but surveys indicated that most Americans wanted larger automobiles and were prepared to pay for them.[93] With the baby boom and the expanding American family, with low-cost gasoline (despite the United States switch from net oil exporter to importer), with vast improvements in the American highway system, with new affluence in the 1950s, American consumers wanted big, showy, powerful cars—and United States automobile makers responded accordingly. Table 5-4 shows the more than doubling in horsepower of American car engines between 1950 and 1957 (from 111 to 237 horsepower). The 1955 Chevrolet was 195 inches long; the 1958 model extended 209 inches.[94] The lengthening (and also the widening) of American cars was general.

As American cars became more comfortable, roomy, powerful, and expensive, they became less competitive in world markets, and, as noted, in 1949 British car exports exceeded American and, in 1956, German foreign sales overtook the British. This did not mean that United States companies gave up foreign markets. Until 1968, the United States was a net exporter in the category of motor vehicles, parts, and engines. Much more important, however, were the huge investments American companies made abroad to provide appropriate automobiles for foreign markets. United States enterprises participated in the growing world markets primarily through direct investments rather than United States exports. In the 1960s as the United States began to show serious balance of payments deficits and as United States Government restrictions were placed on foreign investment outflows, United States corporations were able to continue to expand outside the United States by reinvesting profits and borrowing abroad.[95]

While most American consumers liked the output of Detroit, certain buyers of cars in the United States did not want large automobiles. In

---

92. Motor Vehicle Mfrs. Ass'n, *Facts and Figures 1977*, p. 18 [hereinafter, MVMA, *Facts and Figures*].
93. Nevins and Hill, *Ford: Decline and Rebirth*, n. 32 *supra* at 333.
94. L. J. White, *The Automobile Industry Since 1945* 182 (Harvard Univ. Press, 1971).
95. Wilkins, n. 1 *supra* at 335–336.

TABLE 5-4 Average Horsepower U.S. Automobile Engines 1950–1968[a]

Year	Horsepower
1968	249.0
1967	239.4
1966	232.9
1965	220.3
1964	206.3
1963	195.7
1962	182.9
1961	175.1
1960	188.2
1959	214.2
1958	227.3
1957	236.7
1956	206.8
1955	173.1
1954	150.8
1953	133.0
1952	122.1
1951	116.2
1950	110.9

[a] Weighted average based on estimated percentage of production for each model; for new automobiles only.
Source: American Petroleum Inst., *Petroleum Facts and Figures, 1971,* 326.

the late 1950s, they turned to imports. In 1957, the number of passenger cars imported into the United States exceeded the number exported (see Appendix A *infra*). By 1959, automobile imports, which in 1957 represented a mere 3.5 percent of the United States market, surged to 10.2 percent. Moreover, in 1959, American Motors' Rambler—an economy car—captured 6 percent of the United States market.[96] Among the imports in 1959 were the so-called "captives" (products produced by foreign subsidiaries of United States firms). These cars had been produced for sale abroad. In an emergency, they could fill United States producers' needs at home. Thus, General Motors brought in Opels and Vauxhalls; Ford imported its English Anglia and German Taunus. The rise in imports into the United States coincided with the first drop (in 1956) in the United States tariff since 1934; the tariff declined from 10 percent to 9.5 percent ad valorem—hardly enough to make a significant economic difference (but perhaps a psychological boost to the importer).

Ford, General Motors, and Chrysler responded to the new American demand for economy cars with domestically produced "compact" units.

---

96. White, n. 94 *supra* at 294.

Although they were not small in European terms, they were shorter and narrower than the standard American models. For a limited time, they cut sharply into imported car sales.[97] United States companies did not need to import "captives" when they had their own more suitable United States offerings; foreign producers such as Renault and Fiat which had not built up sales and service organizations in the United States, could not meet the new domestic competition.[98] Volkswagen's rise in sales also slowed.[99]

Then, in response to domestic demand during the 1960s, American cars once more grew in size and power. Gasoline remained cheap in the United States, and the American public still desired the larger, more powerful cars. Innovations in United States industry were in comfort and styling. Indeed, as United States incomes rose, the purchase of new cars represented an even smaller portion of the American family budget; Americans could afford the big car.[100]

Once more, some American buyers were not satisfied with United States products and imports resumed their upward climb, until 1968 when, for the first time since 1906, the dollar value of United States imports of motor vehicles, parts, and engines exceeded the dollar value of such United States exports (see Appendix B *infra* for the actual figures). In 1906, when the dollar value of car imports into the United States had exceeded exports, imports had been the expensive cars; sixty-two years later the imports were primarily economy cars. In 1968, no producer in the United States made a new car that had a manufacturer's suggested list price below $1,800; fully 17 different models of imported cars sold at port-of-entry for under $1,800.[101]

Meanwhile, the United States' automobile tariff had continued to drop, reaching a mere 5.5 percent in 1968.[102] In 1965, the United States and Canada signed the Canadian Automobile Agreement, which removed tariff duties that impeded trade between the two countries in specified motor vehicles and original equipment automotive parts. Its goal was to provide conditions "in which market forces may operate effectively to attain the most economic pattern of investment, production, and trade."[103] The agreement provided the basis for an integrated North American automobile market.

---

97. Appendix A *infra* reflects the rise of imports 1950–1959 and their decline 1960–1961.
98. White, n. 94 *supra* at 185.
99. Based on incremental increase in Volkswagen registrations, given in Nelson, n. 43 *supra* at 333.
100. MVMA, *Facts and Figures 1972*, p. 41.
101. *The Imported Automobile Industry* 44 (Harbridge House, 1976).
102. Tariff schedule from International Trade Comm'n, Wash., D.C.
103. U.S. Sen. Comm. on Finance, *Canadian Automobile Agreement—Eleventh Annual Report* (Wash. 1977), gives good details on the pact and includes a copy of the agreement. Quotation is from p. 3.

Under the Canadian Automobile Agreement, as Table 5-5 and Figure 5-1 indicate, bilateral commerce expanded rapidly. Indeed, comparing Table 5-5 and Appendix B, *infra* one sees that in 1970, 80 percent of American motor vehicle, parts, and engine exports were to Canada and 52 percent of United States imports were from Canada. After 1965, United States passenger car imports from Canada exceeded exports. Although multinational companies refer to a "North American-type car," government regulations continued to prevent the full integration of the United States and Canadian markets.[104]

In the 1960s, because of low United States tariffs and the lower costs of production in Europe, and because of product differentiation, European car makers did not need to invest in manufacturing or even assembly in the United States to reach this market. Companies such as Volkswagen and Daimler-Benz, however, did invest in developing marketing organizations. Volkswagen had done so from scratch, since the mid–1950s.[105] Daimler-Benz had started using the Studebaker-Packard network. (Mercedes-Benz Sales Corporation, Inc., was a subsidiary of the Studebaker Packard Corporation.)[106] In 1965, after Studebaker decided to stop United States production, Mercedes-Benz of North America Inc. was formed to take over the Studebaker-Packard dealer organization.[107]

The United States share of world automobile production declined from about 75 percent in 1950 to 30 percent in 1970.[108] The United States "share" in these figures excludes cars that subsidiaries of United States multinational enterprises produced abroad. The United States share dropped not only because of the growth of European and Canadian automobile manufacture, but because of worldwide industrialization. Japan and Australia developed full-scale automobile manufacturing. Countries that had had prewar assembly operations, among them Spain, Brazil, and Argentina, started to manufacture automobiles. Nations that had never had assembly plants now insisted upon them.[109]

As the United States, Canada, and Western European nations low-

---

104. Duty-free import privileges in Canada (but *not* in the United States) were limited to vehicle manufacturers; individual Canadians who imported U.S.-made cars had to pay a 15 percent ad valorem tariff. The Canadian regulations have resulted in the persistence of higher car prices in Canada than in the United States.
105. Nelson, n. 43 *supra* at 8–10.
106. Schildberger, n. 19 *supra* at 222.
107. Data on the takeover from W. R. Stinnette, Mercedes-Benz of North America, Jacksonville, Fla., Aug. 29, 1975. Studebaker had about 1,200 dealers; Mercedes-Benz terminated all except 300. White, n. 94 *supra* at 17, indicates Studebaker announced it would stop U.S. production in March 1966.
108. MVMA, *Facts and Figures 1972*, p. 66.
109. Automobile Mfrs. Ass'n, *1971 Automobile Facts and Figures*, pp. 12–13 (world production and assembly).

TABLE 5-5 United States–Canada Trade in Automotive Products, 1964; 1970–76 U.S. Imports–Canadian Imports (Millions of U.S. Dollars)

	1964	1970	1971	1972	1973	1974	1975	1976[1]
U.S. exports[2]								
Cars	34	631	985	1,075	1,439	1,657	2,142	2,354
Trucks	23	263	334	504	643	916	922	985
Parts	577	2,019	2,448	2,866	3,552	3,980	4,409	5,550
Subtotal	634	2,913	3,767	4,445	5,634	6,554	7,472	8,889
Tires and tubes	6	23	36	51	92	223	170	116
Total exports	640	2,936	3,803	4,496	5,726	6,777	7,643	9,005
U.S. imports								
Cars	18	1,474	1,924	2,065	2,272	2,595	2,809	3,477
Trucks	4	564	587	713	789	887	917	1,363
Parts	49	1,080	1,481	1,795	2,172	1,997	2,008	2,983
Subtotal	71	3,118	3,992	4,573	5,233	5,479	5,734	7,823
Tires and tubes	5	14	8	22	68	65	67	166
Total imports	76	3,123	4,000	4,595	5,301	5,544	5,801	7,989
Net balance	+563	−196	−197	−99	+426	+1,233	+1,842	+1,016

[1] Preliminary.

[2] Canadian import data. Parts exports (Canadian imports) adjusted to exclude tooling charges in millions of U.S. dollars as follows: 1970–$93; 1971–$80; 1972–$85; 1973–$68; 1974–$188; 1975–$110; 1976–$43.

Note: Data exclude U.S.–Canadian trade in materials for use in the manufacture of automotive parts.

Data are adjusted to reflect transaction values for vehicles.

$1.00 Canadian = $0.925 U.S., 1964; $0.958 U.S., 1970; $0.990 U.S., 1971; $1.009 U.S., 1972; $0.9997 U.S., 1973; $1.02246 U.S., 1974; $.984001, U.S. 1975; $101.41, U.S. 1976.

Source: U.S. Sen. Comm. on Finance, *Canadian Automobile Agreement*, 95th Cong., 1st Sess. (1977), 13.

FIGURE 5-1 United States–Canada trade in automotive products 1965–76

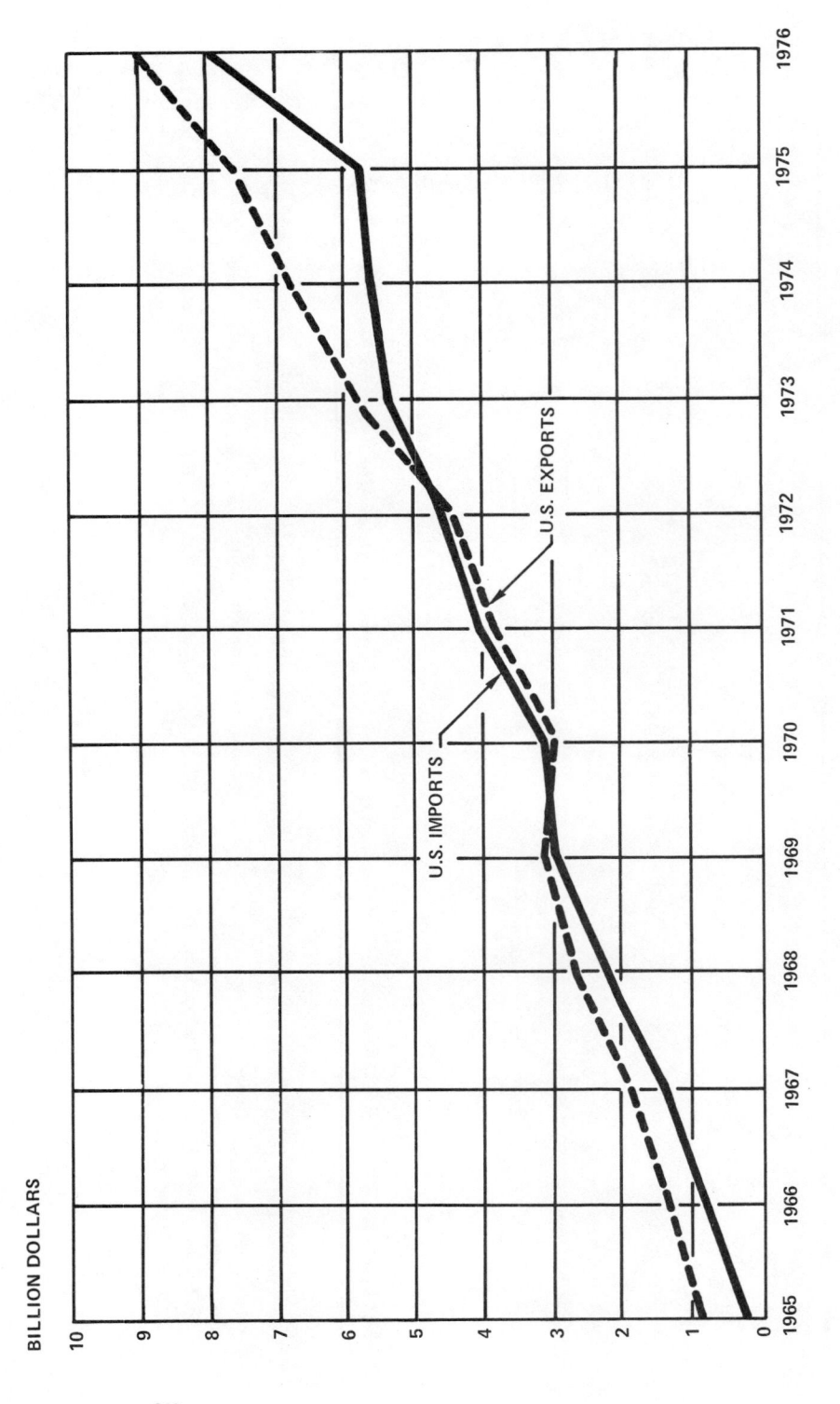

Source: U.S. Senate, Committee on Finance, *Canadian Automobile Agreement*, 95th Cong., 1st Sess. (1977), 14.

ered tariff barriers, governments elsewhere imposed customs duties and other discriminatory measures to protect and encourage national industries. Governments in countries with infant industries pressed for local content in vehicles; import and exchange quotas became common. Around the world, subsidiaries, affiliates, and licensees of large American and European multinational corporations participated in the spread of industrialization and competed in numerous national markets.

Thus, investments in automobile manufacture and assembly reflected and contributed to worldwide economic development. Host government regulations provided the conditions for the creation of new "national" automobile manufacturing and assembling industries. Government was most in evidence in areas of new industrialization. Where industries were well established, tariffs and trade restrictions were reduced.

Table 5-6 indicates the population per car in selected countries. By 1970, western Europe had reached the level of automobile ownership prevailing in the United States in 1929; Japan was above the level of Australia, but below that of Canada in 1929; the major countries in Latin America had roughly the same ratio of persons per car as did western European countries in 1939. Elsewhere worldwide, the ratio of persons to car ownership was far higher—but the automobile was, mainly through the activities of United States and European multinational companies, becoming increasingly ubiquitous.

RECENT TIMES: 1968 TO 1978

The last decade has seen an economically more integrated world automobile industry than ever in history. Manufacturing facilities proliferate. There has been a phenomenal development of Japanese automobile manufacturing. The United States market has become wide open to competition from abroad. Multinational automobile enterprises have expanded in size and scope, and new ones have joined their ranks. The period has seen a transformed world economy: The strength of the yen

TABLE 5-6 Population Per Car in 1970

United States	2	Argentina	16
Canada	3	Venezuela	17
Australia	3	Mexico	41
New Zealand	3	Brazil	43
West Germany	4	Chile	56
France	4	Iran	105
United Kingdom	5	Indonesia	508
Italy	5	Nigeria	817
Japan	12	India	902

Source: MVMA, *Facts and Figures 1972*, 28–29.

and the mark contrasts with the dollar's new weakness; the "oil crisis" has influenced the international automobile industry; government agencies provide new standards on pollution, safety, and fuel efficiency; and, once again, the postwar goals of a liberal trading system seem vulnerable to new protectionism.

The economic integration of the world automobile industry has been encouraged by the product offerings of multinational corporations that have moved away from cars, and more particularly from parts, designed for narrowly circumscribed home markets. In 1972, the European Economic Community's external tariff on passenger cars was reduced to 11 percent.[110] The next year the European Economic Community was enlarged to nine nations with the entry of the United Kingdom, Denmark, and Ireland. The potential for transnational sources of supplies and markets has grown. Even countries in Europe outside the Common Market, Spain for example, can be involved in an integrated market. Ford's Fiesta, introduced in September 1976, is properly called a European car; it is a product of no single country.

Britain's automobile makers have been pummeled by the new competition from continental imports in the British market. The largest enterprise in England, British Leyland, (now BL Ltd.), never developed an effective marketing organization.[111] In 1975, this ailing giant became government owned.[112] Already, by 1968 to 1970, the majority of the "British" passenger car producers were owned by United States multinational firms.[113] British industry has become integrated into world markets, first through United States and now through European multinational corporate action. Indeed, the August 1978 announcement that Peugeot-Citroen (itself a merger of two large French manufacturers)[114] planned to acquire not only Chrysler's British assets (in the former British Rootes Group), but its French ones (in Simca) and its Spanish facilities, in exchange for $230 million in cash and a 15 percent interest in Peugeot-Citroen, represents a new and impressive integration of the European automobile industry. The plan demonstrates the transnational character of the modern automobile industry. Peugeot-Citroen will become Europe's largest automobile company. Chrysler declared that it would participate actively in Peugeot-Citroen through its membership on the Board of Directors and "at other levels."[115] In Europe, also, Fiat is rationalizing production, as it reported in April 1978, "to

---

110. Data from EEC office, Wash., D.C.
111. D. F. Channon, *The Strategy and Structure of British Enterprise* 109 (Harvard Univ., 1973).
112. *Economist*, Aug. 16, 1975, p. 71.
113. Channon, n. 111 *supra* at 105–109.
114. On the Peugeot-Citroen Merger of 1976, see excellent article in *New York Times*, June 5, 1977.
115. Details in *Wall Street Journal*, Aug. 11, 1978.

reinforce the oneness of the European market both internally and internationally in order to obtain economies of scale somewhat closer to those enjoyed by [its] larger extra-European competitors."[116]

The integration of North American markets has also accelerated. In 1965, in connection with the Canadian Automobile Agreement, subsidiaries of United States enterprises in Canada gave the Canadian government "Letters of Undertaking to increase Canadian value added." When signed, the letters had the tacit approval of the United States Government. As our exports to Canada dropped below imports from Canada in 1970, the United States Government withdrew its tacit approval of the Letters of Undertaking; in 1977, the United States Government stated that the letters were not "valid instruments."[117] The consequences of the 1965 Agreement have been described as a "classic case of the substitution of foreign for domestic investment induced by tariff reduction."[118] Even though the dollar value of United States automotive exports to Canada has exceeded imports since 1973, the United States Government has been far from content with the American automobile makers' (actually their subsidiaries') contribution to Canada's efforts to build its national industry. This discontent has grown recently. Assistant Secretary of Treasury C. Fred Bergsten in August 1978 strongly condemned Canadian "subsidies" to lure United States and other automakers to locate plants in Canada. His remarks were provoked by that nation's requirement that Canadian duty reductions on United States-made Volkswagens were "conditioned on larger purchases of Canadian auto parts by Volkswagen plants throughout the world."[119]

The present-day economic integration of the automobile industry belies national identifications. The integration is not only in evidence in Europe and North America; indeed, it has been reported recently that General Motors' Asian subsidiaries were deciding whether to buy transmissions from a General Motors facility in the Philippines or from alternative company sources in the United States or Europe.[120] The decision implies an interchangeability of the transmissions that was impossible in earlier years.[121]

Worldwide in the 1970s, in industrial countries, and even more in developing ones, host governments have pressured enterprises to provide employment by raising local production and exporting. Brazil and

---

116. Fiat, *Reports of the Board of Directors 1977* 8 (Apr. 1978).

117. *Canadian Automobile Agreement*, p. 5.

118. C. F. Bergsten, T. Horst, and T. H. Moran, *American Multinationals and American Interests* 88 (Brookings Inst., 1978).

119. *Statement by C. Fred Bergsten before U.S. H. of Rep. Subcomm. on Int'l Trade, Investment, and Monetary Policy* (Aug. 1, 1978).

120. Bergsten et. al, n. 118 *supra* at 384.

121. For future of economic integration see "The Auto Clash Goes Global," *Dun's Review*, Apr. 1978, pp. 49–53.

Mexico, for example, have imposed export requirements. Multinational corporations have responded, lest they lose their competitive positions in those markets.[122] If companies export parts, there has to be interchangeability. Paradoxically, host government regulations work both for and against economic integration. The government regulations that require export promote it; those that press for local content and protection of local industry restrict it. Often the regulations are one and the same.

Worldwide, multinational companies have built new plants and created new "national" industries. Spain is developing a major automobile industry. Fiat, for example, fears competition in Western Europe from Eastern Europe and from developing countries; yet along with other multinationals Fiat has contributed to the emergence of these very same new automobile industries. Fiat licenses production by the Polish FSO and FSM and by the Yugoslav Z.C.Z. It produces cars in Argentina and Brazil.[123] Table 5-7 indicates passenger car production by country in 1977 and the population per car registered in 1976. It shows the spread of both production and consumption of passenger cars.

Nowhere has this automotive growth been greater than in Japan.[124] Japan is now second only to the United States in automobile production and first in passenger car exports. The Japanese domestic market was protected from outside competition in the 1950s and 1960s by tariff and nontariff barriers; government policy in Japan blocked foreign multinational enterprises from scaling the barriers to trade and gaining protection behind the walls.[125] Like their European counterparts, Japanese producers built cars in a country where all the plant and equipment was of postwar vintage and thus incorporated the latest technology. Gasoline was high priced and gasoline taxes far exceeded those in the United States. The result was that most Japanese-made cars were small, light, and fuel efficient. Throughout the postwar years, the Japanese

---

122. The Brazilian export program is voluntary, but linked with local content requirements; there are major advantages to the manufacturer that participates. In Mexico, 60 percent of the value of imported production material must be compensated for by exports of equal value; in 1979, the figure increases to 100 percent. Data from U.S. Dep't of Commerce, Sept. 1978. See Bergsten et. al, n. 118 *supra* at 422–423, for some of the implications. Note the measures of Canada toward Volkswagen are not unlike those of less developed countries.

123. Fiat, n. 116 *supra* at 24.

124. M. Y. Yoshino, *Japan's Multinational Enterprises* 65 (Harvard Univ. Press, 1976), indicates the rise in production from 100,000 units (1951) to 5 million (1970). In 1977, Japan produced 5.4 million passenger cars per year. MVMA, *Motor Vehicle Facts & Figures '78*, p. 17, for 1977 figure.

125. In the 1950s, Japanese producers did obtain *licenses* to assemble British and French models (those of Austin, Rootes, and Renault) and thus gained experience with small cars. See Y. Tsurumi, *The Japanese are Coming* 23 (Ballinger, 1976).

TABLE 5-7 Passenger Car Production—1977 in 000s of units (In Parentheses Is Population per Car Registered in 1976)

United States	9214 (2)	Brazil	464 (18)
Japan	5431 (6)	Australia	369 (3)
West Germany	3790 (3)	Belgium	300 (4)
France	3092 (3)	Poland	280 (27)
Italy	1440 (4)	Sweden	235 (3)
United Kingdom	1328 (4)	Yugoslavia	231 (13)
USSR	1280 (86)	Mexico	188 (25)
Canada	1162 (2)	East Germany	170 (8)
Spain	989 (7)	Argentina	168 (9)

Source: MVMA, Facts and Figures 1978, 17, 28–31.

have sought to dispel their prewar image of producing cheap and shoddy merchandise. Government regulations have insisted on quality. Owing to the expansion of automobile traffic in Japan, the Japanese government in the 1970s also introduced high standards of emission control.[126]

As noted, foreign multinationals were never in the post–World War II years able to penetrate the Japanese domestic passenger car market. The recent decline in the Japanese tariff has made no difference. The entrenched domestic industry serves as an effective barrier to entry. Moreover, Japanese automotive standards provide a further obstacle to imports. In March 1978, Japan was the first nation to eliminate its tariff on passenger cars since Britain abandoned free trade in 1915. Its zero tariff compares with the 3 percent United States and the 11 percent European Economic Community customs tariff. The dropping of the Japanese automobile tariff, along with the recent steep rise in the value of the yen, has signaled an increase in foreign car sales in Japan. In no way, however, has there been a sizable foreign car entry.[127]

If United States and European multinational corporations failed to penetrate the Japanese market, this did not mean that the phenomenon of multinational enterprise was absent. Quite the contrary, Japanese-headquartered multinational business emerged. Japanese companies first produced for their domestic market. Then, they exported and invested in a marketing organizations abroad to sustain their exports. In the late 1950s, Japanese cars began to appear on the United States market, and in the 1960s Japanese firms in the United States started to integrate vertically, establishing sales and service outlets. Like Volkswagen, and like their American competitors, Japanese companies

---

126. Harbridge House, Boston, Massachusetts, has conducted an excellent research study for the U.S. Office of Technology Assessment. The report has fine data on air pollution regulations in Japan. Henceforth, I will cite this initial draft of the unpublished Harbridge House study as *Harbridge House Study 1977*.

127. *Wall Street Journal*, Aug. 7, 1978.

recognized it was impossible to reach the United States market or any foreign market without a distribution and a service network. After 1968, Japanese car sales in the United States mounted rapidly. In 1974, in units, and in 1975, in dollars, Japanese passenger car imports in the United States surpassed those from West Germany ($1.7 billion v. $1.5 billion in 1975). In 1975, Toyota sold 284,000 cars in the United States, compared with Volkswagen's 268,000. That year, Japan became the world's largest exporter of passenger cars. In 1976, both Toyota and Datsun were outselling Volkswagen in the United States, and the dollar value of Japanese imports of passenger cars in the United States was $2.8 billion, compared with the German total of $1.6 billion.[128]

The opening of the United States market to such imports has been an important feature of the last decade. For the first time since the exceptional year 1959, in 1968, automobiles from abroad (excluding those from Canada) obtained more than 10 percent of the United States market. Late in 1968, United States manufacturers announced they would build "subcompact" cars, which they introduced in 1970 to compete with the imports. A second generation of United States-made subcompacts appeared in 1974 to 1975.[129] By 1977 to 1978, United States industry was again heralding "new generations of fuel-thrifty automobiles."[130] Nonetheless, imports have exceeded 10 percent of United States retail sales in *every* year since 1968, reaching as high as 18.6 in 1977 (see Appendix A *infra*).

The United States automobile tariff has further declined from 5 percent in 1969 to 3 percent in 1972.[131] In August 1971 came the "Nixon shock," when the dollar was devalued. The dollar was devalued again in 1973 and left to float. But it sank. All other things being equal, the effect of the decline in the dollar should have resulted in a reduction in imports, for imports became more expensive vis-à-vis domestic products. Currency declines are equivalent to tariff increases. Other things were not equal, however. In 1973 to 1974, the Organization of Petroleum Exporting Countries (OPEC) hiked the price of oil fourfold. There was also the Arab oil embargo. In 1974, the United States economy moved into a recession. Since automobile imports—despite their rising prices—remained cheaper in initial cost and more economical to operate, Americans continued to buy imports. With the recession in 1975,

---

128. Figures from MVMA, *Facts and Figures 1975*, p. 61, and *ibid.* 1977, p. 81. See *Automotive News 1977*, p. 70 (on level of imports by make). In 1976, the number of Japanese car imports (1.1 million) exceeded the number of Canadian car imports (825,000), although the dollar total of U.S. imports from Canada was still higher than from Japan. MVMA, *Facts and Figures 1978*, p. 81.
129. Harbridge House, n. 101 *supra* at 34, 36.
130. MVMA, *Facts and Figures 1978*, p. 2.
131. Data from International Trade Comm'n, Wash. D.C.

consumers wanted smaller cars, and imports from Japan and Europe obtained a then-record 18.4 percent of the American market.

Among the 1974 to 1975 American subcompacts produced in response to these events were Ford's Pinto MPG, with a 34-mile-per-gallon rating on the EPA highway test and the Chevrolet Chevette, which was 400 pounds lighter than General Motors' earlier subcompact, the Vega. General Motors had already produced versions of this car in Germany, Brazil, and Australia.[132]

Even with the decline in value of the dollar, in 1975 the median price at port of entry of imports from Japan and Europe was $3,000; the median manufacturers' suggested retail price for domestic cars was $4,200.[133] By 1975, imports and domestic subcompacts and compacts obtained a staggering 53 percent of the United States market.[134]

The dollar declined in value against other major currencies from 1976 to 1978; as a consequence, prices of United States imports rose; inflation and spiraling costs in Europe and Japan also contributed to higher prices for imports into the United States. Slowly, sales of imports came to be affected by the realignment in currency values. The gap between the price of domestic cars and of imports narrowed.

In 1973, Volvo decided to build an assembly plant in Virginia to reach the United States market; in 1977, however, it postponed its plant in view of shrinking sales. Volvo found the competition with home-built American automobiles, captive imports, and Japanese products too rigorous.[135] In 1976, Volkswagen concluded that it had to manufacture its "Rabbit" in the United States in order to sustain American sales. Production began in April 1978, but in the summer of 1978 more than 60 percent of the "Made in America" Volkswagen, including engines, was still made abroad.[136] Japanese companies have also reviewed the possibility of plants in the United States, and in August 1978, Toyota announced that it would build a United States assembly plant, while Nissan was reported to be negotiating for a plant site.[137]

Barely five months earlier, at the end of March 1978, American Motors and Renault revealed plans for joint distribution of American Motors and Renault vehicles in the United States and Canada, increased imports into the United States of Renault's Le Car, and eventual produc-

---

132. Harbridge House, n. 101 *supra* at 36.
133. *Ibid.* at 43.
134. *Ibid.* at 37–38.
135. On Volvo's experience, see *European Community*, July–Aug. 1978, p. 10.
136. *Ibid.* at 11–12; *Miami Herald*, Apr. 9, 1978. *Wall Street Journal*, Aug. 22, 1978, gives the 60 percent figure. Earlier anticipated figures were 30 percent.
137. Honda decided to assemble motorcycles in Ohio, *Miami Herald*, Oct. 12, 1977. It indicated it might start U.S. manufacture of cars in "several years." See *ibid.*, Aug. 29, 1978, on Toyota plans, and *ibid.*, Sept. 1, 1978, on Nissan's negotiations with Baltimore and Maryland officials.

tion of Renault passenger cars in American Motors' assembly plants.[138] In April, American Motors indicated that it would assemble a medium-sized Renault car (the R18) at its Kenosha, Wisconsin plant.[139]

American multinationals varied in their approach to the new small car demand in the United States, sometimes presenting automobiles made in this country,[140] sometimes products partially made in the United States, with certain parts imported, and, on occasion, introducing captive imports.[141]

As a consequence of the sharp rise in oil prices after 1973, consumer-nation governments have been jarred into seeking means of increasing energy supplies and of limiting gasoline demand. These have ranged from policies encouraging oil exploration and the search for alternate energy sources, to fiscal policies such as raising taxes on gasoline and progressive taxes on cars by size, weight, and engine capacity; speed limits that conserve gasoline; performance standards for vehicles; public transportation; research on different fuels for use with conventional engines; and new attention to nonconventional power trains with a variety of potential sources of energy. Each nation has developed separate responses to the oil crisis. Multinational automobile companies have reacted with new research and development expenditures, as well as changes in product and engine designs. There has been new use of lighter materials. In Europe and Japan, particularly, taxes on gasoline have soared, further encouraging fuel-efficient cars.[142]

The United States Government in the 1970s has imposed new standards for safety, emission control, and mile-per-gallon performance on cars sold in the United States. The last of these regulations was in response to the energy crisis. Because United States producers are newly burdened with government-mandated costs, their competitive position in world markets appears to have been reduced (the new costs offsetting the effects of the declining dollar). No one, however, worries much about this, for Canada excepted, the American automobile industry has almost given up reaching foreign markets through United States exports although, as Appendix A does indicate, exports are rising. There is some alarm in Europe over United States production of

---

138. *Miami Herald,* Apr. 1, 1978, and *Wall Street Journal,* Apr. 3, 1978.
139. *Miami Herald,* Apr. 14, 1978.
140. The Energy Policy and Conservation Act of 1975 defined a domestically manufactured car as being at least 75 percent (by cost) made in the United States or Canada.
141. On captive imports, 1964–1976, see U.S. Int'l Trade Comm'n, *Automotive Trade Statistics,* Series B., USITC Publication 839 (Wash., Oct. 1977), pp. 66–68 and 30–32.
142. *Economic Report of the President, 1978,* p. 187. *The Harbridge House Study 1977* is detailed and extremely useful on these approaches. According to this study, prices per gallon of regular gasoline at the pump (Jan. 31, 1977) equaled $2.11 (Italy), $1.63 (France), $1.43 (West Germany), and $1.14 (England).

"European-size" cars with low fuel consumption and low pollution levels,[143] and some companies are making new efforts to export.[144] Nonetheless, the issue has arisen primarily as whether the new United States regulations give *imports* an advantage.

Government-mandated costs for American producers clearly make them less able to take advantage *at home* of the declining value of the dollar. The gap between the price of imports and domestic output has not narrowed as rapidly as it otherwise would, since American car prices have risen annually, in part because of the costs imposed by regulations. United States-made automobiles appear to have needed more design changes to comply with American regulations than have imported products. Disc brakes, for example, were standard on imports in the mid–1960s. In 1965 only 2.2 percent of domestic automobiles had them. By the time the standard went into effect (January 1, 1976), United States cars had disc brakes as well, but this meant major design changes.[145] Imports have also had to introduce substantial changes to comply with United States safety regulations.

In March 1966, under the authority of the Motor Vehicle Air Pollution Control Act of 1965, the Secretary of Health, Education, and Welfare issued initial standards on the discharge from exhaust systems of new motor vehicles. The standards were based on the size of engine cylinder displacement, with smaller cars having less rigorous requirements. Since imports were smaller, on average, than cars made in the United States, the latter were more affected and had to undertake more extensive design alterations.

But the costs to United States industry related to meeting government-imposed safety and emission standards seem to have been far less, relative to imports, than the costs of complying with the requirements of the Energy Policy and Conservation Act of 1975. This act provided for annual, mandatory mile-per-gallon standards, with a fleet average of 27.5 miles per gallon to be reached by 1985. For decades, Europeans and Japanese have produced economy cars with mile-per-gallon performance superior to that of United States automobiles. As

---

143. See Fiat, n. 116 *supra* at 8. When in the interwar period, the British horsepower tax forced the redesign of British engines, British economists thought this made the car less competitive in world markets, see above; likewise, the general consensus now is that the added costs of regulation make the U.S. car less competitive, but can it be that the new designs will be more suitable in export markets?

144. Occasionally, there seem to be export opportunities—to Saudi Arabia, for example. The issue of increasing exports is frequently discussed. When I mentioned my pessimism to a U.S. Department of Commerce representative, he disagreed. The U.S. Department of Commerce has been pressing U.S. companies to export. But U.S. exports of passenger cars, excluding those to Canada, were less than 1.2 percent of U.S. production in 1977. Based on data from Appendix A *infra* and MVMA, *Facts and Figures 1978*, p. 8.

145. Harbridge House, n. 101 *supra* at 42.

United States standards are imposed, American cars have required substantial technological changes, leading to reduction in size and weight, and the introduction of more efficient engines; these changes involve high cost. To meet these new regulations means formidable capital expenditures by American enterprises.[146]

The United States Government has been alarmed at this country's dependence on oil imports, which, moreover, hurts the United States balance of payments. Reduction in gasoline consumption by automobiles is one means of stemming oil imports. Paradoxically, measures designed to cut *oil* imports through mandated mile-per-gallon standards have served at least temporarily to raise *automobile* imports.

In 1975, Congress considered legislation that would give buyers of new automobiles tax rebates and would introduce an excise tax system, both designed to encourage the production and purchase of cars with fuel-efficient engines. Congress initially rejected these proposals, at least in part because of its recognition that measures of this sort would have the effect of subsidizing imports. Moreover, a Federal Energy Administration spokesman, Roger W. Sant, testified that if the rebates were limited to domestically produced cars, this would violate Article II, Paragraph 4, of the General Agreement on Tariffs and Trade, to which the United States is a party, and invite retaliatory action by our trading partners.[147] In the national energy plan of the present administration, a "gas guzzler" tax, rewarding fuel-frugal engines was again proposed.[148] In view of the changes in the United States automobile industry between 1975 and 1978, such a tax, which would continue to favor imports, would probably be less harmful to United States producers now than in earlier years. The U.S. Department of Commerce concluded, however, that "the National Energy Program appeared to be a major factor in stimulating imported car sales by focusing attention on their fuel efficiency, which results from their smaller size and lighter weight."[149] The U.S. International Trade Commission felt the Fuel Efficiency Tax and the Fuel Efficiency Rebate in the National Energy Act would favor Japanese imports.[150] Nonetheless, the Act which was signed by President Carter on November 9, 1978, did contain a tax on "gas guzzling" cars to begin with 1980 models.

At least in the short run, United States regulations on safety, emis-

---

146. On this, see for example, *1975 Automobile Facts & Figures*, p. 6.

147. See *testimony of Roger W. Sant, Assistant Administrator for Conservation and Environment, Federal Energy Administration, U.S. Sen. Comm. on Commerce, Automobile Fuel Economy and Research and Development, Hearings*, 94th Cong., 1st sess. (1975), pp. 112–113.

148. *Economic Report of the President 1978*, p. 192.

149. U.S. Dep't of Commerce, *1978 U.S. Industrial Outlook* 148 (Jan. 1978).

150. U.S. Int'l Trade Comm'n, *Fuel Efficiency Incentive Tax Proposal: Its Impact Upon the Future of the U.S. Passenger Automobile Industry, Report to U.S. Sen. Comm. on Finance*, 95th Cong., 1st sess. (1977), p. 4.

sion control, and miles per gallon seem easier for importers to meet than for American producers. No United States policy-maker, however, wants the carrying out of one set of policies to cause deficits in the United States balance of payments by giving an advantage to car imports or worse still, domestic unemployment, by making it advantageous to produce abroad for sale in the United States.

With a world automobile industry, domestic policy measures have systemic implications. The postwar commitment by the United States to a freer, more open world economy has significant present-day consequences. Imports have stimulated competition and technological progress in the United States. In many circles in this country there is now talk of protectionism to safeguard the jobs lost through imports. The International Monetary Fund reports that in 1977 and early 1978 industrial countries made increasing use of antidumping laws and countervailing duties to offset foreign subsidies and commented that "it is often difficult to know whether such measures result from increased sensitivity to long-standing practices or whether they reflect an increased use of price-cutting actions by exporting countries. At least in their initial impact, these measures tend to have a trade retarding effect."[151]

Because the automobile industry is multinational, and because the leading American producers realize that barriers to trade would harm everyone including them, United States automobile makers have not asked for protection of the United States domestic market. By contrast, United States steel makers have clamored for protection, and, of course, to the extent that steel is protected, higher costs are likely to be passed throughout the economy in the form of higher automobile prices, since automobiles are large consumers of steel.[152]

United States Government officials have pressed, at the Tokyo Round of Multilateral Trade Negotiations, for elimination of barriers to trade, whether they be tariffs, state subsidies, government requirements that serve to distort markets, or standards that offer obstacles to commerce. The Tokyo Round has taken place in the context of worldwide fears of protectionism.[153] It is symbolic that after a steady decline in tariffs in the industrial world, it has been 6 years since the United States and the European Economic Community reduced their tariffs on passenger cars, although the tariffs are low at 3 percent and 11 percent, respectively.

Thus far, the main automobile imports into the United States have come from Canada, Europe, and Japan. As nations around the world develop car manufacturing, as their governments press for and subsidize exports, and their costs of production decrease, what is to be the response of the United States? Multinational automobile companies have spread technology worldwide; the automobile industry is interna-

---

151. *IMF Survey,* Aug. 14, 1978.
152. *Finance and Development,* Sept. 1978, pp. 14–15.
153. See *ibid.*

tional. National regulations imposed on an international industry seem inevitable, yet anachronistic.

In conclusion, no novelty exists in regulation of the automobile industry. Whether in the United States or abroad, government regulations of various sorts have had, and will continue in the future to have, an important influence on the industry. What is distinctive today seems to be the new and imposing impact of the particular regulatory measures concerned with safety, pollution, and especially energy, on a thoroughly multinational industry. Likewise, the spectre of varying forms of trade restraint seems present and bound to create distortions in international markets. All these national regulatory actions can have unanticipated consequences, unless policy-makers view them in the context of multinational automobile enterprises operating through investment and licensing as well as trade in an increasingly integrated worldwide automobile industry.

APPENDIX A TO "MULTINATIONAL AUTOMOBILE ENTERPRISES AND REGULATION: AN HISTORICAL OVERVIEW"

U.S. Automobile Imports, Imports as Percentage of U.S. Automobile Sales, and U.S. Automobile Exports

Year	Imports (000 units) Total	Imports Excluding Canada	Imports From Canada	Imports as percentage of U.S. market (excludes Canadian Imports)	Exports (000 units) Total	Exports Excluding Canada	Exports To Canada
1948	16			0.5	140		
1949	12			0.2	120		
1950	16			0.3	217		
1951	21			0.4	141		
1952	29			0.7			
1953	29			0.5	154		
1954	25			0.5	173		
1955	57	57	*	0.7	211	183	28
1956	108	108	*	1.6	175	137	38
1957**	259	258	1	3.5	142	126	16
1958	431	431	*	8.2	122	105	17
1959	668	668	*	10.2	104	79	25
1960	444	444	*	7.8	117	169	27
1961	279	279	*	6.5	104	88	16
1962	375	374	1	4.9	127	109	18
1963	409	408	1	5.1	144	136	8
1964	537	528	9	6.0	166	150	16
1965	559	530	29	6.1	106	62	44

(Cont. on next page)

255
International Trade and Domestic Regulation

	Imports (000 units)			Imports as percentage of U.S. market (excludes Canadian Imports)	Exports (000 units)		
Year	Total	Excluding Canada	From Canada		Total	Excluding Canada	To Canada
1966	913	747	166	7.2	178	64	114
1967	1,021	697	324	9.2	280	43	237
1968	1,620	1,119	501	10.7	330	43	287
1969	1,847	1,156	691	11.7	333	41	292
1970	2,013	1,320	693	15.3	285	39	246
1971	2,587	1,785	802	15.3	387	39	348
1972	2,486	1,644	842	14.8	410	34	376
1973	2,437	1,565	872	15.4	509	57	452
1974	2,572	1,754	818	15.9	601	85	516
1975	2,075	1,341	734	18.4	640	89	551
1976	2,537	1,711	826	14.8	680	107	573
1977	2,790	1,940	850	18.6	698	106	592

* Less than 500.
** Year when imports exceeded exports.

Source: 1948–1954: Imports and imports as per cent of U.S. market from L. S. White, *The Automobile Industry Since 1945* 291, 293 (Harvard University Press, 1971). Exports from G. Maxcy and A. Silberston, *The Motor Vehicle Industry* 228 (George Allen & Unwin, 1959). 1955–1976: Imports and exports from MVMA, *World Motor Vehicle Data*, 1977, 204, 203. Imports (excluding Canada) as percent of U.S. market calculated based on registration data and data from MVMA. 1977 data from U.S. International Trade Commission, *Automotive Trade Statistics 1964–77* 2–3 (May 1978); and MVMA *Motor Vehicle Facts & Figures '78*, 7.

APPENDIX B TO "MULTINATIONAL AUTOMOBILE ENTERPRISES AND REGULATION: AN HISTORICAL OVERVIEW"

Value of U.S. Exports and Imports of Automotive Vehicles, Parts, and Engines—1923–1970 (in millions of dollars)

Year	Exports	Imports
1970	3,652	5,956
1969	3,888	5,346
1968	3,453	4,295
1967	2,784	2,634
1966	2,354	1,910
1965	1,929	939
1964	1,729	767
1963	1,468	586
1962	1,301	521
1961	1,188	383
1960	1,266	633
1959	1,187	844
1958	1,123	555
1957	1,349	339
1956	1,395	145
1955	1,276	85
1954	1,072	53
1953	998	53
1952	1,024	56
1951	1,218	38
1950	746	23
1949	772	13
1948	939	35
1947	1,153	6
1946	556	5
1940	259	1
1939	260	1
1938	277	2
1937	354	1
1936	246	1
1935	232	*
1934	192	*
1933	92	*
1932	78	*
1931	152	1

(Cont. on next page)

Year	Exports	Imports
1930	284	2
1929	547	3
1928	509	3
1927	397	2
1926	328	2
1925	324	1
1924	...	1
1923	...	1

* Less than $500,000.

Source: U.S. Department of Commerce, Bureau of the Census, *Historical Statistics of the United States* 895 (Washington, 1975).

INTERNATIONAL COMPETITION IN THE WORLD AUTOMOTIVE INDUSTRY

Michael C. Pearce, *Head of Automotive Research, The Economist Intelligence Unit LTD.*

The various factors influencing international competition in the world automotive industry are much more complex today than they were a decade ago. In the 1960s, market requirements were the main forces determining international competition, although changes were taking place which have become much more significant during the 1970s.

WORLDWIDE MARKET CHANGES IN THE 1960s

During the 1960s, Japan became a major manufacturing center for vehicles, joining the existing well-established manufacturing blocs in North America and Western Europe. However, the characteristics of each manufacturing center were rather different.

Trends in North America

The North American industry had reached a mature state by the 1960s. However, the large, comfortable cars built to meet domestic requirements had little appeal outside North America. Consequently, exports were minimal. Besides, General Motors and Ford had long since established plants in Western Europe to produce smaller cars to meet requirements there. These smaller cars were also exported in volume. Chrysler acquired Rootes in Great Britain and Simca in France and thus joined General Motors and Ford as a European car producer.

The Big Three also invested in other countries which had established their own automotive industries. Examples include Australia, South Africa, Brazil, Argentina, and Mexico, where high protective barriers successfully kept imports out.

The North American automotive scene was therefore self-contained.

Car ownership had virtually reached saturation level so that emphasis was placed on frequent model changes to sustain a high level of replacement sales. The domestic market was large enough to support the necessary expenditure by General Motors and Ford on frequent tooling for new models. Chrysler, however, the smallest of the Big Three, sometimes found it difficult to finance new investment. American Motors, the fourth-largest producer, operated on a much lower level and tended to pioneer new trends, particularly for smaller cars.

Imported small cars, initially from Western Europe but then also increasingly from Japan, threatened the domestic United States market. New registrations of imported cars reached 1 million units in the United States in 1969. The buying public initially regarded an imported car as a novelty. In a short time, they became aware of the advantages of small cars in their own right. Domestic producers tried to counter the challenge by captive imports and the production of subcompacts, but through the 1960s the mainstream requirement in North America continued to be for large, comfortable cars.

Western Europe

In Western Europe, the main development in the 1960s was the rationalization of the industries in the main producing countries. Various mergers in Britain resulted, finally, in the establishment of British Leyland in 1968. In France, Panhard was absorbed by Citroën. In Germany, Volkswagen acquired Audi and NSU, BMW took over Glas, and Borgward ceased production. A similar trend took place in the German truck industry. MAN acquired Bussing; Daimler-Benz bought Hanomag and Henschel from the Rheinstal Group. In Italy, Fiat acquired Autobianchi and Lancia.

The barriers between West European countries were gradually dismantled with the establishment of the European Common Market. This development was beginning to encourage arrangements across frontiers, although the exclusion of Britain from the European Common Market did much to discourage these developments in the 1960s. Nevertheless, automotive companies began to realize the advantages of pan-European organizations. Ford was an important leader in this development with the establishment of Ford Europe in 1967. This was a logical progression from the decision taken by Ford in 1960 when it bought out the 45 percent minority shareholders' interests in Ford United Kingdom. The reason given by Ford at that time was to "obtain greater operational flexibility and enable us better to co-ordinate our European and American manufacturing facilities and integrate further our product lines and operations on a worldwide basis." Viewed in retrospect, this was a very important step in the internationalization of the automotive industry which set the pattern for other companies to follow.

Ford Europe has proved to be a highly successful venture. The European planning and sourcing concept for automotive component and material procurement could be fully developed once Britain entered the European Common Market in 1973. Ford now regards all Europe as one market and plans its investments, manufacturing facilities, and marketing on this basis. It has major automobile investments in the United Kingdom, Germany, Belgium, and, more recently, in Spain. This gives Ford extensive flexibility in sourcing. In fact, Ford is currently the largest importer of cars in the United Kingdom. However, to the average British motorist a Ford is seen as a British product; few question where it was ultimately assembled.

Fiat also tried to establish the pan-European approach in the late 1960s by obtaining 15 percent of Citroën. They might have succeeded had General de Gaulle not vetoed the Italian company's attempt to gain control. It did increase its holding to 49 percent in the early 1970s, but finally divested itself of the holding. In 1974, heavy losses by Citroën led the French Government to sponsor a takeover of its car operations by Peugeot.

The Emerging Japanese Industry

Japan expanded its vehicle production very rapidly in the 1960s. Japanese car production increased from 165,000 units in 1960 to 3,179,000 in 1970. The domestic market was certainly unable to absorb the rapid expansion of the industry and the Japanese producers began a very active campaign to develop export markets. Japanese car exports increased from a mere 7,000 units in 1960 to 725,000 units in 1970. The Ministry for International Trade and Industry also promoted a rationalization of the industry. Nissan took over Prince Motors and Fuji; the Mitsubishi companies formed one group; and the Toyota group included Daihatsu Motor and Hino.

While rapidly expanding exports, Japan also protected its own domestic market by various open and hidden controls. Japan liberalized its investment code in the early 1970s which allowed American producers to seek links with Japanese producers through investment rather than trade. Chrysler was permitted to take a 35 percent interest in Mitsubishi in 1971; General Motors took a financial interest in Isuzu. Ford also discussed investment in Toyo Kogyo, but the deal fell through and culminated only in a technical and cooperation agreement. These agreements assisted the smaller Japanese producers, enabling them to develop new markets, particularly in the United States. Although the American automobile producers have benefited from the investments, it has certainly not provided increased sales in Japan of either Northern American or European vehicles produced by the Big Three United States automobile producers.

Countries in other areas of the world continued to establish or expand their own automotive industries during the 1960s. Opportunities for exports from Europe thus diminished rapidly, slowing down the growth of the European producers. At the same time, the Japanese were providing increasingly severe competition to European exports. Consequently, the indigenous continental European producers established plants in developing countries to protect their market position. They were also willing to sell their technology to Eastern Europe.

The American-owned producers were less willing to establish investments, perhaps because earlier investments in South America had not provided the return they had anticipated, due to economic and political instability. The Japanese attitude to investment overseas in the 1960s was increasingly governed by the belief that it was necessary if there was no other way of rapidly penetrating a new market.

The trends described above continued into the early 1970s. Then the world automotive industry experienced the traumatic effects of the oil crisis. The impact on revenue was sudden and dramatic as sales fell. This effect was relatively short lived. By 1977, world putput of vehicles had more than recovered the pre-oil crisis level of 1973. The impact on costs was more damaging and long-lasting. Inflated costs severely affected manufacturers' ability to make provision for adequate investment. In addition to investment for commercial needs, the manufacturers have been faced with government pressures to invest in designing vehicles to conserve fuel. The pressures have varied from country to country with, of course, the greatest pressure taking place in the United States.

GOVERNMENT POLICY AS AN EMERGING FACTOR IN THE 1970s

Government intervention of this sort is now the primary influence on the development of the leading automotive industries of the world. The various policies of governments in different countries have profound impact on international competition. These policies are also encouraging the leading automobile manufacturers to develop strategies which maximize the opportunities and minimize the threats of government action in various markets.

In a recently published study by *The Economist* Intelligence Unit[1], the role of government was analyzed in the following way:

> The USA: Government as Legislator
>
> Western Europe: Government as Owner
>
> Japan: Government as Promoter
>
> Developing Countries: Government as Initiator

These policies are having a number of predictable effects on international competition but are also resulting in changes which perhaps legislators did not foresee.

---

1. *Worldwide Automotive Activity 1977 and Outlook 1978/79,* Economist Intelligence Unit Special Report.

The United States Automobile Industry

International Trade and Domestic Regulation

The United States Government's policy as a legislator is well-defined. The initial emphasis was towards an improved environment through emission and noise controls, greater safety, and improved product quality. Since the oil crisis, the further factor of fuel conservation has been introduced by the legislators. The first three factors did little to alter the concept of the typical American car except to increase prices to meet the costs of the various legislative requirements. The intention of the various requirements was not to restrict imports, although in practice they did so. Western European car producers have been faced with the dilemma of investing to conform with United States requirements or to be excluded from the market. Some Western European manufacturers decided to invest; others have found it too costly to conform. Japanese manufacturers were not faced with the same dilemma because similar environmental and safety legislation was introduced in Japan.

Legislation concerning fuel conservation is likely to affect most seriously the competitive position of the United States automotive industry. Legislated fuel economy standards are forcing American automotive producers to redesign their product. The downsizing of cars, for example, brings American cars much closer to those designed in Western Europe and Japan.

The leading American car producers can call upon the vast experience they have gained in "small cars" technology as a result of their investments in Western Europe. General Motors and Ford are utilizing their experience to the full. The policy of the United States Government helps these two giant companies to move towards a world car design policy. What strategies they will adopt in the future to maximize the profit benefits arising from this trend toward world-designed cars remains to be seen.

A transnational company can no longer make its decisions solely on the basis of market factors. In Western Europe, in particular, sociopolitical pressures are becoming increasingly important and these companies will certainly not wish to run down their existing large-scale investments in Western Europe. In developing countries, labor costs could be attractive for the assembly of small cars despite the absence of technical skills and a supporting industrial base. The possible interplay of such factors makes it impossible to speculate on the future policies of General Motors and Ford. However, the fuel conservation policies of the United States Government will certainly have a growing effect on the international investment and trading patterns of General Motors and Ford. These policies will by no means be the only factors which these companies will take into account. Their future overall policies are likely to be directed towards maximum standardization of product and increased flexibility in manufacturing facilities. The Ford Europe concept could be extended to the Ford World concept. Chrysler's decision, for financial reasons, to sell its European interests to Peugeot Citroën has severely weakened its opportunities for a future international marketing strategy. Chrysler now seems to be committed wholly to survival as an independent company in the United States. Its financial participation in Peugeot Citroën is unlikely to be of great benefit to Chrysler. It could, however, be of great assistance in enabling Peugeot Citroën to establish a significant market presence in the United States.

The legislative impact of fuel conservation is an important factor which is encouraging Western European car manufacturers to seek greater involvement in the United States. The downsizing of cars provides the opportunities to utilize quickly existing small car technology. However, other interrelated factors are influencing their decisions. Viewed from Western European eyes, the United States market is the largest single automobile market in the world. Renault took the opportunity of close association with American Motors to ensure that it would have a good distribution system for its cars in the United States. Renault cars may be assembled at some American Motors plants. It also has the opportunity to market Jeeps through its strong distribution system in Europe and other countries. The decision of Renault could well have averted a United States Government decision on whether it should embark upon the same policy as certain Western European Governments in becoming an owner in the automotive industry in order to protect employment.

Volkswagen's policy to invest in the United States was also based upon the decision to maintain a strong presence in the United States market. A further factor was that international exchange movements have made German products increasingly expensive in the United States. The international exchange movements have also prompted several West German component manufacturers to invest in the United States.

British vehicle component manufacturers, who are much stronger than British vehicle producers, are also beginning to invest in the United States but for different reasons. The weakness of the British motor industry has encouraged them to look for new markets. Investment in the United States is likely to provide a better rate of return than it does in the United Kingdom.

So far Japanese automotive producers have not invested in the United States, but increasingly they will be faced with the decision to do so if the yen continues to be such a strong currency.

Foreign companies are therefore taking decisions to invest in the United States because of the opportunities arising from downsizing of cars in the United States to meet fuel economy standards. The possibility of tariff protection may also be in their minds. The United States is a low tariff country. Provided that imported cars meet the same legislative requirements as domestically produced cars, there are no barriers to entry. In fact, small volume producers such as Rolls Royce are able to obtain dispensation from fuel economy standards. However, there are presently lobbying pressures for greater protection against imports.

These pressures could grow with the continuing balance-of-trade deficit for the United States and the fact that imports are damaging other sectors of United States industry. Legislative changes are bringing the design of American cars more in line with cars produced in other world manufacturing centers. An upsurge in imports is not likely in the short term because international exchange rates are making imported cars increasingly expensive. However, economic pressures could lead to protection measures in the longer term future.

Government Policy in Europe

In Western Europe, recent government intervention in the automotive industry has been mainly in the field of employment protection. This has been particularly so since the impact of the oil crisis which severely damaged the profitability of many companies. In the United Kingdom, government intervention has become crucial for the survival of an indigenous motor vehicle industry. The most important example was the takeover of ailing British Leyland by public ownership. Despite a massive injection of public investment and a rapid succession of senior management changes, the company is still in a very difficult position. The present management is taking a very strong line on labor disputes. Whether this action will enable Leyland to make a recovery remains to be seen. Much ground has been lost in meeting international competition. However, the survival of the company is crucial to ensure the maintenance of employment in the Midlands in particular. It is possible that the only long-term solution is for the government to allow Leyland to associate with another automobile manufacturer. There is currently some speculation of a possible link with Renault. The possibility of a link with a Japanese manufacturer should also not be ruled out completely. Japanese companies are currently faced with decisions on how to ensure a long-term presence in Europe. One remedy for the growing pressure in many countries against Japanese cars might be for Japanese producers to invest in Europe. What is important in Britain is to ensure that investment in the British motor vehicle components industry is maintained for employment reasons, and government policy should be directed towards this end.

In this context the decision by Chrysler to sell its European interests to Peugeot Citroën may not further this end. Although there are assurances that Chrysler manufacturing facilities will be maintained, it is difficult to see how the plant in Linwood, Scotland can be made viable. Of more significance to the British economy is the fact that Peugeot Citroën is a highly vertically integrated car producer, and there is no guarantee of the continuing large scale use of some British-made components. National considerations are still very strong. For example, Lucas has been obstructed from gaining complete control of a leading French producer of electrical automotive components by the French Government, which has prevented Lucas from purchasing the financial interest in the company currently held by Bendix. The French Government preferred to see Ducellier as part of a French-owned monopoly group of electrical automotive equipment producers. Another example was the ruling of the German cartel office which prevented GKN from acquiring a leading German automotive components producer, Fitchel & Sachs.

In France itself, Renault has been state-controlled since the end of the World War II. The French Government also assisted in the merger of Peugeot and Citroën after the oil crisis, and is, of course, supporting the acquisition of Chrysler's interests by Peugeot Citroën in France.

In Italy, Alfa Romeo is state-controlled. In Holland, the Dutch Government agreed on a major funding of Volvo's troubled Dutch passenger car operation in early 1978, with the express intention of maintaining employment. Volvo itself is in the process of receiving government participation, though not from the Swedish Government. The Norwegian Government has agreed to take a 40 percent shareholding in Volvo. By so doing it will utilize some of its North Sea oil revenues and also promote some manufacturing of Volvo components in Norway. The Spanish Government has an interest in the largest car producer, Seat, but against the current trend, it is seeking to sell its holding to Fiat.

Government control is not present in the German motor industry. However, the institutional banks play a strong role in German industrial investment. They actively intervened to prevent any further participation when Kuwait took a 15 percent stake in Daimler Benz several years ago. Open intervention would be difficult because of fear of monopolies. However, it is interesting to note that the West German cartel office is not standing in the way of Volkswagen and MAN in their joint project to produce a new medium truck range.

Besides government intervention, the European automotive producers are also increasingly moving towards joint ventures to ensure an adequate basis for investment. Examples include the joint investment in small diesel engines by Societe Franco-Italiana de Motori (Sofim) in which Fiat, Alfa Romeo, and Saviem (Renault) each has a one-third stake. Another example is Franco-Suedoise Moteurs (FSM) which is a joint company formed by Renault, Peugeot, and Volvo to produce a V6, 2 ½ litre petrol engine for cars made by the three companies. The pressures on costs are likely to see further joint ventures between European manufacturers. In August, Sig. Agnelli of Fiat actively spoke of the need for greater Western European cooperation in the automotive sector. Fiat itself is a strong advocate of a pan-European approach but Agnelli appeared to exclude the American-owned companies in Western Europe from any participation. Its truck operation, IVECO, with facilities in Italy, Germany and France, is rapidly emerging as a challenger to Daimler Benz as the leading producer of trucks and buses in Europe.

However, national considerations are not always paramount in Europe. The European Economic Community Commission has legislative functions and is taking the initiative in establishing common standards, type approval, etc. It could become a strong forum for initiating greater safety and environmental controls for the automotive industry in Western Europe. At present, however, this is unlikely as its directives are often based upon the report of working parties on which automotive companies are well-represented. The European Economic Community Commission is taking greater interest in consumer protection and could have a substantial influence in this area in the future.

Japanese Government Policy

The main objectives of the Japanese motor industry have been to expand and export. A third objective could be said to be to keep the domestic market for themselves. In each of these three areas the Japanese Government plays a major role. The Japanese Government has actively promoted Japanese car exports. Exports have also been encouraged to expand through the industry's close relationship with the Japanese financial system and the government's expansion policy. At the same time it gives active encouragement to exports, the Japanese Government has failed to open up its domestic market on a fair trade basis and its construction and use regulations, while benefiting Japan's environment and consumers, have in the past been implemented in a difficult and arbitrary manner for prospective importers. Recently the government and the industry have gone some way in clarifying the testing procedures for imported cars. However, despite these relaxations, imported cars find it difficult to find a suitable distribution system in Japan. In 1977, car imports totalled only 41,500 units out of a 2.5 million market.

Market pressures rather than government action are beginning to have a greater influence on the Japanese automotive industry. Exports are being affected by the strength of the yen. This influence could prove to be a much more important factor in influencing the strategy of the Japanese motor industry in the future. The possibility of Japanese investment in the United States is strong in the near future with Toyota, Nissan, and Honda already looking for sites. Joint ventures in Europe are also a strong possibility.

The *Economist*[2] predicted in a recent article that

> the cheap imported Japanese car is dead. A revolution is under way at Japanese car companies. By the mid-1980s Japan's car makers will be out of high volume, low margin exports and into lower volume higher profit models. Parts of the Japanese motor industry will be dismantled and shifted abroad, where labor costs (even in America) are now lower.

---

2. *Economist*, Sept. 23, 1978.

The arguments are convincing, but if the prediction is correct it will cause a large scale employment problem in Japan.

New Motor Industries in Developing Countries

More and more countries in the world are seeking their own motor industries. The reasons given are to save on imports or to expand their industrial base, but often political pride rather than economic necessity is the main reason. It is relatively easy for government to encourage local assembly; it is often difficult to make the transition to local manufacture because of the lack of a strong supporting industrial infrastructure. To publicize investment in forging and foundry capacity is much less glamorous than to announce the establishment of a motor vehicle plant. In the past, a number of countries have permitted the establishment of too many assembly plants for the size of the domestic market with no hope of exporting the surplus. Increasingly, governments are planning their industries more carefully. Potential investors are also more carefully evaluating the viability of projects and their long-term implications.

Nearly all new production facilities are dependent on the technology of the established manufacturers in North America, Western Europe, or Japan. Although the development of new vehicle industries may be based on political decisions, they nevertheless have an effect on the established manufacturers. First, the potential for exporting is, in general, reduced although companies which do decide to invest often secure a short-term advantage by exporting knocked-down kits, assemblies, and components. Second, the manufacturers' own home markets (and possibly some of their export markets) are potential selling areas for the new industries. A very good example is that Fiat technology helped to build up the Polish and Russian car industries and now Polish and Russian cars of Fiat design are being exported back to Western Europe.

CONCLUSION

From this wide-ranging review of various trends occurring in the world automotive industry several conclusions can be drawn:

1. Government intervention in various forms is playing an increasing role in influencing the pattern of international competition.

2. With the exception of the United States, government intervention tries to aid its domestic motor industry by protecting employment or encouraging investment, or both.

3. The United States Government's policy is to implement legislation to protect the motorist and conserve energy. This does not necessarily help its automotive industry.

4. All the leading automotive producers, whether they are American,

Western European, or Japanese increasingly have to evaluate the various economic and political factors in their marketing strategies. These decisions are increasingly likely to be directed towards investment rather than trade.

Two important questions grow out of this discussion:

1. Will the United States Government be able to continue to pursue its legislative policies without feeling the need to resort to some form of protection for its automotive industry?
2. Will other governments seriously implement similar measures to those being taken by the United States Government on environmental control, safety and fuel conservation? With limited resources some of their vehicle producers would find it difficult to comply and still have sufficient funds for commercial survival.

SUMMARY

The automobile in the United States, in Britain, or in other producing countries can no longer be analyzed, managed, or regulated in terms of competitive forces within the traditional national markets. The industry and its competitive domain now extend worldwide and increasingly its developments in national markets are being shaped by pressures being brought to bear by the actions of governments in the major producing countries. No single government can act independently today and be free of serious international consequences for domestic economic development and employment.

THE INTERNATIONAL PRODUCT LIFE CYCLE AND UNITED STATES REGULATION OF THE AUTOMOBILE INDUSTRY

Louis T. Wells, Jr., *Professor, Harvard Business School*

Regulation of the huge and complex automobile industry is necessarily controversial. There is no comprehensive agreement about the effects of government policy on the industry or about the nature of the response by the United States industry to the changing world environment.

Consider one example. According to some representatives of the United States industry, United States Government policy can be blamed in part for the inroads foreign cars have made into the United States market. Government requirements for improved gas mileage have saddled United States firms with design changes and development costs that foreign firms have avoided. According to this view, regulations concerning pollution have been easier for foreign producers to satisfy. Passenger car diesel engines were already in use abroad, and modifications of the small gasoline engines produced outside the United States were easier than for the large United States engines. According to some foreign firms and governments, however, United States government regulations have been responsible, either by design or as an indirect consequence, for excluding foreign cars from the United States market. Early drafts of the safety regulations for instance, required tail lights to be mounted higher than the rear fenders of some European cars. The standards, therefore, seemed to be designed to favor big cars. The crash test, too, seemed to discriminate against the very small producers and small exporters, for whom sacrificing several cars to the tests represented a proportionately higher cost. Finally, the early pollution regulations seemed inappropriate to foreign manufacturers, who argued that controlling the percentage of pollutants in the exhaust is less appropriate for small cars than the absolute amount of pollutant emitted by a car (or emitted per passenger mile). Moreover, as soon as it became evident that several foreign manufacturers could meet the pollution regulations before the American producers, implementation of the rules was postponed. This took away the advantage foreign firms had been able to acquire.

American producers claim that foreign governments subsidize their home producers, either openly or through mechanisms available when the companies are state-owned. The worst violator, Japan, makes it particularly difficult for American firms to retaliate because of the barriers placed in the way of a seller of imported cars in Japan.

Foreigners, and some Americans, counter by arguing the United States industry has simply been lazy or unresponsive. When the public wanted a smaller car, the American industry did not offer the product until imports had grabbed a significant market share. When the need was for new technologies to meet safety, pollution, and mileage regulations, the United States industry demonstrated its inability to innovate more than new body styles, while foreign firms quickly demonstrated their technical ingenuity.

There is some truth in all these views. But neither individually nor in total do they do justice to the historical development of this industry. A better understanding of the automobile industry is required for appropriate responses by government officials and business managers. Moreover, there are lessons in the history of this industry for regulators and managers of other industries. The automobile industry, like any other, is in some ways a special case. But it also shares certain significant characteristics with some other important industries.

INTERNATIONAL COMPETITIVENESS

Various conceptual models are available by which to predict or explain the competitiveness of a particular United States industry in the world market. The two major models of interest here are (1) the traditional economic model; and (2) the product life cycle model.

In the traditional economic model, industries are classified according to their use of various factors of production; countries are ranked according to their supplies of those factors. Countries will, it is suggested, be competitive in those industries that use intensively their most abundant factors of production. It has been argued that the United States, for instance, ought to be competitive in the world market in industries that are capital-intensive in their production processes, because the United States has a large stock of capital relative to other countries. The automobile industry ranks fairly high in capital intensity. In 1957, it was fortieth out of 122 industries.[1] Thus, one might expect to find the United States automobile industry in a strong trade position.

The traditional economic model is consistent with the data for the early history of the industry. In 1920, the United States exported over

---

1. H. B. Lary, *Imports of Manufactures from Less Developed Countries* 146–177 (National Bureau of Economic Research, 1968).

170,000 automobiles while importing less than 1,000. But the United States has since become a net importer of automobiles. In 1976, the United States exported 680,000 passenger automobiles and imported just over 2.5 million. The weak position of the United States as an exporter is more apparent when United States trade with Canada is eliminated: 573,000 of the exported cars went to Canada,[2] which represents a special case due to the trade agreement between the United States and Canada covering automobiles and parts. A satisfactory model must be able to explain the deterioration of the United States industry in world markets.

The traditional economic model could explain the deterioration of the United States position if there were changes in the relative position of the automobile industry in a ranking of industries by factor use or if there were a shift in factor endowments. It could be that automobiles were more capital-intensive in the list of industries existing in the 1910s and 1920s than in the current list. In fact, it is more likely that the automobile industry has become *more* capital-intensive and has moved higher in the ranking.

One could still retain the traditional economic model by trying to explain the shift in the United States trade position in terms of foreign countries becoming more protective and the United States less protective. The facts suggest that this, too, has not been the case. The figures in Table 5-8 suggest that the trend since 1940 has been toward lower tariffs everywhere. In fact, tariffs in Europe and elsewhere have tended to understate the degree of protection against the United States automobile. Higher gasoline prices, taxes, and insurance based on engine displacement or horsepower have tended to penalize the United States car. There is no evidence, however, that these factors have increased in recent years. In fact, when one adds shifts in exchange rates, the changes might even suggest the possibility of an improvement in the United States trade position in recent years.

To understand the shifts in the United States trade position in automobiles, one must turn to another conceptual model, namely the product life cycle. According to the product life cycle explanation of trade, certain industries follow a predictable pattern that begins with the United States as a net exporter and ends with the United States as a net importer. The model appears to be useful in describing trade in high income or labor-saving products. The automobile has behaved in the way that the model would forecast.

For decades American manufacturers have been faced with a particularly high income market and with a high cost for skilled labor. They have been especially likely, therefore, to innovate products or processes

---

2. Source: *U.S. Trade Statistics.* In fact, imports represent a smaller share of the U.S. market than they represent in some European markets. Imports account for more than 30 percent of car sales in the United Kingdom and Italy and over 20 percent in France and Germany. See *Motor Industry Statistics* (London, HMSO, 1969).

TABLE 5-8 Tariff Rates: Major Markets by Year

	1910	1930	1940	1950	1960	1965	1976
France	8–12%	46%	n.a.	n.a.	31%	22%	11%
Germany	2–3%	spec. tariff, var. by wgt.	spec. tariff, var. by wgt.	35%	13–16%	22%	11%
U.K.	Free	33.3%	33.3%	33.3%	30%	22%	11%
Japan		50%	70%	40%	35–40%	20–40%	6.4%
U.S.	45%	25%	10%	10%	7.5%	6.5%	3%

that are suitable for that kind of market. Once they innovate, American firms have tended to manufacture the new products or to use the new processes first in the United States. Direct production costs may indeed be higher than they would be in some foreign site, but the advantages of foreign production are outweighed by the advantages of manufacturing close to the market. United States production allows close contact between engineering and sales personnel. People in sales and service can recognize service problems and solve them quickly; people in engineering can change models quickly. In addition, United States production has the advantage of having many nearby specialized service and supply firms. At this stage, costs matter relatively little, anyway. The task of the innovator is simply to get the right model out quickly rather than to drive costs to the minimum. The new product has not been standardized, so the consumer can do little comparison shopping.

Exports may begin at this stage in the process, if some foreign demand exists for the innovation. Then as incomes abroad grow, United States exports grow. As foreign markets continue to grow, it becomes tempting for a local firm abroad or a United States competitor to set up a plant in the foreign market to escape tariffs and shipping costs and to take advantage of what has been, until very recently, a supply of labor cheaper than that available in the United States. When the threat becomes apparent, the United States firm may preempt competition by setting up its own subsidiaries. The effect of foreign investment or foreign competition is to reduce the growth of United States exports.

Meanwhile production processes and models will have become standardized. Price competition may increase. Thus, controlling production costs becomes important. As foreign plants grow, they obtain economies of scale and become competitive. They begin to supply third markets that had been supplied in the past from the United States. And American exports continue to be eroded. Eventually, the site of competitive production moves down the ladder of development. Finally, at some point the United States begins to buy from cheaper foreign sources.

The pattern of automotive trade has fit well the forecasts of the product life cycle model. The automobile was invented in Europe. In 1903, French production exceeded United States production. But the mass-produced models were American innovations. The curved-dash Olds and then the Ford Model T were built in America. With mass production came United States dominance of world trade. By 1913, United States production was the highest in the world, ten times the output of France. By 1929, the United States was exporting over 400,000 passenger cars per year, while importing fewer than 1,000. In that year, 80 percent of the automobiles in world trade were American-made (in Canada or the United States).[3]

To defend their foreign markets, United States firms began to set up

---

3. G. Bloomfield, *The World Automotive Industry* 316 (David and Charles, 1978).

plants abroad. Ford went to the United Kingdom in 1911, France in 1913, and Germany in 1926. The initial effect was to increase the export of parts. In 1915, new cars accounted for 87 percent of United States automotive exports. By 1920 the figure was 70 percent; by 1930, it had fallen to 58 percent.[4] Eventually, foreign cars began to make inroads into the United States market.

By 1977, imports had captured almost 20 percent of the United States market. This is not a large fraction compared to European markets, but United States imports were not offset by exports as was often the case in Europe. The industry that had once been a major net exporter became a major net importer.

United States exports of cars to Europe have not been important for years. In 1965 exports to the United Kingdom, France, Germany, and Italy were just under 7,000 cars, the majority of which went to Germany. Nevertheless, the United States continued to supply other markets for some time. In such developing countries as those of Central America with no domestic producers, cars produced before the early 1950s are largely American. But in the 1950s, the shift there was clearly toward European cars. In the 1970s, the Europeans had been displaced by the Japanese. The shares of world trade demonstrate the pattern. In 1953 Europeans had 75 percent; the Japanese, none. By 1963, Europe had 94 percent; Japan 1 percent. In 1973, European share had fallen to 77 percent, while Japan's had risen to 22 percent.[5] According to the model, next will be exports from the richer, more industrialized developing countries, such as Korea.

The result of the product life cycle is not an inevitable disappearance of the United States industry. Only the overly simple version of the product life cycle model suggests that the United States will eventually import all its cars, perhaps from the developing countries. Of course, corporations are not helpless bystanders in international trade. They have strategies designed to prolong or to alter the cycle.

RESPONSES TO THE PRODUCT LIFE CYCLE

Faced with the later phase of the product life cycle, firms have a number of possible strategies. One possibility is to follow the cycle and locate an increasing amount of production facilities overseas. Foreign facilities can be used as sources for exporting to higher-cost areas such as the United States. Another possibility is to innovate. Innovation may be basic, intended to start a new cycle; or it may be designed to isolate the United States market from the rest of the world. A third corporate strategy is to abandon the industry by shifting resources to other activities.

---

4. If Canada is excluded, U.S. exports of parts for assembly were about 6 percent of U.S. exports of new passenger cars in 1910. By 1915, the figure was 30 percent; 1930, 43 percent.

5. Bloomfield, n. 3 *supra* at 316.

United States automobile companies have included, at various times, some elements of each of these strategies in their responses to import competition. But the heaviest investment has been in attempts to isolate the United States market from the rest of the world. That attempt has met with considerable success. However, the success of the strategy was declining by the late 1960s. The emergence of mileage requirements and, perhaps, pollution and safety standards have accelerated the already evident decline in the ability of United States producers to differentiate the United States product from what was already available from the rest of the world. When viewed in the long run, therefore, the effect of government regulation can be seen as a blip in an otherwise steady trend.

RESPONSE TO IMPORTS

United States automobile firms did, for a time, attempt to diversify their activities to lessen their dependence on automobile manufacturing. By 1957, 10 percent of General Motors' and Ford's sales and 8 percent of Chrysler's were nonautomotive. But the strategy was largely abandoned. Although Ford continued to diversify for a period (reaching 11 percent nonautomotive sales in 1966), by 1976 the figures were 5 percent for General Motors, 8 percent for Ford, and 2.7 percent for Chrysler.[6] Apparently, the skills and assets of the automobile firms were not suitable to establish the companies in strong positions in other industries. With reduced emphasis on diversification, United States firms have worked primarily to differentiate the United States product from the product sold in the rest of the world. This strategy has involved selling an increasingly larger car.

It has been argued that American driving conditions demand a larger, heavier, and faster car than do European conditions. Differences between European and American automobiles are thus not a reflection of corporate strategy, it is said, but rather of the demands of the marketplace. The evidence to support this argument is rather weak. Indeed, an examination of purchases in developing countries throws considerable doubt on the validity of the simple explanation. Driving conditions in the Third World have proved to be surprisingly unimportant in determining the kinds of cars purchased. Crowded countries and countries with wide open spaces have behaved pretty much alike. For many years, they bought largely United States automobiles that seemed to be the best buys on the world market. As European costs declined, purchasers shifted to European cars. United States sales continued for longer in markets that were more distant from Europe. Eventually, Japanese cars seemed to offer the best buys, and captured a large market share. Purchases in the developing countries suggest that, over a wide

---

6. 1966 and 1976 figures from company annual reports. 1957 figures from *Barron's* 37 (Sept. 2, 1957) 11.

range of sizes, consumers are influenced more by economics than by driving conditions.

What the American consumer could have been induced to buy if offered a wide range of sizes produced at home will remain a matter of conjecture. The American producers offered little choice. Starting in the mid–1950s, when imports appeared on the United States market, the American car began to grow. The 1950 Chevrolet was 197 inches long, with a wheelbase of 115 inches, and had an engine displacement of about 216 cubic inches (6 cylinders). That compares with the German manufactured G.M. Opel Kapitän with a 106-inch wheelbase and a 151-cubic-inch engine (6 cylinders).[7] By 1958, the low-priced Chevrolet was 10 inches longer and had an engine displacement of almost 1 liter (61 cubic inches) more. Figures 5-2, 5-3, and 5-4 show the changes in size and weight of the inexpensive American cars.

It is important to note that imports could not simply move into the gap in the American market. Most mass-produced cars in Europe at the time had engines less than 1200cc. The American consumer was thus given the choice of a large American car, a very small car (VW Beetle, Renault Dauphine), or a middle-sized import that was produced at low volumes and high costs. Volvo and others did offer cars in the range abandoned by American producers, but they were very expensive. Most imports offered only a very scattered dealership and service network in the United States.

Faced with a very small import or a very large American car, the majority of consumers stuck with the American product. To be sure, they could still choose a smaller engine. Chevrolet continued to offer the 6 cylinder even as the V-8 became so popular. But the increasing weight of the automobile (and, perhaps the advertising messages) made the smaller engine a less attractive choice.

There were a few mass-produced foreign cars larger than the Volkswagen Beetle and Renault Dauphine, but most were manufactured by American firms (Vauxhall and Opel, in particular). United States firms could have imported these products and overcome the parts, service, and representation problems facing other foreign producers of middle-size cars. The United States manufacturers seem to have decided not to follow this alternative strategy after some erratic and half-hearted attempts. In 1956, the Metropolitan and the English Ford appear to have been the only significant captive imports, accounting for 7.3 percent and 4.3 percent, respectively, of imports. At the peak of captive imports (1959) they reached about 24 percent of all imports. This figure includes Mercedes-Benz and DKW-Auto Union, whose United States sales were handled by Studebaker-Packard distributors. By 1976, captive imports had fallen to 8 percent of all imports.[8] Success might well have eroded the markets for United States firms' larger,

---

7. Data from *Automotive Industries*, Mar. 15, 1950, pp. 113, 165.
8. Data from various issues of *Ward's Automotive Yearbook*.

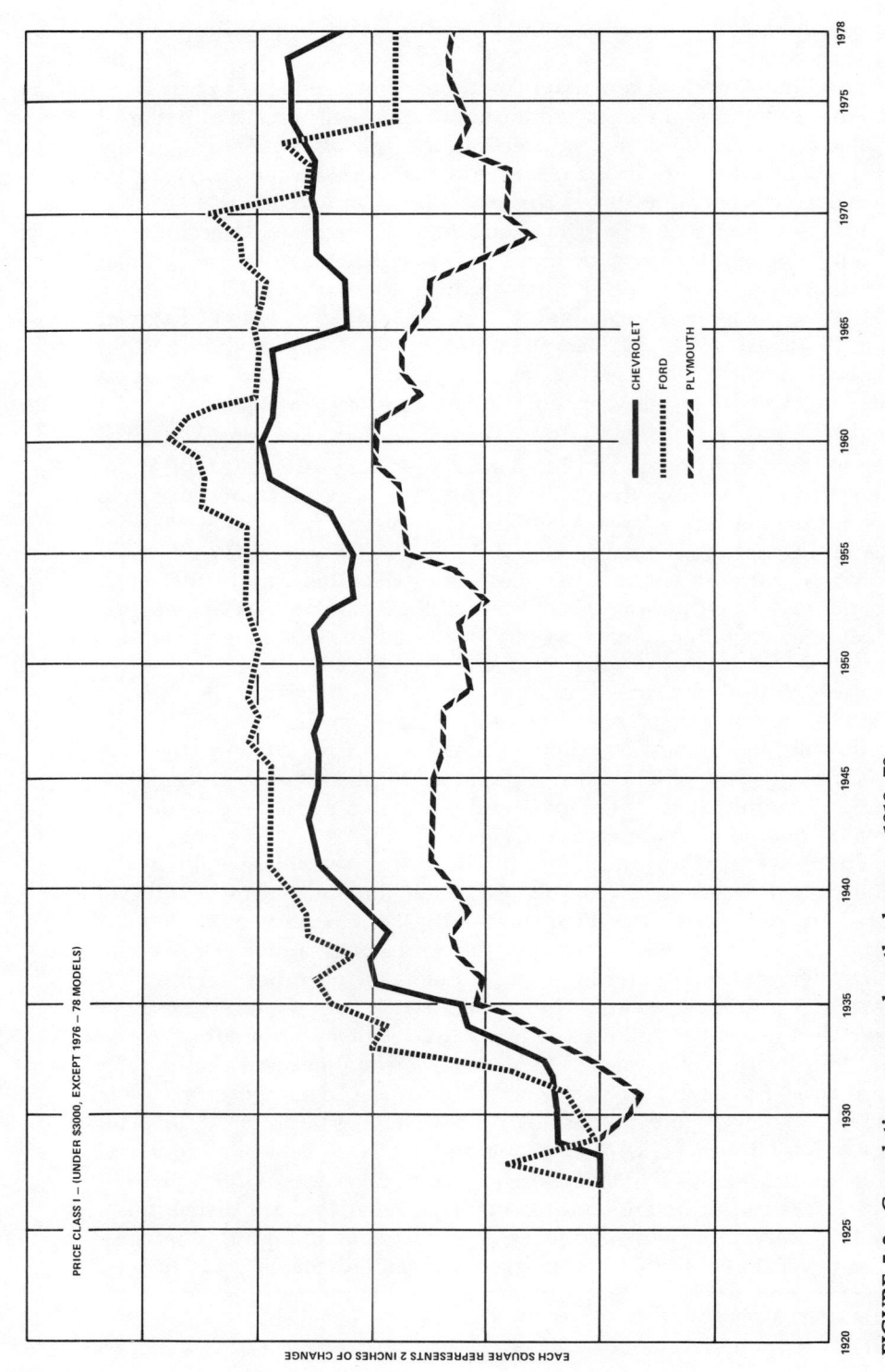

FIGURE 5-2 Cumulative average length changes, 1919–78

279
International Trade and Domestic Regulation

FIGURE 5-3 Cumulative annual weight changes, 1919–78

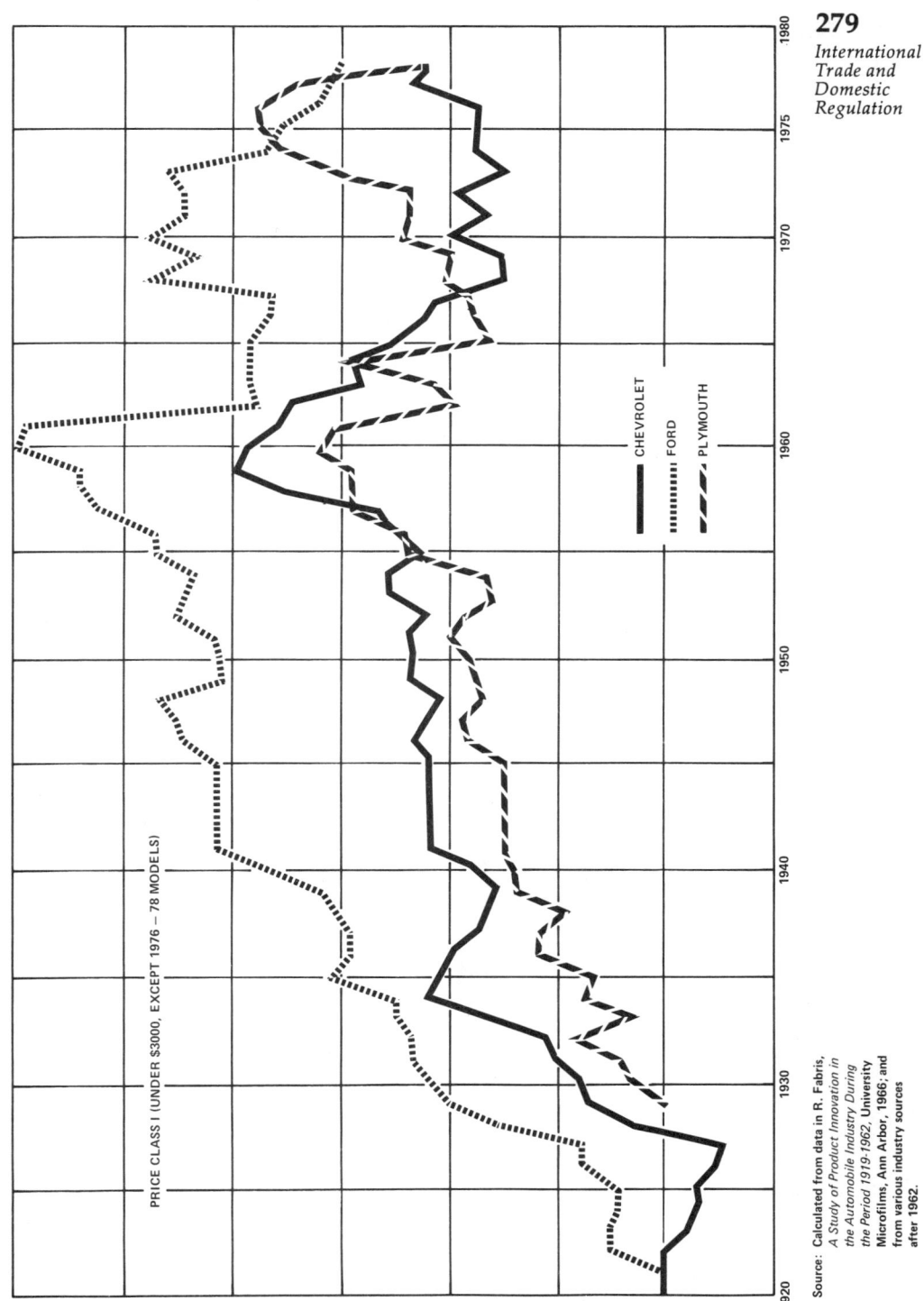

Source: Calculated from data in R. Fabris, *A Study of Product Innovation in the Automobile Industry During the Period 1919-1962*, University Microfilms, Ann Arbor, 1966; and from various industry sources after 1962.

EACH SQUARE REPRESENTS 33.33 POUNDS. UP TO 1962: "UNLADEN" WEIGHT MEASURED. 1963 ON: "CURB" WEIGHT MEASURED.

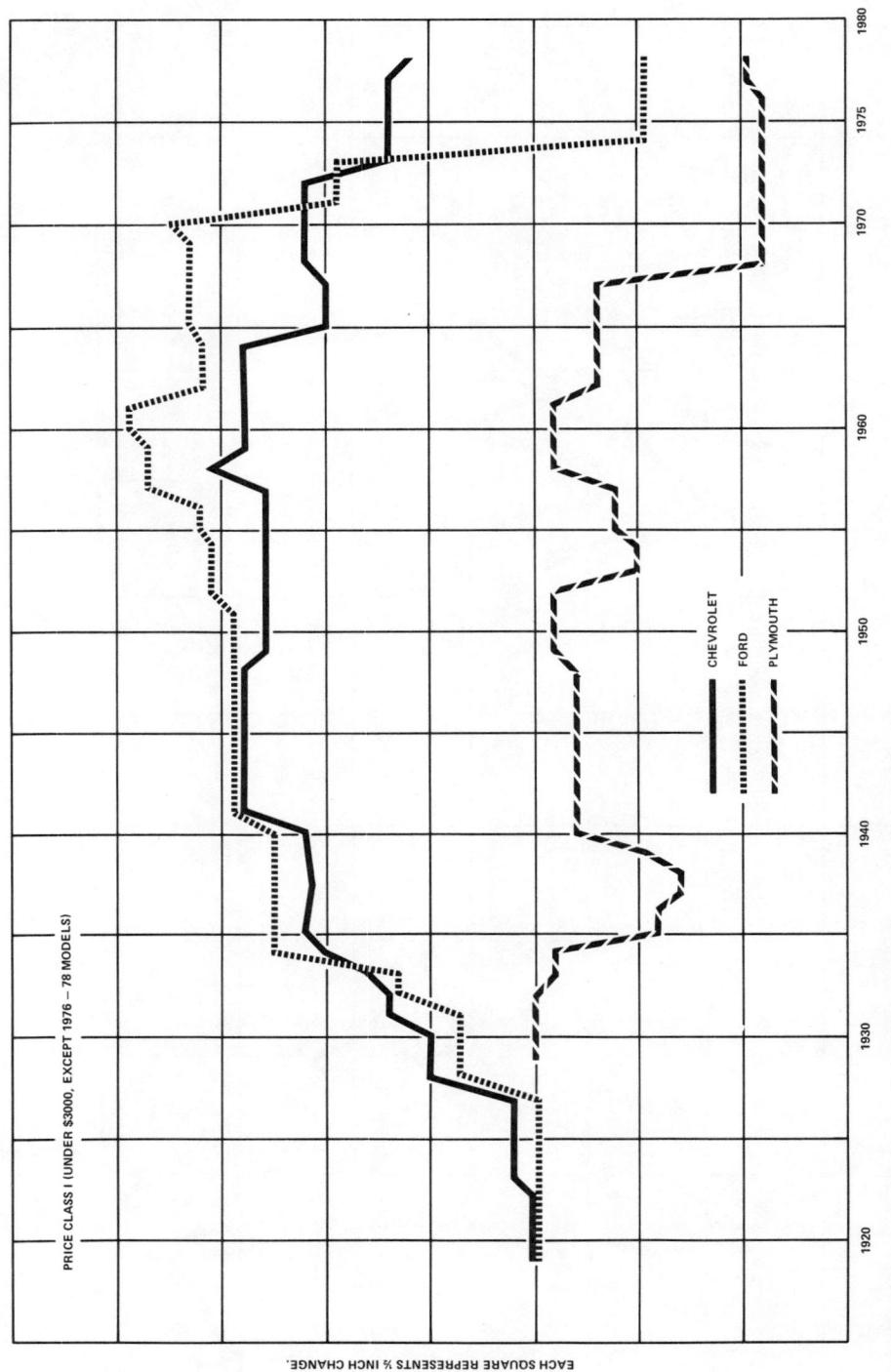

FIGURE 5-4 Cumulative annual wheelbase changes, 1919–78

American-made cars. The result would have been excess capacity in the United States and strains on capacity in European plants that already faced a good home market.

Ford and General Motors did not again import a European car in volume until mileage requirements were introduced. The major import was not a larger European model but a small one. Ford Fiesta sales led to a climb in the share of captive imports to almost 10 percent of all imports in 1977. All indications are that Ford plans to continue selling the Fiesta only as long as its sales count in the calculation of fleet-average gas mileage. Thus, its import seems only an aberration in a well-established policy—one of the "blips," that regulation has caused in a rather steady change in the United States position in the world auto market.

Although small cars provided the vast majority of imports in the 1950s and early 1960s, by the late 1960s the middle gap was being filled by offerings of noncaptive imports. The average car manufactured in Europe was increasing in size, consistent with the higher income levels there. Volkswagen offered a larger model and larger engines in its Beetle (up from 1100cc to 1600cc). Peugeot and Volvo made more larger cars and were selling them in the United States. The 1976 Volvo was 192.6 inches long and had an engine displacement of 2.5 liters, close to the size of the 1950 Chevrolet. Moreover, Japanese manufacturers were beginning to fill the gap.

Apparently recognizing the erosion of the differentiation strategy, American firms offered cars (Pinto, Vega) in the middle range similar in size to the cars of the early 1950s. It was clear that competition would be severe. Rather than offering cars in a market shared only by three major firms, the United States companies were doing battle with a large number of imports in the small car field. Thus, United States firms have continued to complain of low profit margins—or even losses—on their small cars, in contrast to the larger models where they faced no severe competition.

It is no surprise that United States firms preferred to do business in larger cars where competition was weak. But the facts of the international marketplace had meant that by 1970 a continued reliance on producing only large cars would mean a significant loss of market share in the United States. Thus, before the energy crisis in 1973, United States manufacturers had begun to offer smaller cars. Viewed in retrospect, the energy crisis and the mileage requirements simply accelerated a trend already underway. In fact, as shown in Figure 5-5, the effects of this regulatory legislation are hardly noticeable at all.[9]

---

9. For a finer breakdown of sales by size and type of automobile, see Figure 14 of Bloomfield, n.3 *supra*. See also R. L. Carlson, "Seemingly Unrelated Regression and the Demand for Automobiles of Different Sizes, 1965–1975," *The Journal of Business* 246 (Apr. 1978).

*CARS LESS THAN 190 INCHES LONG.

Source: Adapted from Figure 2.1 of Eric J. Toder, *Trade Policy and the U.S. Automobile Industry* (New York: Praeger, 1977).

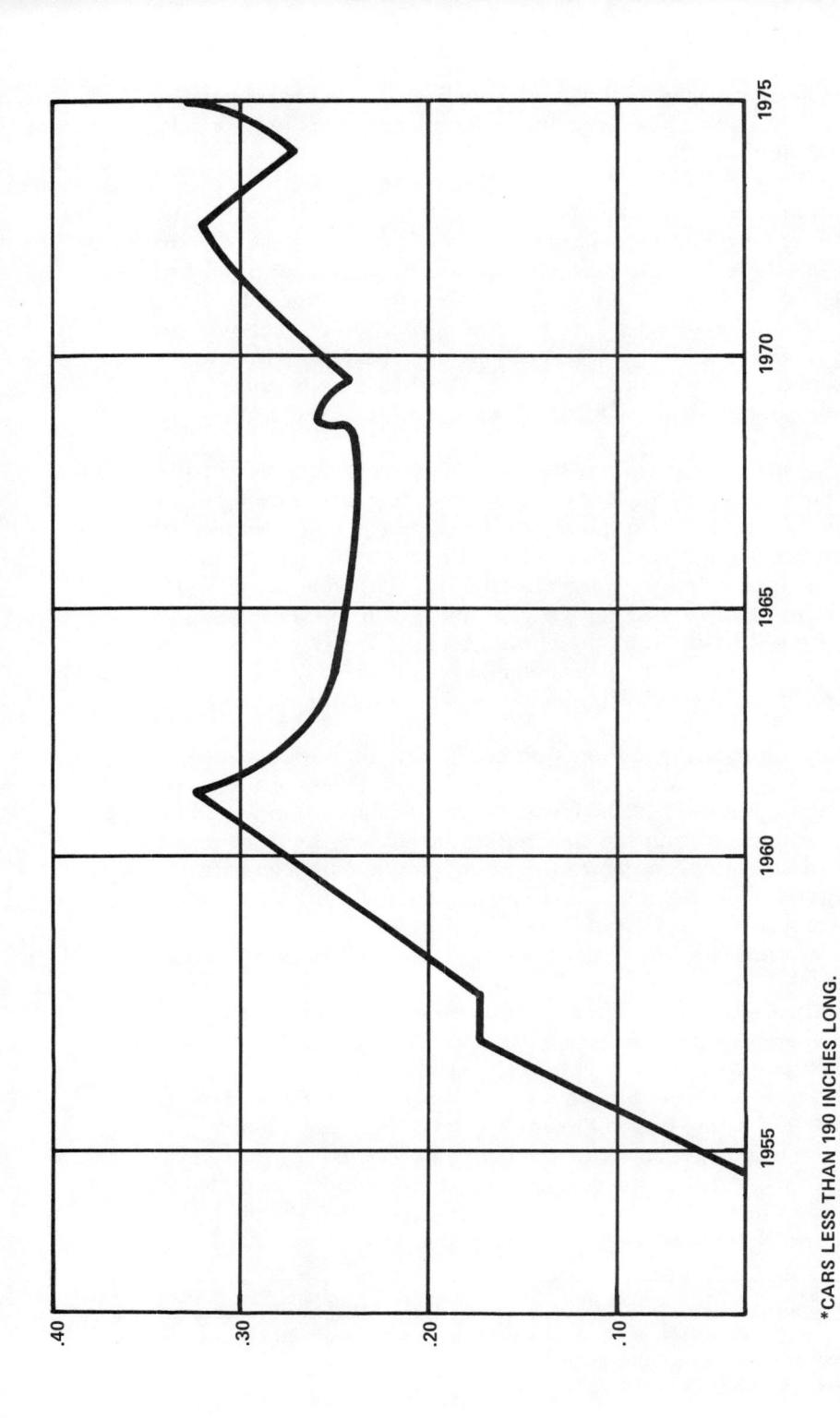

FIGURE 5-5 Small car sales as a percentage of all cars in U.S. 1955–75

TOWARDS A "STANDARD CAR"

The product life cycle model suggests the trend toward an international "standard car." American producers designed strategies to fight against this development. I believe that this strategy was becoming increasingly unsuccessful even before the fuel economy regulation appeared, forcing American manufacturers to design smaller cars.

While the average American car was getting smaller, the average European car was getting larger. In Britain, the share of cars with engines of less than 1000cc decreased from 30.4 percent of the market in 1965 to 19 percent in 1973. The biggest increases were for cars in the 1501cc to 2000cc range, which went from 18.9 percent to 27.7 percent of the market. The move to larger cars in Europe was primarily the result of higher incomes. Meanwhile, in the United States the subcompact and compact cars were gaining market share, probably because of congestion and price. Sales of United States subcompacts and compacts grew from about 7 percent of United States sales in 1968 to almost 17 percent in 1972. By 1975 they had grown, in a steady trend, to about 20 percent. Meanwhile, imports—almost all small cars—grew from about 11 percent to about 17 percent.[10] Cars under 190 inches in length (roughly the size of the 1950 Chevrolet) held about 16 percent of the United States market in 1959. Their share jumped to almost 35 percent with the introduction of the Corvair, Falcon, and Valiant; declined to about 21 percent by 1966; and then grew rather steadily to hold 36 percent by 1975.[11] The market share of the so-called "standard-sized" car in the United States slipped steadily from 40 percent in 1968 to a little under 20 percent in 1975. The trend was a steady one over the seven-year period. Although the averages were still far apart, the area of overlap had increased dramatically. The smaller United States car and the larger European cars hardly differed in usuable passenger room from what the United States consumer had bought eagerly in the early 1950s.

Standardization occurred in features other than size. In the early days of the automobile, the consumer was offered a bewildering choice of mechanical features: Three wheels or four, tiller or steering wheel, gasoline internal combustion or steam engines, and so on. By the 1930s, standardization was still far from complete. The worldwide automobile industry produced, on a large-scale basis, cars of various sizes and drive-train configurations. Cars had the engine in front with front- or with rear-wheel drives, or in the rear over the driven wheels. A few significant producers were still betting on the two-cycle engine through the 1950s.

By the 1970s, there seemed to be a strong move toward a standard configuration. Front-wheel drive was beginning to win its battle for acceptance. Among the 50 best-selling models in world trade, 45 percent

---

10. Gerald Bloomfield, n. 3 *supra* at 68–69.
11. E. J. Toder, *Trade Policy and the U.S. Automobile Industry* (Praeger Publishers, 1978).

of the cars sold were front-wheel drive in 1976. In 1978, 40 percent of all the cars sold in Europe had transverse engines and front-wheel drive, a combination innovated by the British.[12] By 1977, approximately 1 out of every 4 cars produced in the world had front-wheel drive, a 15 percent increase over 1976 (see Figure 5-6).

The laggards have been the American-owned firms and the Japanese manufacturers (see Table 5-9). United States firms clearly have had the available technology. Ford, for example, manufactured its Fiesta abroad as its "world car," and imported it only because of the mileage requirements. General Motors produced a large front-wheel drive car; Chrysler was making a small front-wheel drive product. For some, the strategy was still that of differentiating the United States car from these mass-produced abroad. General Motors, however, appeared to be betting against the front-wheel drive, with its Chevette "world car."

Front-wheel drive may not be the norm of the future.[13] But even if the norm shifts, many producers would make the same type car, whatever the new norm might be.

CHANGES IN COMPETITORS

In several national markets production has become more concentrated (see Table 5-10). Compared to 1955, which may be taken as the year normal industrial production was resumed in Europe and Japan, concentration has increased in every country except Italy. This pattern has worried national authorities concerned with encouraging competition.

On the other hand, more open borders and more producers in other markets have introduced a new element of competition in those very same countries. Imports have provided the consumer with alternative models and prices. Table 5-11 shows the percent of total market held by major domestic producers. The trend in the United States, Italy, and the United Kingdom has been toward a smaller share, due to foreign competition. In Germany and France, imports have substantially offset the effect of growing concentration among domestic producers.

In the United States market, competition has been most intense in the market for smaller size cars, of course. While profit margins have remained high on the models supplied only by the United States producers, they have been squeezed on the smaller sizes.[14] Foreign prices tended to move with exchange rates, and the prices for United States small cars have tended to follow the imports as the only serious compe-

---

12. "Safer, Super Efficient Front-Wheel Drive Cars," *House and Gardens,* Apr. 1978, p. 38.
13. See "Back-to-front Cars," *The Economist,* June 10, 1978, p. 89.
14. See, for example, *the testimony of Ford's Chief Economist, John Deaver, before the Sen. Foreign Economic Policy Subcomm.,* cited in G. H. Farnsworth, "Ford Concedes it Lags in Competition with Imports Despite Dollar's Fall," *New York Times,* June 23, 1978, p. D4.

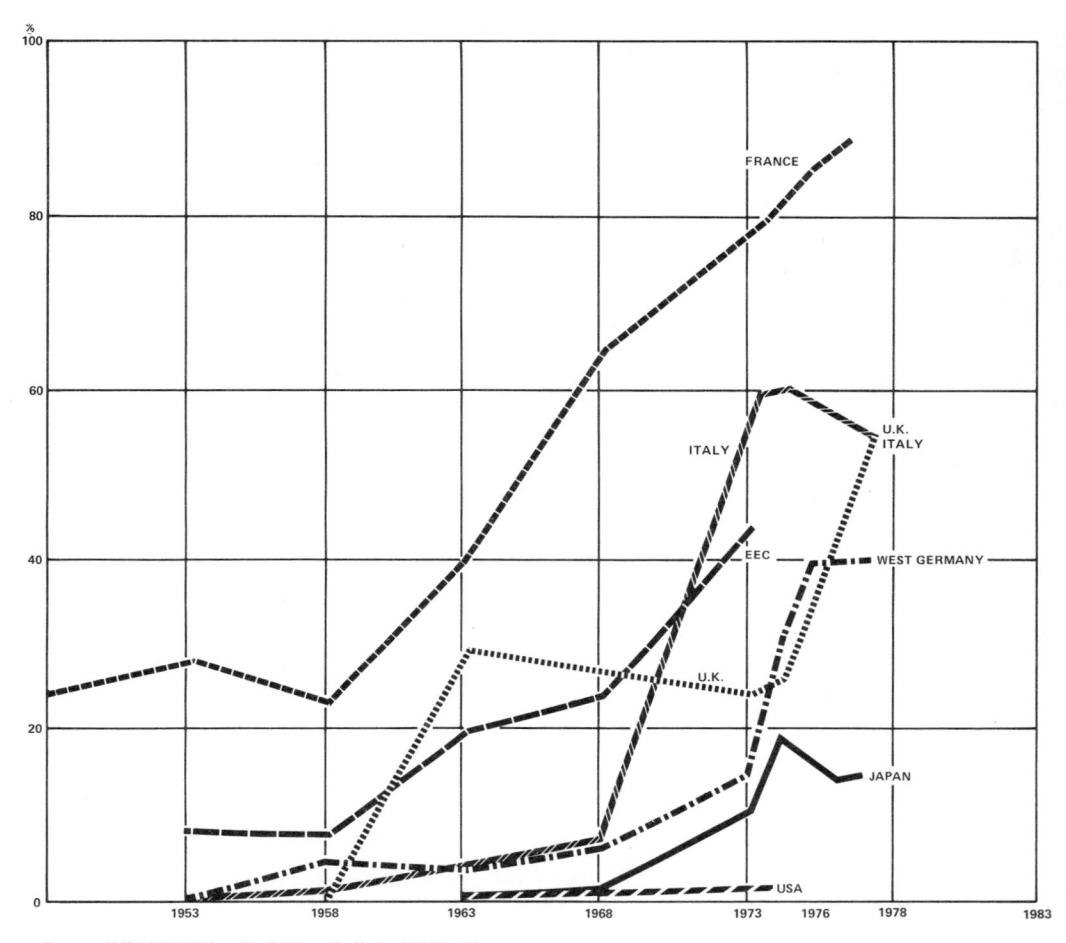

Sources: 1963, 1973, 1974 from *Ward's Automotive Yearbook* 1976, p. 16.
1977 from *Automotive News Market Data Book* 1977, p. 27.
1953, 1958, 1968 from Society of Automotive Engineers, *The Techniques of Front Wheel Drive in Europe*, H. Seznec and H. LaGrange. Report 750013.

FIGURE 5-6 Front-wheel-drive cars as a percentage of all cars produced by major European countries, by year

tition (see Figure 5-7). As the industry moves toward a standard car, the margins of United States manufacturers will probably be further eroded.

United States firms' relative strength abroad has also declined. No longer having a technological edge, United States firms have faced growing competition in countries where they have subsidiaries.[15] In the newly producing countries, United States firms can no longer name their terms. General Motors used to be able to insist on joint ventures, but then European and Japanese firms offered more liberal terms as they expanded abroad. United States firms had to respond, so that today au-

15. For evidence on the influence of competition on bargaining power, see N. Fagre and L. T. Wells, Jr., "Bargaining Power of Multinationals," mimeo.

TABLE 5-9 Percentage of Cars with Front-Wheel Drive 1978, Selected Manufacturers

Manufacturer or brand	Percentage with front-wheel drive
Alfa Romeo	50%
Audi-NSU	100
Austin	All but low volume taxis
Chrysler France	90
Chrysler U.K.	20
Citroën	100
Fiat	About 50
Ford-Spain	100
Ford-Germany	20
Ford-U.K.	15
Mercedes Benz	0
Mini (Leyland)	100
GM-Opel	0
Peugeot	About 66
Princess (Leyland)	100
Renault	100
Saab	100
SEAT	About 33
Triumph (Leyland)	0
GM Vauxhall	0
Volkswagen	90
Volvo	0
Subaru	100
Honda	100
All Japanese	15

Source: Calculated from *Automotive News 1977 Market Data Bank*.

tomobile technology can be obtained by a potential new producer under a simple licensing arrangement.

Other factors have also changed in the international marketplace. One potentially important change that could affect competition is the increasing role of state-owned automobile producers. Into the 1960s, the only important state-controlled producers were Renault and Volkswagen. Evidence on the importance of state ownership to the behavior of Renault is scanty. But Renault has not held a significant share of the United States market since the Dauphine was sold here. Volkswagen, especially under the Christian Democratic Government, seems to have taken most decisions as would a private firm. More recently, the state role in automobile production has grown considerably. The larger share of domestically owned plants in Britain is government controlled. Alfa Romeo of Italy, once largely a sports car manufacturer, has moved into the market for mass-produced cars. Efforts to sell the

TABLE 5-10 Percentage of Production Accounted for by the Top Manufacturers in Major Producing Countries (1946–1977)

	U.S. (3 firms)	W. Germany (4 firms)	France (3 firms)	Italy (2 firms)	Japan (2 firms)	U.K. (4 firms)
1946	84.6%	100%	53.9%	n.a.	n.a. (110 cars)	80.0%
1950	87.0	92.9	76.2	n.a.	83.3%	83.2
1955	95.6	76.4	78.5	99.8%	69.1	87.1
1960	91.2	77.8	76.6	99.7	75.3	87.5
1965	96.3	87.0	80.1	97.6	65.0	91.1
1970	95.7	94.6	83.4	96.9	71.3	87.2
1975	95.0	99.5	99.7*	97.4	75.3	87.2
1976	97.0	99.0	99.7**	99.0	71.0	99.4
1977	98.3	99.0	99.6***	97.2	93.2	99.4

* Citroën included with Peugeot.
** Lancia included with Fiat.
*** "Big 5" includes Triumph Standard.
Source: W. Duncan, *U.S.–Japan Automotive Diplomacy* Appendix B (Ballinger Publishing Co. 1973).

TABLE 5-11 Percentage of Market Held by Domestic Producers (1946–1977)

	U.S. (3 firms)	W. Germany (4 firms)	France (3 firms)	Italy (2 firms)	Japan (2 firms)	U.K. (4 firms)
1946	85.5%					
1950	87.0					
1955	95.2	64.9%				
1960	84.2	62.0	70.3%	83.9%	60.5%	
1965	90.2	72.9	n.a.	80.5	40.6	94.5%
1970	82.2	65.7	70.6	68.6	50.6	85.1
1975	79.9	61.0	79.3	65.8	73.7	64.8
1976	82.6	72.0	76.7	61.6	69.7	61.7
1977	80.0	73.0	77.5	n.a.	71.9	

Source: W. Duncan, *U.S.–Japan Automotive Diplomacy* Appendix B (Ballinger Publishing Co. 1973).

Polish and Russian manufactured Fiats in Western Europe have begun. What the increased role of state firms will mean for international competition remains to be seen. The meager evidence now available suggests that the Western European state-owned firms are behaving in ways similar to the private ones, except with respect to decisions about where to locate factories at home.[16] Intervention could become much greater if European governments were to move further to the left.

---

16. See L. T. Wells, Jr., "Automobiles," in *Big Business and State* 195–254 (R. Vernon, Ed., Harvard Univ. Press, 1978).

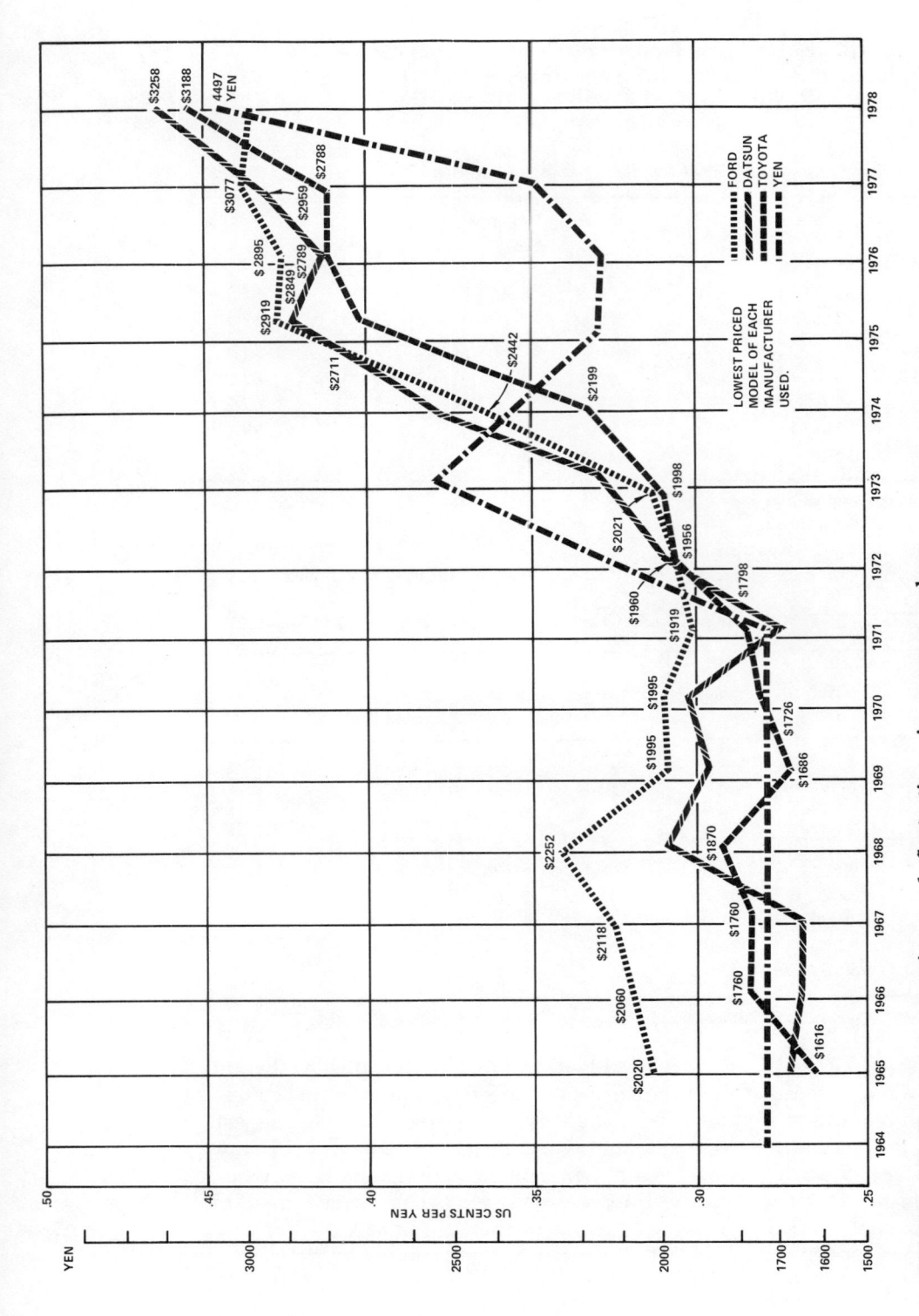

FIGURE 5-7 Passenger car prices and fluctuations in currency values: Japanese import vs. American Ford

While the attention of national authorities remained focused on the number of domestic producers, that focus has become increasingly irrelevant. With open borders, imports provide discipline for the domestic industry, as has been demonstrated in the United States. Three major firms may not provide a basis for intense price competition. But in spite of the efforts of United States firms to isolate the United States market from competition by differentiating the product, they have been forced to respond to imports with new models and competitive prices.

Nevertheless, antitrust authorities cannot relax under an assumption that competition will remain. The task of assuring that competition is not thwarted is a more difficult one when one has to rely on firms of different nationalities. Firms have always had a tendency to work out arrangements to avoid competition. Monitoring and prohibiting those arrangements becomes increasingly complex as the managements span international borders. In Europe the links among firms of different nationalities are multiple. (See text after n. 19 *infra*.) Each link provides the opportunity to communicate plans, to divide markets, and to limit innovation. An expansion of these links, say to include American firms, ought to be of as much concern to United States antitrust authorities as an expansion of links between Ford and General Motors. But the jurisdictional problems of enforcing an antitrust policy in the international area are manifold. Consider a hypothetical joint venture between Ford and, say, Toyota in Indonesia. That joint venture might be encouraged by the Indonesian authorities, because it allows economies of scale; it might be quite acceptable to the Japanese authorities, who have many tools for controlling Japanese firms; but it should be viewed as a major threat to competition by United States authorities.

Until United States antitrust policy faces the reality of the new international competition, it will be unable to deal with such problems. The traditional tool of breaking up large firms is likely to be counterproductive. And the actions that count will be overlooked.

INNOVATION AS A STRATEGY

The competition that drives down profit margins at the end of the product life cycle can be avoided if the American producer can innovate something really new to begin a new cycle. International Business Machines, for example, moved from household gadgets to office machinery to computers as its innovative edge was dulled.

The American producer might, it would seem, be able to innovate something new in the automobile field that would enable it to avoid tough price competition from foreign imports. In fact, the odds of such a response are probably rather low.

First American producers no longer have any unique advantages over their foreign competitors. The automobile has become a commonplace item throughout the Western world. Foreign producers are faced with markets that are likely to be no less stimulating for innovation than that faced by American firms. Thus, an innovation is perhaps equally likely abroad as in the United States.

Second, the existence of many large, technologically competent firms in the world means that any innovation is likely to be copied quickly, if profits appear promising.

Third, a large part of the industry seems to have settled in a mode that discourages innovation. In the United States, Alfred P. Sloan stated General Motors' strategy clearly: "The policy we set was valid if our cars were at least equal in design to the best of our competitors in a grade, so that it was not necessary to lead in design or run the risk of untried experiments.[17]" That statement would, I suspect, still describe the policy of any of the three major United States producers.

In the open Europe of the Common Market, the risks facing any one producer who does not innovate would appear to be higher, in light of the greater number of competitors. In fact, the level of innovation there appears to be higher: The small front-wheel drive car, the small diesel engine, mass-produced cars with four-wheel independent suspension, a safe bumper system with little added weight,[18] and so on. It has been the firms outside the United States that have led in finding ways to meet pollution regulations without the awkward catalytic converter. In 1975, 70 percent of United States Fords, 100 percent of General Motor cars, and 75 percent of Chrysler products had catalytic converters,[19] whereas only 20.3 percent of imports had them. By 1977 only 9.6 percent of imports had them.

The European firms, however, have been rapidly establishing links that will enable them to monitor innovative activities in ostensibly competing firms. In some cases, the link is a joint venture for research and development. In other cases, the links are slightly more subtle. One diagram shows a network of relationships linking Renault, Daimler-Benz, Alfa Romeo, Volvo, Fiat, Ferrari, Lancia, SEAT, Peugeot, Citroën, Volkswagen, Audi/NSU, and Porsche, as well as the European producers of commercial vehicles.[20] One can hardly doubt that these links will be used to restore stability to the industry. Research and development budgets can be cut if one is assured that competitors are not spending much on innovation.

If that were the whole story, one would suspect that innovation is about to end in the industry. In fact, it probably is not. Cross-regional

---

17. A. P. Sloan, *My Years with General Motors* (New York: Doubleday Co., Inc., 1963), cited in Harbridge House, *The Imported Automobile Industry* 39 (Dec. 1976).

18. See Harbridge House, *ibid.* at 40.

19. Constructed from data in *Automotive News 1976–78 Market Data Book*, *Ward's Automotive Yearbook*, various issues; "How the Catalytic Converter Unexpectedly Paid Off," *Business Week*, Oct. 5, 1975, pp. 68–69; and "Automotives get Delay in Meeting Pollution Recks," *Wall Street Journal*, Mar. 1975, p. 6.

20. 1978 Market Data Bank Issue, *Automotive News*, Apr. 26, 1978, p. 12. See also L. T. Wells, Jr., "Automobiles," n. 16 *supra* at 248.

rivalry could sustain innovation if antitrust policies can limit transnational ties. Then European firms might still innovate in competition with American firms. The American firms' policy of avoiding innovations is clear enough, however, so that the Europeans are more likely to conform to it, as soon as they can reduce the rivalry among themselves. It is the remaining "outsiders" that are likely to provide the innovation. In recent years, the Japanese have been important in this role. Eager to obtain a share of the world market, they have introduced the rotary engine (a European product, of course) and the stratified charge engine. A very few years ago, the chairman of a European automobile firm assured me that he knew personally the chief executive officer of every European and American automobile firm. He added that he knew none of the managers of Japanese firms. No doubt, this will change as the Japanese share of the world market increases. In a world of oligopolists, the Japanese will eventually decide that innovation is for them also a losing game. They will become "insiders." But by then, if the industrialized countries' trade policies do not exclude them, the automobile firms of Korea and other developing countries will be trying to break into world markets. Preliminary indications were evident by the mid–1970s. Tata, of India, exported some $10 million of commercial vehicles in 1974. By 1978, it was selling in Turkey, East Africa, and West Africa. Hyundai, of Korea, was beginning an export drive. Korean vehicle exports rose to 48,000 in 1976 from under 500 in 1965. Brazil, whose producers were under the control of major international firms, exported 67,000 vehicles in 1976, up from less than 9,000 in 1972. As these countries just entering the world market strive for exports, innovation may serve as one of the means of competition.

MATURE OLIGOPOLIES

The present automobile industry is best described as a mature oligopoly sharing a number of characteristics with other mature industries. In steel, many petrochemicals, textiles, and airlines, as in automobiles, innovation is not rapid enough for United States firms to maintain a technological lead long enough to insulate them from foreign competition. In fact, innovation in these industries seems to occur abroad as frequently as in the United States. With fixed costs representing a rather high percentage of total costs, producers are tempted to wage price battles on the basis of incremental costs, especially in export markets. New producers, entering the world market from countries that are rapidly industrializing, create a new element of instability. Further, state firms or firms with state support play an important role in the world market. Interested in employment stability and foreign exchange earnings, they may behave in ways that differ from the patterns set by private firms.

Still, the automobile industry differs somewhat from most other mature oligopolies. Unlike steel, petrochemicals, and basic textiles, the product can be differentiated. The American consumer does seem to have some loyalty to the American product, because of brand preference, styling, and other features. Older customers have been reluctant to shift to imported products or even to smaller American products. Thus, for a time, consumer loyalty and preferences grant some protection to the American manufacturer.[21] Similar "consumer" loyalty offers little protection to a petrochemical, steel, or basic textile manufacturer.

The American automobile manufacturer is also somewhat protected from new competition by the large investment in distribution required of a new entrant into the United States market. To sell cars effectively, a supplier must provide a parts and service network that covers the United States. Advertising must be undertaken. Efficiencies are available perhaps only on a national scale. (It is little wonder that the Japanese concentrated their early efforts in Europe on small markets—Belgium, Switzerland, and Scandinavia). On the other hand, products such as textiles, steel, and petrochemicals can be sold effectively on a regional basis.

In addition, automobile manufacturers face considerable transportation costs. One calculation estimates that Japan's cost advantage over United States producers disappears when transportation costs are added.[22] The investment by Volkswagen and the proposed investments by Japanese firms in United States plants further suggest that production cost differences are not overwhelming.

CONCLUSION

In response to the move toward standardization and foreign competition, one would expect a slow, but continuing, erosion of margins and market share for United States firms as they face competition from imports and from foreign firms locating in the United States. With the protection offered by consumer loyalties, product differentiation, entry costs, and transportation one would not expect the United States automobile industry to disappear, however. Forecasts do not suggest the need for a protective policy either: Neither United States Government regulation nor foreign government intervention appears to have been significant enough to influence the pattern greatly. The pressures are the results of increased competition in a mature industry.

The beneficiary of this competition is likely to be the United States consumer. The aim of government policy ought to be to ease the transition, especially for labor that will have to be slowly shifted to other activities, and not to protect United States industry from that competition. Rather than erecting import barriers or encouraging foreign export quotas or state-supported, market-sharing arrangements, the United States government should make sure that United States firms do not build links with foreign competitors that will restrain price competition and reduce rivalry and, thus, innovation.

---

21. See Toder, n. 11 *supra* at 75–77, 213.
22. *Ibid.* at 232.

DISCUSSION

ROBERT V. COLEMAN: Mr. Pearce pointed to Ford's remarkable success in integrating its European operations. As a result of this integration strategy, Ford now produces 25 percent of its motor vehicles in Europe. Its European after-tax return on sales is probably double its United States return on sales. In 1977 it enjoyed a 12.5 percent share in the total Western European market, topped only by Renault with 13.5 percent. With United States cars approaching European cars in size we are on the threshold of a new integration in a worldwide sense. This suggests that General Motors and Ford will be designing cars for production in both Europe and the United States with substantial commonality of parts. This will provide flexibility for sourcing on either continent, thereby increasing each company's economies of scale.

Japanese industries face several dilemmas when planning to relocate some manufacturing to the North American continent. Their growth up to now has been supported primarily by exports. Growth potential in its high-volume markets now seems limited. In its number 1 export destination, North America, which accounted for almost 50 percent of Japan's car exports in 1977, it faces competition with the domestic compacts and subcompacts. Any further increase in its penetration into this country will probably lead to protectionist demands in the United States. Japan already faces protectionist policies in its number 2 market, Europe, which accounts for 22 percent of its car exports (1977). Japan has a favorable position in markets in developing countries, but these markets at present lack the high-volume potential to sustain the Japanese industry's growth rate. Threatened with a future production growth rate of 4-to-5 percent annually, it will be difficult to move some of its manufacturing operations to the United States without creating major unemployment in Japan.

Professor Wells feels that the United States industry has not in the past been innovative relative to the European and Japanese competitors, and that it will not improve in the future. Therefore, he forecasts a long-term gradual erosion in the United States industry's market share in the domestic market. He implies, but does not state, an eventual end to the United States industry. However, the United States industry has been innovative enough over the years to make substantial gains in productivity. Prior to emissions control, safety regulations, and the energy crisis, innovations were directed at customer appeal and reliability, because these advances would promote car sales. Incidentally, it was the industry's high degree of market orientation that has resulted in its present size.

Wells specifically criticizes the awkward catalytic converter and praises the foreign manufacturers for their limited use of this device. Use of converters is basically a function of car weight and engine size; the larger imported cars that correspond to United States cars in weight and engine displacement do use converters.

Finally, I am more optimistic about the United States industry's ability to maintain their market position. Profit margins will be lower. But I expect the United States industry to retain 80 percent and probably 85 percent of the domestic market. I agree with Wells that the United States Government should not pursue a protectionist policy.

KENKICHI KONISHI: I feel strongly that it is necessary to judge the automobile policy of a government or the behavior of individual companies within the historical perspective presented in Professor Wilkins' discussion. Frankly speaking, I felt easier after reading her paper because I found that many of the things for which we Japanese are accused nowadays by other countries and foreign industrialists, are almost identical to those things which our accusers have done themselves at certain stages in their own automobile history.

I agree with Professor Wells' conclusion that the United States consumer will be best served by open competition in the United States automobile market. I think this is a generally accepted point. I tend to disagree, however, with his somewhat simplified application of the product life cycle concept which suggests that the United States firms, due to the maturity of the industry, will face a "slow, but continuing erosion of margin and market share."

Professor Wells argues that the United States makers' originally successful strategy of differentiation, meaning promotion of large cars, has protected the United States companies from the product life cycle and foreign competition, but that now standardization is eroding their market share. I feel that the reverse is the case. Rather it was the United States makers' neglect of a rising small car market that led to the rise in imports. As soon as the United States industry puts its considerable technical and design expertise behind the development of a small car, they will become more competitive with imports, not less. To a certain extent this movement has already taken place, and we can expect it to intensify in the future.

We should also recognize that the Energy Policy Conservation Act fuel economy regulation is a vital factor in changing the competitive structure in the United States car market. I believe it a mistake to characterize this regulation as a "blip" in an otherwise inevitable process. The Energy Policy and Conservation Act tied the sales, and thus the pricing, of the small car to the downsized luxury car. The United States companies will continue to produce luxury cars for an increasingly affluent American public. However, in order to do so they must make a significant investment in the small car market, an investment which may not be justified in terms of the margin received,* but will be justified when that margin is considered together with the margin on the large car sales, which in turn, under the Energy Policy and Conservation Act, depend on the sale of the small car. This radically new concept in car pricing was the direct result of the Energy Policy and Conservation Act. Rather than a "blip," it is a major eruption.

---

* On June 22, 1978, Mr. John Deaver, Manager of the Economics Department at Ford Motor Company, testified before the United States Senate Foreign Economic Policy Subcommittee that "even at present prices Ford is incurring a net loss on small car sales."

It means that imported cars are challenged not only by the new entry of the domestic small cars in the previously almost exclusive market of the imports, but also by the low price of those domestic cars, which, if they were imports, could be the subject of dumping complaints.

In several places Mr. Pearce suggests that the success of the Japanese automobile industry in the United States market, and the failure of Americans to market in Japan, is due to Japanese Government export promotion on the one hand, and to protectionist measures on the other. I think these comments give a misleading impression of the nature of the Japanese automobile industry and the basis for its success.

First, with respect to the suggestion that the Japanese Government has failed to open its domestic market, it is important for one to indicate the time frame to which one is referring. There was indeed a considerable amount of protection of the Japanese automobile industry in the past. These barriers began to be dismantled in the mid–1960s—the time, incidentally, in which exports began to expand—and were progressively reduced so that today there is a zero tariff on imported automobiles, the possibility of 100 percent capital participation by a foreign company in a Japanese automobile manufacturing facility, and special treatment for imported cars in order to speed up the certification process.

Professor Wilkins pointed out in her discussion that by 1970 Western Europe had reached the equivalent level of automobile ownership held in the United States in 1929 (1 car per 5 persons). However, Japan in 1970 was below Canada in 1929 (1 car per 10 persons). Roughly speaking, this means the Japanese auto industry, or the Japanese living standard as shown by auto ownership, was more than forty years behind Canada, and more than fifty years behind the United States.

This being the case, it is not so unusual that Japan protected its domestic market until 1970 because, as Professor Wilkins mentioned, Britain had an 88 percent surcharge on auto imports even in 1919. But Japan has liberalized its policies on auto imports and foreign investment, and reduced the tariff very dramatically: From 17.5 percent for larger cars and 34 percent for small cars in January, 1970 to 10 percent for all cars in

April 1971; finally, after a few further steps the auto tariff became zero in April 1978, making Japan the first country in the world to eliminate the auto tariff.

Nevertheless, some say Japan is not an open market and that it is the most difficult market to penetrate. However, I wonder if those people who say Japan is not an open market really have a firm intention and have tried their best to export their cars to Japan. First of all, did American manufacturers have proper cars to be exported to Japan before the four-door Chevette was built by General Motors for the 1978 model year? Did American and European manufacturers study the demand of Japanese consumers and the peculiarities of the Japanese market? Did they establish a dealer network in Japan as Japanese manufacturers established in this country? Without a thorough study of these questions, which are mandatory for any export of automobiles to a foreign market, it is, I think, a one-sided opinion to say the Japanese market is not open.

Second, there is at least the suggestion that Japan's environmental regulations are an unfair barrier to the Japanese market. Because of rapid economic expansion during the 1960s and thereafter, many pollution problems have arisen in Japan. Hostile public opinion directed against both industrial and governmental negligence in controlling the environment, therefore, forced the government to impose very strict environmental regulation. The automobile emission standard in Japan was no exception. However, it should be pointed out also that Japanese auto emission regulations were strongly influenced by the United States emission-control policy, if not born in the United States.

The Japanese government, like the United States, is applying the same safety and emission regulations to both domestic cars and imported cars. Furthermore, the Japanese government extended the effective date of the 1978 emission standard by three years only for imported cars.

Third, it is suggested in these statements that the Japanese government has fostered the Japanese industry and promoted Japanese exports. There is no question that the Japanese government has long been interested in ensuring a healthy export sector. This has been a matter of survival in a resource-scarce country. However, the Japanese automobile industry has received little if any promotional support from the Japanese government either in terms of developing manufacturing capability or in exporting. Due to this factor the Japanese automobile industry is exceptionally independent of government influence. Mr. Pearce refers to government rationalization of the Japanese automobile industry. In fact, the government for years urged a rationalization of the Japanese automobile industry, and in 1968 in a meeting at Hakone, sponsored an industry resolution not to tie up with foreign capital. Yet shortly thereafter Mitsubishi signed a capital tie-up with Chrysler, followed by Isuzu's agreement with General Motors. The government's attempt to force rationalization of the Japanese automobile industry is more an example of the lack of government influence than anything else. In addition, it is commonly recognized that the success of the Japanese in the United States market is due not to government promotion of exports but to the fact that the Japanese automobile companies studied the United States market and then produced a technologically design-competitive vehicle to meet the need of the United States consumer.

Fourth, a word should be said about the Japanese attitude towards exports compared to that in the United States. As indicated above, the Japanese have had to export in order to survive. Japan's resource structure is the reverse of the United States' in that the vital materials to sustain an expanding industrial strength and standard of living must come from abroad. This has not been the case with the United States, until recently, with its growing dependence on foreign oil.

The United States, in contrast, has seen exports as secondary to a large domestic market. With abundant resources, there has not been the pressure to export, and the government, while concerned over balance-of-payments problems, has not felt it necessary to devise a consistent government approach towards export policy. The United States attitude has always been that exports can take care of themselves, and for many years they did, with significant trade balances in favor of the United States., and any deficits in the balance of payments owing principally to foreign aid and capital outflows.

What concerns us is that while Japan has now liberalized its import policies, the United States may turn in the opposite direction and impose import restrictions to protect employment and its balance-of-trade position.

W. R. WILKINSON: I agree with Professor Wells' assumption of the mature industry and do not foresee that any of the auto manufacturers in the United States will ever be rejuvenated into a major exporter. As Mr. Konishi mentioned, the industry has developed as a protected industry; tariffs have been reduced in individual countries only as the economies of production in that country precluded any high degree of import competition. We see that most recently in Japan, where extremely high tariffs and a subsidiary tax structure existed up until a few years ago. These tariffs have been reduced as the domestic industry demonstrated its ability to compete effectively in the home market against imports. This also has been true in Europe and the United States. A casual look at Third World markets indicates that built-up-vehicle importation is restricted as soon as the country obtains even a semblance of a capability to develop an independent automobile industry. The worldwide trend is to protect the auto industry as a major domestic enterprise because auto imports are too great a drain on a country's balance of payments. The United States, having come full circle on this theory, is now the only really viable import market, with a duty of only 3 percent. Europe also has proven susceptible to Japanese imports, but exchange valuation and actions by the European Economic Community or individual countries is likely to limit Japanese penetration.

The expectation that any nation's industry can attain any significant innovative edge on a national basis is unfounded. Any innovations are rapidly assimilated throughout the world industry.

Mr. Pearce mentioned, and I agree, that all of the regulations other than fuel economy—those concerning safety, damageability, emissions, and noise—have had relatively little impact on the relative position of the major producers. Until now (1978) the only major impact of the fuel economy laws has been that the domestic companies have been preoccupied with meeting the fuel economy standards, while importers have been left relatively free to respond to normal market incentives. As the corporate average fuel economy regulations become more stringent, the United States companies will be forced to price their most fuel-efficient vehicles so as to obtain a steady or increasing share of that market segment, almost irrespective of the economies of producing that individual car line. Thus, as Mr. Konishi noted, domestic producers might be selling small cars at prices that would restrict import volumes. It also suggests that a two-tier domestic price system might be created, in which there would be a price gap between the most fuel-efficient domestic cars and larger, less fuel-efficient vehicles. The importers, facing uneconomic price competition in the small cars where they are presently represented, might move into a mid-tier section with larger cars priced under the North American counterparts. In effect, they could utilize their small car volume, with high-fuel economy, as an umbrella to permit sale of less fuel-efficient larger cars.

It is clear that meeting the fuel economy standards will strain the capital resources of the United States industry and limit its ability to compete in other parts of the world. The example of this is Chrysler, which has simply withdrawn from the European market and is in the process of withdrawing from other non–United States markets as rapidly as possible. Neither Ford nor General Motors will be forced to that extreme in the near future, but our ability to compete will be hampered by the availability of capital resources, and perhaps will result in the loss of our competitive position.

Professor Wells concluded that innovation in the European and Japanese companies has led innovation in the United States; I suggest that his examples of innovation—front-wheel drive, independent rear suspension, etc.—were merely a normal response to local market requirements. Both of the noted features represent substantial cost penalties in a vehicle. Front-wheel drive is attractive in small cars because it is package efficient. To what extent that penalty is justified as cars get bigger is a subject of continuing debate, both in this country and in Europe, where large cars still tend to be rear-wheel drive. Independent Rear Suspension offers a substantial handling advantage on winding European roads, but is of little real advantage on a United States expressway. Front-wheel drive, independent rear suspension, and similar features have been around along time; we could have adopted them if they were considered to be cost-effective. Similarly, automatic transmissions and integral air conditioning have developed in this country (but not in Europe), because of a market demand to which we responded.

WELLS: I had not intended to be critical of the United States industry's ability to innovate. In fact, the United States industry produced a front-wheel drive car, the Accord, in the 1930s. The strategy of the major producers was to refine rather than develop a radical change, which was an appropriate strategy given their position. Radical innovations are brought about by firms trying to break into a market or defend their position.

I agree with Mr. Wilkinson that innovations can arise anywhere. United States, Japanese, and European firms face similar markets; any innovation is likely to be copied very quickly. I am concerned about the links being established between firms, since they can play the role of depressing the innovative activities of the companies. Links allow firms to keep an eye on each other.

The American industry is not going to die; there is a lot of consumer loyalty, and there are high barriers to entering the United States market, such as developing a nationwide distribution system.

WILKINS: I define regulation in the broadest terms as government intervention. Is government intervention going to continue to have a role in the world auto industry or is it, as Professor Wells suggested, simply a "blip" in the product life cycle pattern?

Professor Wells suggests that Korea is going to be the new entrant into the United States import market. What I see is that every single major exporter has had a domestic market before it has had an international market and has gone international in terms of an integrated system.

WELLS: When I use the term "regulation," I use it in a very narrow sense. Government intervention has been terribly important to the industry. The three-wheel car is the product of an odd British rule on taxes and licensing, and it disappeared because of the British export requirement at the end of the Second World War; you could not export the three-wheel, so they added the fourth wheel.

Probably the Korean exports will go first to Third World markets, and eventually enter the United States. The 20 percent of the United States market held by imports is not large compared to European markets where more than 20 percent of the cars sold are imported.

WILKINS: The 20 percent goes up when you include the Canadians.

GOVERNMENT: In other countries, the figure is 20 percent or more, but those countries also export.

WELLS: Yes, it is the balance of trade that is significant.

CONSULTANT: You have to explain import penetration in terms of scale economies and majority tastes. Domestic manufacturers served the majority tastes of the United States consumers and imports have served the minority of consumers who desire the specific features imports offer. In the 1980s when domestic manufacturers will offer both types of these cars, the imports' success is likely to decline.

ACADEMIC: That General Motors first introduced the Chevette in Brazil and later in the United States fits nicely with Professor Wells' hypothesis. Also Volkswagen only produces Beetles in Brazil. The Koreans view themselves as being cost competitive with the Japanese sometime in 1980.

AUTO (U.S.): The entry barriers to the United States market are not as expensive as Professor Wells thinks. Honda's experience shows that developing a dealer network can be quick and inexpensive. Secondly, you need not open dealer networks nationwide, as shown by the Japanese who started in California, where their market penetration is 40 percent and in Hawaii where it is 47 percent. I disagree with [the consultant's] comment; I think the importers will be able to hold their 20 percent penetration.

GOVERNMENT (DOT): That 20 percent of the United States market is huge, as big as Japan's total market, and is significant. The United Auto Workers went after fuel economy regulations as a way to make domestic manufacturers produce cars that would be competitive with imports, and thereby improve domestic auto employment, since the consumer would seek the most fuel-efficient car.

GOVERNMENT (DOT): United States regulation in the safety area has been viewed by European and Japanese manufacturers as a barrier to trade designed to protect our industry. Regulations have also been a catalyst, however, for innovation domestically and overseas. The positive aspects of regulation should be explored.

WILKINS: The regulations may be viewed as barriers, but they have actually penalized the domestic manufacturers more than foreign exporters.

PEARCE: With reference to my observations on the Japanese auto industry, their export performance has been tremendous, they have exploited opportunities as they arise. As to Mr. Konishi's concern over my labeling the Japanese government a promoter, I will restate the relationship. I detect an organic situation between the industry, the government, and financial institutions, who together are all working to one single aim, that is, "How can we assist the industry in improving their position overseas?" This relationship does not exist in the United States or Europe.

On the question of imports into Japan, there has been a complete removal of barriers. But there are specific regulations which the Japanese car manufacturers are in a better position to meet than the importers, and distribution has been so limited to importers that it is difficult to get a distribution network in Japan. There is much more emotion over this point in Europe than in the States; the Italians have cut their quota of Japanese imports, the United Kingdom government has reached certain agreements with the Japanese government, etc.

As to the question of European mergers, British Leyland will have to reach an agreement with someone; in France, Renault is discussing joint ventures with American Motors; and Peugeot-Citroen may have to do some consolidating in the future. Germany has antitrust legislation, however.

ACADEMIC: The development of the Korean industry involves a close relationship between the industry and the government resembling the protectionist policies set up in Japan in the 1950s. Hyundai [Korea] has more inquiries about setting up dealer networks in the United States than they can handle. They will have their vehicle through the certification system and ready to market in the United States, probably in twelve to twenty-four months.

No comment has been forwarded about East European penetration. We know that the marketing arm for most Russian products is in a certification program with one vehicle now and will be able to export in twelve to twenty-four months. They have also started a marketing program in Canada, with 5,000 units predicted the first year.

HONDA'S ENTRY INTO THE WORLDWIDE AUTOMOBILE INDUSTRY

Koichi Shimokawa, *Professor, Hosei University,*
Visiting Scholar, Harvard Business School

FOREWORD

[The entry of new firms into the worldwide automobile industry in the post–World War II era is prohibited by the large economies of scale, enormous capital requirements, the demand for sophisticated management expertise, and the barriers of access to markets as established by the existing giant multinational automobile firms—or so we may hear from economic theorists. But, despite theoretical improbabilities, the Honda Motor Company did it! And without the support of MITI or Japan, Inc.—the government-industry establishment in Japan—or other major automobile firms. Success was not reached in the traditional way, by developing an expensive or high performance product for the affluent. It came through the development of Honda's CVCC, a technically innovative product that sought advances in pollution control as well as fuel efficiency and practical transportation. In the process Honda broke with other major Japanese automobile firms, which resisted stringent pollution-control regulations in Japan, paving the way for legislation that successfully implemented responsible pollution-control standards in Japan before those in the United States.

What characteristics led to Honda's success in this risky venture? Was it marketing skills? Access to less costly skilled labor? Entrepreneurial skill, or luck? Professor Shimokawa, a noted automotive historian with the University of Hosei in Tokyo, describes the characteristics and conditions that underlie this important innovation. It is the classic case of an innovator who is personally in touch with the ingredients for success, with advanced research, the latest production and product concepts, as well as human resources. It is an instructive text for those who believe that innovation in the automobile industry does not pay.—Eds.]

HONDA'S ENTRY INTO THE WORLDWIDE AUTOMOBILE INDUSTRY

Throughout its short and successful existence Honda Motors has pursued original ideas. It has functioned outside of Japan Inc. and, as an independent manufacturer, has been able to develop its own worldwide brand. By establishing its brand worldwide in motorcycles, developing a CVCC engine which was the first to meet Senator Muskie's clean air standards, setting up venture businesses, and pursuing research and development in multiple fields beyond conventional automobile technology, Honda continually provides a model of effective business for the society of automobile industries, which are themselves losing their innovative entrepreneurship. Its own particular business behavior has been reflected from the first in Honda Motors' technological idea and business ideology.[1]

Mr. Honda, the Entrepreneur

Mr. Honda was born near Hamamatsu in central Japan in 1905, the son of a country blacksmith. After graduation from elementary school, he acquired experience as a mechanic and small businessman. During World War II, his small piston ring business incorporated with Toyota Motors. He took out several patents for ring machinery and improved machine tools. Immediately after the war, he sold his small business to Toyota, and, in 1946, he established Honda Motors.

Honda started in 1949 with the so-called motorbike, a bicycle with a 50cc engine. Honda Motors then made a small motorcycle called "Dream D" with a 98cc engine which was later modified by installing a new 146cc OHV engine. As a result, in 1952, Honda gained a 70 percent share of the market for small motorcycles. In 1953, they had 7 billion yen of sales volume, although their capital equity was still only 15 million yen. Honda Motors, not content with this initial success, however, were eager to advance in the world market. To this end, Mr. Honda made his first visit to Europe to observe the international road race on the Isle of Man, and to inspect the technology of the European motorcycle industry. Throughout this trip he compared the most advanced machine tools, and discovered the best to adopt. He decided to import a large volume of the most modern machines and equipment, even though his company's financial condition could hardly afford it.[2] Payment for importing the machinery was 450 million yen. From 1952 to 1954 Honda invested 1,500 million yen compared with the 1,000 million yen invested by Toyota and 300 million yen invested by Nissan in this time. Although Honda was a very small motorcycle company, they were

---

1. S. Honda, *Speed ni ikiru (My Life with Speed)* 15–61 (Jitsugyono nipponsha Tokyo, 1964); N. K. Shinbunsha, 17 *Watashino Rirekisho (My Life and Career)* 247–289 (Tokyo, 1962).
2. T. Sakitani, S. Honda and T. Fujisawa, *Asahi Journal*, Sept. 22, 1978, p. 42.

intent on investing in modernizing their operation before Toyota and Nissan.

After studying the techniques these provided, Honda modified the equipment repeatedly to suit his new manufacturing process and layout. Because of this accumulated technical expertise, Honda Motors entered big motorcycle production, and in 1960 won trophies for all sizes at the TT Race on the Isle of Man. This success established Honda with a world brand.

Honda entered the motor vehicle sector, and met with similar success as a result of their technological sophistication and their world-famous name. The CVCC engine was developed by adapting, on the basis of accumulated technology, the internal combustion engine from small motorcycle engines to large automobile engines.

The Sources of New Technology

It has been said that Japan's gross volume of industrial production involved almost no new invention or development because basic research was ignored in favor of imitative technology. The pattern in Japan was to import and initiate technology from western countries, and then to modify and apply it to Japanese manufacturing problems, and finally to integrate the trial results and use them in a practical way.

The automobile industry was no exception. But Honda's CVCC engine is clearly the product of creative technology and not the product of imitation. What is meant by creativeness in this case? It is not the use of research and development as a symptomatic treatment for the sake only of a speedy response; it is rather a return to basic research. It is combining, as much as possible, original basic research and the fruits of applied research. In developing the CVCC, a most important original idea was implemented. This was to start with analyses of the process in the internal combustion engine, which generated such polluting materials as carbon monoxide and nitrogen oxides, and to remove these polluting materials by more complete combustion within the engine. To proceed along these lines, it was necessary not only to understand mechanical engineering and the physical mechanism of the internal combustion engine, but also to investigate the chemical processes of combustion. Continuous transfer of information between engineers in various fields was essential to the success of the project, as was their teamwork in the trial-and-error applications of the findings of pure research. This established an atmosphere at Honda Motors in which employees could give full play to their individual creativeness in pursuit of their common object. There is no doubt that this kind of atmosphere provided motive and power for the success of the CVCC.[3]

There is a tendency among automotive companies to prefer practical research to basic research which does not lead directly to cost cutting or

---

3. Honda Motors, *Hondano Ayumi (Brief History of Honda)* 79–81 (Tokyo, 1974).

superiority in market competition. This tendency is observable in the United States as well as in Japan. There have been no big changes in the fundamental system of auto production since Henry Ford I established the moving assembly line for his Model T. After World War II, basic patent rights for powersteering and the disc brake came from outsiders such as parts makers or machine makers.[4] The auto makers accepted these innovations quickly after seeing their practical possibility, and merely modified them in adapting them for their own use. We cannot deny that there appeared among big automobile manufacturers an undesirable tendency to adopt easy model changes and cost cutting without sufficient concern for improving quality.

The combination of the practical utility principle and attaching high importance to basic research was further linked to the principle of completeness, which seeks perfection and never does by halves what needs to be done. This basic technological idea soon blossomed for Honda into such successes as winning the Isle of Man race, establishing a worldwide brand, and developing CVCC. This idea was given organizational support through the establishment of an independent technical research center supported by 2.5 percent of Honda's total sales. The technical staff assembled in this center were guaranteed creative research work; Honda Motors applied as much of the results as possible. Members of the research center could be involved totally in creative development projects evolving from basic research, and be released from daily modification research. Under this system, Honda Motors could keep its innovative attitude toward research and development.[5]

Business Philosophy and Management in Honda

Vice President Takeo Fujisawa laid the foundation on which Mr. Honda could build his engineering talents and put in practice his technological idea. The business ideology of Honda Motors in which their technological idea flourished was developed by Mr. Fujisawa. Such a combination of top executives as business-philosopher Fujisawa and freely acting engineer Honda was similar to the combination of Henry Ford I and James Couzen in the early stages of the Ford Motor Company.[6]

The special feature of Honda's business ideology was a human

---

4. L. J. White, *The Automobile Industry Since 1945* 211–213 (Harvard Univ. Press, 1971).
5. H. Nishikiori, *Honda Keiei, Tsuyosano Himitsu (Honda Business, Secret of Its Strength)* 189–191 (Union Shuppan, Tokyo, 1975); Honda Motors, n. 3 *supra* at 36–38.
6. K. Shimokawa, *Ford—Tairyo Seisan, Kanrito Rodo, Soshikito Seuryaku (Ford—Mass Production, Management and Labor, Structure and Strategy)* 21–23 (Toyokeizai Shimposha, Tokyo, 1972). A. Nevins, *Ford—The Time, The Man, The Company* 226–276 (Charles Scribner's Sons, 1954); 1972, pp. 21–23; pp. 330–347; pp. 354–357; pp. 495–499; pp. 546–548; pp. 570–573.

using-to-capacity principle combined with a merit-rating system.[7] For example, in their personnel management, Honda introduced a new system of work evaluation in place of the usual graduation and seniority system. This was made easier, of course, because the average age of employees was still young owing to the company's short history. Honda skillfully combined the using-to-capacity principle with motivation and participation in management at the plant level. For example, they tried improving the manufacturing process and the manufacture and modification of machines and tools at each working step. Honda promoted the quality control circle, as a voluntary and interfunctional circle independent of the company's formal organization. At Honda an atmosphere was created in which employees never thought of their jobs as heteronomous, but worked autonomously with full inventiveness.

This spirit not only pervaded the plant level but penetrated the organization of the company. Even the production workers thought of themselves as engineers, and were expected to become "machine maniacs." The company established a special qualification system under which a worker could be promoted to the same specialist status as a white-collar manager.[8] Furthermore Honda extended its using-to-capacity principle into the recruiting system. They employed the necessary personnel from the outside, without considering at each step of their development the former place of work, status or career.[9] This using-to-capacity principle became established in the fields of production management, engineering and personnel management, but did not at first penetrate the marketing field because Honda's early years were production-oriented.

Marketing

When Honda entered the motor vehicle market, they tried to make their own special sales system by introducing the using-to-capacity principle here as well. Fujisawa's idea and leadership originally organized the system of bicycle shops as motorcycle shops, thereby developing the motorcycle sales system. Thus motorcycle retailing used already established distributing agents. To support motor vehicle sales, however, they needed a new marketing system which could also supply technical service. Other Japanese manufacturers, at that time, used Toyota's so-called *Chokuhan* system (literally: direct selling system), which sold directly through a nationwide distribution organization[10] to a main dealer in each area for each make. Under this system, the distributor stressed a cooperative relationship and personal contact with their

---

7. Nishikiori, n. 5 *supra* at 83–85.
8. Honda Motors, n. 3 *supra* at 95–100; Nishikiori, n. 5 *supra* at 87–89.
9. Honda Motors, *ibid.* at 102–103.
10. *Ibid.* at 68–70; Nishikiori, n. 5 *supra* at 192–195.

dealers through dealerhelps (i.e., dealer assistance in the fields of training, management, and sometimes a guarantee for a bank loan), sales financing, and investment in the dealership. This system tended to curtail dealer independence, though it was well-suited to Japanese group-oriented behavior. Honda, on the other hand, established the so-called *Gyohan* system (literally: business selling system), which entailed selling to *Tokuyakten* (literally: special contract sales store or special-type dealer) through company branch stores.

Under this marketing system, each Honda dealer was permitted to participate. Even small stores such as former bicycle or motorcycle shops could sell freely without territory or franchise. There were no sales quotas, but each dealer had to take full responsibility for payment for the number of cars he ordered. To help small dealers concentrate only on sales activity, Honda established a Honda SF (service factory) as its nationwide technical service network for inspection, maintenance, and repair.[11]

In introducing the using-to-capacity principle into the business management fields of production, personnel, and marketing, Mr. Fujisawa exercised the business leadership which turned Mr. Honda's basic technological idea into the reality of company administration. He helped employees and dealers to give full play to their free individual characters as experts in technology or management. He stressed human respectfulness, and combined harmoniously the traditional Japanese business practices leading to informal group teamwork with the promotion of an individualistic spirit favoring autonomous creative invention.

Honda's Innovation Success with the CVCC

The CVCC success was specifically realized in the situation of a rapidly changing social environment. After 1965 in Japan, parallel to the rapid growth of the automobile industry, there occurred such problems as traffic safety, car recalls, consumerism, congestion in big cities, pollution, and the need to conserve energy resources. Amid the difficulties of the last thirteen years, the CVCC development came in response to the new challenge of government regulation of automobile pollution. Under the auspices of Senator Muskie the Clean Air Act was passed in the United States in 1970. In Japan the schedule for compliance with the Muskie Law was never extended as it was in the United States because pollution was very serious and public opinion would not permit it. Although at first many Japanese automobile makers resisted, hoping for

---

11. Honda Motors, n. 3 *supra* at 64–65. T. Fujisawa, *Taimatsu wa jibunnotede (Light Our Way with a Pine-Torch by Ourselves)* 104–107 (Sangyonoritsutandai Shuppanbu, Tokyo, 1974).

an extension, Honda Motors proclaimed immediately that they would be able to meet the Japanese Muskie Law standards. After that the government set high and clear regulations, and all other Japanese automobile makers followed suit and met them.

The development of the CVCC reflected the deeply serious reaction of Honda's engineers to the N-360's recall; this became a vital turning point in the business history of Honda. When Mr. Honda made his decision to develop the CVCC, the project appeared highly risky and offered little profit. In proclaiming his decision to employees in his company, Mr. Honda declared that he would undertake the CVCC development challenge for the sake of restoring his company's image, which had recently suffered from the recall of the minicar N-360. Responding to his speech, the young group of main engineers expressed their opinion that this project should be tried, not only for business but for society. The new project, therefore, even though it was undertaken by a private company, was promoted from the viewpoint of social responsibility.[12]

In 1969 the car recall problem in Japan affected not only Honda Motors but other automobile makers, and became a problem for the entire Japanese automobile industry. As a newcomer into the automobile market, Honda Motors had the big handicap of being the target of attack by the User Union, a radical consumer group. Its other problems included shortness of lead time and difficulties in the pretest system of the N-360, complications in responding to the User Union, and the alienation of some dealers (*Tokuyakuten*) resulting from rapid changes in marketing method. It was therefore natural that the engineers who were to develop the CVCC should require a great deal of themselves. It was also natural that they should hope to develop the CVCC less for reasons of private enterprise and more for reasons of social responsibility.

After the CVCC got under way, Honda Motors poured 70 percent of their total R&D personnel into the new project and concentrated on its complete success.[13] As a result, the CVCC greatly improved Honda's business. The new engine was well-suited to the changing social environment of the time. Especially after the oil crisis, when energy conservation rapidly became a problem, this new engine acquired a good reputation as a device that not only decreased pollution but also improved energy efficiency. While the CVCC was establishing its reputation, many automobile companies purchased its patent license. Although in the United States market in 1974 Honda Motors' place was twelfth among imports, in 1977 it rose to third.

---

12. S. Mito, "Kigyode dekinaimonowanai (There is nothing impossible for business)," *Diamond Time* 82 (Tokyo, 1975).
13. L. Ronan, "The Honda Motor Company's CVCC Engine," unpublished paper, Harvard Business School, p. 29.

Conclusion: Implication of Innovation Success and Its Future Prospect

Honda's CVCC success could be considered a typical as well as a special case of innovation success, in which the active challenge by government and social demands stimulated technological innovation. This was combined with commercial success in the world market. We could say it was a new type of success which greatly affected the new international competition in technological innovation.

From the long-range viewpoint, however, even Honda's CVCC should be considered only as a temporary and tentative success. Some fifteen years ago, confronting capital liberalization, at the time when the Japanese automobile industry established its base as a mass-production industry and started to be a strategic industry, there was broad optimism in the spread of the car, and in the individual convenience and social efficiency which accompany owning a car. In general, there was underestimation of the negative consequences which were to come with the automobile civilization. No one at the time could have forecast that so many social and environmental problems would suddenly sprout during the next ten years.

Since oil crises, cost inflation, energy conservation, and regulation for automobile safety and pollution have emerged, no one can deny that a turning point has come for the automobile industry, checking its rapid growth. Which way should the industry go in order to keep its status as a national industry and harmonize the claims of the social environment with those of the automobile civilization which it has brought about? The problems in the future of this industry are too big to allow easy responses.

As to social environment change, it is notable that the Japanese Government's attitude, especially its industrial policy which had been committed to the growth of the automobile industry, has changed somewhat. This tendency involves a slight transformation of the Japan Inc. policy. Increasing consideration of the negative aspects of automobile civilization has developed, with a second look at the role of the automobile industry in an era of low growth and a total transportation policy. It seems to have begun in the alteration of Japan's basic MITI and DOT policy, and shows an intention on the government's part to make responding-to-environment-change a strategic target by means of policy inducement.

In this new situation, what prospect does the Japanese automobile industry have and what response should it make? I think the automobile industry will have to rid itself of the business thinking which concentrates only on the "hardware" of mass-producing cars and mass marketing, and will have to turn into a total transportation industry which can take responsibility for the entire automobile civilization, i.e., the "hardware" of motor vehicles supplemented with the "software" on the social uses of the car. The position of the automobile industry in the national economy must be clarified. This involves evaluating car-transport efficiency and use effectiveness in terms of the industry's contributions to the GNP, the consumption of oil and energy resources, and the social cost, and would lead to the allocation of cars, both the number and the type, to various spheres of society within the total transportation system. The total system of the industry must include transportation, distribution, and human living, without sticking to the conventional technological framework centered in mechanical engineering.

This kind of transformation in the automobile industry cannot, of course, be achieved by one quick effort, nor by one private company. What is necessary is an active inducement by public policy with an eye to developing a total transportation system. To realize it, a policy is needed which will endorse a turning point view both internationally and domestically, beyond the Japan Inc. kind of inducement aimed at strengthening the automobile industry's potential for international competition and growth by scale-up. This kind of inducement will have to displace the former easy "mutual leaning" government and business relationship. It will have to promote actively technological innovation and autonomous enterpreneurship with an awareness that the automobile industry's turning point demands a return to the pioneer's earnest spirit.

DISCUSSION

CARL NASH: Honda is an interesting example of what small companies can do. When Honda got into the question of how they were going to respond to the passive-restraint requirements in the early 1970s, they went to the American companies who were developing the various systems and got some of the inflators and air bag systems, and found them to be unacceptable for the kind of car that Honda was building at that time. They decided to take a fresh look at the question, and they came up with an approach as innovative as the CVCC engine in response to the emission-control and fuel economy problems. Honda also has developed a simulator that is quite unique, that tests driver reaction in motor vehicles.

Quality control at Honda is also interesting. The worker is very involved. There are very few quality-control inspectors on the line because the workers themselves perform the quality control.

Honda has made many mistakes, as well. The N360 model was recalled, a cylinder head gasket leakage problem has recently caused another recall, and there is a motorcycle servicing problem.

In Honda, one sees an individual and a management structure which is bold and willing to take chances; as a result Honda has made many advances. Will they continue to do so in the future against Toyota and Nissan? This is uncertain.

SHIMOKAWA: Honda's success came from not only entrepreneurship but also good opportunity.

ACADEMIC: What is the role of the Japanese tax laws in fostering innovation? Does Japan have a program of tax benefits or indirect subsidy that accrue to an automobile firm that puts money in research and development?

SHIMOKAWA: For the most part, no.

AUTO (U.S.): MITI protects the home market. Moreover, the Japanese export their "excess" production. This puts them in a unique position to do their research and development.

AUTO (FOREIGN): We are not closing our market to the outside world. Until 1970, General Motors really did not have a car that could be exported to Japan. Our tendency today is to be open; it looks like you in the United States will be closed. MITI is the chief proponent now to *import* cars.

CHAPTER SIX
The Adversary Relationship: Regulators vs. Industry

EDITORS' NOTE

Much has already been said, in these pages and elsewhere, about the adversary relationship that seems to exist between the newly regulated automobile industry and the government agencies charged with its oversight. Observers of and participants in the regulatory process frequently express regret that this relationship is not more harmonious; all too frequently, they are tempted to assess blame for the situation without going on to analyze its causes, effects, and the possible improvements that could be made in the regulatory process to increase the light and decrease the heat that it generates.

This chapter attempts to advance our understanding of the regulatory process respecting automobiles, and to identify dispassionately some procedural reforms that could be made.

Joan Claybrook is the administrator of the National Highway Traffic Safety Administration, which has responsibility for setting both safety and fuel economy standards. Accordingly, her perception of the industry and its attitude toward and potential for innovation is of particular relevance to the subjects addressed in this chapter.

In their essay on inter-industry cooperative research, Norman Alpert and Eugene L. Holt examine two cases in which they believe promising research efforts were frustrated by government policies. In one instance the traditional antitrust concerns of the Department of Justice are said to have prevented cooperation between the automobile and petroleum industries aimed at helping to meet government standards for automobile emissions and fuel economy. In the other case, congressional distrust of regulatory agency involvement in inter-industry research efforts caused the EPA to withdraw from a cooperative program of the petroleum and automobile industries to control emissions. According to the authors, this congressional sentiment reflected an unwarranted fear among public interest groups that the EPA's independent judgment was being compromised by its participation.

According to Brian Ketchem and Stan Pinkwas, however, the public's role in regulation of the automobile is far too limited. They would like to see not only government support for public participation in decision-making, but also a more holistic approach to transportation policy. Regulation of the automobile, they suggest, should not be a process that merely tinkers with the performance of the product but one that also asks basic questions about our dependence upon automobiles and its implications for other surface modes of transportation and for the shape of our cities.

David Potter argues that although many of the regulations governing automobiles depend explicitly upon scientific premises and research, decisions are too often made upon the basis of what he calls "advocacy-science." In order to enhance the quality and credibility of regulatory decisions, he calls for the establishment of a third-party review procedure that would subject the scientific foundations for regulation to the scrutiny of a neutral body, i.e., one associated with neither the industry nor the regulating agency.

Robert A. Leone and John E. Jackson reject "as myth" both the idea of an independent, strictly professional and apolitical regulatory agency, and the idea that there are strictly policy issues that can be divorced from technical questions and analytic procedures. Accordingly, they would involve the Congress and the President more directly in the regulatory process than the present system of mere oversight implies.

REGULATION AND INNOVATION IN THE AUTOMOBILE INDUSTRY

Joan Claybrook, *Administrator, National Highway Safety Administration*

I would like to focus on one aspect of technology—innovation—by taking a look at the stimuli for innovation within the automotive industry, and what role the government has played in pressing for the application of technological innovation toward socially responsible goals.

Innovations can be brought about by two fundamental mechanisms: (1) A demand for them; and (2) the irresistible attraction of new ideas. These are traditionally referred to as *market pull* and *technology push*, but those terms are too limited to describe the range of conditions that can bring about innovation.

There are at least six forces that influence the rate of auto industry innovation, as well as its focus, and often they interact dynamically with each other:

- Internal stimuli
- Market structure
- Inventions
- Independent research
- Public expectations or crises
- Government regulation

INTERNAL STIMULI

It is important to distinguish between innovation that is needed to fulfill consumer health and safety rights and the kind of innovation that has dominated the auto industry since the 1930s. In industrial automation, styling, and promotion, the auto industry has been quite innovative. But this has not been the case with the subject of all these efforts—the operating motor vehicle itself. Most insider suggestions concern better ways to cut costs and increase productivity. This is where the real incentives are found.

Electronic Assisted Scheduling is cited by William Abernathy[1] in one of his case studies as a continuing area of innovation allowing better utilization of plant, inventory, and labor in the automobile production system while not compromising the variety of offerings or flexibility in production scheduling. It developed out of both technology push in the electronics industry, which has expanded explosively in the last forty years, and market pull by the automobile manufacturer as customer.

This concept is typical of the industry's bread-and-butter innovations—those that reduce cost and promote productivity for the manufacturer as opposed to product innovations that reduce harm or provide other benefits for the purchaser. The industry, as customer for innovative changes, eagerly looks for those that can reduce the cost of building cars and increase its own profits and stability. In recent years, the use of computers for virtually all aspects of the automobile business has vastly increased its design options and the speed and thoroughness with which tasks can be completed, and reduced costs.

An article in *Fortune* magazine in June 1956 entitled "How Strong is GM Research?" concludes:

> Despite the glitter of its new technical center, GM has not yet proved that it has a research laboratory of front rank. Until very recently Detroit had never done much research as scientists understand it. Most of its so-called research achievements have fallen rather under the heading of advanced engineering.

Paul Chenea, vice-president in charge of General Motors' research laboratories, acknowledged as much in his speech, "Innovation, Maturation, and the Automotive Industry,"[2] in which he talked about the evolutionary nature of auto industry innovation. While suggesting that innovation has not declined in Detroit as it does in most industries as they mature, he hastened to point out the barriers: "Making even incremental innovations in automotive subsystems, which have undergone many generations of major design cycles, requires massive investments in technical manpower and facilities."

Professors Nelson, Peck, and Kalacheck, in *Technology, Economic Growth and Public Policy*,[3] are cited in a paper by Professor Mark B.

---

1. W. J. Abernathy, *The Productivity Dilemma, Roadblock to Innovation in the Automobile Industry* 201 (The Johns Hopkins University Press, 1978).
2. P. Chenea, "Innovation, Maturation and the Automotive Industry," speech before the Annual Meeting of the American Assoc. for the Advancement of Science (Jan. 1979).
3. R. R. Nelson, M. J. Peck, and E. D. Kalacheck, *Technology, Economic Growth, and Public Policy* (The Brookings Institution, 1967).

Schupack of Brown University in the 1968 Senate hearings on competition in the automobile industry[4] as pointing out that the auto industry investment in research and development is a very small percentage of its sales. They suggest that, with no size or institutional barriers, the auto industry's superficial product differentiation barrier may well dictate the limits of auto industry research.

Lawrence White, in his chapter in Walter Adams' book, *Structure of American Society*,[5] suggests that since World War II, the big auto companies have tended to rely for advances in technology on their suppliers, who have done much of the pioneering development work on new items like power steering and brakes, ball joints, alternators, and transistorized ignitions. While competition among suppliers has been one stimulus for innovation in the automobile industry, the direction of supplier research and development is fairly rigidly constrained by the priorities of the giant manufacturers. Also, many new items were first used on European cars before the American companies decided to adopt them. The materials suppliers—steel, aluminum, glass, plastics, and paint companies—have done the development work in this area according to White, who points out that the manufacturers have pushed the suppliers to take the risks and absorb the initial costs of developing new technology.

While there are some exceptions, all these factors suggest that historically the domestic automotive manufacturers have had little internal stimulus since the 1920s for development of motor vehicle innovations, and particularly ones concerned with so-called externalities—that is, health and safety items of concern to car users or the public generally but of little concern to manufacturers who suffer no harm from their absence.

MARKET STRUCTURE

One of the continuing debates about the automotive industry is whether the huge size of the companies is conducive or harmful to product innovation. The case has been argued that the stability and resources of these large companies foster broad-scale research opportunities and enhance the possibilities for technological breakthroughs. On the other side, it is argued that the oligopolistic structure of the industry, and its resulting noncompetitive conduct, inhibits new ideas or any activity which might rock the boat. One might recall Judge Learned Hand's description of "the quiet life" of the monopolist.

---

4. M. B. Schupack, "Statement Regarding Competition in the Automobile Industry," Oct. 22, 1968, in *Planning, Regulation, and Competition: Automobile Industry–1968. Hearings on the Question: Are Planning and Regulation Replacing Competition in the American Economy? Before the Subcomm. of the Senate Select Comm. on Small Business*, 90th Cong., 2d Sess. (July 10 and 23, 1968).

5. L. White, "The Automobile Industry," in W. Adams, *The Structure of American Industry* 165 et seq. (Macmillan Publishing Co., Inc., 1977).

Scherer, in his basic text, *Industrial Market Structure and Economic Performance*,[6] argues that large company size does not inspire creativity and innovation. He points out that the early, most imaginative steps in the innovative process require relatively small resource commitments and that the heavy financial commitments do not come until full-scale development begins. He cites approvingly the sixty-one case histories compiled by Jewkes, Sawers, and Stillerman[7] of important twentieth century inventions showing that less than one-third came from industrial research laboratories. Subsequently, Hamberg investigated twenty-seven major inventions introduced in the 1946-through-1955 decade and found only seven originally conceived in large industrial laboratories, while twelve were traced to independent inventors.

Scherer concludes that huge or tiny firms, for different reasons, are not the most conducive to innovation.

> All things considered, the most favorable industrial environment for rapid technological progress would appear to be a firm size distribution which includes a preponderance of companies with sales below $200 million, [Scherer says,] pressed on one side by a horde of small, technology-oriented enterprises bubbling over with bright new ideas, and on the other by a few larger corporations with the capacity to undertake exceptionally ambitious developments.

Consistent with this conclusion is the Office of Management and Budget assessment of the federal responsibility in assuring support of small business through the contracting and procurement process.[8] Their interest is focused on the fact that

> there is considerable evidence that the small proportion of federal research and development work that is being awarded to small technology-based firms is contributing to a serious loss of high technology capabilities to our Nation.

A background paper prepared for the OMB stated:

> Many analysts believe that small firms have a better record for innovation than large firms.... Some believe that managers of small R&D firms have a greater incentive to innovate while conversely, in some cases, the marketing plans of large firms dictate that technical improvements to their products be held to a minimum. There also is a possibility that researchers in large firms tend to overspecialize to a greater extent than researchers in

---

6. F. M. Scherer, *Industrial Market Structure and Economic Performance*, 338 et seq. (Rand McNally College Publishing Co., 1970).

7. J. Jewkes, D. Sawers, and R. Stillerman, *The Sources of Innovation* (St. Martin's Press, 1959).

8. J. Rabinow, et al., *Small Firms and Federal Research and Development*, a report to Office of Federal Procurement Policy (Office of Management and Budget, Ad Hoc Interagency Panel, Feb. 24, 1977) p. 2.

small firms. Mr. Rabinow has observed that, "when one narrows his specialization, he probably comes up with fewer ideas. If one loads the dice in favor of a certain art, one cuts off analogous arts . . . . The more an inventor can pull out of related and unrelated arts, the more original his ideas are likely to be."

Empirical evidence indicates that in a comparison of firms with less than 1,000 employees and those with over 1,000 employees:

> Firms with less than 1,000 employees accounted for almost one-half of major U.S. innovations during 1953–73.

> The ratio of innovations to sales is about one-third greater in firms with less than 1,000 employees.

> Firms of less than 1,000 employees have a ratio of innovations to R&D employment which is approximately four times greater.

> The cost per R&D scientist or engineer is almost twice as great in firms of over 1,000 employees.

As applied to the automotive industry, economist William Shepherd, in *Market Power and Economic Welfare*,[9] suggests that the two primary sources of shared monopoly—the model year change and the dealer-franchising policies—are disincentives to innovation. White points out that with price competition "muted," the manufacturers have focused their attention in rivalry for sales in nonprice areas, such as the annual model change which also serves as a method of encouraging faster replacement and larger sales. As adopted by the automotive companies, the annual model change has consisted primarily of superficial frills and style rather than technological or significant engineering changes, a logical strategy if the objective is minimum risk and cost. The industry has learned how to promote style and design but has not attempted to convey to consumers any sophisticated information regarding automotive technology.[10] With consumers having a difficult time at best judging the merits of technological advances, the decision was made long ago to promote sales based on what the customer could see and feel.

In addition, with technology advances always uncertain, and the lead-time constraints for mass production unyielding except at a large cost, the manufacturers long since abandoned this form of product competition. Having found a successful sales strategy which increased the barriers to entry by competitors, the companies shunned any mention of improvements which might ameliorate the so-called externalities—health and safety damage. They even claimed that any

---

9. W. G. Shepherd, *Market Power and Economic Welfare: An Introduction* 232 et seq. (Random House, 1970).

10. The Congress in 1972 recognized this failing and instructed NHTSA to develop comparative consumer information by make and model on crashworthiness, damageability, and repairability. Funding was acquired for fiscal year 1979 to begin this task.

mention of them might scare customers away! In addition, the cost of the styling and annual model year change—variably estimated at from $200 to $700 per car in pre-1970s dollars—used precious resources in nonproductive ways.

Another explanation for the slow rate of auto industry innovation is the absence of stress in an oligopolistic industry to compete for a position in the marketplace. In a rare public appearance by a chief auto industry executive, George Romney in 1958 told the Kefauver Antitrust and Monopoly Subcommittee hearings on administered prices:[11]

> If you want to keep an industry out of a rut, have enough companies in it so that some of those companies have got the sheer necessity of invention. When you get down to a few—and they are all prospering—millionaires and billionaires don't pioneer.
>
> . . .
>
> Mr. Curtice [of General Motors] has pointed out that above a reasonable minimum, size itself is not an important factor in the ability of a company to compete effectively. This is absolutely true, but there continue to be persistent illusions about the importance of size.
>
> Incidentally, those illusions are promoted and furthered and there is practically a concerted campaign going on in the United States today among the biggest companies in the land to further the illusion that size is an inherent advantage in terms of product value, and it is not true, but it is designed to increase the competitive handicap and difficulty of smaller companies secondarily; primarily, to meet the public concern about this problem of size and economic concentration.
>
> . . .
>
> What I am saying to you is that the product competition in the United States hasn't been sufficient to result in developing automobiles in this country which would permit people to make a free choice from the types of automobiles that people are using . . . .

Two examples indicate how the lack of internal incentive and the fact of external peer pressure can frustrate innovation in health/safety developments in this highly concentrated industry. In 1956, Ford decided to offer a "safety package" to the public consisting of the deep dish steering wheel, padded dash, and safety belts. But it dropped all advertising within several months of the beginning of that new model year because of fears expressed by other companies—primarily General Motors—that discussing safety items would take away customers from the industry as a whole.

In 1969, the Justice Department charged the four American auto

---

11. G. Romney, "Administered Prices," *Hearings Before the Subcomm. on Antitrust and Monopoly of the Senate Comm. on the Judiciary*, 85th Cong., 2d Sess. (Feb. 6 and 10, 1958) pp. 2885, 2847–2848.

companies with conspiring to restrain the development and use of vehicle pollution controls.[12] The memorandum supporting the case disclosed that Chrysler yielded to pressure from Ford and General Motors by not installing its Cleaner Air Package emission control system although it was ready to be put on 1965-model cars. The two giant companies apparently intended to continue their opposition for 1966 models until it became evident that Chrysler's California certification was going to be granted.

INVENTIONS

Auto industry executives have recognized the slow pace of innovation in their industry and the need for engineering progress. More than a decade ago Henry Ford II acknowledged:

> When you think of the enormous progress of science over the last two generations, it's astonishing to realize that there is very little about the basic principles of today's automobile that would seem strange and unfamiliar to the pioneers of our industry . . . . What we need even more than the refinement of old ideas is the ability to develop new ideas and put them to work.

Yet the frustrated inventors who never penetrate the bureaucracy of the auto industry are legion. The government itself has given short shrift to inventors of safety and emission equipment, although occasionally one breaks through the public consciousness through sheer persistence, the interest of a news reporter, or an appearance at Congressional hearings.

The auto industry has been plagued by the NIH (Not Invented Here) syndrome from its early days. The companies do not like to pay royalties to inventors and have been known on more than one occasion to review an inventor's patent and subsequently develop quite similar products on their own—leaving the small inventor to try to sue a company with resources he could never match. On other occasions, the companies have been charged with purchasing an invention and placing it on the shelf.

With venture capital hard to come by for final development and production of an invention, and with a gross imbalance in size and resources between the manufacturers and almost any of the suppliers, there has always been a master-servant relationship between the auto manufacturers and the companies or, on occasions, individuals who provide much of their technological capability. More than one company—and some after servicing the industry for years and years—have been virtually broken by a decision to discontinue their product. Indeed, when controversial auto industry matters arise in the

---

12. *The Congressional Record,* H4070, 71, May 18, 1971.

regulatory/Congressional arena about whether a certain development is feasible and practicable, the suppliers, with a few exceptions, remain silent for fear that stepping out of line might cost them business. The economic pressure of such a relationship is immeasurable, and it clearly has silenced some proponents of readily available product improvements from stepping into the public limelight.

INDEPENDENT RESEARCH

Research by independent organizations and the government can stimulate innovation within the industry in several ways. First, such work can identify critical problems that should be addressed in the design or construction of automobiles. Second, independent R&D can develop new concepts or hardware to solve problems.

Prior to the enactment of the auto safety statute, the prime institutional research outside the auto industry was conducted by the Public Health Service in the Department of Health, Education, and Welfare (HEW). The HEW grant program funded individual researchers who were interested in a particular aspect of vehicle or highway safety. There was little coordination among the different grantees, but there was a small body of expertise built up in the 1950s and early 1960s which was crucial in the debate for enactment of the present law. The auto industry, with HEW, also funded some work during the 1950s at several independent laboratories, such as Cornell Aeronautical Laboratories and the Harvard School of Public Health, on crash injuries. But this work was virtually unknown to the public at large and thus was not a challenge to the auto industry's refusal to give priority to safety in its products.

Liberty Mutual, and then New York State, developed prototype or experimental safety cars, but the work was either not completed or had little impact by the time the new statute was enacted. However, this work did play a major role in the requirement now in the law that the NHTSA must develop experimental safety vehicles—in essence, hardware to challenge traditional industry concepts.

The early experimental safety vehicle program work was crude, and the auto industry made a mockery of it. In the early 1970s, they contracted with the Department of Transportation for $1 to produce their own experimental safety cars. They created Goliaths that weighed in at 5500-plus pounds, one of which was made of such esoteric materials it could not be mass produced. In other words, a safer car cannot be made.

The Department turned to the foreign governments and industry to do what the domestic industry would not. A number of foreign countries with their industries produced first-rate experimental safety vehicles—mostly weighing between 2,000 and 3,000 pounds—which were designed to crash without severe injury or death at 40 to 50 miles per hour. They showed that it could be done—with a small car—and thus gave new credibility and self-confidence to the experimental vehicle program.[13]

The next step—and one still in progress—was the development by the Department of Transportation of attractive, light-weight experimental cars that could be used as the basis for rule-making activity to push the state of the art beyond the basic minimum set in the 1967 standards and still in effect today. Two new vehicles are just being completed—one quite close to the state of the art of present manufacturing but significantly exceeding the safety characteristics of presently produced vehicles, and the other a new concept vehicle whose production would require industry to initiate some retooling. Both are small in weight, high in fuel economy, and with 40- to 50-mile-per-hour crash survivability characteristics. Their purpose is to show the public and the industry that it can be done, that far safer and fuel-efficient vehicles that are attractive and appealing can be manufactured.

Other outside institutional research that has played a role in challenging traditional auto industry mystiques has been done by the Insurance Institute for Highway Safety since it has been headed by Dr. William Haddon, Jr., beginning in 1969. The Institute has played a major role in pushing for reduction in vehicle damageability, in developing an independent data system based on insurance industry information, in discovering and calling for the recall of defective vehicles, particularly those that are badly designed, and in researching and toppling some of the traditional beliefs in automotive and highway safety.[14]

In addition to showing affirmatively that certain health and safety measures can be readily built into cars, the institutional research outside the auto industry pushes the companies to look further into the future rather than focus as they too often do on the next several years. Although the industry constantly reminds the government of its lead-time needs—three years-plus is the usual request—the industry itself has rarely looked very far into the future of advanced technology application, particularly to meet societal needs in motor vehicles. But outside research can do little more than show the way. Absent public recognition and demand, it is merely another possibility—and often one to be ignored.

CONSUMER EXPECTATIONS

Consumer expectations for the design of vehicles to meet societal goals have matured significantly in the last ten to twelve years. The major

---

13. Statement of Soichi Kawazoe, *Hearings Before the Subcomm. on Commerce and Finance of the Interstate and Foreign Commerce Comm.*, 93rd Cong., 1st Sess. (April 1973) pp. 145–152.
14. *Insurance Institute for Highway Safety Status Reports*, prepared and distributed by IIHS, Watergate Six Hundred, Suite 300, Washington, D.C. 20037.

example of consumer impact on vehicle design came with the oil embargo in late-1973 and its influence on the industry to improve fuel economy, which had been dropping steadily for years as the companies made bigger, faster cars in the eternal search for something new—other than new technology. The gasoline lines and the drop in auto sales jolted an industry used to stability and evolutionary changes. It introduced the era of the downsized car, and the opportunity for other cost-reducing innovations.

Since my colleague, Michael Finkelstein, has dwelt at length with the issues of consumer expectations and the need for technical consumer information about vehicle safety, I will not pursue that further except to say we certainly know from the Pinto and Firestone experience that the public will not buy automotive items they perceive to be hazardous, and we know from surveys of public opinion such as the Hart survey[15] and others[16] that the public says it wants greater safety built into cars. The key question is whether this interest will be reflected in marketplace demand if the government supplies technical information to consumers or whether it will only happen if a manufacturer decides to break ranks and produces and sells its safety innovations.

FEDERAL REGULATIONS

In the last decade, a major new factor, federal regulation, has had a substantial influence on the priorities and the performance of the auto industry. The primary purpose of federal regulation is to set minimum levels of performance in safety, fuel economy, and emissions that must be met by all cars sold in the U.S. In each case, the regulations have forced a new look at the basic technology of the motor vehicle:[17]

---

15. P. D. Hart and research associates, *Public Attitudes Toward Passive Restraint Systems*, survey conducted for the National Highway Traffic Safety Administration (Aug. 1978).

16. See, for example, Yankelovich, Skelley, and White, Inc., *A Summary Report of Driver Attitudes Toward Restraints for Greater Safety in the Operation of an Automobile*, prepared for the Motor Vehicle Manufacturers Association of the United States, Inc. (Sept. 1976); G. Gallup, *Public Votes 46 to 37% in Favor of Required Air Bags* (July 1977); Teknekron, Inc., *Final Report, 1978 Survey of Public Perceptions on Highway Safety*, prepared for the National Highway Traffic Safety Administration (Nov. 1978); and L. Harris and Associates, survey carried out for Amtrak (April 1977).

17. A number of innovations have resulted, at least in part, from regulation of the automobile. These include:

> Passive occupant restraint systems. In the late 1960s, Ford (in combination with the Eaton Corp.) and GM began air bag development programs. These programs were designed to provide a better alternative to the active safety belt. In the early 1970s, in response to rule-making to require passive restraints, Volkswagen developed a less expensive and simpler passive belt system, which they have offered on the Rabbit model since 1975.
>
> The combined pressures of environmental and fuel economy requirements led to the

- Safety standards have caused body designers to include crash integrity as an integral factor in the design of frame and body structures. This includes providing a fairly rigid passenger compartment with occupant restraints, energy absorbing interior padding and exterior structures, and safety packaging of the fuel system.

- Emission-control standards have forced engine designers to rethink the fundamental technology of the internal combustion engine as well as the design tradeoffs that had been conventionally made in engines. It also stimulated a substantial amount of work on alternative engine technologies.

- Fuel economy standards have resulted in a complete rethinking of the basic design parameters of automobiles—from special layout and drivetrain configuration to materials and fabrication techniques.

- Regulations, in general, encourage innovation in areas where the market demand is unclear. If manufacturers believe safety does not sell, they will be reluctant to risk innovations in that area, believing they will have a price disadvantage if they do. By levying uniform standards on all companies, this risk is eliminated and the manufacturers are challenged to find the least costly way to achieve the performance required.

These federal regulatory programs are stimulating a level of product innovation that has not been seen since the early days of the industry. And the direction of that activity is no longer only toward near-term marketing objectives such as style and luxury options, but rather it is addressing the serious social, environmental, and resource problems that plague the automobile transportation system.

A secondary benefit, however, has been to stimulate and to advance the art of automotive engineering. The adoption of computers for virtually all aspects of the automobile business has resulted from the need to meet federal requirements without compromising the traditional performance and value of passenger cars. These requirements have also introduced new levels of rigor into the engineering and testing of vehicles, which now must meet objective performance standards, not just best-guess evaluations of perceived consumer desires.

One of the unfortunate side effects of minimum federal standards is that they are often treated as maximum standards by this monolithic

---

development of several innovative engine technologies: The catalytic exhaust converter, stratified charge engines, and electronic engine controls, to name three of the more important recent ones.

Requirements for bumpers that protect automobiles in collisions at up to 5 mph (10 mph car-to-car impacts) have led to a number of innovations in bumper technology such as improved hydraulic shock absorbers and soft-faced plastic systems that have the additional advantage of providing improved pedestrian impact protection.

Innovations in "slippery" lubricants have resulted from the need to improve fuel economy, mostly to meet federal fuel economy standards.

The fuel economy program is resulting in innovations in the configuration of vehicles built in North America (such as front wheel drive) as well as in the use of new materials (such as plastics, aluminum, and high-strength–low-alloy steels).

industry. In such a case, they tend to define a state of the art and are used as an excuse to avoid further innovation in that aspect of the vehicle once the standard is met. The Department of Transportation is attempting to address this difficulty in the future by promulgating technical consumer information requirements that can help make safety, damageability, and maintainability marketplace factors. Competition among automobile manufacturers to achieve high consumer ratings could stimulate further innovation in these areas.

Despite the continuing industry complaints about current regulations, it is quite clear the industry leaders recognize that regulation has had a salutary effect on innovation in the last several years as we prepare for the new models of the 1980s. Numerous industry spokesmen have acknowledged this.

Mr. Charles Heinen, Director of Vehicle Emissions at Chrysler, is an example:

> Much as I hate to admit it, the EPA accelerated the pace at which we studied combustion. The knowledge we've gained is important, whether applied to emission control or fuel economy.[18]

Henry Ford II was even more direct:

> We wouldn't have the kinds of safety built into automobiles that we have had unless there had been a Federal law. We wouldn't have had the fuel economy unless there had been a Federal law, and there wouldn't have been the emission control unless there had been a Federal law.[19]

Among those who are delighted with the challenges from the regulations of the 1980s are industry engineers. For them and the public for the first time in four decades the "new" in "new model year" will refer to new technology and it will be primarily by engineers, not stylists. The engineers are excited. Listen, for example, to Robert B. Alexander, Vice-President, Car Product Development Group, Ford Motor Company, who said last year:

> The lion's share of the burden of meeting these stringent standards and mandates will fall on the shoulders of the engineers. In fact, I like to call this the "age of the engineer"—and I, for one, couldn't be happier.[20]

Or hear the words of Stuart Frey, Chief Vehicle Engineer, Car Engineering Group, Ford Motor Company, who said:

---

18. C. Heinen, as quoted in *Business Week*, Feb. 16, 1976.
19. H. Ford II, *Meet the Press*, television broadcast, Oct. 30, 1977.
20. R. Alexander, speech before the Management Briefing Seminars sponsored by the Mich. Chamber of Commerce and the U. of Mich., Traverse City, Mich., Aug. 4, 1977.

Let me say that the task ahead is the kind that an engineer relishes because it puts a premium on ingenuity and creativity. I believe I speak for all of my colleagues in the industry when I say I'm delighted to be part of the action.[21]

The vehicle manufacturing industries are experiencing a renaissance, driven substantially by federal regulation, taking them from the era of seat-of-the-pants engineering toward the technological forefront of American industry. And this revolution is producing not only direct benefits in the performance of the product, but also significant fallout in improved productivity, enhanced ability to compete in the worldwide automotive market, and a new professional standing for the automotive engineer.

FUTURE TRENDS

The question now is whether, given this renewed regulatory stimulus, the climate is such that the innovations needed for the future will flow in sufficient volume to meet the increasing challenges of the future. Or will the manufacturers stonewall the public, hold suppliers hostage, and refuse to apply their genius and capability for the public's benefit? Will materials be developed that can make the gas turbine or the Stirling engine a reliable, low-cost engine for the cars of the late 1980s and the 1990s? Will we continue to have the kinds of technological inventions that will allow the United States to take advantage of the favorable exchange rates, making the new American-built motor vehicles highly competitive on the international market?

There is a trend that bodes ill in this respect: The overall reduction in the commitment of resources by the country to civilian research and development. This problem has occurred both in industry and in government. Our current budget for motor vehicle research and development is about $21 million, or approximately five hours' of General Motors' gross revenue. While the deaths and injuries continue to climb, the funds available for safety research have decreased nearly $3 million since 1975, and inflation has reduced our purchasing power by another 25 percent. The funds first allocated in 1977 for fuel economy research have remained level ever since. Similarly, although the industry has committed a large amount of capital to programs to meet federal fuel economy requirements in the short term, the commitment of the industry to longer-term research and development for safety, fuel economy, and emissions is tiny, and follows the trends of United States industry generally toward very short-term horizons.

Another factor that discourages innovation is an economic climate of boom-and-bust cycles. High inflation rates usually discourage invest-

---

21. S. M. Frey, speech at the U. of Mich. Management Conference, Traverse City, Mich., Aug. 10, 1978.

ments in the generation of ideas and inventions that are needed for longer-term innovations and changes. High interest rates that result from inflation cause some manufacturers to shorten even more their time horizons, and one of the first casualties is long-term research and development projects.[22]

As the influence of inflation on investment decisions makes evident, therefore, the government's commitment to controlling inflation does not merely help the consumer's pocketbook directly in the short term; It also averts the long-term, secondary effects on the consumer that may be even more damaging. Of course, safety, conservation, health, and environmental regulatory programs also contribute substantially to the control of inflation. Increased hospital costs can be offset by decreased numbers of maimed people and by improvements in the general health of the public. Decreased vehicle damageability can reduce automobile insurance costs just as improved vehicle safety can. Our fuel economy program will have a substantial effect not only on the cost of operating an automobile; it will help to control our enormous appetite for high-cost, inflation-producing petroleum imports.

And the regulatory program also pushes the industry to treat societal goals seriously and not cut them back as the first casualty of a tight market.

We are looking forward with great anticipation to the vehicles of the mid-1980s—the socially responsible automobile and its companion trucks, vans, and buses. We expect these vehicles to contribute not only to our economic and environmental well-being as individuals, but also to the country's well-being.

In conclusion, it is important to distinguish between innovation that is needed to fulfill the consumer health and safety rights and the kind of innovation that merely refines the engineering of the high-compression engine.

Second, innovation becomes more necessary as the passing years expand the gap between the growth of problems and the technology available to solve these problems. Alfred North Whitehead put it with characteristic wisdom: "Duty," he said, "arises from the power to alter the course of events." This is not 1940, when Los Angeles was just beginning to experience photochemical smog from the automobiles' exhausts; this is not 1950, when auto crash casualties were viewed as solely the fault of the "nut behind the wheel;" this is not 1960, when a glutted oil industry was holding down domestic production through state production controls; this is not 1970, when an Administration looked at the auto crisis burgeoning on many consumer and environmental fronts with cool indifference if not outright hostility. This is a

---

22. On the other hand, sometimes inflationary pressures serve as a catalyst for productive cost reductions such as downsizing. Also, the auto industry has been making record profits, and General Motors, for one, rarely borrows money because it has been able to generate money internally.

time of computers and space vehicles, communications satellites and early solar energy—and of motor vehicles that still would not surprise your great-grandfather.

As several auto executives have been saying in recent speeches, the times are changing, consumer expectations are rising higher and going deeper. This is no safety-pin industry with an essentially mature technology. Motor vehicles are an unfinished technology that desparately needs what industry engineering creativity can give it—heavy infusions of humane engineering progress that provide life-saving and economic benefits for consumers.

INTER-INDUSTRY COOPERATIVE RESEARCH AND THE GOVERNMENT: TWO CASE STUDIES

Norman Alpert and Eugene L. Holt, *Exxon Research and Engineering Company*

Cooperative research between the automobile and petroleum industries has had a long and fruitful history, extending back almost sixty years and accounting for several basic advances in the efficient use of the nation's transportation and energy resources. These cooperative inter-industry arrangements have always been subject to all of the traditional antitrust restrictions on anticompetitive behavior, most important of which are the Sherman, Clayton, and Federal Trade Commission Acts. This paper focuses on two recent inter-industry research programs designed to generate necessary information for meeting government regulations that limit automotive emissions and fuel consumption. It will examine the effects of traditional antitrust concerns on these activities, and will also look at the effects of congressional distrust of regulatory agency involvement in inter-industry research efforts.

CRC-APRAC

It became clear to the petroleum and automobile industries before 1920 that the problem of matching the supply and quality of gasoline to the rapidly growing and increasingly sophisticated automobile population required joint action. The Coordinating Research Council (CRC), jointly funded by the American Petroleum Institute and the Motor Vehicle Manufacturers Association, carries on this effort today, with some guidance from the Society of Automotive Engineers, which is a professional association. The CRC pursues the strategies adopted in the early days of the industries: Setting up technical committees composed of representatives from individual companies to identify critical problem areas and either to channel funds to contracting laboratories or to conduct joint research through member laboratories, sharing costs and benefits alike. The technical committees are also responsible for approving reports, which are then made public.

It must be stressed that the areas investigated under CRC sponsorship have been of very broad and general scope. Prime examples are the development of uniform test methods for determining the octane properties of gasoline and surveying the octane requirements of the automotive population. Areas which might afford a direct competitive advantage to a particular member company have never been part of the CRC agenda. For example, development of new automobile hardware such as transmissions, or of improved petroleum processing such as catalytic cracking, have always been pursued on an individual, proprietary basis by member companies quite removed from CRC activities.

The CRC has successfully explored many of the relationships between fuel and lubricant properties and engine performance and continues to do so. By the mid-1960s, however, another area began to grow in importance as the contribution of the automobile to atmospheric pollution came to be recognized. In 1968, the Air Pollution Research Advisory Council (APRAC) was set up within the CRC to direct research efforts aimed at generating broad-based, nonproprietary information in this new field. Research programs were developed to study a variety of engineering, atmospheric, and medical problems. Studies of the composition of automotive exhaust gases, the driving patterns of vehicles in use, and the loss of hydrocarbons from vehicles due to evaporation and displacement of fuel tank vapor by incoming liquid during refueling, were undertaken in the engineering area. Investigations of the fate of various pollutants in the air, their effects on vegetation, and the influence of natural sources of hydrocarbons on pollution levels, have begun to elucidate the role of automotive emissions in atmospheric chemistry. Finally, APRAC-sponsored medical programs, ranging from epidemiological studies of the effects of nitrogen dioxide and carbon monoxide on populations to direct measurements of carbon monoxide effects on humans, have clarified some of the effects of pollutants on health.

Compared to total expenditures on pollution-control research by industry and government, amounting to many hundreds of millions of dollars, APRAC expenditures have been relatively modest, totaling less than $28 million through 1977.[1] By concentrating its efforts on a few key areas, however, the APRAC program has had a significant effect on the national effort to develop an efficient pollution-control program. For example, APRAC-sponsored studies were helpful in generating a standard driving cycle, used in the federally mandated procedure for measuring the level of auto emissions. Other programs led to the development of new measuring techniques for polynuclear aromatic compounds and an understanding of their characteristics as emissions from

---

1. *CRC-APRAC Status Report,* Coordinating Research Council, New York (Jan. 1978).

both gasoline and diesel engines. These latter results are becoming increasingly significant as the debate intensifies over possible emission of carcinogenic compounds from diesel engines. Also, APRAC studies of hydrocrabon loss to the atmosphere during vehicle refueling have been used by the EPA in planning its strategy for controlling such emissions. These are just a few examples of the significant influence that APRAC-sponsored programs have had on the national emission-control effort.

APRAC's parent, the CRC, has a long history of conducting research in cooperation with and on behalf of the government. This was particularly true during World War II, when the CRC was called upon by over 30 military and government agencies to conduct some 300 projects dealing with fuel and lubricant problems. In fact, the Council was given three awards for its wartime service.[2] Similar government cooperation was expected as APRAC began its work on matters of great national concern. Initially the National Air Pollution Control Administration (NAPCA) of the Department of Health, Education, and Welfare, and later the EPA, into which NAPCA was absorbed, took a keen interest in APRAC activities. They participated as members of the Air Pollution Research Advisory Committee itself and on its subcommittees and project groups. They also partially funded programs particularly relevant to regulatory activities.

This arrangement did not please everyone, however; public interest groups, in particular, distrusted the APRAC-EPA cooperative effort, fearing that the EPA's independent judgment was being compromised by participating in APRAC programs. A representative of the Center for the Study of Responsive Law questioned the relationship[3] in 1971, in the course of an EPA public hearing on automobile emission standards. Then Administrator of the EPA, William Ruckelshaus, responded by placing in the hearing record a statement summarizing the benefits achieved by EPA's involvement in APRAC activities. The statement stressed that these joint activities were in neither the strictly governmental domain of regulation nor in the automobile maker's domain of hardware development. Rather, according to Ruckelshaus' statement, the programs provided basic scientific and technical data upon which both regulatory and innovative functions depended. Such joint programs optimized the nation's technical and financial resources in obtaining such data. The statement also pointed out that government prerogatives were protected through such arrangements as full EPA partnership in discussions regarding project planning, direction, and review; EPA selectivity in project support; and full public disclosure of all project results.[4]

---

2. M. K. McLeod, "The Co-Ordinating Research Council," 41 *J. Petroleum*, No. 384, pp. 353–393 (Dec. 1955).
3. *EPA Public Hearing on Automobile Emission Standards* 70–71, 84–86 (May 7, 1971).
4. *EPA Statement for the Record* (June 29, 1971); *EPA Public Hearing on Automobile Emission Standards* (May 6–7, 1971).

There was little public discussion of EPA-APRAC involvement until the issue surfaced again in 1973, at a hearing of the Senate Subcommittee on Air and Water Pollution. APRAC had sponsored studies of the health effects of carbon monoxide. One particular program, jointly financed by the EPA and APRAC, was undertaken to determine the range of carboxyhemoglobin levels in the blood of urban and nonurban populations. It showed that smokers averaged well-above nonsmokers in carboxyhemoglobin levels. The study also found that the *average* level for nonsmokers, even among city dwellers, did not exceed a point considered dangerous by the EPA. It pointed out, however, that a substantial segment of the population in the above-average category did fall into the harmful range.

Different interpretations of the data were possible, however. Chrysler Corporation pointed to the relatively low *average* carboxyhemoglobin levels measured and the significant effect of smoking to claim that the EPA standards were too stringent. Senator Muskie, then Chairman of the Subcommittee, took exception to Chrysler's interpretation and use of the data in newspaper ads to attack the bases of the EPA's air quality criteria and automobile emissions standards for carbon monoxide. Senator Muskie's major concern was the origin of the study in joint EPA-APRAC sponsorship. It seemed to him that EPA was joining APRAC in lending support to Chrysler's claims.[5] He questioned EPA representatives regarding their participation in APRAC. Assurances were made by the EPA people, including Administrator Ruckelshaus, that they were satisfied with the objectivity of APRAC activities, and felt them to be a valuable means of stretching scarce resources to gather needed information. Furthermore, they were comfortable with the fact that various parties interpreted the results in different ways. This was to be expected regardless of the validity of the results or their origin.

Senator Muskie also questioned the *appearance* of the EPA-APRAC cooperative effort. He felt this weakened public faith in the EPA's ability to act as an objective and independent regulatory agency. The Administrator promised to consider the matter. Several months later his successor, Russell Train, formally notified the CRC of EPA's withdrawal from APRAC.[6] In doing so he expressed "considerable personal regret" and repeated his satisfaction that EPA's participation "had been entirely constructive from every standpoint." He expressed his confidence in the "data generated . . . free from bias." He referred, however, to the EPA's need to maintain not only the fact but the appearance of objectivity. Since serious questions had arisen "in the minds of at least some people deeply concerned with environmental matters," it was prudent for EPA and APRAC to sever their working relationship.

---

5. *Hearing Before the Sen. Subcomm. on Air and Water Pollution* (Apr. 8, 1973) pp. 216–239.
6. *Letter from Russell E. Train (EPA) to Milton K. McLeod (CRC)* (Oct. 26, 1973).

Coming as it did toward the end of 1973, EPA's withdrawal had a particularly severe effect on APRAC activities.[7] The oil embargo and resulting recession cut deeply into the ability of many of APRAC's remaining sponsors to maintain their financial commitments. Annual APRAC expenditures fell from $2.9 million in 1973 to only $1.5 million by 1976. In addition, even though some informal contacts were maintained, the various Project Groups of APRAC were denied the technical expertise of EPA personnel in planning and evaluating programs. Thus, the effectiveness of APRAC was impaired, both quantitatively and qualitatively, by EPA's disengagement.

Objections were based on the fact that Chrysler's attack on the EPA standards for carbon monoxide control was grounded on its interpretation of a study partially funded by EPA, thereby possibly lending credibility to Chrysler's claims and weakening the government position. But consider the situation if EPA had been the sole sponsor of the study, a strong possibility since it had been suggested by the National Academy of Sciences. How much more weight could Chrysler's arguments have carried in that case? On the other hand, if EPA had stood aside and let APRAC conduct the work by itself, imagine the protests over EPA's abdication of its responsibility to gather such data, leaving the field to its industry critics. Finally, there could have been concurrent programs by EPA and by APRAC, but that would have been financially wasteful and probably technically impossible because of the scarcity of qualified investigators. Whichever course of action EPA had chosen, they would have been condemned by one group or another.

IIEC

The Inter-Industry Emissions Control Program (IIEC),[8] a somewhat different type of inter-industry cooperative research program involving the automobile and petroleum industries, was also aimed at helping to meet government standards for automobile emissions and fuel economy. Antitrust factors, particularly a consent decree entered into by United States automobile makers, affected this effort, however.

The IIEC was organized in 1967 by the Mobil Oil Company and the Ford Motor Company to conduct long-range research toward the development of low-emission, gasoline-powered vehicles. Like APRAC, the IIEC concentrated on broad research areas, leaving specific development efforts to the proprietary programs of member companies. Unlike APRAC, however, it was oriented toward the interactions of vehicles

---

7. *A Review of the APRAC Program*, Economics and Science Planning, Inc. (Jan. 24, 1977).
8. L. J. McCabe and W. J. Koehl, *The Inter-Industry Emission Control Program—Eleven Years of Progress in Automotive Emissions and Fuel Economy Research*, SAE Paper No. 780588, presented at Soc'y of Automotive Engineers Passenger Car Meeting (June 5–9, 1978).

and components with fuels and lubricants and not toward atmospheric or medical sciences. It also lacked any EPA participation.

The IIEC concept proved a popular one and the original two members were quickly joined by five more United States petroleum companies and four foreign automobile makers. Two more foreign automobile makers, Toyota and Volkswagen, later became affiliated with the IIEC. A 3-year, $7 million program was initiated encompassing 15 projects, carried out in member laboratories and ranging from mathematical modelling to prototype vehicle construction.[9]

The cooperative effort proceeded smoothly until 1969, when two events occurred that altered the IIEC operation. First, it became evident that the originally intended expiration date in early 1970 would not allow completion of work on a number of promising projects. It was agreed, therefore, that the program should be extended. This agreement was frustrated before it could be completed, however, by an unrelated Justice Department action against the United States automobile makers and their trade association, then called the Automobile Manufacturers Association.[10]

In this case the Justice Department had alleged that the United States automobile makers were conspiring to delay the development and introduction of emission-control devices on automobiles. The resulting consent decree specifically prohibited, *inter alia,* (1) agreements restricting any individual company from deciding independently when it would install such devices; (2) agreeing to file joint statements with governmental agencies on automobile emission and safety standards unless expressly authorized to do so; and (3) continuing certain restrictive agreements with regard to patent assignments and licensing. The key provision that eventually affected the IIEC (4) prohibited any agreements with other defendants or with any nondefendant manufacturer with a 2 percent share of the world's cars, trucks, and buses, to exchange confidential information on emission-control devices. In effect, this prevented Ford from undertaking new cooperative research with Fiat and Nissan, two other IIEC members in the 2 percent or more category, in the area of automobile emission control. In order to overcome this problem, Ford petitioned the Justice Department for permission to continue in the IIEC program. This petition was granted, but only to allow completion of ongoing programs, and only to the end of 1970.

---

9. The history of the IIEC and its interactions with the Justice Department are drawn freely from J. F. Socolofsky, *Cooperative Industry Research—Fear of Antitrust Violations as a Deterrent—Case History: Inter-Industry Emission Control (IIEC) Program,* presented at U.S. Dep't of Commerce/Industrial Research Inst. Seminar on Institutional and Legal Constraints to Coop. Energy R&D, Wash., D.C. (Dec. 16, 1974).

10. United States v. Automobile Mfrs. Ass'n, Inc., U.S. Dist. Ct. for the Cent. Dist. of Cal., Civ. Action No. 69075-JWC, (Oct. 29, 1969)—CCH Trade Cas. 72,907 (1970).

One direct result of the Justice Department's stand was the elimination of a cost-benefit analysis of emissions-control technology, which the IIEC had intended to conduct through an outside contractor. Another was to introduce considerable uncertainty about the future of the IIEC program. Without the full participation of a major United States automobile maker like Ford, the effort would not be worth continuing.

Technical progress continued, despite the uncertainty, with prototype concept vehicles demonstrating, by the end of 1970, the feasibility of meeting the IIEC's original emission and durability goals. At the same time, however, the Clean Air Act Amendments of 1970 set up new emission standards even more stringent than these IIEC goals. This raised the question of whether the IIEC program should attempt to continue beyond the 1970 deadline set for Ford. During this time, the prospects of legislative relief, legitimizing cooperative automobile oil company programs on automotive air pollution, were explored by Mobil. The chances for passage of such a bill were slim, and the idea of legislative relief was dropped.

Ford then petitioned the Justice Department to continue in the program beyond the end of 1970. In December of 1970, after receipt of a written judgment by the EPA that such an extension would be in the public interest, permission for 1971 was granted. Because of the late date of this permission, orderly continuation of the program was made more difficult. When Ford filed petitions for extensions into 1972 and 1973, the Justice Department again delayed granting permission until December of the prior years.

By the middle of 1973, the IIEC participants concluded that increasing fuel economy was becoming as important as achieving low emissions. Plans were drawn up accordingly to redirect the program's efforts toward both goals for the three-year period 1974 to 1976. Ford petitioned once again in November 1973 for permission to participate for the full three years. Although interim permission was granted pending a final determination, the resulting uncertainty hindered the 1974 program. The Justice Department's final approval, which did not come until October 1974, covered only the remainder of 1974 and 1975, not 1976. Because of this, some of the longer-range projects had to be abbreviated to accommodate the shorter time scale.

Justice created other problems, too, for the second-phase IIEC program. For example, one condition set by the Justice Department for Ford's continuing role was that any background patent owned by a participant must be made available under suitable license arrangement to all interested parties if it blocked the use of any subsequent patents developed under IIEC sponsorship. One of the programs undertaken by IIEC-2 involved the rotary engine. Toyo Kogyo, manufacturer of the Mazda, was one of the original IIEC participants and a pioneer in rotary engine development. It found the condition unacceptable and dropped out of the IIEC at this point, depriving the group of its technical expertise.

The 1969 Consent Degree also prevented Toyota and Volkswagen, each of which controlled over 2 percent of world motor vehicle sales, from gaining full membership in the IIEC. Instead they were restricted to know-how agreements, giving them access to IIEC results, but were forbidden from taking part in project planning or supplying research results to Ford. Thus, the group was not able to take advantage of the considerable technical expertise of these two companies either. In fact, Volkswagen withdrew altogether at the end of 1972.

The IIEC program continued until the end of 1977, making total expenditures of $32 million. Ford's participation was maintained through the Justice Department's approval of its annual petitions. The decision to terminate the program grew out of the members' view that the state of basic knowledge had progressed by 1977 to the point where further progress lay more in the area of proprietary systems and device development by individual companies than in continued joint and open programs.

During the eleven years of its existence, the IIEC program made a number of noteworthy contributions to the technology of automotive emissions control and fuel conservation. These have been documented in some sixty-five publications, sixteen United States and numerous foreign patents.

CONCLUSION

One can understand, under the circumstances, how the Justice Department's concerns about restraint of trade in emission-control devices might have been sufficiently aroused to justify the original 1969 Consent Decree. A small group of United States automobile makers, who together essentially dominated the United States market, worked closely through their trade association in the development of emission-control devices. Does this mean, however, that the same concerns should have been carried over to groups like CRC-APRAC and the IIEC? Probably not, for the following reasons.

First, the representation of the CRC-APRAC and IIEC groups was much broader than the Automobile Manufacturers Association of the 1969 Consent Decree. In the case of APRAC, a wide variety of engine and component builders, along with the petroleum industry, were associated with the United States automobile makers. The IIEC included only one United States automobile maker, along with a number of foreign car manufacturers and numerous oil companies. Second, all results obtained by these two organizations were made available to the public, thereby promoting the freely competitive use of such information. Finally, the areas explored by both groups were broad and general in nature; specific production-system development was left to the proprietary efforts of individual companies. This latter point is well-illustrated by the proliferation of different emissions-control systems from the various United States and foreign automobile makers.

We understand Senator Muskie's intentions and the antitrust enforcement objectives of the Justice Department. The Senator wished to maintain not only the fact, but also the appearance, of independence in a regulatory agency. The Justice Department wanted to carry out its mandate to promote competition. But in view of the broad-based membership of APRAC and IIEC, the general nature of their programs, and the public availability of all information they generated, perhaps their treatment was harsher than circumstances warranted. The public interest might have been better served by a more sympathetic attitude on the part of Congress and the Justice Department.

DISCUSSION

HAROLD C. MACDONALD: The 1969 Consent Decree has, in large part, outlived any legitimate purpose it may once have served; it continues to inhibit joint activity related to state and federal regulation of motor vehicle safety and emissions, which has a disproportionately adverse effect on smaller companies.

How has the decree affected projects undertaken to advance research and technology? The Motor Vehicle Manufacturers Association study of gas generants was severely handicapped by the inability to get up-to-date data, which the auto makers could not risk disclosing because of the consent decree and the antitrust laws. As a result, the Arthur D. Little and Petell work had to be based largely on out-of-date data and speculation.

IIEC's effectiveness was limited because of our inability to enter into agreement with other IIEC members to allow them to work on proprietary experimental hardware. For instance, the studies on PROCO had to be carried out with obsolete hardware since the current hardware was proprietary; the question of the optimal octane for automotive fuels could not be addressed because the investigation would require disclosure of proprietary information.

APRAC's effectiveness has also been limited by antitrust restrictions. At present, we are unable to undertake a truly meaningful program on the potential health effects of diesel emissions, since we cannot provide the contractors with the hardware that Motor Vehicle Manufacturers Association members currently have under development.

I do not mean to imply that the 1969 Consent Decree is the only problem in these cases. But the Department of Justice really should develop a procedure to allow interested parties to cooperate in advancing the state of technology. Allowing the 1969 Consent Decree to expire as scheduled would go a long way, but more is needed.*

CARL NASH: The question involved in Messrs. Alpert and Holt's discussion—does the smog consent decree stifle innovation in emissions control or safety technology?—is really not an important question. The 1969 Consent Decree really spells out what the antitrust laws of this country mean. If the 1969 Consent Decree were taken away, one would assume that the behavior of the companies would be roughly similar to what it is today, for those things forbidden by the decree are forbidden by the antitrust laws.

This gets us to the real question of R&D effectiveness: What is it that promotes the advancement of technology to help us with the environmental, social, and resource questions that we are facing? We know that high interest rates tend to discourage industrial companies from doing long-term research projects. In effect, high interest rates cause companies to bring their horizons in closer. We also know that research and development is really a small part of the problem of new technology. Commercialization is a major component.

I have seen a couple of cases in which innovations which have obvious value have come along outside the industry and neither the auto makers nor their suppliers have been willing to touch them. My favorite example is Caterpillar Tractor's beadless tire. After seven years of effort, neither Detroit nor the tire manufacturers have been willing to translate the new technology into a commercial product.

---

* On March 30, 1979, the District Court renewed the Consent Decree for an additional ten years. Shortly thereafter, General Motors and Chrysler announced their agreement for General Motors to share certain pollution control engineering with Chrysler, subject to approval by the Department of Justice. Approval was received, and Ford then petitioned the District Court to reconsider its decision to extend the decree. The court agreed to hear argument on reconsideration, and a hearing date was set.—Eds.

ALPERT: The real objective of the cooperative research I talked about is problem definition. The intent in these cooperative programs is not to come up with a product, but the scope of the problems; the innovation part is left to the individual firms. The point of my discussion is that in the kind of cooperative research I talked about there are problems with the overall regulatory climate—not only with antitrust, but also with the views of a congressional body toward a regulatory agency—which can get in the way and hinder this kind of research.

AUTO (U.S.): Mr. Nash implied that United States auto makers are not innovative. I point to the example of air bags. General Motors spent a lot of money on this product. We tooled up to sell 100,000 and scarcely sold 10,000. With regard to engines—you can take $25 million and multiply it 15 times and you have not got what we sunk into the rotary engine. And I hate to tell you how many rotary engines we sold in the last few years. I would strongly defend the record of money and effort spent on R&D by the domestic manufacturers. At the same time, I believe there is value to cooperative research on basic issues, as Dr. Alpert has shown.

ALPERT: Government regulation is having a strong, negative impact on the innovative process. The expense of regulation so preoccupies the management and financial resources of companies that the innovative process is set aside. The more regulation you have, therefore, the less innovative an industry tends to be. We have to move out of an adversary situation to one of more cooperation. In areas where the regulatory climate is more cooperative, such as in Japan, the overall innovative process is encouraged. During World War II, the United States had a period of government-industry cooperation and much innovation occurred.

NASH: In answer to the air foil example, I mention Ricardo's work on the internal combustion engine—an individual effort. And I point out that, despite the fact that Japan has no antitrust laws, Japan's two major automobile companies—Toyota and Nissan—are the least innovative.

BEYOND AUTOCRACY: THE PUBLIC'S ROLE IN REGULATING THE AUTO

Brian Ketcham and Stan Pinkwas, *Citizens for Clean Air, Inc.*

THE POST-AUTOCRATIC STATE

The United States needs to reevaluate its attitudes toward automobiles. This means going beyond the simplistic notion that improving automobiles as consumer products, that making endless technical adjustments, will solve the social problems their use creates. But we will never do this by continuing to rely on the industry for our information, by continuing to accept its mythology, and by continuing to accept its definitions.

As a first step, Congress must investigate the social, economic, and political consequences of our nearly total dependence on automobiles. The attempts that have been made—such as the Office of Science and Technology's report, "Cumulative Regulatory Effects on the Cost of Automotive Transportation" (RECAT),[1] the task force on Motor Vehicle Goals Beyond 1980, and the ongoing National Transportation Policy Study Commission—became as captive of automotive interests as most Americans are of their cars. Instead of helping us understand the consequences of our automobile use, their conclusions were routinely used to thwart further regulation. Meanwhile, government decisions about automobiles continue to be based on inadequate, skewed information and made with little regard for the societal effects of automobiles or the highways they require.

A long-term, decently funded commitment to support public participation in transportation decision-making can help overcome this. But public participation demands technical expertise and few individuals or public organizations can afford its cost; corporations and foundations

---

1. *Cumulative Regulatory Effects on the Cost of Automotive Transportation (RECAT)*, Final Report of the Ad Hoc Comm., Office of Science & Technology, Wash., D.C. (Feb. 1972).

have already proven unwilling. Given the automobile industry's historic dominance of the regulatory process, the federal government would be justified in taking up the slack.

The government can do some of this fairly quickly. For example, NHTSA should expand their demonstration program to support public participation in federal rule-making procedures. Other agencies should begin similar participation programs.

Washington should also encourage the development of a corps of technicians who can independently evaluate such matters as automobile safety, emissions control, fuel economy, public transportation, and transportation planning and land use. There are no experts now available to the public for such work who are not already employed by industry or government. Those experts that are available are understandably reluctant to provide the sustained involvement public participation demands. A modest effort could be funded for $10 million a year (or about 1 cent for every $400 that consumers spend on transportation).

The academic community should also begin to take a greater interest in transportation issues—especially in the social impact of automobiles. Universities have the resources to investigate the problem and provide courses in the externality costs of automobile use. The socio-economics of transportation is a ripe, untapped area for exploration.

Finally, there is a need to investigate and reform the industry's posture toward the media. The trade and enthusiast press is heavily subsidized while the general press is alternately junketed and intimidated. The industry's economic clout with the media is a powerful propagandistic force that it is not afraid to use to shape public opinion or suppress unfavorable comment. For example, when we submitted an article about diesel emissions and public health to *New Engineer* magazine in 1978,[2] a major diesel auto maker threatened to withdraw from advertising negotiations if the article ran. It did, and the manufacturer carried out its threat. The price of *New Engineer*'s integrity was about $100,000.

We have already embarked upon what Robert Heilbroner calls "planned capitalism." Increasingly, its cutting edge will be the environmental impacts of manufactured goods. These impacts, says Heilbroner, "indicate the need for an unprecedented degree of monitoring, control, supervision, and precaution with regard to the economic process."[3] Elsewhere, he is more specific: "In the last quarter of this century the transportation industry will more and more provide the implementation for whatever transportation policy government deter-

---

2. B. Ketcham and S. Pinkwas, "Diesels and Man: Are We Creating a New Environmental Problem by Solving an Old One?" *New Engineer* (Apr. 1978).
3. R. L. Heilbroner, "Reflections: Boom and Crash," *The New Yorker*, Aug. 28, 1978, p. 71.

mines to be in the best interest of national survival."[4] Heilbroner believes this is a welcome and necessary development for the nation and for the private transportation industry; that is, it will help preserve the industry's profit structure for as long as possible.

On the whole, this is an accurate assessment and, although the auto/highway industry fights against every turn of the regulatory screw, it understands where history is leading it. For example, "the country must launch an integrated national planning program now . . . if the country is to meet its post–1990 surface transportation needs," the Highway Users Federation said to its members, adding that "the Federation stands ready to help in this national effort."[5]

Yet transportation still needs to be integrated into the broad range of planning processes the government conducts, particularly those concerning land use and energy. President Carter noted in his 1977 energy message[6] that transportation accounts for 26 percent of all our direct energy costs. But he failed to note that the production of vehicles, spare parts, and fuel, and the building, operation, and maintenance of related facilities account for an additional 17 percent. This brings transportation's share of the energy budget up to 43 percent, as Table 6-1 illustrates. Yet instead of substantive ideas for reducing transportation energy use, President Carter proposed passenger car fuel economy standards that were already law and excise tax rebates and inadequate gasoline taxes that were axed by Congress.

The last years have seen the beginning of a reasonable regulatory process, but automobiles and highways still unreasonably pervade our lives. As Kenneth Schneider, another critic of the industry observed, "unlimited multiplication of anything challenges the worthiness of what is created."[7] Public interest organizations can help devise the saner path we need to follow. More automobiles with better options can no longer substitute for legitimate progress. The myth of infinite resources is dead; conservation and rehabilitation are necessities.

THE MYTHIC OPPOSITION

There is almost no meaningful participation by the public in the automotive regulatory process. However, because certain aspects of the automobile, primarily consumer-related, are coming under regulation, the idea has gained currency that there is a well-organized, well-funded grass roots movement opposing unregulated automobile production and its indiscriminate use. The welter of hearings and committees and

---

4. R. L. Heilbroner, *Business Civilization in Decline* 36–37 (W.W. Norton & Co., 1976).
5. Highway Users Fed'n, *1977 Annual Report,* p. 10.
6. *The National Energy Plan,* Executive Office of the President, Energy Policy and Planning, Wash., D.C. (Apr. 1977).
7. K. R. Schneider, *Autokind vs. Mankind* 226 (W.W. Norton & Co., 1971).

TABLE 6-1 1975 Distribution of Total National Energy Consumption

	Percent of total national energy budget
Direct Tranportation	
Automobile fuel	11.8%
Truck fuel	4.7
Air fuel	3.5
All other transport fuel	5.3
Subtotal	25.3%
Indirect Transportation	
Refining and distribution of fuels and lubricants	5.3%
Construction, operation and maintenance of loading, storage and maintenance facilties for private trucking and all common carriers	4.3
Manufacture and repair of highway vehicles including parts and tires	4.2
Manufacture and repair of air, rail and marine vehicles and support equipment	1.9
Construction and Maintenance of highways	1.7
Subtotal	17.4%
Nontransportation	57.3%

Source: Adapted from "National Transportation, Trends and Choices," Figure II.15, p. 32 (DOT, Jan., 1977).

the general huggermugger of lobbying supports the idea. Unfortunately, no organized movement exists. Although some economic and environmental realities are finally being recognized by the industry, the commercial imperatives of the assembly line still effectively dictate important social policies. In the meantime, the general public remains as excluded as ever from their formulation.

By 1979, there will be about 118 million automobiles and 31 million trucks in the United States, more than 1 vehicle for every licensed driver. Interstate highways and parking lots already determine the shape of our cities and towns, where people live, how they commute, and where they will work. Approximately one-fifth of the labor force performs automobile- and highway-related work. Subways and railroads have atrophied, unable to compete with the automobiles; more than 200 communities have completely abandoned public transit. Hundreds of neighborhoods, primarily urban, have been ruined by unwanted roads. Tailpipe exhaust causes most of our urban air pollution, traffic accidents kill more people under thirty-five than any disease, and the miles we drive cost us virtually all of the oil we import. We can no longer live without automobiles, but neither, it seems, can we afford to live with them.

No one really knows exactly how excessive their costs have grown to be. The true costs of automobile use have always been obscured by a general refusal to include the costs of subsidies the industry demands from the government and the social costs of its products. The best estimate is that it costs the people of this country about $420 billion (in 1978 dollars) a year for mobility. This figure is so large that many refuse to believe it, but a rough documentation exists. As Table 6-2 illustrates, the auto/truck/highway share for 1978 is $352 billion, or 83.3 percent. As we shall see below, another $100 billion should be added to represent the societal costs of automotively induced air and water pollution, congestion, accidents, medical expenses, and government subsidies.

The automobile industry never acknowledges this oppressive side of its nature, preferring instead to posture itself as plagued by regulators and zero-growth environmentalists. Yet, despite its warnings and fulminations, the industry is healthy and growing. Indeed, NHTSA compellingly argues that its regulations have improved both the quality of Detroit's vehicles and the domestic industry's competitive position. Automotive retail sales totalled $144 billion in 1977, which is one-fifth of all the retail sales in the country. Since 1968, the net worth of General Motors and Ford has increased substantially and now exceeds $24 billion; Chrysler's net worth increased modestly during this period. General Motors and Ford's ratio of after-tax profit to net worth also increased; Chrysler's fluctuated.[8] It should be recalled that General Motors, Ford, and Chrysler account for 97 percent of domestic production and nearly one-half of world production through more than 200 facilities in more than 40 other countries.[9]

The automotive regulatory process is administered by the federal government through NHTSA (which is part of DOT), the Federal Highway Administration (FHWA), and the EPA. NHTSA regulates the fuel economy and safety characteristics of vehicles; FHWA regulates highways and roads, which is to say that it administers the Highway Trust Fund; and EPA regulates emissions and noise.

Participation by the public in these decisions has been exceedingly modest, often nonexistent. It has also largely been confined to NHTSA's fuel economy and safety proceedings and EPA's emissions proceedings. Participation in highway controversies tends to occur at the city level and is often not even thought of as an aspect of automobile regulation.

---

8. *The Contributions of Automobile Regulation (Preliminary Report)* 26–31, NHTSA (June 1978).

9. B. C. Snell, *American Ground Transport: A Proposal for Restructuring the Automobile, Truck, Bus, and Rail Industries,* presented to the U.S. Sen. Subcomm. on Antitrust and Monopoly of the Comm. on the Judiciary (Feb. 26, 1974), p. 10.

TABLE 6-2 Direct Consumer Costs for All Modes of Transportation, 1970–1982 (Billions)

	1970	1971	1972	1973	1974	1975	1976	1977*	1978*	1979*	1980*	1981*	1982*
Automobile costs	$92.3	$107.1	$117.9	$129.8	$137.8	$148.2	$172.9	$177.8	$193.3	$210.5	$229.2	$249.5	$271.8
Truck freight costs	69.2	79.3	92.1	102.5	107.7	112.0	130.7	143.6	158.7	175.6	194.4	215.2	238.5
Highway mode subtotal	$161.5	$186.4	$210.0	$232.3	$245.5	$260.2	$303.6	$321.4	$352.0	$386.1	$423.6	$464.7	$510.3
For-hire and all other transportation costs	38.3	41.1	44.3	49.6	56.4	58.0	60.6	64.4	70.5	76.8	83.9	91.5	100.1
Total transportation costs	$199.8	$227.5	$254.3	$281.9	$301.9	$318.2	$364.2	$385.8	$422.5	$462.9	$507.5	$556.2	$610.4
Highway construction and maintenance costs**	$20.8	$22.5	$23.2	$24.2	$26.1	$28.7	$29.8	$32.0	$34.1	$36.4	$38.8	$41.4	$44.1

* Projected from Tables, pages 4 & 5, "Transportation Facts and Trends," July, 1977 and "Quarterly Supplement," Jan. 19, 1978, Transp. Ass'n of Am., using a least-squares exponential regression of the 1965–1976 data.

** Source: *Highway Statistics Summary to 1975*, Report No. FHWA-HP-HS-S75 (Fed. Highway Adm., 1978).

Such regulation demands expertise because the automobile, even as a social problem, is ineluctably grounded in complex technologies. The industry's special interests know this and draw on their corporate members to finance the expertise they need. Organizations such as the National Automobile Dealers Association, the American Petroleum Institute, the Highway Users Federation for Safety and Mobility, the American Trucking Associations, the Motor Vehicle Manufacturers Association, and even the United Auto Workers, potently represent the transportation industry.[10]

They monitor and testify at hearings, contribute to congressional election campaigns, spend millions of dollars on their own research programs, lobby intensively at all levels of government, produce their own publications, place their representatives in influential government positions, subsidize the trade press, and cultivate the general press. Estimates of the automobile industry's lobbying budget are as high as $500 million a year[11] and may well be conservative. For example, General Motors contributes heavily to obvious automobile lobbies but also to the American Public Transit Association and the Railway Progress Association.[12] These are cornerstones of the transit lobby, whose interests might be presumed to differ widely from those of the auto/highway lobby. General Motors, however, also dominates ground transit modes such as locomotives and buses: As Bradford Snell concluded in his landmark report to the Senate Subcommittee on Antitrust and Monopoly, "automakers embrace transit in order to prevent it from competing effectively with their sales of automobiles."[13]

---

10. A full roster of the auto/highway lobby is beyond the scope of this article but even a partial list is enough to illustrate its breadth and strength. Thus, we have: The American Ass'n of State Highway & Transp. Officials; The American Auto. Ass'n; The American Imported Auto. Dealers Ass'n; The American Iron & Steel Ass'n; The American Petroleum Inst.; The American Pub. Transit Ass'n; The American Pub. Works Ass'n; The American Retail Fed'n; The American Road & Transp. Builders Ass'n; The American Soc'y of Civil Engineers; American Trucking Ass'ns, Inc.; The Associated Gen. Contractors of Am.; The Automotive Information Council; The Automotive Legislative Council of Am.; The Automotive Liaison Council; The Automotive Parts & Accessories Ass'n; Automotive Serv. Councils, Inc., and The Automotive Serv. Indus. Ass'n. Also: The Committee for Automotive Dealers; The Diesel Auto. Ass'n; The Highway Users Fed'n for Safety & Mobility (and its 90 state, regional and local chapters); The Independent Dealers Comm. Dedicated for Action; The International Council of Shopping Centers; The Iron & Steel Inst.; The Motor & Equip. Mfrs. Ass'n; The Motor Vehicle Mfrs. Ass'n; The National Ass'n of Indus. Parks; The National Ass'n of Mfrs.; The National Auto. Dealers Ass'n, The National Auto Muffler Ass'n; The National Automotive Radiator Serv. Ass'n, The National Parking Ass'n; National Realty Ass'n, Inc.; The National Merchants Ass'n; The National Tire Dealers & Retreaders Ass'n; The Transportation Ass'n of Am.; The Transportation Research Bd; and the U.S. Chamber of Commerce.
11. Snell, n. 9 *supra* at 95. See 300; Snell cites estimates ranging from $100 million to $500 million.
12. *Ibid.* at 46.
13. *Ibid.* at 46.

The Highway Users Federation, which alone consists of more than 450 individual organizations, and the Motor Vehicle Manufacturers Association have a combined lobbying budget of more than $15 million a year, most of it contributed directly by General Motors, Ford, and Chrysler.[14] Before 1970, the Federation was known as the National Highway Users Conference (NHUC) and was explicitly a creature of the automobile companies. It was founded in 1932 by Alfred P. Sloan, then president of General Motors, who served as its permanent chairman until 1948. Alfred Bradley succeeded Sloan as president of General Motors and as permanent chairman of the National Highway Users Conference through 1956. That year, the conference achieved its greatest success—creation of the Interstate Highway System and the trust fund financing mechanism. One result was that from 1956 through 1970 the federal government spent about $70 billion for highways (and, therefore, automobiles) and only $765 million for rail transit.[15]

Lest anyone imagine this influence to have abated, we have the direct testimony of Secretary of Transportation Brock Adams who told a 1977 gathering of the Highway Users Federation elite that "there is more power here in terms of what the transportation community can do . . . than any other place in the world."[16]

The base of much of this influence is the industry's mastery and distribution of information. The auto/highway lobby, as well as the manufacturers, conducts extensive public relations and advertising campaigns. The National Auto Dealers' Association, for example, launched one in November 1978 "to get more and more Americans to speak up for the automobile."[17] The campaign consisted of slick ads in national consumer and public interest magazines plus television and radio spots. General Motors, Ford, and Chrysler contributed $500,000, the lion's share of the initial financing. Less visibly, the Highway Users Federation in 1977 sent out fifteen separate "Candidate Papers" to all congressional candidates, a "highway transportation information kit" to all newly elected legislators, and a new edition of its *Highway Fact Book* to all senators and representatives.[18]

The materials are slick in form and content. Increasingly, they argue against environmental criticisms by claiming that autos and highways are environmental necessities. The Highway Users Federation, for example, distributes a background document for editors that claims it is vitally important to complete the Interstate Highway System in order to: (1) Improve road safety and reduce accidents; (2) reduce urban traffic congestion and air pollution; and (3) conserve gasoline.[19]

14. *Ibid.* at 45.
15. *Ibid.* at 45.
16. See n. 5 *supra* at 1.
17. "NADA moves ahead with ad campaign to back 'Automobility,' " *Automotive News*, Oct. 23, 1978.
18. See n. 5 *supra* at 1.
19. *Editor's Resource,* Highway Users Fed'n (Oct. 25, 1978).

Except for its scale, all this is no more than the routine politics of business. A study by Common Cause of federal regulatory agencies demonstrated that special interests have ten times more access to administrators than do consumers. The study explained that this is partly because the public has no one to speak for it on many of the issues that come before regulatory bodies.[20] In October 1978, Senator Edward Kennedy concluded from his own observations that special interest influence is so extensive that "representative government on Capitol Hill is in the worst shape I have seen it in my sixteen years in the Senate. The heart of the problem is that the Senate and the House are awash in a sea of special interest campaign contributions and special interest lobbying."[21]

In the automotive arena, special interests have the field virtually to themselves. Although many public interest and environmental organizations could justifiably be involved with transportation issues, none of the major organizations has a funded program dealing with the automobile—not Common Cause, not the Sierra Club, not the National Audubon Society, not the Wilderness Society, not the Environmental Defense Fund, and not even the Nader organizations.[22]

However, the field is not barren: Consumers Union looks after the integrity of the automobile as a consumer product; the Center for Auto Safety, directed by Clarence Ditlow, works to create safer cars and a safer driving environment; and Citizens for Clean Air, directed by Brian Ketcham, strives to identify and reduce the social costs of our dependence on automobiles. The Insurance Institute for Highway Safety is also frequently cited as an effective voice of the public. But its real mission is to reduce the costs of the insurance industry. In fact, the insurance industry funds the Institute and is the special interest it

---

20. *With Only One Ear: A Common Cause Study of Industry and Consumer Representation Before Federal Regulatory Commissions,* Common Cause (Aug. 1977).

21. Sen. Edward M. Kennedy, *Climbing Mountains with Phil Hart,* The Philip A. Hart Lecture, Lake Superior State College, Sault Ste. Marie, Mich. (Oct. 23, 1978).

22. The public interest and environmental community has grown considerably in the last decade but, with the exceptions noted in the text, such organizations do not fund programs dealing with the automobile. A partial roster includes: The American Council on the Environment; The American Lung Ass'n; The American Medical Ass'n; The American Pub. Health Ass'n; The Center for Auto Safety; The Center for Transp. Policy; Citizens for Clean Air, Inc.; Common Cause; Consumer Action Now; the Consumer Fed'n of Am.; Consumers Union; Energy Action; The Environmental Defense Fund; The Exploratory Project for Economic Alternatives; The Highway Action Coalition; The Institute for Policy Studies; and The Institute for Pub. Transp. Also: The League of Women Voters; The National Audubon Soc'y; The National Clean Air Coalition; The National Comm. for Auto Crash Protection; The National League of Cities; The National Wildlife Fed'n; The Natural Resources Defense Council; Public Citizen; The Public Interest Economics Foundation; Public Interest Research Groups; The Public Resources Center; The Sierra Club; The Wilderness Society; and The Urban Land Inst.

represents. But, with or without the Institute, these few groups can hardly compete against the resources of Detroit.

This enormous imbalance has biased the federal regulatory process since its inception. There have been four major attempts to analyze the social impact of the automobile: (1) The 1972 RECAT study; (2) the 1976 study on Motor Vehicle Goals Beyond 1980;[23] (3) the National Transportation Policy Study Commission; and (4) the Congressional Office of Technology Assessment (OTA) Auto Study. Each of these efforts was heavily armored with special interest representation. The conclusions of the first two were so strongly pro-industry that they have been used ever since to argue against regulation.

RECAT, for example, was proposed in relative secrecy and written and released with almost no public involvement or comment. It reflected the automobile industry's assertions that emissions and safety regulations were too harsh and too expensive even as they existed in 1972. Though most of RECAT's conclusions have been discredited, its publication constituted a serious obstacle to standards under consideration at the time.

In 1975, DOT created a task force from the personnel of several federal agencies[24] to prepare a major report on Motor Vehicle Goals Beyond 1980. The task force held four hearings during which it heard thirty-two speakers; thirty represented automakers, taxicab owners, the American Automobile Association, and oil and chemical companies; one represented the Sierra Club; and one represented the California Health Department. In addition, then Secretary of Transportation William Coleman refused to grant a request to incorporate into the study process a professional critique by public interest representatives.[25] The final report understated the impact of the auto, virtually ignored auto-related externality costs, and endorsed diesel engines without so much as a look at their potential problems. Yet the automobile industry criticized the report for not going far enough even as they prepared to use it.[26]

---

23. *Report by the Federal Task Force on Motor Vehicle Goals Beyond 1980*, Wash., D.C. (Sept. 2, 1976).

24. The agencies were: The Council on Environmental Quality; The Department of Commerce; The Department of Defense; The Department of Health, Education, and Welfare; The Department of Labor; The Department of Transp.; The Department of the Treasury; The Domestic Council; The Energy Research & Dev. Administration; The Environmental Protection Agency; The Federal Energy Administration; The Federal Highway Administration; The National Aeronautics & Space Administration; The National Highway Traffic Safety Administration; The National Science Foundation; The Office of Management & Budget; and The Urban Mass Transp. Administration.

25. *Letter from Assistant Secretary of Transportation Hamilton Herman to Brian Ketcham, Vice President, Citizens for Clean Air, Inc.* (Feb. 26, 1976).

26. "Automakers Object to Optimistic View of Task Force Report," *Automotive News*, Nov. 1, 1976.

In 1976, Congress established (under the Federal Aid Highway Act) the National Transportation Policy Study Commission "to report findings and recommendations with respect to the nation's transportation needs, both national and regional through the year 2,000."[27] This commission is still active and consists of six congressmen, six senators, and seven so-called "public citizens." One of these citizens represents an asphalt paving association; another is the chairman of a railroad; another presides over a highway construction company; another over a trucking company; another over an airline; and another over an auto dealership. Several are also involved in real estate investment and land development. The seventh citizen represents the Southern Pennsylvania Transportation Authority, but there is an enormous distinction between operating a transportation company and representing its passengers. Again we find the industry, in mufti, calling the shots.

The OTA Auto Study is similarly flawed and shows the same signs as its predecessor investigations of being unable to grapple with the societal impacts of automobiles and their use.

In each of these instances, the industry's self-interest easily overwhelmed the public interest. Yet the industry never abandons its defensiveness and frequently inveighs against the regulators, environmentalists, zero-growth freaks, and socialists it claims are arrayed against it.[28] Most of these phrases are code words for consumer and public interest advocates who, in reality, constitute a relatively tiny opposition.

As a result, we know far less than is generally believed about the impact of automobiles on our culture. For example:

- How dependent are we on passenger cars as means of transportation? How do we define that dependence? In terms of available alternatives? In terms of costs? In terms of the allocation of natural resources?

- What federal policies and regulations have contributed to the automo-

---

27. *National Transportation Policy Study Commission, Open Meeting,* Fed. Reg., Vol. 42, No. 91, p. 23887.

28. The Diesel Automobile Association, in particular, indulges in such characterizations. Its members strongly attacked Dr. Delbert Barth, then the EPA's Deputy Administrator for Health and Ecology, over the agency's diesel emissions research program (calling it part of a "witchhunt by environmentalists") at a DAA conference at the New York City Statler-Hilton on Nov. 28–29, 1977. Meanwhile, Volume 1, Number 1 of *Diesel Motorist,* the DAA's magazine, charged that energy and environmental regulations were written by "alternate life-style folk running their nonsense through computer banks in agency basements."

When a brief, oral version of this essay was presented at this symposium, Sydney Terry, Chrysler's Vice President for Consumer Affairs, implied that Brian Ketcham was a card-carrying Communist and Maoist sympathizer hiding behind a public interest persona. NHTSA's *The Contribution of Automobile Regulation,* cites other less vituperative criticisms of the regulatory process by Henry Ford II, Lee Iacocca (then with Ford), and Thomas Murphy and John Riccardo of General Motors and Chrysler, respectively.

bile's rise to dominance and the decay of other modes of transit? What policy reforms might bring about a more equitable balance between automobiles and other modes? How can such reforms be effected?

- Is mass transit a viable alternative to automobile use? If so, what kinds of mass transit and under what conditions? If not, what alternatives are viable?
- What are the societal costs of automobile and truck use? How can they be accurately measured and plugged into planning processes?
- What are the impacts of our automotive policies on our foreign policies? On our balance of payments?
- Finally, what will we do in 30 years when we have 200 million autos and trucks and no gasoline: What is the real meaning of impending energy shortages?

Without government encouragement and sponsorship of the public interest, these questions are likely to remain largely unanswered and our economically unhealthy dependence on automobiles will probably increase.

CONSUMING THE AUTO

In a consumer-oriented society it is a basic tenet that consumers have a right to well-made goods. As a result, the public interest has been able to raise an effective if belated voice about automobiles as products.

The relationship between exhaust emissions and fuel economy illustrates the point. For years the industry insisted that low emissions could only be achieved at the expense of mileage. As if to prove this, domestic auto makers selected the cheapest possible approach for controlling emissions for their 1973 and 1974 models. But the approach was technically deficient and the cars of those years are notorious for their poor mileage and performance. The two years linger in Detroit's memory like sour vintage. In the eyes of the public, they discredited emissions controls.

The suddenness of the 1973-to-1974 Arab oil embargo and the gasoline shortages it produced intensified the growing resistance to emissions controls. Automobile makers and their allies blamed EPA and the Congress for forcing them to go with an inadequate control technology and, indeed, the public refused to accept the devices. But the main problem was Detroit's obsession with maintaining a low purchase price regardless of the effect on overall performance. It was a classic instance of a penny-wise, pound-foolish policy that is still costing consumers more in added fuel costs ($10 to $15 billion over the 10-year vehicle life cycle of the 1973-to-1974 cars) than it saved them in initial purchase costs.

In the early 1970s, Dr. William Balgord, now President of Environmental & Resources Technology, Inc., and Brian Ketcham set out to demonstrate that the industry was wrong. In 1973, Dr. Balgord built an

American Motors Matador that operated below the original 1975-to-1976 statutory emissions standards (0.4 hydrocarbons, 3.4 carbon monoxide, 0.4 nitrogen oxides) for 25,000 miles. In January 1974, they installed an advanced catalytic control device similar to the one used in the Matador in a Ford Pinto. Within five days, they had the Pinto meeting statutory emissions standards with a 20 percent *improvement* in fuel economy.

In a related area, Citizens for Clean Air challenged the industry's puffery of diesel technology as a satisfactory substitute for conventional spark-ignition engines. There is considerable evidence that diesels generate and emit carcinogens. While all the evidence is not yet in, there is enough to warrant taking a cautious approach. But portions of the auto industry have rushed to dieselize while insisting that diesels are perfectly safe. In March 1977 and in January 1978, Citizens for Clean Air testified before NHTSA about the evidence against diesel exhaust particulates and about the possible effects on health of the unregulated production of present diesel engines for widespread use in passenger cars.[29] Our intervention prompted the government to undertake its own research program and to begin drafting appropriate regulations for diesels.

Unlike EPA, NHTSA has recognized its need for independent data. As one result, it awarded Citizens for Clean Air a modest contract to develop and test advanced three-way catalyst technology on intermediate-sized cars. This means that we are now in a position to demonstrate more conclusively that clean-running, economical, moderately priced cars are within the industry's capability. Part of Clean Air's research into diesels and its presentations before NHTSA were funded by a NHTSA demonstration project to support public participation in federal rule-making proceedings. The project is an admission of the need for greater public representation in administrative proceedings. Though a model of understatement, the regulations describing it acknowledge that

> [I]t has sometimes been difficult for some consumer, environmental and other groups of citizens that are either widely dispersed or poorly financed to bear the cost of participating in federal regulatory proceedings. By contrast, better financed and organized groups, frequently representative of the regulated industry, are often able to participate vigorously and effectively . . . [and] may have a disproportionate influence on government decision making.[30]

---

29. B. Ketcham, W. D. Balgord, and S. Pinkwas, *Final Report to the National Highway Traffic Safety Administration on Nonpassenger Automobile Average Fuel Economy Standards, Model Years 1980–81*, Citizens for Clean Air, Inc. (Feb. 7, 1978).

30. *Financial Assistance to Participants in Administrative Proceedings. Final Rule and Advance Notice of Proposed Rulemaking*, DOT/NHTSA, Fed. Reg., P. 8, p. 2864 (Jan. 13, 1977).

Unfortunately, NHTSA's program is small and restrictive. For example, it compensates technicians at one-third the rate it compensates lawyers (reflecting the reality that lawyers write such programs). This insures that technical presentations cannot be fully funded. The project also requires applicants to prove their poverty. However, in Catch-22 fashion, payment does not occur until months after all work has been completed. This means that participants must pay all their own expenses anyway; in our case, we took out a loan.

The industry is ambivalent toward consumer improvements. On the one hand, it agrees that we need safer, cleaner, more economical cars. On the other hand, it disagrees with virtually every specific requirement that might make this principle a reality. Existing regulations are, therefore, all products of compromise and negotiation; they are extremely complex and detailed; some overlap, others are ineffective. However, auto makers do not hesitate to cite their faults as a way of discrediting regulation in general.

Yet, auto makers usually benefit from the improvements they have been forced to make. The industry has been driven to make overdue reforms and to monitor more closely the quality of its product. Eugene Bordinat, Ford's chief of styling, has even described for *Newsweek* how "a new safety standard covering bumpers led to a series of styling changes that ultimately resulted in a sweeping redesign of the 1973 Thunderbird—and turned it into a better selling car."[31]

From a consumer's viewpoint, the postregulation automobile is a far better product than the preregulation automobile. It gets better mileage, runs cleaner when tuned, and comes equipped with seat belts and other mandated safety features. NHTSA estimates the added cost of safety features at $250 per car.[32] This is far below the industry's claims. NHTSA also estimates that the safety improvements it has forced Detroit to make have saved 200,000 lives since 1966.[33] Sales, meanwhile, have generally improved over the last years.

The automobile as a consumer product is, therefore, slowly coming under reasonable regulation. The needs of the industry are being served by the demands of its consumers and, though public participation in this process has been exceedingly limited, its input has tended to go a long way.

But the number of public interest organizations that now participate can be counted on the fingers of one hand and, as the industry's more flagrant abuses come under control and the issues become increasingly technical, public participation will become more expensive and more difficult to maintain.

---

31. "A Sculptor on Wheels," *Newsweek*, Oct. 23, 1978, p. 80.
32. NHTSA, note 8 *supra* at ii.
33. *Ibid.* at 32.

Government Technology and the Automobile

THE COSTS NOBODY COUNTS

The genius of the auto industry has been its ability to transform its own need to divide and manufacture into a strategy of regulation by division. Given this impetus—and the natural tendency of a bureaucracy to subdivide as it multiplies—the regulatory process has grown along fragmented and narrowly defined lines. Even now, it functions under the illusion that a complex social force such as the automobile can be productively governed by regulating it only in terms of its component characteristics.

This is regulatory failure—and a major consequence has been that the real costs of automobiles are still poorly understood. The industry denies them, governments do not understand them, no one properly examines them, and the public pays. Since these costs go unrecognized, they also go unregulated.

The sticker price on a new car reflects a small part of the ultimate cost to its purchaser and virtually none of the costs that will be borne by society at large. According to our best estimates these little understood societal costs affecting health, the environment, and urban economies amount to $100 billion each year or, broken down, to about $10,000 added to the sticker price of every new car that is sold.

Traffic congestion is probably the most visible of the automobile's broader impacts. Indeed, it is the common cold of most cities, and as resistant. It also resists costing out. While there are no national figures, the cost for New York City has been estimated at $661 million a year.[34] This includes only the substantial personal time consumed in static traffic and not the increased cost of doing business, which is passed on to consumers.

In 1974, the National Academy of Sciences estimated that automotive-related pollution causes up to 4,000 deaths and 4 million sick days each year. The cost to society for this is $5 billion. Adjusting this 1974 figure for inflation (26.3 percent between 1974 and 1978) raises the bill to $6.31 billion.[35] The chronic noise and stress levels so many people are exposed to by their proximity to or dependence on automotive traffic have been increasing slowly but perceptibly. Their effects on health are real.

Auto accidents have more calculable effects and, regardless of the 55 miles-per-hour speed limit, their casualties still exceed those of many wars. In 1977, this meant more than 47,000 deaths, 4 million injuries, and more than 22 million damaged vehicles. NHTSA estimated their cost at $43 billion, exclusive of pain and suffering.

Automotive water pollution is another of the automobile's environ-

---

34. B. Ketcham, S. F. Wilder and S. Pinkwas, "Table 19: Annual Costs of Weekday Congestion by Mode," *The Cost of Congestion,* App. L, Citizens for Clean Air, Inc. (Oct. 1978).

35. B. Ketcham, *Societal Cost Accounting; A New Tool for Planners—The Auto vs. the City* 7, Citizens for Clean Air, Inc. (Oct. 1976).

mental impacts. It is ignored because it is difficult to quantify. For example, the salt used to quickly de-ice roads contaminates water tables, thus necessitating more expensive water treatment plants. The corrosive properties of road salt are also partly responsible for the structural decay in 100,000 of our bridges.[36] Oil from highway run-off also finds its way into water and eventually onto beaches. The New York State Department of Environmental Conservation estimated that one-third of the oil found in the region's waters comes from this source.[37]

Though the auto/highway lobby likes to pretend that everything is paid for out of various user fees and taxes, automobiles receive considerable government subsidization. According to a FHWA forecast,[38] these extra government-supplied funds came to $10.92 billion in 1978: $1.860 billion from property taxes and assessments; $6.652 billion from general fund appropriations; $1.915 billion from investment income; and $491 million from miscellaneous taxes and fees. These monies were collected at all levels of government—federal, state, county, and municipal—and applied to the automobile, primarily in highway construction and maintenance. Furthermore, user fees do not fully cover such auto/highway-related expenses as police and safety measures; administration, planning and design costs; and the interest payments on highway-related bond issues. These constitute substantial subsidies paid by the general public to motorists and the motoring industry.

One final example: There is now more land in the United States covered with pavement than with housing. This is land that is effectively off the tax rolls, unavailable for taxable growth. New York City's streets and highways cover some of the most valuable realty in the world and add up to about one-third of the city's acreage;[39] but because they provide no direct income of their own and have long since become too expensive to maintain, they now seriously endanger New York's economy.

When such externalities are considered, it is invariably in a context that precludes the industry's culpability. For example, traffic congestion and sprawl are thought of as municipal political problems; air quality as a state responsibility; lung diseases and stress as medical problems; and commuting time as a personal decision. Most of the public efforts to regulate automobiles, therefore, occur at local, state, and regional levels. In fact, many areas have yet to acknowledge explicitly that they

---

36. V. Pappas, "Pittsburgh Is Facing Problem That Once Hit London Bridge," *The Wall Street Journal*, Nov. 18, 1976.
37. Ketcham, n. 35 *supra* at 8.
38. *Income From the Nation's Highways Will Be Almost $35 Billion in 1978*, DOT Press Release, Table HF-11 (Feb. 9, 1978).
39. The developed land has been valued at about $81 billion. Ketcham, n. 35 *supra* at 12.

are attempting to regulate automobiles along with highways, air quality, and congestion.

There are at least twenty areas around the country where new or planned interstate highways actively encroach on municipal budgets and priorities.[40] In these cities, the transportation planning processes have largely bogged down because of the long, bitter controversies that have arisen over auto use and its appropriation of limited capital funds.

It is symptomatic of our growing reliance on technology that most of these struggles revolve around environmental impact statements (EISs). Mandated by the National Environmental Policy Act of 1969, their writing has evolved into a scientific cottage industry. At the same time that they have become indispensable they have also become enormously complicated, technically sophisticated, and expensive to write and review. The upshot is that the public cannot meaningfully participate in issues based on EIS analyses without access to costly expertise.

EISs were originally intended as tools that the public could use to determine a project's anticipated effects on the environment. Instead, they have largely become scientific apologies for political decisions made in disregard of basic environmental and social considerations. In general, they are written to satisfy federal planning and funding requirements and with little or no meaningful contribution by the public. After reviewing more than fifty EISs in the past eight years, we have yet to find one that is not biased in favor of construction.

EISs that relate to automobiles tend to be about highway projects. In New York, for example, we are participating in an effort to trade in for subway rehabilitation funds a proposed 4.2 mile, $1.4 billion real estate/interstate project known as Westway. Backed by the city's construction, realty, and banking interests, Westway has been promoted as the key to New York's rehabilitation. In fact, at more than $5,000 an inch, it will threaten adjacent communities; increase air and water pollution; increase the city's congestion; further erode its already damaged subway system; and appropriate for automobiles the city's meager capital resources.

Though the choice between automobiles and the general population seems absurdly clear in this case, maintaining the technical expertise to defend it has become an overwhelming burden. One of the major obstacles has been the EIS, which the West Side Highway Project (a quasi-public body created to build the interstate) spent $16 million in federal funds to develop. This is more than twice the sum spent to write the EIS for the considerably more expensive Alaska pipeline.

---

40. The Phoenix-Papago Freeway in Ariz.; the Hawthorne-Century Freeway in Calif.; the Rocky Hill-Farmington Freeway and Route 7 in Conn.; the Chicago Crosstown Freeway in Ill.; I-3 in Honolulu; I-93 in Mass.; I-696 in Detroit; Franconia Notch in N. H.; I-78, I-95 and I-287 in N.J.; Westway in Manhattan; I-40 in Durham; I-80 between Allentown and Bethlehem in Pa.; I-476 near Philadelphia; I-40 in Memphis and I-440 in Nashville; I-95 in Va.; I-90 in Seattle; and the Inner Loop in Wash., D.C.

The highway project used about $9 million of its EIS money to create an elaborate mathematical model for predicting traffic levels and air quality. This model has become the basis for many of the crucial hearings involving the project. Unfortunately, it is incomprehensible to almost anyone without a doctorate in mathematics or engineering. As a result, no more than a handful of people in the entire city can even follow the arguments at these hearings, much less understand the level of detail. The general public, meanwhile, is uninformed and outside the decision-making process.

In Connecticut, the highway interests are pressing for an unneeded and unwanted $200 million expressway, known as Route 7, between Norwalk and Danbury. Again, the key analysis is the EIS. As it happens, this particular EIS is unusually poor. Connecticut's Department of Transportation did little or no field testing of its projections; relied on weak and manipulated information; concocted speed and travel characteristics drastically different from those that exist; ignored the development the highway is intended to encourage; ignored its harmful impact on an adjacent AMTRAK commuter line; relied on an antiquated and deficient air quality report; and refused to consider meaningful alternatives. Indeed, the department even admitted that most of its highway planning is totally theoretical. The FHWA found none of these failings serious enough to delay its rubber-stamp approval process.

But Westway and Route 7 are exceptions. Public interest groups have gathered the expertise to prevent their construction. Such expertise is not generally available: Technicians prudently consider their careers before accepting such assignments and few public organizations could afford the expertise were technicians available. This means that most of the urban interstate highway projects now in litigation, about $10 billion worth, will be built without adequate public review.

The regional picture is equally grim. In most areas, the transportation planning process required by the Department of Transportation is carried out behind closed doors. The New York/New Jersey/Connecticut Tri-State Regional Planning Commission, for example, operates as something of an invisible branch of government. As the region's lead planning body, Tri-State is responsible for guiding the flow of hundreds of millions of dollars of federal transportation funding each year. Yet, its meetings are unpublicized, inordinately long, tedious and insubstantial; its documents are difficult to understand; and its very existence is unknown to many of the area's editors and reporters. Although it is routinely criticized for its refusal to encourage public participation,[41] it changes little from year to year. It even ignored its own internally funded study, which recommended that it reach out to the public.[42]

---

41. *Tri-State Regional Planning Commission Programs: Program Audit 4.1.75*, New York State Legislative Comm'n on Expenditure Review (May 5, 1975).
42. M. J. McManus, *The Need for a Major Overhaul of the Tri-State Regional Planning*

Meanwhile, New York (and most other states) is now revising its transportation plans in accordance with the 1977 Amendments to the Clean Air Act. The goal of the Act is to reduce automobile pollution in urban centers by developing reforms that would reduce automobile use and improve public transit.

In New York, such a plan was prepared and adopted in 1973. But it was never implemented. New York State and City encouraged public opposition and Mayor Abraham Beame spent his entire administration fighting the plan in court. Though he lost every hearing, he successfully prevented its implementation. Because of this recalcitrance, the 1977 Amendments instructed New York State to revise both its plan and its attitude toward the public. Late last year, New York began to move. But its new plan and new public participation program appear, as of this writing, to be amateurish and insincere attempts to compress two years' worth of work into less than four months. The general public, meanwhile, is unaware of what is happening and New York's overall hostility to this program has been abetted by the failure of EPA and the Department of Transportation to help the public become involved.

All of these situations demonstrate the importance of seriously regulating the automobile industry, in terms of its products (through emissions, safety regulations, and the like) and in terms of how its products are used (through comprehensive and open planning processes). But this requires a holistic approach: Regulations cannot be made and implemented piecemeal and expected to work.

Given existing conditions, such a holistic approach will be a long time in coming. The public interest community can speed its realization by more actively engaging in the politics of transportation, in particular by working for the internalization of the societal costs of the auto/highway mode. The government, meanwhile, can encourage public participation by helping the public develop the resources and expertise without which it can neither follow events nor represent itself.

To build a public constituency, to help the public understand what is happening, and to help the public have some meaningful say in what is happening all seem to be beyond the pale of the transportation industry's pursuit of profit and the government's ability to support. Yet, without a reasonable input into the country's burgeoning transportation planning processes, the public will never be able to challenge the imperious hold automobiles have on most American cities or even effectively to regulate how passenger cars are used within urban bounds.

Commission, Tri-State Regional Planning Comm'n, New York (Mar. 29, 1977). Both this and the above report cite numerous other critical sources.

DISCUSSION

PETER KINZLER: The auto industry is not as capable of asserting its self-interest as Mr. Ketcham perceives it to be. The progress in enacting and enforcing fuel economy safety, and clean air regulation is clear evidence of this. I am concerned with Mr. Ketcham's proposal to provide public funding for public interest advocacy. Objective analysis can be had without going to that extreme. Congress has increased its own analytic capabilities by greatly expanding the professional staffs of its subcommittees in recent years.

Keeping public advocacy under the auspices of federal agencies ensures more efficient and objective inputs to regulators than would be obtained under a more adversarial advocacy system. Presently, groups providing inputs through existing public interest advocacy funding programs in DOT and the FTC must (1) represent an interest not otherwise adequately represented; (2) represent a viewpoint necessary to a fair determination of the rule-making proceeding; and (3) be unable effectively to participate because of the cost. The agencies themselves, of course, have a large amount of internal expertise in the areas they oversee. Finally, there are private groups that provide objective information, such as the Insurance Institute for Highway Safety.

Expertise is not the problem; sophisticated lobbying is the problem. It must be counterbalanced first by sophisticated internal information systems on the government side. Coalition lobbying also can counter industry lobbying. For example, a coalition of insurance companies, consumer groups, and labor unions was effective in countering industry lobbying against passive restraint systems.

SYDNEY TERRY: I challenge Brian Ketcham's right to claim that he represents consumers in voicing the views that he has. Ketcham would like to deny citizens the right to choose the lifestyles they prefer. Freedom to choose is a paramount consideration in evaluating the solution to the problems we face.

KETCHAM: I do not feel that the consumer today has a choice. The allocation of funds for urban infrastructure has precluded the development of alternative transportation systems. This is certainly true in the case of New York City.

ACADEMIC: Evidence I have seen suggests that other factors, e.g., consumer tastes, industry relocation due to changing technological needs, and so forth may have produced the patterns observed in New York City and elsewhere.

TRADE PRESS: I would like to point out two inaccurate implications of Mr. Ketcham's discussion. First, the automotive press receives no subsidy whatsoever from the industry. Second, tailpipe emissions are not a major source of ambient pollution nationwide, but only a small fraction thereof.

THIRD-PARTY REVIEW

D. S. Potter, *Vice President, General Motors Corporation*

The central problem with regulation, automotive and otherwise, as it is perceived today, is that its presupposes a fundamentally paternalistic role for government. This role is in keeping with the progressive philosophy of government that has dominated political thought since the turn of the century, and which held sway during the 1960s. According to this view, government is the appropriate tool for making social progress; and the concerned parent is the appropriate role model for such a government.

The concerned parent can and, indeed, often must impose his or her will in order to see that the citizen-child thrives and is not endangered. Obviously, this parent-government is more concerned with the needs of the citizenry than with its rights. Given the obvious needs of many United States citizens during the first decades of the twentieth century, the rights of individuals were deemed secondary. Pamphleteers derided talk of individual rights as "the so-called right of the poor to sleep under bridges"; yes, and even as "the so-called right of the individual to fix his own contract with an all-powerful corporation." A regulatory bureaucracy to provide relief for the citizen seemed appropriate for the century's first fifty years. Perhaps fifty years hence, historians will be able to judge whether the social gains achieved under this philosophy outweighed the loss of individual freedom resulting from governmental intrusion into the private lives of the citizenry.

In the 1960s, public attention shifted to the individual and his or her rights. This shift necessarily led to limitations on the powers of regulators. Regulations could no longer be justified simply by such concepts as efficiency. If it is less efficient for welfare recipients to pay their own rent than to have the state pay the landlord directly, so be it; there are other gains to be had, measured in self-reliance, self-respect, and relief from the watchful eye of the parent-government. Perhaps the best example of the move away from paternalism and toward individual rights is the recent legislation "repealing" seat belt interlock regulations. In the present era, scientific data are being used more and more frequently as a basis for socially aimed regulation. Of course, mathematical descriptions, such as medical statistics, have long been used to supply arguments for needed regulation. Gradually, however, regulators began to depend upon so-called objective scientific data to help frame the regulation itself. Unfortunately, we have learned that even the most "objective" scientific data do not inevitably lead to a single conclusion. The data must be interpreted, a step that introduces the possibilities of wide disagreements. And even if the data are completely accurate, it is not always easy for the participants in the regulatory process to discern whether they are complete. For these reasons, it seems appropriate and in the interest of fostering better, more credible regulation, that we establish some neutral mechanism to characterize the various portions of "science" in the data base for controversial regulatory decisions.

To their credit, the NHTSA management has perceived this need. In 1976 they attempted to set up a body within their own ranks to meet it. In detailing the purpose of this group, John Snow, then Administrator of NHTSA, described it as "taking a lead as independent questioner and critic." He added that it "must bring independent and objective scrutiny . . ." to the regulatory process. I intend to illustrate the need for an independent review mechanism with a few examples from my industry's recent past. Such a mechanism will serve the public interest well.

One instance involves the early bumper standards. When these regulations were in the proposal stage, their strongest proponents were in the insurance industry. The major premise on which bumper standards were formulated was that the proposed standard would save the consumer money by reducing the damage caused by low-speed accidents. The regulators had what they believed to be all the appropriate cost and frequency data for low-speed accidents. The insurance data were collected using accepted scientific methodology and seemed to be unbiased and accurate. However, an impartial, third-party referee might also have pointed out that the cost data did not account for the increased costs associated with damage to the new hardware in higher-speed collisions. Had the regulators realized that, they would have been better able to assess the true costs and the probable benefits of the regulation. This omission and the resulting myopia is typical in the use of science in policy-making. Since such advocacy-science is a fact of regulatory life, however, it is appropriate to develop a method for identifying and checking it in the regulatory process.

A neutral third party could advance the public good as well in situations where the regulators are forced to choose between their own and a competing method for interpreting data. Any researcher, whether he or she works for industry or government, has human frailties. Regulators and regulated firms alike should acknowledge the human tendency to believe more strongly in data that support their individual positions rather than data that refute them.

General Motors encountered a problem of this sort during the recent rule-making on passive restraints. Our safety engineers had developed a method for matching automobile accidents so that we could compare real-world accidents in which automobile occupants used different restraint systems, specifically air bags, or no restraints at all. We could thus draw conclusions about the relative effectiveness of various restraint systems in the real world with real people. After the methodology was developed, it was demonstrated to NHTSA staff personnel. They pointed out what they saw as shortcomings in the methodology. Our engineers evaluated the criticism and responded. Eventually, the method was written, submitted, and published by an engineering journal.

Normally, these steps would be sufficient to establish the credibility of a scientific procedure. When we approached the NHTSA again in the rule-making, however, they simply chose to use their own methodology, despite what we believe were obvious shortcomings in it. The more cynical in our business may simply dismiss the agency's action by pointing out that their own methods better supported their own favorite restraint system. NHTSA in their turn, have dismissed our study, stating that "General Motors is a vastly interested party. The positions it adopts are necessarily those of an advocate for a particular result." Surely the credibility of the regulator, the industry, and, most important, eventual regulation would all have been enhanced by a third-party review of alternative analytical methods and an objective determination of their relative validity. And if the General Motors position is judged wanting, so be it.

Although the proposed review process need in no way bind the regulator to exclusive use of one method or the other in all cases, it could indicate to the agency how best to arrive at an intelligent decision. This, obviously, is where the public good lies. One feels instinctively that it would be unreasonable to expect third-party review to eliminate the controversy that surrounds many regulatory decisions. Regulations promulgated in areas where the data are sufficient to indicate clearly both the need for regulation and the appropriate regulatory response do not generate controversy. Controversy comes from those cases where the regulator feels the need to exercise his or her judgment despite insufficient or contradictory data. The nature of judgment will continue to be such that reasonable people may disagree on the decision.

Opinions from disinterested reviewers could nonetheless aid the regulatory process in several ways. Research contracts, which the regulatory agencies let in order to generate data upon which to base their decisions, could be reviewed by an individual or group familiar with research methodology and with contract research. This review procedure would assure the regulator that research efforts and public monies were going into areas that promised to yield the most useful classes of data. It also could insure that the research methodologies, being the most appropriate to the problem at hand, would yield the most credible data.

For example, General Motors and EPA are planning, on an informal basis, experimental programs to resolve the issue of particulate emissions from diesel engines. Our scientific staffs have met and will continue to do so as warranted. Our shared goal is quite simple; by having each team know what the other intends to do and how they intend to do it, we hope to eliminate needless duplication of efforts. We also hope that because of this exchange the results will be free from any unconscious bias. But most of all, we are simply trying to see that all the appropriate research is done, either by the government or by industry. We are trying to avoid the situation in which the issue reaches the rule-making stage only to have somebody point out that a significant area has been neglected. In addition to looking over each other's shoulders during the planning of our respective programs, we have agreed to have both programs evaluated by a panel of referees so that the total program is as complete as it can be. The initial plan calls for General Motors to appoint one referee, EPA another, and for the two appointees together to select a third.

When applied to already completed research, third-party review might advise the regulators as to the probable accuracy and validity of the results, based on the experimental methods and techniques used. Review might also venture an opinion as to the relative quality of the experimental methodology for conflicting data. It might help a regulator assign values to conflicting data bits, for instance, if he knew that one finding had been extracted from a refereed scientific journal while another was found in private correspondence and had never been deemed sufficiently credible to be published within the appropriate scientific discipline. Review might also offer an opinion on the relative completeness of the data base or on areas where additional research might be helpful.

The idea of third-party review is hardly radical. The procedure has precedent not only within the scientific community, but also within the government. Congress, for example, frequently calls upon such organizations as the National Academy of Sciences to provide information appropriate to problems it faces. The underlying premise is that better and more complete solutions to societal problems flow from better and more complete data. Bias, or even the appearance of bias, on the part of any participant in the decision-making process erodes the credibility of all those concerned and can taint the ultimate decision regardless of its intrinsic virtue.

Bias is an appropriate issue to raise in a decision of regulatory advocacy-science. To assume that research efforts, or, for that matter, research personnel, are not at least subtly biased is more than naive. It is also illogical; science conducted to influence regulatory decisions in some way is designed to foster or combat regulation. Consider the following example of the subtlest bias. John Snow, the former Administrator of NHTSA, described the workings of that agency's proposed internal science jury, called the Planning and Evaluation group, by saying that he believed that the new procedure would "enhance the quality of our most important product, rule-making." Some people in our industry, whose most important product is a high-quality automobile, hope deep down inside that science will indicate that regulations are unneeded. Is either view unbiased? Of course not.

Given the emerging attitude of American society, any regulator faces an uphill battle in getting regulations accepted by the public. A system of third-party review of the scientific data used to support regulation could aid the regulator by removing some of the appearance of bias. But more important, third-party review could ensure that the regulator understood both the strengths and the weaknesses of the data base. This could only improve the quality of regulation.

TOWARD MORE EFFECTIVE ORGANIZATION FOR PUBLIC REGULATION

Robert A. Leone, *Professor, Harvard Business School*
John E. Jackson, *Professor, University of Pennsylvania*

Questions of "institutional capacity" and strategy are familiar to both regulators and to private sector managers. For example, when EPA considers whether it has the technical and legal talent necessary to promulgate a set of regulations, it is evaluating its own institutional capacities. Similarly, when managers of automobile firms assess the "fit" between the size, location, and autonomy of dealers or the effects of advertising style and prices on sales, they are addressing questions of corporate capacity and strategy for operating in a specific market environment.

Despite this familiarity with strategic concepts, however, managers in the private sector and policy-makers in the public sector typically lack specific and well-articulated strategies for dealing with regulatory realities. Managers often see regulation narrowly as increased dollar cost and uncertainty, thus failing to recognize the legitimacy, managerial significance, and competitive implications of regulatory actions. Policy-makers, on the other hand, often see regulations narrowly as either an administrative or a policy problem, thus failing to recognize the diversity of legitimate competing interests that are created by regulations and expressed in the dynamic process of economics and politics.

The goal of all studies of institutional capacity is to improve an organization's abilities to use its limited economic and managerial resources to achieve well-defined and socially valued objectives. In the private sector, this means using resources more efficiently by properly matching institutional strengths with corporate goals and market realities. In the public sector, it means adopting regulatory policies that increase the probability of specific government programs fulfilling their reasonable and desired purposes, minimize costs and undesirable side effects, and reconcile any conflicting objectives.

In the closely regulated world of the automobile industry, questions of institutional capacity are basic and pervasive. For example, the administration of a strong emissions-control policy has significant consequences for the individual firms within the industry and for the cost of transportation to consumers. Does the EPA have the necessary political capacity to identify and respond to the legitimate equity interests of the differentially affected firms and citizens? Or is its capacity strictly technical? Do automobile manufacturers, parts suppliers, and consumers have the capacity to identify and to articulate their interests? Or are they so poorly organized and politically unsophisticated that their legitimate interests are poorly articulated and ignored?

Questions of strategy are also basic and pervasive. The discretionary strategic choices managers and policy-makers make today expose their institutions to the effects of future changes in the environments in which they operate. Thus, while all comparable institutions may be simultaneously subject to the same set of external economic and political factors, the relative importance of a particular factor to an individual organization will depend upon its history of strategic decisions.

The lack of attention to issues of institutional capacity and regulatory strategy can be traced, at least in part, to a generally poor understanding of the complex nature of the regulatory process. Therefore, before we can address specific issues of capacity and strategy, we must describe the regulatory process.

PUBLIC NEEDS AND THE REGULATORY PROCESS

Figure 6-1 *infra* presents one characterization of the regulatory process. As it shows, the public's need for collective action and associated conflicts about the extent and effects of that action, are central to the regulatory process. The public's demand for outcomes requiring joint effort—such as clean air—justify and legitimize government intervention in the private economy.[1] Different people place quite different values on collective goals, however; some individuals demand very high quality air and will make large sacrifices to obtain it. Since alternative public policies imply very different distributions of the burden of achieving such a goal, the politics of collective action cannot usefully be disentangled from the economics of collective action.

The debate over effluent taxes as a means of achieving socially desirable levels of automobile emissions illustrates the point. As can be seen from Lawrence White's essay *infra* (at p. 401), most of the arguments for and against effluent fees on automobile emissions relate to questions of economic efficiency. We contend that the debates over the allocational efficiency of effluent fees are incomplete and misdirected. Such debates

---

1. See E. Stokey and R. Zeckhauser, *A Primer for Policy Analysis*, Ch. 14 (W.W. Norton & Co., 1978), for a discussion of why these problems are collective in nature and require government intervention to remedy.

are incomplete if they do not take into account the political realities affecting effluent fees. They may also be misdirected, however, in that much analytical attention that might fruitfully address the distributive consequences of such fees is devoted instead to questions of administration and implementation. Indeed, Congressman Dave Stockman's (favorable) comments on White's discussion reflect his concern for the political and distributional attributes of effluent fees, not merely their efficiency attributes. The Congressman's implicit "model" of the regulatory process thus simultaneously accounts for the political as well as the technical dimensions of regulation.

The differing values placed on outcomes and the distributional effects of alternative policies can create important and legitimate conflicts among individuals, which the political system must attempt to overcome. Two factors, in particular, complicate this process.

First, in addition to the public benefits and costs entailed, every program confers private benefits and imposes private costs, which may accrue to producers, consumers, or even bureaucrats. Producers of emissions-control devices, for example, and consumers whose property's value will rise as a result of having cleaner air in their neighborhood, have a very clear private interest in the emissions-control program. To complicate matters further, however, people may also obtain such private benefits by using the coercive power of government regardless of whether there is a public interest at stake. Thus, if the government mandates air bags on all cars, people who value them can get them more cheaply because of production economies. These people will have used government to obtain a private benefit at the expense of those who did not value the accessory. In any given situation, it is impossible to disentangle public and private motives. The latter often come cloaked in arguments about the public good. One important capacity of public institutions, therefore, is the ability to recognize and respond to conflicts about legitimate public interests while distinguishing the private interests involved.

Second, collective goods—which are the usual objects of public regulation—share the "free-rider" characteristic: It is not possible to deny the benefits of the collective good or outcome to those who refuse to contribute to its provision. Not only is there no incentive for anyone personally to attempt solutions to the public problem, there are strong incentives to avoid even doing one's "fair share" while encouraging others to take the necessary action.

INTERESTS AND INTEREST GROUPS

A natural outgrowth of the interests, both public and private, associated with collective goods and governmental policies are formal organizations to represent and promote these interests. An understanding of the limitations and variations in interest-group influence is therefore critical to an understanding of the regulatory process. For one thing, interest groups encounter the same free-rider problem characteristic of public goods. Since each individual has the incentive not to contribute to the interest group, but to hope that others' contributions and activities will be sufficient to achieve the desired policy, it can be very difficult to organize an effective interest group.

The precise nature of the interests, public or private, bears on the ease with which interest groups can organize, and on their potential effectiveness. Interests that are intensely felt by a highly concentrated group of individuals are easier to organize, and then more influential, than interests that affect each individual less, even though the number of potentially affected individuals may be very large. If the affected population is small, easily identified, and visible to each other, group consciousness may even overcome the free-rider problem.

If the potential gains to collective action for each individual are large, many of them may be induced to pursue the common goal regardless of the fact that noncontributors will also benefit. Interest groups will often frame issues, therefore, in terms designed to generate this type of support. Their appeals are frequently couched in symbolic, moral, and emotional terms so that individuals can feel that a whole way of life or great principles are at stake. (This may indeed be the case: The minority rights, antiabortion, and environmental campaigns are examples.)

Interest groups play a more important role in the political process than merely pursuing the public and private interests of their members. In the adversarial model of regulation it is expected that the conflict and debate among contending interest groups will identify the broader range of public and private interests affected by public action, provide relevant information to the public, and through discussion and compromise yield final policies that reflect the full range of interests. Presumably, even unorganized interests among the public will have their preferences represented and championed by one or another of the organized groups. Thus, while consumer interest groups press demands for energy conservation and safer cars, the automobile industry represents by proxy the interests of those consumers more concerned with automobile performance and cost; the electrical industry perhaps champions an alternative to the internal combustion engine while the petroleum industry defends it and so forth. In theory, the behavior of these groups will leave few of the public's interests unrepresented.

This interest group model of the governmental process has some clear weaknesses. We have already argued that the characteristics of public and private interests inherently favor the formation and influence of some potential interest groups—smaller groups of more intensely affected persons—relative to others. Thus, environmental and consumer groups were slow to form and still face a continuing struggle for membership and resources. The nature of public and private interests and the free-rider problem also bias the choice of activities groups undertake in pursuing their interests. Organizations with economic interests, such as automobile firms, will concentrate their lobbying efforts on those decisions that most directly affect them (e.g., specific decisions made by regulatory agencies), rather than on the broader legislative decisions setting priorities and choosing policies. In this way, firms' successful lobbying efforts are most likely to benefit the organizations doing the lobbying. In contrast, any benefits from lobbying in the legislative arena would likely accrue as well to those who have not directly invested in the political activity. A serious consequence of this response to the free-rider problem, however, is that the interests of the general, unorganized public are poorly represented at the important phase where regulation is authorized.

The biases inherent in interest group politics extend beyond this free-rider problem. Interest groups become concerned with advancing both the status of the organization and the careers of its leaders.[2] Howard Margolis has argued that much of the public's interest in clean air and the efforts to reduce automobile emissions, for instance, was not well-served by the contests between the strong environmentalists and the automobile companies over the terms of the 1970 Clean Air Act.[3] The public would have been better served by the original proposal of a 90 percent emissions reduction effective in 1980 rather than 1975. The environmentalist organizations, however, motivated in part by their need for an absolute moralist position, argued that all pollution was bad, and demanded an immediate end to polluting emissions. The automobile companies, who might have been expected to lobby for the delayed standards, had a more important interest to pursue, given the structure and strategy of the industry. According to Margolis, the primary concern of the American car companies was to preserve the primacy of the internal combustion engine over alternative technologies that would encourage new (possibly foreign) competition, require substantial capital investment, render obsolete much of their current technology and physical capital, and threaten their control of the industry. The earlier deadline, particularly coupled with the pressure on the petroleum companies to market no-lead gasoline, fulfilled this interest. The companies could argue that there was no way to develop and introduce an alternative technology by 1975 and that attaching the catalytic converter, which they had earlier opposed, to the internal combustion engine was the only practical way to meet the standards by then. Furthermore, if the standards could subsequently be delayed one or two years at a time with weaker interim standards, there would be no

---

2. The incentives facing members of interest groups and the incentives facing the potential leaders of these organizations are different. The "policy entrepreneurs" who can successfully build such organizations stand to gain considerable private rewards for their efforts. These rewards need not (although they can) be monetary; they may take the form of public recognition and personal fame, the ability to influence public policy, and the chance for a variety of public offices.

3. H. Margolis, "The Politics of Auto Emissions," *The Public Interest* 3–21 (Fall 1977).

pressure to adopt alternative technologies not controlled by the current industry. We need not agree with Margolis's specific conclusions to see that this is a situation where even many competing interest groups, each pursuing its own institutional objectives and strategies, do not necessarily result in representation of the whole range of public interests.

Currently, there is a trend toward even more specialized interest groups that focus on very specific interests and pursue them with increasing vigor. Very intense, single-issue public advocacy is quite apparent in many social areas such as abortion, gun control, or television advertising to children. General business lobbies, too, such as the Chamber of Commerce and industrywide trade associations, are being replaced by increased activity on behalf of individual firms. Much of this shift can be traced to the effects of regulation on the competitive structure of specific industries. The differential competitive effects of regulation pit firms and industries against each other, making industrywide and private sector-wide political action less attractive.

ESTABLISHING PRIORITIES

The establishment of special priorities and the reconciliation of diverse interests are traditionally assigned to the "political" part of the regulatory process, the first two levels in Figure 6-1. In setting society's priorities among competing objectives, the legislature and executive respond to the public's various demands and interests. As we have seen, however, the competing private interests which collective action sets in motion may be formidable barriers to the making of sound public policy because some but not all of these interests will be articulated and promoted by various interest groups.

Elections, political parties, and the continuing competition among individuals and parties for public office constitute, in theory, another link from the public's interests to the setting of priorities. Thus the political process should dilute the role of particular interest groups. In heterogeneous constituencies, with officeholders elected on a one-vote-per-person basis, politicians and parties must accommodate their behavior and positions to the distribution and intensity of individual preferences within the electorate. Hence, they build coalitions among voters, as evidenced by party platforms and balanced tickets, which should further blunt the effects of interest groups.

This theory increasingly fails to describe reality, however. Congressional representatives are charged with running errands for constituents, spending time seeking media exposure for their own political advancement, and even using the power of office to enrich themselves, rather than focusing on policy-making. Further, organizing and running a political campaign requires considerable resources—money and activists—that only organized interest groups can donate. Thus, elected politicians can be influenced by organized interests, both public and

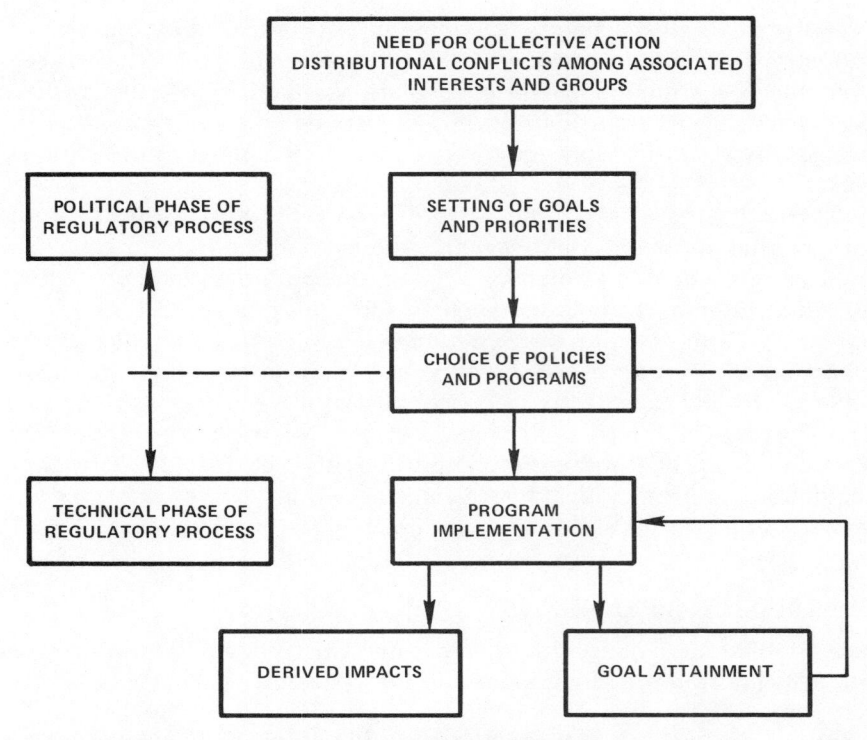

FIGURE 6-1 Simplified view of the regulatory process

private, to an ever greater extent. Political parties could, in principle, counteract the financial and political influence of interest groups, but in fact the decay of party organizations and the weakening of the electorate's party ties are increasing the influence of interest groups.

Congress is responsible for the entire range of public policy issues and, because of its electoral ties to small (especially in the House) or geographically differentiated constituencies, it is very sensitive to the distributive effects of policy and its implementation. The most important distributional concerns are those affecting local employment and economic activity, although there is evidence that representatives are influenced as well by broader constituent interests than economics.[4] The strength of the link between groups of constituents and their representatives is directly related to the importance of the issue within the district or state. Policy will therefore reflect the preferences of the constituencies most concerned about an issue, rather than a simple majority of the electorate or the interest groups within it.

---

4. Leone and Jackson, "The Political Economy of Federal Regulatory Activity," in *Public Regulation of Economic Activity* (G. Fromm, Ed., Nat'l Bureau of Economic Research, 1979). See also O. A. Davis and J. E. Jackson, "Senate Defeat of the Family Assistance Plan," *Public Policy* 245 (1974).

The rise of autonomous congressional committee and subcommittee structures and the decline of the party organizations, both in the Congress and among the electorate, have increased the influence of specific constituency interests, particularly economic ones. Thus, representatives from agricultural districts dominate the committees that make agricultural policies, and shape those policies to their constituents' interests. Recent reforms in the party structures and seniority rules are intended to strengthen the influence of the party leaders in these matters, but we have little evidence of their success. Currently, the influence of particular interests, as exerted through congressional elections and the committee structure, seems to dominate the interests of the unorganized public.

The President, too, has come to play a very important role in priority-setting. Although this role is most apparent in the budgetary process, presidential leadership and influence extend to all facets of the process. Most important legislation originates in the White House (although there are exceptions, such as the Clean Air Act of 1970) and Congress often needs prodding from the President to complete action on a bill.

The President relies on two very different constituencies than does either side of the Congress, however. One of these constituencies is electoral, the other bureaucratic. To be elected, or reelected, the President must collect a majority of the votes in enough states to constitute a majority of the electoral college. Consequently, presidential candidates will be less sensitive to specific regional concerns and interests and more sensitive to how policies affect significant interests across several regions and many states. The President will be highly influenced by interest groups that are organized on a national scale and can either provide support in many states and localities or have ready access to national media sources—such as the AFL-CIO, Nader's organizations, much of the environmental movement, and so forth. As with congressional elections, the decline of party organizations and weakened party identification among the electorate have left presidential candidates dependent upon interest groups for campaign resources and political influence.

The President's bureaucratic constituency is also very important. As head of the executive branch of the federal government, in preparing budgets and legislation, the President must weigh the narrowly focused interests of the many executive departments and agencies. And their interests may deviate substantially from those of the public.

Once regulatory goals or priorities have been set, the next problem is one of policy choice which is too often seen as a strictly technical or administrative matter. One aspect of it is, indeed, the technical analysis of alternative policy instruments and programs, such as predicting the effects of regulation versus effluent taxes or the selection of fleet-weighted rather than minimum mileage standards. These analyses often include cost-benefit, cost-effectiveness, or feasibility studies carried out by lawyers, engineers, and economists employed by the administrative agencies that will be charged with carrying out the chosen policy. Such technical analyses are intended to help Congress and the President to select the most "efficient" means to attain the goals they have set. Efficient, in this context, usually means incurring the least total cost for a given result.

The choice of an adequate policy instrument is extremely sensitive and difficult, and not often amenable to such an efficiency analysis. As a practical matter, the decision to adopt a fleet-weighted average rather than a minimum standard regulation may have little effect on the total costs of mileage regulation; but the effects on different car producers and consumers may be substantial. Domestic assemblers with a well-balanced product line will be favored by fleet-weighted averages over those with a limited product line and buyers of gas guzzlers will still get their cars, although at a substantially higher price. It is incomplete and misleading, therefore, to treat this as an administrative decision to be determined on narrow technical grounds, such as least aggregate cost or legal due process, ignoring the major political implications of these decisions. Politicians do not ignore them and, therefore, policy analysts cannot do so.

IMPLEMENTATION

In conventional theory, good implementation decisions can be based on rigorous analysis of the alternatives and their consequences. It is generally assumed that the major impediment to good decisions is the uncertainty of the outcome. Given this view of implementation, it is not surprising that the regulatory agencies' major strengths are typically their ability to obtain, organize, and use experts in the decision process.

Their assignment to concentrate on the technical and administrative (implementation) aspects of issues, their specialization of functions, and their reliance on expertise have important and predictable consequences for agency behavior. Agencies will tend to define objectives in prescriptive and narrow ways; to isolate problems and analyze alternatives only in terms of its single objective; and to assume that the political and economic world remains constant. This behavior precludes (1) effective consideration of conflicts with other policy objectives assigned to other agencies; (2) sensitivity to the derived effects of regulations which do not affect the agency's stated objective; and (3) any accommodation to the actions of other actors. Legitimate conflict about different policies becomes a bureaucratic conflict among competing agencies—for funds, people, and access within the executive branch. In such cases, the shrewdness, contacts, and institutional expertise of individual agency administrators, rather than the broader public interest, may determine the outcome.

A common characteristic resulting from the agency's focus on a single outcome is the desire to shift any uncertainty associated with a policy and the attainment of the mandated objective to other actors and institutions, such as other agencies, private businesses, or the public. For example, the current automobile emissions program, whereby the EPA sets effluent levels and tests production models to ascertain whether they meet the standards, shifts the uncertainty with respect to achieving clean air onto the automobile manufacturers. Consider the manufacturers' costs if the test vehicles should fail, given that production of that model year's cars has already begun. By contrast, an effluent tax program would put the agency in a more uncertain position: It might end up a year with greater tax revenues and less pollution control than it anticipated.[5]

The more sophisticated implementation plans provide for the monitoring of results by the President and Congress to determine whether policy goals are being attained. In any event, congressional evaluations commonly entail hearings and investigations by the congressional committees responsible for oversight of the particular agency. Congress's legislative and budgetary authority can make the agencies particularly sensitive to the interests expressed by the committee members during oversight. This sensitivity can be harmful to the public's interest, however. The committee system in Congress creates the opportunity for special interests to exert a large influence on policy. The oversight function makes the agencies even more dependent upon these same committees, often on matters which never come to the attention of the full Congress, thus reinforcing agency sensitivity to specific constituency and interest groups' demands.

The main characteristic of the traditional view of the policy process described in Figure 6-1 *supra* is its hierarchical structure. What feedback exists in this model is the product of administrators. This model is inadequate and must be greatly expanded to be of help in understanding the regulatory process.

Economists and political scientists in the public policy field have made two important extensions of the model as shown by the dashed lines in Figure 6-2. The goals set by the political process may not be realized because the original choice of policies was in error, not because their implementation is faulty or underfunded. It also may be the case that new information and experience have caused politicians to reconsider the choice of policies and possibly to try new ones. The first addition, then, on the right side of the chart, shows the reevaluation of the original choice of a policy instrument as part of the overall assessment of a policy's success.

The second extension is the explicit recognition, denoted on the left

---

5. We might illustrate one political problem with effluent taxes here. It seems unlikely that the recipients of the additional revenues will be the same people disadvantaged by the higher pollution levels. This distributional question is an important political matter often ignored by economists' studies.

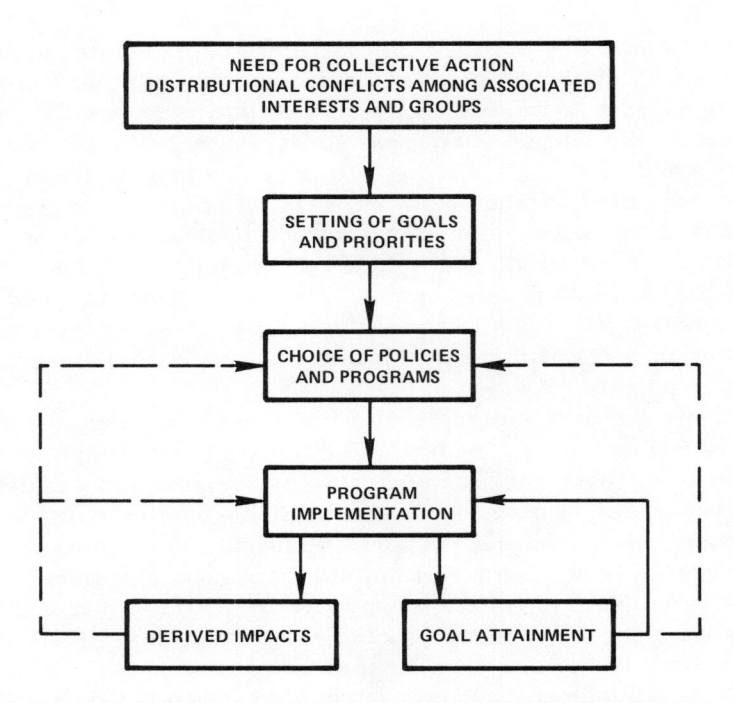

FIGURE 6-2   A more sophisticated view of the regulatory process

side of Figure 6-2, that policy implementation necessarily produces effects beyond those directly related to the policy goal. These derived or secondary effects may conflict with other social goals and are sure to be redistributive in that they create secondary benefits for some people and costs for others. Thus a supplier of seat belts benefits from their being required equipment; the producer of lead-based gasoline additives suffers when we require catalytic converters, which need unleaded gasoline; people in rural areas find they are paying for pollution-control devices from which they receive little benefit; and required safety features add weight that inhibits achievement of mileage goals. These derived effects may equal or exceed the intended effects in magnitude and will always exist because of the interdependent nature of the politico-economic environment and the limitations of our policy instruments. The feedback links from "derived impacts" to "policy choice" and "implementation" represent these effects.

AN EXPANDED MODEL OF THE REGULATORY PROCESS

One critical element is still missing from this more sophisticated model—recognition of the inseparability of the economic and political aspects of regulation. Both the goal-related and the derived impacts affect individual interests, their conflicts, and the process by which social priorities are set and policies selected. These feedback links to the political arena, represented by the dashed and dotted lines in Figure 6-3, arise for a variety of reasons. If the true costs of a program were originally underestimated, new information may cause society to alter its pursuit of certain outcomes. People may then set new priorities, not just adopt different methods for achieving the same ends. Similarly, a policy's potential conflicts with other priorities require continual monitoring and may require adjustment of the priorities, not merely better coordination and administration of existing programs.

The nature of the regulatory process itself may create these important feedback effects: Many of a program's derived impacts are determined by the administrative agency during implementation, and are thus not foreseeable during the initial debate over priorities. These derived impacts may not alter the total cost of the program, but may have substantial distributional consequences that will substantially change the constellation of political forces among the electorate. Individuals bearing an unanticipated burden will want to revise the policy, while those with decreased burdens or unanticipated gains may strongly support the policy.

Whatever agency is authorized to implement the program typically becomes a powerful advocate for its continuation. The policy's implementation may also create new interest groups to promote previ-

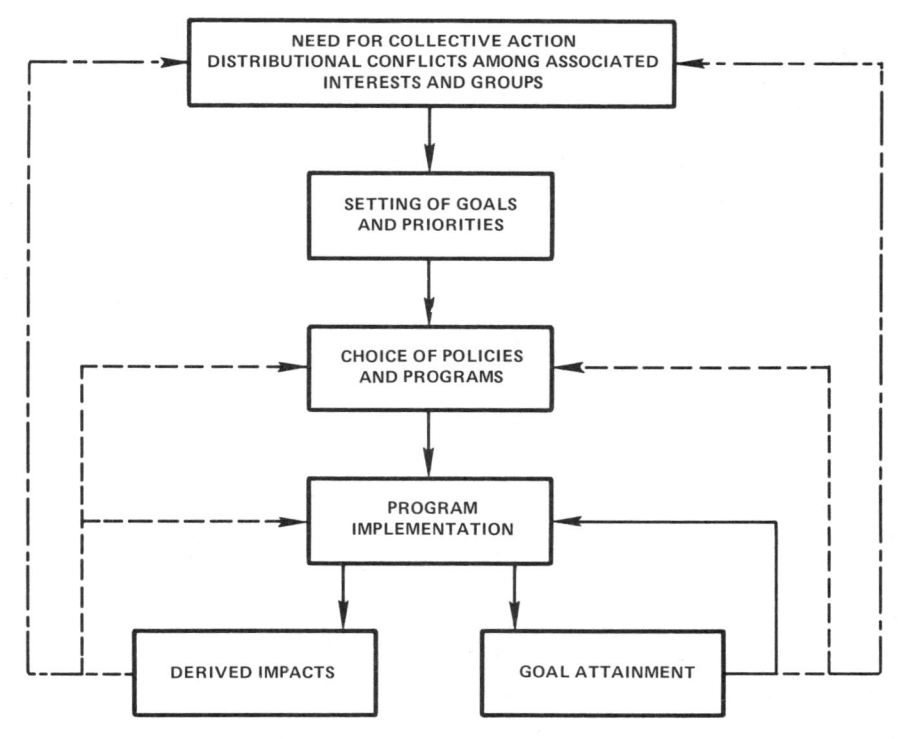

FIGURE 6-3 An expanded view of the regulatory process

ously unorganized interests. In the extreme, the regulations may even eliminate previous interests and groups, for example, by driving marginal firms in an industry out of business, leaving the industry to a different set of firms, perhaps large oligopolists. Thus, the process of developing and implementing policy alters both the interests and the conflicts within society and the processes by which collective needs are translated into public action.

How various individuals, firms, and interests are affected by a policy; how these effects influence preferences and interests; and how they alter the political process require sophisticated political and managerial analyses. These analyses must focus on individual effects at the microlevel. Unfortunately, our limited technical capacities and our narrow conceptualization of the questions means that analysis typically concerns only aggregate costs and benefits, with little or no consideration given to the legitimate equity claims of affected individuals. Yet many decisions with negligible effects on total social costs and benefits have large distributional consequences that merit a public response and that may evoke significant political actions. To illustrate, in a recent analysis of the impact of water pollution regulations on the pulp and paper industry, we found that even slight alterations in the definitions of industry subcategories and in the compliance standards imposed on these subcategories resulted in substantial changes in firm net worth, the level of competition within the industry, and the regional distribution of economic activity.[6]

Clearly, these "technical" decisions affect competitors differentially, given the specific technology and competitive strategy that each firm already has in place. The EPA and other regulatory agencies often have very little capacity to respond to such concerns. Of course, the lack of capacity is sometimes presumed to be beneficial, since it can be a source of immunity from unseemly political pressure. As a practical matter, however, failing to provide a regulatory agency with the capacity to respond to a problem will not eliminate the problem.

A second attribute of the process we have described is that it is not static and instantaneous, but dynamic and evolutionary. The economic and political activities whereby participants continually learn about the technical and political consequences of regulation and, accordingly, develop options, refine goals, and influence public and private policy is an ongoing process. This characteristic is particularly true of regulatory policy which is derived from the continuing decisions of the administrative agency as it promulgates and enforces rules. These ongoing decisions, often hidden from public scrutiny, give affected parties ample opportunity to react to a policy and to change its direction.

The dynamic and evolutionary character of the regulatory process takes on greater significance when we consider that the mass public generally lacks a deep understanding of the issues and has only limited

---

6. R. A. Leone and J. Jackson, n. 4 *supra*.

information about alternative policies. Even in currently debated nontechnical areas, the public may perceive public issues in only broad and symbolic terms, e.g., "Clean Air Is Good." In areas that require sophisticated technical analyses, the public may be quite uninformed. This is not surprising, since many so-called experts cannot agree on the costs and effects of many of the programs proposed, and many public officials and private sector managers, too, react to the symbolic rather than the substantive issues. Public debate is all too often superficial and rhetorical, therefore, doing little to mediate the legitimate conflicts created by regulatory strategies. The political institutions are expected to perform that function.

The importance of these dynamic properties is heightened by our inability to analyze and assess the full effect of proposed regulations and by certain institutional incentives and responsibilities. Specifically, Congress and the regulatory agencies have little incentive or need to consider the costs, even in the aggregate, of achieving a particular goal because the vast majority of the costs will be felt in the private market and do not require congressional appropriation. Nancy Dorfman estimates that only 25 percent of the costs of the environmental programs passed in the early 1970s are borne by the public sector, and even that includes state and local costs.[7] If Congress had to pass tax increases to cover the private as well as the public costs of these and similar programs, there would be a lot more public discussion of their magnitude and incidence, as well as better analysis of their effectiveness. In the environment, Congress often becomes more sensitive to the symbolic aspects of the issues prompting the regulations than to the real trade-offs required in implementing them. Neither they nor the public must bear the costs directly. Indeed, it might be difficult to explain to one's constituents a vote against a program the true costs of which are not readily perceived by the voters.

Finally, and most importantly, the full political process outlined in Figure 6-3 *supra* is interactive, not hierarchical. The interactions are inherently and legitimately political because they involve the weighing of different, conflicting interests among individuals and priorities. Actors in the regulatory process may perform badly, not merely because of their analytical limitations nor because of their failure to see the dynamic and evolutionary aspects of regulation, but because they fail to perceive its interactive nature. One of the major consequences of this failure of perception is the widely held belief that it is possible and permissible to isolate "technical" questions from "policy" issues.[8] Technical issues often refer to efforts to identify and estimate the cost and possible consequences of proposed regulations: Will a given en-

---

7. N. Dorfman with A. Snow, "Who Will Pay for Pollution Control?—The Distribution by Income of the Burden of the National Environmental Protection Program, 1972–1980," 28 *National Tax Journal*, No. 1, pp. 105–115 (Mar. 1975).

8. See, e.g., David Potter's essay, p. 367 *supra*.

gineering modification meet certain emissions standards? What will the modification cost? Does the modification decrease gasoline mileage? Unfortunately, the simple distinction is impossible. All policy questions are both technical and political.

Consider the example of automobile emissions control. When Congress debated emissions standards for automobiles, they often bypassed complex technical questions because they were unresolvable. Indeed, despite obvious facts to the contrary, individual members of Congress repeatedly stated that technical issues were not germane to the debate. In a similar vein, political considerations are often thought to be less relevant when congressionally mandated policy is being administered rather than formulated. Particularly in the case of emissions control, where the EPA administrator was given explicit performance requirements, one might naively expect few political issues to arise in the course of administering the program. As a practical matter, however, the political dimensions of the various administrative decisions that confronted EPA often exceeded the environmental dimensions. The distinction between political and administrative decisions becomes even more obviously hopeless when we recall that many economic interests devote their lobbying activities to influencing the regulatory agencies' decisions rather than to the legislative process.

Deciding which decisions are technical and which ones are political is a futile exercise. The important concerns for both public and private decision-makers are the technical and political effects of each regulatory decision, the various political institutions' capacities to respond to these effects, and how we can capitalize on these capacities to improve public policy.

TOWARD MORE EFFECTIVE PUBLIC REGULATION

We have described a regulatory process that is interactive, dynamic, and very sensitive to micro-level impacts. These characteristics have important implications for the type of analysis required for effective regulation, the structure of public and private institutions, and the behavior and attitude of individual participants in the regulatory process.

It is painfully clear, at least to those of us with an academic bent, that if society is to progress toward more effective public regulation, analysts must develop and refine methods to capture and identify at a very disaggregated level those consequences of regulatory activity that have substantial distributional implications for individuals, firms, and regions of the country. Firms must assess the effects of regulation on their competitive positions, not just its effects on capital and operating costs. Public officials must identify the incidence of regulatory impacts and the resulting political pressures, not just aggregate costs and benefits. To do these analyses, we must increase the sophistication of our micro-level modeling capabilities. Such micro-level modeling is neither cheap nor easy, just necessary.[9]

The improved analyses we seek must also give greater prominence to the dynamic characteristics of the regulatory process. Static analyses based on the assumption of an instantaneous shift from one equilibrium to another are simply inadequate for assessing the effects of a regulatory strategy. At present, however, the tools for disaggregated, dynamic analyses are not available; future research must provide them.

We have attempted to demonstrate that the impact of regulations cannot be divorced from the institutions that promulgate and implement them.[10] Accordingly, when we address the questions of risk and uncertainty associated with any program, we must also consider how specific institutions will respond to that risk. If we accept the premise that managers of organizations—whether public or private—want to reduce the uncertainty associated with their decisions, then we can see how important it is that different regulatory schemes lead to different patterns of exposure to risk. If a regulatory agency has considerable authority, for example, there is less risk of not achieving the performance objective but a greater probability of over-regulation and probably greater cost and uncertainty for producers and consumers. Conversely, leaving more discretion to firms, as in the case of design standards or effluent taxes, might lead to less regulation, but also increase both the risk of not achieving the performance objectives and the uncertainty confronting administrators. Explicit consideration of these risks and how organizations are likely to react to them should be a routine part of regulatory analysis.

Implicit in our call for these improvements in the analytic methods used to evaluate regulatory programs is our underlying belief that understanding is the better part of wisdom. If we are to improve our institutional capacities for regulation, it is essential for each actor in the regulatory process to have a better understanding of that process. We wonder, for example, if the automobile industry had recognized that the public's demand for safer, cleaner cars was both legitimate and likely to be fulfilled, and if they had clearly decided what their strategic competitive interests were, whether they could have avoided their current political problems by engaging in some form of political activity other than the stonewalling efforts characteristic of the 1960s. Similarly, we wonder whether, if policy-makers had fully appreciated the fact that emission-control efforts were not only "forcing technology," as was commonly recognized, but also forcing the competitive strategies of various auto producers, they would have acted differently.

---

9. For example, a recent paper assessing the impacts of water pollution regulations on the paper industry presented a micro-economic model at the level of individual plants for this purpose. (Leone and Jackson, n. 4 *supra*.)

10. See J. Dunlop "New Approaches to Economic Policy," *Regulation* 14 (Jan./Feb. 1979).

The institutional improvements we see as desirable stem directly from the interactive and dynamic nature of the regulatory process. We reject as myth the idea of an independent, strictly professional and apolitical regulatory agency. On the contrary, we feel strongly that regulators are subject to the same political pressures as other federal executives. We similarly reject as myth the idea that there are strictly "policy" issues. Thus, the Congress must also accept its responsibilities for considering technical questions and develop the means for obtaining and processing the requisite analysis. This condition is not impossible to meet: The House Ways and Means and Senate Finance Committees address complicated tax matters in a technically and politically sophisticated manner. Finally, private firms and individuals must accept their role as participants in this political process and be willing to contribute their analysis and arguments about the explicit *public* conflicts of proposed policies and regulations and not confine their arguments to the "technical" issues.

One clear recognition of the adaptive, dynamic, and political nature of the regulatory process would be to institutionalize continuous legislative review, oversight, and direction. Legislation, in our view, should not mandate inflexible constraints on future actions, but should allow means for adapting future regulations and implementation schemes to experience. One model of this process might be the initial House version of the 1972 Amendments to the Federal Water Pollution Control Act. This proposal set out specific short-term goals and criteria for regulation (the 1977 standards), established longer-term objectives without mandating their implementation (the 1983 and 1985 goals), and created a study and review process to assist in appropriate mid-course corrections (the so-called Rockefeller Commission). We might contrast this proposal with the 1970 Clean Air Act. This legislation not only set very specific short- and long-term goals for air quality and auto emissions but also failed to provide an explicit mechanism to insure responsible mid-course corrections in policy. Instead, we have now delayed implementation of standards and must contend with strategies proposed and evaluated on an *ad hoc* basis. This approach has benefited neither producers, environmental interests, nor the public.

The program of monitoring and mid-course corrections we advocate differs from traditional oversight of administrative action in that all decisions and debate would come before the full Congress, follow the traditional legislative process, and go to the President for approval; oversight would not be left to individual committees or subcommittees whose decisions and influences may be confined to a narrow set of interests. Such participatory monitoring of regulation by Congress and the President would create an explicit, adaptive, and dynamic political process, reflective of the feedback links shown in Figure 6-3 *supra*. Note that this proposal differs sharply from the currently popular concept of "sunset" laws. Such laws mandate only periodic reviews of an agency's existence and, consequently, neglect the more nearly continuous evaluation and adjustment of agency decisions that are essential to effective regulation.

Our final set of recommendations concerns the behavior and attitudes of the individual participants in the process. To say that both public and private actors must think and behave strategically perhaps restates the obvious—although we find little evidence of such efforts. For example, most business curricula contain numerous courses training the manager to think strategically about the economic environment, the behavior of consumers, and competitive market forces. We find only fledgling—and sometimes token—efforts to teach strategic thinking about the political environment, the behavior of voters and interest groups, or the competitive implications of government action. Similarly, many programs for public managers give considerable attention to aggregate cost-benefit studies, decision theory, and ways to evaluate and implement given policies. Much less attention is paid to estimating the distributive effects of various policies and the political implications of those effects. If public and private actors will simply recognize the legitimately conflicting interests inherent in many public decisions, and understand the way in which institutions react to shape these interests and express their interests throughout the political structure, we will have advanced our capacity for good public regulation.

We have tried to argue that before they can develop adequate strategies, public and private managers must have better tools of analysis. Our studies suggest, however, that all actors in the regulatory process must also distinguish analysis from decision. Analysis, by itself, no matter how sophisticated, will rarely lead to a unique policy choice. Indeed, the most analysis can ever be expected to do is establish the terms of trade among society's many conflicting objectives. Decision is an explicit statement of preferences, not a mechanistic extension of technical analysis.

All parties to the regulatory process must further distinguish decision from strategy. A policy decision is at least partly an expression of preferences. A policy strategy, by contrast, is a means of marshalling and organizing scarce organizational resources so that over time the cumulative effect of individual decisions will lead to the desired ends. Stated somewhat differently, the strategic choices we make today determine the incremental decisions that we will confront tomorrow. In the regulatory arena, strategy means a careful assessment of where individual actors wish to be when the world around them changes. These are discretionary choices; they are not dictated by markets, laws, or analytical investigations.

DISCUSSION

CARL NASH: Professors Leone and Jackson's discussion brings one question to mind. Periodic review of regulatory policy by the legislative branch would prove extraordinarily time consuming and complex. Would such review really be workable?

A third-party review like that proposed by Dr. Potter, would also prove quite cumbersome. Current court cases on passive restraints and air bags are taking a long time; would we want to institutionalize such delays? Also, if there are parties qualified to make third-party reviews, chances are they are already involved in the regulation process. The quality of reviews will vary with the individuals reviewing—there is no more guarantee of more uniformity or thoroughness and objectivity than under the present system. And review will not correct problems like a lack of information.

DAVE STOCKMAN: Congressional review would prove too time consuming to be feasible. Such a review procedure could never react quickly enough to public discontent. This is already a severe problem that leads to a consumer backlash against regulation, which has caused dislocations in the materials supply channels of the industry, the modal choices of citizens, and in fleet turnover rates.

Dr. Potter's idea of third-party review is fine—if he can find me a neutral person to appoint the third party.

CHAPTER SEVEN
Market Forces in a Regulated Environment

EDITORS' NOTE

In the simplest of world views, markets are either free or regulated. In this most complex of real worlds, however, it seems that some of the best-functioning, most competitive markets—such as those for commodities and capital—are intensely constrained by laws, regulations, association rules, standard contracts, and so on.

The successful marriage of market forces and regulatory goals was the subject of presidential Economic Advisor Charles Schultze's Godkin Lectures at Harvard in 1977. Government, he said, should wherever possible structure regulation so that individuals may pursue their self-interest through market-like transactions. Thus, he would prefer a scheme of marketable "rights to pollute" over one in which each source of pollution is subject to an administratively determined maximum output.

What is the appropriate mix of market forces and regulatory constraint in the context of policies for the automobile? In this chapter, Congressman Stockman argues that there is *no* case for fuel economy standards because market responses to rising oil prices would have induced an appropriate adjustment in fuel economy. He goes on to raise serious questions about automobile emissions-control policies that are applied uniformly to metropolitan and rural areas. These questions are addressed at length by Lawrence J. White, who has long been an articulate advocate of the superiority of automotive effluent fees over our current emissions-control policy.

In the next essay Michael M. Finkelstein considers the role of consumer safety information in the government's policy arsenal. To the extent that consumers have good information about the safety consequences of purchasing a particular model car, the market for safety may make much of the current, equipment-mandating approach to safety regulation unnecessary. Finkelstein argues that there is a consumer demand for safety, contrary to the industry's claims, so that developing a consumer information approach, if practical, would be effective. But "good information" is a difficult concept to apply to a subject as complex as "crashworthiness."

Finally, Robert Berke reports on the responses of fleet owners—a surprisingly large portion of the automobile market—to the regulation-induced changes of the last decade. These buyers have adapted to downsizing with some difficulty, and oppose any further regulatory requirements, although they would like to see automobile manufacturers offer certain safety and monitoring equipment as a matter of business judgment. As he demonstrates, the fleet sector constitutes an unusually good source of information about the economic effects of regulation on consumers: The "fleet manager is a model of the rational car buyer" and he keeps detailed accounts. Indeed, Berke comments that fleets would be a natural testing ground for new technologies, which are often required for the first time on an entire model year's production run; such "bang starts" are a costly way to learn about the in-use characteristics of any device.

ADDRESS

Dave Stockman, *Member of Congress from Michigan*

While I was sitting in the audience listening to the introductory remarks, I began to wonder whether I possessed the expertise necessary to address such a highly trained group of specialists. Two modest qualifications did come to mind, however. First, having done graduate work across the river at the Harvard Divinity School, I know something about the process of divine revelation, which, I would suggest, is relevant to what brings us here today. Second, having been elected to Congress for the first time in 1976, I am neither responsible for nor intimately familiar with the tangled history of how the regulatory laws that led to this symposium got on the books in the first place.

I am led to believe, however, that two epochal events occurring in the first half of this decade prompted these regulatory pressures, which have caused the design, engineering, and cost-accounting departments of the automobile industry to be shifted from Detroit to the banks of the Potomac. While this shift is not necessarily inappropriate, the previews I have been reading of the first fully designed Potomac car—that for the 1985 model year—do not sound reassuring. Apparently, it will be a small aluminum and plastic box equipped with a 4-cylinder engine and auxiliary foot pedals, a box that will cost consumers considerably more while satisfying them considerably less than today's variant, to say nothing of yesterday's. I would suggest, therefore, that before these Potomac cars are actually built, we had better reconsider the revealed authority that inspired them.

The first of these epochal events occurred in August of 1970, when Sir Edmund* went to the mountain and returned clutching a stone tablet decreeing a 90 percent reduction in tailpipe emissions within 5 years.

---

* Senator Edmund Muskie, of Maine—Eds.

This became known subsequently as the "statutory standard commandment" or the ".41/3.4/.4 rule" to the high priests of the environmental temple.

This 1975 deadline for universal compliance with the statutory commandment had a number of obvious implications. First, it was pretty clear that some sort of externally grafted converter would become the chosen instrument of clean-up—as an alternate clean engine could not be developed and produced in the time frame allowed. Second, lead additives would have to be phased out, since they are incompatible with catalytic converters. Third, as a result of lead being unavailable, the petrochemical industry would have to run the carcinogen detector's gauntlet seeking a new additive. Or, failing the discovery of such an additive—which is what has apparently happened—would have to settle for substantially reduced engine performance or revert to very high-cost, crude-intensive, refinery octane boosting processes in order to make automobiles perform satisfactorily. In the latter event, the not inconsiderable fuel penalty of the emissions system itself would be compounded by the octane penalty for these added refinery runs and additional crude inputs.

Legend tells us that while these energy penalties were being sorted out and the theological debate raged in Congress about the precise date for full compliance with the statutory standard commandment, the second epochal event occurred. The villain Yamani emerged from a dust cloud generated by the October 1973 war and declared that henceforth the Kingdom of Saudi Arabia would determine the supply and price of oil in the entire world. This second revelation was also very quickly translated into a sacred formula, this one known as the 27.5 miles-per-gallon rule. Like the earlier rule, it had a number of implications, but in the first instance, I would suggest that only one of the following two propositions could have been true. Number one, Mr. Yamani did indeed know whereof he spoke: That unlike any other commodity, oil's supply, demand, and economic growth elasticities do not exist or they are close to zero; that the potential for fuel substitution is slight; and that there are few significant oil, gas, or other substitute fuel resources remaining to be discovered or produced anywhere in the world outside of OPEC's territorial control. In this case, the real price (1978) of oil would rise to $30 per barrel by 1985, that being the breakeven price for the 27.5 miles-per-gallon mandated standard. That breakeven price, or the price of crude oil at which the lifetime discounted fuel cost savings of a vehicle will exceed the incremental cost of achieving higher fuel economy assumes, I might add, that the ordinary mortals who inhabit the engineering departments in Detroit can produce a 27.5 miles-per-hour fleet at an incremental cost of $1,700 per unit in lost consumer utility or increased sticker price and maintenance cost over the vehicle's lifetime.

Either that proposition was true or the alternative was true: Namely, that like most cartelists, Mr. Yamani was blowing hot air; and that supply, demand, and economic growth and fuel substitution responses around the world would insure that the real price of oil would not rise much beyond $13 per barrel in 1978 dollars by 1985. In that case, Detroit would be well-advised to undertake a crash search for a team of pre-Newtonian physicists and pre-Ricardian economists who could advise it on the design and manufacture of a vehicle that could meet the 27.5 miles-per-gallon formula—nearly double fuel economy—with less than $900 in increased sticker cost, increased vehicle life maintenance cost, and reduced utility combined, $900 being the breakeven point if the real price of oil does not rise between now and 1985.

In my view the chances that Mr. Yamani was blowing hot air are high, and the chances for Detroit finding and employing pre-Newtonian physicists are low, especially since most of them are already employed by the Department of Transportation. The probability that the United States economy will suffer an economic efficiency loss on the order of $10 billion per model year after 1985 is thus considerable.

My point here is that ever since attending Harvard Divinity School and learning that the story of Noah and the Ark was plagiarized from the epic of Gilgamesh, which originated in an earlier Sumerian culture, I have been somewhat skeptical about divine revelation, especially as it pertains to such secular matters as the design of motor vehicles. And I would suggest that the underlying cause of all of these knotty second-, third-, and fourth-, order dilemmas—such as performance standards versus design standards, or emissions versus fuel economy trade-offs—is the first-order fact that most of these problems derive from the two statutory schedules for tailpipe emissions and for fuel economy, which, insofar as I can tell, are largely premised on divine revelation.

I am fairly convinced that this is the case in the instance of the fuel economy standards. To persuade you of that, I would like to have you consider a number of what I think are very reasonable propositions. If you accept these propositions, then you must conclude that mandatory fuel economy standards are not necessary at all.

Proposition 1. Fuel economy is optimized in the fleet being produced today, given the prevailing price of petroleum; the structure of consumer demand for automobiles in terms of various performance and design characteristics that buyers seek; and the incremental cost of improved fuel economy in terms of sticker price increases, utility losses, or life cycle operating and maintenance expense increases that would result if those improvements were made. In short, I would like to suggest that unlike the area of emissions, there are no externalities at work in the case of fuel economy. Both buyers and sellers have an incentive to minimize the life cycle vehicle cost in terms of an optimum split between the cost of producing a car that achieves a given fuel economy, and the expected cost of fuel over its lifetime.

Proposition 2. Given that there are no externalities in the case of fuel economy and that the automobile market works about as well as any other in responding to changing factor prices, in this case oil, there is no reason to believe that the Congress or the Department of Transportation can anticipate future petroleum price changes any more accurately than can this mammoth market of automobile buyers and sellers. In short, an unregulated automobile market would find the breakeven price and appropriate fuel economy level just about as efficiently as the policy-makers who inhabit the congressional committees and the agency charged with implementation. As a matter of fact, I would suggest that the marketplace will establish it even more efficiently in terms of maximizing social or economic welfare because policy-makers tend to have a very narrow, mission-oriented outlook, and to focus only on the one variable that they are charged with regulating. That is true of policy-makers at both the congressional level and the agency level. Where would the Commerce Committee be if we did not have this whole important area of fuel economy standards in which to operate? We would not have the prestige, the influence; we would not have the power; and we would not be in on the action, so naturally we have a vested interest in looking at only one variable—potential fuel savings—and that is what we do. Clearly the same is true in even more heightened degree of the bureaucrats at the Department of Transportation. The success of their performance is measured only by how much fuel they save regardless of effects on the economy and the cost per barrel of fuel conserved.

This was brought home to me by the fuel economy standards that were proposed a few months ago for light trucks. I am sure that someone from the Department of Transportation will take issue with me on this later today, but according to my calculations, using industry figures on the sticker price increases that will be required to meet those standards in the time frame specified, we were looking at spending $40 per barrel of oil saved. It seems to me that that is a pretty dramatic indication of the problem with mission-oriented committees and agencies attempting to outguess the market when there are no externalities in the first place.

Now, that leaves one lame excuse for fuel economy standards, and I think that excuse is fast disappearing. It has been argued that since we are controlling domestic oil production prices substantially below the world level, we must have a policy to impose higher fuel economy performance in order to compensate for the erroneous price signals that are coming out of the controlled petroleum market that Congress created in the first place. That may seem like a roundabout way of dealing with erroneous price signals, but that was one of the arguments that was made. I would suggest to you that that argument will not hold water much longer for three reasons. First, only 18 percent of production going into the petroleum supply system today is coming from the lower tier, $5-per-barrel oil. The lower tier is declining every month due to natural depletion of the reservoirs and, in addition, some is simply "disappearing." Producers and resellers are finding that they can sell lower tier oil directly to utilities for perhaps a higher price—nobody knows—or are finding other ways to unload it outside the price control/entitlement structure. Second, EPCA expires June 1, 1979, and while I do not have any great hope that the Carter Administration will immediately decontrol oil, I think they will do a number of things to raise the average price of domestic output. They will probably have more reasonable, enhanced-oil-recovery pricing incentives; they will probably broaden the stripper exemption; and they may adjust the new oil price. All of these would bring the blended average domestic price closer and closer to the world price, so that actually there will not be much of a difference in a very short time. The third thing is that the world refining industry has enormous excess capacity today, which is driving down the product price to near the variable cost of refining, and so there is not much of a difference at the product price level, which is what counts for user responses, between the domestic product price and the world product price anyway. That is why we are having such a hard time figuring out what to do with entitlements on imported residual oil, for example.

Now, the point here is that as a result of all of these converging factors, within two or three years the price of petroleum products in the United States market will be no different from the world price. So the old argument that we had an artificially depressed gasoline price with need to compensate by means of fuel economy standards will no longer hold.

There are two other alleged externalities involving fuel economy. The first one, which is pure fiction, is the balance of payments problem. Once the domestic petroleum price reaches the world price, and supply and demand have been allowed to equilibrate, you have to be a mercantilist to believe that you can efficiently reduce imports any further. Actually, by forcing the economy to "save" $13 per barrel on the import bill by spending $25 per barrel for domestically produced synthetics or $40 per barrel for "conservation gasoline" via fuel economy standards, the net result will be a loss in national output and income, not a gain. Indeed, the balance of payments argument is really nothing more than a modern version of the old notion that by filling up our harbors with rocks, we can maximize economic welfare by reducing imports.

The other externality, which has to be taken more seriously, is the defense and the security issue. That is a real problem, but it is by no means evident to me that the most efficient countermeasure, given the real security risk inherent in the possibility of a supply interruption, is to disfigure the American automobile, disrupt 10 percent of GNP, and impose a cost burden on the economy that may well be on the order of $10 billion per year.

There might be a more efficient way to cope with that problem, as I will argue from analogy. Today the 80 million American citizens living in a few large cities pose a security problem because they are very vulnerable to strategic nuclear attack by the Soviet Union. We have essentially 3 options available in dealing with the security vulnerability of those 80 million people. One, we could spend a few trillion dollars of our national resources rebuilding all these cities underground, thereby making them relatively secure from nuclear attack. Two, we could spend a few hundred billion, as Mr. Rockefeller once proposed, and set up a very sophisticated civil defense system of shelters, evacuation procedures, and so forth. Or, three, we could spend only a few tens of billions, and perhaps even less, on a strategic deterrent based on the principle of MAD—Mutual Assured Destruction—designed to keep the Soviet Union from launching its missiles in the first place. We have chosen the third option because a counter-threat seems to be the most efficient way of dealing with the threat, given the cost of the alternatives and the uncertainties we are willing to risk.

I would argue that we have pretty much the same logic involved in the case of imported oil, particularly oil from the Persian Gulf. We merely need to put a few billion barrels in strategic reserves to perform the same kind of deterrence function. Moreover, strategic storage has practically no cost, since the value of that stored oil is going to appreciate over time. It would be a far cheaper way of meeting any security threat or responding to any supply interruption than totally disrupting the domestic automobile market and the whole related sector of GNP, to say nothing of all the other areas of the economy—appliances, residential markets, and so forth—that we are also disrupting for the same reason.

So I guess this all sums up to say that I do not think there is any case, economic, security, or otherwise, for the fuel economy standards and the premises that underlie them. By contrast, I would admit that the religious revelation of the emission schedule does have some empirical and logical basis. There is an obvious public health problem. Nobody can deny that. But it is perhaps a case similar to the religious dietary laws on pork. To the extent that they discouraged people from eating contaminated pork, they had a salutary effect. But modern preservatives and refrigeration work far more efficiently than the dietary laws or total abstinence; so we have gone that route.

Nevertheless, I would raise the following serious questions about the prevailing orthodoxy concerning the .41/3.4/.4 rule: First, neither the original nor the recently revised document stating criteria for oxidant control is a model of scientific rigor. Indeed, the case is overwhelming for a significant relaxation of the primary ambient standard for ozone. So I think that we have some pretty serious policy questions and issues to discuss regarding the basic air quality objective before we proceed to implement fully the statutory tailpipe compliance schedule.

Second, since the tailpipe standard was written before the oxidant criteria document was even formulated, and before we knew very much about how oxidants form, it is time to review the connection between the tailpipe emission schedule insofar as it bears on the two contributors—hydrocarbons and oxides of nitrogen—and the primary ambient standard, whether revised or in its present form. This is especially necessary, since, first, we are beginning to find that natural sources, such as winter rain, peat bogs, underground oil field leakage, stratospheric down drafts, and so forth, contribute substantially to oxidant concentration in many areas; and second, it is becoming pretty apparent that those few metropolitan regions which do have heavy oxidant concentrations also have unique air basin characteristics. Therefore, the uniform tailpipe control approach to attaining a questionable oxidant standard could well be grossly inefficient.

Third, we ought to review the carbon monoxide standard. The problem here is limited to high carbon monoxide concentration at peak driving times in limited urban areas. In these cases, the rush-hour surge of vehicles and emissions does generate large carbon monoxide concentrations that clearly are hazardous to health. But the fact is that in most suburban and rural areas, given the number of automobiles on the road, there is no problem at today's emission levels. We might be better able to alleviate the limited problem of peak driving time carbon monoxide concentrations in densely trafficked urban areas in other ways, perhaps through better traffic management, through better highway engineering, or even through restricting traffic flows at those times of the day when the carbon monoxide problem is severe. Perhaps this question reflects a rather parochial point of view, but it is worth asking: Why should my rural constituents have to pay $200 or $400 extra for carbon monoxide control that does absolutely no good where they live?

Finally, once we get a defensible ambient standard for oxidants, once we determine how oxidant loads are formed and controlled, and once we determine the appropriate share of reduction in oxidant formation for the automobile sector, then we might finally consider more efficient means of tailpipe emission reductions, such as the variable tax or even a multicar strategy, recognizing the clear differences in the oxidant problem from one area of the country to another. In any case, it seems to me that one can make a strong argument for a freeze on the current 1978 model year emissions standards until we sort out the issues that I have tried to raise here.

Unfortunately the relevant parties to this whole policy process are not very interested in getting to those basic questions involving the premises on which current regulatory programs rest. EPA and DOT are not interested because they have a vested interest in their current mission, and if we were to scale back the standards and try alternative enforcement or implementation mechanisms, their turf, their responsibilities, and their power might be reduced. The same is true for subcommittees in the Congress. We might have been able to draw on experts, but we find that many of the experts in the country have become like the temple priests. They are more adept at explaining and advising how to comply with the sacred rules than in asking fundamental questions about their relevance or justification. Industry might be another source to stimulate this debate. But I find that industry people are so busy putting out brushfires regarding next year's standards, next year's fleet of automobiles, changes in test procedures, and all the other things that we have discussed, that industry really makes a small contribution to the wider policy debate that I think is needed.

What does this suggest? Total despair? Well, not quite. It leaves only the American public and the American electorate to enter the equation and I would like to suggest in closing that we probably will be hearing from them in a model year or two.

AUTOMOBILE EMISSIONS CONTROL POLICY: SUCCESS STORY OR WRONGHEADED REGULATION?

Lawrence J. White, *Professor of Economics, New York University**

> "They [the Federal Government] can close the plants, put someone in jail—maybe me—but we're going to make [1978] cars to 1977 standards."—E. M. Estes, President of General Motors, quoted in *The New York Times,* October 5, 1976, page 24.

INTRODUCTION

In Washington circles, automobile emissions-control policy is considered one of the success stories in the environmental and safety regulation areas. If this is a success story, the other areas are surely in deep trouble. Any policy that causes the president of the largest manufacturing corporation in the country to issue a statement like the one above must be considered suspect.

Programs that encourage confrontation, bluffing, delay, collusion, poor design, inefficiency, and inequities cannot be considered good policy. Yet that is what our current policy of setting emissions standards and of direct "forcing" of technological improvements in emissions reduction has achieved. The alternative to present policies need not be one of simply allowing uncontrolled automobile emissions. There are superior policies available—notably those centered on effluent fees as a means of discouraging polluting behavior and encouraging research on emissions-reduction technology.

Accordingly, this essay will not dwell at length on specific levels of emissions reduction or on the costs and benefits of those levels. There have been an adequate number of studies that have done that.[1] We will

---

* Professor White is currently with the Council of Economic Advisers.—Eds.

1. *Final Report,* U.S. Ad Hoc Comm. on the Cumulative Regulatory Effects on the Cost of Automotive Transp. (RECAT) (Feb. 1972); D. W. Dewees, *Economics and Public Policy: The Automobile Pollution Case* (MIT Press, 1974); F. P. Grad, A. J. Rosenthal, et al., *The Automobile and the Regulation of Its Impact on the Environment* (Oklahoma Univ. Press, 1975); *Air Quality, Noise and Health,* Report of a Panel of the Interagency Task Force on Motor Vehicle Goals Beyond 1980, DOT

focus here instead on the broader issues of shaping policies designed to achieve emissions reduction. We will argue that current policies have all of the undesirable properties mentioned in the previous paragraph. And we will argue that a program of effluent fees would eliminate most, if not all, of these undesirable characteristics. An effluent fee program would bring to bear all of the favorable properties of the price system—a system that the automobile companies usually espouse but for which they have shown little enthusiasm in the emissions area.

CURRENT POLICIES AND THEIR PHILOSOPHY

The analytical essence of the air pollution problem has by now been absorbed by most individuals concerned with pollution-control policy. Air pollution constitutes a classic case of (in economists' terms) a negative externality. Individuals, as a by-product of their other activities (e.g., driving their cars), are emitting harmful pollutants that cause uncompensated damages to others. Property rights in air are ill-defined, so that, absent some kind of government program, there is no mechanism for adversely affected individuals privately to sue or otherwise collect their damages from the polluters. And, in the case of motor vehicles, even if the property rights were well-defined, the problems and costs of private detection and enforcement might still make private action impractical.

With the major costs of the action borne by others and not directly by the polluter, we cannot expect individuals in a society motivated largely by personal benefit considerations to take pollution-reduction actions voluntarily. Pollution-reduction activities carry costs for the individual undertaking them, while the benefits will be enjoyed primarily by others. Further, in the case of air pollution, the apparent reduction in pollution from any individual's single effort may be so small as to discourage even those whose feelings of altruism might otherwise spur them to reduction efforts. Similarly, in a society in which companies are

(Mar. 1976); *The Report by the Federal Task Force on Motor Vehicle Goals Beyond 1980*, Vol. 2, Task Force Report, DOT (Sept. 2, 1976); D. Harrison, Jr., *Who Pays for Clean Air?* (Ballinger, 1975); D. W. Dewees, "The Costs and Technology of Pollution Abatement," in *Approaches to Controlling Air Pollution* (A. F. Friedlaender, Ed., MIT Press, 1978); D. L. Rubinfeld, "Market Approaches to the Measurement of the Benefits of Air Pollution Abatement," in *Approaches to Controlling Air Pollution* 240–273 (A. F. Friedlaender, Ed., MIT Press, 1978); E. S. Mills and L. J. White, "Government Policies Toward Automotive Emissions Control," in *Approaches to Controlling Air Pollution* 348–409 (A. F. Friedlaender, Ed., 1978); H. D. Jacoby, J. D. Steinbruner, et al., *Clearing the Air: Federal Policy on Automotive Emissions Control* (Ballinger, 1973); L. J. White, "American Automobile Emission Control Policy: A Review of the Reviews," 2 *Journal of Environmental Economics and Management* 231–246 (Apr. 1976); *Air Quality and Automobile Emission Control*, National Academy of Sciences and National Academy of Engineering (hereinafter cited NAS-NAE), prepared for the U.S. Sen. Comm. on Pub. Works (Sept. 1974); *Report by the Committee on Motor Vehicle Emissions*, NAS (Nov. 1974).

largely motivated by the pursuit of profit, we cannot expect these companies voluntarily to provide pollution-reduction devices on automobiles. The devices are costly; the extra costs will have to be reflected in higher prices for the automobiles; and nonaltruistic customers will instead choose to buy automobiles without devices at lower prices.

Accordingly, some kind of government program is necessary to induce individuals and companies to take actions that they would not take voluntarily to reduce emissions. The method chosen has been that of setting specific standards for emissions of specific pollutants from automobiles. At the federal level, these standards have been focused entirely on new automobiles. A few states and local communities have also set standards for automobiles in use, but they are the exceptions rather than the rule.

The federal government first became involved in setting standards for automobiles in 1965, with the passage of the amendments to the Clean Air Act.[2] The Secretary of HEW set specific emission exhaust standards for hydrocarbons (HC) and carbon monoxide (CO) for 1968; in subsequent years the Secretary of HEW and later the Administrator of EPA set more stringent standards for hydrocarbons and carbon monoxide, established nitrogen oxide (NO_x) standards, and set separate standards for evaporative emissions from gas tanks and carburetors.

The original standards were well within the technological capabilities of the automobile companies. In 1970, however, Congress decided to "get tough" with the automobile companies and to "force" the pace of technological improvement in emissions reduction. Congress mandated that by 1975 emissions of hydrocarbons and carbon monoxide from new cars should be reduced by 90 percent from their 1970 levels and that by 1976 emissions of nitrogen oxides should be reduced by 90 percent from their 1971 levels. Further, new cars were required to meet these standards for their first 5 years or 50,000 miles of use, whichever comes first.

In subsequent years, the EPA and the Congress delayed the imposition of these stringent standards at various times. The latest delay, granted in the 1977 Amendments to the Clean Air Act, imposes the 90 percent reduction in hydrocarbons in the 1980 model year, the 90 percent reduction in carbon monoxide in the 1981 model year, and the 90 percent reduction in nitrogen oxides in the 1983 model year. Table 7-1 provides a summary of the applicable exhaust emission standards and qualifications thereto.[3]

Note that these standards have been promulgated in the form of "meet the standard or else. . . ," where the "or else" has been a civil

---

2. Earlier, California had required blow-by emission controls for the 1963 model year and in 1964 required exhaust controls for the 1966 model year.
3. A more detailed discussion of the program is provided in the sources cited in n. 1 *supra*.

TABLE 7-1 Federal Exhaust Emissions Standards (grams/mile)[a]

	HC	CO	NO_x
Uncontrolled car	8.7	87.0	4.0
1968–69	5.9	50.8	—
1970–71	3.9	33.3	—
1972	3.0	28.0	—
1973	3.0	28.0	3.1
1975–76[b]	1.5	15.0	3.1
1977–79[b]	1.5	15.0	2.0
1980[c]	0.41[d]	7.0	2.0
1981–82[c]	0.41	3.4[d]	1.0[e]
1983[c]	0.41	3.4	0.4[f,g]

[a] As measured by the federal constant-volume sampling, cold- and hot-start test.
[b] Interim standards established in 1973 and subsequent years.
[c] Level established by 1977 Amendments to the Clean Air Act.
[d] Original 1975 requirements of the 1970 Amendments to the Clean Air Act.
[e] Subject to waiver for diesel automobiles and the products of small manufacturers.
[f] Original 1976 requirements of the 1970 Amendments to the Clean Air Act.
[g] To be established only if the EPA determines that the public health requires it; otherwise, the standard is 1.0.

penalty of up to $10,000 per car sold and thus has been an implicit threat to close down any company in violation.

Why has the policy of setting standards for new cars been chosen over possible alternative policies? Primarily, I believe, because it provides the *appearance* of certainty. Congress and EPA command; the auto companies will obey. Further, the Congress has always had the attitude that the automotive pollution problem was solely the responsibility of the automobile companies; it was their responsibility to remedy it. And there has been a general belief at all levels of government that the pollution problem was purely a technological problem and that, if pressured hard enough, the companies would develop the proper technological solution.[4] This has, no doubt, been encouraged by the general American belief in the technological prowess of American industry.

In a world of well-known, well-developed, not-too-costly, and non-deteriorating emissions-control technology, the presumption of certainty, of a completely predictable (and completely conforming) response by the automobile companies, is probably a valid one. But, at least since the passage of the 1970 Amendments to the Clean Air Act, we have been in a world of unknown, uncertain, and unpredictable technology. (We will argue *infra* that this was also the case before 1965.) And in this world, the certainty of conformity promised by a policy of standards becomes a chimera. A policy of forcing technological im-

---

[4] For a good development of this theme, see Krier and Ursin, *Pollution and Policy* (University of Calif. Press, 1977).

provements through the setting of possibly unattainable standards may instead, ironically, delay those technological improvements. Further, the emphasis on standards for new cars has meant that other ways of controlling automotive emissions have been neglected, and excessively costly and inequitable policies have been followed.

THE FAILINGS OF THE STANDARDS PROGRAM

Perverse Incentives

In a world in which the technology of emissions reduction is uncertain and yet to be made practicable, a policy of setting standards has some obvious, perverse incentives for the development of that technology. Technologies that might be lower in cost but fail to meet the standards will be ignored. Technologies that might offer greater reductions than the standards require, at relatively modest marginal costs, will also be ignored. If there are standards for multiple pollutants, technologies that might be especially good (and inexpensive) at meeting the standards for some pollutants will nevertheless be ignored if they cannot meet the standards for other pollutants. This has been an obvious problem for the development of diesel-powered automobiles for the American market; it is relatively easier to achieve low hydrocarbon and carbon monoxide emissions, but relatively more difficult to control nitrogen oxide emissions, with a diesel. The only incentive to develop technologies that fail to meet standards would be to influence future policy—revisions of standards. But this is an indirect incentive indeed.

Further, if a company takes the "or else" threat of closure seriously, it will focus on technologies with big probabilities of success, even if they are high cost. Lower-cost technologies with greater uncertainties will be ignored, even if, on an expected value basis, they are a superior alternative.

But the question of whether the company genuinely believes the "or else" sanction needs to be examined more thoroughly. Consider again the quotation at the beginning of this essay. Did Mr. Estes genuinely believe that the General Motors' plants might be closed or that he would be put in jail? Clearly, the federal government is not going to close down large companies. Hence, a large company faces mixed incentives. If it decides to make an all-out, costly effort to develop the technology to meet the standards—and succeeds—it will achieve public relations benefits, curry favor with the policy-makers, and perhaps earn some royalties from licensing its technology to other companies. But, of course, success is not completely assured. If, on the other hand, it delays, drags its feet, and reports that the technology is simply not available, while maintaining enough of a research effort so that it can claim to the EPA, courts, Congress, and/or the public that it has made a good faith effort, it will not be shut down when it fails to meet the standards; instead, it will be given delays in the enforcement date of the standards.

Thus, the standards approach provides an incentive for "brinkmanship" behavior on the part of large companies. If a company actually gets to the brink, it can be fairly confident that the federal government will blink first.

Further, the standards approach encourages collusion among the companies. Though the incentives facing the individual company might lead it to make an all-out effort, it is clear that the incentives for the industry *jointly* are to delay. To the extent that the industry presents a united front and says that the technology is not available, brinkmanship becomes yet easier, delays in standards enforcement become yet more certain, and public relations advantages become yet greater. The policy-makers and the public are dependent to a great extent on the companies to inform them as to the state of technology and its feasibility. In the end, it is the companies that have to build the cars; in the end it is they who can say, "We simply cannot do it." Delaying the development of emissions-control technology and delaying the reporting of information about that technology are clearly in the industry's joint interests.

A History of Delay

The discussion to this point has largely been of a theoretical nature. Let us now examine the history of the automotive emissions-control effort to see how these incentives have, in fact, operated.[5]

After A.J. Haagen-Smit's research of the late 1940s and early 1950s had uncovered the basic process creating photochemical smog and had strongly indicated that motor vehicles were an important contributor to the problem, the automobile manufacturers formed a joint committee to study the problem in December 1953; in mid-1955 they signed a cross-licensing agreement ensuring that all manufacturers had royalty-free access to the emissions-control technology developed by any other manufacturer. Though this agreement may have facilitated the exchange of new knowledge once that knowledge was created, it simultaneously dulled the incentives for each company to pursue research so as to gain a technological lead on its rivals. In January 1969, the Department of Justice brought an antitrust suit against the companies, claiming that the cross-licensing agreement was part of a pattern of collusion among the companies to delay the development and introduction of

---

5. Other reviews of this history are found in L. J. White, *The Automobile Industry Since 1945* Ch. 14 (Harvard Univ. Press, 1971); H. D. Jacoby et al., n. 1 *supra* at 9–14; Grad et al., n. 1 *supra* at Ch. 8; E. O. Stork, "The Federal Statutory Emission Standards," in *Advances in Environmental Science and Technology*, Vol. 7 (J. N. Pitts, R. L. Metcalf, and A. C. Lloyd, Eds., John Wiley & Sons, 1977); Mills and White, n. 1 *supra* at 349–355.

emission-control technology.[6] In September 1969, the suit was settled, without an admission of guilt by the companies, by a consent decree that included the dissolution of the cross-licensing agreement.

Through the 1950s officials from the Los Angeles City and County and California state governments prodded the automobile companies to do something about the pollution problem. The companies responded by saying that pollution was a complex problem that needed more research. And the research proceeded slowly.

Finally, in 1959, blow-by was "discovered" as a major source of emissions. Since the blow-by port had been specifically designed to vent engine emissions from the crankcase; since the technology to control these emissions had been known since the 1930s and had been installed on some commercial and industrial vehicles in the 1940s;[7] and since any untutored observer could peer under a running engine and observe the blow-by fumes escaping, it is a wonder that this discovery took so long. In any event, the automobile companies voluntarily installed blow-by emission controls on all cars sold in California in 1961 (subsequent California legislation made it mandatory) and on all cars sold nationwide in 1963.

In 1962 to 1963, rebounding from a period of financially lean times, Chrysler took a number of aggressive actions in the automobile market. It greatly extended new car warranties on drive-train components to 5 years or 50,000 miles, whichever came first (the standard warranty at the time was 12 months/12,000 miles); it aggressively entered the fleet sales market, slashing fleet prices considerably; and, most important for our purposes, it aggressively touted some modest advances in emissions-control technology and convinced Los Angeles officials that they should make some fleet purchases for demonstration purposes. Chrysler received intense automobile industry criticism for this last action.[8]

In 1963, the California legislature, tiring of the automobile companies' expressions of good intentions and absence of rapid progress, passed legislation requiring that exhaust-control devices be installed on new cars when two such devices had been certified by the state. This opened the field to parts manufacturers, who did not share the automobile companies' interests in delay. In March 1964, the automobile companies told the state that the 1967 model year was the earliest that exhaust-control devices could possibly be installed on new cars. In June 1964, the state certified four devices (all made by independent parts manufacturers), thus making exhaust controls mandatory on the 1966 model cars. In August 1964 the companies announced that they would,

---

6. Some of the Justice Department's evidence concerning the alleged collusion was put into the *Congressional Record* of May 18, 1971, by Representative Phillip Burton. It is reprinted in U.S. Sen. (1973), pp. 445–456.
7. See Krier and Ursin, n. 4 *supra* at 147.
8. R. Nader, *Unsafe at Any Speed* (Pocket Books, 1965).

after all, be able to install exhaust-control devices (of their own manufacture) on the 1966 model cars.

In the spring of 1972 the Ford Motor Company told the EPA that its personnel had improperly maintained the sample 1973 model cars that were being tested so as to be certified to meet the 1973 standards. Ford was required to begin the certification process anew but was allowed to ship cars to its dealers (but not to sell them to the public) before certification was completed. There was little question that EPA was not prepared to shut down the Ford Motor Company.

Also in 1972 the automobile companies first asked the EPA for a one year's delay in the 1975 standards established by the 1970 Clean Air Act Amendments. The EPA denied the request, the companies appealed to the courts, and the question was remanded to the EPA for reconsideration. This time, in April 1973, the EPA granted a year's delay. An important consideration is Administrator William Ruckelshaus's decision was his finding that Chrysler was completely unable to meet the 1975 standards. Its expenditures on emissions control were between one-sixth and one-tenth of the absolute amounts spent by Ford and General Motors and were one-third as much per sales dollar. It had switched catalyst suppliers in September 1972, which apparently delayed its emissions-control program by six months. Ruckelshaus devoted four pages of his decision, plus a six-page appendix, to Chrysler's efforts. He all but accused Chrysler of bad faith and of deliberately dragging its feet and delaying its emissions-control program. But he was not prepared to shut down Chrysler, and he granted the delay.[9]

By the end of 1974, after receiving two delays (one from the EPA in 1973, one from the Congress in mid-1974) of a year each, the companies apparently concluded that the original standards, at that time scheduled for 1977 and 1978, were simply not achievable and slackened their research efforts. This was noticed by an EPA report in February 1975[10] and a National Academy of Science report in June 1975.[11] The companies promptly received another year's delay in the hydrocarbon and carbon monoxide standards in April 1975, this time because of a fear of sulfuric acid emissions from catalysts.

By the fall of 1976 it had become clear to all that the automobile companies were not prepared to meet the original stiff emissions standards, then scheduled for the 1978 model year. Indeed, the companies already had prototype 1978 models on test tracks, beginning the emissions certification process for the 1978 model year, with the sure knowledge that they would fail the 1978 standards. Congress was expected to

---

9. This decision is found in *U.S. Sen. Comm. on Public works, Subcomm. on Air and Water Pollution, Hearings on the Decision of the EPA Adminstrator* 2-51 (Apr. 16–18, 1973).

10. *Automobile Emission Control—The Technical Status and Outlook as of December 1976,* EPA (1975).

11. *Report of the Conference on Air Quality and Automobile Emissions, May 5, 1975, to the Committee on Environmental Decision-Making,* NAS (June 5, 1975).

pass a new set of amendments to the Clean Air Act, delaying the emissions requirements yet again and getting the companies (or the EPA, depending on one's perspective) off the hook. But a filibuster in the Senate at the last minute prevented passage, and Congress adjourned without the legislation. It was this failure to pass new legislation that led to the statement by Mr. Estes that heads this paper.

Eventually, in August 1977, Congress did pass the necessary amendments to the Clean Air Act, establishing the new schedule of standards provided in Table 7-1 *supra*. (In the interim, EPA had to give special permission to the companies to ship their 1978 models to their dealers but not sell them to the public.) But in early 1978, the Ford Motor Company, in its report to the EPA on the status of its emissions-control program, expressed serious doubts as to its ability to meet the stringent standards now scheduled for the 1981 model year.[12] We may not have seen the end of delays in the imposition of the original 1975/1976 standards.

In-Use Emissions

As currently formulated, the standards apply solely to the sale of new cars. Until the 1977 model year, the EPA only tested the prototype cars that the companies provided to it and inspected vehicle assembly lines to ensure that vehicles were being assembled in conformance with those that were certified. In the 1977 model year, the EPA began spot assembly line checks of individual vehicles, but General Motors has recently challenged in court EPA's right to carry out these spot checks.

With testing and enforcement occurring only at the certification level, automobile owners have no incentive to maintain their cars so as to achieve low emissions. Indeed, if they believe that tampering with the emissions-control system may improve the performance of their car (e.g., gasoline mileage, power, drivability), they may well do so. Nothing in the various amendments to the Clean Air Act makes this illegal for individuals; only car dealers, service station personnel, and fleet owners are forbidden to tamper; but without any in-use inspection, even this is unenforceable. A 1975 EPA report provided evidence of significant tampering with emissions-control systems. This evidence is reproduced in Table 7-2. Also, surveillance of in-use emissions (to be discussed *infra*) has revealed that over 10 percent of a sample of owners of 1975 model cars that were not supposed to use leaded gasoline were nonetheless doing so, thus significantly raising hydrocarbon and carbon monoxide emissions.[13]

---

12. *Advanced Emission Control Program Status Report*, Ford Motor Co., submitted to the EPA, (Jan. 1978).
13. A. P. Berens and M. Hill, *Automobile Exhaust Emission Surveillance—Analysis of the FY 1974 Program*, Table 40, p. 61, Emission Control Technology Div., Office of Mobile Source Air Pollution Control, Office of Air and Waste Management, EPA (Sept. 1976).

TABLE 7-2 Results of Antitampering Survey Conducted by EPA, as of 1975

Survey area	% of vehicles with major components of emission control system removed	% of vehicles with missing air/fuel limiter caps*
Washington, D.C.	15	33
New Jersey	15	50
Cincinnati, Ohio	Not Available	17

* Suggests degradation of emission control through poorer control of air-fuel mixture.

Source: EPA, *Progress in the Implementation of Motor Vehicle Emission Standards Through June 1975*, Table II-3, p. 14. (1976).

The incentives for motorists to tamper, to use leaded gasoline, and generally not to maintain their emissions-control system are clearly present. What has this meant for actual emissions from vehicles in use? The EPA has conducted a series of emissions surveillance programs, in which cars in actual private use are tested and their emissions recorded.[14] These data have been used by the EPA primarily as an input into local transportation control plans. (To determine the necessary severity of controls to achieve a particular goal, one has to know the pattern of actual emissions.) These data are reproduced in Tables 7-3, 7-4, and 7-5.

The tables reveal that average actual in-use emissions have frequently exceeded the federal standards by statistically significant amounts (at the 95 percent confidence level, using a 2-tailed test). This has been true for every model year, in every testing period, for carbon monoxide. It has been true for a number of years for hydrocarbons. The problems appear to be especially serious for high altitude areas; average hydrocarbon and carbon monoxide emissions in Denver have never been below the federal standards and have usually been far above. Conformance with the standards does appear to be appreciably better for nitrogen oxides, however, as revealed in Table 7-5. The tables also reveal a definite tendency for emission control to deteriorate with the age (and mileage) of the vehicle.

Another measure of in-use emissions is the percentage of cars in-use that would pass all of the appropriate federal standards. As can be seen in Table 7-6, at all times less than half of the sample in-use automobiles are capable of meeting all of the standards; in some years, none of the sample cars in Denver are capable of meeting all of the standards.

Preliminary tests on very low mileage 1977 model cars indicate a

---

14. Since the selection of these cars involves motorists who are willing to let the EPA test its cars, there may be a downward bias to the reported figures. Owners of particularly "dirty" cars may be embarrassed and reluctant to allow their cars to be tested.

TABLE 7-3 Average In-Use Emissions of Hydrocarbons, grams/miles

Model year	Federal standards	1972[b]	1973[b]	1974[c]	1975[d]	1976[d]
1967 and earlier	—	8.74[e]	8.67[f]	8.65[g]	8.93[h]	8.85[i]
1967 and earlier (Denver)	—	10.16[e]	11.91[f]	9.87[g]	—	—
1968[a]	5.9	5.73	6.18	7.09	6.30	6.37
1968 (Denver)	5.9	7.35*	6.89	7.65*	—	—
1969[a]	5.9	5.25	4.83	6.30	5.98	5.77
1969 (Denver)	5.9	6.32	5.97	7.07*	—	—
1970[a]	3.9	3.77	4.89*	5.07*	5.34	5.78*
1970 (Denver)	3.9	6.72*	5.56*	6.56*	—	6.05*
1971[a]	3.9	3.07	3.94	4.22	5.21*	4.84*
1971 (Denver)	3.9	5.59*	5.19*	5.51*	—	6.91*
1972[a]	3.0		3.02	4.17*	4.23*	3.82*
1972 (Denver)	3.0		4.75*	5.40*	6.53*	5.65*
1973[a]	3.0			3.59*	3.33	3.65*
1973 (Denver)	3.0			4.54*	4.60*	4.71*
1974[a]	3.0			3.08	3.58*	3.97*
1974 (Denver)	3.0			4.19*	5.15*	4.64*
1975[a]	1.5				1.32	1.72
1975 (Denver)	1.5				2.22*	2.37*
1976[a]	1.5					1.34
1976 (Denver)	1.5					2.34*

* Significantly above the applicable Federal Standard at the 95% confidence level.
[a] All cities in sample except Denver.
[b] Chicago, Denver, Houston, St. Louis, and Washington, D.C.
[c] Denver, Detroit, Houston, Newark, and St. Louis.
[d] Chicago, Denver, Houston, Phoenix, St. Louis, and Washington, D.C.
[e] 1957–1967 cars.
[f] 1966–1967 cars.
[g] 1967 cars.
[h] 1965–1967 cars.
[i] 1966–1967 cars.

Sources: J. A. Rutherford, *Automobile Exhaust Emission Surveillance—Analysis of the FY 75 Program*, Table 25, pp. 50–52, Emission Control Technology Div., Office of Mobile Source Air Pollution Control, Office of Air and Waste Management, EPA (1977); A. P. Berens and M. Hill, *Automobile Exhaust Emission Surveillance—Analysis of the FY 1974 Program*, Table 11, p. 42, Emission Control Technology Div., Office of Mobile Source Air Pollution Control, Office of Air and Waste Management, EPA (1976); J. Bernard, P. Donovan, and H. T. McAdams, *Automobile Exhaust Emission Surveillance—Analysis of the FY 73 Program*, pp. 41, 58, 60, Certification and Surveillance Div., Office of Mobile Source Air Pollution Control, Office of Air and Waste Management, EPA (1975).

TABLE 7-4 Average In-Use Emissions of Carbon Monoxide, grams/mile

| Model year | Federal standards | \multicolumn{5}{c}{In-use testing year} |
		1972[b]	1973[b]	1974[c]	1975[d]	1976[d]
1967 and earlier[a]	—	86.5[e]	93.5[f]	108.3[g]	108.5[h]	110.1[i]
1967 and earlier (Denver)	—	126.9[e]	141.0[f]	146.1[g]	—	—
1968[a]	50.8	69.3*	64.6*	74.8*	82.6*	87.1*
1968 (Denver)	50.8	109.2*	101.4*	97.0*	—	—
1969[a]	50.8	60.0*	62.4*	67.7*	78.5*	70.0*
1969 (Denver)	50.8	76.4*	97.8*	104.6*	—	—
1970[a]	33.3	47.6*	53.2*	65.0*	63.9*	75.0*
1970 (Denver)	33.3	94.8*	87.5*	105.2*	—	85.4*
1971[a]	33.3	39.6*	51.1*	51.5*	52.7*	56.1*
1971 (Denver)	33.3	88.1*	80.3*	96.9*	—	94.4*
1972[a]	28.0		36.9*	56.7*	51.8*	50.6*
1972 (Denver)	28.0		80.4*	90.5*	84.5*	71.6*
1973[a]	28.0			47.0*	45.3*	49.1*
1973 (Denver)	28.0			84.7*	81.0*	82.8*
1974[a]	28.0			35.9*	41.8*	52.2*
1974 (Denver)	28.0			79.0*	83.7*	81.4*
1975[a]	15.0				22.9*	27.4*
1975 (Denver)	15.0				48.5*	47.9*
1976[a]	15.0					18.3*
1976 (Denver)	15.0					45.1*

Source and footnotes: See Table 7-3, *supra.*

similar pattern for these vehicles, although the high altitude problems may have been resolved.[15]

The Problem of Phasing

An essential part of the standards program is that the standards have been phased in gradually. As revealed in Table 7-1 *supra,* a set of standards usually apply unchanged for two years, after which one or more of the standards is tightened. This gradual phasing is intended to achieve some interim emissions reductions and to reassure the EPA and Congress that progress in emissions control is indeed being made. If a strict set of standards were simply mandatory, say, five years in the

---

15. J. T. White, III, *An Evaluation of Restorative Maintenance on Exhaust Emissions from In-Use Automobiles,* Table 3, p. 5, Society of Automotive Engineers, Technical Paper Series, No. 780082 (1978).

TABLE 7-5 Average In-Use Emissions of Nitrogen Oxides, grams/miles

Model year	Federal standards	1972 [b]	1973 [b]	1974 [c]	1975 [d]	1976 [d]
1967 and earlier[a]	—	3.54[e]	3.34[f]	4.04[g]	2.89[h]	2.83[i]
1967 and earlier (Denver)	—	1.89[e]	2.03[f]	2.22[g]	—	—
1968[a]	—	4.44	4.32	5.21	3.60	3.49
1968 (Denver)	—	2.20	2.86	3.21	—	—
1969[a]	—	5.45	5.08	5.56	4.25	4.13
1969 (Denver)	—	2.59	2.93	3.76	—	—
1970[a]	—	5.15	4.35	4.95	3.66	3.50
1970 (Denver)	—	2.78	3.32	3.22	—	2.73
1971[a]	—	5.06	4.30	4.83	3.90	3.84
1971 (Denver)	—	3.05	2.74	3.18	—	2.58
1972[a]	—		4.55	4.80	4.03	4.03
1972 (Denver)	—		3.08	3.29	2.68	2.74
1973[a]	3.1			3.47*	3.01	2.97
1973 (Denver)	3.1			1.96	2.06	2.20
1974[a]	3.1			3.08	2.89	2.90
1974 (Denver)	3.1			1.81	1.85	2.03
1975[a]	3.1				2.44	2.59
1975 (Denver)	3.1				1.62	1.81
1976[a]	3.1					2.56
1976 (Denver)	3.1					1.82

Source and footnotes: See Table 7-3, *supra*.

future, with no interim standards, the opportunities for brinkmanship by the companies would be yet greater.

But the price that must be paid for this gradualism is that the companies are denied the learning curve benefits (and possibly the full amortization of capital equipment) from a long experience with one set of standards. Costs are inevitably higher than they would be with longer periods of fixed standards.

Gradualism is normally considered good policy. Here we see the costly consequences of gradualism.

A Summary

Progress had definitely occurred in emissions-control technology. New model cars today emit fewer pollutants than did new model cars of a decade ago. But this progress has been slower than it need have been. It

TABLE 7-6 Percentage of Cars In-Use that Would Pass All of the Appropriate Federal Standards

Model years	In-use testing year			
	1973[b]	1974[c]	1975[d]	1976[d]
1972[a]	39%	21%	24%	19%
1972 (Denver)	3	3	0	0
1973[a]		15	19	13
1973 (Denver)		3	0	11
1974[a]		42	22	14
1974 (Denver)		0	0	0
1975[a]			37	30
1975 (Denver)			6	4
1976[a]				47
1976 (Denver)				14

Footnotes: See Table 7-3, *supra.*

Sources: J. A. Rutherford, *Automobile Exhaust Emission Surveillance—Analysis of the FY 75 Program,* Tables 16, 22, pp. 41, 47, Emission Control Technology Div., Office of Mobile Source Air Pollution Control, Office of Air and Waste Management, EPA (1977); A. P. Berens and M. Hill, *Automobile Exhaust Emission Surveillance—Analysis of the FY 1974 Program,* Tables 18, 19, pp. 46, 47, Emission Control Technology Div., Office of Mobile Source Air Pollution Control, Office of Air and Waste Management, EPA (1976); J. Bernard, P. Donovan, and H. T. McAdams, *Automobile Exhaust Emission Surveillance—Analysis of the FY 73 Program,* pp. 8, 38–40, Certification and Surveillance Div., Office of Mobile Source Air Pollution Control, Office of Air and Waste Management, EPA (1975); and M. E. Williams, J. T. White, L. A. Platte, and C. J. Domke, *Automobile Exhaust Emission Surveillance—Analysis of the FY 1972 Program,* p. 6, Certification and Surveillance Div., Office of Mobile Source Air Pollution Control, Office of Air and Water Programs, EPA (1974).

has been more costly than it need have been. The inflexibility of the standards approach discouraged the introduction of diesels and other alternative engines. The inflexibility of the standards in 1973 and 1974 alone probably meant $7 billion in excess costs.[16] Cars in use have generally not been attaining the certification standards. And more delays in attainment of strict standards are on the horizon.

These findings must be ascribed to the standards approach. This approach has not brought the certainty of attainment and enforcement that it is supposed to bring. Instead, it has brought delay and evasion.

INSPECTION AND MAINTENANCE

Recognition that vehicle maintenance is important to the emissions control effort has been growing. The 1970 Clean Air Act Amendments instructed the EPA to work with the states to develop mandatory inspection and in-use standards programs; this charge was repeated and strengthened in the 1977 Amendments. But both the EPA and the states

---

16. See Mills and White, n. 1 *supra* at 398.

have been laggard in this. Only a few states and local communities currently have mandatory inspection and in-use standards programs. Maintenance in fact is not being greatly encouraged.

The EPA is likely to put greater pressure on the states in the future. If history is any guide, it will encounter severe political resistance. The New Jersey inspection program was delayed for two years because of motorist objections. In 1965, California tried to make the retrofit of blow-by devices on older cars mandatory; but motorists objected, and the program was rescinded.[17] In 1973 to 1975, California tried to make the retrofit of exhaust-control devices mandatory on older cars; again motorists objected, and again the program was rescinded.[18]

In part, motorists object to the imposition of another set of costs; we would all like to have cleaner air without having to pay for it. In part, they seem to fear being caught with an automobile that simply cannot pass the in-use standards, or that will require devices that are too costly, or might severely impair the performance of their cars.

Ironically, the required inspection and in-use standards, with the required maintenance implied thereby, may be too late to play their proper role. On top of expensive required emissions devices on new cars, the required maintenance may simply be too expensive for the extra emission-reduction benefits that it brings.

Some recent EPA restorative maintenance surveys appear to point in this direction. In 1976, EPA selected a total sample of 300 in-use 1975 and 1976 model year cars in Chicago, Detroit, and Washington, D.C. Emissions tests were administered before and after a series of maintenance procedures were performed on the cars. Seventy-four percent of the vehicles had at least one malperformance of an emissions-related component or system. The before and after emissions levels are given below in Table 7-7.[19] Fuel economy increased slightly, from 13.74 to 13.95. But the estimated maintenance costs (with labor valued at $15 per hour and replacement parts valued at retail prices) were $41.44 per car.[20] The only substantial reduction was in carbon monoxide emissions, and

---

17. Except that retrofit was made mandatory at the time of transfer of title. See Krier and Ursin, n. 4 *supra* at 148–153.
18. Again, retrofit was made mandatory at the time of transfer of title. See Krier and Ursin, *ibid.* at 240–247.
19. J. C. Bernard and J. F. Pratt, *An Evaluation of Restorative Maintenance on Exhaust Emissions of 1975–1976 Model Year In-Use Automobiles*, Emissions Control Technology Div., Office of Mobile Source Air Pollution Control, Office of Air and Waste Management, EPA (Dec. 1977).
20. R. Gafford and R. Carlson, *Evaluation of Restorative Maintenance on 1975 and 1976 Light-Duty Vehicles in Detroit, Michigan*, App. G, Emission Control Technology Div., Office of Mobile Source Air Pollution Control, Office of Air and Waste Management, EPA (May 1977); D. R. Liljedahl and J. Terry, *Evaluation of Restorative Maintenance on 1975 and 1976 Light-Duty Vehicles in Chicago, Illinois*, App. G, p. 33, Emission Control Technology Div., Office of Mobile Source Air Pollution Control, Office of Air and Waste Management, EPA (Jan. 1977).

TABLE 7-7 Pre- and Post-Maintenance Performance Levels in 300 EPA-Selected Sample of 1975 and 1976 Model Year Cars

	Pre-maintenance (grams/mile)	Post-maintenance (grams/mile)
Hydrocarbons	1.32	0.87
Carbon monoxide	20.27	7.65
Nitrogen oxides	2.82	2.55

the costs to achieve it may be too high. With over 140 million motor vehicles on the road, $41 per vehicle comes to a total of over $5.7 billion.

Unfortunately, the studies cannot tell us about subsequent deterioration and hence they cannot tell us if this is a one-time-only expenditure to achieve permanently the carbon monoxide emissions reductions or whether expenditures of this magnitude would be necessary, say, annually to achieve those emission reductions. If the former, they are probably worthwhile; if the latter, certainly not. Also, they cannot tell us anything about older cars, for which the emissions might be greater but for which the maintenance costs would also be greater.

In short, in this area as in all others, some careful cost-benefit analysis should be done to see if the extra emissions reductions are worth the extra costs. It may well be the case that required inspection, in-use standards, and the consequent required maintenance, on top of the expensive required emission-control devices on new cars, is an idea whose time has passed.

AN EFFLUENT FEE PROGRAM

The basic logic underlying an effluent fee is that polluters ought to be made to pay the marginal social costs of their polluting activities. By keying fees paid to actual emissions, such a policy allows individuals to take the most efficient actions open to them. If pollution avoidance is inexpensive, individuals will have an incentive to undertake avoidance actions; if pollution avoidance is expensive, they will choose instead to pay the fee. But, if the fees are properly structured to represent the marginal social costs of pollution, either choice represents an efficient outcome.

A thorough effluent fee program would involve fees levied on all motor vehicles in use and on all easily measured harmful pollutants.[21] Fees would be based on short emissions tests conducted annually, similar to the tests and procedures currently done by the State of New Jersey. The total fee paid would be based on the mileage driven in the previous year, the emissions reported on the test, and the particular fee

---

21. Ideally, the fees on motor vehicles would be in conjunction with fees on stationary sources.

schedule. Fee schedules would vary geographically according to the severity of the local pollution problem. Urban areas with serious pollution problems would likely levy stiff fee schedules; rural areas with less severe problems would levy lower schedules. The direct costs of annual testing would probably be modest, particularly if the testing were done in conjunction with annual safety inspections.[22]

Let us examine the consequences of such a fee program. Individuals would have an incentive to seek out and maintain "clean" cars. The companies would have a direct incentive to build "clean" cars and to advertise that fact. The mix of cars would be adjusted so that the "dirtier" cars were shipped to the low-fee areas, where pollution problems were less severe, and the "cleaner" cars were shipped to the high-fee areas, where pollution problems were more severe. The proper balance between devices and maintenance effort would be found. The durability of the devices would become an important consideration for motorists and the companies. Further, the companies would have a clear incentive to develop new emissions-reduction technology. The incentives for brinkmanship and for collusion to delay the introduction of new technology would no longer be present. The strengths of the price system—motivating private individuals and corporations to pursue their own self-interests in finding efficient ways to reduce costs and maximize benefits—would be brought into play.

Even an effluent fee system that only applied to new vehicles (again, levied at the local geographical area, with fees based on estimated lifetime emissions), though a far inferior second-best policy because of the absence of incentives for maintenance, would nevertheless be a far superior policy to our current standards approach. Again, the same motivations (except for maintenance effort) would be present.

Three possible objections to effluent fees need to be laid to rest. First, there is the question of equity. Will a fee system pose undue hardships for low-income individuals? The answer is that, compared to the current uniform standards approach, it would likely lessen the average burden on low-income individuals. As numerous studies have shown, the current standards program is far from costless.[23] Current new cars cost roughly $200 more because of emissions-control equipment, plus a present discounted cost of about $100 in extra maintenance and decreased fuel economy. The 1980s models, embodying tighter standards, will cost appreciably more. The 1973 and 1974 model cars were especially costly, because of the decreased fuel economy caused by the exhaust gas recirculation necessary to meet the nitrogen oxide standards of those years. These costs eventually filter through to the used car market. Low-income individuals do not escape them, regardless of whether they are new car or used car buyers. In fact, as Harrison and

---

22. A complete, feasible, and practical fee schedule and program has been presented by Mills and White, n. 1 *supra* at 385–393.
23. See the studies cited in n. 1 *supra*.

Dorfman[24] have demonstrated, the distribution of costs of the present emissions standards program is regressive; i.e., low-income households pay a higher percentage of their incomes to cover the costs of emissions control than do higher-income households.

At the same time, the benefits from emissions reduction seem to be distributed relatively uniformly among income classes. Though low-income households are relatively overrepresented in central cities, where pollution problems are serious and, consequently, where the benefits from emissions reduction are high, they are also overrepresented in rural and semirural areas, where pollution problems are considerably less severe and hence where the benefits from emissions reduction are low. On a net cost-benefit basis, the impact of the current standards program is regressive.

By contrast, an effluent fee program with different fees for different geographical areas would mean that low-pollution areas could charge lower fees and thus cause less emissions reduction and less costs in those areas. Not only would this be more efficient than the present uniform national standards, but, because of the overrepresentation of poor households in rural and semirural areas (where private autos tend to be used more and public transportation to be used less than in urban areas), the lower costs in these areas would improve overall equity.

A second possible objection to effluent fees is that different fee schedules in different geographic areas will pose administrative burdens for governments and marketing burdens for the automobile companies.[25] This need not be the case, however. State and local governments currently levy taxes and fees at rates that differ among them. There surely is some evasion and fictitious residency claims as a consequence, but these have not posed such a large administrative burden as to cause the states and local governments to conclude that uniform tax rates and fees are superior. The same would surely be the case for differential effluent fees. As for the companies, they are quite good at altering production mixes in response to consumer demand. The addition of consumer demands based on effluent fees would not add appreciably to their burden.

Third, there is the question whether research and development programs and efforts at technological change by the automobile companies will respond to the incentives of an effluent fee program. We have abundant evidence that individuals and companies do respond to eco-

---

24. D. Harrison, Jr., "Controlling Automotive Emissions: How to Save More Than $1 Billion Per Year and Help the Poor Too," 25 *Public Policy* 527–533 (Fall 1977); N. S. Dorfman, "Who Will Pay for Pollution Control?—The Distribution of the Burden of the National Environmental Protection Program, 1972–1980," 28 *National Tax Journal* 101–115 (Mar. 1975).

25. Similar objections are raised by the Panel on Air Quality, Noise and Health (DOT, 1976, pp. 5–54 to 5–58) to an expanded two-car strategy in which high pollution areas require stringent controls (as does California currently), while the remainder of the country requires less stringent controls.

nomic incentives in their choices of goods and of inputs into production processes, substituting capital for labor, etc. The question of technological change responding to economic incentives is somewhat different: The usual evidence is concerned with relatively short-run substitutions, whereas technological change is concerned with longer-run dynamic processes. Nevertheless, we need not rely on the old saw that there are hundreds of engineers in Detroit who would sell their grandmothers for the opportunity to save a dollar per car. There is a small but growing empirical literature that does indicate that technological change in the private sector responds to economic incentives.[26] One cannot expect instant technological discoveries in response to an effluent fee program. But the incentives are clearly there. The companies would surely respond.

SUMMARY AND CONCLUSIONS

Our current emissions-control program has definitely brought progress. But that progress has been too slow, too costly, and too inequitable. An alternative program based on effluent fees could have brought faster, less costly, and more equitable progress—and still could do so for the 1980s and 1990s, if enacted today.

Yet, none of the branches of government has shown serious interest in effluent fees. No governmental review of the automotive emissions program has considered it a serious alternative.[27] The latest such report, compiled by the Federal Task Force on Motor Vehicle Goals Beyond 1980, dismisses it with a single reference as a possible alternative but never explores it in any depth;[28] the background panel report for the study did not even mention it.[29]

Legislators have been equally uninterested. Questions about effluent fees rarely arise in congressional hearings.[30] In the Senate Hearings on the 1977 Clean Air Act Amendments, the question was raised a few times but quickly dropped.[31] It was never raised in the House hearings.[32]

---

26. For summaries of this literature, see B. Gold, Ed., *Research, Technological Change, and Economic Analysis* (D. C. Heath, 1977); H. P. Binswanger, V. W. Ruttan, et al., *Induced Innovation* (Johns Hopkins Univ. Press, 1978); L. J. White, *Is Technological Change Responsive to Economic Incentives?*, Working Paper Series, No. 77-98 (New York Univ., Faculty of Business Administration, Dec. 1977) which also contains some new evidence on this question.
27. See the government studies cited in n. 1 *supra*.
28. DOT (1976b), p. 17-2.
29. DOT (1976a).
30. L. J. White, "Effluent Charges as a Faster Means of Achieving Pollution Control," 24 *Public Policy* 111–125 (Winter 1976).
31. *U.S. Sen. Comm. on Environmental and Pub. Works, Subcomm. on Environmental Pollution, Clean Air Act Amendments of 1977—Hearings* (1977), Pt. 1.
32. *Progress in the Implementation of Motor Vehicle Emission Standards Through June*

Equally distressing is the automobile companies' seeming lack of interest in effluent fees. In response to the few questions that were raised, the auto company representatives were baffled and disinterested. Some had never heard of the concept before.

The automobile companies are quick to tout the strengths of the price system in other areas, such as fuel economy regulation.[33] Yet, as we have shown, an effluent fee program would bring these same strengths of the price system to bear on the pollution problem. If the companies mean what they say about the price system, it is time that they consider seriously and endorse an effluent fee approach as the way to deal with the nation's air pollution problems.

1975, EPA (1976); U.S. H. of Rep. Comm. on Interstate and Foreign Commerce, Subcomm. on Health and the Environment, Clean Air Act Amendments of 1977— Hearings (1978).

33. H. L. Duncombe, Jr., *Statement of General Motors Corporation to the Energy Resource Council on the Draft Report by the Federal Task Force on Motor Vehicle Goals Beyond 1980,* Mimeo (Oct. 21, 1976); C. M. Kennedy of Chrysler, *Statement at the Hearing on the Report of the Federal Task Force on Motor Vehicle Goals Beyond 1980 6,* Mimeo (1976).

DISCUSSION

CARL NASH: Economic models seem not to be politically acceptable. I would like to see some research into the reasons for this—obviously there must be something wrong with economic models if they so seldom are acceptable to most citizens.

I wonder also if current laws are as unresponsive to consumer preferences as White implies. Regulations are reviewed and often revised as the need arises.

DAVE STOCKMAN: Larry White's discussion shows an admirable regard for economic efficiency and for the power of the market system. I have one problem with it, though. That is that the criteria used for setting the tax rate are problematical, since the health effect of ambient pollution and the contributions of the automobile to ambient pollution have not been determined with any reasonable certainty. The present standards are not based on current techniques or evidence. They must be reevaluated before we discuss specific pollution policies that are to be based upon them. Also, a tax rate should not be imposed uniformly nationwide, but varied according to regional needs.

Nonetheless, a tax would put regulators back in touch with public desires, and would add flexibility to the regulatory process.

ACADEMIC: Dr. White, how is a nationwide system to determine the taxes to be imposed on vehicles any more efficient than the currently proposed I/M [in-use maintenance] systems?

WHITE: The problems with I/M systems are slight. I argue that their value could be greatly enhanced if combined with the administration of an effluent tax. Compensating for regional variations in optimal emission levels would not be that difficult.

ACADEMIC: One should never fool with standards governing dangers to the public's health. Reexamination of standards should not be manipulated in the casual manner that would be possible under your proposal.

WHITE: Air pollution is not the critical health problem that you make it out to be. It's not as if small and temporary miscalibrations of the tax level would result in scores of deaths.

AUTO (U.S.): White's idea is a good one. The government certification procedure has grown to monstrous levels of complexity. A tailpipe tax would allow us to self-certify, by reacting to consumer demand as modified by the tax. It would also allow us to buy time, at a price, to phase in risky new developments.

GOVERNMENT: We've considered effluent taxes before, but felt that certainty of effect in abating pollution was more important than theoretical elegance. One cannot predict in advance what level of economic incentives would work.

AUTO (U.S.): Certainty is a desirable quality from the standpoint of industry as well.

ACADEMIC: I agree that uncertainty is the salient consideration in regulation of pollution. The OECD recommended a tax approach, however, because it felt we could better concentrate our efforts on stationary emitters, and use a less sure but less cumbersome method of controlling mobile emitters while still curing the overall pollution problem.

AUTO (U.S.): Field testing of vehicles is expensive. It may not be worth the effort, since autos contribute only 4 percent of total man-made pollution. In fact, controlling emissions from cars may cost more than it is worth by any method.

TRADE PRESS: There is no test available that approximates emission performance under actual driving conditions; thus such testing as is feasible at present provides no fair basis for the imposition of an effluent tax.

GOVERNMENT: Despite its problems, testing has worked well in New

York City. We produced improvements in safety, pollution, and fuel economy there at a cost of $40 dollars a car, which is good cost-effectiveness in my book.

ACADEMIC: The effluent tax is a dead horse, [although] we would all love to see it work. The problem is that such a proposal is an economic solution to an inherently political problem. The efficiency of economic solutions lies in the establishment of parameters in a decentralized fashion. But the tax rate in White's proposal must be set in a political fashion; thus his proposal is not really a market solution at all.

CONSUMER SAFETY INFORMATION AS A GOVERNMENT POLICY TOOL

Michael M. Finkelstein, *Associate Administrator for Rulemaking, National Highway Traffic Safety Administration*

The government's traditional approach in dealing with health and safety matters has been to impose requirements on an industry via regulation. The National Motor Vehicle and Traffic Safety Act of 1966, for example, provides for government intervention in the marketplace through the establishment of minimum levels of safety performance as stated in federal motor vehicle safety standards promulgated by NHTSA. A producer must meet each safety standard in order to sell a motor vehicle in the United States.

Title II of the Motor Vehicle Information and Cost Savings Act calls for government intervention of a very different type. This Act authorized NHTSA to rate the comparative performance of automobiles with respect to crashworthiness, damageability, and ease of maintenance, and to provide information on each of these factors to the public. But the government would only provide the consumer with safety information; it would not impose any requirements on manufacturers to change their products.

An examination of the consumer information program authorized by the Cost Savings Act should start with the Vehicle Safety Act, which preceded the Cost Savings Act by six years. The 1966 legislation requiring the issuance of motor vehicle safety performance standards was a political reaction to an increasing number of traffic deaths and a belief that the motor vehicle industry was all but ignoring safety. In part, the manufacturers' posture was said to be predicated on their belief that "safety does not sell cars." If this assertion is correct, then of what use is safety information to consumers and what influence can such information have on their auto purchase decision? A useful point of departure for this discussion, then, is to reexamine the oft-cited, but untested proverbial wisdom that safety does not sell.

In extensive studies[1] conducted since enactment of the Cost Savings Act, consumers *say* that they are concerned about vehicle safety. One important reason for buying a large car is their belief that it is safer than a small car. The studies go on to state, however, that the vast majority of consumers assume that all cars within a size class are equally safe. At the same time, a recent survey done by Peter Hart for the Department of Transportation[2] found that the public's understanding of technological alternatives that can improve safety was surprisingly deep and that the public's desire for additional information was strong.

To date, the public has had little access to information about differences among cars. Obviously, an industry is never anxious to advertise the fact that its products can fail. It is much more desirable to focus on the utility of cars, the pleasure associated with their use, and the status associated with the owner of such a solid product. In spite of this, Ford was advertising itself as the safety manufacturer in the late 1950s, promoting seat belts as options.[3] Volvo[4] and Mercedes[5] still try to sell safety to the motoring public. And as recently as the September 24th, 1978 National Football League telecast of the Washington Redskins and New York Jets game, General Motors was using films of simulated crashes in their commercials.

In all likelihood, the entry of the federal government into the safety regulation of automobiles in the 1960s led the public to believe that cars were thereby made uniformly safe. While complaining about the cost of federal regulation, the automobile manufacturers certainly try to give the impression that this same regulation also serves as a governmental seal of approval. The public is becoming increasingly aware, however, that federal safety standards establish minimum requirements that manufacturers can and, in some cases, do exceed. Recent Mercedes ads[6] have clearly shown that safety measures beyond those required by government standards are now being built into their cars.

It is time for the government to make such points as strongly. With Title II of the Cost Savings Act, the government has the authority to inform the public that some cars perform better than others, as well as to dispel the notion that all cars within a class are equally safe. Title II authorizes the Secretary of Transportation to determine the relative crashworthiness of automobiles and to communicate this information

---

1. National Analysts (a division of Booz-Allen), "Consumer Reaction to Title II Interpretations," *Final Phase I Report—The Automobile Consumer Information Study*, App. D (1975).
2. Peter Hart Associates, *A Survey of Private Citizens to Obtain Information on Passive Restraint Systems* (1978).
3. Ford ad, *Saturday Evening Post*, 1956.
4. Volvo ad, *Car and Driver*, Sept. 1977, p. 36.
5. Mercedes ad, "Germany Special Supplement," *Allegheny Airlines Flightline Magazine*, Oct. 1978.
6. Mercedes ad, *Business Week*, Sept. 11, 1978, pp. 106–107.

to the public to aid them in their decision to purchase an automobile. Crashworthiness is intended to measure the relative likelihood of a vehicle occupant being killed or severely injured in a crash. The statute requires that the information be made available in a simple and readily understandable form to ease consumer comparisons.

But the statute was enacted in 1972. Where, then, is the rating system today, six years later?

Congressman Bob Eckhardt, Chairman of the Consumer Subcommittee of the House Committee on Interstate and Foreign Commerce—the Committee that wrote the Cost Savings Act—asked Joan Claybrook precisely this question in May 1977, less than one month[7] after she assumed the position of NHTSA Administrator. Claybrook testified that the program had been terminated. After spending almost $3 million, it had been determined that predictive crashworthiness ratings for new cars were beyond the state of the art. Since NHTSA was unable to predict crashworthiness, the program had been abandoned.

Claybrook committed the agency to begin where previous work left off and develop comparative crashworthiness ratings based upon the performance of recent model cars. In part, this recognized that there are twice as many used car transactions as new car sales each year. This policy was aimed as much at the automobile industry as the consumer, however. The increasing number of citizens who are concerned about the safety of the automobiles they drive should have access to reliable information about the track record of the manufacturers. Companies having a record of producing safer cars should be able to benefit from it.

What will happen when consumers have adequate information to conclude that not all cars within a given class are equally crashworthy?[8] We have had several natural experiments that may help us answer the question. With the 1978 summer of the Pinto and the Firestone 500 behind us, we may now see how consumers responded to two widely publicized defect investigations. Another case worth reviewing, one in which NHTSA had a very minor role, is the Consumer Union's assertion that the Chrysler Corporation's Omni/Horizon was unacceptable because of poor handling.

Ford Pintos built between 1971 and 1976 were found to have fuel tanks designed so that in rear-end collisions the likelihood of fire was significantly higher than for other cars. Subsequent to the 1976 model, under a much stricter federal standard, the performance of Ford Pintos was no longer much worse than their class. However, the finding that fuel tanks on over 1.5 million 1971-to-1976 cars in use were unsafe was the basis for requiring Ford to recall these vehicles and to remedy the

---

7. *Motor Vehicle and Cost Savings Act of 1972—Oversight Hearings, Subcomm. on Consumer Protection and Finance, House Comm. on Interstate and Foreign Commerce*, 95th Cong., 1st Sess. (May 2 and 9, 1977).

8. The available evidence suggests that most consumers now believe that all vehicles within a market class are equally safe. National Analysts, n. 1 *supra* at App. D(13).

situation. While this investigation was underway, a California jury awarded $125 million in punitive damages to the young survivor of a Pinto crash who received burns over 90 percent of his body. The judge later reduced the award to $3.5 million, but the initial judgment, combined with the potential cost of the recall to Ford and the spectacular nature of fire accidents, put this issue onto the front page of most newspapers.

While, as mentioned, the 1978 Pintos were materially better than the 1976 version, during the month of the recall (June), Ford could hardly give them away. Even with a $325 incentive to dealers to sell Pintos, there was a 40 percent drop in June sales, followed by a 34 percent decline in July and a 5 percent fall in August. By the beginning of September, Ford had a seventy-eight-day supply of unsold Pintos, compared to Chevrolet's forty-six days for the Chevette.[9] Although not yet reflected in the retail values, used Pinto wholesale prices were down 25 to 40 percent.[10]

The Firestone 500 case is another instance where a major product line of a major manufacturer was found by NHTSA to be unsafe. Firestone 500s were the top-of-the-line passenger car tires manufactured by Firestone Tire and Rubber Company until they were phased out of production and replaced by the Firestone 721 beginning in 1977. (However, some 500s were still being manufactured in January 1978.) NHTSA received reports indicating that a disproportionate number of Firestone 500s were failing in use, causing serious crashes in many instances. An investigation was opened and an initial determination was made on July 7, 1978, that a safety-related defect existed in the Firestone 500.

Three factors made the Firestone 500 case a story for the front pages. First was the potential size of the recall, reaching possibly 15 million tires with an estimated cost to Firestone of $500 million. Second, there were congressional hearings on the subject, chaired by Congressman Moss, and NHTSA public hearings, chaired by Administrator Claybrook. Third, the combative attitude adopted by Firestone made the issue much more newsworthy. It should be noted that, again, the defective product was no longer being produced; in this case, even the name had been changed. As with the Pinto, however, Firestone passenger car tire sales dropped during the year ending October 31, 1978.

The last case mentioned was Consumer Union's "unacceptable" rating for the Omni/Horizon. This was announced at a press conference June 14, 1978 that received national publicity. Officials of both the United States and the Canadian Governments tested the car and found no handling problems. While the impact on Chrysler sales was not as

---

9. J. L. King and P. Lienert, "Pinto is Big Problem as Ford Shoots for '79 Sales Increase," *Automotive News*, Sept. 18, 1978, p. 2.

10. J. L. King, "Used Pinto Prices Go Pfft; Sales Still Dry Up," *Automotive News*, Sept. 25, 1978, p. 62.

pronounced as the impact of the Pinto recall on Ford sales, it was noticeable. The June sales for the Omni/Horizon totaled 15,991, dipping to 14,808 in July. By August, sales figures were up to 19,442, although they fell to 15,837 in September. At the start of September, Chrysler had a 78½ day supply of unsold Horizons and an 82½ day supply of Omnis.[11]

In early September 1977, Chrysler experienced a similar sales loss following widespread publicity about possible Aspen/Volare defects. August 1977 Aspen/Volare sales totaled 47,608; overall, Chrysler sold 105,584 cars during that month. By September the Aspen/Volare sales were down to 39,975 and the overall car sales were 92,633. The October sales figures did show improvement, however, with 49,585 Aspen/Volares being sold; total sales for Chrysler were 113,508 for that month.

While it is not apparent from the foregoing discussion that safety sells, a good argument can be mounted that a perceived lack of safety costs sales. Moreover, when faced with serious safety hazards, the industry is unsure of what to do to offset their effect on sales. In the case of the Pinto, Ford reverted to its mid-1950s approach and advertised the safety features in the 1978 Pinto fuel tanks. While not acknowledging the defects in the 1971 to 1976 models, they did refer to the new improved fuel tank in the 1978s. Firestone, on the other hand, ignored the issue of the 500, but began offering an unheard of two-year warranty on the 721 that replaced it. Further, Firestone was going to spend an unspecified sum to hire Jimmy Stewart the movie star as the spokesman for their company to project an image of corporate integrity. Finally, Chrysler went so far as to publish the Canadian Government's positive findings with respect to the handling quality of the Omni/Horizon.

The point of this examination is clear. When consumers have what they believe to be safety-related information that allows them to differentiate among products, they act on it. Moreover, manufacturers respond to this consumer behavior in their advertising.

The purpose of the United States Government in disseminating consumer information is to have consumers react in the marketplace to safety differences and to encourage companies to respond to the consumers' desire for safety by upgrading products. We realize that providing complicated, technical information to consumers about the crashworthiness of an automobile is a difficult task. Although we believe that consumers react to questions of safety, most of the cases where a shift of buying can be observed result from straightforward, negative publicity. Can consumer information based on qualitative ratings of the relative crashworthiness of a car create the same reaction as well-publicized, life-threatening situations? This is a question that we hope to answer in the course of our development of an automotive ratings program.

---

11. J. L. King and P. Lienert, n. 9 *supra* at 58.

Obviously, the presentation and the availability of the ratings are going to be important in gaining consumer acceptance. A brochure which states that the chances of crash survival are 25 percent greater in Car A than in Car B *when* involved in a head-on collision, *when* wearing a seat belt, *when* sitting in the rear left seat, *and when* the occupant is between the ages of 30 to 50, will be meaningless. The data must be presented in a form that is easily understood, yet is not so simplified as to be meaningless or misleading. In addition, we know from previous consumer surveys and in-depth group interviews that people are interested in knowing how the information was developed and specifically what the magnitudes of differences are among automobiles. We also know from testing promotional messages in the previous work that the information should be stated directly and that gimmicks will not effectively "sell" crashworthiness ratings.

In terms of the data and methodologies available, we are better able to provide relative ratings: Car A is "better than average," and Car B is "worse than average." Will consumers accept "better than average," "average," and "worse than average" as a rating scheme for crashworthiness? National Analysts[12] told us in 1974 that "average" is meaningless and that the most acceptable form of crashworthiness ratings was a probability score—the probability of sustaining a fatal or serious injury. So we have here another question that must be examined before an elaborate rating scheme is developed.

The measurement and understanding of consumer attitudes is central to the development of crashworthiness ratings under Title II. We plan to generate the rating data while further exploring the attitudes of the potential users. We plan to conduct surveys and group interviews as we examine and refine the data necessary for the ratings. We anticipate that we will be able to develop meaningful comparisons of recent car performance and ultimately predict the crashworthiness of new cars. What would we then expect to happen? How does this program mesh with NHTSA's other regulatory activities? And lastly, how does a consumer information program relate to the subject of industrial innovation?

We view the consumer information program authorized by Title II of the Cost Savings Act with an open mind. It is clear that consumers react to information that indicates that a product poses a serious safety hazard. We are hoping to see similar consumer reactions to more positive crashworthiness ratings. We hope that consumers gravitate to safer models and that manufacturers of models rated less safe see a decline in sales.

Over time, if these shifts in sales occur, we would expect that manufacturers would react to the market and exploit crashworthiness. For this to happen, the government must develop valid ratings, ratings in which the consumer can believe.

---

12. National Analysts, n. 1 *supra* at App. D(19).

The more that we in the government can keep this information before the public, the more market pressure the industry will feel to develop innovative safety improvements. For unlike most of our regulations, which are directed at a very specific safety problem or a well-defined component of a vehicle, crashworthiness ratings are all-encompassing. Thus, the manufacturers will have almost complete freedom with respect to improving the crashworthiness of the products they manufacture. With a measurable objective, a profit incentive, and almost total freedom of approach, it is hard to imagine a more fertile environment for innovation.

Finally, a crashworthiness rating program which deals with the overall performance of the vehicle and which, at least in theory, rewards manufacturers who excel, would appear to complement a safety-promoting regulatory scheme that sets minimum performance requirements in very narrowly defined areas. Currently, we are concerned that the present regulatory scheme inhibits innovation and pushes the design of vehicles toward the lowest common denominator, which is in many cases the federal standard. A 30-miles-per-hour rear crash test to assure the integrity of fuel systems may really ensure that cars will not exceed the standard but will be designed only to meet that test.

Generalized crashworthiness ratings at their best should invigorate the industry and get their competitive juices flowing in an area that will provide real value to the consumer.

Over the next few years, this will be an area worth watching. The federal government must develop a meaningful rating system and only then will the consumer be able to bring to bear positive pressure on the industry to improve safety.

DISCUSSION

PETER KINZLER: One way of using information more efficiently would be for NHTSA to allow test marketing of new designs in small areas to determine new features' effectiveness before mandating their installation on a national scale. But making information available may not have much effect in the absence of market incentives to use that information. For example, current fault insurance, because it protects the assets of the driver against damage he may cause another person, encourages people to buy cars that will inflict less damage on others. Thus, the system rewards people who drive lighter, less safe vehicles. No-fault, which pays drivers for their own damages, takes into account the driver loss-incurring potential. This means that no-fault can reward the driver for owning a safer, more defensible automobile by lowering his insurance premium. Thus, information on vehicle safety would be much more valuable to drivers under no-fault than under fault insurance.

SYDNEY TERRY: Making more information available to consumers would benefit industry and consumers alike. The problem is, how do you get the public to read and use information, and how do you keep the information free of bias?

An example [of the bias problem] is the recent controversy over the Chrysler Omni. A consumer advocacy group began a campaign to prove that the car was unsafe. We went to NHTSA and asked them to evaluate the accusations themselves; NHTSA found the accusations to be unwarranted. They saved our bacon in this instance; if they had not intervened, our efforts to market this perfectly sound vehicle would have been ruined. It is that sort of consumer advocacy that works against the public interest.

AUTO (FOREIGN): We do not know how to test car performance realistically in an accident. How is information to be generated before a new product is introduced?

FINKELSTEIN: Obviously, it can not be. We tried and failed. However, useful data can be gathered on the field performance of a car shortly after it is introduced.

ACADEMIC: It seems to me that auto companies have done little to sell cars on the basis of safety. How much latent consumer demand for this has yet to be exploited?

TERRY: Selling after-crash safety was tried and it did not work. The benefits perceived by the consumer have to be greater than the extra cost involved to make any extra-cost feature worthwhile. Further, when all companies have essentially the same safety features, there is no basis for the brand differentiation that would make the selling of safety worthwhile.

ACADEMIC: Then it seems likely that a campaign to make the public more safety conscious would raise the value to manufacturers of advertising on the basis of vehicle safety.

THE RESPONSE OF FLEET OWNERS TO REGULATION-INDUCED TECHNICAL CHANGES IN CAR DESIGN

Robert Berke, *Executive Director, National Association of Fleet Administrators, Inc.*

Within the past ten years the automotive industry and its customers have participated in a veritable revolution involving all areas and components of the automobile, partly as a result of regulation of the industry. First came the vehicle safety standards developed by NHTSA; then enactment of the Clean Air Act with its various amendments covering emission controls to reduce the air pollution caused by automobiles; then the passage of statutes governing use of gasoline and the mandated improvement in gasoline mileage spurred by the oil embargo of 1973 to 1974.

The effects of all these changes are difficult to assess; field studies involving many automobiles and drivers are complex and costly. The managed fleets of automobiles, an important part of industry and government transportation, on the other hand, provide a rich source of important data about the effectiveness of regulation-induced changes in the automobile and an index to the purchasing behavior of an especially knowledgeable class of automobile buyers.

THE FLEET SEGMENT

The passenger car fleet market is a highly significant but generally unrecognized segment of the total automotive market consisting of millions of vehicles (the exact number is a matter of interpretation) used by every industry and by all levels of government for the efficient conduct of its business. According to a recent survey by the National Association of Fleet Administrators (NAFA), 73 percent of the fleet vehicles are used for sales purposes, 23 percent for service calls, and 4 percent for delivery.[1]

---

1. *Fleet Use and Maintenance Practices Survey,* NADA (Apr. 1977). Prepared for testimony presented to U.S. Fed. Trade Comm.

Corporations and government agencies maintain fleets to provide transportation required by their employees and executives. They are not in business to operate fleets of vehicles. Consequently the vehicles are a cost of doing business and must be operated as efficiently and effectively as possible.

The basic source of data on fleet car registrations is R. L. Polk & Co., Detroit, Michigan. They classify fleet sales as purchases by companies or government agencies that register ten or more new units in one of two consecutive years. During the period 1968 through 1977, fleet sales have ranged from a low of 9.3 percent of total new car sales in 1971 to a high of 14.7 percent in 1977. The low point in number of cars purchased for fleet use was 955,000 units in 1975; the high point was in 1977 when fleet sales totaled 1,343,365 units. Table 7-8 is a record of the total automobile sales by year, sales to fleets buying ten or more units, and their percentage of the total.[2]

Accurate estimates of the total number of vehicles used for business—including individually owned or leased cars and those in fleets of fewer than ten units—are very difficult to gather because of varying state registration procedures. Bobit Publications, Inc., for example, has estimated the total business car population to be more than 10 million units. Nevertheless, the most recent figures furnished by the Fleet and Leasing Sales Activity of the Ford Motor Company permit us to update the estimate for 1977 shown in Table 7-8.

Fleets purchasing ten or more new units generally fall into four categories: 1) Commercial accounts or company-owned units; 2) leasing and rental companies; 3) state and local governments, and 4) the federal government. In 1977, commercial accounts registered 196,668 new passenger cars; leasing and rental companies, 1,026,446; state and local governments, 97,512; and the federal government, 22,739. Of the leasing and rental group's total registrations, 65 percent are estimated to go to leasing companies for long-term service (more than 1 year) and 35 percent to daily rental firms.[3]

FLEET VEHICLE SELECTION

The corporate fleet manager is a model of the rational car buyer. A top executive of one of the nation's leasing and fleet management service companies summed this up recently:

> We take a far more rigorous view of the automobile than the average customer. The responsibility to make the right cost-saving car recommen-

---

2. D. Shonka, "Characteristics of Automotive Fleets in the U.S.," Oak Ridge Nat'l Laboratories (June 1978).
3. Statistics provided by Fleet & Leasing Sales Activity, Ford Motor Co. (Aug. 1978).

TABLE 7-8 Shonka Estimates of Yearly Fleet Purchases, 1968–1977

Year	Total automobile sales (in thousands)	Sales of 10 or more units to fleets (in thousands)	Percentage of total sales
1968	9,656	985	10.2%
1969	9,583	1,093	11.4
1970	8,405	1,009	13.0
1971	10,250	1,098	9.3
1972	10,950	1,105	9.9
1973	11,439	1,291	11.6
1974	8,867	1,083	13.7
1975	8,200	1,070	13.1
1976	10,111	1,154	11.8
1977	9,124	1,219	13.4

dations to our clients is not one we take lightly. We want cars that are economical to operate. We need adequate space for at least four passengers and we need a trunk to carry samples and tools. We want safety, especially as cars become smaller; however, that doesn't mean we want air bags. For the money we are spending, we will insist on a quality product . . . sloppy manufacturing and massive recall campaigns will not be tolerated. And, of course, we want style because style goes hand in hand with resale value.[4]

The desire to maximize economy of operation and to minimize depreciation is borne out by survey after survey of fleet administrators and leasing company executives. These 2 factors account for at least 75 percent of total fleet costs. According to the *Guidelines: 1979 Fleet Vehicle Specifications*, written for professional fleet managers:

The proper selection of vehicles is still the first and most important decision in fleet management. The vehicles selected must be equal to the demands of the job, be economical to operate, bring a high return on the used car market, and at the same time satisfy the operator.[5]

In its annual New Car Acquisition Survey, NAFA asks its members to rank the most important factors in their fleet car selection. Depreciation/resale value was the most important consideration according to the 1979 Survey. In the three previous surveys it had ranked

---

4. Presentation by A. Samuel Penn, Senior Vice President, Peterson, Howell & Heather, Inc., and President, Fleet Management Services, Baltimore, Md., to University of Michigan seminar (Aug. 1978).
5. *Guidelines: 1979 Fleet Vehicle Specifications*, A. J. Cavalli, Vice President and Director, client service, C.I.T. Service Leasing, New York, N.Y. (June 1978).

second to economy of operation, which has now dropped to second place.[6]

Choosing a vehicle "equal to the job demands" usually involves considerations of trunk space or carrying capacity. Fleet administrators are aware that most 1979 models offer three different types of spare tires: The conventional full-size tire; a "space saver," which is a collapsible tire requiring inflation for use and deflation for storage; and the "tempa spare," a smaller, permanently inflated tire that can be used for approximately 2,000 miles. The type of spare tire can be a major factor in deciding on a car with specific trunk capacity, and must be measured against cost, the high mileage usage of a fleet car, and safety. This is one example of the multiple factors involved in making the proper fleet car buying decision.

MANAGEMENT PROCEDURES

Management procedures in professional fleet administration cover a wide area. They include instructional car manuals issued to drivers of company-provided cars, reports and recommendations to management, proposed budgets, and data processing systems that record every facet of the vehicle's operation. The widespread use of computer technology to record and check vehicle expenses has dramatically reformed management procedures. So-called "exception reporting," for instance, automatically flags cars that exceed specific parameters and suggests proper corrective action. This makes great savings in maintenance and downtime possible.

Three forms provided by C.I.T. Service Leasing Corp. (Table 7-9) are examples of the management services offered by leasing companies to their clients. These forms provide individual vehicle operating data with appropriate comments, a vehicle operating summary, and a consolidated report for all units a company has in service.

Reasons for the development of sophisticated performance monitoring systems are immediately obvious in the following statistics. In 1968, the average fleet car cost approximately $3,000 and gasoline was 35 cents per gallon. The price of a typical mid-size 1978 model fleet car was more than $5,200 and the required unleaded gasoline cost more than 65 cents per gallon. Operating or running expenses which, according to NAFA's Recommended Classification of Automobile Expenses, include fuel, oil, tires, maintenance, and repair, excluding accident repairs, were less than 4 cents per mile 10 years ago. In 1977, they were nearly 6½ cents per mile. The total cost to a company to keep a business car on the road has thus increased in these past 10 years from $159.81 a month in 1968 to $264.65 a month in 1977.[7]

---

6. "Annual New Car Aquisition Survey," NAFA *Bulletin* (Aug. 1978).
7. *U.S. Composite Fleet Performance Report,* compiled by Peterson, Howell & Heather, Inc., Baltimore, Md.

TABLE 7-9 Individual Vehicle Operating Data (top); Vehicle Operating Summary (bottom); Consolidated Operating Data (next page)

MAY 1978 — INDIVIDUAL VEHICLE OPERATING DATA

CLIENT AND UNIT NUMBER	YEAR AND MAKE	OPERATOR	MONTHS IN SERVICE	MONTHS REPORTED LIFETIME	MONTHS REPORTED Y.T.D.	PROJECTED REPLACEMENT DATE	STATE
51432-66456	77 CUTLASS	JOHNSON	19	18	5	2-79	VA

	GAS	OIL AND LUBE	TIRES	NORMAL REPAIRS	TOTAL RUNNING EXPENSES	ACCIDENT REPAIRS LESS RECOVERIES	MISC.	RENTALS	ADJ. TO RESERVE	INSURANCE	TOTAL	LESS PERSONAL USE CHARGE	NET TOTAL
LIFETIME													
DOLLAR COST	1,527	27	116	122	1,792		332	3,134			5,258	917	4,341
AV. DOLLAR COST/MONTH	85	2	6	7	100		18	165			283	51	232
CENTS COST PER MILE	4.5	.08	.3	.4	5.3		1.0	8.6			14.9	2.7	12.2
S.L.C. YEAR AND MAKE AVERAGE	4.1	.10	.4	.6	5.2								
YEAR TO DATE													
DOLLAR COST	457	14	98	50	619		35	819			1,473	355	1,118
AV. DOLLAR COST/MONTH	91	3	20	10	124		7	164			295	71	224
CENTS COST PER MILE	4.6	.14	1.0	.5	6.2		.4	8.3			14.9	3.7	11.2
S.L.C. YEAR AND MAKE AVERAGE	3.9	.10	.4	.6	5.0								

REMARKS: Y.T.D. GAS COST ABOVE S.L.C. AVERAGE Y.T.D. RUNNING EXPENSE ABOVE S.L.C. AVERAGE
LIFETIME AND Y.T.D. M.P.G. BELOW S.L.C. AVERAGE

	TOTAL MILES REPORTED	BUSINESS MILES REPORTED	PERCENT BUSINESS MILES	AV. MONTHLY MILEAGE	GAS GALLONS	AVERAGE COST PER GALLON	MILES PER GALLON	S.L.C. YEAR AND MAKE AV. M.P.G.
LIFETIME	34,351	20,085	58.4	1,908	2,380.7	.64	14.4	17.1
YEAR TO DATE	9,851	4,857	49.3	1,970	687.7	.66	14.3	19.2
CURRENT	1,957	1,245	63.6		122.3			

CLIENT NUMBER 51432 — MAY 1978 — VEHICLE OPERATING SUMMARY

UNIT NUMBER	YEAR, MAKE AND OPERATOR	PROJECTED REPLACEMENT DATE	MONTHS IN SERVICE	MONTHS REPORTED	TOTAL MILEAGE REPORTED	MILES PER GALLON	GAS	OIL-LUBE	TIRES	NORMAL REPAIRS	TOTAL
60252	75 CHEVELLE MALIBU ROBINSON	5-78	38	35	41,818	10.6*	5.7*	0.03	1.0	1.3	8.3*
				5	5,932	10.7*	5.0*	0.02	1.2	5.9	12.9*
60798	75 CHEVELLE MALIBU MINEY	9-77 S	36	34	65,949	14.0	4.4	0.10	0.5	0.7	5.7
				4	6,494	15.2	4.4	0.06		0.1	4.6
60883	76 MONARCH HANDSCHUH	9-78	24	24	43,459	12.1	5.1	0.15	0.5	1.0	8.3
				4	7,180	12.2	5.3	0.13	0.1	0.3	5.8*
60944	76 TORINO B HALLA	2-79	30	30	39,030	9.0*	6.5*	0.17	0.5	3.7	10.9*
				5	6,001	10.4*	6.5*	0.28	2.2	3.9	12.9*
63892	76 MONARCH J ZARING	2-79	28	28	40,726	13.0	4.8	0.17	0.3	1.1	6.4
63920	76 CHEVELLE MALIBU R RUDD	5-78	25	24	48,168	12.5	5.3	0.38	0.7	1.7	8.1*
65924	77 CUTLASS C OFFEN	5-79	13	12	23,234	15.9	4.1	0.19	0.5	0.3	5.1
				5	10,467	16.8	3.9	0.11	0.2	0.5	4.7
66346	77 CUTLASS COTE	9-78	19	18	42,180	16.6	4.1	0.09	0.3	0.3	4.8
				3	11,050	16.3*	4.3	0.03		0.7	5.0
66456	77 CUTLASS JOHNSON	2-79	19	18	34,351	14.4*	4.5	0.08	0.3	0.4	5.3
				5	9,851	14.3*	4.6*	0.14	1.0	0.5	6.2*
66676	77 CUTLASS KNAPP	11-78	18	17	37,905	15.3	4.2	0.25	0.3	1.1	5.9
				5	9,617	14.4*	4.5*	0.27	1.0	3.5	9.3*
68394	77 CUTLASS SAVAGE	12-79	13	13	51,031	14.9	4.1	0.19	0.5	0.5	5.3
				5	7,095	14.6*	4.2	0.13	0.2	1.3	5.8*
70112	78 GRANADA R RUDD		5	4	5,795	14.2	4.8*	0.07	0.1	0.1	5.1
				4	5,795	14.2	4.8*	0.07	0.1	0.1	5.1

"S" DESIGNATES SOLD VEHICLE.
"*" DENOTES OUT OF LINE CONDITION. REFER TO "INDIVIDUAL VEHICLE OPERATING DATA."
FIGURES IN SHADED AREA ARE YEAR TO DATE.

437

TABLE 7-9 (cont.)

MAY 1978   CONSOLIDATED   OPERATING DATA

CLIENT NUMBER: 51400

											MONTHS IN SERVICE LIFETIME	MONTHS REPORTED LIFETIME	MONTHS REPORTED YEAR TO DATE	MONTHS IN SERVICE YEAR TO DATE
											14233	13136	3104	3374

LIFETIME	GAS	OIL AND LUBE	TIRES	NORMAL REPAIRS	TOTAL RUNNING EXPENSES	ACCIDENT REPAIRS LESS RECOVERIES	MISC.	RENTALS	ADJ. TO RESERVE	INSUR-ANCE	TOTAL	LESS PERSONAL USE CHARGE	NET TOTAL
DOLLAR COST	1041757	33342	99133	232112	1406344	27138	86338	2021258	109		3541185	437688	3103497
AV. DOLLAR COST/MONTH	79	3	8	18	108	2	7	142			259	33	226
CENTS COST PER MILE	4.5	.14	.4	1.0	6.0	.1	.4	8.1			14.6	1.9	12.7

YEAR TO DATE													
DOLLAR COST	240767	8316	31737	72174	352994	14319	26399	453543	40346-		806909	102688	704221
AV. DOLLAR COST/MONTH	78	3	10	23	114	5	9	134	13-		249	33	216
CENTS COST PER MILE	4.8	.15	.6	1.3	6.6	.3	.5	7.7	.7-		14.4	2.0	12.4

VEHICLES IN SERVICE

NUMBER OF UNITS – 632

	TOTAL MILES REPORTED	BUSINESS MILES REPORTED	PERCENT BUSINESS MILES	AV. MONTHLY MILEAGE	GAS GALLONS	AV. COST PER GALLON	AV. MILES PER GALLON
LIFETIME	23,144,120	16,500,001	71.2	1,762	1,642,547.9	.63	14.1
YEAR TO DATE	5,414,335	4,141,224	76.4	1,744	369,079.6	.65	14.7
CURRENT	1,285,796	967,306	75.2		84,700.4		

Table 7-10 shows the total monthly costs of a business car for the past ten years, as well as the monthly operating expenses, business miles driven, and miles per gallon. It should be noted that business mileage increased from 1968 through 1973 and then dropped sharply. Last year it was practically at the same level it was in 1968. The average business car is using 30 gallons of gasoline less per month now than in 1973, and 12 gallons of gasoline less than in 1969. This conservation, which is a result of improved gasoline mileage and the professional fleet managers' wise selection of economic vehicles, has partially offset the impact of inflation and increased costs on fleet expenses.

FLEET RESPONSE TO CHANGE

The professionally managed corporate fleet responded to increases in vehicle costs and operating expenses in three separate but interrelated ways: (1) Reductions in size and weight of the car used in fleets; (2) better cost control systems; and (3) increased "charge-back."

According to the NAFA's annual New Car Acquisition Surveys, during the 1971 model year the predominant fleet vehicle was the so-called "standard" size car with a 119- to 121-inch wheelbase weighing more than 4,000 pounds. This car accounted for 72 percent of the new car acquisitions in that model year. The declining number of acquisitions in this category began before the oil embargo and the

TABLE 7-10 Operating (or Running) Expenses per Month

Year	Miles per gallon	Business miles per month	Cents per mile	Dollars per month	Cost per month (dollars)	Cost per mile (cents)
1968	13.2	1,879	0.0369	79.87	159.81	0.0738
1969	12.9	1,875	0.0392	85.51	171.42	0.0786
1970	12.6	1,891	0.0412	91.60	185.45	0.0833
1971	12.5	1,919	0.0438	98.51	192.58	0.0857
1972	12.2	1,932	0.0448	102.15	203.33	0.0891
1973	11.8	1,933	0.0470	106.99	213.29	0.0938
1974	12.2	1,805	0.0609	129.09	234.13	0.1106
1975	12.3	1,863	0.0631	138.41	238.55	0.1087
1976	13.0	1,880	0.0630	140.10	243.98	0.1097
1977	13.6	1,880	0.0642	142.61	264.65	0.1192

Total cost to company per car per month

Source: U.S. Composite Fleet Performance Report prepared by Peterson, Howell & Heather, Inc., Baltimore, Maryland.

government's mandated fuel economy standards; it continued until 1978, as shown on Table 7-11.

The typical fleet vehicle today is the so-called "mid-size" car with a 106- to 114-inch wheelbase weighing between 3,000 and 3,500 pounds. These mid-size cars will account for 71 percent of the new car acquisitions during the 1979 model year. Large cars (more than 114-inch wheelbase and weighing more than 3,500 pounds) will take 23 percent of the new car orders while small cars (less than 106-inch wheelbase and weighing under 3,000 pounds) take 6 percent.[8]

With the switch to smaller, lighter cars has come a gradual shift to smaller engines; first to smaller 8-cylinder engines and now to 6-cylinder engines. In 1970, at least 90 percent of the fleet cars were equipped with 8-cylinder engines; today only 60 percent are ordered with 8-cylinder engines and approximately 40 percent are ordered with 6-cylinder engines and this percentage is increasing.

The second response to increased expenses was to develop better cost-control systems to monitor growing automotive expenses. These cost controls, often automated, enable the fleet manager to receive frequent reports on performance and costs, to maintain accurate records, to spot problems quickly, and to take corrective action. These sophisticated records provide data on comparative makes and models to assist the fleet manager in his efforts to acquire vehicles that are both economical to operate and high in resale value.

The third response was to increase the personal-use "chargeback." In almost all sales and service fleets, the car operator is permitted to use

---

[8]. NAFA *Bulletin, supra* n. 6.

TABLE 7-11 Trends (Percent) in New Car Acquisitions by Fleets

Car size	Model year									
	1970	1971	1972	1973	1974	1975	1976	1977	1978	1979
Compact or small	4	1	2	1	2	22	31	29	4	6
Intermediate or mid-size	26	27	38	49	58	72	61	62	81	71
Standard or large	70	72	60	50	39	6	6	8	15	23

For the surveys through the 1977 model year, car categories were based on wheelbase: *Standard* size cars were those with 119-inch or longer wheelbase; and *intermediate* was a car with 112-118-inch wheelbase, while a *compact* was a car with less than 112-inch wheelbase.

For the 1978 and 1979 model year surveys, NAFA adopted a new classification system in order to keep pace with the introduction of the new models from General Motors and later from other manufacturers. It categorized cars by both wheelbase and weight. The new categories are *large*—over 114-inch wheelbase, weight more than 3,501 pounds; *Mid-Size*—106-to-114-inch wheelbase, weight between 3,000 and 3,500 pounds; *Small*—under 106-inch wheelbase, weight under 3,500 pounds. If a car does not fit both wheelbase and weight category, weight is then used to determine the category it is placed in.

These data were developed from the annual New Car Acquisition surveys conducted by NAFA.

the car for personal driving after working hours, on weekends, and on vacations. The great majority of companies always charged for this use and in recent years increased the charges substantially.

In conjunction with these cost-controlling actions, the NAFA and its members undertook in 1975 a major market research project to develop a set of guidelines for the automobile manufacturers who wished to serve the fleet market. This project, known as NAFCAR, produced the first realistic data on current fleet vehicles, requirements for future vehicles in terms of size, weight, equipment, safety, carrying capacity, and other desirable features (primarily technological improvements). Two years later, in 1977, the survey was repeated to determine if the manufacturers had made any progress in meeting the fleet requirements.

The major problem areas were the same in both surveys: Protection from rust and corrosion, wheel alignment, shock absorbers, weather stripping, paint, and gasoline mileage. Unfortunately, in four of these problem areas—wheel alignment, paint, weather stripping, and protection from rust and corrosion—the degree of dissatisfaction expressed by fleet administrators increased as the size of the vehicle decreased. In other words, the smaller their cars, the greater their level of dissatisfaction. Only in gasoline consumption was this trend reversed.

The fleet administrators expressed a strong preference for today's mid-size car—a vehicle with a wheelbase between 106 and 114 inches weighing between 3,000 and 3,500 pounds. However, they felt that current models in this size range had inadequate rear leg room and trunk space.

Features the fleet administrators would like to see built into future vehicles include fluid level indicators, improved cold-start performance, brake wear indicators, on-board diagnostic equipment, standardized instrument panels, and an antiskid device.[9]

FUTURE CHANGES

In contemplating future passenger car developments, the fleet administrator basically has two choices: (1) He can anticipate the trends and move to smaller cars that meet his needs as soon as they are available; or (2) he can stay with the larger cars he is currently using until he is forced to make a change because they are no longer being manufactured. This choice is not as simple as it might appear to be. There is always resistance to change. As the advantages of the change to smaller, lighter cars become apparent, resistance tends to diminish. Nevertheless, downsizing will create substantial problems for fleets. As pointed out earlier, one of the considerations in fleet car selection is to "satisfy the operator." It will take a great deal of persuasion to convince the company employee that he will be satisfied with a smaller and smaller car.

---

9. *NAFCAR I and II*, research projects sponsored by NAFA (1975 and 1977).

In many cases, the corporate employee uses his car as his office. The car assigned to the employee is thus a symbol of that employee's status in the company. Another problem arises from the normal use of the business car. Table 7-8 *supra* points out the extremely high mileage use of fleet cars. Comfort and safety must be considered as well as efficiency and economy.

Although the managers of fleets are concerned about the effects of further downsizing, they are sure that the development and continued improvement of diagnostic equipment, both in the vehicle and the service station, will improve vehicle operation and reduce maintenance costs. The ability to identify, remove, and replace faulty components on the basis of electronic diagnostic devices rather than a mechanic's trial and error will be a great step forward. But it will not be without its cost. For many years the industry and public have complained about a shortage of skilled mechanics who are able to repair complicated components, or even to locate the source of trouble. The development of diagnostic equipment may help eliminate some of the need for these skilled mechanics, but will greatly increase the demand for more skilled technicians, trained to use sophisticated electronic diagnostic equipment.

THE ROLE OF PROFESSIONAL FLEET MANAGERS IN REGULATORY PROGRAMS

In looking to the future, it is essential that we realize that the automobile is, and will continue to be, the dominant mode of transportation in the United States. No form of mass transit will replace it, particularly for business use. In all probability, the internal combustion engine, at least in a form similar to what is now in use, will continue to be the power plant in the foreseeable future. There is nothing in sight to replace it.

There is no doubt that existing regulations have contributed to safer, more economical vehicles that are less offensive to the environment. Most fleet operators would be opposed to additional "regulation-induced" changes, however. The industry and its fleet customers are still struggling to comply with regulations promulgated by DOT, the Department of Energy, and the EPA that at times seem to be contradictory and confused.

At the present time the need is not for additional regulations, but for enforcement of the existing ones and the development of a cooperative spirit between regulatory bodies that will eliminate conflict and counterproductive actions between them.

In the creation of new regulatory programs, we suggest that greater use be made of professionally managed fleets. They can serve a dual purpose: They are a natural testing ground for new developments because of the high mileage use of fleet cars; and they can provide accurate data based on the extensive record-keeping systems employed in their cost-control systems. The members of the NAFA have cooperated willingly—and will continue to do so—with the industry and government agencies in such programs.

The automobile industry has made substantial progress in the past five years developing new vehicles that are smaller, lighter, more economical to operate, safer, and cleaner. If the industry is permitted to operate under existing regulations it is our belief they will continue to improve their product and meet the needs of the general public as well as those of the fleet segment.

DISCUSSION

CLARENCE DITLOW: I noticed one contradiction in Mr. Berke's position, which was that fleet owners wanted many features such as breakwear indicators, diagnostics, antiskid breaks, smaller car size, and so on, but disliked regulation. How can fleetowners expect to benefit from new features in the absence of regulation when in fact most automobile improvements have been made in response to regulatory pressures?

The bumper standard has been cited as an example of the adverse effects of regulation. It is claimed that the standard resulted in heavier bumpers, but all manufacturers are now moving toward lighter, more efficient designs. Regulation must be relied upon to produce most of the changes that consumers would find desirable.

BERKE: Fleet owners are not opposed to a regulation; rather, we wish to give manufacturers more time to respond to current regulations adequately.

GOVERNMENT: Let us look at the question of what consumers want in an automobile.

BERKE: The fleet owners' goal is to get a high resale value on used fleet cars. They find that options and luxury appointments can compensate for small car size.

PUBLIC INTEREST: Consumers form many subgroups, most of which are not very well informed about the product they are buying.

GOVERNMENT: One thing consumers want is more horsepower, but they are not getting it.

ACADEMIC: Is it true that "business users" account for about 60 percent of car sales?

AUTO (U.S.): 25 percent of Fords are sold to fleets.

BERKE: 13 percent of General Motors cars are sold to fleets.

ACADEMIC: So business users would be very substantial. If the actual figure even approaches 60 percent, then tax incentives to business for buying innovative vehicles could be a strong market incentive to manufacturers.

LUCIEN NEDZI: Many business cars are bought in the same less rational mode found among individual private consumers.

AUTO (U.S.): If fleets are as sizeable a market as they seem to be, when the allowable number of large cars on the road becomes extremely limited, fleets may come to own most big cars and turn that segment of the market into an automobile futures market subject to all manner of instabilities.

DAVE STOCKMAN: I foresee a huge consumer backlash long before the 1985 standards are enacted. Consumers will rebel around 1980 or 1981 and there will be a rollback of the standards. Tragically, this will occur only after the industry has spent billions of dollars unnecessarily.

AUTO (U.S.): If our rate of innovation continues apace, we will be able to meet the 1985 standards with an acceptable car. The problem is, it will cost consumers and the industry a bundle. Is the price worth paying?

ACADEMIC: I disagree with the Congressman's scenario. There was a trend toward small cars before regulation began; other countries downsized via market responses, without regulation. There is no indication that regulation will cause a backlash.

SUPPLIER: But the trend in Europe today is toward larger cars.

Appendix 1

SYMPOSIUM PARTICIPANTS*

Abernathy, William J.
Professor of Business
Harvard Business School

Agnelli, Umberto
Vice Chairman and President
FIAT

Alpert, Norman
Manager
Environmental Health Programs
Exxon Research & Engineering Company

Amato, Ignazio
Professor
Director of Research and Development, Italy
FIAT

Ashford, Nicholas A.
Professor of Technology and Policy
Center for Policy Alternatives
Massachusetts Institute of Technology

Aurich, Wolfgang
BMW

Ayers, Ruston F.
Manager
Sales Administration
ITT Automotive Electrical Products Division

Balle, Freddy
Long Range Planning Director
Renault

Berke, Robert
Executive Director
National Association of Fleet Administrators, Inc.

Blumer, James W.
Group Vice President
Marketing and Technical
Libbey Owens Ford Company

Boston, Gerald W.
Associate Counsel
Office of the General Counsel
Ford Motor Company

Bower, Joseph L.
Professor of Business
Harvard Business School

Boyd, J. Hayden
Senior Research Associate
Charles River Associates

Boylan, Myles G.
Policy Analyst
National Science Foundation

Bradley, Stephen P.
Professor of Business and Associate Director of Research
Harvard Business School

Brower, E. S.
President
Automotive Products Division
Allied Chemical Corporation

* Affiliations as of the date of the Symposium, October 19–20, 1978

Bunch, Howard M.
Manager
Transportation Research Projects
Highway Safety Research Institute
University of Michigan

Businaro, U. L.
Professor and
  Director of Research Center
FIAT

Callahan, Joseph M.
Editor and Radio Commentator
Automotive Industries Magazine and Station WJR

Claybrook, Joan
Administrator
National Highway Traffic Safety Administration
U.S. Department of Transportation

Coleman, Robert V.
Automobile Specialist
Bureau of Domestic Development
U.S. Department of Commerce

Condit, E. C.
Director
Marketing Planning
Libbey Owens Ford Company

Coonley, Philip
Economist
Transportation Systems Center
U.S. Department of Transportation

Costantino, James
Director of Transportation Systems
Transportation Systems Center
U.S. Department of Transportation

Curley, Kathleen Foley
Harvard Business School

Davis, Richard
Administrative Assistant to the Vice President
Environmental Activities Staff
General Motors Corporation

Devereaux, William J.
Chief
Standards Modification Division
National Highway Traffic Safety Administration
U.S. Department of Transportation

Ditlow, Clarence
Center for Automobile Safety

Duchesneau, Thomas D.
Professor of Economics
University of Maine, Orono

Dugoff, Howard
Deputy Administrator
National Highway Traffic Safety Administration
U.S. Department of Transportation

Edwards, Allen L.
Vice President
Automotive Sales
Sheller-Globe-Corporation

Eltinge, Lamont
Director of Research
Eaton Corporation

Erickson, Walter W.
President
Gelco Services

Evans, Thomas
Chief Engineer
Research and Development
Rockwell International

Falberg, Edward O.
Executive Vice President
Staff
Gulf & Western Manufacturing Co.

Fearnsides, John J.
Deputy Under Secretary
U.S. Department of Transportation

Feuer, Seymour S.
Group Vice President
McCord Group
Ex-Cell-O Corporation

Finkelstein, Michael M.
Acting Associate Administrator for Rulemaking
National Highway Traffic Safety Administration
U.S. Department of Transportation

Frazier, M. L.
Director of Marketing
TRW, Inc.

Freeman, Cy
Director of Marketing
ITT Automotive Products Group

Fukuda, Minoru
Executive Director
Management Intelligence Co., Ltd.

Gage, James F.
Vice-President
Engineering
Prestolite Electrical Division

Gillespie, L. H., Jr.
Plastic Products and Resins Department
E.I. du Pont de Nemours & Co.

Ginsburg, Douglas H.
Assistant Professor of Law
Harvard Law School

Glaspie, James D.
Sales Manager
The Budd Company

Glynn, Edward F., Jr.
Deputy Assistant Director
Bureau of Competition
Federal Trade Commission

Goodson, R. Eugene
Institute for Interdisciplinary Engineering Studies
Purdue University

Green, Robert
Technical Director
North American Automotive Group
ITT

Hanson, Kirk O.
Harvard Business School

Hauth, Willard E.
Program Manager
Automotive Electronics Systems
Motorola, Inc.

Hirsch, Robert L.
General Manager
Petroleum Exploratory Research
Exxon Research & Engineering Company

Hogan, C. F.
Chairman
McCord Corporation

Hoge, Robert R.
Executive Director
Business Development
The Bendix Corporation

Holt, Eugene
Exxon Research & Engineering Company

Howard, Robert M.
Legislative Assistant to Congressman John D. Dingell
House Interstate and Foreign Commerce Committee

Itoh, Kunihiko
Administrative Manager
Toyota Motor Company

Jackson, John
Professor of Political Science
University of Pennsylvania

Jenkins, C. L.
Director
Government Relations
General Motors Corporation

Jenny, Larry
Project Leader
Transportation
Office of Technology Assessment
U.S. Congress

John, Richard
Chief
Energy Programs Division
Transportation Systems Center
U.S. Department of Transportation

Kahn, Helen
Bureau Chief
Washington Automotive News

Kasper, Daniel M.
Professor of Business
Harvard Business School

Kawano, Jiro
General Manager
Toyota Motor Company

Kehrl, Howard
Executive Vice President
Technical Staffs and Corporate Product Planning
General Motors Corporation

Ketcham, Brian
Vice President and Chief Engineer
Citizens for Clean Air

Kinzler, Peter
Counsel
Consumer Protection and Finance Subcommittee
U.S. House of Representatives

Konishi, Kenkichi
Director
Japan Automobile Manufacturers Association

Kotyk, Michael
Division Chief
Sheet Products
U.S. Steel

Kramer, Larry
The Washington Post

Kuhlman, Kay R.
International Trade Specialist
Office of International Economic Research
U.S. Department of Commerce

Kwoka, John
Economist
Federal Trade Commission

Lapham, Edward
Financial Editor
Automotive News

Leeth, B. Timothy
Professional Staff Member
Committee on Appropriations
U.S. Senate

Leone, Robert A.
Professor of Business
Harvard Business School

Lindquist, Terry K.
Vice President
Engineering
Transportation Equipment Group
Borg-Warner Corporation

MacDonald, Harold C.
Vice President
Research and Engineering Staff
Ford Motor Company

MacKay, Michael L.
Director
Product Development
Gould Inc.
Engine Parts Division

Makowski, M. P.
Director of Gould Materials
Research Laboratory
Gould Inc.

Mallon, Paul B.
Industry Specialist
Merrill Lynch Pierce Fenner, & Smith, Inc.

Maxwell, Robert L.
Group Manager
Transportation
Office of Technology Assessment
U.S. Congress

McAllister, Thomas E.
Marketing Manager
Automotive
Aluminum Company of America

McCabe, Robert J.
Director
Treasurer's Office
Administration Section
General Motors Corporation

McCarthy, Kevin B.
Counsel
U.S. House of Representatives
Committee on Interstate and Foreign Commerce
Subcommittee on Transportation and Commerce

McCraw, Thomas K.
Professor of Business
Harvard Business School

Messinger, Richard D.
Vice President
Research & Development
Cincinnati Milacron Inc.

Meyer, John R.
Professor of Business
Harvard Business School

Meyer, W. A. P.
Technical Consultant
Gulf Science & Technology Company

Mills, D. Quinn
Professor of Business
Harvard Business School

Minor, Wendell L.
Vice President
North American Tire Subsidiaries
The Goodyear Tire & Rubber Company

Misch, Herbert L.
Vice President
Environmental & Safety Engineering
Ford Motor Company

Moller, John V.
Assistant Director
Government Affairs Division
Motor Vehicle Manufacturers Association

Morrison, Allan
Visiting Professor of Law
Harvard Law School

Nash, Carl E.
Special Assistant to the Administrator

National Highway Traffic Safety Administration
U.S. Department of Transportation

Nave, Charles H.
Technical Planning Manager
NARO
Ford Motor Company

Nedzi, Lucien N.
Member of Congress

Negro, Alberto
Director
Research and Development, USA Branch
FIAT

Nulty, Timothy
Senate Committee on Commerce, Science and Technology
Science and Transportation Subcommittee

O'Day, Paul T.
Deputy Director
Bureau of Domestic Business Development
U.S. Department of Commerce

Orski, C. Kenneth
Vice President
The German Marshall Fund

Palmer, James
Administrator
Research and Special Programs Administration
U.S. Department of Transportation

Pearce, Michael C.
Head of Automotive Research
The Economist Intelligence Unit Ltd.

Pettifor, Andrew H.
National Science Foundation

Plourde, Albert M.
Director
Planning
Carter Carburetor Division of ACF Industries, Inc.

Popovich, Frank T.
Director
Automotive Services Group
Data Resources, Inc.

Potter, David S.
Vice President
Environmental Activities Staff
General Motors Technical Center
General Motors Corporation

Powell, Samuel F., III
Acting Chief
Technology Assessment Division
National Highway Traffic Safety Administration
U.S. Department of Transportation

Racey, L. J.
Group General Manager
ITT North America Automotive

Randall, Donald
Washington Representative
Automotive Service Councils

Reistrup, John
Chief
Division of Consumer Affairs
U.S. Department of Transportation

Ricci, Robert C.
Chief
Energy Demand Analysis Branch
Transportation Systems Center
U.S. Department of Transportation

Roberts, Louis W.
Director of Energy and Environment
Transportation Systems Center
U.S. Department of Transportation

Ronan, Arthur P.
President
On-Highway Group
Automotive Operations
Rockwell International

Ronstadt, Robert
Professor of Business
Babson College

Rosenbloom, Richard S.
Professor of Business and Associate Dean for Research and Course Development
Harvard Business School

Rozendaal, Jan W.
Owner/President
Nordic Ford-Toyota-BMW

Rubinger, Bruce
Senior Operations Research Analyst
Transportation Systems Center
U.S. Department of Transportation

Schmidt, Rudiger
Department Manager
Volkswagenwerk AG

Schultz, Walter F.
Vice President
General Manager
Doehler-Jarvis Castings

Scott, Will
Vice President
North American Governmental Affairs
Ford Motor Company

Seiffert, Ulrich
Chief Safety Engineer
Volkswagenwerk AG

Shackson, Richard H.
Director
Environmental Research Office
Ford Motor Company

Shapiro, William
Manager
Regulatory Affairs
Volvo of America Corporation

Shelton, Joanna R.
International Economist
U.S. Department of the Treasury

Shimokawa, Koichi
Visiting Professor of Business
Harvard Business School

Silbergeld, Mark
Director
Washington Office
Consumers Union

Smaglick, Paul W.
General Sales Manager
A.O. Smith Corporation

Smick, A. Edward
Professional Staff Member
Committee on Commerce, Science and Transportation

Speck, Paul
Technical Writer
General Motors Corporation

Stockman, David
Member of Congress

Stork, Eric O.
Visiting Fellow in Technology and Public Policy
A. A. Potter Engineering Center
Purdue University

Strombotne, Richard L.
Director
Office of Automotive Fuel Economy Standards
National Highway Traffic Safety Administration
U.S. Department of Transportation

Suzuki, Yasuhiko
Vice President
External Relations
Nissan Motor Corp. in U.S.A.

Terry, Sydney L.
Vice President
Public Responsibility & Consumer Affairs
Chrysler Corporation

Tessieri, John E.
Vice President
Research & Technical Department
Texaco

Thornton, Raymond
Member of Congress

Tourney, Russ
Accounts Manager for the Chrysler Corporation
National Steel Corporation

Triplett, William C., II
Washington Representative
American Honda Motor Company, Inc.

Utterback, James M.
Research Associate
Massachusetts Institute of Technology

Van Rennes, A. B.
Associate Director
Bendix Research Laboratories

Veraldi, Lewis C.
Vice President
Advanced Vehicles Development
Ford Motor Company

Vernon, Raymond
Professor of Business
Harvard Business School

von Hulsen, Hans-Viggo
Head, Foreign Legal Dept.
Volkswagenwerk AG

Webber, Melvin
Professor
Institute of Urban and Regional Development
University of California at Berkeley

Weiss, Elliott J.
Professor of Law
Cardozo School of Law

Wells, Louis T., Jr.
Professor of Business
Harvard Business School

White, Lawrence J.
Professor of Economics
New York University

Whitford, Robert K.
Deputy Director
Transportation Systems Center
U.S. Department of Transportation

Wilkins, Mira
Professor of Economics
Florida International University

Wilkinson, W. R.
Executive Director
Product Strategy Development
Corporate Strategy & Analysis Staff
Ford Motor Company

Winsauer, Richard
Director of Planning
Automotive Products Division
Motorola, Inc.

Wolek, Francis W.
Deputy Assistant Secretary for Science and Technology
U.S. Department of Commerce

Administrative

Curhan, Joan P.
Research Administrator

Rinehart, Margaret
Symposium Secretary

Research Assistants

Oberhofer, George

Ronan, Lawrence

Simonson, Gael

Appendix 2

BIBLIOGRAPHY

GENERAL

Books

Abernathy, William J. *The Productivity Dilemma: Roadblock to Innovation in the Automobile Industry.* Baltimore: Johns Hopkins University Press, 1977.

Bloomfield, Gerald. *The World Automotive Industry.* North Pomfret, Vermont: David and Charles, 1978.

Capron, William M., Ed. *Technological Change in Regulated Industries.* Washington: The Brookings Institution, 1971.

Grad, F. P., et al. *The Automobile and the Regulation.* Norman, Oklahoma: Oklahoma University Press, 1975.

Honda Motors. *Hondano Ayumi (Brief History of Honda).* Tokyo, 1974.

Kahn, A. *The Economics of Regulation.* New York: John Wiley & Sons, 1971.

Maxcy, George and Aubrey Silberston. *The Motor Industry.* London: George Allen & Unwin, 1959.

Nelson, Walter Henry. *Small Wonder, The Amazing Story of the Volkswagen.* Boston: Little, Brown and Co., 1950.

Nevins, Allan and Frank Ernest Hill. *Ford: The Times, The Man, The Company.* New York: Charles Scribner's Sons, 1954.

———. *Ford: Expansion and Challenge 1915–1933.* New York: Charles Scribner's Sons, 1957.

———. *Ford: Decline and Rebirth, 1933–1962.* New York: Charles Scribner's Sons, 1963.

Rousseau, Jacques. *Histoire Mondiale de l'Automobile.* Paris, 1958.

Schneider, Kenneth R. *Autokind vs. Mankind.* New York: W. W. Norton & Co., 1971.

Toder, Eric J. *Trade Policy and the U.S. Automobile Industry*. New York: Praeger Publishers, 1978.

White, Lawrence J. *The Automobile Industry Since 1945*. Cambridge: Harvard University Press, 1971.

Wilkins, Mira and Frank Ernest Hill. *American Business Abroad: Ford on Six Continents*. Detroit: Wayne State University Press, 1964.

Monographs

Abernathy, William J. and Balaji S. Chakravarthy. *Government Intervention and Innovation in Industry: A Policy Framework,* presented to the American Association for the Advancement of Science, Washington, February 15, 1978.

Common Cause. *With Only One Ear: A Common Cause Study of Industry and Consumer Representation Before Federal Regulatory Commissions*. Washington, August 1977.

Ford Motor Company. *State of the U.S. Automobile Industry*. Detroit, 1978.

Goodson, R. Eugene. *Federal Regulation of Motor Vehicles*. West Lafayette, Indiana: Purdue University, 1977. (A report prepared for the U.S. Department of Transportation.)

———. *Federal Regulation of Motor Vehicles: A Summary and Analysis*. West Lafayette, Indiana: Purdue University, 1977.

Ketcham, Brian. *Societal Cost Accounting: A New Tool for Planners—The Auto vs. The City*. New York: Citizens for Clean Air, Inc., 1976.

McLean, Robert F. *Lightweight Versus Heavyweight—The Contest of the Future*. SAE Transportation Paper, No. 770809. Society of Automotive Engineers, Passenger Car Meeting, September 1977.

National Analysts (a division of Booz-Allen). "Consumer Reaction to Title II Interpretations." *Final Phase I Report—The Automobile Consumer Information Study,* 1975.

Snell, Bradford C. *American Ground Transport: A Proposal for Restructuring the Automobile, Truck, Bus, and Rail Industries,* presented to the Subcommittee on Antitrust and Monopoly of the Committee on the Judiciary, U.S. Senate, Washington, February 26, 1974.

U.S. Congress, Office of Technology Assessment. *Technology Assessment of Changes in Future Use and Characteristics of the Automobile Transportation System*. Washington, 1978.

U.S. Department of Transportation, NHTSA. *The Contributions of Automobile Regulations*. Washington, 1978.

U.S. Department of Transportation. *Report by the Federal Task Force on Motor Vehicle Goals Beyond 1980*. Washington, 1976.

U.S. Office of Science and Technology. Ad Hoc Committee on the Cumulative Regulatory Effects on the Cost of Automotive Transportation (RECAT). *Final Report*. Washington, 1972.

Articles

Leone, Robert. "The Real Costs of Regulation." *Harvard Business Review* (November-December 1977), 57–66.

────── and **John J. Jackson.** "The Political Economy of Federal Regulatory Activity." *Public Regulation of Economic Activity.* Ed. G. Fromm. National Bureau of Economic Research, 1979.

Linden, L. H. and David Iverack. "The American System of Regulating the Automobile." *Regulating the Automobile.* Ed. John Heywood, et al. Energy Lab Report, MIT-EL-77-007. Cambridge: MIT, November 1977.

Wells, Louis T., Jr. "Automobiles." *Big Business and the State.* Ed. Raymond Vernon. Cambridge: Harvard University Press, 1974.

White, Lawrence J. "A Proposal for Restructuring the Automobile Industry." *Antitrust Law and Economics Review,* 7 (1975), 89ff.

FUEL ECONOMY

Monographs

Dato, Tasuka, Shizuo Yagi, Akina Ishizuya and Isao Fujii. *Research and Development of The Honda CVCC Engine.* SAE Transportation Paper, No. 740605, 1974.

Ketcham, Brian, William D. Balgord, and Stan Pinkwas. *Final Report to the National Highway Traffic Safety Administration on Nonpassenger Automobile Average Fuel Economy Standards, Model Years 1980–81.* New York: Citizens for Clean Air, Inc., 1978.

Ronan, Lawrence and William J. Abernathy. *The Honda Motor Company's CVCC Engine: A Case Study of Innovation.* Working Paper, No. HBS 78-43. Boston: Division of Research, Harvard Business School, 1978.

──────. *The Development and Introduction of the Turbocharger: A Case of Innovation in Response to Fuel Economy Regulation.* Working Paper, No. HBS 78-44, Boston: Division of Research, Harvard Business School, 1978.

Articles

"Conferees Agree to Penalize Makers of Gas Guzzlers." *Congressional Quarterly Weekly Report,* September 30, 1978, p. 2714.

Goldmuntz, Lawrence. "The Public Interest in Auto Fuel Efficiency." *Automobile Fuel Efficiency,* Vol. 2. Ed. M. Meader. McLean, Va.: Mitre Corp., 1978.

McLeod, M. K. "The Co-Ordinating Research Council." 41 *J. Petroleum,* No. 384 (December 1955).

Government Documents

U.S. Department of Transportation, Energy Panel. *Research and Development Opportunities for Improved Transportation Energy Usage.* Report No. DOT-TSC-OST-73-14. September 1972.

U.S. Department of Transportation, NHTSA. *First & Second Annual Reports to Congress.* Washington: Automotive Fuel Economy Program, January 1977 and January 1978.

U.S. Department of Transportation, NHTSA. *Data Analysis for 1981–1984 Passenger Automobile Fuel Economy Standards.* Washington, February 1977.

U.S. Department of Transportation, NHTSA. *Rulemaking Support Paper Concerning the 1981–1984 Passenger Auto Average Fuel Economy Standards.* Washington, July 1977.

Wharton EFA, Inc. *An Analysis of the Automobile Market: Modeling of the Long-Run Determinants of the Demand for Automobiles,* prepared for U.S. Department of Transportation, Transportation Systems Center, Cambridge, February 1977.

EMISSIONS CONTROL

Books

Dewees, D. W. *Economics and Public Policy: The Automobile Pollution Case.* Cambridge: MIT Press, 1974.

Grad, F. P., A. J. Rosenthal, et al. *The Automobile and the Regulation of its Impact on the Environment.* Norman: Oklahoma University Press, 1975.

Harrison, D., Jr. *Who Pays for Clean Air?* Cambridge: Ballinger Press, 1975.

Jacoby, H. D., J. D. Steinbruner, et al. *Clearing the Air: Federal Policy on Automotive Emissions Control.* Cambridge: Ballinger Press, 1973.

Krier, James E. and Edmund Ursin. *Pollution and Policy.* Berkeley: University of California Press, 1977.

Monographs

McCabe, L. J. and W. J. Koehl. *The Inter-Industry Emission Control Program—Eleven Years of Progress in Automotive Emissions and Fuel Economy Research.* SAE Transportation Paper, No. 780588. Society of Automotive Engineers, Passenger Car Meeting, June 1978.

National Academy of Science. *Report by the Committee on Motor Vehicle Emissions.* Washington, November 1974.

——— and **National Academy of Engineering.** *Air Quality and Automobile Emission Control,* prepared for the Committee on Public Works, U.S. Senate, September 1974.

Polinsky, A. Mitchell. *Notes on the Symmetry of Taxes and Subsidies in Pollution Control.* Discussion Paper, No. 515. Harvard Institute of Economic Research, 1976.

Socolofsky, J. F. *Cooperative Industry Research—Fear of Antitrust Violations as a Deterrent—Case History: Inter-Industry Emission Control (IIEC) Program.* Presented at U.S. Department of Commerce/Industrial Research Institute Seminar on Institutional and Legal Constraints to Cooperative Energy R&D, Washington, December 16, 1974.

Articles

Dewees, D. W. "The Costs and Technology of Pollution Abatement." *Approaches to Controlling Air Pollution*. Ed. A. F. Friedlaender. Cambridge: MIT Press, 1978.

Margolis, Howard. "The Politics of Auto Emissions." *The Public Interest* (Fall 1977), 6.

———. "Another View of the Politics of Auto Emissions Control." *Regulating the Automobile*. Ed. John Heywood et al. Energy Lab Report, MIT-EL-77-007. Cambridge: MIT, November 1977.

Mills, E. S. and Lawrence J. White. "Government Policies Toward Automotive Emissions Control." *Approaches to Controlling Air Pollution*. Ed. A. F. Friedlaender. Cambridge: MIT Press, 1978.

Stork, Eric O. "The Federal Statutory Emission Standards." *Advances in Environmental Science and Technology*, Vol. 7. Eds. J. N. Pitts, R. L. Metcalf, and A. C. Lloyd. New York: John Wiley & Sons, 1977.

White, Lawrence J. "The Auto Pollution Muddle." *The Public Interest* (Summer 1973), 97.

———. "American Automobile Emission Control Policy: A Review of the Reviews." in Vol. 2, *Journal of Environmental Economics and Management*, April 1976, p. 231.

———. "Effluent Charges as a Faster Means of Achieving Pollution Control." *Public Policy* (Winter 1976), 111.

Government Documents

Berens, A. P. and M. Hill. *Automobile Exhaust Emission Surveillance—Analysis of the FY 1974 Program*. Ann Arbor: Emission Control Technology Division, U.S. Environmental Protection Agency, September 1976.

Bernard, J. C. and J. F. Pratt. *An Evaluation of Restorative Maintenance on Exhaust Emissions of 1975–1976 Model Year In-Use Automobiles*. Ann Arbor: Emissions Control Technology Division, U.S. Environmental Protection Agency, December 1977.

Gafford, R. and R. Carlson. *Evaluation of Restorative Maintenance on 1975 and 1976 Light-Duty Vehicles in Detroit, Michigan*. Ann Arbor: Emission Control Technology Division, U.S. Environmental Protection Agency, May 1977.

Liljedahl, D. R. and J. Terry. *Evaluation of Restorative Maintenance on 1975 and 1976 Light-Duty Vehicles in Chicago, Illinois*. Ann Arbor: Emission Control Technology Division, U.S. Environmental Protection Agency, January 1977.

U.S. Environmental Protection Agency. *Automobile Emission Control—The Technical Status and Outlook as of December 1976*. Washington, 1976.

U.S. Environmental Protection Agency. *Progress in the Implementation of Motor Vehicle Emission Standards Through June 1975*. Washington, 1976.

U.S. Interagency Clean Car Advisory Committee. *Report on Low Emission Vehicle Certification Program Under Section 212 of the Clean Air Act,* submitted to the Low Emission Vehicle Certification Board, November 1974.

SAFETY

Books and Monographs

Lorange, Philip A. and **L. H. Linden.** *Automobile Safety Regulation: Technological Change and the Regulatory Process.* Energy Lab., MIT-EL-77-036. Cambridge: MIT, October 1977.

Nader, Ralph. *Unsafe at Any Speed.* New York: Pocket Books, 1965.

Peltzman, Sam. *Regulation of Automobile Safety.* Washington: American Enterprise Institute, 1975.

U.S. Department of Transportation, NHTSA. *The Contributions of Automobile Regulation (Preliminary Report).* Washington, June 1978.

Index

Abernathy, William J., 29, 71, 320
Accidents:
 counted 1977, 360
 externalities of, 12–13 (*See also* Externalities)
Accident statistics:
 downsizing's effect, 172
 scenarios, 175–177
Adam Opel A. G., 231
Adams, Brock, 144, 353
Adams, Walter, 129, 321
Administered prices, 324
Administrative Procedure Act, 73, 122–123, 127
Advertising, and car safety, 425
Air bags, 29, 328n.17, 345, 369, 374
 Eaton's regulatory experience, 53
 effect on fatalities, 177 (*See also* Fatality rates)
 as passive restraint, 79, 81
 product liability, 93 (*See also* Product liability)
Aircraft industry, and government sponsored research, 37
Air pollution (*see* Pollution control)
Air Pollution Research Advisory Counsel, purpose, 335
Alaska pipeline, 362

Alexander, Robert B., 330
Alpert, Norman, 344–345
Aluminum industry, 189–190, 192
 downsizing's effect, 172
American Law Institute, Restatement (Second) of the Law of Torts, 91
American Motors Corporation:
 capital expenditures, tables, 209–210
 debt position 1985, tables, 207–208
 financial position 1985, table, 206
 geographical markets, 153
 light truck fuel standards, 132–133 (*See also* Fuel economy; Light trucks)
 Renault, joint distribution, 249–250
American Petroleum Institute, 334, 352
American Public Transit Association, 352
American Trucking Association, 352
Antidumping laws, 253
Antilock brakes, regulation barriers, 53
Antiskid brakes, 29

461

Antiskid brakes (*Cont.*):
  fleet cars, 441
  product liability, 93 (*See also* Product liability)
Antitrust law:
  Big Four consent decree, 339, 341, 343–344, 406–407
  effect on research and development, 7
  international competition, 289
Arab Oil Embargo of 1973, 120, 144, 248, 328, 357, 394, 433
Arbitration, suggested in product liability cases, 101–102
Army, Tank Automotive Command, 60
Asbestos, 112, 115
Ashford, Nicholas, 112–115
Aspen/Volare, 428
Assumption of risk, narrowly construed, 100
Ault v. International Harvester, 94n.11
Austin car, 228
Australia, auto industry between wars, 232
Autobahn, 236
Automobile industry:
  barrier effect of regulation, 52–54
  Big-Three's innovation criticized, 129
  capital-intensive, 272
  changes in operation, 146
  collusion, 17–18, 28, 339, 341, 343–344, 406–407
  computers, 320, 329
  concentration's implications, 17–19
  conditions for entry into, 305
  consumers and safety information, 428–430
  deconcentration arguments, 19–21, 36
  fleets (*see* Fleet vehicles)
  foreign business of major producers, table, 222

Automobile industry (*Cont.*):
  fuel economy standards, reactions, 121 (*See also* Fuel economy)
  government relationships, 74–75
  Japan, 312–313 (*See also* Honda Motors; Japan; Toyota)
  lobbies, 352–354
  mature oligopoly, 291
  organizational changes, 158–159
  posture toward media, 347
  small car sales, 151
  Spain's development of, 246, 266
  suppliers, 211
    major multinational, 221n.1
  transnational character illustrated, 244
  United States, 263–265
  vehicle model variety reduction, 150
  world economic integration, 244, 245
  (*See also* Corporations, Industrial; Innovation; Invention; Research and development; Technology)
Automobile Manufacturers Association, 149
Automobiles:
  costs, sticker *and* societal, 360
  crashworthiness, 425–427 (*See also* Crash testing; Testing procedures)
  externalized costs and benefits, 11–17 (*See also* Externalities)
  Office of Technology Assessment study, 8
  ratings program, 428–430
  regulatory prescriptions, 11
  social and dollar costs, 349–351
  social impact, four analyses, 346, 355–357
Automotive engineering, regulation's stimulus to, 329

Automotive fuel economy standards:
  measures to implement, 199
  simulation model of impact on Big Four, 198–210
  (*See also* Fuel economy)
Automotive products, United States–Canada trade, tables and figures, 241–242
Automotive water pollution, 360–361

"Bad man" theories, 18
Balance of payments, 397
  Japan and United States compared, 8
  regulation's impact, 135–136
  United States deficits, 237
Balgord, William, 357–358
Barker v. Lull, 92n.3
Barrier effect, regulation and innovation, 52–54, 60
Battery industry, 190
Beame, Abraham, 364
Bench trial, suggested in products liability cases, 102–103
Bergsten, C. Fred, 245
Berke, Robert, 444–445
BL Ltd., 244
  foreign business, table, 222
Black Americans, auto industry employment, 132
Black box, 181–182
Blow-by discovered, 407
Bobit Publications, Inc., 434
Bordinat, Eugene, 359
Bradley, Stephen P., 212–213
Brinkmanship, 405–406
Brower, E. S., 211
Buildings:
  codes, 65–66
  regulatory instruments, types, 66–67
Bullock Committee of Parliament, 25n.45

Bumpers, 329n.17, 359, 368, 444
Bunch, Howard, 178–179
Bureaucracy, 157
Business judgment rule, 21

Calculators, prices schematically shown, 49
California:
  automotive exhaust standards, 41
  emissions devices, inspection, 415 (*See also* Emissions control; Pollution control)
Canada, Ford's early penetration, 226–227
Canadian Automobile Agreement, 239–240, 245, 272
Capital expenditures, Big Four, tables, 209–210
Capital investments, 163
Capron, William B., 50–51
Carbon monoxide, 307, 335, 399, 403, 408–412
  Clean Air Act Amendments, 124 (*See also* Clean Air Act)
  in-use emissions, table, 412
  (*See also* Fuel economy; Nitrogen oxides)
Carcinogens, 358, 394 (*See also* Diesel engines; Dieselization)
Car owners 1939, comparisons by country, 232
Catalytic converter, 146, 162, 190, 192, 290, 294, 358, 394
"Catch 22," 186, 359
Caterpillar Tractor, beadless tire, 344
Center for Auto Safety, 354
Center for the Study of Responsive Law, 336
Chakravarthy, B. S., 71
Chemical companies, and product liability cases, 112–113
Chenea, Paul, 320
Chevette, 130, 151, 152, 249, 284

463
Index

464
Index

Chokuhan marketing system, 309–310 (*See also* Honda Motors; Japan; Toyota)
Chrysler Corporation:
  Aspen/Volare, 428
  CAFE's effect on geographical markets, 153 (*See also* Corporate average fuel economy; Fuel economy)
  capital expenditures, tables, 209–210
  cleaner air package, 325
  debt position 1985, tables, 207–208
  electronic engine controls, 181 (*See also* Electronic engine controls)
  emissions control touted, 407–408
  European divestiture, 54, 212–213, 244, 263–264, 265
  financial position 1985, table, 206
  foreign business, table, 222
  fuel standards, impact, 134–135
  Jefferson Avenue plant, Detroit, 131, 156
  light truck fuel standards, 133 (*See also* Light trucks)
  Omni/Horizon criticized, 426–428, 431–432
  overseas suppliers, 136
  product characteristics, 147
  product mix, 152
  threatened by CAFE standards, 155
Citizens for Clean Air, Inc., 128–129, 354
C.I.T. Service Leasing Corporation, fleet forms, 436–438 (*See also* Fleet vehicles)
Claybrook, Joan, 145, 426
Clean Air Act:
  automotive exhaust reduction, 41
  electric vehicles certification, 59,

Clean Air Act (*Cont.*):
  60, 62 (*See also* Electric vehicles)
  1970 Amendments, 16, 119–120, 340, 364, 376, 379, 404–405, 408
  emission numerically valued, 124
  executive and congressional duties compared, 123
  Federal Water Pollution Act contrasted, 388
  1977 Amendments, 183, 403
Clean air standards, Japan, 310–311
Coatings industry, 190
Coleman, Robert V., 293–294
Coleman, William, 355
Collusion:
  emissions control consent decree, 339, 341, 343–344, 406–407
  standards as promoting, 406
Command and control strategies, 14, 36
  consequences of, 15
  consumer information as alternative, 36
  unanticipated features of, 15–19
Commerce Department, Domestic Policy Review Committee, 7–8
Common Cause, 354
Common Market (*see* European Economic Community)
Compacts, 283
Comparative negligence, 101–102
Competition:
  changes in competitors, 284–287, 289
  concerns, regulated product, 147
  fuel standards effect, 139
  models to explain:
    product life cycle model, 272, 274–275

Competition (*Cont.*):
   traditional economic model, 271–272
   public policy process, 148–149
   state-owned auto producers, 286–287
Computers, 320, 329
   fleet management, 436 (*See also* Fleet vehicles)
Congress, constituencies, 378–379
Connecticut, Route 7, 363
Consent decree, Big Four collusion to delay emissions control, 339, 341, 343–344, 406–407
Consumer information, as alternative to command and control, 36
   safety information, 428–430
Consumer markets, manufacturer's disclaimers in, 107–108
Consumer Price Index, fuel standards effect, 134
Consumer protection, European Economic Community Commission, 267
Consumer Protection Agency Bill, 157
Consumers, safety information, 428–430
Consumers Union, 354
   Chrysler's Omni/Horizon, 426–428, 431–432
Contextual uncertainty, 197–198
Contingent fees:
   advantages and disadvantages, 104–105
   British and American compared, 104
Contracts, in product liability cases, 106–108
Contrarino, Michael, 38
Contributory negligence, 97–98
Coordinating Research Council, purpose, 334–335

Cornell Aeronautical Laboratories, 326
Corporate average fuel economy (CAFE):
   alternatives to, 144
   downsizing GM's line, 153–154
   geographical markets, 153
   initiation, 144
   organizational changes in auto industry, 158–159
   passenger car standards, table, 145
   product mix, effect, 151
   strategies to counter, 155–156
   (*See also* Fuel economy)
Corporate social responsibility movement, 23
Corporations, industrial:
   federal chartering arguments, 21–24, 36
   model and real world contrasted, 21–22
   public directors on Board, 24–26
   (*See also* Automobile industry; Innovation; Invention; Research and development; Technology)
Couzen, James, 308
Crash testing, 79–80, 326–327
   crashworthiness, 425–427
   rating schemes, 429–430
   GM's simulation in ads, 425
   regulations, 270
   (*See also* Testing procedures)
Cross-licensing agreement, emission control technology, 406–407

Daihatsu Motor, 261
Daimler-Benz, 223
   foreign business, table, 222
Daimler Manufacturing Company, 225
Damages:
   and comparative negligence, 102

Damages (Cont.):
"pain and suffering" awards, 103
Dealer-franchising policies, 323
Deconcentration arguments, 19–21, 36
Defense Department:
  epochal innovation, support for, 50, 60, 62
  fuel economy improvements, 125–126
Defining a scenario, 198
de Gaulle, Charles, 261
Delaunay-Bellville, 223
Delaware corporation law, 22–23
Denver, Colorado, hydrocarbon and carbon monoxide emissions, 410–412
Design defect:
  definitional problems, 92, 94
  determining "unreasonably dangerous," 99
Design standards, 55–58, 147
  performance standards differentiated, 70–72, 75
  performance standards preferred, 65–66
  performance supplemented, 69–70
  (See also Performance standards)
Diesel engines, 147, 186, 336
  GM/EPA cooperation, 370
  GM's success, 154
  Societe Franco-Italiana de Motori, 266
  trends, 192 (See also Carcinogens; Dieselization)
Dieselization, 129, 138, 149, 158
  carcinogenic effects, 358, 394
Differentiation, United States strategy, 276, 281
Directors, automobile manufacturing corporations, 24–26
Direct selling systems, 309–310
Disc brakes, 251
Ditlow, Clarence, 178, 187, 354, 444

Diversification, as response to product life cycle, 275–276
Dodge v. Ford Motor Co., 21n.30
Dole, Robert, 7
Domestic Policy Review Committee, 7–8
Downsizing, 163
  fatalities and accidents, tables, 176–177
  fleet vehicles, effects, 441–442
  foreign investment in United States, 264
  GM's head start, 146, 150, 153–154
  industry's attitudes, 172
  motor vehicle weight reduction, 138
  risk of, table, 149
  rubber industry, 192
Drivers, 1995 profiles, 172–173
Driving conditions, American and world compared, 276
Drugs, regulations' effect on innovation, 51
Duesenberg Motor Company, 226
Duncombe, Henry, 121, 128–129, 130n.25, 147

Eaton, air bag development, 53
Eckhardt, Bob, 426
Economic practicality, 133–134
Economic risk scenario, Big Four, 209–210
Economies of scale:
  Fiat, 245
  GM's advantage, 147
  interchangeable parts, 237
Economist, 267
Economist Intelligence Unit, government's role, analysis, 262
Effluent fees, 373–374, 381
  consequences, 417
  objections to, 417–419
Elastic yardsticks, and performance standards, 67–69

Electric and Hybrid Vehicle Research, Development, and Demonstration Act, 120
Electric vehicle, 58–59, 60–62, 192
  Federal Electric and Hybrid Vehicle Program, 60–61
Electronic Assisted Scheduling, 320
Electronic engine controls, 180–188
  components of, 181–182
  maintenance, 182
  testers, 184–186
Elliptical tire, 156
Emergency Loan Guarantee Board, Lockheed investigation, 26
Emissions control, 386
  antitampering survey, table, 410
  bibliography, 401n.1
  brinkmanship promoted, 405–406
  Chrysler's aggressive actions, 407–408
  effluent fees, 416–420
  emissions vs. fuel economy, 180–181
  history, 406–409
  inspection and maintenance, 414–416
  in-use measurements, 409–412
  maintenance performance, table, 416
  perverse incentives to achieve, 405–406
  phasing's consequences, 412–413
  standards:
    setting described, 124–125
    table, 404
  (*See also* Pollution control)
Energy, distribution of consumption, table, 349
Energy Department, fuel economy research, 32

Energy Policy and Conservation Act, 16, 32, 120, 124–125, 127, 128, 133, 144, 180, 196, 251, 295
  political strategies of auto makers, 156
Energy Reorganization Act, 120
Energy Resources Council, 126
Energy Supply and Conservation Act of 1974, 126
Entrenchment, regulation's effect on innovation, 54–55, 60
Entrepreneurs, epochal innovation, 48
Envelopment, regulation's effect on innovation, 55–59, 60
Environmental & Resources Technology, Inc., 357–358
Environmental Defense Fund, 128, 354
Environmental impact statements, 362
Environmental Protection Agency, 336, 350
  Clean Air Act, 16 (*See also* Clean Air Act)
  electronic engine controls, 185 (*See also* Electronic engine controls)
  fuel economy improvements, 125–126
  innovation competition, 32
Epochal innovation, envelopment's effect, 58–59, 60–61
Epstein, Richard, 100
Equipment performance standards, 124
Escola v. Coca-Cola Bottling Co., 91n.1
Estes, Elliot M., 130, 401, 405, 409
Europe, fuel economy regulations, 82
European Economic Community, 221, 260, 290
  impact on auto industry, 235–236

European Economic Community Commission:
  legislative functions, 267
Excise tax:
  and fuel economy standards, 122
  gas guzzlers, 144, 155–156, 252
Executive branch, fuel economy activities 1970–1976, 141–142
Experimental safety cars, 326–327
Exports:
  British and German, 237
  Japanese growth, 261–262
  new cars, table, 229
  origin in product life cycle model, 274
  United States, 224, 227
    auto exports, table, 255–256
    history, 271–272, 274–275
    1920's and 1930's, 228
    value of exports, table, 257–258
Externalities, 321
  air pollution as negative, 420
  costs and benefits, 11–13
    command and control strategy, 14–17
    reinternalization of, 13–14
  and fuel economy, 395–397
  social costs of automobiles, 361

Fairmont, 151
Falcon, 146
Fatality rates:
  downsizing, tables, 176–177
  figures, 41–43
  small and large car studies, 171
Federal Aid Highway Act, 356
Federal chartering (*see* Corporations, industrial; Federal Corporate Chartering Act)
Federal Corporate Chartering Act, 23
Federal Electric and Hybrid Vehicle Program, 60–61 (*See also* Electric vehicle)
Federal funds, disadvantages, 6
Federal Highway Administration, 350
Federal Motor Vehicle Safety Standards, 79, 81
Federal Register, 73, 127
Federal regulation (*see* Regulation)
Federal Task Force on Motor Vehicle Goals Beyond 1980, 419
Federal Water Pollution Act (1972 Amendments), 1970 Clean Air Act contrasted, 388
Fiat, 244–245
  foreign business, table, 222
  Poughkeepsie plant, 225–226
Figures (*see* Tables and figures)
Financial module, 201–202
Finkelstein, Michael M., 328, 432
Firestone 500, 328
  consumer and industry reaction, 426–428
Fleet vehicles:
  buying the right car, 434–436
  costs, 436
  industry characterized, 433–434
  management procedures, 436–441
  NAFCAR, 441
  operating data, tables, 437–438
  trends in new car acquisition, table, 440
  yearly purchases, table, 435
Ford Europe, 260–261, 263
Ford, Gerald, 144
  fuel economy, 126
Ford, Henry, I, 308
Ford, Henry, II, 44, 155n.11, 325, 330
  and Volkswagen, 234
Ford Motor Company:
  Canadian operations, 226–227
    (*See also* Canadian Automobile Agreement)
  capital expenditures, tables, 209–210
  competition's future costs, 54–55

Ford Motor Company (*Cont.*):
  debt position 1985, tables, 207–208
  electronic engine controls, 181–182 (*See also* Electronic engine controls)
  exhaust systems, 41
  Fiesta, 244
  financial position 1985, table, 206
  fleet sales, 445
  foreign assembly and manufacturing plants, 228
  foreign business, table, 222
  fuel standards impact, 134–135
  geographical markets, 153
  light truck fuel standards, 133 (*See also* Light trucks)
  Model T, 226–227
  Model Y, 230
  Pinto, 25, 69, 115, 426–428
  product characteristics, 146–147
  product mix, 151–152
  reaction to fuel economy standards, 121
  safety campaign 1956, 41–42
  safety package 1956, 324
  volume production, 224
Ford United Kingdom, 260
France:
  auto industry between wars, 230
  government auto policy, 266
  nineteenth-century automobiles, 223
  post–World War II growth, 234
Free enterprise, 155, 157
Free-rider problem, 375–376
Frey, Stuart, 330
Front-wheel drive, 283–284, 300
  percentages, table, 285–286
Fuel economy:
  achievements, schematically, 203–204
  auto industry's reactions to standards, 121

Fuel economy (*Cont.*):
  automotive standards, table, 197
  command and control strategy, 14–15 (*See also* Command and control strategies)
  congressional bills, table, 121
  cost-benefit analysis suggested, 137, 162
  DOT/EPA 1974 Report to Congress, 126–127
  "economically practical" standards, 133–134
  effects on market segments, 149–150
  electronic engine controls, 180–188
  Energy Policy and Conservation Act, 16
  European and NHTSA regulations contrasted, 82
  excise taxes, 122, 144, 155–156
  executive and congressional duties compared, 123
  executive branch activities 1970–1976, 141–142
  fleet weighted vs. minimum mileage regulations, 379–380
  gas guzzler tax, 120–122, 144, 155–156, 252
  goals by year 2000, 38
  government sponsorship of research and development, 27
  history of program, 125–133
  increases since 1973, 39
  incremental innovation as basis for improvement, 43–46
  innovation competition, 32
  legislation, 120–122
  legislative impact, 264
  NHTSA's responsibilities, 127
  national policy, 12
  1985 goals, 11n.1, 41, 68, 120, 126, 138, 251, 394–395
  passenger cars, Big Four testimony, 130

Fuel economy (*Cont.*):
　performance standards as targets, 74
　prospects beyond 1985, 140
　research and development, 331
　rule-making:
　　activities FY 1977 summarized, 143
　　light trucks, 131–133
　　passenger cars, 128–131
　　process described, 127–128
　standard setting described, 125
　standards as deterrent to innovation, 138–139
　synthetic fuel development, 162–163, 165–166
　tax approach rejected, 15, 19, 35–36
　transfer of technology accelerated, 138
　United States policy, impact, 263–264
　Voluntary and Mandatory Programs, 126
Fuel economy module, 200–201
Fuel efficiency rebate, 252
Fuel efficiency tax, 252
Fuji, 261
Fujisawa, Takeo, 308

Gage, James, 84
Gas guzzler tax, 120–122, 144, 155–156, 252
GATT, 252
General Motors Corporation:
　capital expenditures, tables, 209–210
　debt position 1985, tables, 207–208
　electronic engine controls, 181
　exhaust systems, 41
　financial position 1985, table, 206
　fleet sales, 445
　foreign assembly and manufacturing plants, 228

General Motors Corporation (*Cont.*):
　foreign business, table, 222
　full-line policy, 227
　geographical markets, 153
　light truck fuel standards, 132–133
　Opel operations, 231
　open style policy, 158, 164
　passenger car rule-making, 128–130
　product characteristics, 146–147
　product mix, 151–152
　reaction to fuel economy standards, 121
　redesigned cars to 1985, 174
　research and development efforts, 35
General Services Administration, low-emission vehicle development, 59
Geographical markets, 153
Germany:
　auto industry between wars, 231
　auto policy, 266
　industrial patents confiscated, 6
　nineteenth-century cars, 223
　post–World War II, 234–235
Ginsburg, Douglas H., 36–37
Glass industry, 190, 192
Goodenough v. Omaha Porkers, 93n.10
Goodson, Eugene, 73
Government:
　Britain's auto policy, 265
　interest group model, 374–377
　Japanese auto policy, 267–268, 297–298
　role analyzed, 262
　United States policy, 263–265
　Western European policies, 265–267
Great Britain:
　auto industry between wars, 229–230
　contingent fee system, 104

Great Britain (*Cont.*):
    government auto policy, 265
    nineteenth-century cars, 224
    post–World War II growth, 234
Greenman v. Yuba Power Prod. Inc., 91n.2
Gross National Product, fuel standards effect, 134
Gyohan marketing system, 310

Haagen-Smit, A. J., 406
Haddon, William, Jr., 327
Hand, Learned, 98–99, 113, 321
Handywagons, 5
Hanson, Kirk O., 36, 166
Hart, Peter, 425
Hart survey, 328
Harvard Godkin Lectures 1976, 122, 397
Harvard School of Public Health, 326
Head injury criterion, 79
Hearings:
    light truck rule-making, 131–133
    passenger car rule-making, 128–130
Heilbroner, Robert, 347–348
Heinen, Charles, 330
Highway Fact Book, 353
Highway fatality trends, 41–43 (*See also* Fatality rates)
Highway Users Federation, 348, 352
    activities, 353
Highways:
    Route 7, Connecticut, 363
    Westway, 362–363
Hino, 261
Hitler, Adolph, auto and road construction, 231
Holden Motor Body Builders Ltd., 232
"Hold harmless" clauses, 107

Honda Motors:
    business ideology, 308–309
    CVCC engine, 39, 41, 44, 58–59, 307–308, 310–311
    early motorcycles, 306–307
    established, 306
    N-360 minicar recalled, 311, 314
    personnel management, 309
Honda, S., biographical sketch, 306
Horsepower, average United States engines, table, 238
Horsepower race, 41–42
Horsepower tax, Great Britain, 229–230
Hydrocarbons, 399, 403, 408–411
    Clean Air Act Amendments, 124
    in-use emissions, table, 411
Hyundai of Korea, 291

Imports:
    Honda's CVCC in United States, 311 (*See also* Honda Motors)
    Japan's barriers, 261, 267, 271, 296–297
    United States:
        auto imports, table, 255–256
        growth, 238–239
        history, 272, 274–275
        response to, 276–277, 281
        value of imports, table, 257–258
Incremental innovation, 43–46, 60 (*See also* Innovation; Inventions)
Independent garages, 183–184
Inflation, 157
    effect on research and development, 331–332
    regulation as causal factor, 135–136
Injuries:
    rates discussed, 43
    reduced-weight fleet's effect, 172

Inner cities, federal regulation's impact, 134
Innovation:
  barriers to, 320
  company size as conducive or harmful, 321–326
  competition recommended, 30–31
    disadvantages, 31–33
  epochal, 46–51, 60
  forces influencing rate, 319
  incremental, 43–46, 60
  mechanisms, 319
  model year change as disincentive, 323
  pollutant emissions, 73
  regulation's effect, 51–52
    barrier effect, 52–54, 60
    entrenchment, 54–55, 60
    envelopment, 55–59, 60
    negative impact, 345
    stimulus to, 328n.17
  response to product life cycle, 275–276
  strategy, 289–291
  (See also Invention; Research and Development; Technology)
Institutional capacity, 372–373
Insurance, product liability, 93
  (See also Product liability)
Insurance industry, downsizing's effect on, 172
Insurance Institute for Highway Safety, 327, 354–355
Interchangeable parts, 237, 245–246
Inter-Industry Emissions Control Program, purpose, 338–339
Internal combustion engine, legislation to ban, 120
Internal science jury, 371
International Business Machines, 289
International Monetary Fund, 253
Interstate Highway System, 353
Intrinsic uncertainty, 197

Inventions:
  barriers to, 325–326
  constitutional provisions, 5–6
  Domestic Policy Review Committee, 7–8
  Europe, 290
  federal regulation's impact, 8–9
  Honda Motors, 312 (See also Honda Motors)
  incentives, 6
  reduction's consequences, 8
  strict liability as disincentive, 92
  (See also Innovation; Research and Development; Technology)
Isle of Man, TT race, 306–307, 308
Isuzu, 261
Italy:
  government auto policy, 266
  production process innovation, 219

Japan:
  American investment in, 261
  auto industry between wars, 232
  automotive growth, 246–247
  barriers to imports, 261, 267, 271, 296–297
  future dilemmas, 293–294
  government policy, 267–268
  United States trade compared, 8
  zero tariff on cars, 247
Japan, Inc., 305–306, 312–313
Jeeps, 153, 264
John, Richard, 11, 164–165
Judicial review, innovation competition, 32
Jury trials, alternatives to in products liability cases, 102–103
Justice Department:
  electronic engine controls, 185
  and Inter-Industry Emissions Control program, 339–341

Kasper, Daniel M., 115–116
Kennedy, Edward, 354
Ketcham, Brian, 354, 357–358, 366
Kinzler, Peter, 365–366, 431
Konishi, Kenkichi, 294–299
Korean automobile industry, 291, 303
Kreps, Juanita, 136

Legal fees (*see* Contingent fees)
Legislation:
　environmental, 119–120
　Federal Electric and Hybrid Vehicle Program, 60–61
　fuel economy, 120–122
　motor vehicle regulatory standards, table, 119
　National Traffic and Motor Vehicle Safety Act, 65–66
　University and Small Business Patent Procedures Act, 7
Leone, Robert, 149
Letters of Undertaking (Canada), withdrawn, 245
Liberty Mutual, 326
Licensing agreements, 285–286
Light trucks:
　growing importance, 192, 211–212
　rule-making, 131–133, 156
　trends, 192
Lobbies:
　activities, 352–354
　auto/highway lobbies listed, 35n.10
Lockheed, 26
Lovdal, Michael, 144
Low-income households, federal regulation's impact, 134
Lucas, 265–266

MacDonald, Harold C., 343–344
Machine-tool manufacturers, product liability cases, 106–107 (*See also* Product liability)

MAD (Mutual assured destruction), 398
Mandatory Fuel Economy Program, 126
Managerial autonomy, 157
Manufacturing defects, strict liability and negligence differentiated, 99
Manufacturing risk, 207–208
Margolis, Howard, 73, 376
Marketing, Honda Motors, 309–310 (*See also* Honda Motors)
Marketing module, 200–201
Marketing organization:
　Britain's failure to build, 244
　Japan's development, 247–248
Markets:
　Japan, 261–262
　North American trends, 259–260
　percentages, table, 287
　performance-oriented and established mass, 50
　thin specialty markets, examples, 48–51, 60–61
　Western European trends, 260–261
Market segments:
　effects of fuel standards, 149–150
　types, 150
Marshall v. Barlow's, Inc., 26n.47
Mass production:
　Canada and Europe, 229
　France, 230
　Germany, 231
　Great Britain, 230
　United States, 225, 226
Matador, 358
Maverick, 146
Mazda, 340
McCabe, Robert, 35, 37, 162–163, 166
Media, auto industry's posture towards, 347
Medical devices, product liability's effect on, 92

473

Index

Mellon, Robert P., 157
Mercedes, 225
Mercedes-Benz, Studebaker-Packard taken over, 240
Mills, D. Quinn, 84–85, 87
Minicar N, 360
  recalled, 311, 314
Minority unemployment, federal regulation's impact, 134
Misch, Herbert, 130n.25
MITI (Japan), 305, 315
Mitsubishi, 261
Mobil Oil Company, 338
Mobile Source Air Collection Control, EPA testing procedures, 68
Model T, 226–227, 274, 308
Model Y, 230
Model year change, as disincentive to innovation, 323
Monte Carlo simulation, 196
Morris-Cowley car, 226
Morris, William Richard, Morris-Oxford car, 226
Morrison, Alan, 84–86
Morton, Rogers, 126
Motorcycle helmets, 12n.5
Motorcycles, Honda Motors, 306–307 (See also Honda Motors)
Motor Vehicle Air Pollution Control Act 1965, 251
Motor Vehicle Goals Beyond 1980, 346, 355–356
Motor Vehicle Information and Cost Savings Act, 127, 424
Motor Vehicle Manufacturers Association, 149, 333–334, 352, 353
Murphy, Thomas, 155, 157
Muskie, Edmund, 342, 393
  Clean Air Act Amendments, 120, 306, 310–311
  EPA-APRAC cooperation, 337
Mustang, 146

Nader, Ralph, 23–24, 36, 354
  Unsafe at Any Speed, 118
NAFCAR, 441
Nash, Carl, 314, 344–345, 390, 421
National Academy of Sciences, 360, 370
National Aeronautics and Space Administration, fuel economy improvements, 125–126
National Air Pollution Control Administration, 336
National Analysts, 429
National Association of Black Social Workers, Inc., 132
National Association of Fleet Administrators, acquisition survey, 435–436, 439 (*See also* Fleet vehicles)
National Audubon Society, 354
National Automobile Dealers Association, 157, 352
  lobbying activities, 353 (*See also* Lobbies)
National Energy Plan, 121
National Energy Program, 252
National Environmental Policy Act of 1969, 362
National Highway Traffic Safety Act of 1966, 119
National Highway Traffic Safety Administration, 16–17, 32, 54, 63, 86, 122, 124, 145, 350
  crashworthiness rating, 426 (*See also* Crash testing; Testing procedures)
  downsizing, 172
  fuel economy regulations, 82 (*See also* Fuel economy)
  passenger car fuel standards, 128
  passive restraints, 79, 81
  planning and evaluation groups, 368, 371
  public participation in rule-making (*See also* Rule-making)
  responsibilities, 127–128

National Highway Users Conference, 353
National Motor Vehicle and Traffic Safety Act of 1966, 65–66, 122–123, 424
National Transportation Policy Study Commission, 346, 355–356
Nedzi, Lucien, 445
Negligence:
 comparative, 101–102
 contributory, 97–98
 doctrine described, 90, 97
 Hand (Judge Learned) formulation, 98–99, 113
 strict liability differentiated, 99
Negotiated settlement, suggested in product liability cases, 101–102
New Detroit, Inc., 132
New Engineer, 347
New Jersey, emissions devices, inspection, 415
New York City:
 traffic congestion, 360
 Westway, 362–363
New York Times, on Clean Air Act Amendments, 120
Nilov engine, 59
Nissan Motor, 261
 foreign business, table, 222
Nitrogen oxides, 158, 307, 335, 399, 403, 405
 Clean Air Act Amendments, 124
 (See also Carbon monoxide; Catalytic converter; Emissions control; Pollution control)
No-fault and fault insurance, 431
Noise standards, effect on weight reduction, 195
Nordhoff, Heinz, 235
Norway, government auto policy, 266
Nulty, Timothy, 35–36, 163–164

Office of Management and Budget, 322–323
Office of Science and Technology, 346, 355–356
Office of Technology Assessment, automobile policy study, 8, 355–356
Oil, strategic storage, 398
Oil crisis, 262
Oil industry, 190
Olds (1902), 224, 274
Oligopoly, 291
Omni/Horizon, 426–428, 431–432
OPEC (*see* Organization of Petroleum Exporting Countries)
Opel, GM acquires, 231
Organization of Petroleum Exporting Countries, 248

Pain and suffering awards, 103
Pan-European Marketing, 261, 266
Panhard and Levassor, 223
Passenger car:
 birthplace, 223
 decline in material to produce, 193
 fleets (*see* Fleet vehicles)
 inertial weights, 149–150
 length changes, table, 278
 model variety reduction, 150
 1995 figures, 173
 prices and currency fluctuation, table, 288
 production by country, table, 247
 redesigning, 173–174
 rule-making, 128–131 (*See also* Rule-making)
 size mix, tables, 190–191
 small car sales, table, 282
 suppliers, 211
  major multinationals, 221n.1
Passive restraints, 328n.17, 369
 deaths and injuries, impact, 177
 effect on weight reduction, 195

Passive restraints (Cont.):
  Honda Motors, 314 (See also Honda Motors)
Patents:
  federal funds to develop, 6–7
  government policy, 33
  uniform patent policy, 7
  University and Small Business Patent Procedures Act, 7
  (See also Innovation; Invention; Research and Development)
Peak, V. Lonnie, Jr., 132
Pearce, Michael C., 303
People v. Fries, 13n.5
Performance code, 66
Performance standards, 55–58, 147
  basic argument favoring, 67
  design standards differentiated, 70–72, 75
  equipment, 124
  financial risk consideration, 68–69, 72–73, 85
  limitations, 67–69
  new car fleet fuel economy, 125
  preferred, 65–66, 82
  reevaluation recommended, 82
  as targets, 74
  (See also Design standards)
Performance statements, three elements of, 70
Personnel management, Honda Motors, 309 (See also Honda Motors)
Petroleum, savings through fuel standards, 139
Peugeot, 223
Peugeot-Citroen, 136
  Chrysler's divestiture of European interests, 54, 212–213, 244, 263–264, 265
  foreign business, table, 222
Pharmaceuticals, product liability's effect on, 92–93
Pinto, 25, 69, 115, 151, 249, 328
  Belgord's emission's device, 357–358
  fire hazard charge, effect, 152, 426–428

Plant rejuvenation and modernization:
  fuel standards effect, 139
Plastics industry, 190, 192–193
  downsizing's effect, 172
Plumbing industry, regulation developments, 70
Pocket calculators, 48–49
Political coalitions, auto industry's use of, 156–157
Political party organization, decline, 378–379
Political strategy, 154–158
Pollution control:
  air pollution as negative externality, 12, 402
  automotive exhaust:
    improvements listed, 41
    reductions, 41
  automotive water pollution, 360–361
  Big Four conspiracy to restrain, 325, 339, 341, 343–344, 406–407
  command and control strategy, 14 (See also Command and control strategies)
  effluent fees on emissions, 88, 373–374, 416–420
  electronic engine controls, 183
  executive and congressional duties compared, 123
  government sponsorship of research and development, 27
  incremental innovation as basis for improvement, 43–46
  Japan, 297
  legislation, 119–120
  reinternalizing externalized costs, 13–14
  tax approach rejected, 15, 19, 35–36
Popovich, Frank T., 211
Population, 1995 profiles, 172–173
Population per car, table, 243
Posner, R., 98
Potomac car, 393
Power train efficiency, 138

Index

President of the United States:
  constituents, 379
  1971 statement of government patent policy, 33
Price module, 200–201
Pricing:
  CAFE's effect, 152–153 (*See also* Corporate average fuel economy)
  relative pricing strategies, 152
Prince Motors, 261
"Probability case," 198
PROCO (Programmed combustion) engine, 147, 149, 150, 186
Product liability:
  chemical company's aversion to, 112–113
  collateral source income, 105–106
  comparative negligence as improvement on, 101–102
  contingent fee system, 103–105
  contractual protection, 106–108
  defenses to:
    safety standards, 109
    state-of-the-art, 108–109
  depressing effect on innovation, 92
  jury trials, alternatives, 102–103
  manufacturer's liability expanded, 100–101
  "pain and suffering" awards, 103
  Pinto case, 115 (*See also* Pinto)
  United States Interagency Task Force on, 92–93, 95
Product life cycle model, 295
  innovation as strategy, 289–291
  international competitiveness explained, 272, 274–275
  international standard car suggested, 283
  strategies to cope, 275–276
Production, percentages, table, 287
Pro Forma Generator module, 201–202

"Proposition 13," 157
Protectionism, 272, 292
  Japan, 296–297
  United States, 269
Public interest, as automobile industry objectives, 155
Public interest advocacy, 365–366
Public Interest Campaign, 128
Public Interest Economics Foundation, 128
Public interest groups:
  fuel economy standards, 128–129
  listed, 354n.22
Public policy process, competition in, 148–149

Rabinow, Jacob, 6
Railway Progress Association, 352
Rambler, 238
Randall, Don, 178, 187–188
Raw materials, costs compared, 193
Redesigned cars, fuel economy standard's effect, 173–174
Red Flag Law, 223, 224
Regulation:
  administering agencies listed, 350
  advantage to imports? 251–253
  adversarial model, 375
  analysis and decision distinguished, 389
  automotive regulations of last decade, 55
  buildings, regulatory instruments, 66–67
  characterized, 378, 382–383
  decision and strategy distinguished, 389
  defined, 301
  Europe post–World War II, 235
  fleet manager's opinions, 442–443
  industry concentration, implications for, 17–19
  innovation-related, 8–9

Regulation (*Cont.*):
  innovations resulting from, 328n.17
  Japan's construction and use regulations, 267
  moratorium urged, 157, 187
  negative impact on innovation, 345
  paradox, 46, 60
  as paternalism, 367
  performance and design standards, 55–58 (*See also* Design standards; Performance standards)
  plumbing industry, 70
  pre–World War I, 223–227
  primary purpose, 328
  promulgation procedure, 73
  regulatory failure, 360
  rule-making procedures recommended, 83
  thin specialty markets, effect on, 51, 60
  third-party review, 367–371
"Relative impact," 199
Relative pricing (*see* Pricing)
Renault, 153, 223
  foreign business, table, 222
  nationalized, 234
Research and development:
  aggregate industrial spending, table, 40
  antitrust law's effects, 7
  current budget for motor vehicles, 331
  federal funds, disadvantages, 6–7
  General Motors' efforts, 35
  government sponsorship of, 27–30, 35–36, 60
  Honda's CVCC engine, 310–311 (*See also* Honda Motors)
  innovation competition recommended, 30–33
  nonautomobile industry sources of, 27–30, 37
  private sector conditions, 5

Research and development (*Cont.*):
  regulatory intervention's effects, 44–46, 60
  size of innovative firms, 323
  (*See also* Innovation; Invention; Technology)
Ricardo, Henry, 44
Risks:
  financial risk and fuel standards, 139–140
  manufacturing risk, 207–208
  market risk's importance, 147–148
  risk analysis:
    described, 196
    different scenarios, 208–210
    economic risk scenario, 209–210
    normal scenario, 202–208
    simulator model, 201
  sample risk matrix, table, 149
  technological risk, 207–208
R. L. Polk & Co., 434
Road salt, 361
Rockefeller Commission, 388
Rockwell International, 53
Rolls Royce, 228n.37, 264
Romney, George, 324
Ronan, Lawrence, 38
Rootes, 259
Rosengart vehicles, 230
Rotary engine, 291, 340, 345
Rozendaal, Jan, 111–112
Rubber industry, 190, 192
  downsizing's effect on, 192
Ruckelshaus, William, 336, 408
Rule-making:
  fuel economy activities FY 1977 summarized, 143
  light trucks, 131–133 (*See also* Light trucks)
  National Highway Traffic Safety Administration, 358–359
  process described, 127–128
  public participation in, 347

Safety:
　command and control strategy, 14–15 (*See also* Command and control strategies)
　consumer reaction to information, 428–430
　crash testing, 79–80 (*See also* Crash testing; Testing procedures)
　does it sell? 424–430
　executive and congressional duties compared, 123
　fatality rates, 41–43 (*See also* Fatality rates)
　government sponsorship of research and development, 27
　incremental innovation as basis for improvement, 43–46
　independent research on, 326–327
　legislation, 118–119
　National Highway Traffic Safety Administration, 16–17
　National Traffic and Motor Vehicle Safety Act, 65–66
　new technologies listed, 41
　research and development, 331
　small and large car studies, 171
　standard-setting described, 122–124
　standards in product liability cases, 109
　tax approach rejected, 15, 19, 35–36
　Volvo and Mercedes efforts to sell, 425
　(*See also* Product liability; Strict liability)
Sant, Roger W., 252
Saudi Arabia, 394
Sawhill, John, 121
Scherer, F. M., 322
Schneider, Kenneth, 348
Schultze, Charles, Harvard Godkin Lectures 1976, 122, 391
Schumpeter, Joseph, 46, 58
Schupack, Mark B., 320–321
Seat (Spain), 266
Seatbelts, 14, 368
　interlocks, 29, 53
　NHTSA standards, 79, 81
　product liability, 93–94
　usage rate, 87
Secrest, Fred, 121
Segmentation (*see* Market segments)
Seiffert, Ulrich, 85–86
Sensors, 181–182
Service stations, 183–184
Shareholder democracy, 23
Shepard, William, 323
Sierra Club, 354
Simon v. Sargent, 13n.5
Sloan, Alfred, 151, 290, 353
Small car sales, CAFE's effect, 151
Smith, Gerald, 132
Snell, Bradford, 352
Snow, John, 368, 371
Société Renault, 223
Soltys, Terry Cauthon, 144
Southern Pennsylvania Transportation Authority, 356
Spain, automobile policy, 266
Spark plugs, 192
Special contract sales store, 310
Specification (design) code, 66
Speed limits, 41–43
"Standard car," 283–284, 285
　fleet vehicles, 439
State-of-the-art defenses, 108–109
State-owned auto producers, effect on competition, 286–287
State v. Mele, 13n.5
State v. Pack, 12n.5
Steel industry, 189, 192
Stepp, Marc, 134
Stewart, Frederick, 130n.25
Stockman, David, 374, 390, 421, 445
Stonewalling, 154, 387
Stork, Eric, 75

480
Index

"Straight-line" fuel economy proposal, 144
Strategy, 373
Stratified charge engine, 59, 291
Strict liability:
  doctrine discusses, 98–101
  negligence differentiated, 99
  philosophical formulation, 91
  Restatement (Second) of the Law of Torts:
    Section 402A, 91
  safety incentives for victims, 100
Strombotne, Richard, 62–63, 211–212
Studebaker-Packard, Mercedes-Benz takeover, 240
Subcompacts, 283
  United States entry into, 248
Sunset laws, 388
Sweden, automobile policy, 266
Swine Flu program, liability provisions, 92–93
Synthetic fuel development, 162–163, 165–166

Tables and figures:
  antitampering survey, 410
  after-tax profit and net cash inflow, 204–205
  average horsepower U.S. engines, 238
  before and after maintenance, emission devices, 416
  Big Four:
    debt position 1985, 207–208
    financial position 1985, 206
  calculator prices, 49
  car prices and currency fluctuation, 288
  carbon monoxide in-use emissions, 412
  cars in-use meeting standards, 414
  consumer costs for transportation, 351
  corporate political strategy, 161

Tables and figures (*Cont.*):
  crash testing, 80
  driver age and accident type, 175
  energy consumption distribution, 349
  envelopment of established technology, 56
  executive and congressional duties compared, 123
  exhaust emission standards, 404
  exports of new cars, 229
  fatality rates, 41–43
  federal initiatives, effects, 45
  fleet operating data, 437–438
  fleet purchases, 435
  foreign business of major car producers, 222
  front-wheel drive, 285–286
  fuel economy:
    achieved, 203–204
    congressional bills, 121
    standards, 197
  GMC body redesigning, 174
  hydrocarbon in-use emissions, 411
  industrial spending for auto research, 40
  legislation, motor vehicle regulation, 119
  length-of-car changes, 278
  licensed drivers and population, 173
  light truck fuel standards, 133
  market percentages of domestic producers, 287
  material profile, passenger cars, 193
  miles-per-gallon averages, 146
  motor vehicle-related standards, 78
  passenger cars:
    fuel standards 1981–1984, 130
    production by country, 247
    size mix, 190
  population per car selected countries, 243

Tables and figures (*Cont.*):
  potential technological competitors, 57
  product cost improvement patterns, 47
  product liability insurance, 114
  production percentages, 287
  regulation's effect on innovation, 52
  regulatory process, 378, 382–383
  risk analysis simulator model, 201
  sample risk matrix, 149
  seven army innovations, 61
  small car sales, 282
  structure of motor vehicle regulatory standards, 123
  tariff rates, 273
  total vehicle mix, 191
  trends in new car acquisition by fleets, 440
  truck/bus sales by weight, 191
  tuneups by shop size, 184
  U.S. auto imports and exports, 255–256
  U.S.–Canada trade, 241–242
  value of U.S. imports and exports, 257–258
  vehicle weight-sales weighted mix, 194
  weight changes, 279
  wheelbase changes, 280
Tail lights, regulations, 270
Targets, performance standards as, 74
Tariffs, 272
  early U.S., 224, 227–228
  European Economic Community 1972, 244
  France, 230
  Great Britain, 229
  Japan, 246–247, 296–297
  rates, table, 273
  United States:
    1968, 239
    1972, 248
Tata of India, 291

Technological risk, 207–208
Technology:
  actions creating, 44
  current and projected innovations, 137–139
  divergence of core technologies, 43
  electric vehicle, 58–59, 60–62, 120, 192
  electronic engine controls, 180–188
  incremental and epochal innovation, 46–51, 60
  licensing agreements to obtain, 285–286
  life cycle model, 46–52
  new technologies listed:
    fuel economy, 39, 41
    pollution control, 41
    safety, 41
  pull and push, 44–46, 60, 319, 320
  rate of change discussed, 43–46
  regulatory intervention's effects, 44–46
  regulatory paradox, 46, 60
  (*See also* Emissions control; Fuel economy; Innovation; Invention; Pollution control; Safety; Technology)
Terry, Sidney, 130n.25, 366, 431–432
Testing procedures:
  crash testing, 79–80 (*See also* Crash testing)
  electronic engine controls, 184–186 (*See also* Electronic engine controls)
  Ford's concern, 148
  and performance standards, 67–69 (*See also* Performance standards)
Thalidomide, 104
Tires:
  beadless, 344
  elliptical, 156
  Firestone 500, 328, 426–428

Tokuyakten, 310, 311
Tokyo Round of Multilateral Trade Negotiations, 253
Torts, Restatement (Second) of the Law of Torts, Section 402A, 91
Toxic substances, 112
Toyo Kogyo, 340
Toyota Motor:
  foreign business, table, 222
  Inter-Industry Emissions Control, 339
  marketing system, 309
  United States assembly plant, 249
Tracey, Karen, 144
Trade:
  foreign barriers to, 228–229, 231–232
  shares of world trade, 275
  United States position, 272
Traffic congestion, 360
Train, Russell, 337
Transportation Department:
  air bags, 53 (See also Air bags; Passive restraints)
  electronic engine controls, 185
  energy conservation study 1971, 125
  experimental safety cars, 326–327
  innovation competition, 32
  planning process, 363
  Transportation Systems Center, 128, 196
Transportation policy:
  Japan, 312–313
  National Transportation Policy Study Commission, 356
Traynor, Judge, 91
Treaty of Rome (see European Economic Community)
Tri-State Regional Planning Commission, 363
Trucks:
  Fiat, 266
  Germany, 260
  sales by weight, table, 191
  (See also Light trucks)

TT Race, 306–307
Tuneups, 183–184
Turbochargers, 39, 41, 44, 138, 149, 190, 192
  California's regulations, 53

Uncertainty, contextual and intrinsic, 197
Unemployment, 157
  fuel standards effect, 134
Unions, Italy, 219
United Auto Workers, 134, 352
United States:
  auto industry characterized 1950's and 1960's, 237–240
  foreign car assembly plants in, 249
  foreign investment in, 264–265
  government auto policy, 263–265
  Japan's trade compared, 8
United States Constitution, authors and inventors provisions, 5–6
United States Interagency Task Force on Product Liability, 92–93, 95
United States v. Automobile Manufacturers Association, Inc., 17n.20
United States v. Carroll Towing Co., 98n.1
University and Small Business Patent Procedures Act, 7
Useful Life clauses, 107–108
User Union (Japan), 311
Using-to-capacity principle, 309–310
Utterback, J., 50

Variable cost module, 200–201
Vehicle Safety Act, 424
V-8 engine, 51
Volkswagen:
  foreign business, table, 222

Volkswagen (Cont.):
  Inter-Industry Emissions Control, 339
  manufacturing in U.S., 249
  origins, 231
  post–World War II growth, 234–235
Voltaire, 16
Volume production, 224
Voluntary Fuel Economy Program, 126
Volvo, 266
  exhaust system, 41
  foreign business, table, 222
  United States assembly plant planned, 249

Wages, United States and Europe, 225
Water pollution, automotive, 360–361
Weight:
  changes, table, 279

Weight (Cont.):
  reduction's effect on injuries, 172
Wells, Louis T., Jr., 294, 295, 301–302
Westway, 362–363
Wharton EFA model, 200
Wheelbase, changes, table, 280
White, Lawrence, 28, 321, 373–374, 422
Whitehead, Alfred North, 332
Wilderness Society, 354
Wilkins, Mira, 301–302, 303
Wilkinson, W. R., 299–301
Windshield defrosting and defogging systems, NHTSA standards, 67
Wright, Marshall, 53

Yamani, 394–395
Yen's strength, 267

Zinc industry, 190